The Legal, Administrative and Managing Framework for Spatial Policy, Planning and Land-Use. Interdependence, Barriers and Directions of Change

The Legal, Administrative and Managing Framework for Spatial Policy, Planning and Land-Use. Interdependence, Barriers and Directions of Change

Editors

Maciej J. Nowak
Giancarlo Cotella
Przemysław Śleszyński

MDPI • Basel • Beijing • Wuhan • Barcelona • Belgrade • Manchester • Tokyo • Cluj • Tianjin

Editors
Maciej J. Nowak
West Pomeranian University of Technology
Poland

Giancarlo Cotella
Politecnico di Torino
Italy

Przemysław Śleszyński
Polish Academy of Sciences
Poland

Editorial Office
MDPI
St. Alban-Anlage 66
4052 Basel, Switzerland

This is a reprint of articles from the Special Issue published online in the open access journal *Land* (ISSN 2073-445X) (available at: https://www.mdpi.com/journal/land/special_issues/Spatial_Policy).

For citation purposes, cite each article independently as indicated on the article page online and as indicated below:

LastName, A.A.; LastName, B.B.; LastName, C.C. Article Title. *Journal Name* **Year**, *Volume Number*, Page Range.

ISBN 978-3-0365-2365-1 (Hbk)
ISBN 978-3-0365-2366-8 (PDF)

Contents

About the Editors

Maciej J. Nowak (born 1982), is a professor at the West Pomeranian University of Technology, head of the Real Estate Department, and member of the Presidium Committee for Spatial Economy and Regional Planning, Polish Academy of Sciences. Author of over 200 works in this field, including more than 30 monographs. Participant in several dozen grants and projects, realized for the National Science Center, polish ministries and central institutions and regional/local governments. Member of government teams developing changes in the spatial management system in Poland. Author of recognized legal commentaries on spatial planning regulations. Legal advisor participating in numerous court and administrative cases related to spatial planning. In the implementation of projects and publications, extensively cooperated with representatives of other countries (including the Czech Republic, Slovakia, Latvia, Ghana and Germany).

Giancarlo Cotella is an Associate Professor of spatial planning at Politecnico di Torino. His research focuses on the comparison of spatial governance and planning systems in Europe and beyond, and on the mutual influence between the EU and the Member States in that field. He has been widely published in the international scientific literature and participated in several international research projects, including the ongoing ESPON METRO and the recently concluded ESPON SUPER, COMPASS, URRUC and ReSSI. He has actively been involved in the activities of the Associations of European Schools of Planning since 2006, and he coordinates the AESOP Thematic Group on Transboundary Planning, Policy Diffusion, Planning Cultures.

Przemysław Śleszyński (born 1973), is a professor at the Institute of Geography and Spatial Organization of the Polish Academy of Sciences, member of committees of the Polish Academy of Sciences: Committee of Geographical Sciences PAS (scientific secretary), Committee of Demographic Sciences PAS, Committee on Migration Research PAS and Spatial Management Committee of PAS. Vice-Chairman of the Polish Geographical Society and chairman of its Commission on the Geography of Settlements and Population, member of the Main Urban Planning and Architectonic Commission and the Society of Polish Town Planners, chairman of the Task Committee of the Geographical Olympics. He deals with socio-economic geography and spatial management, including the spatial structures of population and enterprises, urban and regional development, migration, transport geography, spatial planning, landscape aesthetics. He is the author of over 400 works in this field, including more than 20 monographs (including about 100 works in English). He has been the coordinator of and participant in several dozen grants and projects, realized for international institutions (among others, ESPON, INTERREG programs) and central and local governmental public entities, including 15 years as the coordinator of government reports on the state and progress of planning works in municipalities. He is also the author of the "List of medium cities, losing their social and economic functions" and other solutions, which are included in the key strategic documents of Poland: The Concept of National Spatial Development 2030 (2011) and the Strategy for Responsible Development (2016).

land

Editorial

The Legal, Administrative, and Governance Frameworks of Spatial Policy, Planning, and Land Use: Interdependencies, Barriers, and Directions of Change

Maciej Nowak [1,*], Giancarlo Cotella [2] and Przemysław Śleszyński [3]

1 Department of Real Estate, Faculty of Economics, West Pomeranian University of Technology, 70-310 Szczecin, Poland
2 Interuniversity Department of Regional and Urban Studies and Planning (DIST), Politecnico di Torino, 10125 Torino, Italy; giancarlo.cotella@polito.it
3 Department of Urban and Population Geography, Institute of Geography and Spatial Organization, Polish Academy of Sciences, 00-818 Warsaw, Poland; psleszyn@twarda.pan.pl
* Correspondence: Maciej.Nowak@zut.edu.pl

Abstract: The article provides an overview of the legal and administrative aspects of spatial governance and planning and of the related challenges. The legal dimension of spatial planning, administrative spatial planning traditions, as well as different frameworks and conditions for the governance of territorial regions are briefly introduced. On this basis, the various contributions that compose the special issue are framed and presented to the readers. In conclusion, a number of directions for further research are identified. Overall, the article serves as an editorial introduction and the various issues it touches upon are further specified in the individual contributions the compose the special issue.

Keywords: spatial policy; spatial planning; territorial governance; land use; law

Citation: Nowak, M.; Cotella, G.; Śleszyński, P. The Legal, Administrative, and Governance Frameworks of Spatial Policy, Planning, and Land Use: Interdependencies, Barriers, and Directions of Change. *Land* **2021**, *10*, 1119. https://doi.org/10.3390/land10111119

Received: 11 October 2021
Accepted: 18 October 2021
Published: 22 October 2021

1. Introduction

Spatial planning research presents numerous overlaps with several other disciplines due to the heterogeneity and interdisciplinarity of its practices [1]. One key variable determining how spatial planning works in a specific context concerns the relation between spatial planning and the legal system that allows it to function. Exploring this relationship is a relevant research challenge that concerns issues related to the enactment and implementation of spatial development strategies, land-use planning, regulation tools, and all other devices and administrative decisions that influence space. Moreover, spatial planning is a path-dependent activity [2] that is developed and consolidated through time due to several different elements such as the mentioned legal system, the administrative tradition that characterizes a country, and the so-called spatial planning tradition. Finally, spatial planning practices are constantly subject to the influence of previously developed solutions. Instead of leading to convergence, however, policy mobility episodes increase the overall variety, borrowing arrangements that need to be tailored to the new context to function within new conditions [3,4]. For these reasons, the practice of spatial planning is extremely heterogeneous worldwide, embedded as it is in geographical and historical conditions that characterize each place [5]. Additionally, spatial planning systems are difficult to analyze and compare.

Against these multiple complexities, this Special Issue gathers contributions concerning a broad range of research issues. These include the economic and legal aspects of spatial planning and urbanization processes; the implementation pitfalls that may characterize strategies and instruments and the costs of misfunctioning spatial planning tools; the instruments dedicated to steering and regulating land, and the role of propriety rights in land use policy, etc. The collected papers approach these issues from different perspectives and concern different areas of the world. It is worthwhile to analyze the cases that they present and then try to position them in the context of broader theoretical and practical formulations.

To open this Special Issue, the following sections further characterize outline the conceptual issues introduced above. These issues include the legal dimension of spatial planning, the role of administrative and spatial planning traditions, and the different frameworks and conditions that influence territorial governance. After that, the various articles that compose the Special Issue are introduced as a helpful guide for the readers. Finally, the contribution is rounded off by the proposal of a preliminary agenda intended to guide other scholars interested in developing further research on these matters.

2. The Legal Dimension of Spatial Planning

The relationship between spatial planning and law has been repeatedly addressed in the literature. Several thematic directions are distinguished. Among others, Buitelaar [6] addresses the problem of flexibility in planning, reducing the objectives of planning regulations to minimize future risks. Plans that are binding acts and plans with a more strategic function pursue this goal differently. The choice of a specific spatial planning formula over others determines (and is determined by) how the role of law and, more in general, of propriety rights [7] is understood in a given country. In regulatory planning systems, legal certainty is critical; in discretionary systems, flexibility is key [8,9]. Thus, one can distinguish between plan-based and development-based systems, conformative, performative, neo-performative systems, or even state-led and market-led systems [10–12]. While each configuration grants many specific benefits, none is exempt from risks. Overly regulatory plans may result in a development lock. On the other hand, overly flexible planning may result in excessive discretionality and the prevalence of the market's interest to the expense of the public good. Moroni et al. [13] rightly emphasize that the law does not guarantee a specific effect per se; it can only contribute to its achievement when it manages to fit and interpret the particular contextual conditions within which it is enforced. Moreover, as these conditions continuously vary, any law should be capable of considering further socio-economic, territorial, and institutional challenges and trends that emerge and manifest over time [14].

When considering the pitfalls of plan-based and development-based systems—and any configuration positioned in between these two ideal extremes of the spectrum—it is important to note that no legal framework on its own can guarantee that the goals of spatial planning are achieved [12]. It is impossible to present universal regulations that can be adopted successfully by every country, which is why the role of administrative and spatial planning cultures and traditions plays a crucial role in the equation. Consequently, positive results in achieving spatial planning goals are often achieved by balancing regulatory and strategic or development-led planning activities that depend on actual needs [15]. For instance, especially in countries characterized by a high level of spatial chaos, a transitional, a more regulatory formula may be required to grant a minimum level of legal certainty and, in turn, grant control over development outcomes. At the same time, systems should be flexible and reflexive enough to incorporate changing socio-economic and territorial conditions into spatial planning continuously. It would allow one to accommodate and balance the various instances of public and private actors that, altogether, contribute to shaping development trends [16].

3. Administrative Spatial Planning Traditions

The way spatial planning operates is intertwined with the particular administrative cultures and traditions that characterize different countries and regions [17]. Following the work of Hesse and Sharpe [18], which distinguish northern European, Anglo-Saxon, and Napoleonic countries based on the degree of local autonomy, Lidström [19] divided the northern European group into two categories: Scandinavian welfare democracies and

Middle European countries, characterized by different local government systems. Taking a different path, Goldsmith [20] classified the basic types of local government systems. Differences were distinguished between a so-called patronage model, primarily concerning southern European countries, where local politicians aim to ensure that the interests of their community are well promoted and defended at higher levels of government, and a welfare state model, concerning northern European countries, where efficient services' delivery has shaped local government over time. Finally, Loughlin and Peters [21] proposed a more complex analysis, which defines four different 'state traditions' based on different aspects of state and political features (political and administrative culture, state organization, state-society relationship, etc.). These aspects determine the conditions within which democracy is understood and practiced. When it comes to spatial planning systems, fewer classifications have been produced over time [22]. The first examples concern the already introduced relationship between planning and law and produce rather schematic classifications of the legal and administrative systems within which planning operates [23–25]. In contrast, following a metaphor adopted by Reimer et al. [26], the legal system represents the main corridor along which planning practice can move. From the end of the 1990s, various contributors argued that spatial planning practices are also shaped by equally important socio-economic, territorial, and cultural conditions [27]. As a consequence of this acknowledgment, many more nuanced classifications were produced that consider additional variables. Following Loughlin and Peters' [21] approach to the analysis of public administration systems, the EU Compendium of Spatial Planning Systems and Policies [28] used several different criteria to define four 'spatial planning traditions', a term that emphasizes how spatial planning is deeply embedded in the complex historical conditions of a place. It was used to help distinguish planning systems, together with six other variables. These variables were: (i) the scope of the system in terms of policy topics covered; (ii) the extent of national and regional planning; (iii) the locus of power or relative competencies between central and local government; (iv) the relative roles of public and private sectors; (v) the maturity of the system or how well it is established in government and public life; and (vi) the apparent distance between expressed goals for spatial development and outcomes. Based on these criteria, four major spatial planning traditions were proposed and then updated in 2007, including countries that had entered the EU as it expanded eastwards [29].

The most recent comparative analysis of the spatial planning systems that characterize the European continent—the ESPON COMPASS research project [1]—accounts for even higher heterogeneity. The conceptualization of spatial governance and planning systems as 'institutional technologies', through which public authorities allocate rights for land use and development [30] was used by Berisha et al. [31] to reflect on the capacity of public control of spatial development embedded in each system. In particular, their analysis points out the lower capacity of public control intrinsic in the traditional 'conformative' models operating in southern European countries, especially in comparison to the 'performative' models that characterize Anglo-Saxon countries [10]. However, it also shows that, whereas most northwestern and eastern European countries have been progressively moving towards 'neo-performative' [18], the results achieved as a consequence of this shift are highly variable. It confirms their dependence on the actual contextual conditions within which each system is embedded.

4. Different Frameworks and Conditions for the Governance of Territorial Regions

An additional variable that influences the configuration and effectiveness of spatial planning is the particular administrative-territorial organization within which it develops and functions. Modern administrative-territorial units are highly heterogeneous in terms of their names and territorial scope (federal states, regions, provinces, districts, prefectures, counties, municipalities, etc.). Similarly, actual socio-economic and territorial phenomena vary from country to country. Hence, a question arises on whether and how administrative boundaries are compatible with geographical and functional phenomena and how this affects spatial governance and planning.

A practical approach to the conceptualization of the above dilemma within a broader conceptual–theoretical framework is the economic region theory of K. Dziewoński [32] that distinguishes between three classical interpretations of a region: (i) the subject region as a cognitive object; (ii) the statistical region as a tool of research; and (iii) the administrative region as a tool of action. Whereas statistical regions often overlap with administrative ones because the organization of statistical services directly refers to the system of state power, these two regions rarely fully overlap with the first type. It leads to differences in how they are included and studied. Additionally, there is a mismatch between cognitive results and application expectations. A notable example here is the functional areas of cities, which objectively exist but are not statistically defined and often lack territorial boundaries with established authorities. Only a few examples of specific objective regions exist, e.g., daily urban systems [33] and urban functional areas [34], which are subject to "objective" delimitation that overlaps with units of territorial administration. It usually applies to the largest and most complex urban agglomerations, i.e., metropolitan areas, which have been provided with administrative status in many European countries (France, Italy, Portugal, and Spain). However, even when an attempt has been undertaken to establish more or less institutionalized metropolitan areas to govern functional urban phenomena, the mismatch remains, as the boundaries of the created administrative units may not include the entire commuting zone (e.g., Barcelona, Lyon, and Milan) or, on the contrary, concern territories that by far exceed the actual functional relations (e.g., Turin and other Italian metropolitan cities) [35].

This incompatibility between functional and administrative areas has severe implications for spatial governance and planning, as the latter should cover as much as possible of a homogeneous socio-economic area that is functionally interconnected [36]. This principle seems to be entirely fulfilled in the case of national and, to a relatively large extent, local spatial planning systems. The former covers entire countries (although even here, one may have doubts due to the growing role of cross-border links). The latter covers local communities such as villages, settlements, and neighborhoods. In contrast, significant discrepancies seem to exist at the intermediate levels, including regions, provinces, or metropolitan areas.

The implications of this mismatch for territorial governance and planning effectiveness are highly relevant; for example, the mismatch between places of residence, work, and public services in general, even under conditions of increasing digitalization, causes excessive mobility and transport intensity. This problem is increasingly recognized, mainly through the concept of functional urban areas (FUAs) [37]. Over time, this problem has led to experimental variable forms of inter-municipal cooperation, with groups of local authorities joining forces concerning selected issues, often in the form of flexible planning activities (as opposed to more 'rigid' zoning, regulatory planning). However, the results of these actions have often been ineffective [38], and in some cases, even lead to the escalation of old socio-historical conflicts [39].

In summary, the question is whether the higher stability of an administrative-territorial division positively influences spatial planning, and subsequently, the rationality and efficiency of spatial development. Or, on the contrary, is further flexibility needed to give an account of territorial complexity in the planning activity and allow for a continuous shift in spatial configurations and instruments guided by the issues to be addressed? The above problem is still unsatisfactorily addressed both within the theoretical and practice discourse. This situation is likely to worsen with the aftermath of the COVID-19 pandemic and the challenges that the pandemic will bring along with it.

5. Exploring Practices from Europe and Beyond: A Roadmap for the Reader

Positioned within the above debate, this Special Issue discusses the implications of legal, administrative, and governance frameworks for spatial planning activities. At the same time, the various contributions that have been collected touch upon other possible inferences that arise from these implications in selected countries worldwide. In their article, Solly et al. [40] deal with sustainable urbanization and, particularly, sustainable land-use practices in European cities and regions. They provide a solid basis to compare and discuss the instruments and practices used in different contexts to steer and regulate land use. Zaborowski [41], on the other hand, argues that the urban planning system is strongly influenced not only by the regulations themselves but also by the way they are interpreted, which varies across countries. Additionally, Górna and Górny [42] adopt a comparative approach in their study, discussing the relationship between the legal framework underpinning spatial planning and the practice of urban agriculture in the two equatorial cities of Singapore and Kigali. In their contribution, De Olde and Oosterlynck [43] point out that contemporary assessments of urban growth management strategies often take the form of quantitative measures of land values and housing prices. In this regard, they argue that these evaluations must also be extended to analyze the policy formulation and implementation process, as it is in phases when the institutions and discourses in which growth management strategies are embedded, are (trans)formed. Myga-Piątek et al. [44] reflect on the differences that emerge when comparing administrative metropolitan areas concerning geography and landscape. Once more, they underline how in most cases, the mismatch between socio-economic and territorial phenomena and the authorities that are deputed to tackle them may hamper the effectiveness of spatial planning.

The objective of the study by Śleszyński et al. [45] was to demonstrate geographical (interregional and functional) regularities related to the economic (financial) effects of adopting local plans. They also aimed to identify the financial effects of implementing local plans in municipalities, i.e., their size, the structure of income (revenue) and expenditure relating to municipal budgets, and the population living in municipalities. Their contribution shows that boroughs often do not obtain adequate revenues from spatial development, and the inappropriate policies of local governments cause heavy burdens that threaten to upset their financial balance. Additionally, Chen et al. [46] examine the relationships between the legal system, spatial planning, and economy. In particular, using panel data from Chinese cities from 2014 to 2017, their analysis indicates that legal provisions can favor the increase in financial credit and foreign investment, in turn determining an increase in housing prices. Similarly, Lityński and Hołuj [47] draw attention to the role of financial instruments, which can play a decisive role in stimulating the creation of compact spatial structures. In this group, attention should be paid to indirect instruments, such as tax exemptions or reliefs for new locations of compact housing. Local self-governments should receive compensation from the state budget for the reduction in income resulting from such tax exemptions or reliefs. Liu et al. [48] highlight that local governments' green management behavior can help promote the implementation of new development concepts from a knowledge management perspective. They argue that the effects of knowledge spillover have a significant impact in the later stage of green governance processes, leading to learning and knowledge synergies and cooperation value-added income, in turn promoting local government green governance into a positive-peer state. Chang and Chen [49] present directions to optimally shape the relationship between economic development and environmental protection while exploring possible solutions to make Chinese urbanization processes more sustainable. Similarly, the results of Meng et al. [50] indicate that innovation-oriented land-use transformation in four dimensions—human capital, physical capital, urban functions, and administration—is conducive to reducing industrial emissions in the region, but not the spillover effect. Finally, the contribution by Sun et al. [51] explores the issue of path-dependency and the impact of historical events on spatial processes, with a particular focus on the development of the Beijing green belt and its legacy.

6. The Legal, Administrative, and Governance Frameworks of Spatial Policy, Planning, and Land Use: Towards a Research Agenda (GC, PŚ, MN)

The issues outlined in the introduction and addressed in the contributions included in this Special Issue highlight how spatial planning activities continue to face serious challenges that have not yet been satisfactorily addressed. Specifically, from the papers included, a scarce correlation emerges between the legal regulations that allow and shape spatial planning activities and the socio-economic and territorial challenges that those activities should tackle. It is often a consequence of the path-dependent influence of the traditional administrative and spatial planning configuration, which presents an inertial resistance to change that is hard to overcome. A similar situation concerns the mismatch mentioned above between 'objective' and 'territorial' units, with the system of judicial–territorial administration that does not always coincide with the boundaries of the fundamental administrative division of a country, in turn leading to an overall deterioration of the conditions within which all actors involved in spatial development operate.

Several overarching research questions and challenges arise here. How can one reconcile economic efficiency with quality of life? How can one effectively protect the values of the natural and human environment? How can one counteract economic polarization and social inequalities? How can one reconcile individual land-use rights with the common good? Finally, perhaps the most crucial question that must be asked in the face of all the highlighted complexity is: how should different spatial planning functions—regulation, steering, development, and communication—coexist within the overall systems and what should their multiple relations be to allow for an unambiguous, effective, and over-regulated planning action?

All these questions are posed in a situation where our knowledge of spatial planning systems is still insufficient. While a good deal of research that focuses on western Europe, North America, and Southeast Asia exists, knowledge about Latin America and especially Africa and the Middle East is still fragmented and is virtually nonexistent relating to territories whose status is contested due to the presence of territorial conflicts. Considering this, we conclude this introductory contribution by proposing a preliminary research agenda that draws from our editors' experience and the thoughts that have emerged in the composition of this Special Issue. It consists of a list of research tasks that scholars may decide to address in their future studies on the matter. As such, it is undoubtedly incomplete and biased by our approach and perspective; still, we hope that it will encourage more in-depth analysis:

- To explore how different types of legal cultures and traditions around the world have an impact on the way spatial planning is understood and practiced.
- To investigate how the relation between law and planning—and its manifestation through the processes that assign development and land-use rights—evolves through time as a consequence of the evolution of the framework conditions, but also bound by path-dependency.
- To discuss whether spatial planning, intended as a framework deputed to allow a more or less coercive public control over spatial development, is actually needed and whether in its absence societies may develop alternative models of self-regulation.
- To reflect whether, in a world where the public sector is less and less capable of planning in isolation, and where there is a growing influence of private actors in decision making, spatial planning is actually representative of and acting towards the common good, or is increasingly an activity favoring specific elites over other groups.
- To analyze and compare the trigger, the functioning, and the outcomes of non-statutory planning activities, i.e., all these activities that develop outside any dedicated legal framework—for instance, voluntary strategic planning, ad hoc inter-municipal cooperation, and other grassroots practices.
- To explore the contamination between different contexts due to the circulation of models and practices, more or less favored by international organizations, and to understand the benefits and the pitfalls hidden along the way.

- To give an account of the emerging attempts to reach a cooperative agreement between functional phenomena and the more or less formal institutions deputed to manage them, their results, and their potential for generalization and diffusion.

To add further complexity to the picture, these questions also need to be contextualized within the ongoing COVID-19 pandemic, its socio-economic and territorial implications, and the challenges that will emerge in its aftermath. Whereas at first, the pandemic may have been seen as a solid motivation to rebuild the world [52], thus prompting policy- and decision-makers to consider new opportunities for spatial planning and its action, through time, as the pandemic unfolded in all its complexity, these initial discussions proved somewhat naïve and illusionary. Additional research will undoubtedly be required to understand how new post-pandemic spatial behaviors will influence spatial development and planning.

Author Contributions: Conceptualization, M.N., G.C. and P.Ś.; methodology, M.N., G.C. and P.Ś.; validation M.N., G.C. and P.Ś.; formal analysis, M.N., G.C. and P.Ś.; investigation, M.N., G.C. and P.Ś.; data curation, M.N., G.C. and P.Ś.; writing—original draft preparation, M.N., G.C. and P.Ś.; writing—review and editing, M.N., G.C. and P.Ś.; supervision, M.N., G.C. and P.Ś. All authors have read and agreed to the published version of the manuscript.

Funding: This research received no external funding.

Institutional Review Board Statement: Not applicable.

Informed Consent Statement: Not applicable.

Data Availability Statement: Not applicable.

Conflicts of Interest: The authors declare no conflict of interest.

References

1. Nadin, V.; Fernández Maldonado, A.M.; Zonneveld, W.; Stead, D.; Dąbrowski, M.; Piskorek, K.; Sarkar, A.; Schmitt, P.; Smas, L.; Cotella, G.; et al. *COMPASS—Comparative Analysis of Territorial Governance and Spatial Planning Systems in Europe. Applied Research 2016–2018 Final Report*; ESPON: Luxembourg, 2018.
2. Cotella, G. How Europe hits home? The impact of European Union policies on territorial governance and spatial planning. *Géocarrefour* **2020**, *94*, 3. [CrossRef]
3. Cotella, G.; Stead, D. Spatial Planning and the Influence of Domestic Actors: Some Conclusions. *disP-Plan. Rev.* **2011**, *47*, 77–83. [CrossRef]
4. Cotella, G.; Janin Rivolin, U.; Santangelo, M. Transferring good territorial governance in Europe: Opportunities and barriers. In *Territorial Governance across Europe: Pathways, Practices and Prospects*; Schmidt, P., Van Well, L., Eds.; Routledge: London, UK, 2015; pp. 238–253. ISBN 978-1-138-86087-2.
5. Healey, P.; Williams, R. European Urban Planning Systems: Diversity and Convergence. *Urban Stud.* **1993**, *30*, 701–720. [CrossRef]
6. Buitelaar, E. The Fraught Relationship between Planning and Regulation: Land—Use Plans and the Conflicts in Dealing with Uncertainly. In *Planning by Law and Property Rights Reconsidered*; Hartmann, T., Needham, B., Eds.; Routledge: London, UK; New York, NY, USA, 2012; pp. 207–218, ISBN 9781315600710.
7. Munoz-Gielen, D. Urban governance, property rights, land redjustment and public value capturing. *Eur. Urban Reg. Stud.* **2012**, *21*, 60–78. [CrossRef]
8. Tarakçı, S.; Turk, S.S. Shaping of flexibility in urban renewal legal sources in Turkey and its effect on practices. *ICONARP Int. J. Archit. Plan.* **2020**, *8*, 652–671. [CrossRef]
9. Savini, F. Don't blame public law: The legal articulation of certainty in Amsterdam land-use planning. *Town Plan. Rev.* **2016**, *87*, 459–479. [CrossRef]
10. Janin Rivolin, U. Conforming and Performing Planning Systems in Europe: An Unbearable Cohabitation. *Plan. Pract. Res.* **2008**, *23*, 167–186. [CrossRef]
11. Munoz-Gielen, D.; Tasan-Kok, T. Flexibility in planning and the consequences for public value capturing in UK, Spain and The Netherlands. *Eur. Plan. Stud.* **2010**, *18*, 7. [CrossRef]
12. Berisha, E.; Cotella, G.; Rivolin, U.J.; Solly, A. Spatial governance and planning systems in the control of spatial development: A European typology. *Eur. Plan. Stud.* **2021**, *29*, 181–200. [CrossRef]
13. Moroni, S.; Buitelaar, E.; Sorel, N.; Cozzolino, S. Simple planning rules for complex urban problems: Toward legal certainty for spatial flexibility. *J. Plan. Educ. Res.* **2020**, *40*, 320–331. [CrossRef]
14. Nadin, V.; Stead, D.; Dąbrowski, M.; Fernandez-Maldonado, A.M. Integrated, adaptive and participatory spatial planning: Trends across Europe. *Reg. Stud.* **2020**, *55*, 791–803. [CrossRef]

15. Solly, A.; Berisha, E.; Cotella, G.; Janin Rivolin, U. How sustainable are land use tools? A Europe-wide typological investigation. *Sustainability* **2020**, *12*, 1257. [CrossRef]
16. Schmitt, P.; Van Well, L. Revisiting Territorial Governance: Twenty Empirically Informed Components. In *Territorial Governance across Europe: Pathways, Practices and Prospects*; Schmitt, P., Van Well, L., Eds.; Routledge: London, UK; New York, NY, USA, 2016; pp. 221–237. ISBN 9781315716220.
17. ESPON. *Tango—Territorial Approaches for New Governance. Scientific Report*; ESPON Coordination Unit: Luxembourg, 2014.
18. Hesse, J.J.; Sharpe, L.J. *Local Government and Urban Affairs in International Perspective. Analyses of Twenty Western Industrialised Countries*; Nomos: Baden-Baden, Germany, 1991; pp. 603–621.
19. Lidström, A. Commuting and citizen participation in Swedish city-regions. *Political Stud.* **2006**, *54*, 865–888. [CrossRef]
20. Goldsmith, A.A. Institutions and planned socioeconomic change: Four approaches. *Public Adm. Rev.* **1992**, *52*, 582–587. [CrossRef]
21. Loughlin, J.; Peters, B.G. The State Traditions, Administrative Reform and Regionalization. In *The Political Economy of Regionalism*; Keating, M., Loughlin, J., Eds.; Routledge: London, UK, 1997; ISBN 0415564506.
22. Nadin, V.; Stead, D. European spatial planning systems, social, models and learning. *Plan. Rev.* **2008**, *44*, 35–47. [CrossRef]
23. Davies, H.; Edwards, D.; Hooper, A.; Punter, J. *Planning Control in Western Europe*; HMSO: London, UK, 1989.
24. Newman, P.; Thornley, A. *International Competition, National Systems and Planning Projects*; Routledge: London, UK, 1996; p. 304. ISBN 9780203427941.
25. Cotella, G. Central Eastern Europe in the global market scenario evolution of the system of governance in Poland from socialism to capitalism. *J. Entwickl. XXIII* **2007**, *1*, 98–124. [CrossRef]
26. Reimer, M.; Getimis, P.; Blotevogel, H. *Spatial Planning Systems and Practices in Europe: A Comparative Perspective on Continuity and Changes*; Routledge: New York, NY, USA, 2014; p. 336. ISBN 1317919106.
27. Nadin, V. International comparative planning methodology: Introduction to the theme issue. *Plan. Pract. Res.* **2012**, *27*, 1–5. [CrossRef]
28. CEC. *European Spatial Development Perspective: Towards Balanced and Sustainable Development of the Territory of the EU Commission for the European Communities*; Office for the Official Publications of the European Communities, Coordination Unit: Luxembourg, 1999.
29. ESPON. *Governance of Territorial and Urban Policies from the EU to Local Level. Scientific Report*; ESPON Coordination Unit: Luxembourg, 2007.
30. Rivolin, U.J. Global crisis and the systems of spatial governance and planning: A European comparison. *Eur. Plan. Stud.* **2017**, *25*, 994–1012. [CrossRef]
31. Berisha, E.; Cotella, G. Territorial Development and Governance in the Western Balkans. In *Governing Territorial Development in the Western Balkans. Advances in Spatial Science (The Regional Science Series)*; Berisha, E., Cotella, G., Solly, A., Eds.; Springer: Cham, Switzerland, 2021. [CrossRef]
32. Dziewoński, K. The theory of the economic region. *Przegląd Geogr.* **1967**, *39*, 33–50.
33. Berry, B.J.L. *Functional Economic Areas and Consolidated Urban Regions of the US. Final Report of the Social Sciences Research Council Study of Metropolitan Area Classification*; Social Sciences Research Council: New York, NY, USA, 1967.
34. Castells-Quintana, D.; Royuela, V.; Veneri, P. Inequality and city size: An analysis for OECD functional urban areas. *Pap. Reg. Sci.* **2020**, *99*, 1045–1064. [CrossRef]
35. ESPON. *METRO—The Role and Future Perspectives of Cohesion Policy in the Planning of Metropolitan Areas and Cities; Interim Report*; ESPON EGTC: Luxembourg, 2021.
36. Śleszyński, P. Problemy delimitacji miejskich obszarów funkcjonalnych w Polsce Delimitation problems of functional urban areas in Poland. *Rozw. Reg. I Polityka Reg.* **2015**, *29*, 37–53.
37. Antikainen, J. The concept of functional urban area. Findings of the ESPON project 1.1.1. *Inf. Raumentwickl.* **2005**, *7*, 447–452.
38. Salet, W.; Thornley, A.; Kreukels, A. *Metropolitan Governance and Spatial Planning. Comparative Case Studies of European City-Regions*; Spon Press: London, UK, 2003; ISBN 9780415274494.
39. Szmytkowska, M.; Kubiak, Ł.; Śleszyński, P.; Korcelli-Olejniczak, E. The making of the Bydgoszcz-Toruń partnership area as an example of a bipolar conflict. *Eur. Plan. Stud.* **2021**, *29*, 2017–2037. [CrossRef]
40. Solly, A.; Berisha, E.; Cotella, G. Towards sustainable urbanization. Learning from what's out there. *Land* **2021**, *10*, 356. [CrossRef]
41. Zaborowski, T. It's all about details. Why the polish land policy framework fails to manage designation of developable land. *Land* **2021**, *10*, 890. [CrossRef]
42. Górna, A.; Górny, K. Singapore vs. the 'Singapore of Africa'—Different approaches to managing urban agriculture. *Land* **2021**, *10*, 987. [CrossRef]
43. De Olde, C.; Oosterlynck, S. Taking implementation seriously in the evaluation of urban growth management strategies: "Safeguarding the Future" of the Antwerp City-Region. *Land* **2021**, *10*, 159. [CrossRef]
44. Myga-Piątek, U.; Żemła-Siesicka, A.; Pukowiec-Kurda, K.; Sobala, M.; Nita, J. Is there urban landscape in metropolitan areas? An unobvious answer based on corine land cover analyses. *Land* **2021**, *10*, 51. [CrossRef]
45. Śleszyński, P.; Nowak, M.; Sudra, P.; Załęczna, M.; Blaszke, M. Economic consequences of adopting local spatial development plans for the spatial management system: The case of Poland. *Land* **2021**, *10*, 112. [CrossRef]
46. Chen, J.; Zhang, H.; Zhou, Q. Rule by law, law-based governance, and housing prices: The case of China. *Land* **2021**, *10*, 616. [CrossRef]

47. Lityński, P.; Hołuj, A. Macroeconomic perspective on urban sprawl: A multidimensional approach in Poland. *Land* **2021**, *10*, 116. [CrossRef]
48. Liu, H.; Yao, P.; Wang, X.; Huang, J.; Yu, L. Research on the peer behavior of local government green governance based on SECI expansion model. *Land* **2021**, *10*, 472. [CrossRef]
49. Chang, B.; Chen, L. Land economic efficiency and improvement of environmental pollution in the process of sustainable urbanization: Case of Eastern China. *Land* **2021**, *10*, 845. [CrossRef]
50. Meng, Y.; Wang, K.; Lin, Y. The role of land use transition on industrial pollution reduction in the context of innovation-driven: The Case of 30 provinces in China. *Land* **2021**, *10*, 353. [CrossRef]
51. Sun, L.; Fertner, C.; Jørgensen, G. Beijing's First Green Belt—A 50-year long Chinese planning story. *Land* **2021**, *10*, 969. [CrossRef]
52. Florida, R. The Geography of Coronavirus, What Do We Know So Far about the Types of Places That Are More Susceptible to the Spread of COVID-19? In the U.S., Density Is Just the Beginning of the Dtory. City Lab. 2020. Available online: https://www.bloomberg.com/news/articles/2020-04-03/what-we-know-about-density-and-covid-19-s-spread (accessed on 15 September 2021).

land

MDPI

Article

Is There Urban Landscape in Metropolitan Areas? An Unobvious Answer Based on Corine Land Cover Analyses

Urszula Myga-Piątek *, Anna Żemła-Siesicka, Katarzyna Pukowiec-Kurda, Michał Sobala and Jerzy Nita

Faculty of Natural Sciences, University of Silesia, 41200 Sosnowiec, Poland; anna.zemla-siesicka@us.edu.pl (A.Ż.-S.); katarzyna.pukowiec@us.edu.pl (K.P.-K.); michal.sobala@us.edu.pl (M.S.); jerzy.nita@us.edu.pl (J.N.)
* Correspondence: urszula.myga-piatek@us.edu.pl; Tel.: +48-32-3689-361

Abstract: The recent increase in urban areas has stimulated landscape urbanization. One of the ways to study this process is an analysis based on the structure of land cover. The aim of this paper is to assess the intensity of the urban landscape on the basis of the CORINE in the seven largest metropolitan areas in Poland and in the Ruhr Metropolis in Germany. To this end, an urban landscape intensity indicator (ULII) was used based on Corine Land Cover at three levels of detail: the metropolitan area, municipalities and hexagons. There are similarities in landscape structure in areas with similar origin (industrial function) and spatial organization (mono- and polycentric agglomerations). The landscape of the Upper Silesia-Zagłębie Metropolis differs from the landscape of other metropolitan areas in Poland and simultaneously shows similarities to the landscape of the Ruhr Metropolis. The results of the ULII also revealed a dependency: the dominance of rural and transitional landscapes in a majority of the study areas. Urban landscapes occur only in the central zones of the metropolitan areas. This proves that determining the range of a metropolitan area in terms of landscape factors is different from doing it with formal or legal ones.

Keywords: landscape urbanization; metropolises; agglomeration in Poland; urban landscape intensity index

Citation: Myga-Piątek, U.; Żemła-Siesicka, A.; Pukowiec-Kurda, K.; Sobala, M.; Nita, J. Is There Urban Landscape in Metropolitan Areas? An Unobvious Answer Based on Corine Land Cover Analyses. *Land* **2021**, *10*, 51. https://doi.org/10.3390/land10010051

Received: 20 November 2020
Accepted: 5 January 2021
Published: 8 January 2021

Publisher's Note: MDPI stays neutral with regard to jurisdictional claims in published maps and institutional affiliations.

1. Introduction

Urbanization has accompanied humankind since antiquity and is a fundamental feature in every civilization. Urbanization refers both to built-up agglomerations and ways of life and describes the process of rural areas transforming into urban ones [1]. During the period of industrialization in the nineteenth century, urbanization processes began to acquire a fast rate and, since then, have become a common phenomenon in expanding cities [2]. The increase in the number of people living in urban areas means that in some European countries this phenomenon affects almost 80% of the population [3]. In addition, some researchers say that by 2030, 75% of all Europe's landscapes will be urban in nature [4]. The constant growth of urban areas is visible mainly around areas of large agglomerations and is related to the processes of suburbanization and urban sprawl [5,6].

The above processes change the structure of the landscape. In this paper, landscape is understood as a combination of different types of land cover [7]. Thus, along with an increase in the degree of urbanization of the landscape, urban areas increase and natural, rural and/or transitional areas decreases. The processes of landscape urbanization have a fundamental impact on its structure and physiognomy and depend on the intensity of changes and technological progress. Thus, in the cities one can speak of an urban landscape, but is this really evident? An urban landscape is understood to be an existing landscape of urban settlements and their surroundings, but with marked types of use of the city and without administrative restrictions [8]. The authors understand the urbanization of landscape as the process of differentiation and concentration of the internal spatial structure of cities and the quantitative increase in the area of landscapes of urban types. This is a result of spatial expansion (urban sprawl) or the transformation of other types of landscapes (suburban, agricultural, forest, etc.) into an urban one. This process is always associated with an increased human impact (or an increase in the gradient of anthropopressure). One important aspect of the urban landscape is its complexity and multidimensionality, which means the living environment of the societal, cultural, historical and economic contexts and a matrix for further development [9].

At the same time as constant socio-economic development, some cities can gain a special hierarchical position in relation to other cities, transforming into metropolises [10]. Therefore, one of the possible ways for the urban landscape to evolve is through the growth of the metropolitan landscape [11]. Metropolises are a unique type of urban complex. Due to the dynamic processes of not only urbanization but also metropolization, the concept of metropolitan landscape is more often considered in landscape geography and in landscape architecture to be a unique type of urban landscape [12]. The concept of metropolitan landscape is related to the fact that the terms "city" and "urban" landscape are inadequate in describing the fullness and enormity of the roles played by urban networks, spaces, environments and processes. They extend far beyond the city area to the peripheral areas around it, both rural and urban [13]. Beunen [14] believes that metropolitan landscape is like an urban field encompassing built-up and open areas within urban centers.

The urban landscape is characterized by the complexity of its aspects, but also by the dynamics resulting from continuous transformation processes [15]. In Poland, the processes of landscape metropolization are in the initial stages; therefore, it is first necessary to recognize the directions of change and the dynamics of urban landscapes. Taking into account the complexity of the concept of urban landscape, it can be considered from many angles and at many research levels [3]. In terms of geography, it means the spatial organization of its individual elements, which are patches of land cover. Their analysis enables the examination of the landscape structure and its identification.

There are various methods in the literature for determining the degree of landscape urbanization. These are mostly based on land cover analysis and land use change. These methods have been tested in various regions, aspects and spatial relationships by many researchers. In the area of Central Europe, studies on the degree of urbanization were carried out by Inostroza et al. [16]. The aim of their work was to perform a spatially explicit quantification of urbanization degrees across the landscape. Dadashpor et al. [17] analyzed land cover changes in the Tabiz metropolitan area in Azerbaijan using the dispersion of urban lands as the landscape indicator. Changes in land cover due to urbanization were also analyzed by Aguilera et al. [18] and Reis et al. [19] using landscape metrics to analyze urban land cover in expanding cities. Tate et al. [20] assessed the impact of urbanization on the natural environment using the multimetric urban intensity index based on variables related to land cover as well as its management and socio-economic status. A similar set of variables was used by McMahon et al. [21] who examined the relationship between the degree of urbanization and the quality of surface waters in areas with high dynamics of urban processes. The relationship between urbanization processes and type of land cover was studied by Li et al. [22] in the Beijing area and Weng [23], who analyzed the urban gradient in Wisconsin. Huang et al. [24] dealt with the problem of converting rural landscapes into urban ones based on land cover analysis using statistical methods—the regression model. Fuzzy set theory was used to identify the transition zone between the urban and rural landscape in Olsztyn and Sieradz (Poland) [25,26]. The types of coverage analyzed on the basis of satellite images allowed trends in the urbanization of Eastern European cities to be identified [27]. The landscape of some metropolitan areas in Poland was assessed, e.g., Trójmiasto (Gdańsk-Gdynia-Sopot, Marciniak) and Poznań [28,29].

The latest research by Naranjo Gómez et al. [30] concerned the analysis of land cover types and changes that took place in the Canary Islands. In this work, the CORINE land cover was used as the basic research material. The CLC database consists of an inventory of land cover in 44 classes. It covers 39 countries, comprising the European Environment Agency (EEA) members and cooperating countries, including the members of the European

Union. This fact is crucial if comparing of land cover in different countries is the aim of the study. The CLC database supports broad spatial analyses because the data describing land cover in Europe are characterized by spatial continuity and enable non-ambiguous identification of various land-use types. Cieślak et al. [31] also used the same database in their analyses to assess the urban sprawl process. Similar research was carried out in by Solecka et al. [32], who assessed this process in the suburban area of Wrocław on the basis of the CORINE database. Benito et al. [33] also based their research on the CORINE model in determining land cover changes in the Mediterranean area. Research on the relationship between urban pattern and land cover was conducted in the Toronto agglomeration. For this purpose, researchers used the NDVI index as well as the urban patterns and socio-economic variables [34].

The aim of the article is to assess the intensity of the urban landscape on the basis of the CORINE database for seven metropolitan areas in Poland and one in Germany. To this purpose, the Urban Landscape Index (ULII) was introduced according to the formula presented by Matuszewska and Będkowski [26]. This index is based on the classification of land cover types in terms of their urban, transitional and rural character proposed by Biłozor [35]. The analyses were conducted at three levels of research details and comparisons made across the cities. The intensity of the urban landscape was calculated at the level of entire metropolitan areas, for administrative units (municipalities) and basic fields in the form of hexagons with an area of 4 km^2.

In this paper, we consider a metropolitan area as an area established based on administrative decisions. Simultaneously, it is an area that aspires to be a metropolis in the future. The pace of development of metropolis depends on many factors, but one of them is the presence of urban landscapes, surrounded by non-urban landscapes. Delineating of metropolitan areas in Poland is based on administrative decisions. These decisions take into account varied criteria, such as functional and economical. Their importance is currently discussed in the scientific literature. Landscape criteria have not been taken into account in these decisions so far. It should be expected that delineating metropolitan areas using landscape criterion would result in a completely different spatial extent of metropolitan areas. Since the administratively established metropolitan areas in Poland are characterized by the presence of urban, rural, and urban–rural municipalities, it can be assumed that non-urban landscapes will also occur within the metropolitan areas. It seems to be a paradox. Hence, the following questions may be posed: how many urban landscapes are in metropolitan areas, and how much city is in a city?

In Poland, only one of metropolitan areas is a polycentric agglomeration (Upper Silesia-Zagłębie Metropolis—US-ZM), while the rest are monocentric agglomerations. Presumably, the US-ZM should be distinguished in terms of landscape due to both the polycentric form of agglomeration and the matter of its origins, because it is the only metropolitan area in Poland whose formation is associated with the mining industry. For the sake of comparison, the Ruhr Metropolis was analyzed, assuming that due to the same genesis, the area might be similar in terms of landscape to the US-ZM.

The metropolitan areas in Poland were not compared in terms of urban landscape so far, although they were studied in terms of agriculture [36]. Additionally, the topic of theirs administrative and landscape dissociation was not raised. The need for landscape studies assessing the intensity of the urban landscape results from the dynamics of processes related to urbanization (suburbanization, urban sprawl, metropolization). The dynamism of these processes generates the need to monitor the areas subject to them.

2. Materials and Methods

The research procedure can be divided into several basic stages (Figure 1). The first step of the research was the selection of the metropolitan areas. According to the classification of urban centers in Poland [37], the largest seven metropolitan areas in Poland were chosen based on the criterion of population. The other criterion of comparison was the origins of metropolitan area, thus the Ruhr Metropolis (RM) in Germany was chosen.

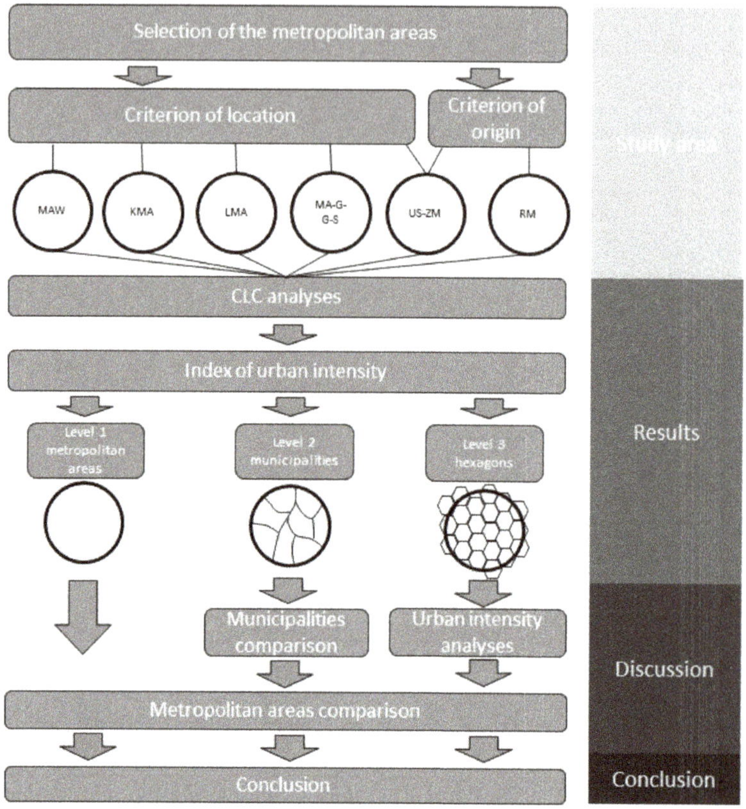

Figure 1. Schematic diagram of the research procedure. Symbols of the metropolitan areas—see Table 1.

Next, the delimitation and classification of land cover types in terms of their urban character were provided. For each land cover type, a value M (the degree of belonging to the urban landscape) was established, showing the urban–rural character of the type. Next, the urban landscape intensity index (ULII) was calculated on three levels of research (top-down approach): ULII value for each metropolitan area (to compare the degree of urban intensity of all studied areas), for each municipality within metropolitan areas (to shows the spatial differentiation and structure of landscape in each metropolitan area), and for geometric basic units—hexagons (to indicate regularities in the metropolitan areas in more detail). After obtaining the index, all metropolitan areas were compared in terms of the spatial distribution of urban, rural and transitional landscapes.

2.1. Study Area

The study area includes: The Metropolitan Area of Warsaw (MAW), the Upper Silesia-Zagłębie Metropolis (US-ZM), the Kraków Metropolitan Area (KMA), the Poznan Metropolitan Area (PMA), the Metropolitan Area of Gdańsk-Gdynia-Sopot (MAG-G-S), the Wrocław Metropolitan Association (WMA) and the Łódź Metropolitan Area (LMA) and the Ruhr Metropolis (RM, Germany) (Figure 2, Table 1). The majority of the studied metropolitan areas are monocentric agglomerations. Only US-ZM and RM have a different spatial character (polycentric). Furthermore, both US-ZM and RM have an industrial (mining) origin, similar polycentric character and high population density (the value of the population density index: 904 and 1163) [38].

Table 1. Basic characteristics of analyzed metropolitan areas.

Symbol	Name	Legal Act/Document	Population [mln]	Number of Municipalities	Area [km^2]
MAW	Metropolitan Area of Warsaw	development strategy	3.08 [1]	72	6206
US-ZM	Upper Silesia-Zagłębie Metropolis	legally established metropolitan association	2.30 [2]	41	2545
KMA	Kraków Metropolitan Area	spatial development plan	1.51 [3]	51	4060
PMA	Poznań Metropolitan Area	spatial development plan	1.33 [4]	45	6198
MAG-G-S	Metropolitan Area Gdańsk-Gdynia-Sopot	Municipalities association, draft act	1.50 [5]	56	6667
WMA	Wrocław Metropolitan Association	spatial development plan/municipalities association	1.20 [6]	44	6719
LMA	Łódź Metropolitan Area	development strategy/spatial development plan	1.10 [7]	28	2496
RM	Ruhr Metropolis	Municipalities association	5.10 [8]	33	4385

[1] Strategy of development of the Metropolitan Area of Warsaw until 2030, 2015. [2] https://metropoliagzm.pl. [3] Krakow Metropolitan Area in 2011–2015, 2016. [4] Delimitation of Poznan Metropolitan Area, WBPP (http://www.wbpp.poznan.pl/opracowania/POM/POM.html). [5] www.metropoliagdansk.pl. [6] Spatial development plan of Lower Silesian voivodship. [7] Strategy of development of Łódź Metropolitan Area 2020+. [8] https://metropole.ruhr.

In this article, administrative criterion of delimitation of metropolitan area was adapted, based on diverseofficial documents (Table 1) [39–46]. The borders adopted in official documents delimit very large areas. It must be emphasized that according to these administrative bases, metropolitan areas may also include rural communities. The structure of the types of communities in Polish metropolitan areas is presented in Figure 3. Analyzing this characteristic, only in US-ZM in Poland urban municipalities dominates.

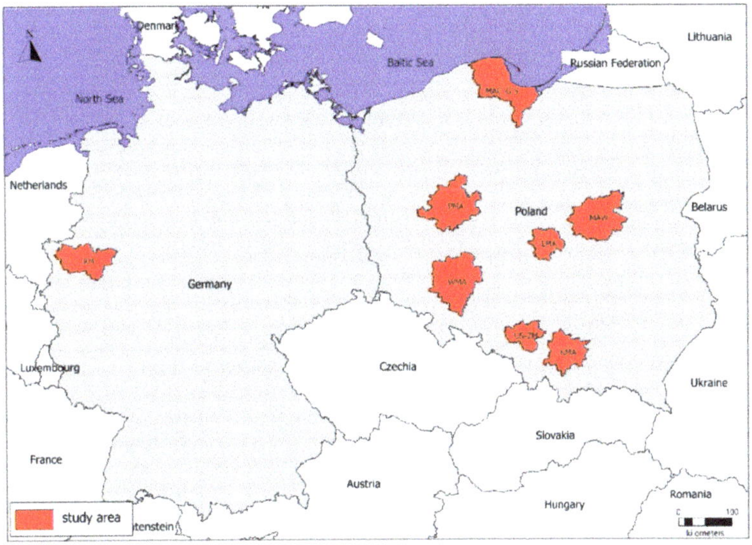

Figure 2. Study area. Symbols of the metropolitan areas—see Table 1.

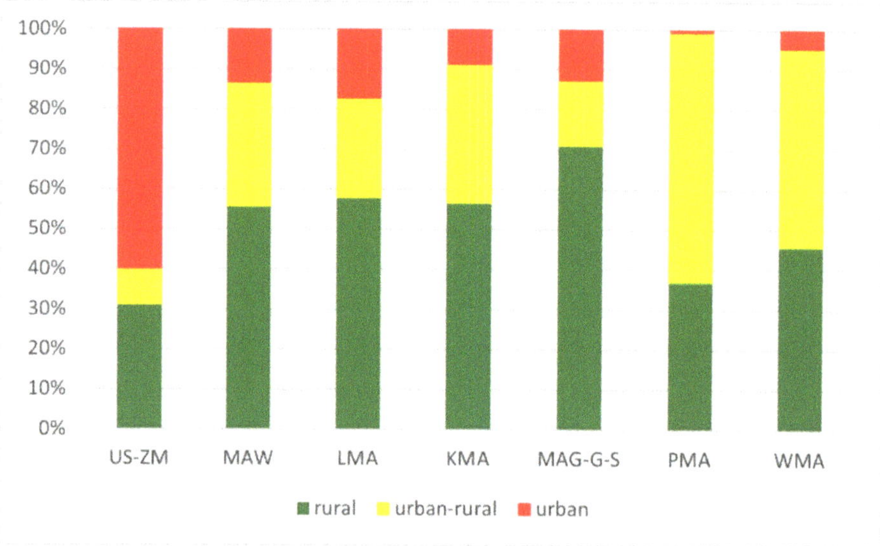

Figure 3. Percentage of administrative types of communities in Polish metropolitan areas.

2.2. Materials

In the presented study, the Corine Land Cover (CLC) database from 2018, Chief Geodesy and Cartography Office (GUGiK), and OpenGeodata of Nordrhein-West walen data were used. The analyses were conducted using the MapInfo Pro 17.0.

It must be emphasized that studies relying on CLC data have certain limitations, such as the detailed nature of the input data and a high degree of generalization. The CLC is a far more useful resource for small-scale studies, but it is a less reliable tool for analyses conducted on a larger scale [47].

The CLC has its own nomenclature that is consistent over the databases from different years and for the whole area. The nomenclature consists of 3 hierarchical levels, which are called standard levels. There are five main classes of land cover (level 1 and 2):

1. Artificial surfaces—built-up areas, including residential areas, commercial and industrial areas, mines, and green urban spaces.
2. Agricultural areas—arable land, permanent crops, meadows, pastures, and land principally occupied by agriculture with significant areas of natural vegetation.
3. Forests and semi-natural areas—forests, shrubs and open areas with little or no vegetation.
4. Wetlands—inland marshes, peatbogs, salt marshes, salines, and intertidal flats.
5. Water bodies—inland waters and marine waters.

Different land-use types within each of the above groups are specified at the second and third levels of the inventory. In the presented study, level 3 was chosen (see Table 2 in Section 2.3). The CLC uses a Minimum Mapping Unit (MMU) of 25 hectares (ha) for areal phenomena and a minimum width of 100 m for linear phenomena. The CLC vector layers were downloaded from the Pan-European datasets of Copernicus Land Monitoring Services.

Table 2. The values of the degree of belonging of land cover to the urban landscape.

Land Cover according to CLC—Level 3	Degree of Belonging of Land Cover to the Urban Landscape (M)
111 Continuous urban fabric	1.00
112 Discontinuous urban fabric	0.69
121 Industrial or commercial units	0.97
122 Road and rail networks and associated land	0.82
123 Port areas	0.82
124 Airports	0.82
131 Mineral extraction sites	0.64
132 Dump sites	0.64
133 Construction sites	0.64
141 Green urban areas	0.68
142 Sport and leisure facilities	0.66
211 Non-irrigated arable land	0.09
212 Permanently irrigated land	0.09
213 Rice fields	0.09
221 Vineyards	0.26
222 Fruit trees and berry plantations	0.26
223 Olive groves	0.26
231 Pastures	0.09
241 Annual crops associated with permanent crops	0.26
242 Complex cultivation patterns	0.26
243 Land principally occupied by agriculture, with significant areas of natural vegetation	0.09
244 Agro-forestry areas	0.09
311 Broad-leaved forest	0.20
312 Coniferous forest	0.20
313 Mixed forest	0.20
321 Natural grasslands	0.35
322 Moors and heathland	0.35
323 Sclerophyllous vegetation	0.35
324 Transitional woodland-shrub	0.35
331 Beaches, dunes, sands	0.35
332 Bare rocks	0.35
333 Sparsely vegetated areas	0.35
334 Burnt areas	0.35
335 Glaciers and perpetual snow	0.35
411 Inland marshes	0.35
412 Peat bogs	0.35
421 Salt marshes	0.35
422 Salines	0.35
423 Intertidal flats	0.35
511 Water courses	0.20
512 Water bodies	0.20
521 Coastal lagoons	0.20
522 Estuaries	0.20
523 Sea and ocean	0.20

2.3. Methods

In the spatial analyses of the intensity of urban landscapes, understood in this case as land cover, the essential step is the delimitation and classification of land cover types in terms of their urban character. The problem was what types of land cover can be described as urban and what types as rural. Furthermore, how to evaluate them to describe the urban landscape intensity? Furthermore, there are some transitional landscapes, which are difficult to be definitely assigned to urban or rural character. Therefore, the authors decided to use a fuzzy theory. Fuzzy logic is applied in the cases of complex, unclear phenomena and can define and present unspecified, uncertain information [48]. This theory was used by Biłozor et al. [25] for identification of transitional zone between urban and rural area. In this work, a classification of 24 forms of space use was proposed and the value of the degree of belonging of land cover to the urban landscape (M) has been defined for each of them. These values were adopted and adjusted to different types of land cover (Table 2). The value of the M is set between 0 and 1, where 0 indicates rural land cover, and 1 urban land cover.

The value of belonging of land cover to the urban landscape was the basis of the Urban Landscape Intensity Index (ULII). This is represented by the following equation:

$$ULII = \sum_{i=1}^{n} fiMi \quad (1)$$

ULII—Urban Landscape Intensity Index, *fi*—share of *i*-th form of land use in the area of the metropolis/municipality/hexagon, *Mi*—the degree of belonging of land cover to the urban landscape, *n*—number of forms of land cover

Analyses of the obtained ULII were conducted at three levels of research: metropolitan area, municipality and hexagon (the area of hexagon was set as 4 km^2). After calculation this index, at level 2 (municipalities) and 3 (hexagons), the values of ULII were divided and classified in terms of landscape types using classification proposed by Matuszewska and Będkowski [26]:

- The urban type of landscape includes units where $0.5 < \text{ULII} \leq 1.0$;
- The transitional type of landscape includes unit types where $0.3 \leq \text{ULII} \leq 0.5$;
- The rural type of landscape includes units where $0 \leq \text{ULII} < 0.3$.

3. Results

3.1. Metropolitan Areas Level

The values of ULII calculated for each metropolitan area are low (Figure 4). The lowest urban intensity was observed for PMA and WMA (0.18). It is interesting to note that the Warsaw metropolitan area is not the most urban one in Poland. The highest values of ULII are achieved by metropolitan areas which are similar in terms of function and structure, RM (0.34) and US-ZM (0.33). MAW was in third place with much lower ULII value (0.26). The results of ULII show a connection with population density (Figure 5).

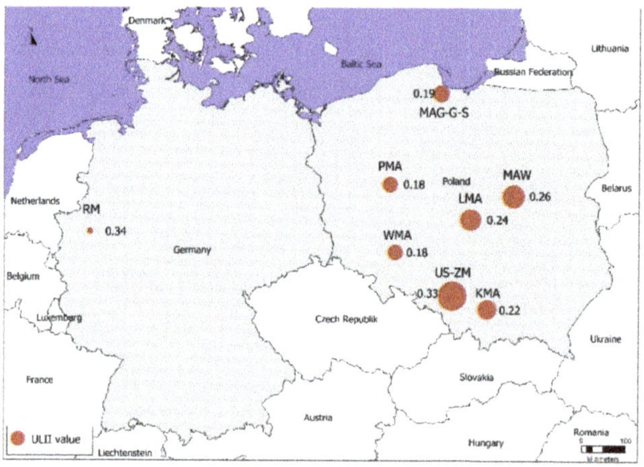

Figure 4. The value of urban landscape intensity indicator (ULII) in the metropolitan areas.

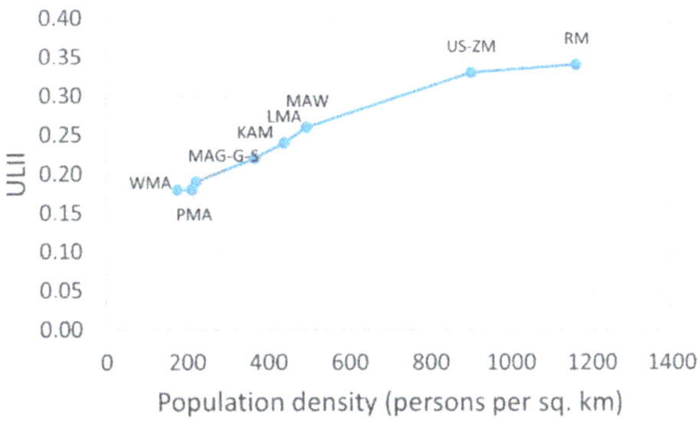

Figure 5. Relation between the value of ULII and population density.

3.2. Municipalities Level

The values of ULII at the level of municipalities show spatial differentiation. The highest ULII for a municipality varies between 0.46 (in WMA) and 0.66 (in US-ZM). It is worth noticing that in the case of the metropolitan areas with the highest ULII, i.e., US-ZM, RM and MAW, the municipalities with the highest ULII value (Świętochłowice for US-ZM, Herne for RM and Piastów for MAW) are not the biggest or main cities of the metropolitan areas (Supplementary Materials, Figure S1).

The medians of ULII in particular metropolitan areas vary between 0.17 (MAG-G-S, PMA, WMA) and 0.29 (USZM, RM) (Figure 6). The median is also high in the case of MAW (0.24). These values of median are typical of rural types of landscape. The values of ULII in the interquartile range in US-ZM, LMA, MAW and RM are typical of rural and transitional types of landscape. In other metropolitan areas, all values of ULII in the interquartile range are typical of rural types of landscape.

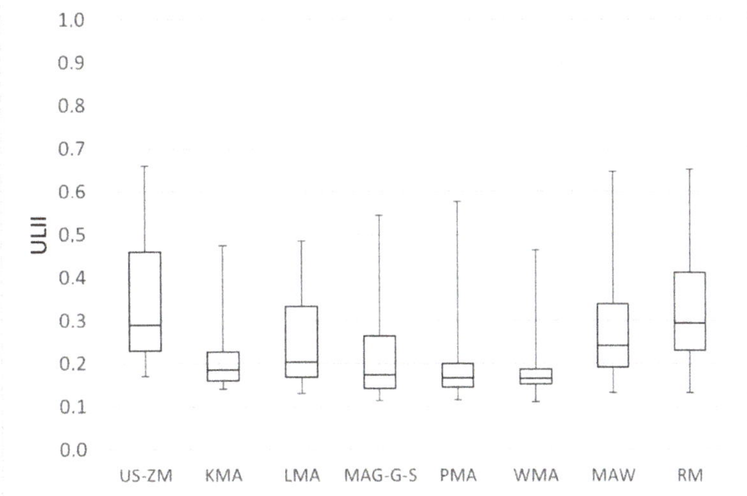

Figure 6. The distribution of the values of ULII on the municipalities level.

The values of ULII in the interquartile range are low. The distribution of values of ULII is characterized by right asymmetry, which means that the municipalities with lower values of ULII are dominant. The highest ULII were noted in US-ZM (0.66—Świętochłowice),

RM (0.65—Herne) and MAW (0.65—Piastów). Municipalities characterised by urban landscape (ULII > 0.5) are located in five metropolitan areas: MAW (7 municipalities: Piastów, Legionowo, Pruszków, Mińsk, Mazowiecki, Ząbki and Warszawa), RM (6 municipalities: Herne, Gelsenkirche, Oberhausen, Bochum, Essen and Duisburg), US-ZM (5 municipalities: Świętochłowice, Chorzów, Siemianowice Śląskie, Sosnowiec and Bytom), MAG-G-S (4 municipalities: Malbork, Pruszków Gdański, Puck and Tczew), and PMA (Luboń and Kościan) (Figure S1). The other municipalities are typical of transitional and rural types of landscape. In turn, the lowest ULII are 0.11–0.14. Only US-ZM stands alone in terms of having the lowest ULII value (0.17 in Zbrosławice) (Figure S1). These low values of ULII occur in municipalities located in the outskirts of metropolitan areas. The lowest values of ULII (0.11) are in Jordanów Śląski and Domaniów, in WMA, and in Lichnowy, in MAG-G-S (Figure S1).

The highest differentiation of ULII in the interquartile range occurs in RM, MAW and US-ZM. A large differentiation also occurs in LMA and MAG-G-S. The other metropolitan areas are characterized by higher similarities of ULII values in the interquartile range. The highest values of ULII in the interquartile range occur in municipalities in US-ZM and RM. MAW also stands out on this score.

In the spatial analysis of the ULII distribution for municipalities, RM and US-ZM clearly stand out. For both areas, the municipalities with high values of ULII are arranged in a wide strip with an east–west direction. The values of ULII are diversified. In addition, in MAW the municipalities are differentiated but the structure is concentric with stellar features. The highest values of ULII are located beyond the center. Other metropolitan areas also have a concentric character. For KMA, LMA and WMA, the highest ULII is present in the main cities. In WMA, the main city (Wrocław) is dominated by municipalities of a low value of ULII with the exception of Oleśnica and Oława (Figure S1). PMA and OMG-G-S also have a concentric character, but the highest values of ULII are in a few small cities spread across the area (Figure 7).

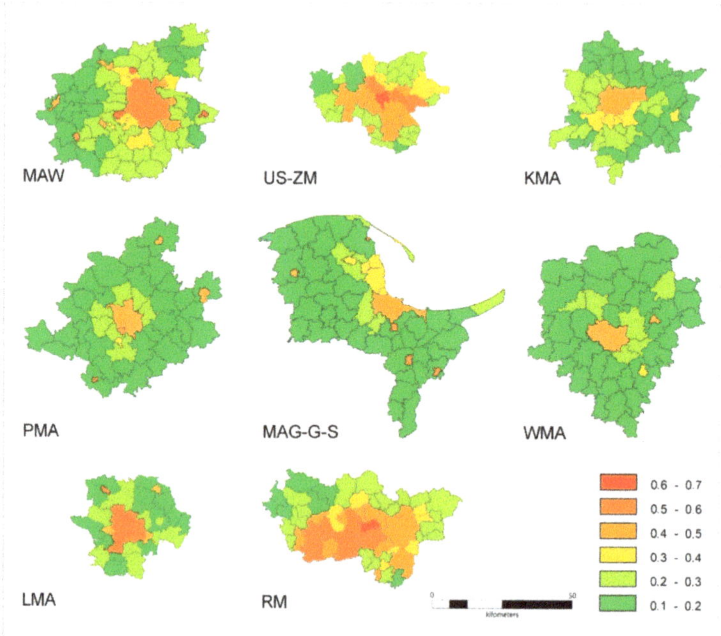

Figure 7. The values of ULII in the municipalities.

The spatial structure of the urban–rural area is differentiated (Figure 8). It should be emphasized that the urban type occupies small parts of metropolitan areas. The largest area of the urban type is present in RM and takes up only 18.74% of the space. Urban type municipalities form a core of 6 municipalities there (Bochum, Herne, Gelsenkirchen, Essen, Oberhausen, Duisburg) (Figure S1). US-ZM has a similar structure of types of municipalities. The urban core (9.11%) is also formed by several cities (Sosnowiec, Siemianowice Śląskie, Świętochłowice, Chorzów and Bytom, Figure S1). In the case of MAW, the urban areas of Warsaw city are almost surrounded by transitional types. In PMA, MAG-G-S, KMA, WMA and LMA, the biggest cities are of the transitional type. Moreover, in KMA, LMA and WMA the urban type of municipality is not present at all. WMA, PMA and MAG-G-S have the most rural areas (above 90% of this type). Between municipalities which form wide rural areas, there are also a few urban ones. The main city (WMA) or the main city with the neighboring municipalities (KMA and LMA) form a transition zone surrounded by a rural zone with individual municipalities of the transitional type.

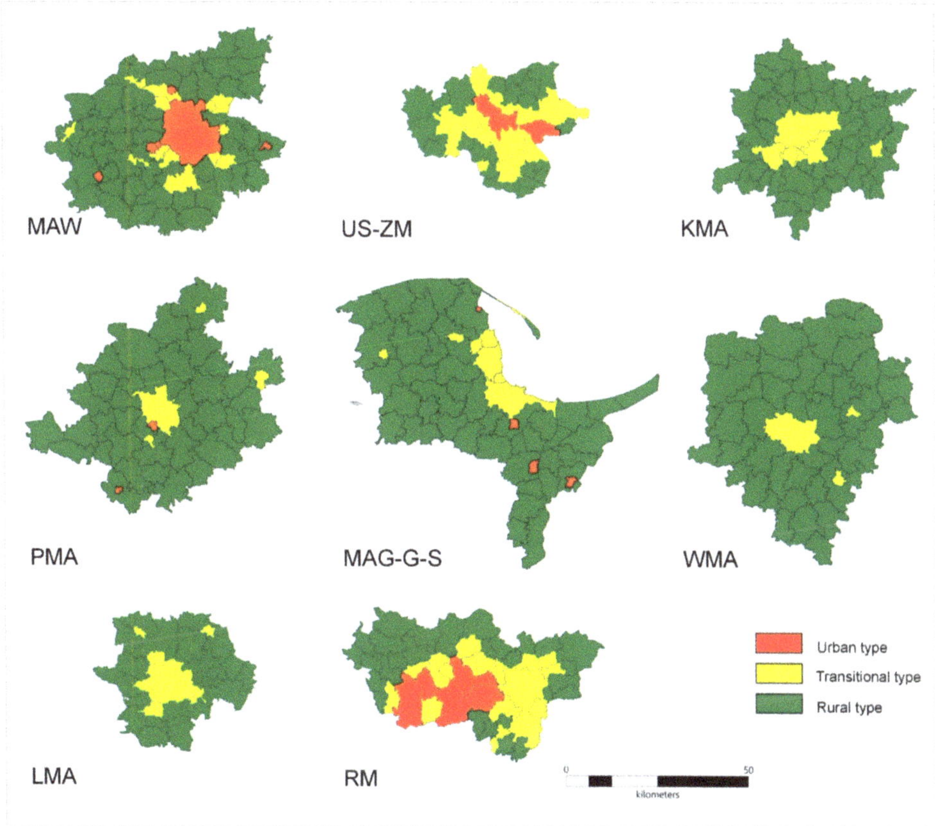

Figure 8. Types of landscape in municipalities in accordance with ULII.

3.3. Hexagon Level

The ULII for hexagons gives more detailed results. Medians of ULII in particular metropolitan areas vary between 0.15 and 0.25 (Figure 9). These median values are typical of rural types of landscape. The median in US-ZM is higher than in other metropolitan areas (by 0.05 than in MAW and by 0.1 than in PMA). Simultaneously, this is the same value as in RM. The values of ULII in the interquartile range only in US-ZM and RM are typical of rural and transitional types of landscapes. In other metropolitan areas, all values of ULII in the interquartile range are typical of rural types of landscape.

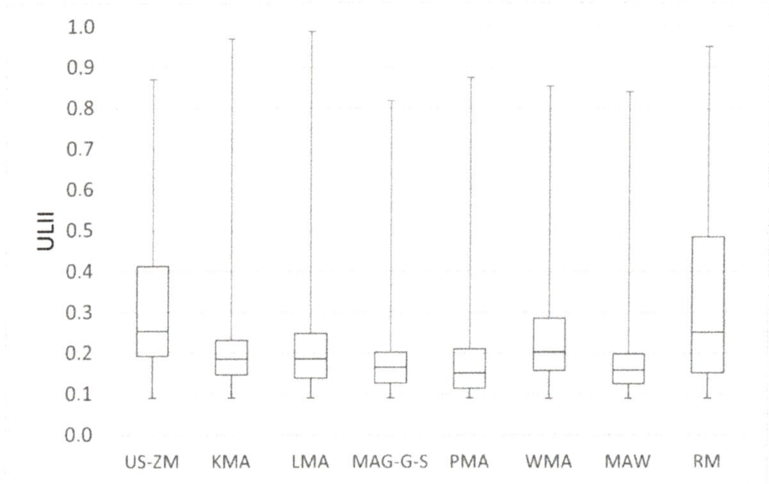

Figure 9. The distribution of the values of ULII on the hexagons level.

The values of ULII in the interquartile range are low. The distribution of values of ULII is characterized by right asymmetry, which means that the hexagons with lower values of ULII are dominant. The highest ULII were noted in LMA (0.99) and KMA (0.97). These hexagons occur in midtown in Łodź, where continuous urban fabric and road and rail networks and associated land dominate, and in Kraków Nowa Huta where there are industrial or commercial units. Simultaneously, these metropolitan areas are characterised by the highest differentiation of ULII. In the case of RM, the maximal ULII is 0.95 in Essen, where industrial or commercial units dominate and continuous and discontinuous urban fabric, road and rail networks and associated land, and green urban areas occur. This value is higher than in US-ZM, where the maximal ULII is 0.87 in Katowice-Bogucice, where industrial or commercial units occur, but there are also broad-leaved forests. In turn, the lowest ULII in all metropolitan areas is the same (0.09). This concerns the outskirts of metropolitan areas where non-irrigated arable land predominates and, in some parts, pastures occur.

The highest differentiation of ULII in the interquartile range occurs in RM, US-ZM and MAW. The other metropolitan areas are characterized by a higher similarity of ULII values in the interquartile range. The highest values of ULII in the interquartile range occur in RM and US-ZM. MAW also stands out on this score. RM is characterized by the highest differentiation of ULII in the interquartile range, which is similar to US-ZM. The maximal values of ULII in the interquartile range in RM are higher than in US-ZM. However, the lowest values of ULII in the interquartile range are lower than in US-ZM.

Spatial analyses show the concentration of high values of ULII in the center of the metropolitan area in KMA, PMA, LMA, WMA (Figure 10). In KMA, the structure of types of hexagons is evenly concentric with a few exceptions. The intensity pattern of the ULII related to the layout of the main roads is visible there. PMA forms a concentric character, stretching to the east (with Swarzędz and Kościan, Figure S1) with numerous small isolated, spotted, scattered high value units and a stronger satellite formed by Gniezno (Figure S1). In LMA there is a clear concentration of the highest values of the ULII in the center of Łódź. High values are also reported in Pabianice, Zgierz and Koluszki (Figure S1), forming a triangular system related to the railway line. In WMA, the main city (Wroclaw) is surrounded by municipalities with a low value of ULII. A few small isolated, spotted, scattered high value units are present, and a small satellite is formed by Oleśnica (Figure S1). In the case of MAW, the structure is stellar and high ULII values are present along the main roads leaving the city. In MAG-G-S, a concentration of high values of ULII is visible along the coast on the line Gdansk-Gdynia-Sopot, with Gdynia taking on a more concentric character, and Gdansk having a more even structure. US-ZM and RM urban areas form a wide strip in an east-west direction. In US-ZM, the core is more compact, while in RM the highest value of ULII is more dispersed.

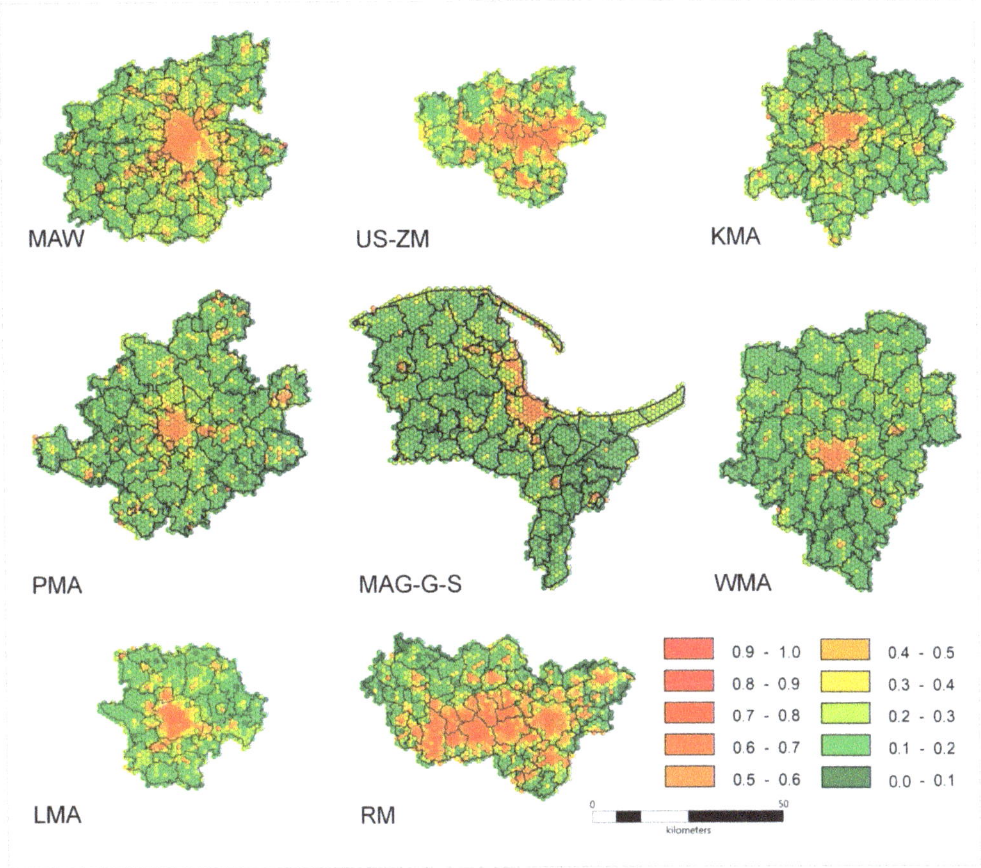

Figure 10. The values of ULII in the hexagons.

Spatial analyses of the urban–rural type show the domination of the rural type in most of the research areas (Figures 11 and 12). This domination is especially visible in WMA, where the urban type is concentrated in a small area of the main city with a thin border of the transitional type. Outside the main city, the urban and transitional types are present in a few small spots. A similar situation is observed in MAG-G-S, with urban types located in three main cities and single, dispersed, isolated urban hexagons located in the whole area. Often, they are related to tourist functions (Łeba, Władysławowo, Jastarnia, Kuźnica, Chałupy). It is significant that, administratively, Chałupy and Kuźnica are villages. A smaller difference in proportions between urban and rural areas is visible in KMA, LMA and PMA. In PMA, the urban type is concentrated in Poznań, but there are also numerous urban and transitional units dispersed all over the area with a more concentrated spot in Gniezno. In KMA, the urban type of Krakow is surrounded by the transitional type. In the east, Bochnia has a characteristic concentric arrangement of urban and transitional types. In LMA, the urban type located in Lodz has a wide border of transitional units. Urban units are also present in Pabianice, Zgierz and the more isolated Koluszki. For US-ZM, a compact east-west urban core spills over into Tychy, Knurów, Ożarowice and Tarnowskie Góry (Figure S1). The largest share of urban type units is present in RM. The urban core forms a wide strip of units located in several municipalities between rivers: Emsher and Ruhr (i.e., Dortmund, Bochum, Essen, Oberhausen, Herne, Gelsenkirchen and Gladbeck, Duisburg). Numerous urban units are also present in Hamm, Hagen and Marl (Figure S1).

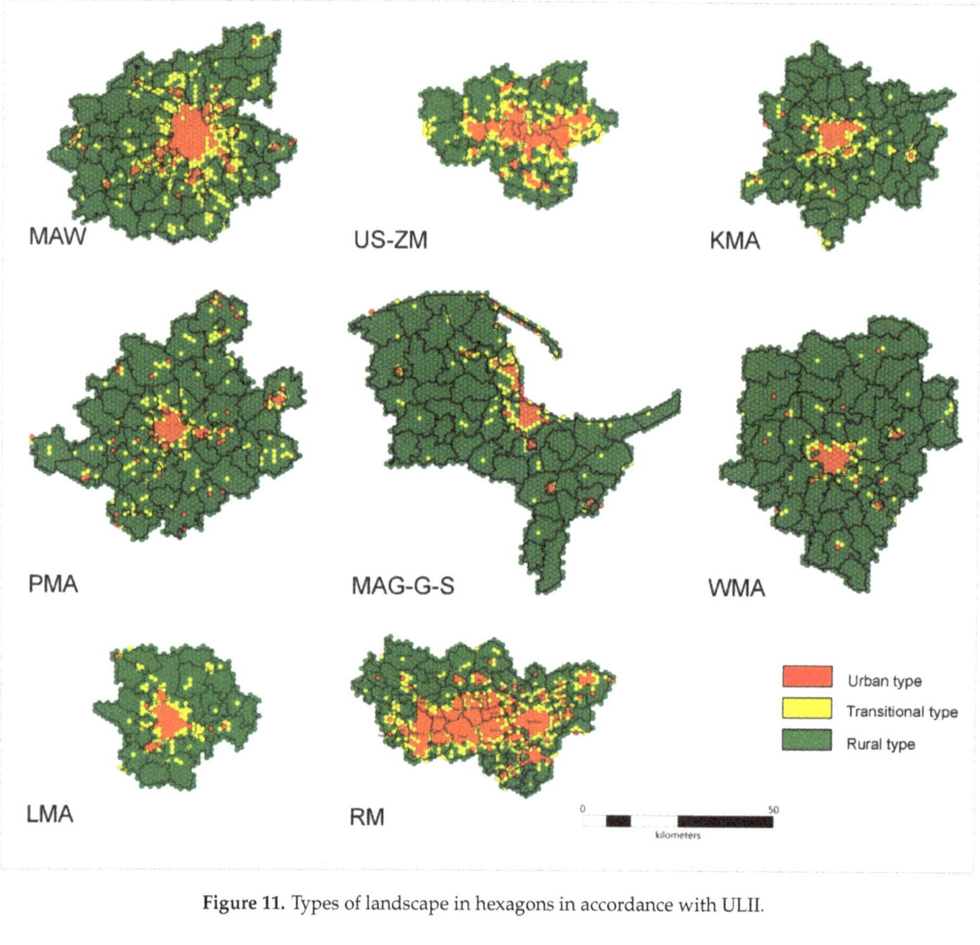

Figure 11. Types of landscape in hexagons in accordance with ULII.

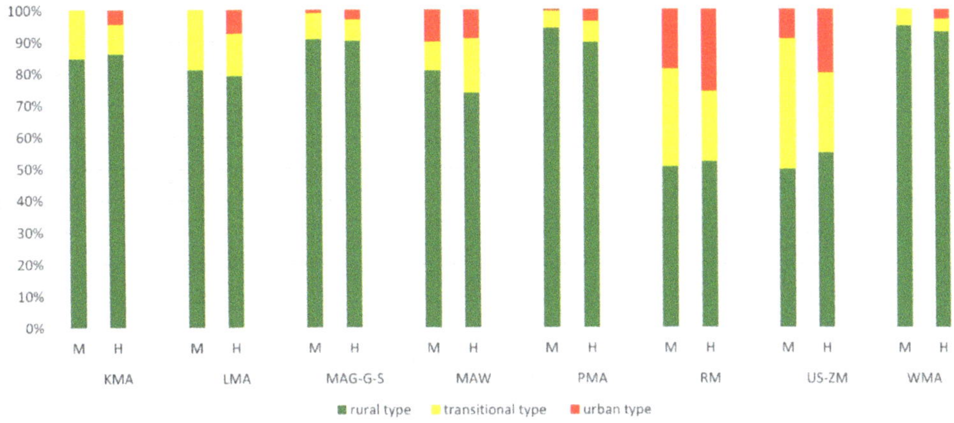

Figure 12. Landscape types in municipalities (M) and hexagons (H).

4. Discussion

In this paper, the intensity of the urban landscape for seven metropolitan areas in Poland was assessed. Additionally, the landscape of RM in Germany was examined as a comparative area for US-ZM—the only polycentric agglomeration in Poland. The use of the ULII index showed that the landscape of the US-ZM differs from the landscape of other metropolitan areas in Poland (higher average values of ULII). At the same time, the landscape of the US-ZM shows some similarities to the landscape of RM (similar values of ULII). Moreover, MAW also shows some similarities to the US-ZM in terms of landscape diversity. What is more, the study showed that urban landscapes occur only in the central zones of the metropolitan areas that were delineated on the basis of official documents. In turn, rural and transitional landscapes predominate as far as percentage of their surface is concerned.

The similarity of the US-ZM and RM landscapes may result from the similar factors that influenced development of these metropolitan areas. In both cases, the mining industry was a factor in the location and development of cities [49]. Moreover, the spatial nature of the agglomeration, polycentric in the case of US-ZM and RM, and monocentric in the case of other metropolitan areas, has an influence on the landscape differentiation and similarities which occur [50]. The value of ULII could also be influenced by a degree of industrialization. High values of ULII occur in former industrial districts such as Nowa Huta (Kraków), Bałuty, Fabryczna (Łódź), Psie Pole, Kowale (Wrocław) and Młyniska (Gdańsk).

The value of ULII could be influenced by many different factors. The initial comparison of the spatial distribution of ULII indicates that among these factors transport network systems and their density, and the spatial organization of metropolitan areas (polycentric or monocentric) can be distinguished [51]. The occurrence of raw materials is also of great importance as they stimulate the economic development of metropolitan areas (this is in the case of US-ZM and RM) [52], and their primary and secondary functions [53,54]. Furthermore, the natural environmental conditions are crucial [55]. They may be favorable (hydrographical network, access to the sea, favorable topoclimatic conditions) or unfavorable (high mountain areas, boggy areas, proximity of protected areas) for the spatial development of metropolitan areas [56–58]. The crucial factor that should be taken into account when interpreting the value of ULII is the process of changes on the border of metropolitan areas in official administrative documents. This process is connected with decisions about incorporating particular municipalities that are of different types: rural, urban or urban–rural. Furthermore, economic potential [59], spatial policy and land prices [60–62] may have an influence as well. Many aspects of urbanization are interpreted through globalization [63].

Nevertheless, the most visible aspect is the relations between the values of ULII and transport network systems and industrial districts. However, this issue requires further recognition in our study area through the statistical analysis of the correlation that occurs between these variables and the construction of a regression model that would allow the occurring relationships to be quantified. Such analyses were conducted by Conway and Hackworth in the Greater Toronto Area [34]. A detailed analysis of landscape urbanization in the context of driving forces in our study area will be the subject of a separate study by the authors. Nevertheless, some basic conclusions could be drawn. The analysis of the hexagons level reveals a star-shaped pattern of the urban landscape in MAW. Additionally, in US-ZM and RM the intensity of the urban landscape is visible in a linear pattern. This is due to the emergence of the urban sprawl process along the transport network which is typical of other metropolitan areas [64–66]. In MAW, the urban landscape is visible along the A2 motorway, and the S8 and S7 expressways along the east-west and north-south routes. The main railway lines to the capital run parallel to the road network. In US-ZM and RM, the intensity of the urban landscape increases along the east-west line, which is connected with the railway between Gliwice and Mysłowice and the A4 motorway in Poland, and the A2 and A42 motorways in Germany. The relationship between the development of the road network and the processes of suburbanization has been confirmed by Garcia-Lopez [67] who, based on the example of Barcelona, stated that the construction of new road infrastructure generates urban sprawl processes. Baum-Snow [68] puts forward the thesis in a similar way, examining the relationship between suburbanization and road development in the United States. Moreover, it is worth noting that the ULII is influenced by the types of urban coverage, which include residential buildings related to urban sprawl processes, as well as industrial areas and large-surface communication junctions. Thus, the transport network influences the level of ULII both directly and indirectly.

Similar research has already been carried out in Olsztyn and Sieradz (Poland) [25,26]. The areas classified as urban in Olsztyn cover only 24% of the city's area. In turn, in Sieradz non-urban areas also prevail. The percentage of agricultural areas within the boundaries of metropolitan areas in Poland was studied by Sroka et al. [36]. Their study shows that 49.9% of the areas administratively belonging to metropolitan areas are occupied by farms. Similar comparative studies conducted for RM and US-ZM showed that agricultural areas cover 39.2% of the RM area and 42.7% of the USZM [38]. These values are lower than the results presented in this paper (81% of seven metropolitan areas in Poland are covered with rural landscapes, 52% in RM, and 55% in US-ZM, respectively). However, the differences result from the different classifications of rural landscapes. In this paper, rural landscape includes arable land, pastures and forests. Hence, this landscape type in our paper has a broader scope. The applied approach allowed the assessment that only in the US-ZM and RM is it possible to distinguish the core of a metropolitan area, in which urban landscapes have the largest percentage among all the analyzed areas. A comparison of landscape types in municipalities and hexagons shows differences in the accuracy of the results. In accordance with the adopted criteria, there are no urban landscapes in KMA, LMA and WMA at the level of municipalities, while at the level of hexagons their occurrence is visible. On average, the share of rural and transitional landscapes is higher at the municipality level than at the hexagon level. Hexagons illustrate with greater accuracy the spatial distribution of landscape types enabling the justification of the existing layout of urban landscapes and further spatial analyses, e.g., related to the study of urban development in terms of driving forces. Moreover, research at the hexagon level is objective and based on mathematical logic, as opposed to the level of boundaries of municipalities and metropolitan areas, whose scope is determined administratively.

As already mentioned in the introduction, many authors use the CORINE database for landscape analysis [30–32]. Nevertheless, it is worth noting that despite many advantages, this database has some limitations [69]. However, this database is imperfect in small-scale studies, while in landscape analysis it is an appropriate source [33]. Admittedly, there are many other databases that may be used in such studies. For instance, in Europe, higher resolutions have Urban Atlas maps—a project developed as part of Global Monitoring for Environment and Security. Nevertheless, maps are created only for selected areas around large cities, so they do not cover the entire EU territory [69]. Another example of the increase in the spatial resolution are the "fourth-level" CLC maps, however, they were prepared only in some countries and classifications used in them are inconsistent with each other. This paper confirms the statement that the CORINE database is useful in landscape analyses, both in relation to administrative units (municipalities, metropolitan areas) and geometric basic fields. It is a particularly reliable source in studies of urban areas undergoing constant change [31]. It must be emphasized that the value of ULII could be influenced by many different factors e.g., different types of a dataset, map scale, type of basic units (their size and shape). While using ULII these limitations must be taken into account.

5. Conclusions

In this paper the intensity of the urban landscape for seven metropolitan areas in Poland and one in Germany was assessed. The analyses were conducted at three levels of detail: the metropolitan area level, municipalities level and hexagons level. The conducted research allows the following conclusions to be drawn:

1. The landscape of the US-ZM differs from the landscape of other metropolitan areas in Poland and shows some similarities to the RM landscape. These areas are polycentric agglomerations. Nevertheless, the landscape of MAW shows some similarities to the US-ZM one despite the fact that this area is a monocentric agglomeration. This may be connected with the capital function of Warszawa that has an influence on the urbanization level.
2. Rural and transitional landscapes predominate within the metropolitan areas delineated according to official documents and administrative affiliation, while the typical urban landscape is characteristic only of the central zones of metropolitan areas. This conclusion may be considered controversial because it proves that in determining the features of a metropolitan area the landscape approach differs from the formal and legal approaches and also based on area and demographic criteria.
3. Basic landscape analysis on an administrative level gives a distorted spatial picture. Therefore, the use of basic units (in this case, hexagons) for the assessment of metropolitan landscape diversity is recommended. Only by using this analysis can all the complexity and diversity of the internal structure of the metropolitan areas landscape be shown.

The conducted studies give new research prospects concerning landscape analysis in metropolitan areas such as driving forces. Furthermore, the changes in ULII value in particular time periods may be also analyzed. Nevertheless, it must be emphasized that the same dataset must be used to make the results comparable. It is connected with the fact that the value of ULII could be influenced by many different factors such as different types of dataset, map scale, type of basic units. Monitoring landscape changes based on the CLC update and the use of the indicators presented in this article, and predicting the directions of landscape transformation as a result of driving forces are some of the most important challenges of contemporary interdisciplinary research. The results of the research may be useful for regional policy, e.g., in the preparation of urban planning documents and spatial development strategies.

Supplementary Materials: The following are available online at https://www.mdpi.com/2073-445X/10/1/51/s1, Figure S1: Administrative division of metropolitan areas.

Author Contributions: Conceptualization, U.M.-P.; methodology, A.Ż.-S., K.P.-K. and M.S.; software, J.N.; formal analysis, A.Ż.-S., K.P.-K. and M.S.; investigation, A.Ż.-S., K.P.-K. and M.S.; resources,

J.N.; writing—original draft preparation, U.M.-P., A.Ż.-S., K.P.-K. and M.S. All authors have read and agreed to the published version of the manuscript.

Funding: This research received no external funding.

Institutional Review Board Statement: Not applicable.

Informed Consent Statement: Not applicable.

Data Availability Statement: Publicly available datasets were analyzed in this study. This data can be found here: Corine Land Cover: https://land.copernicus.eu/pan-european/corine-land-cover, Chief Geodesy and Cartography Office (GUGiK) data: https://mapy.geoportal.gov.pl/imap/Imgp_2.html, OpenGeodata of Nord-rhein-Westwalen data: https://www.opengeodata.nrw.de/produkte/ (accessed on 19 November 2020).

Acknowledgments: We gratefully acknowledge three anonymous reviewers for their constructive comments.

Conflicts of Interest: The authors declare no conflict of interest.

References

1. Antrop, M. Background concepts for integrated landscape analysis. *Agric. Ecosyst. Environ.* **2000**, *77*, 17–28. [CrossRef]
2. Pacione, M. *Urban Geography: A Global Perspective*; Routledge: London, UK, 2001.
3. Antrop, M. Landscape change and the urbanization process in Europe. *Landsc. Urban Plan.* **2004**, *67*, 9–26. [CrossRef]
4. Seto, K.C.; Güneralp, B.; Hutyra, L.R. Global forecasts of urban expansion to 2030 and direct impacts on biodiversity and carbon pools. *Proc. Natl. Acad. Sci. USA* **2012**, *109*, 16083–16088. [CrossRef] [PubMed]
5. Champion, T. Urbanization, suburbanisation, counterurbanisation and reurbanisation. In *Handbook of Urban Studies*; Paddison, R., Ed.; Sage: London, UK, 2001; pp. 143–161.
6. Hennig, E.I.; Schwick, C.; Soukup, T.; Orlitová, E.; Kienast, F.; Jaeger, J.A. Multi-scale analysis of urban sprawl in Europe: Towards a European de-sprawling strategy. *Land Use Policy* **2015**, *49*, 483–498. [CrossRef]
7. Chmielewski, T.J. *Systemy Krajobrazowe. Struktura, Funkcjonowanie, Planowanie*; PWN: Warszawa, Poland, 2012; pp. 1–408.
8. Breuste, J.H. Decision making, planning and design for the conservation of indigenous vegetation within urban development. *Landsc. Urban Plan.* **2004**, *68*, 439–452. [CrossRef]
9. Enache, C.; Popa, A. Decoding the Urban Landscape. *Postmodern Openings* **2019**, *10*, 272–279. [CrossRef]
10. Zuzańska-Żyśko, E. *Procesy Metropolizacji. Teoria i Praktyka*; PWN: Warszawa, Poland, 2016; pp. 1–432.
11. Wheeler, S. The Evolution of Built Landscapes in Metropolitan Regions. *J. Plan. Educ. Res.* **2008**, *27*, 400–416. [CrossRef]
12. Bosselmann, P.; Ruggeri, D. *The Future Metropolitan Landscape*; Pratt Institute University of California, Berkeley College of Environmental Design: Berkeley, CA, USA, 2019.
13. MacKenzie, A. *Understanding Metropolitan Landscapes*; Routledge: London, UK, 2020.
14. Beunen, R.; Van Ark, R.; Van der Valk, A.; Jaarsma, R. Planning nature conservation in Dutch metropolitan landscapes. In *Planning Metropolitan Landscapes—Concepts, Demands, Approaches*; Tress, G., Tress, B., Harms, B., Smeets, P., Van der Valk, A., Eds.; DELTA Series 4; DELTA: Wageningen, The Netherlands, 2004; pp. 166–177.
15. Kijowska, J.; Kijowski, A.; Rączkowski, W. Politics and landscape change in Poland 1940–2000. In *Landscape Through the Lens Aerial Photographs and Historic Environment*; Cowley, D.C., Standring, R.A., Abicht, M.J., Eds.; Oxbow Books: Oxford/Oakville, UK, 2010; pp. 155–166.
16. Qureshi, S.; Hamstead, Z.; Spyra, M.; Qureshi, S. Beyond urban–rural dichotomies: Measuring urbanisation degrees in central European landscapes using the technomass as an explicit indicator. *Ecol. Indic.* **2019**, *96*, 466–476. [CrossRef]
17. Dadashpoor, H.; Azizi, P.; Moghadasi, M. Land use change, urbanization, and change in landscape pattern in a metropolitan area. *Sci. Total Environ.* **2019**, *655*, 707–719. [CrossRef]
18. Aguilera, F.; Valenzuela, L.M.; Botequilha-Leitão, A. Landscape metrics in the analysis of urban land use patterns: A case study in a Spanish metropolitan area. *Landsc. Urban Plan.* **2011**, *99*, 226–238. [CrossRef]
19. Reis, J.P.; Silva, E.A.; Pinho, P. Spatial metrics to study urban patterns in growing and shrinking cities. *Urban Geogr.* **2015**, *37*, 246–271. [CrossRef]
20. Tate, C.; Cuffney, T.F.; McMahon, G.; Giddings, E.M.P. *Use of an Urban Intensity Index to Assess Urban Effects on Streams in Three Contrasting Environmental Settings*; American Fisheries Society Symposium: Bethesda, MD, USA, 2005; Volume 47, pp. 291–315.
21. McMahon, G.; Cuffney, T.F. Quantifying urban intensity in drainage basins for assessing stream ecological conditions. *JAWRA J. Am. Water Resour. Assoc.* **2000**, *36*, 1247–1261. [CrossRef]
22. Li, G.; Sun, S.; Fang, C. The varying driving forces of urban expansion in China: Insights from a spatial-temporal analysis. *Landsc. Urban Plan.* **2018**, *174*, 63–77. [CrossRef]
23. Weng, Y.-C. Spatiotemporal changes of landscape pattern in response to urbanization. *Landsc. Urban Plan.* **2007**, *81*, 341–353. [CrossRef]

24. Huang, B.; Zhang, L.; Wu, B. Spatiotemporal analysis of rural–urban land conversion. *Int. J. Geogr. Inf. Sci.* **2009**, *23*, 379–398. [CrossRef]
25. Biłozor, A.; Czyża, S.; Bajerowski, T. Identification and Location of a Transitional Zone between an Urban and a Rural Area Using Fuzzy Set Theory, CLC, and HRL Data. *Sustainability* **2019**, *11*, 7014. [CrossRef]
26. Matuszewska, M.; Będkowski, K.M. Analysis of the development of the city Sieradz based on the interpretation of aerial imagery and valorisation of the space using elements of fuzzy sets theory. *Acta Scientiarum Polonorum Administratio Locorum* **2019**, *18*, 381–395. [CrossRef]
27. Taubenböck, H.; Gerten, C.; Rusche, K.; Siedentop, S.; Wurm, M. Patterns of Eastern European urbanisation in the mirror of Western trends—Convergent, unique or hybrid? *Environ. Plan. B Urban Anal. City Sci.* **2019**, *46*, 1206–1225. [CrossRef]
28. Marciniak, M. Wybrane aspekty oceny krajobrazu obszarów metropolitalnych. *Biul. Pol. Akad. Nauk. Kom. Przestrz. Zagospod. Kraju* **2015**, *259*, 159–174.
29. Kamiński, J.; Podgórska, A. Krajobraz w poznańskim obszarze metropolitalnym–delimitacja, typologia i zasady ochrony. *Metropolitan. Przegląd Nauk.* **2016**, *2*, 46–63.
30. Gómez, J.M.N.; Lousada, S.; Velarde, J.G.G.; Castanho, R.A.; Loures, L. Land-Use Changes in the Canary Archipelago Using the CORINE Data: A Retrospective Analysis. *Land* **2020**, *9*, 232. [CrossRef]
31. Cieślak, I.; Biłozor, A.; Szuniewicz, K. The Use of the CORINE Land Cover (CLC) Database for Analyzing Urban Sprawl. *Remote. Sens.* **2020**, *12*, 282. [CrossRef]
32. Solecka, I.; Sylla, M.; Świąder, M. Urban Sprawl Impact on Farmland Conversion in Suburban Area of Wroclaw, Poland. *IOP Conf. Ser. Mater. Sci. Eng.* **2017**, *245*, 072002. [CrossRef]
33. Benito, P.R.; Cuevas, J.A.; Bravo de la Parra, R.; Prieto, F.; Garcia del Barrio, J.M.; Zavala, M.A. Land use change in a Mediterranean metropolitan region and its periphery: Assessment of conservation policies through CLC and Markov model. *For. Syst.* **2010**, *19*, 315–328.
34. Conway, T.M.; Hackworth, J. Urban pattern and land cover variation in the greater Toronto area. *Can. Geogr./Le Géographe Can.* **2007**, *51*, 43–57. [CrossRef]
35. Biłozor, A. Application of Fuzzy Logic to the Identification and Localization of the Fringe Areas of the Cityand the Village. *Acta Sci. Pol. –Adm. Locorum* **2005**, *4*, 37–51. (In Polish)
36. Sroka, W.; Mikolajczyk, J.; Wojewodzic, T.; Kwoczynska, B. Agricultural Land vs. Urbanisation in Chosen Polish Metropolitan Areas: A Spatial Analysis Based on Regression Trees. *Sustainability* **2018**, *10*, 837. [CrossRef]
37. Smętkowski, M.; Jałowiecki, B.; Gorzelak, G. *Obszary Metropolitalne w Polsce: Problemy Rozwojowe i Delimitacja*; Uniwersytet Warszawski: Warszawa, Poland, 2018; pp. 1–98.
38. Sroka, W.; Pölling, B. The Potential and Significance of Urban Agriculture on the Basis of the Ruhr Metropolis and the Upper Silesian Metropolis. *Probl. World Agric.* **2015**, *15*, 180–193.
39. ISAP. The Council of Ministers Regulation of 26 June 2017 on the Establishment of the Following in Silesian Voivodship of the Metropolitan Association Called upper Silesia-Zagłębie Metropolis (Journal of Laws of 2017, Item 1290). Available online: http://isap.sejm.gov.pl/isap.nsf/DocDetails.xsp?id=WDU20170001290 (accessed on 19 November 2020).
40. Strategy of Development of the Metropolitan Area of Warsaw until 2030, Strategia Rozwoju Obszaru Metropolitalnego Warszawy do Roku 2030. Available online: http://omw.um.warszawa.pl/wp-content/uploads/2015/09/Strategia-Rozwoju-Obszaru-Metropolitalnego.pdf (accessed on 19 November 2020).
41. Resolution, No. XV/174/03 of 22 December 2003 on the Adoption of the Spatial Development Plan for the Małopolska Voivodship. Available online: https://bip.malopolska.pl/umwm,a,748635,uchwala-nr-xv17403-sejmiku-wojewodztwa-malopolskiego-z-dnia-22-grudnia-2003-r-w-sprawie-uchwalenia-p.html (accessed on 19 November 2020).
42. Spatial Development Plan for the Poznań Metropolitan Area, Attachment No 2.0 to Resolution No. V/70/19 of the Sejmik of the Wielkopolska Region of 25 March 2019. Available online: https://bip.umww.pl/artykuly/2824952/pliki/20190328121632_70.pdf (accessed on 19 November 2020).
43. Draft Metropolitan act of Metropolitan Association for Pomerania Voivodship. Available online: https://www.metropoliagdansk.pl/upload/files/66uch.pdf (accessed on 19 November 2020).
44. Spatial Development Plan of Lower Silesian Voivodship. Available online: https://www.irt.wroc.pl/strona-128-plan_zagospodarowania_przestrzennego.html (accessed on 19 November 2020).
45. Strategy of Development of Łódź Metropolitan Area 2020+. Annex to Resolution No 2/2016 of the Association Council of the Łódź Metropolitan Area of 24 March 2016. Available online: http://lom.lodz.pl/wp-content/uploads/Strategia-Rozwoju-%C5%81OM-2020-_-24.03.20161.pdf (accessed on 19 November 2020).
46. Gesetz zur Stärkung der Regionalen und Interkommunalen Zusammenarbeit der Städte, Gemeinden und Kreise in Nordrhein-Westfalen Normstruktur. Available online: https://recht.nrw.de/lmi/owa/br_vbl_detail_text?anw_nr=6&vd_id=3669&vd_back=N96&sg=0&menu=1 (accessed on 19 November 2020).
47. Jucha, W.; Kroczak, R. Comparison of land use data from the CORINE Land Cover program with data obtained from orthophotomaps. In *Socio-Economic and Spatial Transformation of Regional Structures*; Kaczmarska, E., Raźniak, P., Eds.; Oficyna Wydawnicza AFM: Kraków, Poland, 2014; pp. 123–136. (In Polish)
48. Zwick, R.; Zimmermann, H.-J. Fuzzy Set Theory and Its Applications. *Am. J. Psychol.* **1993**, *106*, 304. [CrossRef]

49. Pierenkemper, T. Entrepreneurs in Heavy Industry: Upper Silesia and the Westphalian Ruhr Region, 1852 to 1913. *Bus. Hist. Rev.* **1979**, *53*, 65–78. [CrossRef]
50. Lan, F.; Da, H.; Wen, H.; Wang, Y. Spatial Structure Evolution of Urban Agglomerations and Its Driving Factors in Mainland China: From the Monocentric to the Polycentric Dimension. *Sustainability* **2019**, *11*, 610. [CrossRef]
51. Clark, W.A.V. Monocentric to polycentric: New urban forms and old paradigms. In *A Companion to the City*; Bridge, G., Watson, S., Eds.; Blackwell: Oxford, UK, 2000; pp. 141–154.
52. Gollin, D.; Jedwab, R.; Vollrath, D. Urbanization with and without industrialization. *J. Econ. Growth* **2016**, *21*, 35–70. [CrossRef]
53. Scott, A.J. Resurgent Metropolis: Economy, Society and Urbanization in an Interconnected World. *Int. J. Urban Reg. Res.* **2008**, *32*, 548–564. [CrossRef]
54. Pukowiec-Kurda, K.; Myga-Piątek, U.; Rahmonov, O. The landscape profile method as a new tool for sustainable urban planning. *J. Environ. Plan. Manag.* **2019**, *62*, 2548–2566. [CrossRef]
55. Ebeke, C.H.; Etoundi, S.M.N. The Effects of Natural Resources on Urbanization, Concentration, and Living Standards in Africa. *World Dev.* **2017**, *96*, 408–417. [CrossRef]
56. Miller, R.B.; Small, C. Cities from space: Potential applications of remote sensing in urban environmental research and policy. *Environ. Sci. Policy* **2003**, *6*, 129–137. [CrossRef]
57. Maciukenaite, J.; Povilaitienė, I. The Role of the River in the City Centre and its Identity. *J. Sustain. Arch. Civ. Eng.* **2013**, *4*, 33–41. [CrossRef]
58. Kline, J.D.; Moses, A.; Alig, R.J. Integrating Urbanization into Landscape-level Ecological Assessments. *Ecosystems* **2001**, *4*, 3–18. [CrossRef]
59. Piao, Y.; Ma, K.M. Economic driving force of urban built-up area expansion in Beijing. *Nat. Res. Econ. China* **2006**, *7*, 34–37. (In Chinese)
60. Wu, Y.; Zhang, X.; Skitmore, M.; Song, Y.; Hui, E.C. Industrial land price and its impact on urban growth: A Chinese case study. *Land Use Policy* **2014**, *36*, 199–209. [CrossRef]
61. Ayazli, I.E. An Empirical Study Investigating the Relationship between Land Prices and Urban Geometry. *ISPRS Int. J. Geo-Information* **2019**, *8*, 457. [CrossRef]
62. Burian, J.; Macků, K.; Zimmermannová, J.; Kočvarová, B. Spatio-Temporal Changes and Dependencies of Land Prices: A Case Study of the City of Olomouc. *Sustainability* **2018**, *10*, 4831. [CrossRef]
63. Wei, Y.D.; Ye, X. Urbanization, urban land expansion and environmental change in China. *Stoch. Environ. Res. Risk Assess.* **2014**, *28*, 757–765. [CrossRef]
64. García-Palomares, J.C. Urban sprawl and travel to work: The case of the metropolitan area of Madrid. *J. Transp. Geogr.* **2010**, *18*, 197–213. [CrossRef]
65. Duranton, G.; Turner, M.A. The Fundamental Law of Road Congestion: Evidence from US Cities. *Am. Econ. Rev.* **2011**, *101*, 2616–2652. [CrossRef]
66. Li, C.; Gao, X.; He, B.-J.; Wu, J.; Wu, K. Coupling Coordination Relationships between Urban-industrial Land Use Efficiency and Accessibility of Highway Networks: Evidence from Beijing-Tianjin-Hebei Urban Agglomeration, China. *Sustainability* **2019**, *11*, 1446. [CrossRef]
67. Garcia-López, M.-A. Urban spatial structure, suburbanization and transportation in Barcelona. *J. Urban Econ.* **2012**, *72*, 176–190. [CrossRef]
68. Baum-Snow, N. Did Highways Cause Suburbanization? *Q. J. Econ.* **2007**, *122*, 775–805. [CrossRef]
69. Śleszyński, P.; Gibas, P.; Sudra, P. The Problem of Mismatch between the CORINE Land Cover Data Classification and the Development of Settlement in Poland. *Remote Sens.* **2020**, *12*, 2253. [CrossRef]

land

MDPI

Article

Macroeconomic Perspective on Urban Sprawl: A Multidimensional Approach in Poland

Piotr Lityński and Artur Hołuj *

Department of Spatial Management, Faculty of Economy and Public Administration, Cracow University of Economics, 27 Rakowicka St., 31-510 Cracow, Poland; litynskp@uek.krakow.pl
* Correspondence: holuja@uek.krakow.pl

Abstract: There are important relationships between the urban sprawl process and economic growth. They are usually expressed through spatial relations and changes taking place in the local, regional and national economy. The temporal and spatial dimension, including dispersed location, are the determinants of development and economic growth. Therefore, the urban sprawl phenomenon and the related location, hypothetically conditioning economic growth, should be subject to macroeconomic research. The article examines how urban sprawl affects the national budget and national economic growth. Unlike many studies where urban sprawl is studied by scattering the population around cities, we undertake more complex examination using buildings' location. Urban sprawl, as we understand it, is a spontaneous spread of buildings around cities. To assess the spontaneity, we use a grid of squares with a side of 500 m. The squares are used to calculate the morphological indicators of urban sprawl. Therefore, quantified urban sprawl is one side of the equation; on the other side are macroeconomic variables. In this way, we examine the relationship between urban sprawl and the national budget and economic growth of Poland. The conclusions obtained are, e.g., urban sprawl does not have a negative effect on the national economy and the budget. This is a different conclusion from those thus far. There are also different conclusions on the regional level. Based on the research results, we formulate recommendations for national economic policy and spatial policy.

Keywords: urban sprawl; macroeconomics; externalities; budget; spatial policy; economic policy

Citation: Lityński, P.; Hołuj, A. Macroeconomic Perspective on Urban Sprawl: A Multidimensional Approach in Poland. *Land* **2021**, *10*, 116. https://doi.org/10.3390/land10020116

Academic Editor: Fabrizio Battisti

Received: 23 December 2020
Accepted: 23 January 2021
Published: 26 January 2021

1. Introduction

Urban sprawl has been a phenomenon discussed in literature since the middle of the last century [1]. This phenomenon is usually identified with a chaotic reorganization of spatial structure of suburban communes with a simultaneous low impact of local spatial policy [2]. The result of this process is the dispersion of buildings in the suburban area, the edge of the city, the metropolitan area or functional area of the core city [3]. Scattering of buildings is associated with the composition of specific, negatively valued morphological features, which include: low building density, lack of spatial continuity, lack of concentration of buildings, lack of buildings' clustering, spatial decentralization, polynuclearity, and lack of mixed land use, lack of proximity [4]. Moreover, it is important from the cognitive point of view to describe the factors that trigger urban sprawl. Despite the fact that the intensity, distribution or parity will have an individual impact on the selected space, some similarities and features are noticeable in them [5]. The urban sprawl process is influenced by local, spatial, historical and economic conditions. Therefore, several groups of related factors can be distinguished. A commonly identified factor in urban sprawl is the process of social development, which is the source of favorable population changes in the city. The reason for the indicated changes is the natural increase and intensified migration to the urban area [6]. The indicated process of social development is reflected in the local and regional economy. Therefore, another group of urban sprawl factors is distinguished in micro and macroeconomic terms. In the first case, the main role is played by: household preferences in terms of place of residence, as well as financial possibilities and constraints.

The macroeconomic context of urban sprawl related to a country's economic growth usually comes down to the distribution of the economic base in the region. Another group of factors is related to the form and decision-making possibilities of entities from the real and regulatory sphere of the economy. The importance of territorial entities is usually reduced to the role played by spatial policy entities in a given country. The authorities at the central level create the general framework (legislation, rules of conduct, etc.) necessary to conduct spatial policy (development policy), while the municipal authorities are responsible for indicating the destination and spatial development at the local level (location policy, investment policy in the field of real estate trading, etc.). Independence, equity and compliance with the guidelines for making decisions by the indicated entities are important here. Also, resistance to the influence of other actors operating in the space for which the generally available and currently binding standards and regulations are not satisfactory. The last important group of urban sprawl factors is closely related to the suburban local investment and speculative conditions of land, including geographic and environmental conditions as well as technical infrastructure.

In parallel to the discussion on the specificity of urban sprawl, the economic consequences of urban sprawl have already been discussed [7]. The economic costs are first and foremost, the increase of public expenses covering construction, extension, and maintenance of infrastructure and public services, extended commuting distance; the consumption of energy and market-related negative influence on the city center [8–12]. The negative impact of sprawl on household budgets is associated mainly with the extension of the use of cars. Economic consequences of the phenomenon manifested in the increased number of vehicles per household, which led to an increase in expenditure on: fuel, insurance, maintenance of vehicles, the periodic purchase of new vehicles [13]. There are also conclusions in the literature about the potential economic benefits of urban sprawl. O'Toole (2009) has argued that sprawl, thanks to the automobile, gave rise to affordable suburban neighborhoods for middle-class and lower-class individuals [14]. The studies cited are micro- or mesoeconomic assessments, while research on macroeconomic consequences is rarely undertaken. Therefore, we can pose the question of how urban sprawl affects the national economy, its growth or the condition of the state budget?

When discussing the national macroeconomic perspective, economic growth is usually disaggregated into dimensions: sectoral, temporal and spatial [15]. The impact of urban sprawl is, therefore, a component of economic growth in both spatial and temporal dimensions. This influence is expressed in spatial relations and changes taking place in the local, regional and national economy. Mankiw et al. they indicate that the location and the environment understood as anthropogenic conditions are a significant determinant of economic growth [16]. The location, especially the scattered one, is an inherent feature of urban sprawl. Therefore, the urban sprawl phenomenon, while theoretically determining economic growth, should be subject to macroeconomic research. On the other hand, the surroundings of the location extend the discussion on the macroeconomic effects of urban sprawl to include externalities. Research and analyzes presented in the literature on external effects focuses on the dependencies caused in local and regional systems and at the institutional level, in the absence of analysis concerning a macroeconomic perspective [17–21]. In the light of this literature, the externalities of urban sprawl justify the formulation of public policy, including economic and spatial, influencing this phenomenon. Apart from a few exceptions, the macroeconomic urban sprawl and its relation with public policy are not widely undertaken in Poland [22].

Taking into account the current state of knowledge, and in particular the gap in the macroeconomic assessment of urban sprawl, the aim of the study is to identify the costs and benefits of urban sprawl at the level of the national economy. As the macroeconomic perspective of urban sprawl permeates the literature with the assessment of externalities, and then with the undertaken spatial policy, the theoretical part explains: the essence of urban sprawl externalities, its macroeconomic costs and benefits, and the instruments of influencing sprawl. Two hypotheses were proposed in the research part: H(1): Urban sprawl adversely affects the financial situation of the national budget; H(2): Urban sprawl slows down the growth rate of the local and national economy. However, the summary presents the results of the research against the background of the literature and formulates recommendations for public policy.

2. Urban Sprawl Externalities as the Basis for Public Intervention

2.1. The Essence of Urban Sprawl Externalities

Since the middle of the last century, cities have been subject to many dynamic and multidirectional changes, i.e., urbanization, metropolisation, decentralization, revitalization, re-urbanization [23]. This evolution of spatial structures is a derivative of pro-or anti-urban behavior and views [24,25]: from urban concentration, through suburbanization to non-metropolitan changes [26]. The variety of trends and phases of development triggers various external effects, which are the premises for state interventionism, including spatial policy.

Economists argue that externalities are generated when an individual imposes costs on or brings benefits to others, and they have no economic incentive to accept these costs or benefits [27–30]. As a result, we observe positive and negative externalities, generated during consumption or at the stage of production itself. Externalities can, therefore, be generated during spatial management, i.e., during the aforementioned trends in city transformations. Therefore, we identify the complexity of the process, magnified by the variety of causes that result in a given effect. The observed reasons are mainly problems with identifying the ownership rights of public and private goods, as well as complementary and substitute goods. Moreover, in identifying externalities, the form of using goods and benefiting from them is important. Therefore, it is reasonable to conclude that when externalities occur, state intervention will not always be needed. Externalities leading to socially acceptable costs will not be a prerequisite for formulating public policy. We must remember that state interventions also generate externalities [31].

Externalities of urban sprawl should be equated with the effects of private and public activities. In regard to private entities, externalities occur when the location of the development of one side improves or worsens the situation of another party, however, until the party generating external effects does not bear the costs of its activities. On the other hand, in regard to public entities, externalities are associated with the improvement or deterioration of the situation of entities operating in space, due to the low degree of control of spatial processes by the local government sector. The behavior of the local government sector entities is sometimes completely uncontrolled, unconscious, or even irrational.

Moreover, public intervention is used in the preferential treatment of certain entities. It is a derivative of the activities performed in the field of providing public goods. Preferential solutions come down to displacing market mechanisms by administrative determination of the costs of production factors, prices and methods of distribution of certain goods [32]. Externalities of urban sprawl are also identified in the area of the emerging relationships between individual users of suburban space. As a consequence, we can see externalities being to a large extent the aftermath of the implemented spatial policy. These effects have specific forms, such as: external benefits and costs; monetary and non-monetary, i.e., technological; unilateral and multilateral, and private transferable and public non-transferable [33].

2.2. Macroeconomic Costs and Benefits of Urban Sprawl

Special attention should be paid to the losses and spatial benefits resulting from the urban sprawl process. Spatial losses are reduced (incurred damage) or unattained (lost opportunities) social benefits from the use of resources and values of space. Moreover, we observe that the phenomenon of transferring some of the costs resulting from space development processes to third parties, usually residents, is a common process. The current and future prosperity of the local community, understood as the quality of life in space, is depreciated. The relationships between the private and social optimum also seem to be important, because they can generate measures of pure intervention.

The proposed approach to the problem does not eliminate other, non-market concepts of losses, e.g., natural or ecological losses. As a result, irreversible damage to the natural environment occurs. This damage is covered by direct market reactions, and spatial benefits are equated with positive effects. They occur simultaneously with the launch of the intervention process limiting the sources of space depreciation. Losses always accompany diminished natural resources. Losses and spatial benefits in the theory of economics are included as external costs and benefits. On the other hand, the use of the values of the environment with a simultaneous downward trend in creating new sources of benefit is expressed through environmental external costs. Taking into account macroeconomic conditions, direct losses can be presented as negative spatial consequences expressed as a reduced environmental potential and indirect ones resulting from spatial development, where there is a division into social and economic losses.

Urban sprawl causes a number of threats, in the natural, social and cultural area. These threats are characterized by a varied scale and form of externalities closely related to the local conditions of socio-economic processes. The lack of urban development planning can be equated with the unplanned and successive growth of urban areas [34]. The observed direct effect of this are monofunctional spatial structures embedded in discontinuous functional and territorial systems. Therefore, the question arises whether urban sprawl processes should not be treated as one of the stages in the development of highly urbanized space? The scientific literature of the last decades has ambiguously interpreted the existing settlement patterns [35]. The space in which man functions is characterized by various features, and one of them is resistance. The resistance of space should be identified primarily with the costs of transport, the costs of moving people, goods, information services. Common internal migrations, their dynamics and the method of analysis are also important.

There are numerous theories discussing demographic and spatial patterns, current and historical trends, or even conflicting interpretations of them. In almost each of them, the problems of the core city, suburbs and rural areas are assessed [36,37]. Typically, these studies focus on the "target" space where relatively most external effects of the urban sprawl process are identified. Depending on various local factors, also on the availability of input data or sometimes research interests, the analysis also covers circular migrations and the morphology of rural areas [38,39]. Some studies show that counter-urbanization has entered a new phase characterized by a new destination of the observed flows [40]. It is characterized by a significant differentiation in individual countries in terms of causes, intensity of trends, etc. It can also be considered in a variety of perspectives, from local, to regional and national [41,42]. The process of counter-urbanization has been observed since the 1960s in Western Europe [43,44] and the USA [45,46]. Its identification sometimes requires interdisciplinary knowledge, as evidenced by research carried out in the disciplines of geography, economics or sociology. One interpretation of this concept points to a faster growth of suburban areas than urban areas. We see a similar situation in non-metropolitan and metropolitan spaces. Ref [42] Contrurbanization generates diversified circulation of resources in the city-village and village-city space. However, the most frequently indicated in the research is the migration of the population towards the areas characterized by a lower concentration [47]. There are many reasons for the migration of people to rural areas, it can be generally stated that it is a search for better living conditions, closer to nature [41,48]. Nevertheless, urban migrants (related to counter-urbanization) in a sense give up their permanent relationship with the city. They choose areas further away from the city/metropolitan core. They give up the current comfort of the impact of the urban fabric, its resources and amenities. They are usually wealthy and not of retirement age [49]. Considering the migration theme, they should be considered as voluntary migrations. In this context, we can observe a clear difference between the processes of counter-urbanization and suburbanization, where in the case of the latter, along with the migratory movements of the urban population to rural areas, important professional, infrastructural, educational, etc. Ultimately, most researchers have both valid and incomplete research results because the structure chosen has not received sufficient attention [50]. Because urban sprawl can take many forms, the effects it generates may have a diverse structure, reach and audience. Burchell et al. (2005) indicate that urban sprawl processes are characterized by an unfavorable macroeconomic impact [51]. Irreversible loss of agricultural land generates negative externalities that are transferred to the neighboring agricultural activities, where productivity, quality of crops, etc. will be limited. There will be problems in the use of mechanized agricultural technologies, including the necessary biological and chemical care of plants. Over time, restrictions are set for other farmers, limiting their functioning. And farmers will limit production for fear that this process will not be profitable. The pressure generated by the users of residential areas in the aftermath of urban sprawl will also increase: various conflicts of interest, for example in the case of the need for water necessary for functioning in housing and agriculture. Burchell et al. (2005) also indicate that the loss of the agricultural function is not compensated for by the amount of a one-off purchase and sale transaction of agricultural land for housing development. There are also studies with different conclusions, which indicate that urban sprawl does not have a negative impact on the national economy [25,52,53]. However, in the case of the local level, not very resistant to dynamic changes or economic fluctuations, the situation seems to be more complicated. Economic growth is the result of various stimulating and destabilizing conditions, causing the state of the local economic crisis [52,54]. In this context, one should bear in mind the course of business cycles and the inevitable economic crises. The recent crisis in southern Europe should undoubtedly be mentioned as a painful example of this. Its most important factors include a very high level of investment risk, social polarization and an economy that intensively exploits natural environment resources [55]. The crisis in Spain caused a direct fracture of the housing bubble resulting from failures in spatial planning and irrational land management [56,57]. As additional reasons for the state of affairs, one should apply to the management method, the implementation of spatial and economic data and relations with local communities (e.g., social guarantees). Spatial planning and development issues have been discussed earlier, it is worth paying attention to the attitudes and beliefs of the local population (including social participation). It is the residents, their attitudes and respect for and commitment to the available space that a lot depends on [58]. There is also a question, whether they will be willing to stay and function in the city, or will they be forced to move to the suburban area to look for the desired social conditions (both will result in financial losses [59]). The observed evolution of the rural spatial structure generates socio-economic changes in local and regional systems. Rural restructuring, identified with its urbanization, was originally attributed to a positive assessment of this process. However, as research shows, urbanization of rural areas also triggers undesirable phenomena causing depreciation in the field of technical infrastructure and spatial structure of villages. There are also unfavorable depopulation phenomena and negative changes in socio-economic structures. The result of the restructuring of rural areas in Poland was a significant increase in the dispersion of buildings and the development of rural areas with large-scale production and housing units [60]. Rural areas are highly diversified in terms of their concentration and compactness, functions, morphology or the pace of urbanization. They have various natural, landscape, cultural conditions, etc. It should also be noted that thanks to the restructuring of rural areas in many countries, e.g., in Poland, Spain, agricultural areas within the metropolitan area gained new economic and tourist functions, etc., and the lifestyle of their inhabitants was changed. However, it cannot be unequivocally concluded that these changes completely restructured the village [61]. Moreover, how much influence will the neoliberal economy implemented in many countries have on urbanization processes? Its effects often have very serious consequences affecting planning and functioning in space [55,62].

2.3. Instruments for Influencing Urban Sprawl

The basic instrument for influencing urban sprawl is an efficient spatial policy, which is based on the legal and administrative requirements of the commune and the state. It is a regulatory approach serving to create the legal as well as regulatory and organizational basis affecting urban sprawl. Such instruments include: acts and regulations, standards, land use plans, geodetic divisions, zoning, construction and town planning standards and various administrative decisions of a permitting, mandating, prohibiting and penal character. On the basis of formal and legal documents, various coercive measures as well as incentive or discouraging measures are generated, affecting directly or indirectly on space users, investors, economic entities, etc. The indicated spatial policy is based primarily on operational, action, structure, development, sectoral plans, pilot; local and regional strategies of development, infrastructure projects, etc.

Land development can be indirectly influenced by operational economic instruments, i.e., discounts, taxes and subsidies. The forms of direct aid take various forms, including [63]: preferential land prices, loans or loan guarantees, differentiation of the property tax rate, subsidizing infrastructure investments, transport, etc. Another group of effective instruments are solutions for material profiling of space. The authorities, especially the local ones, may influence spatial decentralization by the appropriate location of technical infrastructure and social infrastructure. The potential advantage of location is a common argument, especially when making decisions on residential investments, carried out by private individuals and developers. There are instruments of "soft" impact on urban sprawl, but their effectiveness is not always predictable. These are various activities of entities, development agencies, corporations, development banks, etc. operating on the basis of delegating the powers of public authorities in the field of spatial management. It will also be important to influence the behavior of space users based on urban marketing and various information materials; promotion, location ads, built "genius loci", outdoor meetings, promotional gadgets, campaigns in social media, etc.

The aforementioned territorial entities have various causative powers, as well as various impacts on the development of space and urban sprawl processes. This fact results from the heterogeneity of the instruments of influence assigned to them. The scope of their duties is subject to arrangements with government and local government administration bodies (in accordance with the relevant provisions of the Code of Administrative Procedure). In most cases, planning studies at the local level are subject to supervisory control conducted by representatives of the regional government (sometimes representatives of the central administration). Moreover, the decisions of local and regional commissions of appeal may be the subject of a matter before the substantively competent administrative courts. The spatial development law systems in Europe are also varied in terms of the way public authorities are coordinated at the local level. The basic difference comes down to the formula of this coordination which accepts, inter alia, the form of planning documents, legal acts or agreements.

When implementing spatial policy, we must take into account the needs of the local community, including social ones. Some scientific studies provide a valuable analysis of the issues of social exclusion and threats identified in urban structures [58]. Residents have the right to actively participate in the space management process, and their role definitely grows when their legal interests are violated.

The use of operational and "soft" instruments influencing urban sprawl in spatial policy depends on the planning system in the country, for example: British, Germanic, Napoleonic, Scandinavian and Central and Eastern European countries. As Newman and Thornley [64] indicate, these systems are built independently, however, in accordance with applicable standards and generally recognized good practices. Therefore, they are universal and open to local planning challenges. Following the standards of planning procedures, the current form of development is subject to legal protection, necessary verification and positive assessment by the local authority. The lowest-level public administration units have planning powers. The aim of the planning decisions made is to achieve optimal solutions that serve the interests of the general public and the interest of the individual. The potential "optimum" is achieved by defining target, precise and justified local conditions of land development.

The indicated forms of spatial planning as the main goal of their activities set, among others rational and efficient spatial management and preventing urban sprawl. The Germanic system used in Germany, Switzerland, Austria and partly in Eastern Europe, e.g., in Poland, incorporates the land-use plan "Flachennutzunsplan" at the municipal level. In Poland, it is "a study of the conditions and directions of spatial development in a commune". These studies determine the local spatial policy. In order to detail the development conditions, a development plan "Bebaunsplan" is prepared; in Poland it is "the local spatial development plan of the commune". The British system (England, Wales, Scotland and Ireland) uses a document in the space management process that allows for activities in the space called "planning permission", issued by districts and unitary authorities.

On the other hand, the Napoleonic system is used in: France, Luxembourg, the Netherlands, Italy, Portugal, Belgium, Spain and Greece. It is a system in which statutory law takes precedence, on the basis of which detailed legal norms are established, and the principles of spatial planning are defined comprehensively. The local level is legally required to have spatial planning acts, but there is no clearly defined level of accuracy of these studies. For example, in the spatial planning system in Spain, despite the established core of the planning procedure for individual autonomies, there is no obligation to agree on the provisions of planning documentation between neighboring municipalities. In the case of the Scandinavian system in force in Denmark, Sweden, Norway and Finland, based on transparent and uncomplicated legislation, it draws different proportions from the Napoleonic and Germanic systems. For example, in Sweden, the implementation of spatial policy was based on the development of comprehensive plans "oversiktsplaner" and on the local level detailed spatial development plans "praktjpla" and "conditions for spatial development of the area". It is worth emphasizing that the local (bottom-up) level is the most important element in the Swedish planning system.

The implementation of spatial policy in the discussed countries is associated with the ongoing process of spatial management. This process is directly influenced by the form of spatial management and the specificity of real estate markets, including their location (urban, suburban and rural areas). The price of the property plays a leading role in making the decision. It is the result of many factors (location, building method, availability of technical infrastructure, surroundings, labor market, etc.). Therefore, the dynamics and methods of land use, the recomposition of functions in selected spaces and the costs and benefits generated by the reorganization of planning functions are important. They depend on the specificity of the spatial planning tools used. Also, from the administrative division of the country, for example in Spain, the law obliges the plan to cover the entire area of the commune (there may be several). In Poland, the local plan is prepared optionally (in a commune there may be even several dozen plans, a situation in which not a single document will be prepared is also acceptable). Apart from that, as a rule, in Poland there is one type of local and regional plan. They are dedicated to urbanizing and urbanized areas, as well as typically agricultural areas. On the other hand, in Spain there are as many as nine types of plan, five of which are used for urban design and four for territorial planning [65]. From the planning point of view, these countries seem to be similar due to the levels of administration. There is a municipal level in both countries. The province in Spain corresponds to the regional level, and the voivodeship in Poland. In both cases, the principles of the country's spatial policy are prepared at the national level, together with recommendations for the regional and local level. There are more similarities and analogies between the European Union (EU) countries in terms of spatial planning [66]. It is necessary to pay attention to detailed conditions, including issues that determine the effectiveness of the designated spatial policy. Effective land management based on efficient legislation will also be important. In order to efficiently influence spatial processes, including urban sprawl, skillful land structuring is needed (in Spain, land is divided into three classes: I for urbanization; II intended for urbanization; III with no possibility of urbanization). In Poland, an effective solution for specifying the intended use of land is a local plan, which is also local law. Areas not included in this document may be, with minor inclusions (e.g., legally protected areas), freely developed, especially when it comes to housing development on agricultural land. This fact results in the intensification of urban sprawl. Procedures can be simplified, local communities can be significantly involved in the planning process, and policies aimed at optimizing the development of available land can be sought. Various functions can be combined within the planning system, including the expansion of the control system. However, their effectiveness should be considered individually. Interest in space by its users, and thus the observed population density will be determined each time by local possibilities and needs. As research shows, the available technical infrastructure is of great importance, as well as the form of spatial structure development resulting, among others, from the demand for residential or industrial areas [67,68]. Gomez-Antonio and Hortas-Rico [2014] prove that urban sprawl is taking place in Spain [69]. They also indicate that the emergence of urban sprawl in the communes surrounding the city intensifies when sprawl occurs in a neighboring commune. The morphological specificity of urban sprawl in Mediterranean regions is manifested in low urban densities, high losses of non-urban land covers, depopulation of the metropolitan inner core, increasing importance of single housing and the expansion of transportation infrastructures [70,71]. Apart from technological factors and the development of road transport, geographical factors, such as topography and the area's technical infrastructure, play an important role in the escalation of urban sprawl [72,73].

The practice of space management, unfortunately, highlights its various shortcomings, the source of which is still, among others, insufficient knowledge and competences, lack of respect for space and its users, or actions deliberately aimed at quick and short-term profit.

Generally, the availability of instruments, including legal ones, to counteract urban sprawl processes to a large extent depends on the planning system of a given country, applicable standards and commonly used good practices. The available spatial data, without which a diagnosis is difficult, are also important and, therefore, the selection of instruments for influencing the space becomes problematic [74].

3. Materials and Methods

The adopted research objective, which is to identify the macroeconomic costs and benefits of urban sprawl, results from the ambiguity of the current state of knowledge regarding the effects of the process in question. In order to achieve the goal, the verification of two hypotheses supposing a negative macroeconomic impact of urban sprawl was assumed, i.e.:

Hypothesis 1 (H1). *Urban sprawl adversely affects the financial situation of the national budget;*

Hypothesis 2 (H2). *Urban sprawl slows down the growth rate of the local and national economy.*

To verify both hypotheses, studies were proposed in regard to the area affected by the urban sprawl phenomenon in Poland, described by Lityński and Hołuj [75]. This area is presented in Figure 1 and consists of communes located around the capitals of regions or core cities in Poland. Communes in the zone external to the capitals and cores are: 50 cities, 221 villages, 99 town-villages. It should be mentioned that there are three types of commune in Poland: urban, that is cities; rural, i.e., a village with a low degree of urbanization; urban–rural, i.e., a city surrounded by rural areas. It should be explained that the analyzed urban areas have the same administrative status and are among the most important in Poland, as they are the areas surrounding the capitals of the regions. However, not all urban areas in Poland were analyzed, i.e., urban areas that belong to a lower level in the hierarchy of the Polish settlement system were not analyzed. Despite this, the area taken for research covers 15% of the territory of Poland, where 25% of the country's buildings are located. It seems to be a representative sample. For the 370 indicated communes, Lityński [6], using the urban morphology indicators defined by Galster et al. [4], calculates variables: density (Diu), continuity (Ciu), concentration (COViu), clustering (CLUSiu), decentralization (CBDdist), urbanization pressure (UPj→i). This area and quantified morphological are the starting point for research into the economic consequences of urban sprawl.

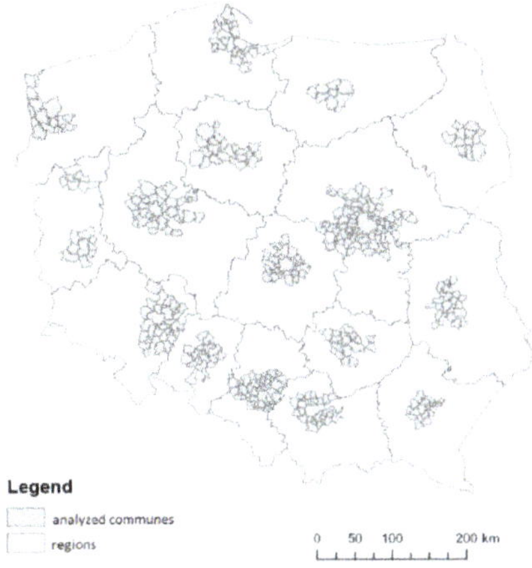

Figure 1. Analyzed area. Source: own based on Lityński & Hołuj [6,75].

Lityński [6] proves that urban sprawl occurs in the analyzed urban areas, which are subject to population migrations from central cities to the suburbs. The physical manifestation of urban sprawl is the remoteness of residential buildings from the core city. New residential buildings are located in agricultural areas, which has been described pejoratively as urbanization pressure. Despite the fact that the buildings are far from the core cities, the composition of the buildings is dense and clustered, maintaining spatial continuity. However, this composition results from the vicinity of new residential buildings with old agricultural buildings. Lityński [6] also emphasizes the significant differentiation of the morphological specificity of urban sprawl between regions, i.e., in selected urban areas other morphological indicators dominate.

The urban sprawl assessment can be presented in an international context. For example, an Organization for Economic Cooperation and Development (OECD) report [76] dealing with the issues of assessing urban sprawl in OECD countries draws attention to this. This report indicates that Polish urban areas are characterized by a higher density than the OECD average. In the light of the measures of the spatial structure of Lityński [6] using the building density, this conclusion can be confirmed. It can also be partially confirmed in the report's conclusion that Polish urban areas are less polycentric than in other OECD countries. This is partly because, as previously signaled, Lityński [6] generally indicates a monocentric character, but in Poland urban areas differ significantly in this respect. The report also indicates that Polish urban areas are less fragmented than the OECD average, which can also be confirmed through the prism of continuity, concentration and clustering indicators. However, the report does not attempt to assess the specificity of spatial development, i.e., its filling, and the presented assessment of urban sprawl, show high urbanization pressure on agricultural areas. These results make it possible to compare the specificity of the Polish sprawl with other OECD countries, to search for similarities and differences. According to the OECD report [76], similar conditions to the Polish urban sprawl can be attributed to Spain. From the morphological side of urban sprawl, both countries show a higher density. Despite this density, building clusters are more fragmented than in other OECD countries. The difference between the two countries is centralization, which in Spain shows the proximity of buildings to core cities, and in Poland its remoteness.

The study was divided into three stages. The first stage consists of assessing the urban sprawl phenomenon in each of the analyzed communes. The purpose of such an assessment is to identify communes with a high and low degree of disorder in the spatial structure that is attributed to urban sprawl. Identifying communes with a high degree of urban sprawl is important in examining economic consequences and verifying hypotheses. For this purpose, Lityński's morphological indicators were synthesized [6] based on the Perkal method:

$$P_i = \frac{1}{p}\sum_{j=1}^{p} z_{ij}$$

where:

z_{ij}—normalized variable: $z_{ij} = (x_{ij} - \overline{x}_j)/s_j$ for stimulant or $z_{ij} = (\overline{x}_j - x_{ij})/s_j$ for destimulant

$\overline{x}_j$—average value of variable j

x_{ij}—value of variable j for the commune i

s_j—standard deviation of variable j

p—number of variables

The Urban Sprawl Index, built on the basis of the Perkal (Pi) method, ranges from −3 to +3. Communes with a high degree of spontaneous spatial structure will show values below 0, areas with a moderate degree of the phenomenon will oscillate around 0, and the area with a relatively low degree will record values above 0. Similar areas are considered to be those with similar index values. Identification of communes for which P(i) < 0 will allow to indicate in the research communes the specificity of the disorder of the spatial structure, which is attributed to urban sprawl. With regard to these communes, research on the economic impact of urban sprawl will be continued.

The second stage involves a verification of H(1). It was decided to verify the hypothesis based on the canonical analysis. The value of the canonical analysis is the assessment of the relationship between two sets of variables. In the case of the presented research, it will be a comparison of morphological variables with fiscal variables. Morphological variables are the aforementioned: D(iu), C(iu), COV(iu), CLUS(iu), CBD(dist), UP(j→i). These variables are referred to in the literature as urban sprawl features [3,4]. Fiscal variables are three types of state budget expenditure for communes: supplement to the general subsidy (SGS); subsidies for own current tasks (SOCT); subsidies for own investment tasks (SOIT).

It should be noted that in Poland there is an extensive system of transfers from the national budget to the budgets of communes. Among the many types of transfer, from the point of view of the subject of this research, SGS is important. It is an expenditure of the national budget for selected communes with income and expenditure disproportions. It pertains to the high costs of implementing communes' own tasks (e.g., building communes' roads), the implementation cost of which is higher than in other units due to specific conditions. On the other hand, SOCT and SOIT are funds transferred from the national budget to communes for the implementation of previously specified tasks in the field of roads, education and sport. The difference between SGS and SOIT is that SOIT is generic, while SGS must be spent on a specific task and unused funds must be returned. In this context, it should be emphasized that the spontaneous location of buildings accompanying urban sprawl generates specific spatial conditions, and thus increased costs of infrastructure construction and maintenance. An example is the elongated streets and sewage system due to the inability to implement the investment along the shortest line. Therefore, the national budget suffers losses due to the need to transfer additional funds to communes for infrastructure in areas with spontaneous development.

The canonical analysis was proposed for four variants of grouping the analyzed communes V(i). V(1) are external communes, meaning all communes around the core cities, regardless of the commune status. V(2) are all external communes for which P(i) < 0. Therefore, it is a collection of external communes where urban sprawl is intense. V(3) includes only external communes which have the status of a rural commune. These are the units where urban sprawl is most commonly recognized in Poland whereas V(4) are those rural communes for which P(i) < 0; ie villages with intensified urban sprawl. V(4) are therefore units with extreme conditions for urban sprawl. Variation of the canonical analysis aims to observe and increase the accuracy of the assessment of the impact of urban sprawl on the national budget.

In the study, the conclusions from the canonical analysis were made on the basis of the canonical weights and the canonical correlation R(k). The canonical weights indicate the direction of the relationship between the accepted substitutes from the two sets through the signs (+) and (-). Moreover, the significance of a pair of canonical variables was assessed using the Barlett significance test. In contrast, R(k) represents the general correlation index between two sets of variables, thus indicating the level of relationship between the spatial structure and budget transfers.

The third stage of the research involves verification of H(2). The basic method of hypothesis verification is standardized mean difference (SMD). SMD is based on a quasi-experimental approach that uses the synthetic control method. The essence of such tests is to identify the control group against which the test group is assessed. It was proposed that the study consisted in comparing the local GDP(per capita) for communes with high urban sprawl with the local GDP(per capita) for the control group.

$$SMD_n = \frac{\varphi_{(\alpha)} - \varphi_{(\beta)}}{s}$$

where:

φ—GDP(per capita)
α—assessed group
β—control group
s—standard deviation

In Poland there is no aggregated GDP at the local level. The lack of GDP at the local level forces a substitution measure. In Polish study tax revenues of municipalities are used interchangeably [77]. Zaucha et al. indicates substantive argument that taxes are associated with the production arising in the territory [77]. In this light, it would be the most appropriate measure of corporate income taxes (CIT). However, the complexity of the Polish tax system prevents such an approach for several reasons: (a) taxes are paid at the place of headquarters and not at the site of product/service; (b) the existence of tax exemptions (e.g., special economic zones); (c) the ability to cover losses from one year to the next tax year. In contrast, personal income taxes (PIT) despite the fact that it has some shortcomings (e.g., the discharge of the tax in place of registration and not in a product/service) have less interference. In addition, Zaucha et al. proposes to add to the revenue the sum of PIT revenue and agricultural tax due to the fact that agricultural holdings do not pay PIT only agricultural tax (AT) [77]. Moreover, Lityński [78], using PIT and AT for research on the local economy, indicates that such an approximation is correlated with GDP at the level of r = 0.98 (p = 0.00). Therefore, in this study, an approximation of GDP(per capita) was proposed according to the formula:

$$\varphi_{(i)} = \frac{\sum_{i=1}^{n} \frac{\left[pit_{(i)} + at_{(i)}\right]}{N}}{n}$$

where:

N—population of the commune i
n—number of communes

As the analysis is dynamic, i.e., it concerns the years 2010–2019, the index of the medium-term rate of changes was used for the dynamics:

$$\overline{T}_{(n)} = \left(\sqrt[n-1]{\left(i_{\left(\frac{n}{n-1}\right)} * \ldots * i_{\left(\frac{2}{1}\right)}\right.} - 1 \right) * 100\%$$

All budget data comes from the collections of the Local Data Bank of the Central Statistical Office in Poland.

4. Results

Figure 2 shows the Urban Sprawl Index in each of the analyzed communes, which is the implementation of the first stage of the research. As the aim of the first stage of the research is to identify communes with a high and low degree of spatial structure disorder, attention should be paid to the intervals P(i). Communes with a chaotic spatial structure are those for which $P(i) < 0$. All communes for which $P(i) < 0$ are in the range (0; −1), which means a moderate degree of spatial structure disorder. The study did not identify communes with a high degree of disorder ($-1 < P(i) \leq -2$) and a very high degree of disorder ($-2 < P(i) \leq -3$). However, most communes for which $P(i)>0$ are in the range (0; 1). These communes are characterized by a moderate degree of space compactness. Only one commune is characterized by a very compact spatial structure, for which $P(i) = 2.13$ and it is a rural commune of Wielka Wieś.

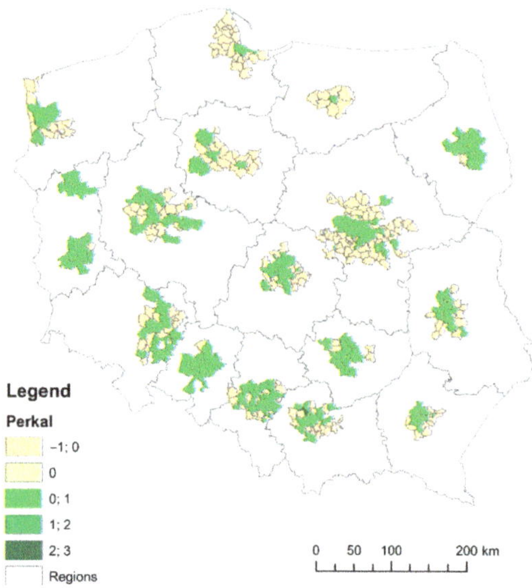

Figure 2. Urban Sprawl Index in the analyzed communes based on the Perkal method P(i). Source: own study based on Lityński [6].

In Poland, the spatial structure of endangered urban sprawl assessed by P(i), is in the range (−1; 1), with one exception. This means that the spatial structure of Polish communes is relatively similar in terms of morphological features of urban sprawl. The level of urban sprawl is not high, but it is also impossible to indicate that the spatial structure is compact. There are no communes in Poland with an absolutely high urban sprawl level. There is also no group of communes with a compact spatial structure. The only exception here is one commune whose spatial structure is very compact.

The second stage of research, which involves verification of H(1), was based on the canonical analysis. As part of the canonical analysis, four variants of the relationship between the suburban structure and transfers from the national budget were tested. Table 1 shows the results of testing four variants. The most satisfactory results are provided by V(4), for which the canonical correlation reaches the highest values of $R(k) = 0.46$. This means that rural communes with a high degree of spatial structure disorder ($Pi < 0$) have the greatest impact on transfers from the state budget.

Table 1. Canonical analysis between budget transfers and urban sprawl.

Variants	$R_{(k)}$	Chi^2	p	N
$V_{(1)}$: External communes	0.31	64.61	0.00	370
$V_{(2)}$: External communes; $P_{(i)}<0$	0.33	42.18	0.00	200
$V_{(3)}$: Villages	0.44	54.38	0.00	221
$V_{(4)}$: Villages; $P_{(i)}<0$	0.46	47.98	0.00	141

The further part of the canonical analysis refers only to V(4), because this variant provides the most favorable results for the verification of the adopted hypothesis. Table 2 presents the results of testing the significance of pairs of canonical variables based on the Barlett test. The assessment of the significance of pairs of canonical variables, based on the critical values of the significance level (p), indicates that at the significance level (α) > 0.00 only the first pair of variables is significant. The remaining pairs of variables are so high (p) that the conclusion was abandoned.

Table 2. Barlett test for $V_{(4)}$.

Element Removed	$R_{(k)}$	$R_{(k)}^2$	Chi^2	Df	p
0	0.46	0.21	47.98	18.00	0.00
1	0.25	0.07	15.44	10.00	0.12
2	0.22	0.05	6.43	4.00	0.17

Based on the results presented in Table 3, it can be indicated the greatest positive relationship between the SGS variable and D(iu). There is no statistically significant negative relationship in the study, i.e., indicating that a higher value of budget transfers is accompanied by a lower level of the morphological variable. Thus, the results of the canonical analysis do not indicate a negative impact of urban sprawl on the state budget.

Table 3. Canonical weights for $V_{(4)}$.

	Right Set				Left Set		
	Elem. 1	Elem. 2	Elem. 3		Elem. 1	Elem. 2	Elem. 3
SGS	0.67	−0.48	−0.58	$D_{(iu)}$	0.97	−1.02	0.25
SOCT	−0.63	−0.76	−0.18	$C_{(iu)}$	0.11	0.68	0.55
SOIT	−0.34	0.54	−0.77	$COV_{(iu)}$	0.24	−1.42	0.26
				$CLUS_{(iu)}$	−0.02	0.22	1.06
				$CBD_{(dist)}$	−0.10	0.01	−0.70
				$UP_{(j\rightarrow i)}$	0.05	1.42	0.00

Therefore, the conclusions from the canonical analyzes carried out indicate that it cannot be said that the disorder of the spatial structure accompanying the urban sprawl phenomenon has a negative impact on the national budget. Thus, it has not been proven that national expenditure is related to negatively valued morphological features, e.g., lower building density. Based on the results of the research, it is not possible to confirm the hypothesis H(1) that urban sprawl adversely affects the financial situation of the national budget.

The third stage of the research, which assumed the verification of H(2), was based on the SMD method. As the hypothesis takes two territorial levels: local and national, two SMD analyzes were carried out. It was assumed that the assessed group are communes with the highest degree of spatial structure disorder, i.e., rural communes for which P(i) < 0. The assessed group in Table 4 is marked as (α). For the assessment of the local impact, the control group is marked as (β1) and consists of rural communes for which P(i) $\geq$ 0. On the other hand, the control group at the national level is marked as (β2) and they are all communes in Poland.

Table 4. Approximation of GDP (per capita) in the assessed group and control groups, Polish currency (PLN).

	2010	2011	2012	2013	2014	2015	2016	2017	2018	2019	$\overline{T}_{(n)}$
$\varphi_{(\alpha)}$	496	548	604	654	702	767	832	915	1038	1164	11%
$\varphi_{(\beta1)}$	555	611	670	711	768	835	905	993	1140	1275	11%
$\varphi_{(\beta2)}$	628	685	727	768	826	892	957	1040	1175	1293	9%

Table 4 presents raw data on the approximation of GDP(per capita) for the assessed group and control groups. It points out the same $\overline{T}_{(\alpha)}$ and $\overline{T}_{(\beta1)}$. This means that the economic growth was the same both in communes with high urban sprawl rates and in spatially compact communes. On the other hand, a lower $\overline{T}_{(\beta2)}$ means that the national GDP(per capita) grows slower than in communes with urban sprawl.

In Table 4 lower values of $\varphi_{(\alpha)}$, than $\varphi_{(\beta1)}$ and $\varphi_{(\beta2)}$ also draw attention. This means that in communes with high urban sprawl rates, the level of GDP (per capita) is lower than in communes with a more compact spatial structure or in the country. This level was assessed using the SMD method, the results of which are presented in Table 5 The SMD values in the range 0.2–0.5 are marked in gray, which means a moderate effect. The study did not identify a large or very large effect.

Table 5. Assessment of the impact of urban sprawl on local and national economic growth using the standardized mean difference (SMD) method.

	2010	2011	2012	2013	2014	2015	2016	2017	2018	2019
$SMD_{(\beta1)}$	−0.21	−0.21	−0.22	−0.18	−0.20	−0.19	−0.19	−0.18	−0.21	−0.21
$SMD_{(\beta2)}$	−0.46	−0.46	−0.42	−0.36	−0.38	−0.35	−0.33	−0.30	−0.29	−0.25

$SMD_{(\beta1)}$, which assesses the impact of urban sprawl on the local economy, is moderately negative. This allows to conclude that the impact of urban sprawl on the local economy is negative. Moreover, changes in $SMD_{(\beta1)}$ in 2010–2019 show a stabilized negative trend, which means that urban sprawl communes are not catching up with communes with a more compact structure. Therefore, it can be concluded that urban sprawl slows down economic growth and economic development. This impact can be assessed as negative at a moderate level. It is possible to confirm the hypothesis that urban sprawl slows down local economic growth.

$SMD_{(\beta2)}$, which assesses the impact of urban sprawl on the national economy, is also moderately negative. The tendency of changes in $SMD_{(\beta2)}$ in 2010–2019 indicates a reduction of the negative impact, but the impact is still moderate. This reduction results from the higher $\overline{T}_{(\alpha)}$ than $\overline{T}_{(\beta2)}$. Thus, the impact of urban sprawl on the national economy is not clearly negative. Even though $SMD_{(\beta2)}$ is negative at a moderate level, the trend of changes indicates a clear improvement. Therefore, the hypothesis about the impact of urban sprawl on the slowdown of the national economy cannot be clearly confirmed.

Two main conclusions can be drawn from the above results. The first is that urban sprawl adversely affects the local economy and its growth. The second, urban sprawl, does not adversely affect the national economy. It also has no negative impact on the national budget. These conclusions are essential for spatial policy. Sprawl does not harm the national economy and the national budget, but communes with a compact structure are important for the dynamization of economic development. The research results confirm that compact communes represent a higher economic level than the national level, and thus have a positive impact on the national economy. For the national economy, the cost of sprawl is the lack of utilization of the development potential of the suburban space. Therefore, spatial policy should not be guided by absolute limitation of urban sprawl, because it has no detrimental effect on the national economy. Policy should focus on guiding the sprawl. This direction should consist in stimulating the formation of suburban housing estates with a compact structure. In the light of research, spatially compact communes dynamize economic development. Therefore, an important role should be played by instruments stimulating positive spatial phenomena, and not restrictive ones preventing sprawl. The formation of compact structures will contribute to the use of the growth potential not only for the economies of the communes themselves, but also for the country.

5. Conclusions and Discussion

The contribution of the research in the development of the current state of knowledge can be noticed in the methodical and theoretical dimension, according to the set hypothesis. The added value in the methodological layer is the measurement of the impact of urban sprawl on national budget, taking into account the morphological variables. It fills the gap in the current state of knowledge regarding the explanation of the mechanism of linking the spatial and budgetary structure. It is significant for the spatial economy and public finances. Determining this mechanism allows for the formulation of spatial and fiscal policies or the integration of spatial planning with socio-economic planning. The conducted research shows that from the macroeconomic point of view, urban sprawl is not a process generating direct costs. However, it is a process that slows down economic growth, and communes with a compact structure are important to accelerate the pace of economic growth. As the assessment of urban sprawl losses is not unequivocally negative, the spatial policy should not focus on the absolute reduction of urban sprawl, but on stimulating the formation of suburban housing estates with a compact structure. We must bear in mind that urban sprawl can have either a positive or negative impact on the space and its other users, which will be equated with benefit or costs. However, the determination of externalities and their size is extremely difficult due to the existing market failures and the impact of this market on the processes taking place in it. What is significant, however, is that the inducers of urban sprawl may not even realize that they are producers of externalities. On the other hand, the remaining entities operating in space experience the resulting external effects [79]. Therefore, according to Papandreou [80], spatial policy should take into account the behavior of entities causing urban sprawl. Taking this into account, on the basis of research results, should be based on the use of instruments stimulating positive spatial phenomena. This means that entities deciding to build should be encouraged to locate among the existing buildings, creating a compact spatial structure. However, restrictive instruments to prevent urban sprawl should not be used, as sprawl is not a macro-economic loss-making process.

The presented conclusion, in light of the literature, justifies the need to combine spatial policy of the national level with the local level. This combination is expressed not only in the coherence of spatial plans, the assumptions of which would focus development into compact spatial structures. It pertains primarily to equipping local government by central authorities with operational instruments for implementing spatial plans. Stimulating compact development at the local level requires financial as well as organizational and legal resources. For the correct functioning of a coherent planning system, active participation of residents along with an efficient public administration system will be important. Here it will be necessary to implement a common, acceptable spatial policy resulting in efficiency resulting from the cooperation of space users. Policy creating conditions for the exploitation of the identified development potentials in suburban areas [81,82].

It seems that financial instruments can play a decisive role in stimulating the formation of compact spatial structures. In this group, attention should be paid to indirect instruments such as exemptions or tax breaks for new compact housing locations. Local self-government should receive compensation from the national budget for the reduction of revenues, which takes place through the application of such understood tax exemption or relief. Another, indirect financial instrument could be a public fund offering credit facilities for the implementation of compact housing investments. There are no such instruments in Poland.

On the other hand, among direct financial instruments, a higher level of subsidizing infrastructure investments is proposed, which would result in the emergence of compact development. In Poland, there are so-called earmarked subsidies, which are a transfer from the national budget to local budgets to secure infrastructure investments. The transfer limit is generally 80% of the cost. There is, therefore, a range of an additional 20% that could be allocated to suburban communes.

The use of stimulating financial instruments creates the risk of an externality, which may be increasing the range of urban sprawl [51]. This may be the case of the anticipatory approach of local authorities to shaping undeveloped suburban space, including equipping it with attractive technical infrastructure. In our perspective, however, the use of stimulating financial instruments should be reserved only for supplementing the development between existing buildings. The point is to transform the current disordered structure of space into a compact form. The creation of completely new suburban housing estates on greenfields should not be stimulated by the public sector, but rather be subject to appropriate planning and implementation control. Control and planning on greenfields should be strengthened with legal and organizational instruments, i.e., organizational standards and administrative decisions. Strengthening the regulatory function of spatial planning, especially through organizational standards, would allow for effective and sustainable land use (e.g., in terms of protection of areas particularly suitable for agricultural production); compliance with the principles of environmental and landscape protection; compliance with safety rules; use the dimensions of buildings in accordance with the urban and architectural requirements [51]. In the case of administrative decisions made at the lowest level of public administration, we see the importance of skills, knowledge and intuition. In agreement with Śleszyński et al. [83] we believe that the spatial policy implemented at the commune level, despite the standardized organizational norms, will be able to produce individualized positive externalities of urban sprawl with appropriate use of administrative decisions.

Stimulating compact development encounters difficulties resulting from the acceptance of costs on the part of society, as indicated by Meade [84]. Then, these costs may, to a limited extent, constitute the basis for verification of the conducted spatial policy and the introduction of restrictive instruments. Hence, we agree with the finding of Baumol et al. [85], that it is necessary to evaluate the effectiveness of national intervention by comparing the potential benefits of reducing social costs with the generated effects for the national budget. Our conclusions about the lack of macroeconomic net costs of urban sprawl justify that, from the point of view of the country, one should be cautious about applying restrictive instruments. The absence of these losses for the economy as a whole means that the government does not have strong arguments for restrictive treatment of urban sprawl in public policy, especially when social losses are accepted. Therefore, there is no justification, for example, to reduce budget transfers for infrastructure investments resulting in the dispersion of buildings. It is true that in Poland there is no such reduction in transfers; however, this example demonstrates the difficulty of creating a compact spatial structure. Since the central authorities does not have an economic interest in preventing urban sprawl, it will be even more difficult to stimulate compact spatial structure. Hence, more important is the appropriate design of the system of financial instruments to stimulate compact development.

The research results are an extension of the current state of knowledge on the macroeconomic impact of urban sprawl. However, like many original concepts, they may have some limitations, which sometimes makes it difficult to formulate universal conclusions for the international scale. Firstly, the impact of sprawl on the financial situation of the national's budget was based on subsidies for communes specific to Polish public finances. Both the types of subsidies and the mechanisms for granting them are strictly defined in Polish law. Therefore, the conclusions about the impact on the national budget are, first of all, adequate for Poland. These conclusions may be valid for countries where the system of transfers from the national budget to the communes' budgets distinguishes subsidies related to co-financing the costs of infrastructure investments due to specific geographic conditions. Second, the impact of urban sprawl on the growth rate of local and national economies was determined on the basis of regional capitals. These are the most important cities in Poland, but there is still a remaining group of medium-sized and smaller cities in the hierarchy of the national settlement system. There is also urban sprawl around smaller towns. It should be noted that the aforementioned limitations also set the directions for future research. An extension of the presented conclusions could be the assessment of the impact of urban sprawl in the configuration of the urban system, e.g., monocentric vs. polycentric; regional vs. subregional cities. It is also possible to adopt a different impact on the national budget than through transfers, which would be a country-specific approach. It seems that due to the different legal structures of the system of income and expenditures from the national budget, it is difficult to build an internationally universal research model.

Author Contributions: Conceptualization, P.L. and A.H.; methodology, P.L.; software, P.L. and A.H.; validation, P.L. and A.H.; formal analysis, P.L.; investigation, P.L. and A.H.; resources, P.L. and A.H.; data curation, P.L.; Writing—Original draft preparation, P.L. and A.H.; literature review A.H.; Writing—Review and editing, P.L., and A.H.; visualization, A.H.; supervision, P.L. and A.H.; All authors have read and agreed to the published version of the manuscript.

Funding: This research was funded by the National Science Centre, Poland; grant no. UMO-2016/23/D/HS4/02961, ("Financial Mechanisms in the Economy Resulting from the Phenomenon of Urban Sprawl") and Cracow University of Economics, Poland, POTENTIAL Program No.52/GGR/2020/POT. ("Cities, suburbs and peripheries in the theory and in the empirical studies").

Institutional Review Board Statement: Not applicable.

Informed Consent Statement: Not applicable.

Data Availability Statement: Publicly available datasets were analyzed in this study. Fiscal data was obtained from Central Statistical Office in Poland https://bdl.stat.gov.pl/BDL/start; spatial data was obtained from the appendices in the book [6].

Acknowledgments: Not applicable.

Conflicts of Interest: The authors declare no conflict of interest.

References

1. Whyte, W.H. *The Exploding Metropolis: A Study of the Assault on Urbanism and How Our Cities Can Resist It*; A Doubleday Anchor Book: New York, NY, USA, 1958.
2. Perrsky, J.; Wiewel, J. Urban Decentralization, Suburbanization, and Sprawl: An Equity Perspective. In *Urban Economics and Planning*; Brooks, N., Donaghy, K., Knaap, G.J., Eds.; Oxford University Press: New York, NY, USA, 2012; ISBN 978-0195380620.
3. Arribas-Bel, D.; Nijkamp, P.; Scholten, H. Multidimensional urban sprawl in Europe: A self-organizing map approach. *Comput. Environ. Urban Syst.* **2011**, *35*, 263–275. [CrossRef]
4. Galster, G.; Hanson, R.; Wolman, H.; Coleman, S.; Freihage, J. Wrestling sprawl to the ground: Defining and measuring an elusive concept. *Hous. Policy Debate* **2001**, *12*, 681–717. [CrossRef]
5. Lityński, P.; Hołuj, A.; Zotic, V. The Polish Urban Sprawl: An Economic Perspective. *J. Settl. Spat. Plan.* **2015**, *6*, 95–105.
6. Lityński, P. *Budżetowe Konsekwencje Żywiołowego Rozprzestrzeniania się Miast dla Samorządów Gminnych (Urban Sprawl and the Budgetary Consequences Form Municipal Governments)*; Uniwersytetu Ekonomicznego w Krakowie: Kraków, Poland, 2019; ISBN 978-83-7252-782-0.
7. Mumford, L. *The City in History: Its Origins, Its Transformations, and Its Prospects*; Harcourt Brace: New York, NY, USA, 1969; ISBN -13 978-0156180351.
8. McHarg, I.L. *Design with Nature*; Natural History Press: New York, NY, USA, 1969; ISBN -13 978-0471114604.
9. Jackson, K. *The Crabgrass Frontier: The Suburbanization of the United States*; Oxford University Press: New York, NY, USA, 1985; ISBN -13 978-0195049831.
10. Downs, A. *New Visions for Metropolitan America*; The Brookings Institution: Washington, DC, USA, 1994; ISBN -13 978-0815719267.
11. Fulton, W.; Pendall, R.; Nguyen, M.; Harrison, A. *Who Sprawls Most: How Growth Patterns Differ across the United States*; The Brookings Institution: Washington, DC, USA, 2001; Volume 23, pp. 428–434.
12. OECD. *Compact City Policies: A Comparative Assessment*; OECD Green Growth Studies; OECD Publishing: Paris, France, 2012; ISBN 9789264167841.
13. Young, M.; Tnguay, G.A.; Lachapelle, U. Transportation cos and urban sprawl in Canadian metropolitan areas. *Res. Transp. Econ.* **2016**, *60*, 25–34. [CrossRef]
14. O'Toole, R. *Gridlock: Why We're Stuck in Traffic and What to Do about It*; CATO Institute: Washington, DC, USA, 2009; pp. 1–277.
15. Pipień, M.; Roszkowska, S. *Empirical Macroeconomics and Statistical Uncertainty: Spatial and Temporal Disaggregation of Regional Economic Indicators*; Routledge Studies in the European Economy: New York, NY, USA, 2020; ISBN 13 978-0367456719.

16. Mankiw, N.G.; Romer, D.; Weil, D. A Contribution to the Empirics of Economic Growth. *Q. J. Econ.* **1992**, *107*, 2. [CrossRef]
17. Capello, R. Spatial Spillovers and Regional Growth: A Cognitive Approach. *Eur. Plan. Stud.* **2009**, *17*, 5. [CrossRef]
18. Gruber, J. *Public Finance and Public Policy*, 4th ed; Worth Publishers: New York, NY, USA, 2012; ISBN -13 978-1429278454.
19. Irwin, E.; Bockstael, N. Land use externalities, open space preservation and urban sprawl. *Reg. Sci. Urban Econ.* **2004**, *34*, 705–725. [CrossRef]
20. Nijkamp, P.; Verhoef, E.T. *Externalities in the Urban Economy*; Tinbergen Institute Discussion Paper; Vrije Universiteit: Amsterdam, The Netherlands, 2003; TI 2003-078/3.
21. Treacy, J. Smart methods for environmental externalities: Urban planning, environmental health and hygiene in the Netherlands. *Irish Geogr.* **2014**, *46*, 3. [CrossRef]
22. Kowalewski, A.; Markowski, T.; Śleszyński, P. *Kryzys Polskiej Przestrzeni. Źródła, Skutki i Kierunki Działań Naprawczych*; Polska Akademia Nauk, Komitet Przestrzennego Zagospodarowania Kraju: Warsaw, Poland, 2020; ISBN 978-83-63305-83-3.
23. Bromley, R.D.F.; Tallon, A.R.; Roberts, A.J. New populations in the British city centre: Evidence of social change from the census and household surveys. *Geoforum* **2007**, *38*, 1. [CrossRef]
24. Colomb, C. Unpacking new labour's *Urban Renaissance* agenda: Towards a socially sustainable reurbanization of British cities? *Plan. Pract. Res.* **2007**, *22*, 1–24. [CrossRef]
25. Turok, I.; Mykhnenko, V. The trajectories of European cities, 1960–2005. *Cities* **2007**, *24*, 165–182. [CrossRef]
26. Cheshire, P.C.; Gordon, I. Resurgent cities? Evidence-based Urban Policy? More Questions than Answers—Special issue. *Urban Stud.* **2006**, *43*, 8.
27. Pigou, A.C. *Economics of Welfare*; Macmillan Company: London, UK, 1952.
28. Samuelson, P.A. *Zasady Analizy Ekonomicznej*; PWN: Warsaw, Poland, 1959.
29. Krugman, P.; Wells, R. *Economics*, 2nd ed.; Worth Publishers: New York, NY, USA, 2009; ISBN -13 978-0716771616.
30. Gruber, J. *Public Finance and Public Policy*, 5th ed; Worth Publishers: New York, NY, USA, 2015; ISBN 13 978-1464143335.
31. Hołuj, A. Ekonomiczne i ekologiczne efekty zewnętrzne w planowaniu przestrzennym. Acta Universitatis Lodziensis. *Folia Oeconomica* **2018**, *4*, 336. [CrossRef]
32. Markowski, T. Planowanie przestrzenne i instrumenty jego realizacji w świetle teorii ułomnych rynków. In *Zarządzanie Rozwojem Przestrzennym Miast*; Lorens, P., Martyniuk-Pęczek, J., Eds.; Wydawnictwo Urbanistyka: Gdańsk, Poland, 2010.
33. Żylicz, T. *Ekonomia Środowiska i Zasobów Naturalnych*; PWE: Warsaw, Poland, 2004; ISBN 83-208-1521-5.
34. *EEA Report, Urban Sprawl in Europe. The Ignored Challenge. No 10/2006*; European Environment Agency: Copenhagen, Denmark, 2006; ISSN 1725-9177.
35. Albrecht, D.E. Nonmetropolitan population trends: Twenty first century updates. *J. Rural Soc. Sci.* **2010**, *25*, 1–21.
36. Sant, M.; Simons, P. The conceptual basis of counterurbanisation: Critique and development. *Aust. Geogr. Stud.* **1993**, *31*, 113–126. [CrossRef]
37. Dahms, F.; McComb, J. Counterurbanization, interaction and functional change in a rural amenity area—A Canadianexample. *J. Rural Stud.* **1999**, *15*, 2.
38. White, P. Labour migration and counter-urbanization in France. In *Labour Migration: The Internal Geographical Mobility of Labour in the Developed World*; Johnson, J., Salt, J., Eds.; David Fulton Publishers: London, UK, 1990; ISBN 978036703458-1.
39. Phillips, M. Counterurbanisation and rural gentrification: An exploration of the terms. *Popul. Space Place* **2010**, *16*, 6. [CrossRef]
40. Jauhiainen, J.S. Will the retiring baby boomers return to rural periphery? *J. Rural Stud.* **2009**, *25*, 25–34. [CrossRef]
41. Bijker, R.; Haartsen, T.; Strijker, D. Migration to less-popular rural areas in the Netherlands: Exploring the motivations. *J. Rural Stud.* **2012**, *28*, 490–498. [CrossRef]
42. Champion, A.; Vandermotten, C. Migration, counterurbanisation and regional re-structuring in Europe. In *People, Jobs and Mobility in New Europe*; Blotevogel, H., Fielding, A.J., Eds.; John Wiley: Chichester, UK, 1997; pp. 69–90.
43. Champion, A.G.; Watkins, C. *People in the Countryside: Studies of Social Change in Rural Britain*; Paul Chapman: London, UK, 1990; ISBN -10 1853961280.
44. Beale, C.L. A further look at nonmetropolitan population growth since 1970. *Am. J. Agric. Econ.* **1976**, *58*, 953–958. [CrossRef]
45. Berry, B.J.L. The counterurbanization process: Urban America since 1970. *Urban Af-Fairs Annu. Rev.* **1976**, *11*, 17–30.
46. Mithell, C.J.A.; Briant, C.R. Counterurbanization. In *International Encyclopedia of Human Geography*; Kitchin, R., Thrift, N., Eds.; Elsevier: Maynooth, Ireland, 2009; ISBN 9780080449104.
47. Wamsley, D.J.; Epps, W.R.; Duncan, C.J. Migration to the New South Wales north coast 1986–1991: Lifestyle motivated counterurbanisation. *Geoforum* **1998**, *29*, 105–118. [CrossRef]
48. Steenbekkers, A.; Simon, C.; Veldheer, V. *Thuis op het Platteland: De Leefsituatie van Platteland en Stad Vergeleken*; Sociaal en Cultureel Planbureau: The Hague, The Netherlands, 2006; ISBN 90-377-0229-5.
49. Geyer, H.S.; Kontuly, T. A theoretical foundation for the concept of differential urbanization. *Int. Reg. Sci. Rev.* **1993**, *15*, 2. [CrossRef]
50. Docampo, M.G. Theories of Urban Dynamics. *Int. J. Popul. Res.* **2014**, *2014*, 11. [CrossRef]
51. Burchell, R.W.; Downs, A.; McCann, B.; Mukherji, S. *Sprawl Costs. Economic Impacts of Unchecked Development*; Island Press: Washington, DC, USA, 2005; ISBN 978-1559635707.
52. Beale, C.L.; Fuguitt, G. Decade of pessimistic nonmetro population trends ends on optimistic note. *Rural Dev. Perspect.* **1990**, *6*, 14–18.

53. Couch, C.; Karecha, J.; Nuissl, H.; Rink, D. Decline and sprawl: An evolving type of urban development-observed in Liverpool and Leipzig. *Eur. Plan. Stud.* **2005**, *13*, 117–136. [CrossRef]
54. Haase, A.; Kabisch, S.; Steinfuhrer, A.; Bouzarovski, S.; Hall, R.; Ogden, P. Emergent spaces of reurbanisation: Exploring the demographic dimension of inner-city residential change in a European setting. *Popul. Space Place* **2010**, *16*, 5. [CrossRef]
55. Méndez, R. Crisis, vulnerabilidad y nuevas desigualdades territoriales en España. *Sistema* **2015**, *239*, 45–63.
56. Burriel, E.L. Subversion of land-use plans and the housing bubble in Spain. *Urban Res. Pract.* **2011**, *4*, 232–249. [CrossRef]
57. García, M. The Breakdown of the Spanish Urban Growth Model: Social and Territorial Effects of the GlobalCrisis. *Int. J. Urban Reg. Res.* **2010**, *34*, 967–980. [CrossRef]
58. Lois, R.C.; Piñeira, M.J. The revival of urban social and neighbourhood movements in Spain: A geographical characterization. *Die Erde* **2015**, *146*, 127–138.
59. Lityński, P.; Hołuj, A. Urban Sprawl Costs: The Valuation of Households' Losses in Poland. *J. Settl. Spat. Plan.* **2017**, *8*, 11–35. [CrossRef]
60. Heffner, K. Czynniki Osadnicze Wpływające na Potencjał Rozwojowy Obszarów Wiejskich. In *Wieś i Rolnictwo 2*; IRWIR PAN: Warsaw, Poland, 2002; pp. 27–48.
61. Hoggart, K.; Paniagua, A. The restructuring of rural Spain? *J. Rural Stud.* **2001**, *17*, 63–80. [CrossRef]
62. Hołuj, D.; Hołuj, A. Mechanisms of Densification of the City in the Neoliberal Economy—A Case Study: The Surroundings of the Eastern Part of the Former Airport Runway Rakowice-Czyżyny in Cracow. *Bull. Geogr. Socio-Econ. Ser.* **2015**, *27*, 81–93. [CrossRef]
63. Słodczyk, J. Gospodarka przestrzenna—pojęcia podstawowe. In *Podstawy Gospodarki Przestrzennej—Wybrane Aspekty*; Korenik, S., Słodczyk, J., Eds.; Wrocław University of Economics: Wrocław, Poland, 2005.
64. Newman, P.; Thornley, A. *Urban Planning in Europe: International Competition, National Systems, and Planning Projects*; Psychology Press, Routledge: London, UK; New York, NY, USA; 1996; ISBN 0-203-73618-4.
65. OECD. *Land-Use Planning Systems in the OECD: Country Fact Sheets*; OECD Publishing: Paris, France, 2017; ISBN 978-92-64-26857-9.
66. Reimer, M.; Getimis, P.; Blotevogel, H. (Eds.) *Spatial Planning Systems and Practices in Europe. A Comparative Perspective on Continuity and Changes*, 1st ed.; Routledge: New York, NY, USA, 2014; ISBN 9780415727242.
67. Zambon, I.; Cerdà, A.; Gambella, F.; Egidi, G.; Salvati, L. Industrial Sprawl and Residential Housing: Exploring the Interplay between Local Development and Land-Use Change in the Valencian Community, Spain. *Land* **2019**, *8*, 143. [CrossRef]
68. Serra, P.; Vera, A.; Tulla, A.F.; Salvati, L. Beyond urban–rural dichotomy: Exploring socioeconomic and land-use processes of change in Spain (1991–2011). *Appl. Geogr.* **2014**, *55*, 71–81. [CrossRef]
69. Gomez-Antonio, M.; Hortas-Rico, M.; Li, L. The Causes of Urban Sprawl in Spanish Urban Areas: A Spatial Approach. *Spat. Econ. Anal.* **2014**, *11*, 2. [CrossRef]
70. Catalán, B.; Saurí, D.; Serra, P. Urban sprawl in the Mediterranean? Patterns of growth and change in the Barcelona Metropolitan Region 1992–2000. *Landsc. Urban Plan.* **2008**, *85*, 174–184. [CrossRef]
71. Torrens, P. A toolkit for measuring sprawl. *Appl. Spat. Anal. Policy* **2008**, *1*, 5–36. [CrossRef]
72. Saiz, A. The geographic determinants of housing supply. *Q. J. Econ.* **2010**, *125*, 1253–1296. [CrossRef]
73. García-López, M.A. Urban spatial structure, suburbanization and transportation in Barcelona. *J. Urban Econ.* **2012**, *72*, 176–190. [CrossRef]
74. Śleszyński, P.; Gibas, P.; Sudra, P. The Problem of Mismatch between the CORINE Land Cover Data Classification and the Development of Settlement in Poland. *Remote Sens.* **2020**, *12*, 2253. [CrossRef]
75. Lityński, P.; Hołuj, A. Urban Sprawl Risk Delimitation: The Concept for Spatial Planning Policy in Poland. *Sustainability* **2020**, *12*, 2637. [CrossRef]
76. OECD. *Rethinking Urban Sprawl: Moving Towards Sustainable Cities*; OECD Publishing: Paris, France, 2018.
77. Zaucha, J.; Brodzicki, T.; Ciołek, D.; Komornicki, T.; Mogiła, Z.; Szlachta, J.; Zaleski, J. *Terytorialny Wymiar Wzrostu i Rozwoju. Spójność, Potencjały i Użyteczność [The Territorial Dimension of Growth and Development. Consistency, Potentials and Utility]*; Difin: Warsaw, Poland, 2015; pp. 120–121. ISBN 978-83-7930-939-2.
78. Lityński, P. *The Correlation between Urban Sprawl and the Local Economy in Poland*; Urban Challenge, Urban Planning Institute of the Republic of Slovenia: Ljubljana, Slovenia, 2016; Volume 27, pp. 86–96.
79. Nowak, M.J. *Niesprawność Władz Publicznych a System Gospodarki Przestrzennej*; KPZK, PAN, Studia, CLXXV: Warsaw, Poland, 2017; ISBN 978 8363563 301.
80. Papandreou, A.A. *Externality and Institutions*; Clarendon Press: Oxford, UK, 1994; ISBN 978-0198287759.
81. Bourne, L.S. *Urban Systems: Strategies for Regulation*; Clarendon Press: Oxford, UK, 1975.
82. Mickiewicz, P.; Nowak, M.J.; Mickiewicz, B.; Zvirbule, A. Environmental protection and integrated development planning in local spatial policy on the example of Poland. *Ann. Univ. Apulensis Ser. Oeconomica* **2020**, *22*, 11–17.
83. Śleszyński, P.; Kowalewski, A.; Markowski, T.; Legutko-Kobus, P.; Nowak, M. The Contemporary Economic Costs of Spatial Chaos: Evidence from Poland. *Land* **2020**, *9*, 214. [CrossRef]
84. Meade, J.E. External Economies and Diseconomies in a Competitive Situation. *Econ. J.* **1952**, *62*, 245. [CrossRef]
85. Baumol, W.; Oates, W. Externalities: Definition, significant types, and optimal-pricing conditions. In *The Theory of Environmental Policy*; Cambridge University Press: Cambridge, UK, 1988; pp. 14–35. [CrossRef]

land

MDPI

Article

Taking Implementation Seriously in the Evaluation of Urban Growth Management Strategies: "Safeguarding the Future" of the Antwerp City-Region

Clemens de Olde * and Stijn Oosterlynck

Department of Sociology, Faculty of Social Sciences, University of Antwerp, Stadscampus-Building M, St-Jacobstraat 2, 2000 Antwerp, Belgium; stijn.oosterlynck@uantwerpen.be
* Correspondence: clemens.deolde@uantwerpen.be; Tel.: +32-32655344

Abstract: Contemporary evaluations of urban growth management (UGM) strategies often take the shape of quantitative measurements of land values and housing prices. In this paper, we argue that it is of key importance that these evaluations also analyse the policy formulation and implementation phases of growth management strategies. It is in these phases that the institutions and discourses are (trans)formed in which UGM strategies are embedded. This will enable us to better understand the conditions for growth management policies' success or failure. We illustrate this point empirically with the case of demarcating urban areas in the region of Flanders, Belgium. Using the Policy Arrangement Approach, the institutional dynamics and discursive meanings in this growth instrument's formulation and implementation phase are unravelled. More specifically, we explain how the Flemish strategic spatial planning vision of restraining sprawl was transformed into one of accommodating growth in the demarcation of the Antwerp Metropolitan Area, epitomised by two different meanings of the phrase "safeguarding the future." In conclusion, we argue that, in Antwerp, the demarcation never solidified into a stable policy arrangement, rendering it largely ineffective. We end by formulating three recommendations to contribute to future attempts at managing urban growth in Flanders.

Keywords: urban growth management; urban sprawl; land use planning; zoning; strategic spatial planning; institutionalism; discourse; Antwerp; Flanders

Citation: de Olde, C.; Oosterlynck, S. Taking Implementation Seriously in the Evaluation of Urban Growth Management Strategies: "Safeguarding the Future" of the Antwerp City-Region. *Land* **2021**, *10*, 159. https://doi.org/10.3390/land10020159

Academic Editor: Fabrizio Battisti
Received: 29 December 2020
Accepted: 29 January 2021
Published: 5 February 2021

1. Introduction: Evaluating Growth Management

Compact settlements are beneficial in terms of the cost of mobility and providing public services as well as safeguarding valuable agricultural land and nature. Therefore, planning strategies have been developed throughout the twentieth century in order to guide growth and protect open space [1]. Urban growth boundaries are arguably the most famous instrument used in these growth management strategies. Early examples are found as Greenbelts in the United Kingdom and, from the 1950s, as statutory lines around cities in the United States. In any form, growth boundaries support "The key idea that imposing a defined boundary around a city beyond which development will be prohibited (at least up to some other jurisdiction) will simultaneously prevent sprawl outside the boundary and promote higher density inside it" [2].

From the second half of the twentieth century, urban growth management (UGM) instruments developed from 'simple' urban containment boundaries into comprehensive plans including a wider array of policy measures to restrain urban growth and promote selective development. Recently, smart growth policy packages have centered more on (dis)incentives than direct regulation. Thereby, the perception of urban growth has evolved from a problem to be contained, to an opportunity to fix past development errors and guide new developments to address current social issues [2–4]. As Calthorpe and Fulton state,

> "A multifaceted policy can reinforce a development tendency toward more compact communities, support efficient infrastructure investments, preserve open space, and encourage the revitalization of many declining areas [5]".

Despite the recognition that UGM instruments are multifaceted, Knaap and Nelson already noted three decades ago that, "Although UGBs are multi-objective instruments, most research on the effects of UGBs has focused on land values" [6]. This also holds true for the evaluative literature published in subsequent decades, which focuses primarily on analysing the effects of growth management strategies on land values and housing prices [7–11]. Additionally, there are many reviews of the effects of urban growth management on urban development patterns [12–16] and mobility [17,18].

We argue that a majority of these contributions evaluate growth management strategies by using quantitative indicators of surface areas, retail sales, land values, building lot sales transactions and traffic. Studies often identify growth management policies—without further elaboration—as independent variables tied to a particular geographical location, in order to evaluate their effects [19,20]. New contributions to the body of work generally suggest improvements in measurement methodology or add new case studies. These quantitative evaluations thus often implicitly assume that growth management policies are executed as they were intended, after which effects can be measured. This approach of evaluating UGM stresses the final stage of the policy cycle [21] and creates a blind spot regarding the events and decisions of earlier stages in which policy is conceived, formulated, and implemented. Furthermore, it is striking that there is hardly any work on the public support for growth boundaries.

Therefore, we argue that there is a need to look beyond the measurement of effects of urban growth management instruments and consider the institutional and discursive conditions in which they are formulated and implemented. This aim is supported by occasional contributions to the literature that do at least recognize the importance of cultural factors and institutional settings on the formulation and implementation processes of urban growth measures. After their statistical analyses of growth boundary effectiveness, Jun [12] and Gennaio, Hersperger and Bürgi [16] refer to the pertinence of political debates and circumstances on these policies, though they refrain from delving deeper into them. In other studies, the data on the broader context *is* there, but it is not given a prominent place in the analysis (e.g., Reference [7]). Moreover, Bengston et al., distil the key lesson that "implementation is critical" [22] because it determines effectiveness.

Other authors also point out the importance of institutional and discursive factors for the success of urban growth management. Margerum produces criteria for the evaluation of collaborative planning processes applied to the implementation of growth management strategies in South East Queensland, Australia [23] and Denver, Colorado [24]. The main conclusions of these studies are that growth management collaborations lead to an increased sensitivity to spatial problems on a regional scale, as well as to increased communication between governments. The studies also, however, find a weak political and community input into growth management projects, and stress the importance of these contributions. Knaap [25] points at the importance of citizens' perceived self-interest in growth management for its public support and Knaap and Nelson [6] also note the role of political tension in their evaluation of the Oregon land use program,

> "The construction and implementation of UGBs in other urban areas is a protracted political process. Turf battles often arose between city and county governments and, in the larger metropolitan areas, between city governments [6]".

Finally, various authors call for more context-specific studies and nuanced analytic frameworks of the policy environments and governance structures in which UGM policies are situated [2,3]. In the words of James et al.,

> "Efforts to manage urban growth tend to occur within the frameworks, conventions, and requirements of government structures—from the municipal to

> the national. However, this very much depends upon associated political and cultural systems [26]".

These contributions show that there is a broad awareness of the importance of the institutionalisation of growth management instruments for their success or failure. Yet, the analysis of the policy formulation and implementation phases is still rare in evaluations of growth management strategies. This paper aims to contribute to the body of work by focusing on the institutional and discursive context in which urban growth policies are formulated and implemented. To illustrate the importance of such a perspective, we analyse the growth management instrument of demarcating urban areas in the Belgian region of Flanders using the Policy Arrangement Approach (PAA). Section 2 outlines our research approach.

2. Analysing the Institutional and Discursive Dimensions of UGM

The PAA [27] describes the structure and institutionalisation of policy arrangements. These are defined as "the temporary stabilisation of the content and organisation of a particular policy domain at a certain policy level or over several policy levels" [28]. Through daily interactions between policy actors, patterns emerge that are more or less stable and that may include the "substantive delineation of the problem at stake and of possible solutions, but also the processes of give-and-take between the actors and the formal and informal rules according to which these processes take place" [29]. The Flemish spatial demarcation instrument analysed in this study is one such policy arrangement intended to restrain urban sprawl.

By distinguishing four dimensions of policy arrangements, the PAA analyses institutional patterns of change and stability:

1. The first dimension of *actors and coalitions* include governments, departments, private citizens, firms, and NGOs with a stake in the policy process.
2. The second dimension is *rules of the game*, defined as mutually agreed formal procedures and informal routines of interaction within institutions. These rules select the shape in which social interactions take place. For instance, procedures to involve citizens in the planning process lead to a certain kind of participation which may or may not have the intended effect and may or may not be satisfactory for those participating.
3. Thirdly, *resources and power* can mean material resources such as land and finances, but also knowledge and expertise. Funding agencies, incumbents of political office, and experts all possess particular resources in spatial planning which lead to the possession of various types of power and influence to affect the outcome of a policy process.
4. Fourth, policy arrangements are analysed in terms of *discourses*. This is a substantive dimension, as opposed to the former three, which are organisational dimensions of a policy arrangement. Discourses include the views and narratives of the actors involved in a policy process. Discourses contain and reflect norms and values, problem definitions, and preferred solutions to problems. The PAA draws a distinction between macro-level governance discourses and those at the level of the concrete policy issues at hand. These discourses may overlap or be at odds. For instance, in spatial planning, the strategic aims of a plan at the regional level plan can be opposed to the interpretations of citizens whose property is affected by it.

As Figure 1 shows, the four dimensions of policy arrangements are linked and their analysis only makes sense when all four are taken into account in their interconnectedness. Changes in one dimension are likely to cause changes in the others as well. For instance, the redefinition of a policy problem (discourses) may cause regulations to be altered (rules), different stakeholders to become involved (actors), and other knowledge and funding channels to become relevant (resources). This makes the PAA a starting point for an encompassing and dynamic analysis of policy processes.

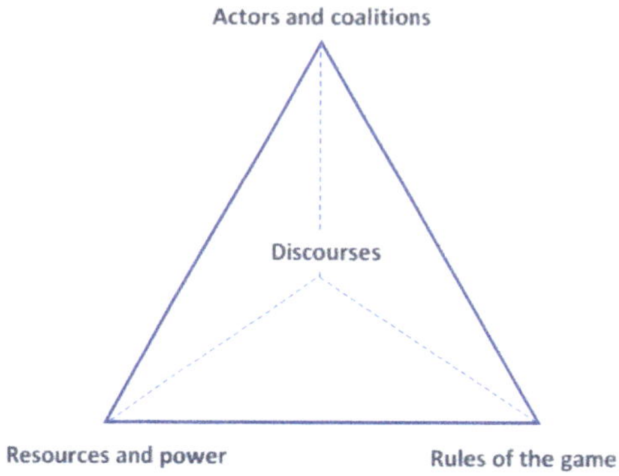

Figure 1. Schematic representation of a single policy arrangement. Adapted from Liefferink in Reference [29].

In this paper, the policy arrangement approach is used to highlight the institutional dimensions of urban growth management strategies. By taking this perspective, we can shed light on the conditions under which the Flemish instrument of demarcating urban areas was formulated and implemented in the Antwerp Metropolitan Area.

3. Case Study: Demarcating Urban Areas in Flanders

3.1. The Belgian and Flemish Spatial Planning System

Modern spatial planning in Belgium can be traced back to the Belgian law on town planning of 1962. This introduced a system of land use planning that led to the development of 48 national zoning plans covering the entire territory. Due to a liberal distribution of areas for housing and other functions in these plans, the landscape became increasingly fragmented. As a part of the federalisation of the Belgian state into semi-autonomous regions, authority over spatial planning in Flanders was devolved to the Flemish region in 1980. Under Flemish rule, further regulations stimulated fragmentation, but the land use planning system introduced in 1962 was kept intact [30].

Within the region, three levels of planning authority operate, each with their respective executive and administrative bodies. At the top, there is the regional level consisting of the Flemish government and the planning administration. The provincial deputation and planning office operate at the intermediate level. Locally, planning is handled by the municipal College of the Mayor and Aldermen and the municipal planning office. Between these levels, a relation of subsidiarity exists. The municipal level is concerned with local planning tasks, the provincial with matters that transcend municipal borders, and the regional with issues that concern the region as a whole. Appeals against decisions are possible from the local to the provincial, and ultimately, the Flemish level [31].

In part due to the adverse effects of the land use planning system on the region's spatial pattern, a new planning system was introduced in the Flemish region in the second half of the 1990s. Now, competent authorities on all three levels were tasked with developing a structure plan containing an overarching strategic planning vision, and spatial plans[1] with decisions to implement this vision.

In the terminology of the most recent comparative study of European spatial planning systems—the ESPON COMPASS project—the Belgian[2] spatial governance and planning system (SGPS) is categorised as one in which market-led development is prevalent. This means that market actors regularly and informally influence spatial policy decision making to pursue their private goals. Additionally, building permits are oriented towards protecting private property, which makes the implementation of comprehensive spatial policy

[1] In Dutch: ruimtelijke uitvoeringsplanning or RUPs.

[2] The COMPASS typology merges insights about the three independent planning systems in Belgium into one national type.

more difficult. Along with the SGPS of 12 Mediterranean and Eastern-European countries, and more so than most other Northern and Western European countries, Belgium leans towards a conformative planning model, where binding general plans determine land use and development rights to a large degree [32]. The legacy of the national zoning plans can clearly be seen here. However, gradual modifications are possible, which is illustrated by interventions made to the zoning plans by the Flemish RUPs at all three levels.

3.2. Restraining Sprawl in Flanders

As a result of its spatial planning history, Flanders is one of the most densely urbanized regions in Europe with a built-up area of 33% [33]. The region is characterized by many of the problems accompanied by such a condition: the fragmentation of nature posing a threat to biodiversity, heavy congestion, a high traffic mortality rate, noise and air pollution, high public expenditures for building and maintaining extensive road and utility networks, insufficient water infiltration leading to flood risk, and finally, the unfavourable aesthetics of a fragmented landscape [34–36].

Because the growth of spatial fragmentation and its problems have long been recognised as an undesirable trend in Belgium [37,38], in 1997, the Spatial Structure plan for Flanders (Dutch: Ruimtelijk Structuurplan Vlaanderen, henceforth: RSV[3]) was developed, accompanied by new planning legislation.[4] The RSV contains an explicit growth management strategy for Flanders[5]. Starting from a vision represented in the metaphor "Flanders Open and Urban", the RSV "(...) strives for a selective concentration of the growth of living, working and of the other social functions in the cities and the nuclei of the countryside" [40]. Therefore, 60% of new housing in Flanders is projected to be realised in demarcated "urban areas" and a maximum of 40% outside them, thereby freezing the areal distribution of urbanization as it was in 1991 and halting the proliferation of urban sprawl. In order to achieve these goals, the RSV distributes quotas of land to be zoned for housing and other functions (industry, services, agriculture, nature) among the Flemish provinces and urban areas, which are to be realized by 2007.

As a part of this strategy, 13 larger and 44 smaller cities designated in the plan are subject to a spatial demarcation instrument that includes a statutory line drawn at plot level around them and parts of their fringe municipalities. Within these urban areas, a concentration and densification of residential and economic functions is envisioned. As a comprehensive growth management strategy, the demarcation process also aimed to promote cooperation between the political, administrative, and societal actors of the urban and suburban (fringe) municipalities to develop a shared vision of the development of the urban region. Within the demarcated area, a number of planning regulations are in effect, the most important being a minimum housing density of 25 units per hectare[6]. The line itself does not change any existing zoning or administrative borders as the new planning regulations only apply to new building permits [7].

Though there are some positive examples, the demarcation of the urban areas is generally regarded very critically in Flanders [41,42]. The structure planning framework in Flanders did not manage to reduce the large amount of residentially zoned areas in Flanders that has existed since the 1970s [38,43]. By not meeting attempts at spatial concentration

[3] This text adheres to the original Dutch acronyms of the planning documents to cater to those familiar with planning in Flanders.

[4] For more information on the RSV's design and implementation, see [30,39].

[5] In addition, there was a set of policy measures aimed at urban revitalization and making cities more attractive places to live; however, as this falls under the policy domain of Domestic Affairs rather than spatial planning, these are left outside the purview of this analysis.

[6] The prescribed minimum density in the rural areas outside the urban growth boundary was 15 units per hectare.

[7] While the demarcations of urban areas in Flanders have some characteristics of smart-growth strategies, they completely lack the involvement of market actors as well as redistribution of development opportunities via transferable development rights (TDR). Furthermore, despite initial intentions, municipalities and provinces were not treated as equal partners in the process. The demarcations are, therefore, discussed here as a classic growth management strategy that in Bae's [2] typology can be characterised as an example of an urban growth boundary with accompanying minimum density zoning, infill and residential unit ordinances and a limitation on new residential development outside the growth boundary.

with a reduction of supply in the suburban and rural parts of the region, the demarcations proved largely inconsequential for the region's spatial pattern.

The intended city–regional cooperation was only achieved in the smaller and "less complex" urban regions and land use logic has emerged as dominant over a more open-ended structure planning approach [44,45]. Reflecting a decade after the approval of the RSV, one of its main authors concludes that demarcation plans have become nothing more than "an inter-municipal local land use plan" which is "an improper use, more strongly, a misuse of the [demarcation] concept that leads to the undesired further juridification of spatial planning" [46]. This raises the question about the conditions of the demarcation instrument's formulation and implementation.

3.3. *Demarcating the Antwerp Metropolitan Area*

Our analysis focuses on the spatial demarcation process of Antwerp. Because it is the largest demarcation process in the Flemish region, it provides the richest selection of findings to analyse the implementation of the growth management policy [8]. The Antwerp urban growth boundary covers parts of 19 different municipalities, two of which lie outside the province of Antwerp in the neighbouring province of East-Flanders. The map in Figure 2 shows land coverage in the greater Antwerp area in 2015. Superimposed on the map is the demarcation line of the Antwerp Metropolitan Area. The map illustrates that Antwerp is a concentrated urban core with a fringe characterised by urban sprawl and ribbon development, both inside and outside the demarcated urban area. Next to the demarcation line, the plan includes 24 areas to be rezoned in order to achieve the quota set for the various spatial functions outlined in the RSV.

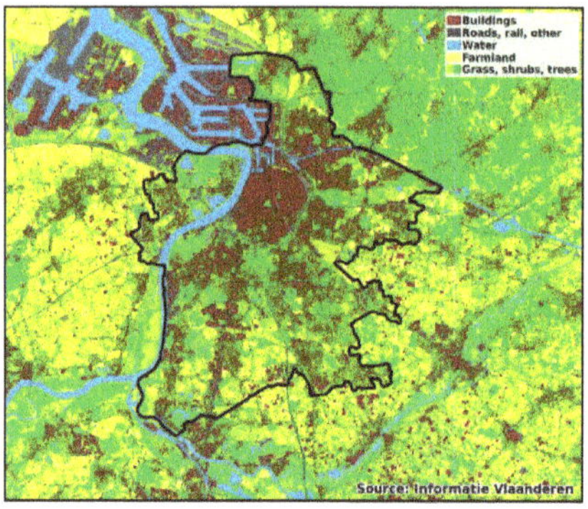

Figure 2. Land coverage in the greater Antwerp area 2015 including the Metropolitan Area demarcation [48,49].

Planning regulations for the urban area are recorded in a regional spatial plan (Gewestelijk Ruimtelijk Uitvoeringsplan or GRUP) for the Antwerp Metropolitan Area [50]. It was designed by a private spatial planning firm, finalized by the regional planning administration and approved by the Flemish government. The timeline in Table 1 shows that this process spanned a period of six years (2003–2009), excluding the legal procedures that followed.

8 The demarcation process of the Flemish urban area surrounding Brussels is arguably even more complex and hence rich in empirical terms. However, as Brussels is a separate region within Belgium, its demarcation is strongly characterised by communitarian politics [47] and is, therefore, not typical of the demarcation processes in Flanders in general.

Table 1. Demarcation of the Antwerp Metropolitan Area: Timeline.

Period	Event
April 2003	Start of demarcation process, round of exploratory talks with municipalities conducted by planning firm led by a former provincial official.
June 2004–April 2005	Three "steering group" meetings of Flemish officials, provinces and municipalities, leading to various iterations of a metropolitan vision.
15 April 2005	Final report concluding the vision process. Contains proposal of demarcation and areas to be rezoned. End of assignment for planning firm.
2007[9]	Process restarted by administration. August 23rd plenary meeting on the design of the regional spatial plan (GRUP).
April–June 2008	Environmental and safety assessments completed.
1 July 2008	Minister of Spatial Planning presents the spatial demarcation to mayors of municipalities involved in plenary meeting.
5 September 2008	Preliminary approval of the Flemish Government of the demarcation Antwerp Metropolitan Area, press release.
October–December 2008	Public inquiry. Objections considered by the Flemish Committee of Spatial Planning (Vlacoro).
8 April 2009	Report of the Flemish Committee of Spatial Planning.
19 Jun 2009	Definitive approval of regional spatial development plan of the demarcation Antwerp metropolitan area.
2009–2012	Council of State hears several procedures against the demarcation GRUP.

3.4. Data

The following empirical analysis is based on a study of the officially published plans and policy documents. From 2015 to 2018, in-depth interviews were conducted with 17 planning experts and officials at the regional level (designated E#), 3 local planners (A–S#), 5 politicians (A–P#), and 4 citizen-activists (A–A#).[10] These interviews were all transcribed and coded. The private planning firm granted access to its archives, while several key respondents provided documents from their personal archives. An analysis of 84 articles in the local newspaper mentioning the demarcation between 1997 and 2017 provided additional context. In the public inquiry on the Antwerp demarcation, the Flemish Committee of Spatial Planning (Vlacoro)—consisting of planning experts, government representatives, and civil society actors—summarized and advised on more than 6000 objections to the preliminary GRUP bundled in petitions, 2100 individual objections, and 12 recommendations by local and provincial governments. The responses in the resulting report [51] were coded by the researchers to show the argumentations for accepting or rejecting the objections. Finally, policy evaluations of various other demarcation and city–regional cooperation processes were drawn upon [42,44,45,47,52,53].

4. Analysis: Safeguarding the Future

Table 2 provides a schematic summary of the analysis of four phases of policy formulation and implementation in the demarcation process. By distinguishing the four dimensions of the PAA in each phase, we show how the land use logic gradually overtook the vision of combating urban sprawl. Each phase is explained in the subsections below.

9 Politicians in Flanders are allowed to have concurrent seats in both local and regional bodies, creating close ties between local and regional politics. Therefore, the process was halted between 2005 and 2007 pending the outcome of local elections taking place 8 October 2006.

10 There were more interviews conducted with local planners, politicians and citizens since the demarcation of the urban area surrounding the city of Mechelen was also researched. As this paper only reports on the Antwerp case, these are not included here.

Table 2. Policy arrangement analysis of the demarcation of the Antwerp Metropolitan Area.

Phase PAA Dimension	1. Counteracting Fragmentation 1996–1997	2. Increasing Tension 2003–2005	3. Economic Engine for Flanders 2007–2008	4. "Coordinating Objections" 2008–2009
Actors and Coalitions	Designers Spatial Structure Plan for Flanders Private urban planning firm designing demarcation methodology.	Private urban planning firm (attempts to maintain original vision). City of Antwerp (disinterested). Fringe municipalities and Flemish Region (oppositional). "Lack of a figurehead".	Spatial Planning administration turns proposal into preliminary plan. Minister of Spatial Planning and his cabinet influence content of the preliminary plan. Fringe municipalities (opposition and political struggles).	Flemish Committee of Spatial Planning adjudicates objections. Citizens, organisations and municipalities (object in public inquiry). Flemish Government decides on final spatial plan, not bound to follow advice.
Rules of the Game	New structure planning framework with the ambition to move beyond legalistic land use planning tradition.	Strategic structure planning approach shackled by land use planning status quo. Fear of a demarcated "urban area" as prelude to municipal mergers. "Procedural process".	Goal: meeting quantified targets laid out in earlier plans. Rising stakes: demarcation starts to function as guideline for distribution of resources in other public sectors, leading to power plays.	Rules of the public inquiry procedure of central importance. Previous plans, regulations, legislation both objected to and used as basis for recommendations.
Resources and Power	Offer sectoral targets for growth to ensure political support for RSV.	Little fringe capacity to handle demarcation process, sufficient capacity in the city. Links between local and regional politics influencing the plan. Resources for consultation process withheld.	Designating land for development to ensure stakeholder support. Metropolitan functions. Administration and Minister possess power of summary viz. earlier steps in the process.	Objections over zoning decisions. Lack of legal, financial and temporal resources to file objections for most citizens.
Discourses	Deconcentrated clustering to safeguard rural areas from urban development.	Antwerp region as a checkerboard of fragmentation, reduce pressure on the countryside. Ambition for city–regional cooperation: "from Antwerp to the Antwerp region". Negative connotation of "urban area".	Space for expansion: Safeguarding the future by enabling development. The plan creates "new space" and the possibility to build new houses. Quantified targets versus threat to local liveability.	Making technical recommendations. Quantitative targets take precedence over spatial quality. "In what way are *our* [citizens] interests represented?"

Between the original vision of the demarcation instrument and the way it is presented in the preliminary version of the spatial plan for the Antwerp Metropolitan Area, a major discursive shift occurred. On 5 September 2008, a press release titled "Antwerp's future safeguarded by the demarcation process of the metropolitan area" marked the Flemish

Government's preliminary approval of the demarcation plan. The plan is promoted as creating new development opportunities, states that it "provides new space" and includes a list of amounts of land area (re)zoned for housing, nature and industry, which is translated in Antwerp's local newspaper as: "the GRUP enables the construction of 8249 houses" [54]. Additionally, the press release mentions decisions on a number of "metropolitan functions" such as regularising a golf course, finding a location for a soccer stadium and the expansion of the local airport. The minister of spatial planning is quoted,

> "Today we have arrived at a balanced proposal in which we safeguard the future of the Antwerp region and make the Antwerp metropolitan area even more attractive for working, residing and living [11]".

The discourse of a press release may be expected to present the ultimate legitimation for a spatial plan to the broader public. Here, it shows a dominant logic of land use planning with land and building opportunities represented as resources made available through zoning. This discourse is almost the opposite of the vision of the Spatial Structure Plan for Flanders under which the demarcation instrument was introduced. Its focus has changed from safeguarding rural areas from development, to safeguarding the future by making development possible. Why did the authors of the press release and their political superiors opt to present the plan in terms of the land use logic dominant in Flanders throughout the second half of the twentieth century, instead of in the terms introduced in the Spatial Structure Plan for Flanders ten years earlier?

4.1. Phase 1: Counteracting Fragmentation (1996–1997)

Despite a discourse that underlines the necessity to counteract urban sprawl, the tension between land use logic and strategic planning is already present in the two documents that lie at the root of the demarcation processes. These are a preparatory study to determine a methodology for demarcating urban areas, commissioned with a private urban planning firm [55][12], and the Spatial Structure Plan for Flanders itself.

The preparatory study mentions the spatial fragmentation of the Flemish settlement structure explicitly as the main reason for developing an urban growth management instrument. It states that, in Flanders, there is currently no clear separation between "urban" and "open space" and it introduces the ambition to break with the trend of a primarily land use-oriented spatial policy. The study presents this intent as the:

> "(...) directed interweaving and bundling of functions and facilities, among which the economic functions, within the urban areas, above all absolute priority is to use and manage the existing urban structure as well as possible (...) the preservation and where possible strengthening and expansion of open space. (...) This breaking of the trend aims for the protection of open space, counteracting the fragmentation, and the separation of open space and urban areas [55]".

In the RSV itself, this is translated into the central strategic spatial policy concept of deconcentrated clustering: striving for a greater bundling of activities within Flanders' decentralized urban structure. The principle is positioned explicitly as a means of combatting urban sprawl:

> "Deconcentrated clustering goes against unbridled suburbanisation and fragmentation and thus reduces the pressure on the countryside [39]".

Combatting sprawl in order to reduce—or at least restrain—the growing negative effects on mobility, environment and cost of public services was, hence, originally one of

---

[11] All quotes from interviewees, press and policy documents are translated from Dutch by the authors.

[12] In Flanders, these firms perform a mix of architectural, urban planning and research work with some of their staff moving freely in both academic and practitioners' circles. In fact, one of the firm's directors played an important role in developing the RSV itself. Furthermore, building private sector capacity through developing expertise regarding the new structure planning framework was a deliberate strategy of those designing the RSV to improve the quality of its implementation [1].

the main goals of this first overarching spatial plan for the Flemish region. The demarcation of urban areas was to be the prime instrument to realise this:

> "The demarcation of the urban areas is considered an essential policy measure in order to stop the urban flight and ribbon development, to be able to realise a "supply policy" regarding additional housing and space for economic activities and safeguard the rural areas from urban development ([39], p. 212)".

This discourse is found in the vision section of both documents and, as such, outlines a number of "grand goals" for the future without going too deeply into particulars. The documents also show that the original methodology to arrive at a demarcation proposal (delineating an urban area and identifying certain areas for rezoning to create a supply of well-situated development areas) was a rich one that considers many socio-spatial indicators before proposing a desired spatial structure.

In terms of actors, the process was supervised by the Flemish regional authorities, though shaping a vision for the urban area itself was considered a task for the municipalities. Therefore, the intent was to give provinces and municipalities the opportunity to provide their input at various moments in the process.

However, this method stood in a tense relationship with the customary practice of land use planning. The newly introduced planning system had to operate against the background of the preceding generation of zoning plans that fix the permitted use of every plot of land in the Flemish region and that continue to shape the spatial-political reality up to this day. While the new planning system preferred a more open strategic "structure planning" process over the existing "passive" national zoning plans, many actors were used to a rule-based practice oriented to the legal certainty of zoning. One of the designers of the RSV mentions the tension between these two paradigms:

> "We were not always very happy with that. Because what we wanted to do was partly at odds with the traditional zoning plans. Those are aimed primarily at legal certainty (. . .) while we would have preferred to depart from a vision and then see which technical, juridical conditions were necessary to transform those interventions in reality (E2)".

There was a keen awareness among the promotors of the RSV (actors) that the success of its strategic spatial planning vision depended on discursive and institutional support of other public and private actors. As part of that strategy, zoning logic did serve a purpose as a resource to ensure their cooperation when implementing the RSV's policy goals by promising them possibilities of future spatial expansion. Thus, the preparatory study already recognizes the importance of sectoral targets for housing, industry, et cetera, when it states that "the translation of these [targets] to an urban area is precondition to establish a demarcation." While concluding that vision is important to achieve the desired spatial structure, the study emphasizes that:

> "The spatial concepts for an urban area have to be aimed at possibilities for expansion. Especially the targets regarding housing and commercial areas have to be translated to the terrain [55]".

Despite the presence of this tension, the vision of counteracting spatial fragmentation was carried forward into the Antwerp demarcation process by a key actor: the same urban planning firm that had produced the preparatory study was commissioned to produce the demarcation proposal for the Antwerp Metropolitan Area.

4.2. *Phase 2: Increasing Tension (2003–2005)*

While the private planning firm could be considered a champion for the new structure planning approach, when the time came to demarcate the Antwerp Metropolitan Area, it quickly ran into other actors: a disinterested City of Antwerp and opposition from both its fringe municipalities and the Flemish Region. This would lead to a loss of resources for broad consultation and the development of city–regional coordination. Lack of formal political support seriously weakened the vision of safeguarding the future through combating urban sprawl and provided room for the land use paradigm to come to the fore.

As a first step towards a demarcation plan for the Antwerp Metropolitan Area, the private planning firm drew up a proposal in a consortium formed with subcontractors responsible for communication and citizen participation. Subsequently, an extensive formal consultation programme was planned. The proposal's discourse reflects the RSV's evaluation of space in Flanders, characterising the Antwerp Area as a "checkerboard of fragmentation", a network city, or a "polycentric whole of fragments, of poles, of dense and less dense places" [56]. To guide development, the proposal aims to realise a supply of development areas within the metropolitan area of Antwerp; it reads:

> "The pressure on the countryside can only be controlled by catering to the spatial needs for housing and commercial activities in the urban area ([56], p. 13)".

In order to realise these aims, a demarcation line is drawn and proposals are made to activate some (residential, industrial and commercial) reserve areas, while eliminating others. The document also includes proposals for infrastructure renewal, investments in housing and culture, regional, transnational and global networking, and the creation of a metropolitan green structure as goals accompanying the demarcation exercise. Finally, by explicitly extending mentions of "Antwerp" to "the Antwerp region"[13], the demarcation proposal repeatedly underlines that this is an effort to be made not just by the city of Antwerp, but by all of the municipalities involved (discourse). It states that cooperation can be realised in a "strong and coherent metropolitan framework" which could be pursued by a potent planning administration on metropolitan level or "a platform that supports the metropolitan policy" ([56], pp. 35, 51, 149).

However, the ambitious vision of counteracting sprawl through the development of a spatially concentrated city-region laid out in the demarcation proposal was impeded by other actors: the Antwerp fringe municipalities and the Flemish Region itself. First, the complex and time-consuming policy context in the Antwerp region restrained working towards city–regional cooperation. The relationship between the city and the fringe municipalities is historically fraught with tensions as far as spatial planning is concerned (see Chapter 2 in Reference [57]). As a part of these tensions, fringe municipalities often self-identify as rural, to stress their independent character as opposed to the (urbanised) City of Antwerp [58]. Therefore, the discursive concept of "urban area" quickly acquired a negative connotation, which, in turn, resulted in political and public resistance to the planning process. There was also fear in some fringe municipalities that the demarcation would be a prelude to future mergers, causing local politicians to start attending meetings originally intended for Flemish and local planning officials. The planning firm reported, nonetheless, that support for the metropolitan area was growing steadily at this time. Various respondents still recall a two-day workshop with stakeholders held in an abbey in one of the fringe municipalities, which acted as "neutral ground" outside Antwerp city limits according to one respondent (A-P5).

The early involvement of local politics was initially welcomed by the Flemish administration as an opportunity to generate support for the project. At the same time, though, the regional level had a low estimation of municipal expertise—also found in other demarcation processes [45]. Building up municipal planning capacity as a resource was another aim of the RSV, but it had not advanced very far at the time of the Antwerp demarcation. When asked about the time available to occupy oneself with the demarcation process, one fringe municipality planner responds:

> "Yes, very limited you know? The main task is handling permits, planning is a task at the side. So, I didn't really treat it very substantially (A-S2)".

[13] This sounds more subtle in Dutch: een verruiming van "Antwerpen" naar "het Antwerpse" (p. 37). A formulation with sufficient vagueness not to be politically threatening.

At the Flemish level, in 1999, a Liberal Party Minister had taken the place of Christian-Democrat and Socialist predecessors who had initiated the RSV and the new planning framework. From this moment, measures aimed at restraining growth outside the urban areas were weakened. In terms of rules, this resulted in a failure to meet the envisioned supply policy in the urban areas with a restrictive land development policy beyond them [30,59]. The planning firm was also not granted permission by the Flemish administration to execute the public consultation part of the assignment and was not paid for work already performed. Consequentially, little resources were spent on promoting an agenda of city–regional cooperation. The private planning firm also noted the lack of a key public figure (actor) to support the strategic spatial planning vision behind the demarcation process. The then mayor of the city of Antwerp was approached to fulfil this pioneering role, but declined because he felt that involvement of his office would fuel distrust in the fringe municipalities.

In fact, the City itself took a back bench in the demarcation process. As one city planning official summarized the attitude: "We'll do it because Flanders is doing it. But we'll decide for ourselves what exactly we'll have to do" (A-S1). For any rezoning it wanted to initiate, it had ample planning resources to organise itself and it was, therefore, not interested in the Flemish rezoning exercise. Interviewees also report a direct link between city politicians and ministers of their party in the Flemish Government. This "vertical connection" functioned as a resource to influence important decisions and resulted in the private planning firm and regional planning officials being taken out of the loop for all the important dossiers regarding the city.

Though discursively still representing the vision of the RSV, the tension between this vision and the land use logic is already visible in the 2005 final demarcation proposal. The erosion of the RSV's vision can be seen where the text explicitly states that it does not want to interfere with the borders, plans and powers of the individual municipalities and does not aim to create new administrative authorities. Despite repeatedly stressing the need for city–regional cooperation, the text mentions the low levels of support and enthusiasm for the demarcation process. The approach, lacking resources for the consultation programme, is recontextualised as an approach through "predominantly informal contacts". The goal of working towards city–regional cooperation was henceforth abandoned in favour of what one interviewee calls a much more "procedural process" (A-S1). Another city official recalls:

> "Although the planning firm started from the ambition of the RSV, from a demarcation line to a programme for the Antwerp region, they were not allowed to work like that, they had to return to the old way of rezoning and -colouring. In effect this is almost a zoning plan (A-P5)".

4.3. *Phase 3: Economic Engine for Flanders (2007–2009)*

When the preliminary demarcation plan was published in 2008, its discourse had transformed into one of "creating space" for expansion, omitting completely the RSV's aim of counteracting unbridled suburbanisation and fragmentation and reducing pressure on the countryside. The prime discursive legitimation presented in the preliminary plan is the continued development of the Antwerp area's position as metropolis and economical engine for Flanders. This, was argued, requires improvement of the quality of the locations for employment, housing, metropolitan services, natural and landscape structures, roads and public transport [50]. The preliminary plan only contains two cursory mentions of the spatial fragmentation of the Antwerp area before moving on to discuss quantified targets for housing and industrial development. The land use logic that already played a role in the earlier phases of policy formulation—both as the legal inheritance of the previous planning system and as *resource* to ensure stakeholder support—takes centre stage in this phase. Thus, the process reflects the exact political-institutional dynamics of land development leading to the spatial fragmentation that the initiators of the RSV sought to transform and contain. Reflecting critically on the process, one city official concludes that the demarcation was reduced to "a number of banal zoning changes" but not to a serious action plan, that, for instance, also included a mobility policy (A-S1).

The Flemish spatial planning administration processed the demarcation proposal into a regional spatial plan. This means that administration and the cabinet of the Minister were the actors that possessed the power to represent and foreground certain voices and arguments from the previous stage and filter out others. Possessing this "power of summary" [60] without the obligation to offer legitimation, the regional administration could also make a different selection of areas for rezoning. Indeed, at this stage, several areas proposed for rezoning and development in the previous phase were left out. Others were added that were not included in the earlier demarcation proposal, either because they were deemed unfit for development by the private planning firm or because they were advised negatively by the City. Eliminating the already existing zoning of a number of areas is no longer mentioned. Finally, some areas for "metropolitan functions" are inserted into the plan. These provide zoning for a water purification installation, a soccer stadium, regularization of a golf course and a commercial area attached to the local airport. Zoning interventions like these were not conceived as part of the demarcation instrument though it could be argued that finding locations for these kinds of supra-local functions is not contrary to the vision of developing a coherent metropolitan area. Yet various interviewees felt these metropolitan functions to be the result of political deals between the City and the Flemish Government and the lobbying of private market parties. In particular, the minister who was elected in the Antwerp constituency and hence had a local political stake in the demarcation process (E3, A-S1, A-P5). Overall, we can thus conclude that, in this phase, the growth management logic of drawing development to some zones in order to prevent it in others was dropped. Despite their caution, the municipalities had been fairly constructive partners during the production of the private planning firm's demarcation proposal. This changed when the classification of urban areas was adopted by other policy sectors as a criterion (rule) for the allocation of public resources such as healthcare facilities and cultural centres[14]. This raised the stakes of (not) falling within an urban area and led to "power plays" between the stakeholders involved reminiscent of the turf battles described by Knaap and Nelson [6]. Similar to the strategy of the city, politicians from fringe municipalities attempted to safeguard their municipality's interests at the Flemish level by exerting influence through "vertical" party lines as well. Furthermore, the animosity between city and fringe came to a head. One interviewee in the Flemish Administration describes the process as:

> "How can I as a city gain power over the adjacent municipalities, and how can I as fringe municipality keep the power of the city out? That's what it came down to. And absolutely nothing more, no cooperation (E1)".

In some municipalities the demarcation became the subject of local political struggles. Opposition parties politicized the demarcation dossier and attempted to co-opt citizens' protests (see also Coppens, Van Den Broeck and Van Wymeersch [53]). One mayor viewed the opposition's stirring up of fears of being absorbed by the city as a strategy of keeping the majority on its toes (A-P3). However, majority politicians resisted the demarcation as well, in sometimes fateful *discourse*. A local alderwoman is quoted in the press:

> "Because of the plans, some farms will be doomed to disappear since the area will have become unliveable (Gazet van Antwerpen, 21 November 2008)".

4.4. Phase 4: "Coordinating Objections" (2008–2009)

Spatial plans in Flanders, like that of the demarcation, are subject to a public inquiry prior to approval by the government. In this last phase of the policy implementation

[14] A point interesting in its own right. The adoption of planning categorizations by other policy sectors could be regarded as a desirable intent of a strategic spatial planning instrument. In the Flemish case, however, this led to struggle and dissatisfaction which expressed itself in a lack of cooperation at the local level that then extended to the Flemish regional level.

process, it becomes clear that the ambition to realise the demarcation in line with the original strategic spatial planning vision has completely withered away and has been replaced by a predominant focus on distribution of resources and rules of the game. In this step in the process, the public inquiry instrument acts as a "regulative device" [60] that takes up some voices and neutralises others. It marks a genre-shift in the planning process from formulating (beneficial) spatial policy to responding to objections. The responses formulated by the Flemish Committee of Spatial Planning to the objections made in the public inquiry were analysed by the researchers. Figure 3 shows the types of the 1375 arguments used[15].

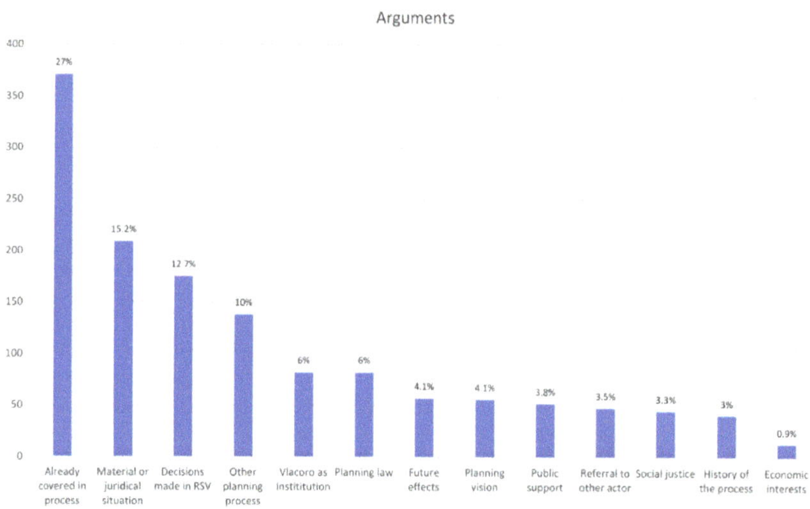

Figure 3. Arguments used in the responses to objections (including internal references).

Overall, the original strategic spatial vision of restraining sprawl in Flanders played no significant role in the objections to the plan. With only 4.1% of responses referring in one way or another to the spatial vision, it was not a major argument in the responses of the committee either (Figure 3). Nor did the chairman of the Committee consider adjudicating objections on the basis of the original planning vision its task. They rather took a rule-based view where the Committee is mostly focused on "coordinating technical objections" so the plan could ultimately be approved:

> "The objections had to be coordinated and then we expect from Vlacoro a technical recommendation. (. . .) Yes, it was a technical committee. So, in principle you have to depart from the RSV that was approved by parliament. Vlacoro did not judge that. It's more about: How shall we propose to solve these technical objections? (E4-1)".

The public inquiry rather triggered responses of citizens and other parties who felt their (landed) interests to be threatened by the urban policy within the demarcation line. This can be seen in the numerous objections that focus on land use type as a resource (re)distributed by the plan:

> "The regulations for the natural area are unclear, can I build a stable for animals, does the area need to be fenced in, can the terrains be grazed, . . . ([51], p. 14)".

[15] These numbers include "internal references": responses to objections that refer to previous responses in the report.

"The 33 ha of the industrial zone is too little considering the high target number. One wonders whether the site doesn't have the potential to incorporate more ([51], p. 33)".

"Why is the Fort of Kruibeke included in the demarcation and not that of Zwijndrecht? The fort of Kruibeke also needs to be excluded from the demarcation ([51], p. 33)".

There are also many procedural challenges to previous plans, regulations, urban planning legislation, and the authority of the Flemish Government to make zoning decisions usually made by municipalities. Most of these, however, have a clear aim of stopping or promoting zoning decisions. The resource-oriented focus of the way urban growth management was implemented through this regional spatial plan was also noted by the committee in its general remarks:

"The plan is strongly based on the obligation to realize the quantitative targets, which means that there is sometimes less attention left for the spatial quality of some proposed urban developments ([51], p. 102)".

Although the public inquiry instrument is designed to allow the voice of citizens and interest groups to be heard, it functions as a regulative device where the "right kind" of discursively and institutionally framed objections (predominantly of a rule-oriented legal nature) are more likely to succeed. In fact, most objections are rejected, or—another example of the power of summary mentioned in Section 4.3—recontextualised and referred to the committee's general remarks (Figure 4). One citizen-activist who led a local group that opposed the inclusion of his neighbourhood in the demarcation summarizes the difficulty of mobilizing the resources and knowledge to phrase objections:

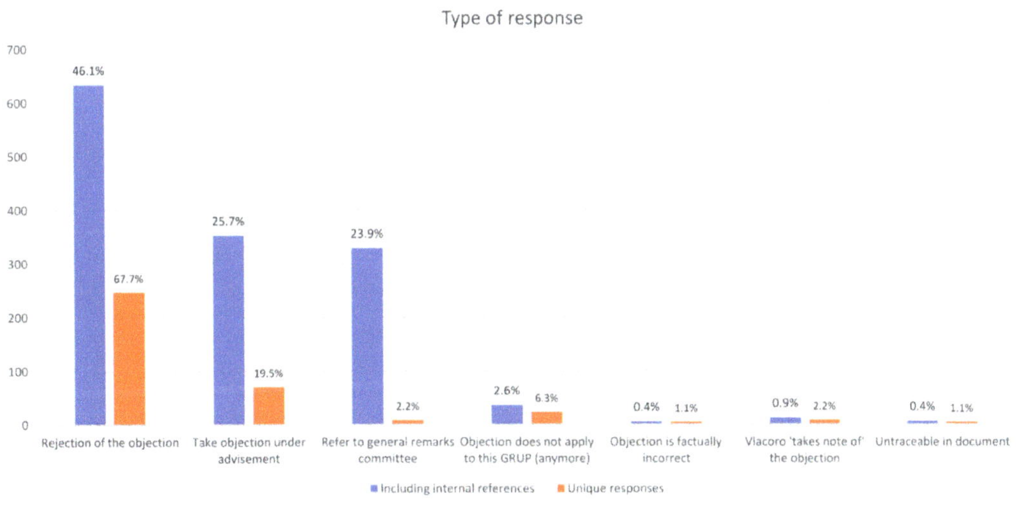

Figure 4. Responses considered in the public inquiry.

There is no capacity. It's almost impossible as a citizen nowadays to object properly against a complex plan. And then you have to know the procedures too. Planning law is tremendously complex. You can't know that as a citizen, you have to hire a very expensive specialised lawyer. There is no money for that. Who is going to gather that? Who will pay for that? And you have to do all of that within a month. That's practically impossible! (A-A1).

Ultimately, the public inquiry led to the elimination of three of the twenty-seven areas to be rezoned. A fourth area was retracted by the Flemish Government a year after the approval of the final demarcation plan in 2009. Four lawsuits were filed with the Council of State, but these only aimed to annul parts of the metropolitan area developments due to local concerns and did not pertain to a larger strategic spatial planning vision. As mentioned by the respondents, filing lawsuits requires resources that only specific actors are able to mobilize: time, knowledge and skills to construct a well-documented dossier and the financial means to hire specialized legal counsel. This left most citizen-activists disillusioned with the process and the value of filing objections:

> And apart from the number of objections you filed, or the number of signatures you collected, that is of no import. The law is the only thing of import. [Politicians say] we belong in the urban area so we can't say no [to development]. –Yes, but what about *our* arguments? In what way do you represent *our* interest? The interest of the common citizen, of the current residents? And there is absolutely no answer to that (A-A2).

Thus, the public inquiry instrument could not ensure the implementation of the original policy vision of restraining sprawl, but served instead as a regulative device to address public participation in a way that maintained the tried and true practice of zoning logic with its emphasis on rules and resources. The result is captured by one rather disillusioned planning official:

> And what it became in the end is at its Belgian, right? Something very administrative, something legal-technical, zoning, securing, putting it into concrete. Was that the intent? I don't think so, but oh well. That's the only thing people know in Flanders right: securing, juridical (knocks on table). Which rights do I have, up to which plot? And that entire structure planning philosophy is translated in demarcations at the plot level, property titles yet again. What is allowed, what isn't? That uncertainty of "in time, what could this become??" A Fleming doesn't want that (laughs) (E3).

5. Conclusions

Despite a broad recognition in the literature that "implementation is critical" [22], contemporary evaluations of growth management strategies still mostly take the shape of quantified measurements of effects such as land values and housing prices, where it is often implicitly assumed that policy was implemented as it was intended. In this paper, we argue that understanding the formulation and implementation phases of these spatial policy instruments is of key importance to gain insight into the conditions of success and failure of growth management strategies.

This argument is illustrated by the analysis of the formulation and implementation of an urban growth management strategy in Flanders, Belgium. Using the Policy Arrangement Approach, it was shown how the institutional dimensions of actors, rules, resources and discourses in the demarcation of the Antwerp Metropolitan Area interrelate to produce an outcome almost diametrically opposed to the original planning vision of reducing urban sprawl. This vision collapsed during implementation where the new structure planning framework was mostly recontextualized in terms of its still active land use predecessor. The orientation towards the protection of private property characteristic of the Belgian spatial governance and planning system, as noted in the ESPON COMPASS classification, can be seen here. This is illustrated by the discursive presentation of land as a resource for new developments and a concomitant focus on the legal aspects of land use planning. In the Antwerp Metropolitan Area, the intent to create a sensitivity to spatial problems on a city–regional scale was eclipsed by antagonistic relations between public actors, resulting in turf battles. Other stakeholders mainly showed disinterest in the process and measures to restrain development outside of the urban growth boundaries were never implemented. Weak community input and the fact that citizens' self-interest did not coincide with the strategic spatial vision led to objections and disillusion, captured by local politics. The dissolution of the original vision is reflected in the discursive metamorphosis of the meaning of the phrase "safeguarding the future" from counteracting urban sprawl into safeguarding it by guaranteeing further development opportunities.

In the Antwerp case, the demarcation of the urban area never solidified into a stable policy arrangement for creating a metropolitan area and combatting urban sprawl on a city–regional scale. Instead, the substantive delineation of the problem, as reflected in the discourse of the Minister, shifted throughout the process from combatting sprawl to creating future development opportunities and solving a number of problematic spatial dossiers. The give-and-take between policy actors and interest groups was profoundly disturbed by strategic behaviour intended to safeguard individual interests. This left a focus on the 'rules of the game' according to which the demarcation process ought to take place. The foregrounding of these rules can be seen from the second stage of the process onward with a "procedural process" taking the place of strategic cooperation, a focus on meeting the quantitative targets for rezoning, the self-perception of the Committee of Spatial Planning as a "technical committee", and finally, in the lawsuits following the demarcation's approval. These findings show that the results of UGM instruments should not only be evaluated from the perspective of their measurable effectiveness, but as part of a project of institutional, discursive, and therefore, sociocultural change. Since a successor to the structure planning framework is currently in development [61], we can ask how a repetition of history may be prevented. The findings in this paper strongly suggest that future planning initiatives aimed at counteracting urban sprawl in Flanders need to take into account three elements. First, Flanders needs to free itself from the historical legacy of the Belgian land use planning system in order for new planning frameworks to have a chance at being successful. The legalistic focus on extensive land use rights established in a growth-centred era hamper any ambitious sustainable spatial development perspective for the region.[16] Secondly, the historical animosity between cities and suburban fringe municipalities will not disappear if planning processes are merely centred on achieving quantitative targets and rely too much on the voluntary participation of these parties. Withdrawing the means for consultation or co-creative processes is a sure way of undermining any local support for city regional cooperation that might exist at the outset of a new planning initiative. Therefore, a strong planning vision and policy implementation on the Flemish regional level is needed to give direction to new initiatives for city–regional planning cooperation. The new Flemish "policy planning" framework is characterised by more elements of smart-growth strategies, including the active involvement of market parties and transferable development rights (TDR). Yet, it is our contention that these strategies will not work if the Flemish government does not adopt a directing role. In addition, political interlinkages between the local and the Flemish regional level need to be regarded with caution. They may aid to promote local support, but also carry the danger of too strong a representation of local interests on the regional level. Finally, public inquiry processes should not solely be treated as "technical coordination" of objections. Spatial planning in urban areas like these revolves around the distribution of scarce spatial resources, which implies that not every actor can be satisfied. However, more constructive ways of handling objections and creating public support need to be found if a new planning framework is to be successful.

Author Contributions: Conceptualization, C.d.O. and S.O.; methodology, C.d.O. and S.O.; formal analysis, C.d.O.; investigation, C.d.O.; data curation, C.d.O.; writing—original draft preparation, C.d.O.; writing—review and editing, C.d.O. and S.O.; visualization, C.d.O.; supervision, S.O.; project administration, C.d.O. Both authors have read and agreed to the published version of the manuscript.

Funding: This research received no external funding.

[16] We are not alone in reaching this conclusion. Various Flemish planning experts argue for and propose ways of abolishing the national zoning plans [62,63].

Institutional Review Board Statement: Ethical review and approval were waived for this study as it did not meet the criteria of the risk analysis table provided by the Ethics Committee for the Social Sciences and Humanities of the University of Antwerp. The identities and contact details of the respondents are only known to the researchers and are not shared with other parties, no vulnerable parties were interviewed and no sensitive information was asked.

Informed Consent Statement: Informed consent was obtained from all subjects involved in the study.

Data Availability Statement: The data presented in this study are not publicly available due to the requirement to protect the participant identities. The data are available from the corresponding author only after the participants' consent.

Acknowledgments: The authors wish to thank all participants in the study for their insights, contributions and time.

Conflicts of Interest: The authors declare no conflict of interest.

References

1. Hack, G. Shaping Urban Form. In *Planning Ideas That Matter*; Sanyal, B., Vale, L., Rosan, C., Eds.; The MIT Press: Cambridge, MA, USA, 2012; pp. 33–64.
2. Bae, C.-H.C. Containing Sprawl. In *Incentives, Regulations and Plans: The Role of States and Nation-states in Smart Growth Planning*; Knaap, G.-J., Haccoû, H.A., Clifton, K.J., Frece, J.W., Eds.; Edward Elgar Publishing: Cheltenham, UK, 2007; pp. 36–53.
3. Chapin, T.S. Introduction: From Growth Controls, to Comprehensive Planning, to Smart Growth: Planning's Emerging Fourth Wave. *J. Am. Plan. Assoc.* **2012**, *78*, 5–15. [CrossRef]
4. Janssen-Jansen, L.B. Smart Growth Strategies as a Challenge for Dutch Developmental Planning Policies. In *Incentives, Regulations and Plans: The Role of States and Nation-States in Smart Growth Planning*; Knaap, G.J., Haccoû, H.A., Clifton, K.J., Frece, J.W., Eds.; Edward Elgar Publishing: Cheltenham, UK, 2007; pp. 233–252.
5. Calthorpe, P.; Fulton, W. *The Regional City: Planning for the End of Sprawl*; Island Press: Washington, DC, USA, 2001.
6. Knaap, G.J.; Nelson, A.C. The effects of regional land use control in Oregon: A theoretical and empirical review. *Rev. Reg. Stud.* **1988**, *18*, 37–46.
7. Cunningham, C.R. Growth Controls, Real Options, and Land Development. *Rev. Econ. Stat.* **2007**, *89*, 343–358. [CrossRef]
8. Pendall, R. Do land-use controls cause sprawl? *Environ. Plan. B Plan. Des.* **1999**, *26*, 555–571. [CrossRef]
9. Mathur, S. Impact of Urban Growth Boundary on Housing and Land Prices: Evidence from King County, Washington. *Hous. Stud.* **2014**, *29*, 128–148. [CrossRef]
10. Jaeger, W.K.; Plantinga, A.J.; Grout, C. How has Oregon's land use planning system affected property values? *Land Use Policy* **2012**, *29*, 62–72. [CrossRef]
11. Dawkins, C.J.; Nelson, A.C. Urban containment policies and housing prices: An international comparison with implications for future research. *Land Use Policy* **2002**, *19*, 1–12. [CrossRef]
12. Jun, M.-J. The Effects of Portland's Urban Growth Boundary on Urban Development Patterns and Commuting. *Urban Stud.* **2004**, *41*, 1333–1348. [CrossRef]
13. Wassmer, R.W. Fiscalisation of Land Use, Urban Growth Boundaries and Non-central Retail Sprawl in the Western United States. *Urban Stud.* **2002**, *39*, 1307–1327. [CrossRef]
14. Jun, M.-J. The effects of Seoul's greenbelt on the spatial distribution of population and employment, and on the real estate market. *Ann. Reg. Sci.* **2012**, *49*, 619–642. [CrossRef]
15. Dempsey, J.A.; Plantinga, A.J. How well do urban growth boundaries contain development? Results for Oregon using a difference-in-difference estimator. *Reg. Sci. Urban Econ.* **2013**, *43*, 996–1007. [CrossRef]
16. Gennaio, M.-P.; Hersperger, A.M.; Bürgi, M. Containing urban sprawl—Evaluating effectiveness of urban growth boundaries set by the Swiss Land Use Plan. *Land Use Policy* **2009**, *26*, 224–232. [CrossRef]
17. Anas, A.; Rhee, H.-J. When are urban growth boundaries not second-best policies to congestion tolls? *J. Urban Econ.* **2007**, *61*, 263–286. [CrossRef]
18. Brueckner, J.K. Urban growth boundaries: An effective second-best remedy for unpriced traffic congestion? *J. Hous. Econ.* **2007**, *16*, 263–273. [CrossRef]
19. Kline, J.D.; Thiers, P.R.; Ozawa, C.P.; Yeakley, J.A.; Gordon, S.N. How well has land-use planning worked under different governance regimes? A case study in the Portland, OR-Vancouver, WA metropolitan area, USA. *Landsc. Urban Plan.* **2014**, *131*, 51–63. [CrossRef]
20. Nelson, A.C.; Moore, T. Assessing growth management policy implementation. *Land Use Policy* **1996**, *13*, 241–259. [CrossRef]
21. Jann, W.; Wegrich, K. Theories of the Policy Cycle. In *Handbook of Public Policy Analysis: Theory, Politics, and Methods*; Fisher, F., Miller, G.J., Sidney, M.S., Eds.; CRC Press: Boca Raton, FL, USA, 2007; pp. 43–62.
22. Bengston, D.N.; Fletcher, J.O.; Nelson, K.C. Public policies for managing urban growth and protecting open space: Policy instruments and lessons learned in the United States. *Landsc. Urban Plan.* **2004**, *69*, 271–286. [CrossRef]

23. Margerum, R.D. Evaluating Collaborative Planning: Implications from an Empirical Analysis of Growth Management. *J. Am. Plan. Assoc.* **2002**, *68*, 179–193. [CrossRef]
24. Margerum, R.D. Collaborative growth management in metropolitan Denver: "Fig leaf or valiant effort?". *Land Use Policy* **2005**, *22*, 373–386. [CrossRef]
25. Knaap, G.J. Self-Interest and Voter Support for Oregon's Land Use Controls. *J. Am. Plan. Assoc.* **1987**, *53*, 92–97. [CrossRef]
26. James, P.; Holden, M.; Lewin, M.; Neilson, L.; Oakley, C.; Truter, A.; Wilmoth, D. Managing metropolises by negotiating urban growth. In *Institutional and Social Innovation for Sustainable Urban Development*; Mieg, H., Töpfer, K., Eds.; Routledge: Abingdon, UK, 2013.
27. Van Tatenhove, J.; Arts, B.; Leroy, P. (Eds.) *Political Modernisation and the Environment*; Springer: Berlin/Heidelberg, Germany, 2000.
28. Arts, B.; Leroy, P. (Eds.) Institutional Dynamics in Environmental Governance. In *Institutional Dynamics in Environmental Governance*; Springer: Dordrecht, The Netherlands, 2006.
29. Liefferink, D. The Dynamics of Policy Arrangements: Turning Round the Tetrahedron. In *Institutional Dynamics in Environmental Governance*; Arts, B., Leroy, P., Eds.; Springer: Dordrecht, The Netherlands, 2006.
30. Van den Broeck, P.; Moulaert, F.; Kuhk, A.; Lievois, E.; Schreurs, J. Spatial planning in Flanders: Serving a bypassed capitalism? In *Spatial Planning Systems and Practices in Europe*; Reimer, M., Getimis, P., Blotevogel, H.H., Eds.; Routledge: London, UK; New York, NY, USA, 2014; pp. 169–188.
31. Vandevyvere, W. Van het Decreet van 18 mei 1999 houdende de Organisatie van de Ruimtelijke Ordening tot de Vlaamse Codex Ruimtelijke Ordening in 2009. In *Handboek Ruimtelijke Ordening en Stedenbouw*, 2nd ed.; Hubeau, B., Vandevyvere, W., Debersaques, G., Eds.; Die Keure: Brugge, Belgium, 2010.
32. Berisha, E.; Cotella, G.; Rivolin, U.J.; Solly, A. Spatial governance and planning systems in the public control of spatial development: A European typology. *Eur. Plan. Stud.* **2021**, *29*, 181–200. [CrossRef]
33. Poelmans, L.; Janssen, L.; Hambsch, L. *Landgebruik en Ruimtebeslag in Vlaanderen, Toestand 2016*; Study Executed on Behalf of the Flemish Planning Bureau for the Environment, Flemish Department of Environment: Brussels, Belgium, 2019.
34. Grietens, E. *Vlaanderen in de Knoop: Een Uitweg Uit de Ruimtelijke Wanorde*; Academic and Scientific Publishers: Brussel, Belgium, 2009.
35. Vermeiren, K.; Poelmans, L.; Engelen, G.; Broekx, S.; Beckx, C.; Nocker, L.D.; Dyck, K.V. *Monetariseren van de Impact van Urban Sprawl in Vlaanderen*; Study Executed on Behalf of the Flemish Department of Environment: Brussels, Belgium, 2019.
36. Meeus, B.; De Decker, P. *De Geest van Suburbia*; Garant: Antwerpen, Belgium, 2013.
37. Mustafa, A.; Teller, J. Self-Reinforcing Processes Governing Urban Sprawl in Belgium: Evidence over Six Decades. *Sustainability* **2020**, *12*, 4097. [CrossRef]
38. De Decker, P. Understanding Housing Sprawl: The Case of Flanders, Belgium. *Environ. Plan. A Econ. Space* **2011**, *43*, 1634–1654. [CrossRef]
39. Albrechts, L. Planners as catalysts and initiators of change. The new structure plan for Flanders. *Eur. Plan. Stud.* **1999**, *7*, 587–603. [CrossRef]
40. Vlaamse Overheid. *Ruimtelijk Structuurplan Vlaanderen, Gecoördineerde Versie 2011*; Departement Ruimtelijke Ordening Woonbeleid en Onroerend Erfgoed, Ed.; Flemish Government: Brussels, Belgium, 2011.
41. Leinfelder, H. 'Gevallen'-planning en hoe moeilijk het is om daden in gedachten te vertalen. In *Ruimte Maken: Gebundelde Papers en Bijlagen PlanDag 2015*; Bouma, G., Vanempten, E., Eds.; VRP/BNSP: Antwerpen, Belgium; Amsterdam, The Netherlands, 2015; pp. 133–142.
42. Voets, J.; De Peuter, B.; Vandekerckhove, B.; Broeckaert, D.; Le Roy, M.; Maes, P.; De Decker, P.; Bervoets, W.; Van der Heijden, R.; Blummel, P. *Evaluerend Onderzoek naar de Effectiviteit van de Uitvoering van het Ruimtelijk Beleid in Vlaanderen*; KU Leuven: Brussels, Belgium; SumResearch: Brussels, Belgium; Hogeschool voor Wetenschap en Kunst Sint-Lucas: Brussels, Belgium; Radboud Universiteit Nijmegen: Brussels, Belgium; Study executed on behalf of the Flemish Department of Spatial Planning, Housing Policy, and Heritage: Brussels, Belgium, 2010.
43. Boussauw, K.; Boelens, L. Fuzzy tales for hard blueprints: The selective coproduction of the Spatial Policy Plan for Flanders, Belgium. *Environ. Plan. C Gov. Policy* **2015**, *33*, 1376–1393. [CrossRef]
44. Cabus, P.; Rynck, F.D.; Voets, J.; Verhetsel, A.; Ackaert, J.; Miermans, W. *Een Sterke Stad en Een Sterke Stadsregio: Verslag en Aanbevelingen op Basis Van Stadsregionale Gesprekken*; Onderzoek Uitgevoerd in Opdracht van de Vlaams Minister van Binnenlands Bestuur, Stedenbeleid, Wonen en Inburgering: Brussel, Belgium, 2009.
45. Boucké, T. *Samenspraak op Stadsregionaal Niveau: Verkennend en Inventariserend Onderzoek*; Kenniscentrum Vlaamse Steden: Brussel, Belgium, 2015.
46. Vermeersch, C. *Structuurplanning Vandaag: Oneigenlijk Gebruik en Misbruik*; Published by the Author. Brugge, Belgium, 2008. Available online: https://nl.wikipedia.org/wiki/Charles_Vermeersch (accessed on 4 February 2021).
47. Boussauw, K.; Allaert, G.; Witlox, F. Colouring Inside What Lines? Interference of the Urban Growth Boundary and the Political–Administrative Border of Brussels. *Eur. Plan. Stud.* **2013**, *21*, 1509–1527. [CrossRef]
48. Informatie Vlaanderen. *Bodembedekkingskaart (BBK), 1m Resolutie, Opname 2015*; Informatie Vlaanderen: Brussels, Belgium, 2015.
49. Vlaamse Overheid. *Afbakeningen van de Stedelijke Gebieden in Uitvoering van het Ruimtelijk Structuurplan Vlaanderen—Toestand 2019*; Vlaamse Overheid-Departement Omgeving: Brussel, Belgium, 2019.

50. Vlaamse Overheid. *Gewestelijk Ruimtelijk Uitvoeringsplan Afbakening Grootstedelijk Gebied Antwerpen*; Ruimte Vlaanderen: Brussel, Belgium, 2009.
51. Vlacoro. *Advies Ontwerp Gewestelijk Ruimtelijk Uitvoeringsplan: Afbakening Grootstedelijk Gebied Antwerpen*; Flemish Committee for Spatial Planning: Brussels, Belgium, 2009.
52. Voets, J.; Peuter, B.D.; Rynck, F.D.; Herck, B.V.; Laat, W.D.; Vloebergh, G.; Broeck, P.V.D. *Onderzoek Naar de Voor het Vlaams Ruimtelijk Beleid Relevante Vormen van Intergemeentelijke Samenwerking*; Instituut voor de Overheid—KU Leuven: Brussels, Belgium; Departement HABE, Hogeschool Gent: Brussels, Belgium; IDEA Consult: Brussels, Belgium; OMGEVING: Brussels, Belgium; Study executed on behalf of the Flemish Department of Spatial Planning, Housing Policy, and Heritage: Brussels, Belgium, 2012.
53. Coppens, T.; Van Den Broeck, J.; Van Wymeersch, E. *Een Evaluatie van Subsidies Voor de Projectcoordinatie van Strategische Projecten in Turnhout en Aalst*; Study Executed on Behalf of the Flemish Department of Environment: Brussels, Belgium, 2016.
54. Van Baelen, J. *Plaats om te Bouwen*; Gazet van Antwerpen: Antwerpen, Belgium, 2009.
55. Omgeving. *Methode voor de Afbakening van Stedelijke Gebieden*; Studiegroep Omgeving: Antwerpen, Belgium, 1996.
56. Studiegroep Omgeving & Buck Consultants International. *Voorontwerp Afbakening Grootstedelijk Gebied Antwerpen*; Study Executed on Behalf of the AROHM Ministry of the Flemish Community: Brussels, Belgium, 2005.
57. Van den Broeck, J.; Vermeulen, P.; Oosterlynck, S.; Albeda, Y. *Antwerpen Herwonnen Stad? Maatschappij, Ruimtelijk Plannen en Beleid. 1940–2012*; Die Keure: Brugge, Belgium, 2014.
58. De Olde, C.; Oosterlynck, S. "The countryside starts here": How the urban-rural divide continues to matter in post-urban Flanders. 2021, Manuscript submitted for publication.
59. Broeck, P.V.D.; Verachtert, K. Whose Permits? The Tenacity of Permissive Development Control in Flanders. *Eur. Plan. Stud.* **2015**, *24*, 387–406. [CrossRef]
60. Fairclough, N. *Analysing Discourse: Textual Analysis for Social Research*; Routledge: London, UK, 2003.
61. Departement Omgeving Vlaanderen. *Strategische Visie Beleidsplan Ruimte Vlaanderen*; Flemish Department of Environment: Brussels, Belgium, 2018.
62. De Olde, C.; Boussauw, K.; Ryckewaert, M. *Draagvlak voor de Betonstop Groter Maken?* Vlaamse Overheid Vergroot Enkel een Vastgoedzeepbel; Knack: Brussels, Belgium, 2020. Available online: https://www.knack.be/nieuws/belgie/draagvlak-voor-de-betonstop-groter-maken-vlaamse-overheid-vergroot-enkel-een-vastgoedzeepbel/article-opinion-1677389.html (accessed on 3 February 2021).
63. Coppens, T.; Vloebergh, G.; De Decker, P.; Leinfelder, H. Hoe Kunnen we het Gewestplan Afschaffen? *Ruimte* **2020**, *47*, 24–29.

land

MDPI

Article

Economic Consequences of Adopting Local Spatial Development Plans for the Spatial Management System: The Case of Poland

Przemysław Śleszyński [1], Maciej Nowak [2], Paweł Sudra [3], Magdalena Załęczna [4] and Małgorzata Blaszke [2,*]

1 Department of Urban and Population Geography, Institute of Geography and Spatial Organization, Polish Academy of Sciences, 00-818 Warsaw, Poland; psleszyn@twarda.pan.pl
2 Department of Real Estate, Faculty of Economics, West Pomeranian University of Technology, 70-310 Szczecin, Poland; Maciej.Nowak@zut.edu.pl
3 Department of Housing and Urban Renewal, Institute of Urban and Regional Development, 03-728 Warsaw, Poland; psudra@irmir.pl
4 Department of Investments and Real Estate, Faculty of Economics and Sociology, University of Lodz, 90-255 Lodz, Poland; magdalena.zaleczna@uni.lodz.pl
* Correspondence: mblaszke@zut.edu.pl

Abstract: The spatial management system in Poland struggles with serious costs as a consequence of local planning. The problem is the lack of appropriate value capturing mechanisms and cost compensation for municipalities, along with significant burdens. Private property is subject to special protection, but the public good is less valued. The article attempts to assess the situation in Poland, recalling also the experiences of spatial management systems from other European countries. It combines legal, economic, and geographical perspectives. The specific objectives were demonstration of geographical (interregional and functional) regularities related to the economic (financial) consequences of adopting local plans and identification of financial effects resulting from the implementation of local plans in communes, i.e., in particular, their size, structure of revenues (income), and expenditures, in relations with the budgets of municipalities and the population living in communes. First, the determinants of spatial policy were defined in the context of institutional economics and the real estate market. Then, a unique database of forecasted and realized budgetary revenues and expenditures of 2477 communes in Poland related to spatial development (infrastructure construction, land transformation, purchase, etc.) was analyzed statistically. Additionally, for five selected communes of different functional types, this issue was examined in detail. It has been shown that municipalities do not derive adequate income from spatial development, and improper policy of local self-governments results in heavy burdens, threatening to disturb their financial balance. The formulated conclusions regarding the legal, economic, and spatial mechanisms may contribute to building tools (instruments) for more effective spatial management in various countries.

Keywords: local development; local law; budgets of local units; financial consequences of spatial chaos

Citation: Śleszyński, P.; Nowak, M.; Sudra, P.; Załęczna, M.; Blaszke, M. Economic Consequences of Adopting Local Spatial Development Plans for the Spatial Management System: The Case of Poland. *Land* **2021**, *10*, 112. https://doi.org/10.3390/land10020112

Received: 29 December 2020
Accepted: 21 January 2021
Published: 25 January 2021

1. Introduction: Assumptions and Goals

The spatial management system and the use of spatial policy tools must always be related to the conditions existing in the real estate market. These institutions are interdependent with each other. The legislator should be able to notice this in every country, appropriately balancing interests of "actors" interested in creating legal solutions in this respect. Much depends on the specific institutional framework, both formal and informal, relating to planning practice. Geographical areas (territories) should be covered by legal acts regulating land destination principles, and the use of the local planning practice should complement their function. If this regulatory role of spatial planning is not fully realized, there is a scope for spatial conflicts to arise [1].

Difficulties in building an appropriate institutional framework result from two ways of sharing the good of limited space: public and private ones. On the one hand, there is a need to conduct an active spatial policy on a local scale, which should effectively protect the area's values related to spatial order; on the other hand, real estate market participants, especially owners, would like to benefit from their rights. Against this background, contradictions occur that are sometimes difficult to reconcile [2–4]. Failure to properly fulfill the regulatory role also means a waste of resources present in space. Improper allocation means a lack of optimal use, e.g., irrational land use and suboptimal distribution of various functions based on these resources [5–8]. The consequences of spatial conflicts are wide and cover all spheres of human activity in geographical space.

That is why the role of local spatial development plans (from now on referred to as local plans) is so important. They are key (regulatory) tools of spatial policy, which are, at the local level, most responsible for determining the land use. Local plans significantly affect the value of real estate and the real estate market. The local plans are subject to research as signals that can influence the decisions of interested actors [9,10] and impact of the process of preparing planning framework [11]. The results of some analyses indicate increase of real estate value in consequence of adoption of local plans [12,13]. Among other directions of research, the impact of planning acts on the supply and prices of housing shall be mentioned [14,15]. However, the use of local plans in European countries is different: they have a different scopes and legal effects. In some spatial management systems, it is the impact of plans on the value of a property that determines the frequency of preparation of plans due to the costs of their implementation for public actors.

Less frequently discussed issues include the economic consequences of spatial regulations influencing real estate market participants' behavior. In this context, Poland seems to be an interesting example because of the complicated and inefficient spatial planning system, generating costs estimated at the level of at least EUR 20 billion per year [16]. They also include the impact of spatial chaos on the real estate market.

Against this introductory background and problem formulation, the objectives of the article are

- the demonstration of geographical (interregional and functional) regularities related to the economic (financial) consequences of adopting local spatial development plans, and
- the identification of financial effects resulting from the implementation of local plans in municipalities (communes), i.e., in particular, their size, structure of revenues (income), and expenditures, in relation with the municipal budgets and the population living in communes.

To achieve these goals, the article first defines the conditions of the spatial policy in the context of governance failure and the real estate market, combining these issues with the problems of spatial management systems in Europe, which are discussed in the literature. Against this background, we present Polish experiences concerning the economic consequences of adopting local plans, which make up the essential empirical part of the article. The focus is on the regularities related to the effects of implementation of local plans on the municipal budgets, according to the functional types of communes. In this context it is worth to add a terminological clarification. *Gmina* is a basic local administrative unit (LAU) in Poland. It corresponds to the former NUTS-5 level, that is, the LAU-2 level, according to the classification of Eurostat. The term "commune" is used commonly for an English synonym of gmina as the smallest territorial division for administrative purposes in Poland. Therefore, it will be used interchangeably in the text with the universal term "municipality".

Against this background, a thesis is formulated that improper regulations, combined with governance failure in the spatial management system, result in a burden on budgets of communes. Estimating the economic effects of local plan arrangements is important both from the viewpoint of rationalizing the local spatial policy and the sustainability of communes' public finances. We associate it with the optimization process, i.e., reaching the best spatial management decisions [17,18]. The tool used to achieve this goal is the forecast of the economic effects of the adoption of a local spatial development plan (from now on referred to as the forecast), the implementation of which in Poland is an obligatory element of the procedure for developing a draft local spatial development plan. The Polish spatial management system belongs to the systems classified as protecting real estate owners' rights in particular. Its detailed analysis is important for several reasons:

- there are clear regulations regarding the compensation of a reduction in the value of real estate by local plans; therefore, it is much easier than in many other countries to determine municipal expenditure related to spatial planning;
- these expenses can therefore be compiled as a whole and compared with the incomes of communes resulting from the adoption of local plans; on this basis, individual types of communes can be distinguished; and
- the results of these comparisons constitute an important point of reference, which will provide several detailed materials for the discussion of the legitimacy of the application of individual Value Capturing instruments and the consequences of an excessively liberal approach to property owners' rights.

The article combines (and unifies) the economic, geographical, and legal perspectives. Developing an approach combining the showed perspectives and enabling the achievement of research objectives with their careful consideration should be a new contribution to the literature dealing with spatial planning and development issues. In the literature on the subject, the issues of economic consequences of spatial planning are considered limited in the dimension relating to all municipalities in a given country. Such an analysis in this publication makes it possible to distinguish groups of communes with different trends in this respect, which also entitles wider conclusions.

In our literature review, we identified the conditions and the problems of the role of local plans and of the economic consequences of spatial planning in European countries. We have highlighted the specificity of the Polish system against this background. Then, we analyzed all communes in Poland in relation to the following issues: forecasted revenues and expenses resulting from adoption of the local plans and realized revenues and expenses relating to the above forecasts. In the Discussion, we applied the conclusions resulting from the research to a wider discussion on the economic consequences of spatial planning.

2. Research Method and Source Materials

For the purpose of exploring the diversification of the financial implications of local planning, data from a survey "Spatial planning in the commune" (carried out by the ministry responsible for the "spatial management" public affairs sector and the Central Statistical Office under the Public Statistics Research Program) were used. This survey consists of collecting responses from all communes in Poland (2477 units in 2019) on the following issues:

- forecasted revenues and expenses related to the adoption of local plans, which are specified in the obligatory documents entitled "Financial impact forecast of a local spatial development plan", and
- realized revenues and expenses relating to the above forecasts.

We used the latest available data for 2019, showing the current implementation of local plans' provisions. In terms of revenues (forecast and realized), these were revenues to communal budgets resulting from (1) planning fee, (2) increase in property tax, (3) tax on civil law transactions, and (4) category of "other" costs. In terms of costs, we took expenses of local budgets into account, which are related to (1) construction of communal roads, (2) purchase of land for roads, (3) construction of technical infrastructure, and (4) other costs included in the "other" category.

Responses have been obtained from a different percentage of communes in the country, depending on the thematic group of the questions (forecast, current status, income, and expenses)—it was 49.5–63.0% of local governments. Out of 2299 communes with local plans,

915 (39.8%) answered questions from all four groups, another 309 (13.4%)—questions from three groups, and 386 (16.8%)—questions from two groups, and 136 (5.9%) to questions from one group. In 1746 communes (75.9%), at least one answer was given. It was possible to collect comprehensive and unique material that allows analyzing and testing the economic effects related to the adoption of local plans on a very detailed spatial scale, and thus to conclude on impacts of spatial planning on the real estate market.

Datasets from the Local Data Bank of the Central Statistical Office for 2017–2019 were used as regards the information on communal budgets. Taking the three-year period into account was aimed at averaging the data in order to avoid local governments' financial indicators' volatility over time. The analyses used the indicator of total communes' income and their self-income ratio. Total revenues of municipalities in Poland include their own revenues, as well as general subsidy (which is a form of redistribution of state revenues, e.g., from taxes) and specific subsidies from the state budget. Own revenues include local taxes (on real estate, means of transport, small business, inheritance and donations, civil law, agricultural, and forestry activities) and revenues from local fees (stamp duty, market fee, maintenance fee, spa fee, etc.).

The division of communes in Poland into types, the so-called functional classification, has been developed specifically for spatial planning monitoring purposes [19]. It distinguishes ten types of communes based on the administrative and functional hierarchy of cities and towns (voivodeship capitals, sub-regional, and local centers), specific locations of communes (suburban zones and transport corridors), and economic functions (tourism, agriculture of various intensity, etc.). To obtain proper generalization, the communes were aggregated to 10 types. Table 1 includes basic information about the distinguished types.

Table 1. Basic information about the analyzed categories of communes.

Type of Gminas (Communes)	Number of Entities	Area (Thous. ha)	Population (Thous.)	Number of Local Plans	Coverage (%)
A—functional urban areas of voivodeship capitals	33	500	9563	4529	47.5
B—their external zones	265	2759	4873	12,181	44.4
C—functional urban areas of sub-regional centers	55	340	4322	3402	56.5
D—their external zones	201	2147	2452	5040	39.1
E—multifunctional urban centers	142	1027	3783	4606	31.8
F—communes with developed transport functions	137	1996	1435	2615	31.1
G—communes with other developed non-agricultural functions (tourism and large-scale functions, including mining)	222	3386	1817	5695	28.6
H—communes with intensively developed agricultural functions	496	6297	3048	4949	26.6
I—communes with moderately developed agricultural functions	665	8653	5179	9119	33.2
J—extensively developed communes (with forests or nature protection areas)	261	4166	1910	3490	19.4
Total	2477	31,271	38,383	55,626	31.2

Source: [13].

3. Literature Review

Local land use plans have different scope and consequences in different countries. Therefore, they should be compared with great caution. Despite even similar legal regulations, the planning practice may differ [20–23]. However, common features and consequences can be distinguished. They mainly concern

- the issues of public capacity to control spatial development and the optimal scope of such control [24,25],
- possible and potential land development limitations included in local plans and the related understanding of the ownership right, and
- changes in real estate value due to local plans, the consequences of compensation, and instruments related to the above issues.

The article focuses primarily on the last two issues. However, their interdependence should be emphasized. The limited ability to control spatial development in a given system entails several negative consequences associated with governance failure [26–30]. It also significantly influences the real possibilities of limitations in land development [31,32] and the relationship between local plans and real estate value. In the latter context, many studies can be distinguished, concerning, among other things, the impact of planning acts on the supply and prices of housing [14,15,33,34] and the impact of protection of urban greenery in the spatial plans on the residential real estate value [35–37]. There are publications that broaden the discussion about the role of local plans in shaping the value of real estate. Nestico et al. [13] draw attention to the link between the process of housing development, and planned environmental and socio-economic conditions. Rebelo [9], considering possible institutional changes, emphasizes the importance of social determinants when considering the economic consequences of spatial planning. Cho et al. [12] show that the impact of spatial planning on the value of real estate also depends on the level of development of civil society in a given area.

In the literature on the subject, various classifications of spatial management systems have been made. By limiting ourselves to European countries' comparisons, one can cite classifications distinguishing regional economy planning, integrated planning, land use planning, and urban planning [38]. This gave rise to further classifications, in which the criteria considered included, among others, linking the development with real opportunities existing in the given area (i.e., access to technical infrastructure), the arbitrariness of local authorities in terms of shaping space, as well as the degree of linking planning processes with legal regulations [39–42]. Applying individual regulations is influenced by planning practice that varies in individual countries, resulting from social, cultural, or economic conditions. From the perspective analyzed in this article, the key seems to be the classification of spatial management systems into systems based on local plans (e.g., Spain, partly Italy, France, and Belgium) and systems based on development planning (Great Britain) [43]. Thus, it can be assumed that both the overall concept of the spatial management system and individual solutions are important. From the perspective of this article, important is the classification made by R. Alterman [31]. It distinguishes groups of countries from the perspective of understanding of the property rights in the spatial management system and the scope of compensation rights. The group with minimum compensation rights includes the United Kingdom and France, and the group with extensive compensation rights includes Germany and Poland. As indicated above, individual countries differ in many respects (legal regulations, planning practice, and degree of integration of development planning with spatial policy).

However, the functions of local development plans can be compared. In the United Kingdom, planning acts define the spatial development strategy, which the public administration interprets when issuing building permits. Thus, British local plans are a combination of Polish "studies of land use conditions and directions" (which will be introduced further on) and local zoning plans. In addition to the basic strategy, they specify land use and the areas whose development is crucial. They also contain guidelines for assessment when issuing building permits [44,45]. In France, local urbanistic plans are acts defining in detail the local development principles. They define the general directions of local policies related to spatial policy and define specific actions (important from an environmental perspective). They also define the detailed conditions for the development of individual areas [46,47]. In Germany, there is a land use plan and a development plan on the local level. The former, which is drawn up for the entire municipality, is a preparatory building plan that defines the general use of land. The development plans are directly binding on the property owners in terms of development parameters and land development [45,48]. Thus, the local plans' functions are understood in different ways, and, in the selected countries, the individual plans contain a "strategic" part and a part with direct guidelines. Therefore, the scope of limitations of property owners' rights and the financial (compensation) consequences of adopting plans can be considered in different variants. Moreover, for this reason, solutions of individual countries related to the economic consequences of spatial planning should be of particular interest for the researchers, as well as (irrespective of the above) cases of countries shall be investigated where extensive compensation rights are provided for.

It is worth to introduce a few individual solutions concerning spatial planning's economic consequences in different countries. In some European countries, model solutions relating to the discussed sphere have been developed. First, the concept of Value Capturing can be invoked. According to it, public entities' planning decisions transfer the costs of public infrastructure and social housing to private entities, whose property value has increased [49]. The above solutions are justified, among others, by the reasons related to the need to reimburse costs incurred by public entities, taking over some negative costs by private entities creating them, as well as the need to mitigate the impact of new investments on the environment [50–53]. The effectiveness of this process depends on several variables. From the investors' perspective, the key is the certainty of specific solutions and public authorities' flexibility to adapt to their concepts (in this case, the authorities' flexibility should not be confused with opportunism). In this perspective, there may be greater investor uncertainty in Great Britain than, for example, in Spain. This uncertainty may determine the failure of specific investments [43]. From the perspective of considering the consequences of reducing real estate value, the literature indicates non-financial compensation options [54]. One of them may be the TDR principle adopted in the United States and disseminated in Europe (e.g., in Italy), including the "transfer of development rights", i.e., a specific "transfer" of the possibility of a certain development to another area [55,56]. One can also cite the concept of spatial concentration of development rights related to TDR (Klaus 2020). In individual European countries, the scope of financial compensation depends on understanding property rights and the degree of possibility of limiting it. For example, in Great Britain, local plans may introduce restrictions without any compensation [44,55]. However, in some countries, there are large irregularities, the most famous of which are mismanagement and simple fraud in setting up the so-called land banks [57], i.e., in the land banking system developed in the last half-century and provided for in the planning and investment procedure [58]. It is worth pointing out that these institutions, essentially intended to counteract the fragmentation of agricultural land, were gradually also directed, e.g., in the Netherlands and Germany, towards implementing public goals [59].

It has been indicated above that apart from individual solutions concerning the economic consequences of spatial planning in European countries, it is worth noting the case of a country classified in the literature as providing for extensive compensation rights in the spatial management system. This country is Poland. It should be pointed out that in post-socialist countries undergoing political transformation after 1989, a common problem is a too liberal approach to the role of property owners in the spatial management system. It results, to a significant extent, from a kind of rebound after the period of centrally controlled economy, which included excessive control of the private property (including numerous cases of takeovers by the state). As early as at the beginning of the first decade of the transformation (1990s), there were still voices that the flawed real estate market system inherited from communism, including the disordered ownership structure, will be a serious burden for a smooth transition to a free market system [60], including society's understanding of the rational principles governing the relationship between private property and the common good. As a result, many countries in this bloc are still, after three decades of transformation, diagnosed with problems of uncontrolled development, misunderstanding what the public interest is, and spatial chaos [61–63].

The spatial management system of Poland is the subject of numerous critical analyses [64–67]. In the opinion of the vast majority of the representatives of the literature on the subject, it does not fulfill its role by not ensuring sufficient protection of the spatial order, nor by stopping the negative spatial trends (including urban sprawl, uncontrolled development, increasing costs of spatial chaos in the settlement, environmental, or transport dimensions [16]). The key tools of spatial policy exist at the commune (local) level. "Studies of land use conditions and directions" (pol. Studium) are documents of directional and strategic nature which are mandatory in every commune; however, they do not directly bind property owners and investors. They may be described as specific equivalents of the former "structure plans" in Great Britain. On the contrary, local spatial development plans (pol. Plan miejscowy), which are equivalent to zoning plans, constitute local law acts but are not obligatory—the commune authorities may adopt them at their discretion (consequently, most of the country is not covered by these plans—the coverage of the territory of Poland with binding local plans in Poland at the end of 2019, which was only 31.2%). Development in areas without adopted local plans is carried out based on administrative proceedings related to the issuance of an individual decision on development conditions [68]. A huge number of decisions issued leads to the aggravation of negative phenomena related to uncontrolled development.

The financial consequences of adopting a local spatial development plan (increasing and decreasing real estate value) have been included in the Act on spatial planning and development from the 27 March 2003. According to Art. 36–37 of the Polish Act, if the local plan restricts the existing possibilities of developing the property in a way that the current development cannot be continued, the commune, by adopting this plan, is obliged to pay the owner of the property compensation equal to the damage suffered. As soon as the property's value decreases and the owner disposes of it within five years of the plan's entry into force or its amendment and has not previously benefited from compensation, he/she has the right to demand compensation equal to the loss value. On the other hand, in a situation where the local plan extends the possibilities of real estate development relating to the previous possibilities and causes an increase in its value, there are no adequate consequences [69]. If the owner of such real estate sells it equivalently within five years from the local plan's effective date, he/she will pay a special fee, the so-called planning rent (a zoning-change fee). Depending on the communal authorities' discretion, it may amount up to 30% of the increase in the property's value (the rate should be included in the plan). It is a specific value capturing mechanism.

4. Financial Effects of Local Plans in Poland

4.1. Forecasted Revenues

According to the data obtained from 1757 communes (75% of those having valid local plans), the state shown according to the forecasts prepared in the years 2003–2019 was as follows. The projected revenues resulting from local plans' adoption were shown for PLN 69.4 billion (PLN 1 billion ≈ EUR 240 million in 2019). The most important share were the proceeds from "other" category (PLN 26.2 billion) and from the increase in property tax (PLN 24.7 billion), followed by the planning fee (PLN 16.3 billion) (Table 2; Figure 1). It should be emphasized that the vast majority of forecasts do not have a specific time horizon: neither minimum nor maximum.

The highest revenues were forecasted in large urban centers, including voivodeship capitals (type A)—PLN 22.3 billion, and in neighboring communes belonging to Functional Urban Areas of voivodeship cities—PLN 14.7 billion. In cities with poviat (county) capital status and generally sub-regional cities (type C), total revenues were expected to amount to PLN 9.1 billion. For the remaining types of communes, a significantly lower sum of incomes was forecasted, including the lowest one in the group of extensively developed communes, which have a high share of forests and protected areas (type J)—PLN 1.5 billion, in intensively agricultural communes (type H)—2.0 billion PLN, and in communes related to the function of communication nodes (type F)—PLN 2.4 billion.

Table 2. Basic quantitative information on the forecasted and realized incomes and expenditures related to adopting local spatial development plans in 10 types of communes, for the year 2019.

Type of Communes *	Revenues (mln PLN)		Expenditures (mln PLN)		Balance (mln PLN)	
	Forecasted	Realized (Obtained)	Forecasted	Realized (Incurred)	Forecasted	Realized
A	22,328	760	44,452	3680	−22,124	−2919
B	14,737	4572	21,208	6910	−6470	−2338
C	9079	4081	13,363	4495	−4285	−415
D	4176	1911	6096	1851	−1921	59
E	5495	1628	8577	3437	−3083	−1809
F	2427	290	2544	824	−117	−533
G	3183	1136	4236	1754	−1053	−619
H	2030	354	2772	693	−741	−339
I	4499	1028	8770	2109	−4271	−1081
J	1470	292	2343	904	−874	−612
Total amount	69,423	16,052	114,361	26,658	−44,938	−10,606

* abbreviations of types of communes explained in Table 1. Source: based on unpublished data of the Ministry of Development and Statistical Office of Poland.

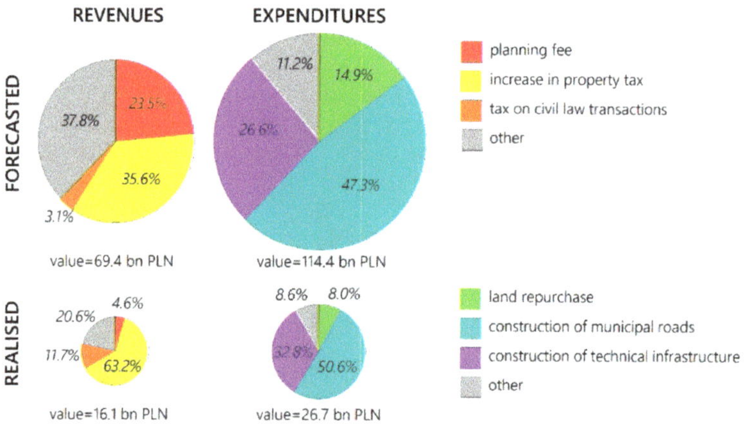

Figure 1. Structure of forecasted and realized revenues and expenditures of communes as a result of local plans enacted, for the year 2019. Source: based on unpublished data of the Ministry of Development and Statistical Office of Poland.

The highest projected revenues were found in Warsaw (PLN 4.9 billion). It was about 7% of the total for the whole country, which is more or less similar to the population potential of the 1757 communes studied. Due to land prices in the capital, this value seems relatively low. Moreover, high income was expected in Szczecin (PLN 3.9 billion), and over PLN 1 billion in Sosnowiec, Cracow, Gdynia, Rzeszów, Gliwice, and Poznań. The high concentration of quotas in a relatively small number of communes draws attention. Half of the local binding plans' forecasted revenues were concentrated in only 3.6% of the communes that reported any amounts (64 out of 1757 local government units).

Despite the obvious differentiation of forecast impacts between large urban centers and peripheral communes, such drastic disproportionality may prove inconsistency and different methodological approaches in forecasting. It is possible both to overestimate the expected revenues and to lower them. Another probable cause of the observed disproportions is inconsistently conducted, ineffective financial management in some communes. In any case, it can be stated that there is some irrationality in the spatial management.

4.2. Forecasted Expenditures

The projected expenditure was shown at the end of 2019 at PLN 114.4 billion, of which over 38% (PLN 44.5 billion) was allocated to voivodeship cities. Among the anticipated costs, primarily the costs of construction of communal roads were indicated (PLN 54.1 billion) and, second, the costs of other technical infrastructure (PLN 30.4 billion). The purchase of land for the construction of communal roads was forecast at PLN 17.0 billion. Still, this amount is probably underestimated by including these expenses partially under the item "construction of communal roads".

The forecasted expenditure was concentrated in particular in two voivodeships: Mazowieckie (PLN 24.9 billion) and Zachodniopomorskie (PLN 14.1 billion). Suppose we recalculated them relating to the number of people. In that case, it gives an amount per capita of 4.6 thousand PLN in the first voivodeship and as much as PLN 8.3 thousand—in the second (national average—PLN 3.0 thousand). However, these calculations do not consider that no data was obtained for over 35% of communes.

It is visible that the burden on communes' budgets due to the adoption of local plans may be significant. In fourteen communes, the forecasted amounts exceeded PLN 1 billion—the highest was in Szczecin (PLN 12.3 billion), Warsaw (PLN 10.6 billion), Poznań (PLN 3.8 billion), and Cracow (PLN 2.8 billion), but high also in smaller communes, especially those located within functional urban areas of voivodeship centers, such as Radzymin (PLN 1.5 billion) and Lesznowola near Warsaw (PLN 1.4 billion), Wieliczka near Cracow (PLN 1.0 billion), and Oleśnica near Wrocław (PLN 2 billion).

A high concentration of forecast expenditure amounts was observed in a relatively small number of communes. The first ten communes concentrated as much as 33.6% of the projected expenditure in the whole of Poland, and in the first 50 communes, it was as much as 53.6%. It again indicates the need for in-depth research to verify the methodology of financial forecasts; the adoption of local plans, including the link with the planning coverage; and the content of documents in terms of land allocation structure. Considering the median of the projected costs in communes (PLN 11.1 million) and multiplying it by about 2000 communes, shown for Poland's whole, the total result obtained from the questionnaires (PLN 114.4 billion) may be up to five times overstated. On the other hand, it cannot be ruled out that a significant number of communes underestimated the cost of the financial consequences of adopting the plans.

4.3. Realized Revenues

By the end of 2019, the proceeds realized from adopting local plans amounted to PLN 16.1 billion (for 1832 communes out of 2326 where there was at least one good local plan and provided relevant data). Thus, it was over four times less than the forecasted revenues. The following communes generated the highest incomes: Włocławek (PLN 1502 million), Kobierzyce near Wrocław (PLN 558 million), Piaseczno near Warsaw (PLN 410 million), Lesznowola near Warsaw (PLN 383 million), and Ostrów Wielkopolski (PLN 375 million). The most important item in total was the proceeds from the increase in property tax (PLN 10.1 billion, i.e., 62.1%).

The realization of revenues showed a greater variation by region. The largest revenues were recorded in the following voivodeships: Mazowieckie (PLN 2.2 billion), Wielkopolskie (PLN 2.1 billion), Kujawsko-Pomorskie (PLN 1.9 billion), Dolnośląskie, and Śląskie (PLN 1.8 billion). This occurred because of the exceptionally high income of only a few local governments in the region. In the voivodeships, Mazowieckie, this applies in particular to Piaseczno and Lesznowola (suburban area of Warsaw), Wielkopolskie—Ostrów Wielkopolski, Kujawsko-Pomorskie—Włocławek, and in Dolnośląskie–Kobierzyce (suburban area of Wrocław). The units with the highest incomes from local plans are both medium-sized, poviat cities (e.g., Włocławek—the former capital of the voivodeship), and rural communes within reach of large agglomerations, where a policy of intensive management of previously agricultural land for housing, industry or services (Kobierzyce, Lesznowola).

Although the highest amount of income was forecasted in voivodship cities, the implementation of local plans in communes belonging to their functional areas and sub-regional cities (poviat or with more than 50,000 inhabitants) brought income 5–6 times higher. In total, these two categories of communes (type B and type C) concentrated 36% of the obtained income. The lowest incomes were generated (as for forecasts) in extensively developed communes, e.g., forestry type of communes and in the ones with the leading functions of intensive agriculture and transport junctions. On the other hand, the amounts obtained in communes with a moderately agricultural function (type I) were greater than those of the three previously mentioned types (F, H, and J). Still, it must also be said that there is the highest number of moderately agricultural communes in Poland (30% of the total). A similar total level of income was obtained in tourist communes (type I), half higher in small towns located outside the functional areas (type E), and twice as high in external FUA (Functional Urban Area) communes of sub-regional cities (type D).

Among the realized incomes, attention is drawn to a small, even in many cases trace, amount resulting from the planning rent. A detailed analysis of the obtained statistical data shows that, especially for cities with poviat rights status, the provisions enabling the collection of planning fees are practically not applicable. It is a complex problem, partly related to the fact that communes set a zero rate of this fee (with a maximum allowable amount of 30%) and various case laws. As a result, the amounts obtained from the planning rent and the total receipts in individual communes vary greatly.

4.4. Realized Expenditures

The total expenditure under the existing local plans by the end of 2019 amounted to PLN 26.7 billion, and thus they accounted for 23.3% of the forecasted expenditure. The outlays were distributed in the following proportions (Figure 1): construction of communal roads—PLN 13.5 billion (50.6%), construction of technical infrastructure—PLN 8.8 billion (32.8%), purchase of land for road construction communes—PLN 2.1 billion (8.0%), and other expenses—PLN 2.3 billion (8.6%).

The largest expenditure was spent on investments in communes belonging to the functional areas of voivodeship centers (PLN 6.9 billion), then in sub-regional cities (PLN 4.5 billion), then in voivodeship cities (PLN 3.7 billion) and other communes (PLN 3.4 billion), and at last, which may be somewhat surprising, in intensively agricultural communes (PLN 0.7 billion), which are particularly numerous in western and northern Poland. The analysis of the structure of expenditures by administrative categories of communes shows that in rural communes the highest costs are related to the construction of technical infrastructure (apart from roads)—they accounted for 47.2% of the total expenditures in these units. Nevertheless, the total costs of building communal roads and purchasing land for roads were almost the same amount. In urban communes, communal roads' construction was the most absorbed in the expenditure structure—47.7% of the total. Its share is even more pronounced in cities with poviat status, where it amounted to 60.9%. Land purchase costs for communal roads were relatively the highest as a category of expenditure in poviat cities (12.6%).

The realized costs related to the enactment of local plans differed significantly in individual regions. In the light of the data obtained, the highest costs were incurred in the following voivodeships: Małopolskie (PLN 3.8 billion), Mazowieckie (PLN 3.6 billion), and Pomorskie (PLN 3.1 billion). Expenses exceeding PLN 2 billion were recorded in three more voivodships. The lowest amounts were recorded in Lubuskie (PLN 0.39 billion), then in Podkarpackie (PLN 0.46 billion) and Świętokrzyskie (PLN 0.61 billion). Among all the communes that replied to the budgetary costs incurred, the largest expenditure was made in Gdańsk (PLN 910 million), Jelenia Góra (PLN 857 million), Cracow (PLN 642 million), Piaseczno (PLN 495 million), Tarnów (PLN 491 million), and Białystok (PLN 471 million). The costs incurred in some communes influenced significantly the total balance of expenditures for a given region (e.g., Jelenia Góra in Dolnośląskie voivodship—32%). In the whole country's scale, the first ten communes generated over 19% of all expenses. It means a very high concentration, which hinders the unequivocal interpretation of the results and causes that conclusions regarding the situation on a national scale should be cautious.

4.5. Forecasted vs. Realized Revenues and Expenditures

The balance of economic effects of adopting local plans is negative, both when we consider the forecasted revenues relating to the forecasted expenditure and the realized results, which can also be observed when converting the amounts to the number of inhabitants of communes (Figure 2). The comparison of income (receipts) and expenses (costs) shows several important regularities. First, neither the expected nor the realized income so far outweighs the expenses. On a national scale, revenues constitute approximately 60% of the reported costs.

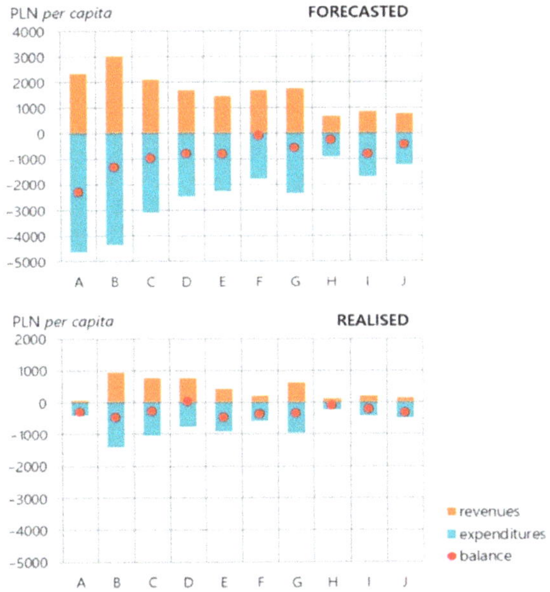

Figure 2. Structure of forecasted and realized revenues and expenditures of communes per capita by types of communes as a result of local plans enacted, for the year 2019. Source: based on unpublished data of the Ministry of Development and Statistical Office of Poland.

The most favorable balance was recorded for the realized income relating to the expenditure by the end of the year in the type D of communes, i.e., in the external zones of functional areas of sub-regional cities. It was slightly positive there, amounting to PLN 59 million. In the remaining categories of communes there are lower balances for financial turnover. In absolute numbers, the most negative balance concerns the ratio of projected revenues to costs in voivodeship cities (PLN −22.1 billion, thus it was assumed that 50% of revenues would offset expenditure). Simultaneously, the percentage ratio of revenues to costs was also the least favorable in voivodeship cities, but only in terms of their implementation (only 20% of revenues offset expenditure). It means that in larger urban centers, the implementation of the economic effects of adopting local plans takes longer. On the other hand, this balance percentage was also very low in the most intensively developed communes, including forest communes (type J), where the income balanced the expenditure by 32%.

On the country scale, there is almost the same rate of obtaining (realizing) revenues to those forecasted (23.1%) compared to incurred and forecasted expenses (23.3%). It can be concluded that both obtaining funds and incurring expenses resulting from adopting local plans are considerably stretched in time.

The most balanced financial situation related to the implementation of the provisions of local plans was found (apart from the already mentioned functional zones of sub-regional cities, where the balance was minimally positive) in the sub-regional cities themselves, i.e., mainly poviat cities. The negative balance there accounted for 9% of all expenditure, while in voivodship cities the amount of negative balance accounted for almost 80% of realized expenses, in smaller towns (type E) it was 53%, and in the most intensively developed communes (type J)—68% of the costs incurred.

The maps show the spatial mosaic nature of the anticipated and realized balances of incomes to expenditures per capita throughout Poland. However, the forecasted balances show clear regional differentiation (Figure 3). More favorable balances of forecasts are observed in the Western and North Territories, including Lower Silesia and northern Poland (Pomerania, Masuria, Warmia) than in the south-eastern part of the country (Lesser Poland, Subcarpathian region), characterized by a greater fragmentation of the agrarian structure and land properties, but also by significant coverage with local plans (the case of the Lublin region). Despite this, many communes from the Lublin region did not provide any data (they did not provide the completed forms during the survey). The balances for implementing local plans (Figure 4) show spatially full mosaic character, where communes with a negative balance dominate throughout the country, but communes with a positive balance are also scattered throughout Poland. The ratio of the expected balances to the communes' incomes (Figure 5) again shows a more favorable situation in the northern, western, and south-western parts of the country than in central, eastern, and north-eastern Poland.

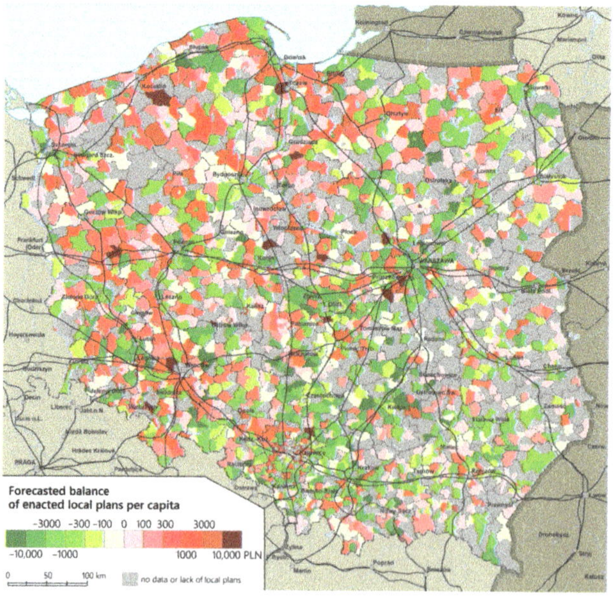

Figure 3. Forecast balance of revenues and expenditures per capita by communes, for the year 2019. Source: based on unpublished data of the Ministry of Development and Statistical Office of Poland.

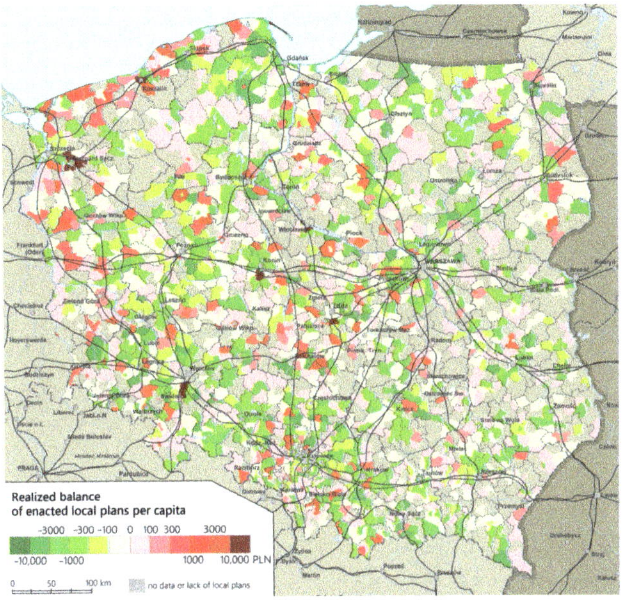

Figure 4. Realized balance of revenues and expenditures per capita by communes, for the year 2019. Source: based on unpublished data of the Ministry of Development and Statistical Office of Poland.

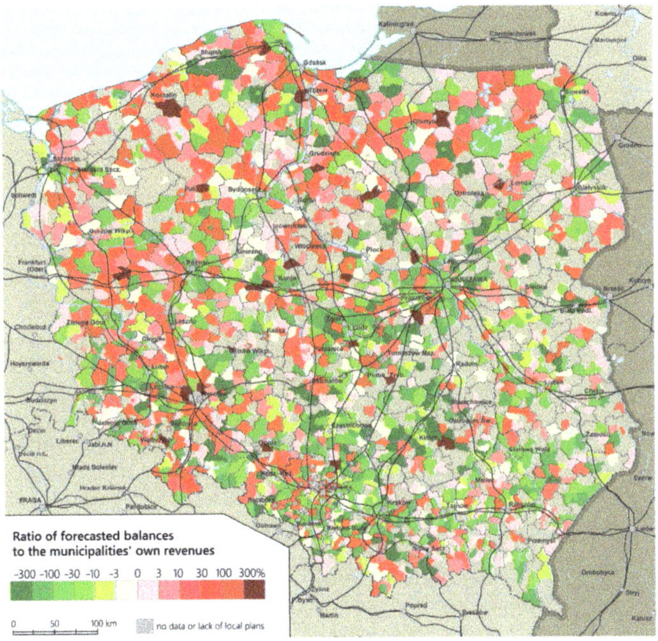

Figure 5. The ratio of forecasted balances to the communes' own revenues, for the year 2019. Source: based on unpublished data of the Ministry of Development and Statistical Office of Poland.

4.6. Examples of Municipalities with Unsustainable Financial Management

The analysis presented in the previous subsections would not be complete if it was not illustrated with examples from specific municipalities. Such a comparison is contained in Table 2, in which information about five municipalities located in different types of municipalities and regions of Poland is collected. They were selected from among 126 communes in Poland, for which, at the same time, there were full financial data available (on the forecasted and realized revenues and expenditures), and the area of these communes is nearly completely covered by the binding local plan (more than 95% of the municipality area). In all of these communes, there were high values of areas for which land use was changed from agricultural to non-agricultural.

All the analyzed municipalities were rather moderately prosperous, as for Polish conditions (municipalities' budgets in the range of 922–1021 EUR per capita, average in Poland-1208 EUR, median 1045 EUR in 2019), including the share of own income (mainly from local taxes and fees) which fluctuated between 31% and 51%. All the municipalities had a negative balance of projected revenues and expenditures due to the adoption of local plans (the highest number in the Michałowice in Cracow Metropolitan Area-106 million EUR) (Table 3). In three of them, revenues were projected mainly from fees and taxes (92–100%), while in the remaining ones the sale of building plots was most likely to be the source of profits. Interestingly, the latter mechanism did not apply to places where the land was most expensive, i.e., Michałowice and the Udanin (commune located by the A4 motorway). One can be almost certain that the tool in the form of "land bank" was not used in those communes. While in Michałowice there may have been a problem with the land ownership structure (most or all of the real estate being in private hands for a long time), the A4 motorway route has been known for a long time and it seems "puzzling" that the commune did not buy land along the motorway when plans to modernize the A4 route in 2002–2006 were known (in the commune there are two exits from the motorway: "Udanin" and "Jarosław").

As far as expenditures are concerned, according to the forecasts, they are to be spent mainly on the construction of infrastructure (together with the purchase of land). The amounts for these purposes account for 83–100% of the expected expenditures in the five municipalities.

In total, all the municipalities are forecast to have a negative balance of forecasted revenues and expenditures, with the largest number of them in the municipality of Michałowice near Cracow (−91 million EUR). Interestingly, this commune has a positive balance. This is, however, quite a peculiarity, as the commune invests little compared to the needs resulting from the rapid population growth due to suburbanization processes (in the years 2003–2019, the balance of recorded inflows and outflows was positive and amounted to 2.7 thousand people, i.e., 37% of the population in 2003). It is also worth noting that the commune has an exceptionally unbalanced budget: the planned expenses are as much as 19 times more than its own annual income (1902%). In the remaining communes this indicator is also high, ranging from 75% (Kiernozia) to 370% (Janów Lubelski).

The examples given show quite clearly how serious the problem of the lack of mechanisms is to ensure the financing of investments related to spatial planning in communes. It concerns both the situation in which the commune is an area of new population inflow (Chełm, Michałowice) and a typical depopulation commune (Kiernozia, Udanin). It is particularly unfavorable that despite the latter premise, related to the decrease in population, the communes do not look for savings in better spatial organization and concentration of buildings (in order to, for example, achieve better consistency ("fit") for services), but allow for a strong supply of new investment areas (in the suburban and depopulated communes of Michałowice and Kiernozia it was about 1.5 thousand sq. m of land per capita).

Table 3. Data on the forecasted and realized revenues and expenditures in the 5 selected communes in Poland. As of 31 December 2019.

Name	Chełm	Janów Lubelski	Kiernozia	Michałowice	Udanin
Locality and character	the suburban commune around the middle town, not far from the border with Ukraine	touristic commune in eastern Poland	peripheral agricultural commune in central Poland about 100 km north of Łódź	suburban commune in the Cracow Metropolitan Area	commune on the A4 motorway route (between Wrocław and Legnica)
Population (thous.)	15.0	15.9	3.4	10.8	5.1
Registered migration balance (number, 2000–2019)	2099	−695	−131	2705	−322
Area (sq. km)	221.8	178.7	76.2	51.1	110.9
Number of local plans	27	11	3	6	70
including change of land use from agricultural to non-agricultural use (ha)	897	728	479	1714	385
sq. m per capita (2019)	597	459	1423	1593	757
Revenues of municipal budgets (mln euro)	13.8	14.6	3.4	10.8	5.0
per capita	922	923	1021	1007	976
own revenues (%)	34.4	40.2	31.3	51.2	41.1
Forecasted revenues (mln euro)	1.5	19.8	0.4	14.6	2.6
including tax type revenues (%)	45.0	52.0	92.0	100	98.0
Forecasted expenditures (mln euro)	4.7	21.8	0.8	105.6	5.7
including construction of infrastructure (%)	90.2	83.6	90.9	100.0	93.5
Realized revenues (mln euro)	1.6	1.9	0.01	8.9	0.01
including tax type revenues (%)	99.8	10.2	0.0	100.0	100.0
Realized expenditures (mln euro)	5.0	7.2	0.5	7.5	3.2
Balance of forecasted revenues and expenditures (mln euro)	−3.2	−2.0	−0.4	−91.0	−3.2
Balance of realized revenues and expenditures (mln euro)	−3.4	−5.3	−0.5	1.3	−3.2
Realized revenues (% forecasted)	110.2	9.8	1.0	60.9	0.01
Realized expenditures (% forecasted)	106.4	33.2	66.0	7.1	55.9
Balance of revenues and expenditures per capita (euro)	−223	−334	−162	125	−628
Forecasted expenditures as a share of own revenues (%)	98	370	77	1902	280

Source: based on unpublished data of the Ministry of Development and the Central Statistical Office of Poland.

5. Discussion

The presented research covers the whole country. Until now, the literature was dominated by research based on case studies, often related to individual investments. It did not ensure good comparability of the results. It is worth pointing out that our research is representative of a relatively large European country.

The basic empirical information resulting from the conducted research is the generally negative financial balance of spatial economics at the local level. It results from not using the instruments provided for in the law, including, in particular, obtaining very low fees based on the increase in the value of the real estate (planning rent mechanism). On the other hand, the costs associated with land use changes are high (land purchase, construction of roads, and other infrastructure costs). The balance of income and expenditure in Poland remains negative. It is different from other countries, which generally acquire a financial surplus due to land conversion [59].

In the context of the second aim, it should be concluded, that the research also revealed a very much mosaic (diverse) pattern of communes' regional structure in terms of balances resulting from spatial management. This lack of regularity may prove that the planning law is very "loose". Some communes in their "width" and "freedom" can rationally and profitably conduct spatial and land management, while others are characterized by a negative balance. As shown on the maps, these are often neighboring communes. Meanwhile, the situation is slightly better in the west of the country and worse in the eastern part. It can be hypothesized that this may result from the greater dispersion of settlement in the country's eastern and central parts [70]. On the other hand, the neighboring with each other of the communes with diametrically different financial results cannot be easily explained. However, it seems that the explanation may be cautiously related to the nature of the local economy and local development, based on the strong influence of local communities and elites.

It is worth noting that the research identified groups of communes with the highest incomes obtained based on the indicated types of incomes (these are communes belonging to the functional areas of voivodeship capital cities and sub-regional cities) and communes where the incomes balance the expenses related to local spatial development plans (mainly communes from the external zones of functional areas of sub-regional cities). This research direction will be continued. As indicated above, most income is related to the increase in property value caused by the local zoning plans.

As far as the second objective of the article is concerned, it is important to note the very wide range of expected financial results. Quite often they exceed the annual budgets of municipalities, and there are situations where this ratio exceeds 300%. Thus, it can be a source of big profits, but also a danger because of the problems related to the lack of funds for investments. In this case, the example of large agglomerations shows how diametrically different it is:

- Warsaw, Łódź, Poznań, Cracow agglomeration: the balance is generally negative, often in relation to the budgets of municipalities over 30% and per capita minus 300 PLN and more;
- Szczecin and Wrocław agglomeration: a positive balance, often in relation to the budgets of communes over 30% and per capita plus 300 PLN and more.

This confirms those research results which indicate financial instability of self-governments as a serious barrier of development, especially in post-communist countries [71–74].

Despite the diagnosed serious problems in this respect in the Polish spatial management system (which is also presented below in the context of governance failure), the research results lead to the conclusion that these problems can be reduced. Therefore, it is possible to analyze further regularities against this background, particularly the premises for differentiating communes in this respect.

Despite the rich conceptual, theoretical, and implementation achievements in public control and management support in real estate markets (in the broadly understood spatial management system), there is still a wide field for new solutions that help optimize investment and location processes changes in land allocation. Identifying further regularities in this regard seems to be essential for the whole concept of value capturing.

Based on the research, it is also possible to clarify the issue of public governance failure in the spatial economy system. Other areas of it have been identified, which may also be noticeable in other countries. High expenses, which are a consequence of adopting local plans in large part of communes, are a serious factor deterring communes from an active spatial policy. These expenses are usually a consequence of the actions of real estate market participants. It can be indicated that the government failure is noticeable in various cases, including the planning and investment procedure in the land banking system [58]. Apart from the accusations of mismanagement, there were spatial conflicts concerning the very role of land banks (e.g., in the Netherlands farmers objected to giving land banks new functions). Therefore, the doubts concerned the form of use and exploitation of public resources (which inherently fits with the dilemmas concerning the concept of value capturing itself). In Poland, serious allegations of mismanagement and fraud appeared, especially in the re-privatization of land in the City of Warsaw [75]. On the other hand, when discussing Poland's local plans' economic consequences, such allegations (on such a scale) were not often expressed.

The creation of binding planning documents may be fraught with the "credible commitment dilemma" [76]. The local community members may not perceive the plans as a solution that is beneficial to them and may not support their implementation. Likewise, local politicians may not be convinced of the political and economic benefits of creating and applying planning documents. Therefore, they will not be interested in creating and implementing them. It is largely related to the understanding of property rights (which varies between countries).

In Poland, this understanding is closer to that of the United States, which more broadly emphasizes the need for compensation for planning restrictions in development [77] and the approach from the Netherlands, emphasizing the rights of the landowner to its increased value because of the provisions of spatial plan [78]. Ultimately, however, it leads to budget problems of public authorities [54], of which the presented situation in Poland is the best example. Non-financial compensation is implemented to a negligible extent and is limited only to selected procedures related to urban regeneration. It is a bad sign for the development of governance in this respect [79]. The solutions from the concept of governance (management through networks, negotiations) not applied in this case allow, together with non-financial compensation (assuming problems related to their application, known for example, from the United States), to limit expenses in this respect. The above confirms that it is necessary to develop an optimal planning style in many European countries [61].

Problems with balancing income and expenditure (and problems with the vast predominance of expenditure) also result from an incorrectly constructed planning rent (fees on the increase in the value of the real estate, i.e., a solution that would implement the Value Capturing concept in Polish conditions). Its optionality, low amount, and the possibility of differentiating its rate are an expression of not only incorrect legislation. As indicated in the literature [48], outside the legal framework, the planning practice determines the implementation of goals which are specific from the spatial management system's perspective. It may come down to informal solutions.

In the case at hand, social pressure led to disseminating informal solutions unfavorable from the spatial management system's perspective: the depreciation of this fee's rates by the communal authorities themselves. It is an interesting example of the public authorities limiting the effects which are positive for them. It should also be added that the possibility of extreme differentiation of rates by public authorities may give rise to allegations of corruption. Such allegations and doubts are noticed (as indicated above) in Western countries. This problem concerns various spheres. Decisions concerning both the spatial development system and the real estate market (i.e., with an impact on real estate value) are discretionary. Discretion in this area as such cannot be eliminated: it would, for example, block the development of planning flexibility.

It is worth paying attention to one more manifestation of public governance failure in the spatial management system identified in the research. It is a severe differentiation of projected and realized expenditure and revenues. From the spatial management system perspective, this significantly hampers rational, planned activities (and this is the standard when implementing the value capturing idea in a significant part of countries). On the one hand, the discrepancies result partly from defective legal bases and, on the other hand, also from the practice of public authorities. From the perspective of communal authorities, sometimes the amounts of income and expenditure in forecasts are justified more by political and pragmatic reasons.

The described phenomenon exacerbates the uncertainty indicated in the literature which is related to European spatial management systems in implementing investments related to the Value Capturing instruments [43]. If we add to this the poor flexibility in terms of changes in planning arrangements (and a much greater risk of opportunistic actions), the more understandable are the problems of the Polish spatial management system and the failure of even sector-based urban agreements. It should be emphasized that the overall formal and procedural uncertainty in the Polish spatial development system deepens the speculative actions of investors and a kind of confusion among local authorities.

As indicated in the literature review, local plans in different countries have different formulas and functions. Individual instruments for the economic consequences of spatial planning are also adapted to these plans in different ways. The presented results lead to the reflection that the definition of extensive compensation consequences in the system, combined with the lack of developed individual instruments for the economic consequences of planning, contributes to a gross reduction of control by public authorities of the spatial development (identified in the literature as a key function of plans). Such control—with different legal solutions—is possible to a greater extent, even when local plans are not legal acts (as in the UK). The example of the French system (considering the compensatory consequences of spatial planning to a negligible extent) also leads to the conclusion that the liberal understanding of property owner's rights developed in post-socialist countries (also in Poland) can be repaired even when applying the regulations of the European Convention on Human Rights. This Convention, despite numerous discussions on it, does not only require such an understanding of property rights as in the Polish spatial planning system [31].

6. Summary

In the study, we presented empirical evidence to support the thesis that spatial planning and spatial development relating to Poland's real estate market have serious drawbacks, leading to mismanagement and losses. The lack of certainty in the real estate function will be maintained, and the non-transparency of decisions made by local authorities affects the overall market. We compared it to the situation in other countries, concluding that Poland, compared to other countries, is characterized by a deeper degree of public governance failure. The lack of certainty and consistency in legislative solutions, and questionable planning practice, together lead to the domination of expenditures over incomes constituting the economic consequences of adopting plans and to the creation of a large mosaic of communes' regional structure in terms of balances resulting from spatial management. There is no wider use of tools related to the concept of governance in this respect, especially in-depth negotiations before planning decisions. There is also a lack of an objectively indicated scope of changes in the local plan that the public authority may conduct on the occasion of such potential negotiations (and such scopes are, e.g., distinguished in the systems of other countries).

Therefore, the lack of a wider implementation of local plans with poor planning practice perpetuates the negative phenomena (spatial chaos). The compensation claims provided for in the Polish system make it difficult to repair it more broadly. Interestingly, in the context of the concept of Value Capturing, even communal authorities deepen these trends, often not taking advantage of the (limited) possibilities of determining and collecting planning rent. There is also definitely a lack of other value capturing solutions, such as the transfer of the right to build (although it must be noted that even sectoral substitutes for value capturing solutions have not been adopted, an example of which is the urban agreement in the urban regeneration process—provided for in the regulations but not applied). Value capture instruments, which can be used by municipalities when the value of real estate increases due to the constructions of infrastructure from public funds, are also not often used in practice.

The conducted analyses indicate several important regularities related to financial effects on the binding local spatial development plans in Poland. Inflows and expenses related to the effects of adopting local plans constitute a high percentage of total revenues and expenses of communes' budgets. A relatively permanent phenomenon is the generally negative result of the effects of adopting local plans (a positive balance occurred only in two out of sixteen voivodeships).

The very heterogeneous financial policy of communes is noteworthy, both in terms of spending funds and obtaining income to implement local plans. It also results from a large diversification of communes' activity in the field of spatial planning—relating to the number, area of coverage, and functions of the adopted plans (dominant use of areas, exclusions from buildings, etc.). The functioning system's serious problem is the occasional occurrence of typical income mechanisms provided for in the Act on Spatial Planning and Development (2003), especially related to the planning fee (rent).

As a result of adopting local plans, there is a strong stratification of local governments' income and cost situation. The observed strong concentration of high revenues and expenses in a small part of communes, both forecasted and realized, implies considerable heterogeneity and generally diverse policies of communes in the field of spatial planning. The observed lack of significant regularities—statistical, functional, and spatial—makes us critically evaluate the local spatial policies, which often brings benefits to some local governments in similar socioeconomic realities and geographical locations, and to others it brings (in most cases) losses.

As the projected burden on local government budgets related to the implementation of local plans (due to expenditure on infrastructure, public roads, land purchases, compensation for owners) often does not balance the revenues (from taxes and local fees and real estate trade), communes often suspend works on spatial development plans. It leads to the development of uncontrolled urbanization based on administrative decisions on building conditions, resulting in spatial chaos and has a limiting effect on local development, with serious financial consequences. They are related particularly to the purchase of land, infrastructure construction, and its maintenance in the future. These "extra" costs, increased due to dispersed, chaotic development, are estimated at EUR 20 billion per year [16].

To sum up, rational spatial management is one of the most underrated endogenous growth impulses of economy in Poland. The high amounts of financial turnover related to implementing spatial plans, when related to many communes' budgets, indicate that spatial planning could be a driving force for local economies. Meanwhile, in many cases, due to negative balances, it threatens to destabilize public finances.

In conclusion, it can be said that for local politics and local law, compared to other countries, the Polish model has not proved successful, as it gives too much freedom in determining income and costs as well as the methods of obtaining and spending them, and thus generating not profits, but mostly losses. In this respect, the presented research provides an illustrative and symptomatic lesson for other countries on how not to proceed in spatial planning on real estate markets.

Author Contributions: Conceptualization, P.Ś. and M.N.; methodology, P.Ś.; software, M.B.; validation, M.B. and M.N.; formal analysis, P.Ś. and M.N.; investigation, P.Ś., M.N., P.S. and M.Z.; resources, P.Ś. and P.S.; data curation, P.Ś. and P.S.; writing—original draft preparation, M.N., P.Ś., P.S. and M.Z.; writing—review and editing, M.N. and P.Ś.; visualization, P.Ś., P.S. and M.B.; supervision, M.N.; project administration, P.Ś. and M.N.; funding acquisition, P.Ś. All authors have read and agreed to the published version of the manuscript.

Funding: This research received no external funding.

Institutional Review Board Statement: Not applicable.

Informed Consent Statement: Not applicable.

Conflicts of Interest: The authors declare no conflict of interest.

References

1. Dühr, S.; Colomb, C.; Nadin, V. (Eds.) *European Spatial Planning and Territorial Cooperation*; Routledge: London, UK; New York, NY, USA, 2010; pp. 360–371, ISBN 978-0-415-46774-2.
2. Bogetoft, P.; Pruzan, P. *Planning with Multiple Criteria: Investigation, Communication and Choice*; Elsevier Science Pub.: Amsterdam, The Netherlands, 1991; pp. 117–123, ISBN 044488999X.
3. De Groot, R. Function-analysis and valuation as a tool to assess land use conflicts in planning for sustainable, multi-functional landscapes. *Landsc. Urban Plan.* **2006**, *75*, 175–186. [CrossRef]
4. Pacione, M. Private profit, public interest and land use planning—A conflict interpretation of residential development pressure in Glasgow's rural–urban fringe. *Land Use Policy* **2013**, *32*, 61–77. [CrossRef]
5. Morrill, R.L.; Symons, J. Efficiency and equity aspects of optimum location. *Geogr. Anal.* **1977**, *9*, 215–225. [CrossRef]
6. Mäntysalo, R. Learning from the UK: Towards market-oriented land-use planning in Finland. *Hous. Theory Soc.* **1999**, *16*, 179–191. [CrossRef]
7. DeVerteuil, G. Reconsidering the legacy of urban public facility location theory in human geography. *Prog. Hum. Geogr.* **2000**, *24*, 47–69. [CrossRef]
8. Rajakallio, K.; Cuthbertson, R.; Pulkka, L.; Junnila, S. Creating urban platforms—Opportunities and challenges for innovation in commercial real estate development. *Cities* **2018**, *77*, 92–103. [CrossRef]
9. Rebelo, E.M. Land betterment capture revisited: A methodology for territorial plans. *Land Use Policy* **2017**, *69*, 392–407. [CrossRef]
10. Hopkins, L.D.; Knaap, G.J. Autonomous planning: Using plans as signals. *Plan. Theory* **2018**, *17*, 274–295. [CrossRef]
11. Immergluck, D. Large redevelopment initiatives, housing values and gentrification: The case of the Atlanta Beltline. *Urban Stud.* **2009**, *46*, 1723–1745. [CrossRef]
12. Cho, G.H.; Kim, J.H.; Lee, G. Announcement effects of urban regeneration plans on residential property values: Evidence from Ulsan, Korea. *Cities* **2020**, 97. [CrossRef]
13. Nesticò, A.; Endreny, T.; Guarini, M.R.; Sica, F.; Anelli, D. Real Estate Values, Tree Cover, and Per-Capita Income: An Evaluation of the Interdependencies in Buffalo City (NY). In Proceedings of the International Conference on Computational Science and Its Applications, Cagliari, Italy, 1–4 July 2020; Springer: Cham, Switzerland; Amsterdam, The Netherlands, 2020; pp. 913–926.
14. Ehrlich, M.V.; Hilber, C.A.L.; Schöni, O. Institutional settings and urban masl: Evidence from Europe. *J. Hous. Econ. Elsevier* **2018**, *42*, 4–18. [CrossRef]
15. Debrunner, G.; Hartmann, T. Strategic use of land policy instruments for affordable housing—Coping with social challenges under scarce land conditions in Swiss cities. *Land Use Policy* **2020**, *99*, 104993. [CrossRef]
16. Śleszyński, P.; Kowalewski, A.; Markowski, T.; Legutko-Kobus, P.; Nowak, M. The Contemporary Economic Costs of Spatial Chaos: Evidence from Poland. *Land* **2020**, *9*, 214. [CrossRef]
17. Domański, R. Accessibility, Efficiency, and Spatial Organization. *Environ. Plan.* **1979**, *11*, 1189–1206. [CrossRef]
18. Pennington, D.N.; Dalzell, B.; Nelson, E.; Mulla, D.; Taff, S.; Hawthorne, P.; Polasky, S. Cost-effective land use planning: Optimizing land use and land management patterns to maximize social benefits. *Ecol. Econ.* **2017**, *139*, 75–90. [CrossRef]
19. Śleszyński, P.; Komornicki, T. Klasyfikacja funkcjonalna gmin Polski na potrzeby monitoringu planowania przestrzennego [Functional classification of Poland's communes (gminas) for the needs of the monitoring of spatial planning]. *Przegląd Geogr.* **2016**, *88*, 469–488. [CrossRef]
20. Reimer, M.; Getimis, P.; Blotevogel, H. Spatial planning systems and practices in Europe: A comparative perspective. In *Spatial Planning Systems and Practices in Europe. A Comparative Perspective on Continuity and Changes*; Reimer, M., Getimis, P., Blotevogel, H., Eds.; Routledge: New York, NY, USA, 2014; pp. 170–176, ISBN 9780415727242.
21. Nadin, V.; Stead, D. European spatial planning systems, social, models and learning. *Disp Plan. Rev.* **2008**, *44*, 35–47. [CrossRef]
22. Nadin, V. International comparative planning methodology: Introduction to the theme issue. *Plan. Pract. Res.* **2012**, *27*, 1–5. [CrossRef]
23. Reimer, M.; Blotevogel, H. Comparing spatial practice in Europe: A plea for cultural sensitization. *Plan. Pract. Res.* **2012**, *27*, 7–24. [CrossRef]
24. Berisha, E.; Cotella, G.; Janin-Rivolin, U.; Solly, A. Spatial governance and planning systems and the public control of spatial development: A European typology. *Eur. Plan. Stud.* **2020**, *29*, 181–200. [CrossRef]
25. Lindholm, G. Land and Ladscape; Linking Use, Experience and Property Development in Urban Areas. *Land* **2019**, *8*, 137. [CrossRef]
26. Levačić, R. Markets and government: An overview. In *Markets, Hierarchies and Networks: The Coordination of Social Life*; Thompson, G., Frances, J., Levačić, R., Mitchel, J., Eds.; SAGE: London, UK, 1991; pp. 35–47, ISBN 978-0803985902.
27. Wolf, C. *Markets or Governments: Choosing between Imperfect Alternatives*, 2nd ed.; MIT Press: Cambridge, MA, USA, 1993; pp. 140–151, ISBN 9780262231725.
28. Webster, C.J. Public choice, Pigouvian and Coasian planning theory. *Urban Stud.* **1998**, *35*, 53–75. [CrossRef]
29. Bertaud, A.; Malpezzi, S. Measuring the costs and benefits of urban land use regulation: A simple model with an application to Malaysia. *J. Hous. Econ.* **2001**, *10*, 393–418. [CrossRef]
30. Brueckner, J.K. Government land use interventions: An economic analysis. In *Urban Land Markets: Improving Land Management for Successful Urbanization*; Lall, S.V., Freire, M., Yuen, B., Eds.; Springer: Dordrecht, The Netherlands, 2009; pp. 3–23, ISBN 978-1-4020-8862-9.

31. Alterman, R. Takings International: A Cross-National. In *Takings International. A comparative Perspective on Land Use Regulations and Compensation Rights*; Alterman, R., Ed.; American Bar Association: Chicago, IL, USA, 2010; pp. 1–75, ISBN 978-1-60442-550-5.
32. Majewska, A.; Denis, M.; Krupowicz, W. Urbanization Chaos of Suburban Small Cities in Poland: 'Tetris Development'. *Land* **2020**, *9*, 461. [CrossRef]
33. Glaeser, E.L.; Ward, B.A. The causes and consequences of land use regulation: Evidence from Greater Boston. *J. Urban Econ.* **2009**, *65*, 265–278. [CrossRef]
34. Kok, N.; Monkkonen, P.; Quigley, J.M. Land use regulations and the value of land and housing: An intra-metropolitan analysis. *J. Urban Econ.* **2014**, *81*, 136–148. [CrossRef]
35. Irwin, E.G.; Bockstael, N.E. The problem of identifying land use spillovers: Measuring the effects of open space on residential property values. *Am. J. Agric. Econ.* **2001**, *83*, 698–704. [CrossRef]
36. Anderson, S.T.; West, S.E. Open space, residential property values, and spatial context. *Reg. Sci. Urban Econ.* **2006**, *36*, 773–789. [CrossRef]
37. Morano, P.; Guarini, M.R.; Tajani, F.; Di Liddo, F.; Anelli, D. Incidence of Different Types of Urban Green Spaces on Property Prices. A Case Study in the Flaminio District of Rome (Italy). In Proceedings of the 19th International Conference on Computional Science and Its Applications (ICCSA 2019), Saint Petersburg, Russia, 1–4 July 2019; pp. 23–34.
38. European Commission. *The EU Compendium of Spatial Planning Systems and Policies*; Regional Development Studies; European Commission: Brussels, Belgium, 1997; Volume 28, pp. 47–80.
39. Newman, P.; Thornley, A. *Urban Planning in Europe. International Competition, National Systems and Planning Projects*, 1st ed.; Routledge: London, UK; New York, NY, USA, 1996; pp. 28–41, ISBN 9780415111799.
40. Janin-Riviolin, U.; Faludi, A. The hidden face of European spatial planning: Innovations in governance. *Eur. Plann. Stud.* **2005**, *13*, 195–215. [CrossRef]
41. Larsson, G. *Spatial Planning Systems in Western Europe: An Overview*; IOS Press: Amsterdam, The Netherlands, 2006; pp. 21–49, ISBN 978-1-58603-656-0.
42. Stein, L. *Comparative Urban Land Use Planning: Best Practice*; Sydney University Press: Sydney, Austria, 2017; pp. 330–337, ISBN 9781743324677.
43. Muñoz-Gielen, D.; Tasan Kok, T. Flexibility in planning and the consequences for public value capturing in UK, Spain and the Netherlands. *Eur. Plan. Stud.* **2010**, *18*, 1097–1131. [CrossRef]
44. Nadin, V.; Stead, D. Spatial planning in the United Kingdom 1990–2013. In *Spatial Planning Systems and Practices in Europe: A Comparative Perspective on Continuity and Changes*; Reimer, M., Getimis, P., Blotevogel, H., Eds.; Routledge: New York, NY, USA, 2014; pp. 198–214, ISBN 9780415727242.
45. von Schumacher, J.; Werk, K. *Raumordnungsgesetz, Kommentar*; Kommunal—und Schul-Verlag: Wiesbaden, Germany, 2012; ISBN 3829308571.
46. Geppert, A. Vae Victis! Spatial planning in the rescaled metropolitan governance in France. *Raumforsch. Und Raumordn. Spat. Res. Plan.* **2017**, *75*, 225–241. [CrossRef]
47. Geppert, A. France, drifting away from the "regional economic" approach. In *Spatial Planning Systems and Practices in Europe*; Routledge: London, UK; pp. 129–146, ISBN 9781315852577.
48. Blotevogel, H.; Danielzyk, R.; Münter, A. Spatial planning in Germany: Institutional inertia and new challenges. In *Spatial Planning Systems and Practices in Europe: A Comparative Perspective on Continuity and Changes*; Reimer, M., Getimis, P., Blotevogel, H., Eds.; Routledge: New York, NY, USA, 2014; pp. 77–101, ISBN 9780415727242.
49. Muñoz-Gielen, D. Urban governance, property rights, land readjustment and public value capturing. *Eur. Urban Reg. Stud.* **2014**, *21*, 60–78. [CrossRef]
50. Alterman, R. Land use regulations and property values: The "Windfalls Capture" Idea Revisited. In *The Oxford Handbook of Urban Economics and Planning*; Brooks, N., Donaghy, K., Knaap, G.J., Eds.; Oxford University Press: Oxford, UK, 2012; pp. 755–786, ISBN 978-0-19-53-8062-0. Available online: https://papers.ssrn.com/sol3/papers.cfm?abstract_id=2309571 (accessed on 10 December 2020).
51. Muñoz-Gielen, D.; Salas, I.M.; Cuadrado, J.B. International comparison of the changing dynamics of governance approaches to land development and their results for public value capture. *Cities* **2017**, *71*, 123–134. [CrossRef]
52. Suzuki, H.; Murakami, J.; Hong, Y.H.; Tamayose, B. *Financing Transit-Oriented Development with Land Values: Adapting Land Value Capture in Developing Countries*; The World Bank: Washington, DC, USA, 2015; pp. 37–39, 45–46, ISBN 978-1-4648-0149-5.
53. Kim, M. Upzoning and value capture: How US local governments use land use regulation power to create and capture value from real estate developments. *Land Use Policy* **2020**, *95*, 104624. [CrossRef]
54. Van der Veen, M.; Spaans, M.; Janssen-Jansen, L. Using compensation instruments as a vehicle to improve spatial planning: Challenges and opportunities. *Land Use Policy* **2010**, *27*, 1010–1017. [CrossRef]
55. Colavitti, A.M.; Serra, S. Non financial compensation for the redevelopment of the historic urban landscape: The case study of Villasor in Sardinia (Italy). *City Territ. Archit.* **2020**, *7*, 1–15. [CrossRef]
56. Machemer, P.L.; Kaplowitz, M.D. A Framework for evaluating transferable development rights programmes. *J. Environ. Plan. Manag.* **2002**, *45*, 773–795. [CrossRef]
57. Goldman, M. Speculative urbanism and the making of the next world city. *Int. J. Urban Reg. Res.* **2011**, *35*, 555–581. [CrossRef]
58. Flechner, H.L. *Land Banking in the Control of Urban Development*; Praeger Publishers: New York, NY, USA, 1974; pp. 45–52.

59. Van Dijk, T.; Kopeva, D. Land banking and Central Europe: Future relevance, current initiatives, Western European past experience. *Land Use Policy* **2006**, *23*, 286–301. [CrossRef]
60. Węcławowicz, G. *Contemporary Poland*; Space and Society; UCL Press: London, UK, 1996.
61. Nadin, V.; Fernández Maldonado, A.; Zonneveld, W.; Stead, D.; Dąbrowski, M.; Piskorek, K.; Sarkar, A.; Schmitt, P.; Smas, L.; Cotella, G.; et al. *COMPASS—Comparative Analysis of Territorial Governance and Spatial Planning Systems in Europe Applied Research 2016–2018 Final Report*; ESPON: Luxembourg, 2018; Available online: https://www.espon.eu/planning-systems (accessed on 10 December 2020).
62. Alrock, U.; Guntner, S.; Huning, S.; Peters, D. Spatial Planning and Urban Development in the New EU Member States—Between Adjustment anf Reinvention. In *Spatial Planning and Urban Development in the New EU Members States; From Adjustment to Reinvention*; Alrock, U., Gunter, S., Huning, S., Peters, D., Eds.; Routledge: London, UK; New York, NY, USA, 2016; pp. 1–18, ISBN 9781138273214.
63. Maier, K. Changing Planning in the Czech Republic. In *Spatial Planning Systems and Practices in Europe*; Routledge: London, UK, 2014; pp. 215–235, ISBN 9780415727235.
64. Kowalewski, A.; Markowski, T.; Śleszyński, P. *Studia nad Chaosem Przestrzennym, Tom III: Synteza*; Uwarunkowania, skutki i propozycje naprawy chaosu, Studia KPZK PAN: Warszawa, Poland, 2018; Volume 182. Available online: http://journals.pan.pl/skpzk/125269 (accessed on 10 December 2020).
65. Gorzym–Wilkowski, W. Spatial Planning as a Tool for Sustainable Development. Polish Realities. *Barom. Reg.* **2017**, *15*, 75–85. Available online: http://br.wszia.edu.pl/zeszyty/pdfs/br48_07gorzym.pdf (accessed on 10 December 2020).
66. Parysek, J.J. Asking about the future of spatial management in Poland (thirteen years on from the 2003 legal regulation). *Ruch Praw. Ekon. I Socjol.* **2016**, *78*, 37–58. [CrossRef]
67. Kowalewski, A.; Mordasewicz, J.; Osiatyński, J.; Regulski, J.; Stępień, J.; Śleszyński, P. *Raport o Ekonomicznych Stratach i Społecznych Kosztach Niekontrolowanej Urbanizacji w Polsce*; Fundacja Rozwoju Demokracji Lokalnej, IGiPZ PAN: Warszawa, Poland, 2013; pp. 4–6. Available online: http://obserwatorium.miasta.pl/wp-content/uploads/2016/08/Raport-Ekonomiczny-29.10.2013-calosc.pdf (accessed on 10 December 2020).
68. Nowak, M. The Stakeholders and Municipal Authorities in the Spatial Competition. *Biul. Kpzk Pan* **2017**, *265*, 22–35. Available online: http://journals.pan.pl/Content/100772/PDF/Biuletyn+KPZK+265+3-M.Nowak.pdf?handler=pdf (accessed on 10 December 2020).
69. Mickiewicz, P.; Nowak, M. Environmental protection and integrated development planning in local spatial policy on the example of Poland. *Ann. Univ. Apulensis Ser. Oeconomica* **2020**, *22*, 11–18. [CrossRef]
70. Śleszyński, P.; Gibas, P.; Sudra, P. The problem of mismatch between the CORINE Land Cover data classification and the development of settlement in Poland. *Remote Sens.* **2020**, *12*, 2253. [CrossRef]
71. Swianiewicz, P. *Local Government Borrowing: Risks and Rewards: A Reporton Central and Eastern Europe*; Local Government and Public Service Reform Initiative, Open Society Institute: Budapest, Hungary, 2004; p. 427.
72. Szarowská, I.; Majerová, I.; Šebestová, J. Indicators of financial stability for needs of municipalities [Indikátory finanční stability pro potřeby obcí]. *Český Finanční Účetní Časopis* **2018**, *1*, 25–45. [CrossRef]
73. Ushakova, E.; Pak, H.; Kuprin, A. Problems of assessing the financial stability and security of municipalities. *Matec Web Conf.* **2018**, *170*, 2. [CrossRef]
74. Aleksandrova-Zlatanska, S.K. Evaluating the factors for fiscal stability of rural municipalities: The case of Bulgaria, Problems of Agricultural Economics. *Zagadnienia Ekon. Rolnej/Probl. Agric. Econ.* **2019**, *360*, 156–170. [CrossRef]
75. Górczyńska, M.; Śleszyński, P.; Niedzielski, M. Impact of property rights and ownership on the development of Warsaw's contemporary city centre. *Eur. Plan. Stud.* **2019**, *27*, 160–180. [CrossRef]
76. Dixit, A.K. *The Making of Economic Policy: A Transaction-Cost Politics Perspective*; MIT Press: Cambridge, MA, USA, 1998; pp. 200–206, ISBN 9780262041553.
77. Jacobs, H.M. The Future of the Regulatory Takings Issue in the United States and Europe: Divergence or Convergence? *Urban Lawyer* **2008**, *40*, 52–72. Available online: https://www.harveymjacobs.com/wp-content/uploads/2018/06/Jacobs-2008-Regulatory-Takings-Urban-Lawyer.pdf (accessed on 21 December 2020).
78. Muñoz-Gielen, D. Improving Public—Value Capturing in Urban Development. In *Innovative Land and Property Taxation*; Sietchiping, R., Ed.; United Nations Human Settlements Programme (UN-Habitat): Nairobi, Kenya, 2011; pp. 148–169, ISBN 978-92-1-132407-5.
79. Nowak, M. Niesprawność władz publicznych a polityka przestrzenna w Polsce. *Zarządzanie Publiczne* **2016**, *2*, 94–106. Available online: http://bazhum.muzhp.pl/media//files/Zarzadzanie_Publiczne/Zarzadzanie_Publiczne-r2016-t-n36_(2)/Zarzadzanie_Publiczne-r2016-t-n36_(2)-s94-106/Zarzadzanie_Publiczne-r2016-t-n36_(2)-s94-106.pdf (accessed on 10 December 2020). [CrossRef]

land

Article

Towards Sustainable Urbanization. Learning from What's Out There

Alys Solly *, Erblin Berisha and Giancarlo Cotella

Interuniversity Department of Regional, Urban Studies and Planning (DIST), Politecnico di Torino, Viale Mattioli 39, 10125 Turin, Italy; erblin.berisha@polito.it (E.B.); giancarlo.cotella@polito.it (G.C.)
* Correspondence: alys.solly@polito.it

Abstract: The incremental recognition of the importance of land as a finite resource has led to the adoption and implementation of an increasing number of sustainable land use practices in European cities and regions. This paper reflects on these experiences, building on the evidence collected in the framework of the ESPON SUPER pan-European research project. In particular, the authors look at the project's database, which includes 235 examples of sustainable urbanization interventions gathered from all around Europe. In doing so, they reflect on the outcomes of these interventions, focusing on both their scope and objectives and the types of instruments that were adopted in their implementation. The objective of this contribution is to critically analyze the rich set of practices collected throughout the project and to provide guidance for decision and policy makers aiming at promoting a more sustainable use of land. In this light, it suggests a number of recommendations and warnings, bearing in mind that no "right instruments" or "right targets" exist that could prove successful for all European cities and regions.

Keywords: sustainable land use; urbanization; spatial governance and planning; Europe; ESPON

Citation: Solly, A.; Berisha, E.; Cotella, G. Towards Sustainable Urbanization. Learning from What's Out There. *Land* **2021**, *10*, 356. https://doi.org/10.3390/land10040356

Academic Editor: Jefferey M. Sellers

Received: 22 February 2021
Accepted: 23 March 2021
Published: 1 April 2021

1. Introduction

Over the years, and especially since the Second World War, land transformation has become more and more intense, leading to the overexploitation of land and to the progressive recognition of its finite nature. More recently, the COVID-19 crisis has further warned us about the importance that a present and future sustainable built, as well as natural, environment, could have in facing unexpected emergencies more resiliently [1]. There is, therefore, an increasing need to find and adopt integrated solutions to make present and future development more sustainable [2]. Thus, it is essential for policy and decision makers to take careful decisions on urbanization and land use management, approaching the latter not only as a political and technocratic decision but as one that affects our society's well-being and quality of life [3].

This perspective is well acknowledged at the European level, with the European Union (EU) which, through time, has introduced a growing number of policies and actions aiming at promoting a more sustainable approach to development and urbanization [4]. In particular, the EU is trying to halt excessive land transformation with its objective to achieve zero net land take by 2050 [5] and, more recently, the European Green Deal has stressed the need to make Europe climate neutral by 2050 [6]. As a result, in the last few years, policy and decision makers at all territorial levels have started to dedicate increasing efforts to pursue urbanization and land use models that are more sustainable, thus leading to the consolidation of an increasingly heterogeneous set of interventions and practices aiming at this direction [7]. At the same time, it should be noted that this has happened from both the top-down and the bottom-up levels, in the context of both urbanized and depopulated remote rural areas [8,9].

Research and studies on sustainable urbanization and land-use have also increased through time, often stemming from different definitions and interpretations of "sustainability". When focusing on the use of land, the most recent definitions of sustainable urbanization perceive the latter as the "design of future urban development as well as the re-development of existing ones in an environmentally friendly and resource-efficient manner" [10] (p. 1). In particular, sustainable land use seems to depend both on the socio-economic processes that trigger spatial development and on the effectiveness of the instruments that regulate these processes [3]. Adopting a similar perspective, the recently concluded ESPON SUPER project (Sustainable Urbanization and land-use Practices in European Regions, 2018–2020; https://www.espon.eu/super (accessed on 15 March 2021)) reviewed the multiple approaches put in place in different European cities and regions towards the achievement of a more sustainable urbanization, bearing in mind that there are no "right instruments" or "right targets" that could possibly fit all territorial contexts, also due to the high heterogeneity that characterizes the European continent in terms of socioeconomic development, administrative culture and spatial governance and planning [11,12].

The present contribution builds on the results of the SUPER project to develop guidance for decision and policy-makers aiming at promoting a more sustainable urbanization of their territories. It does this through a critical analysis of the rich set of practices collected throughout the project and, in particular, exploring the variable degree of success that characterizes interventions aiming at different goals, as well as adopting different types of instruments. After this introduction, the second section introduces the theoretical framework of the SUPER project, before section three describes the methodology that it adopted to collect and analyze sustainable urbanization and land use practices throughout Europe. Section four constitutes the core of the paper; it provides a quantitative overview of the collected interventions, in particular in relation to their localization and degree of success, to then discuss more in depth their results in relation to their scope and objectives (i.e., densification, regeneration, containment, governance and sectoral policies), as well as to the types of instruments that they have employed (i.e., visions and strategies, rules and legal devices, land use regulations, programs and projects). Finally, a concluding section rounds off the contribution, summarizing its main messages and the implications for decision and policy makers and introducing a number of avenues for future research.

2. Theoretical Framework

Despite its rather long history, sustainability as a concept is still characterized by multiple interpretations and rather blurred boundaries. [13]. The term was coined by the International Union for Conservation of Nature and Natural Resources (IUCN) in the early 1980s, and then adopted by the Brundtland Report a few years later, to indicate "development that meets the needs of the present without compromising the ability of future generations to meet their own needs" [14] (p. 54). As a result, during the last three decades, sustainable development has been at the center of the international research agenda [15]. Indeed, it has increasingly taken a central position in recent EU regional and urban politics, as evidenced for example by the decision to undertake the ESPON SUPER project. Nevertheless, although there is a "vast array of available best practices, little is known about the ways in which best practice is constructed, used, and contested, or of its implications for urban sustainability" [16] (p. 1029). Drawing on the consolidated literature on the topic, the ESPON SUPER project understands sustainability as characterized by three main aspects: temporal, thematic and institutional balance (see Figure 1). In particular, the *temporal balance* refers to the capacity to maintain long-term sustainable development for future generations and to enable the satisfaction of their needs [17]. Although often underestimated, certain factors, such as a governance quality and the durability of policies (e.g., the stability of funding), seem to effectively enhance sustainable urbanization processes [18] (p. 2). Moreover, among the characteristics that support the effectiveness of urban regeneration processes are those policies that envisage long-term sustainable targets, and which are supported by a strong political will (e.g., the UK brownfield targets, see Section 4.1.2). On the other hand, the *thematic balance* refers to three dimensions generally referred to as the "three Es" (i.e., economy, ecology, equity) [19] or the "three Ps" (i.e., people, planet, profit) of sustainability [20]. According to the literature, any intervention faces the challenge of reconciling and enabling the coexistence of these dimensions [21]. Consequently, each of these dimensions has to be fulfilled without sacrificing the others, in order to achieve a development trajectory that is truly sustainable [22]. Finally, sustainability also depends on the *institutional balance*. For various reasons, institutional sustainability is a challenging issue for those working towards the development and implementation of sustainable urbanization policies. In fact, decisions and actions should be implemented through transparent and effective mechanisms, in line and coherent with the overall institutional framework in which they are adopted [23]. Thus, sustainable development can also be seen as a "social and political construct and, as such, the study of the operationalization of sustainable development through the implementation of specific policies provides the critical focus for research" [24] (p. 1).

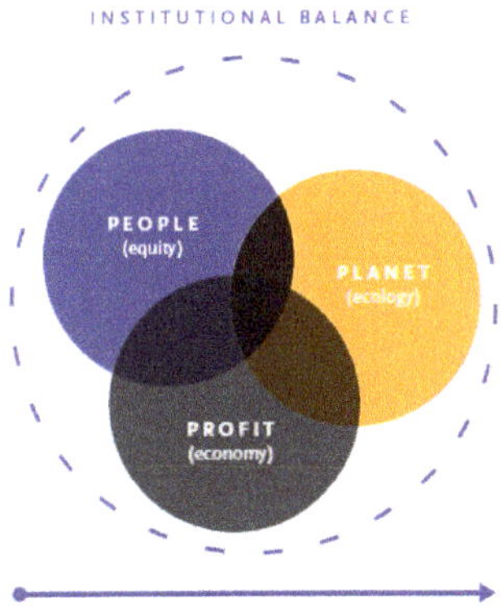

Figure 1. Understanding sustainability (source: [25] (p. 11)).

When it comes to understanding urbanization as a phenomenon that can occur more or less sustainably, the SUPER project does not merely refer to the movement of population to cities or the expansion of the built-up area, but to all physical developments that may affect land (homes, roads, construction sites, playgrounds, airports, business parks, etc.) and to the way they are continuously influenced by policies aiming at regulating and steering development and land-use [26]. In this light, the SUPER project did not measure urbanization in Europe only in quantitative terms but also had the ambition to conceptualize it as the outcome of the countless collective and individual decisions made by humans every day about where and how they want to live, work and play within the constraints of what they can afford and what they can access. In particular, whereas urbanization patterns can be quantitatively described on the basis of key drivers like demography, economic development and society/technology (e.g., [27]), the crucial decision to convert a site from a non-urban use to an urban use is governed by the payoffs and interests of the various actors involved, which, over time, can be described as development practices. Various drivers at the macro level, including institutional and policy drivers, create (dis)incentives at the micro level to create a "local regulatory regime" or "rules of the development game" [28]. Key agents with decision-making authority, those with legal rights or economic or political clout, then interact to produce a decision on land use.

To do this, the SUPER project has designed a conceptual framework that illustrates the main cause and effect relationships that influence urbanization and land-use change mechanisms (Figure 2). The left side represents the key drivers (e.g., demography, economic development, society and technology) of urbanization and land-use patterns. In this respect, the project aimed at highlighting the drivers of change (demand) that affect land use and the institutional aspects that affect urbanization (supply). The right side of the diagram indicates the physical outcomes of land-use decisions (which then impact on the economy, society and environment) in the different European regions, which can be measured through the use of satellite imagery and monitored over time through quantitative datasets and qualitative evidence. In order to link the drivers of urbanization and land-use and their outcomes in European regions, the research gathered and analyzed multiple examples of land use interventions throughout the European countries, in so doing aiming at opening the black box of those local practices that actually contribute to shape land-use through time.

Figure 2. The Sustainable Urbanization and Land-Use Practices in European Regions (SUPER_ conceptual framework (source: [25] (p. 15).

In particular, the project acknowledges that the degree of success of any intervention aiming at steering urbanization in a specific direction is context-dependent (as certain forms of urbanization might be more sustainable than others in the different contexts) and that certain spatial governance and planning systems seem to be better equipped in relation to the promotion of sustainable urbanization than others [29]. In this light, it adopted a practice-oriented approach to explore how sustainable urbanization and land use is pursued in the different European countries and regions, thus developing a database of interventions that were explored in relation to their objectives and scopes, the types of instruments they employed, and their degree of success.

3. Methodology

3.1. Data Gathering

In order to collect sustainable urbanization and land-use practices from all around Europe, four main methodological steps were identified:

(i) first, a preliminary list of interventions was identified on the basis of the knowledge and experience of the SUPER consortium partners;
(ii) this list was complemented with examples retrieved from the national questionnaires of another ESPON applied research project [30];
(iii) then an online survey was created ad hoc, to reach out to experts from a number of pan-European organizations;
(iv) finally, the database was complemented and enriched through a thorough analysis of the scientific literature (e.g., articles, international research reports, national laws and regulations), in order to fill as much as possible the geographical and information gaps.

Throughout the project, the database underwent a number of quality control steps, performed by both the consortium partners and the Project Support Team, so it was subject to incremental fine-tuning. The online survey provided the highest number of results, generating over 160 responses. It was completed by national experts covering all the EU countries, as well as the EU candidate countries (i.e., Albania, North Macedonia,

Montenegro, Serbia and Turkey) and the remaining countries of the Western Balkans (i.e., Bosnia and Herzegovina and Kosovo). The experts were selected on the basis of a variety of different profiles: academic and scientific (e.g., universities, research centers) and more administrative roles (e.g., national, subnational, local agencies). The survey was then disseminated to the ESPON national contact points and members of the monitoring committee, as well as to the members of various academic and professional associations, such as the Association of the European Schools of Planning (AESOP), the European Council of Spatial Planners (ECTP-CEU) and the International Society of City and Regional Planners (ISOCARP). At a later stage, it was also circulated to experts through the use of social media (ResearchGate, as well as the AESOP and ESPON newsletters).

The survey focused on the current state of urbanization processes in the various countries. To facilitate the experts, it started with the following definition of sustainable urbanization and land use: "Sustainable land use means using and managing land assets in a way that does not compromise the livelihood of future generations. It implies a balanced consideration of social, economic, and environmental goods and services provided by the land uses in a certain region. It also implies a careful consideration of long-term attributes of resilience and robustness of the underlying ecosystem." [31] (p. 3). After that, it required the respondents to answer a short set of questions concerning the level of sustainability of urbanization and land-use in their country, the main impediments to the latter, and some examples of interventions affecting the sustainability of urbanization and land use in the practice (Table 1). Importantly, each expert was required to identify up to three interventions responsible for influencing the overall sustainability of urbanization and land use and, for each intervention, to point out the degree of success in terms of sustainable land use.

Table 1. Questions composing the SUPER online survey (source: author's own on the basis of [31] (p. 3)).

1.	In which country do you work?
2.	In which sector do you (mainly) work?
3.	We'd like to know if you think urbanization and land use in your country has become more or less sustainable (1 = much less sustainable, 5 = much more sustainable). Please explain why.
4.	We want to learn about interventions (from territorial governance and spatial planning) that affect urbanization and land-use, for example policies, regulations, subsidies or strategies. These can be at the national or regional but also at the local level. The effects could be intentional or unintentional and could lead to sustainable or unsustainable outcomes. Could you provide some examples of these? Please include the name, the location, a short description and your assessment of its success (max. 3 examples).
5.	What do you consider to be the most important impediment(s) to sustainable urbanization and land-use in your country? Please, briefly motivate your answer. Respondents could choose between: (i) lack of political will and/or declared policy aims in this direction; (ii) scarce effectiveness of the existing territorial governance and/or spatial planning instruments; (iii) other issues (e.g., corruption, lack of resources, lack of knowledge and data etc.).
6.	Do you have any additional suggestion for our research team? (e.g., good sources or case studies to look into, or some additional insight from your region).

3.2. Data Analysis and Intervention Assessment

After the data were collected, the intervention database was compiled and the collected interventions were further analyzed by reviewing available online documentation. The knowledge and the different skills of the consortium partners, as well as a careful analysis of the literature, helped to fill missing information and data. The interventions were then classified according to various categories and a number of analytical fields (see Table 2).

Table 2. Fields adopted in the analysis of the interventions (source: author's own elaboration on the basis of [31] (p. 4)).

Categories	Fields
Basic information	• Name of the intervention • Year (or time frame) • Country • Location • Scale (on the basis of NUTS classification) • Type(s) of EU territory involved (Urban, Rural, Functional area, Coastal area, Mountain region, Peripheral border, Cross-border, scarcely populated, Other) • Urban typology (if urban: Monocentric, Polycentric, Dispersed, Linear, Coastal)
Characteristics	• Scope and objectives (Densification, Regeneration; Containment, Governance, Sectoral priorities (transport, environment, rural development) • Type of instrument (Visions and strategies, Rules and legal devices, Land use regulations, Programs, Projects) • Status (Statutory and mandatory, Statutory and non-mandatory, Non-statutory) • Level of coercion (Non-binding, Self-binding, binding for public actors, Binding for all actors) • Intervention inspired by the EU (Yes/No)
Effects	• Description (scope, goals and functioning) • Description (in terms of how it works) • Degree of success—according to the goal of the intervention • Degree of success with respect to sustainable urbanization • Temporal sustainability: does the intervention prevent economic, social or environmental costs from being passed on to future generations? • Thematic sustainability: does the intervention advance values in the economic, social or environmental dimension without sacrificing those in other dimensions? • Institutional sustainability: is the intervention financially and politically sustainable over time? • Implementation quality—with respect to traditional evaluation criteria (is the intervention efficient-extent to which resources are well-spent, effective-extent to which goals were achieved, and relevant—for identified needs and problems?).

Particularly relevant in the context of this paper is the categorization in relation to the scope and objectives of the interventions and the instruments that they adopted in order to achieve these objectives. More in detail, according to their scope and objectives, the collected interventions were subdivided as aiming either at promoting *densification* (e.g., up-zoning, infill development), fostering the *regeneration* of unused and/or problematic sites (e.g., land redevelopment, urban renewal), the *containment* of urbanization processes (e.g., green belts, urban growth boundaries), the introduction of specific *governance* models and mechanisms (e.g., cross-sectoral integration, integrated plans) or the achievement of specific *sectoral policies* (e.g., related to transport, environment or rural development). At the same time, the collected interventions were also subdivided in relation to the different types of instrument that were employed in each case in order to achieve the identified objectives, as for instance through the joint development of *visions and strategies* (e.g., strategic plans, guidance documents, etc.), *rules and legal devices* (e.g., national and regional laws), *land use regulations* (e.g., zoning, local plans), *programs* (e.g., economic incentives and other types of funds) and *projects* (e.g., single spatial transformation actions and initiatives).As shown in Table 2, the success of the interventions gathered through the above steps was then assessed in relation to both their explicit goals as well as to their ability to come to terms with the different dimensions that characterize sustainable urbanization and land-use—i.e., temporal, thematic and institutional sustainability. This assessment has contributed to develop an understanding of the factors that determine the success of an intervention or the possible reasons behind its failure, in so doing providing interesting evidence upon which to develop guidance for decision and policymakers aiming at promoting sustainable urbanization and land-use.

4. Results and Discussion

Through the described methodology, it was possible to collect and analyze as many as 235 practical examples of how, in the various European countries, actors active at the different territorial levels try to achieve a more sustainable urbanization and land-use (Figure 3). First of all, it is important to highlight that the collected sample is representative but certainly not exhaustive in describing the ongoing urbanization processes and the interventions put in place to address and steer the latter throughout Europe. In particular, whereas the database includes interventions from as many as 39 European countries, the number of interventions collected for the various countries is rather uneven and, whereas this may depend on the differential attention devoted in the various contexts to the issues at stake, it is also influenced by the localization of the consortium partners and of the respondents—with Germany, Italy and the Netherlands featuring a higher number of interventions. For the countries that were less represented in the sample, specific members of the ESPON Monitoring Committee and Contact Point were contacted multiple times in order to indicate additional potential respondents, who were then contacted and engaged, thus contributing to partially rebalancing the database. Overall, even though certain countries are better represented than others, the collected interventions provide a rich and rather comprehensive overview of the recent efforts put in place to promote sustainable urbanization in Europe.

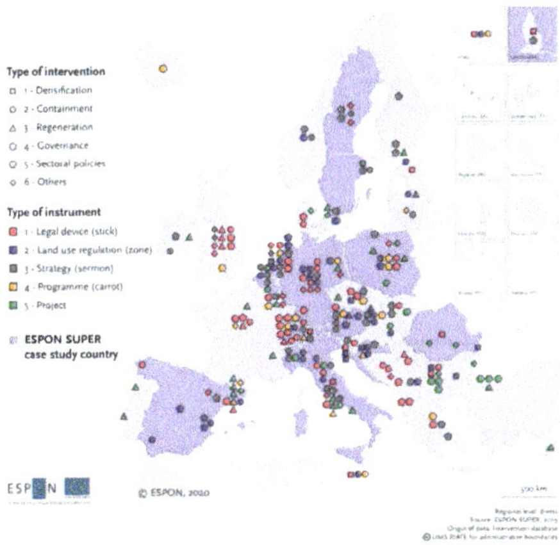

Figure 3. The localization of the SUPER intervention throughout Europe (source: [25] (p. 35)).

As mentioned, each intervention was qualitatively assessed in relation to its success in promoting a more sustainable use of land. This assessment phase was based on the responses of the country experts to the online survey and further verified through desk research (e.g., analysis of scientific articles and reports retrieved through the web). By crossing the level of success with the other variables, it was possible to reflect on which goals and which types of instrument have been more successful, and to further explore the reason behind the success [3] (p. 4). In particular, as shown in Table 3, for each category of the chosen variable, the interventions show varying degrees of success in relation to their ability to achieve a more sustainable urbanization.

Table 3. Degree of success of the analyzed interventions in relation to their scope and goals and to the type of instrument they adopted (source: authors' own elaboration).

Type		Degree of Success				
		1	2	3	4	5
Scope and goals	Densification	9%	0%	41%	36%	14%
	Regeneration	3%	7%	28%	28%	34%
	Containment	7%	7%	32%	34%	20%
	Governance	5%	2%	59%	25%	9%
	Sectoral policies	12%	0%	28%	40%	20%
Type of instrument	Visions and strategies	4%	2%	40%	38%	17%
	Rules and legal devices	11%	5%	42%	29%	14%
	Land use regulations	10%	3%	44%	31%	13%
	Programs	4%	13%	13%	35%	35%
	Projects	21%	6%	26%	21%	26%

The degree of success is related to the interventions' ability to promote sustainable urbanization and land-use (1 = unsuccessful; 2 = scarcely successful; 3 = mixed success, 4 = almost successful; 5 = successful).

As regards their scope and goals, the interventions that promote regeneration seem to be the most successful: in fact, the majority of interventions (62%) are graded four and five, and 28% are graded three. On the contrary, interventions that promote containment seem often scarcely successful: 14% of the interventions are graded one and two. As far as the types of instruments are concerned, programs seem to be the most effective: a high number of interventions (70%) are graded four and five, and 13% are graded three. On the contrary, projects often produce outcomes which are scarcely successful: in fact, 26% of the interventions are graded one and two.

Starting from these first results, the next section carries out an in-depth exploration of the causes that might influence the level of success of the interventions that adopt: (i) different scopes and objectives, and (ii) different types of instruments. The results provide interesting reflections and insights for all those stakeholders who are appointed to take decisions and who are involved in the technical drafting of policies aiming at a more sustainable urbanization.

4.1. Scope and Objectives of the Analysed Interventions

This subsection looks at a number of interventions that seem to promote sustainable land use, as well as limiting land take effects. The interventions are presented in relation to their scope and objective (densification, regeneration, containment, governance and sectoral policies) and, for each of them, the effectiveness and the level of success is discussed. As pointed out in the methodology section, the majority of the examples are based on the experts' responses to the online survey. In some cases, additional sources were investigated in order to verify the information and gather further knowledge.

4.1.1. Densification

In general, densification strategies seem to encourage different typologies of urban development (e.g., compact, polycentric). The results of the intervention database show that densification types of interventions, which promote up-zoning and in-fill development mechanisms, are usually successful in encouraging more sustainable urbanization processes.

Certain characteristics, such as the adoption of long-term sustainable aims and objectives, seem to support the effectiveness of these types of strategies. This can be seen in the Croatian Spatial Plan of Primorje-Gorski Kotar County (available at: https://zavod.pgz.hr/en/plans_and_reports (accessed on 15 March 2021)), which aims to limit future urban growth by promoting a more effective management of land use. To limit urban growth, a number of criteria for determining the size of building areas of settlements, regulating population density, were set. For example, the maximum surface area of building areas in each municipality was derived from the projected population and the minimum density of the inhabitants of the urban area. However, the intervention also seems to have had negative effects since, in an attempt to limit future urban growth, non-residential facilities seem to have been driven further away. Thus, it is important for the local administrations to adopt tangible and short-term objectives when trying to promote a long-term sustainable development.

Other characteristics, such as an increased cooperation between the various stakeholders, also seem to improve the effectiveness of these interventions. For example, the success of the Royal Seaport eco-district in Stockholm (Sweden) is attributable to the constant dialogue and negotiation between the various actors (e.g., public and private) during the various phases of the project. The project shows how the City of Stockholm (which has limited space for greenfield development) has managed to promote densification measures in order to be able to accommodate population growth, as well as to find the most effective environmental solutions [32].

The implementation of legal binding instruments often seems to improve the successfulness of these types of interventions. This is the case of the general development plan of the City of Stara Zagora and its adjacent territories (Bulgaria). For the expert reporting this intervention in the survey, it is one of the most effective tools to fulfil its limitation functions. In fact, the objectives and targets of the plan, including the upper limits of the development indicators, are compulsory and the failure to comply with them is illegal.

Data, knowledge and technical capacity are other characteristics that seem to promote more effective sustainable development. For example, the Infrastructural Cost Calculator, a strategy set up in the region of Lower Austria (Austria), supports municipalities in pre-assessing the financial costs (e.g., municipal infrastructural costs and tax revenues) of urban expansion and related population increase [33]. Thus, the strategy tries to assess the municipal consequences on where and how new inhabitants are settled. However, the effectiveness of the intervention seems to vary in relation to its implementation and a certain level of discretionality seems to characterize its implementation.

4.1.2. Regeneration

Urban regeneration is another goal which frequently concerns interventions aiming to promote sustainable urbanization and land use. A number of characteristics, such as those that envisage the concept of reuse, support the effectiveness of this type of intervention. This can be seen in many urban regeneration processes, such as: Gründachstadt Linz (Austria), the transformation of green roofs [34]; Réinventer Paris (France), the renovation of underutilized areas; Dublin Docklands (Ireland), the regeneration of brownfield areas [35]; the transformation and renewal of vacant areas in Berlin (Germany)unused since World War II.

Among the characteristics that promote urban regeneration are also those that envisage long-term sustainable targets. For example, since 1998 the United Kingdom has been applying brownfield targets (with at least 60% of new housing to be built on brownfield land by 2008), under the banner of an "urban renaissance" [36].

Improved multilevel cooperation between stakeholders also seems to strengthen the effectiveness of these types of interventions [37]. In Italy, the community-led regeneration process in Casoria produced very positive results in relation to the rehabilitation of abandoned areas and the enhancement of public participation. As stated by the expert reporting this intervention, the vision for the regeneration of a former sulfur mine (the Solfatara) in Manziana, through a collaborative and inclusive stakeholder participation in the context of common land ownership and management, is another interesting Italian initiative. On the contrary, the regeneration and rehabilitation of parts of the Taht-el-Kale Quarter in the City of Nicosia (Cyprus) was perceived as less successful. The initiative was part of a wider sustainable integrated urban regeneration strategy and worked in synergy with various social and cultural projects already implemented in the area. Nevertheless, the intervention was considered as less effective, according to the expert, mainly due to the scarce level of public participation.

The adoption of legally binding instruments often improves the successfulness of regeneration interventions. This is the case of the 2007 zero-growth plan of Cassinetta di Lugagnano (Italy) [38], which prohibits urban expansion in order to keep agricultural land as intact as possible. To do this it facilitates the repurposing of existing buildings and the regeneration of industrial areas. Finally, the adoption of an integrated approach also seems to help interventions to be more successful. This can be seen in the 22@Barcelona (Spain) regeneration program [39], which was well-integrated with the restructuring process of the metropolitan area and the urban policies framework.

It is important to highlight that speculation mechanisms can worsen the level of success of these interventions. Indeed, in contrast to the above cases of successful regeneration processes, some of Istanbul's housing renewal projects (Turkey) were criticized by the expert reporting this intervention for being driven by speculation, leading to high-rise housing in peripheral areas, without social infrastructure and transport facilities.

4.1.3. Containment

In the last decades, many containment interventions have been implemented in Europe with the objective of reducing land take. As a consequence, a number of sustainable strategies and green belts have been designed (e.g., the Grüner Ring in Leipzig, Corona Verde in Torino) to limit and control urban growth. Numerous interventions of this kind have proven successful in promoting sustainable development. For example, the Corona Verde strategy [40] envisages an ecological 'crown' around the metropolitan area of Torino (Italy), and brings together different intersectoral policies in order to reduce urban land consumption and to increase the quality of the rural–urban environment (e.g., through the mitigation and renaturation of infrastructural barriers, the conservation of the rural heritage).

Certain characteristics, such as the support of a strong political will and the adoption of long-term visions, seem to improve the implementation of these interventions. For example, the German government set the 30 hectares' target, with the ambitious goal of reducing annual land consumption to 30 hectares per day nationwide by 2020 (Umweltbundesamt—UBA, German Environment Agency: www.umweltbundesamt.de/en/ (accessed on 15 March 2021)). Cooperation that goes beyond municipal boundaries is another characteristic that often improves the successfulness of containment interventions. This is the case of Vision Rheintal (Austria) [41]. For the expert informant, its success is partly due to intra-municipal cooperation, as well as engagement with a heterogeneous group of experts (thus, promoting the transfer of expert knowledge) and the adoption of a holistic approach.

The adoption of legal binding instruments also seems to improve these interventions. For example, the 2014 Tuscany Regional Law on soil consumption (Italy) requires municipalities to delimit the borders of their more densely urbanized areas and to promote the urbanization of empty plots through simplified regulations and incentives. Non-residential transformations outside urbanized areas, which involve the consumption of new land, are only allowed if the co-planning conference provides a favorable opinion (Legge Regionale Toscana 65/2014). Similarly, the 2009 Law for the City of Sofia (Bulgaria), which works together with the city's General Urban Development Plan (GUDP), is considered to have produced positive outcomes, in particular by stating that "the designation of existing green plots or parts thereof in the urbanized territories, created according to the development plans cannot be changed" (art. 9). The GUDP, however, seems to have been less successful. In fact, inconsistencies seem to exist between the plan's overall goals and some of its measures and implementation tools [42]. Thus, certain interventions, if not implemented correctly, might lead to a discrepancy between the desired objectives and the actual outcomes. This might also be exacerbated by a lack of political will, technical capability and scarcity of economic resources.

Moreover, certain containment initiatives may turn out to be counterproductive for the promotion of sustainable land use. This seems to be the case of the Cork Area Strategic Plan (Ireland), which provides a long-term vision for the development of the Cork City-Region up to 2020. The expert reporting the intervention noted that, even though it aims to reduce urbanization in the countryside, an overexploitation of natural resources still occurs, and that the strategy is based on a pro-growth approach.

4.1.4. Governance

Governance interventions that try to improve the mechanisms through which governmental stakeholders manage urban and rural areas seem to influence the ways sustainable development is carried out at regional and local levels. However, these types of interventions seem to have produced results that are more varied than those presented above.

Certain characteristics, such as when interventions promote a long-term sustainable development perspective and adopt an integrated approach, are usually more effective. For example, in Stockholm (Sweden), the urban transformations and modalities of integrated planning are considered successful cases of integrated land use, housing and transport planning. Nevertheless, multi-level collaboration in Stockholm's urban transformations favoring the integration of local actors has had to face challenges, such as the intervention of the central government [43]. In Helsinki (Finland), the agreements on land use, housing, and transport (MAL) for the 2016–2019 period are also perceived as successful. In fact, the intervention promotes a more effective land use management and cooperation between municipalities.

As regards the adoption and implementation of urban plans, governance interventions seem to have had diverse impacts in the different cities and regions. In general, multilevel collaboration seems to improve the effectiveness of these types of interventions. In Poland, the 2016 planning law and housing policy of the Warsaw metropolitan area is a positive intervention, which has contributed to improving the spatial structure of both the city and its surrounding area, in the light of long-term sustainable development (e.g., green corridors, protecting green areas, reducing sprawl). Likewise, the Tri-City metropolitan area planning (Poland) aims to promote a harmonious development of the coastal area of Gdansk-Gdynia-Sopot, enhancing public transport. The intervention is generally perceived as successful due to the integrated governance structure it set up; however, despite its good potential, more time is still needed to fully assess its success. On the contrary, the attempt to promote bottom-up, integrated metropolitan planning led to the approval of the Poznań metropolitan area planning law (Poland) that, despite identifying areas that are important for environmental protection (e.g., degraded areas that require urgent revitalization actions), failed to achieve the expected results in terms of municipal coordination.

4.1.5. Sectoral Policies

Sectoral policies that refer to transport (e.g., mobility), environment (e.g., air, soil, water) and rural development (e.g., agriculture) seem to have different impacts on sustainable land use. Overall, as can be seen in the interventions presented in this subsection, it seems that the adoption of a more integrated policy approach, as well as a long-term strategy or vision, leads to a more sustainable development.

As regards transport policies, the Urban Mobility Plan of Barcelona (Spain), introduced "the superblock model" [44,45], an intervention that is considered very successful since it reduced air pollution levels. In the United Kingdom, the Mini-Holland in Waltham Forest (www.walthamforest.gov.uk/content/creating-mini-holland-waltham-forest (accessed on 15 March 2021)) is another successful intervention that supports urban mobility, reducing motorized transport and creating segregated cycle lanes on the model of Dutch-style infrastructure. The results of the Slovenian Sustainable Urban Mobility Plans (SUMPs) seem to be less successful, according to the expert informant, even though the country adopted the "EU Sustainable mobility for a prosperous future" strategy in order to manage urban mobility more effectively. In fact, only one third of the municipalities adopted the SUMPs and their poor acceptance by local political leaders seems to be one of the main challenges. Since SUMPs are not an obligatory instrument, providing financial support seems to be the best way to encourage their implementation. Another intervention whose success is open to question is the City of Sofia's underground metro (Bulgaria) that seems unable to integrate its mobility goals with achieving a more integrated land use approach. The Lyon–Torino high-speed railway and tunnel project (between France and Italy) is also considered a less successful intervention due to the constant delays and conflicts it has generated [46,47]. In fact, the project has been contested by environmental associations over its potential impacts on the environment (e.g., consumption of land, exploitation of natural resources).

As regards environmental and rural development policies, in Germany, the expert informant considers the BOKS—Soil Protection Concept as a positive example of sectoral intervention, which promotes a higher level of environmental quality and aims to reduce soil consumption. Another interesting intervention is the Lower Austrian spatial planning ordinance for wind energy utilization, which sets up a framework to manage wind-park development up to 2030. It identifies areas where wind turbines are allowed and where development is severely restricted. The expert informant deems it a positive intervention because it promotes the safeguarding of the natural environment; however, the construction of wind turbines in green areas (e.g., in forestry areas) seems to be a controversial topic in the country. It is also worth mentioning the 2007–2013 Green cross-border area—investment in nature project (between Bulgaria and Serbia) which has enhanced environmental awareness, as well as an exchange of knowledge and good practices. On the contrary, in Austria, for the expert informant, the Soil Enhancement Plan has the potential to support sustainable urbanization and land use (e.g., it tries to retain high-quality soil), but is rarely applied. The flood management system along the Tisza River in Hungary is also considered by the expert informant as an unsuccessful intervention due to a lack of coordination between the authorities and financial mechanisms.

4.2. *Adopted Instruments*

Experience has shown there is no ideal tool to be used for managing land use. On the contrary, sustainable urbanization and land use could be achieved through the implementation of a variety of instruments. Examples are discussed below in relation to visions and strategies, rules and legal devices, land use regulations, programs and projects.

4.2.1. Visions and Strategies

Visions and strategies are future-oriented and non-mandatory instruments that set out the main directions for development. One of the characteristics of successful visions and strategies is establishing ambitious, future-oriented objectives and, even more importantly, identifying realistic ones; while conversely, underfunded, incoherent or unrealistic strategies can erode credibility and commitment [25]. On the basis of the examples gathered, strategies introducing an ambitious target that have influenced the use of land include the Vision Rheintal of Vorarlberg (2004, update in 2017) in Austria and the Tri-City metropolitan area planning (2007) in Poland. The objective of the former is to create an interconnected polycentric region, promoting cooperation within it, supporting cross-border cooperation and creating an interconnected living space, fostering and enhancing regional awareness and regional identity, while the objective of the latter is to have a harmonious, complete and dynamic development of the metropolis of Tri-City (Gdańsk, Sopot and Gdynia). Both initiatives promote a more integrated approach to urban containment by facilitating investment on e-mobility transportation, encouraging densification along public transport routes and improving intercity connections within the region. Another successful case is the Corona Verde in Italy where 81 municipalities banded together to promote a new and alternative vision of the territory based on the quality of the environment and high quality of life [40]. The success of the strategy is demonstrated by its capacity to mobilize substantial funds for implementing short-term projects within a wider long-term strategy. Another interesting strategy is the Kooperationsplattform Stadtregion (2014) of Salzburg in Austria. For the expert informant the strategy recognizes the negative impact of diffuse urbanization on quality of life and that is why it aims to limit fragmented settlement and commercial development in the suburban belt of the main cities. To promote containment, the strategy implemented a regional green belt approach using development compensation measures to guarantee equal benefits for participants. At the national level, one clearly successful strategy is the zero-growth goal for car traffic (2018) applied in Norway that aims to introduce non-motorized models of transport [48].

However, visions and strategies are not always successful and face various challenges in addressing sustainable land use. This has proved the case for a number of strategies for European cities, which were challenged by sustainability trade-offs, implementation difficulties and lack of institutional will and capability. For example, the new Finger Plan of Copenhagen (2016–2019) to promote a more efficient transport network paved the way for sacrificing valuable green areas in the countryside [49]. Similarly, the Cork Area Strategic Plan in Ireland (2001–2020) aimed to reduce the loss of agricultural land, but in actual fact rural land consumption increased. Again, while the Athens Master Plan of 2014 introduced innovative concepts, it failed to combine its attention to environmental causes due to a lack of public consultation processes [50,51], while the Sustainable Metropolitan Plan of Rome Capital City 2003 has never been implemented due to limited political and institutional will [52]. Similarly, at the central level, the Climate Adaptation Program in Portugal shows that the success of this type of intervention can be undermined by a lack of political will at the local level [53].

4.2.2. Rules and Legal Devices

Sustainable land use can be addressed by establishing specific legal devices, such as binding laws and bylaws, to create a supportive institutional framework. Decision and policy makers can activate a plethora of different legal devices that can be mandatory or non mandatory—allowing authorities a certain level of flexibility. Sustainable land use can be promoted by introducing ad hoc laws and norms (for land use or environmental protection), as well as by promoting disincentive measures (fees, ad hoc taxes). Based on the experiences gathered, legal devices are not always successful. Contradictions emerge, for instance, in the case of the Poznan Metropolitan Area Planning Law (Poland) [54], which, despite having the merit of introducing concepts like "compact city" and "energy-efficient spatial structure", does not offer enough legal clarity to enforce them.

Sustainable land use can also be achieved by introducing successful economic disincentives or compensation mechanisms. Thus, various initiatives to disincentive excessive land use consumption have been widely experimented in Europe. Among others, it is worth mentioning the cases of the Development and Maintenance Fee applied in the region of Upper Austria (Austria), the double urbanization fee in Emilia Romagna (Italy) and the soil compensation account introduced in Dresden (Germany) [55]. In the Austrian case the initiative establishes that the infrastructure fee is the responsibility of the owner, in order to limit urban expansion, while the Emilia Romagna region decided (by resolution No. 186/2018), on the one hand, to double urbanization fees for projects that convert agricultural land into built up area and, on the other hand, to decrease these by at least 35% (local administrations are allowed to reduce them to 100% if necessary) for projects aiming at regenerating abandoned areas. Finally, the soil compensation account of Dresden aims to confine built-up land for settlements and traffic to 40% of the total urban land, as well as to force investors to carry out compensation measures by themselves or to pay a compensation fee.

An example of a successful land use initiative taken in Europe is the referendum to limit land take (2013) in Switzerland. The aim of the referendum was to curb urban sprawl and promote internal development, forcing municipalities to limit urban expansion. In fact, additional land can only be zoned if there is a real need for it [25]. This kind of direct democracy instrument is typically used for enhancing citizens' awareness on the issue and obtaining political legitimation for sensitive issues like land consumption. Even though not easily replicable—due to institutional mechanisms and cultural attitudes—the importance should be taken into consideration of responsibilizing citizens towards land use, which can be done at a central, as well as at a local level, by increasing participatory mechanisms.

Another restrictive example of land use from Switzerland is the Weber Law (2012). This initiative is interesting from two different perspectives. Firstly, it aims to fight land consumption by limiting the construction of second homes to preserve Switzerland's natural landscape from overbuilding by pursuing containment objectives. Secondly, it establishes measurable targets: no more than 20% of a municipality's housing can be second homes otherwise there will be building restrictions. This is particularly useful for preserving touristic destinations from being overexploited and thus reducing the diffusion of empty or temporarily occupied building structures.

4.2.3. Land Use Regulations

Land use regulations establish binding principles, usually through zoning, that define how land can or cannot be transformed. Historically, this occurs through dedicated local land-use planning tools, aiming at regulating physical development or, in some cases, to forbid development and to leave the land as it is [56]. Based on the experiences gathered, plans are shown to act in different directions according to their final objective. Some plans may promote policies aiming at reducing land exploitation or increasing its optimal use (e.g., Municipal Operative Plans of Reggio Emilia and Bassa Romagna). In both cases, the decision was taken to reduce the buildable surface by 30% and 50%, respectively, to guarantee a more sustainable use of land, while preventing landowners from paying higher taxes on buildable land.

In relation to the overestimation of buildable areas, the municipal operative plan of the City of Reggio Emilia (Italy) was employed to reduce the number of areas which had been zoned for urban uses but remained unbuilt. Since landowners pay taxes based on the value of the zoned land, stripping development rights also yields a financial benefit. The cooperation between municipalities and landowners has succeeded in downzoning over 135 ha of potential urban land to rural functions since 2015. A second phase has so far removed an additional 70 ha from potential urbanization. In so doing, the municipality takes back the possibility of (re)organizing its territory without having any restriction or impediment to changing its planning trajectory. Similarly, the Province of Utrecht (Netherlands) is experimenting with the de-zoning of urban areas back to agricultural use via the imposed land-use plan, primarily regarding unbuilt office space [25].

Land use regulation can also contribute to reducing spatial competition, which has been recognized as one of the main drivers of diffuse urbanization among municipalities. In this respect, the Municipal Structural Plan of the Union of Municipalities (2009) of Bassa Romagna in Italy offers a good example of what can be done to limit competition among municipalities [57]. Based on a cooperative approach and the predisposition of an appropriate institutional arrangement, nine municipalities decided to come together in drafting planning tools to better address sustainable land use. The adopting of the new plan and the further consolidation of the "Union" as a level of administration have contributed to limit the potential negative impact of the divergent interests, through the introduction of a system of compensation across municipalities.

Other land use plans, instead, may focus mainly on protecting and improving existing agricultural land like the Territorial Action Plan of the Huerta de Valencia (2018) in Spain and the Rural Park South (1990) in Milan (Italy), or limiting urban expansion as done by the Physical Environment Special Plan Protection (1980) of the Andalucía Region in Spain.

However, land use regulations cannot guarantee per se the achievement of sustainable land use objectives. In some cases, plans can increase land transformation to respond to market mechanisms (see the Sofia General Urban Development Plan of 2007 in Bulgaria and the Spatial Plan of Zone Chalupkova of 2009 in Bratislava, Slovakia) [42]. Land-use regulations can also promote, indirectly, the explosion of informal development due to their rigidity or lack of clear implementation mechanisms. The Urban Development Plans (starting from 1999) of Prishtina in Kosovo, are an example that, despite their original intentions, led to urbanization processes outside formal rules [58]. Similarly, even if the aim of the Outside Development Zones of 2006 in Malta is to safeguard the integrity of rural areas, they have been accused of justifying speculative initiatives as construction limits are easily exceeded.

4.2.4. Programs

Programs are policy packages aiming at a particular objective. They can be used to create economic conditions (financial schemes, direct investments, allocation of developing funds) for sustainable land use. Throughout Europe, these initiatives have been mainly implemented to create the economic conditions for the renewal of industrial areas (e.g., 22@Barcelona implemented in Spain since 2000), the protection of environmental quality (e.g., the Re-creation of Lake Karla in Thessaly in Greece since 1999 and the Enjoy Waltham Forest program of 2014 in the UK), as well as for promoting cross-cutting initiatives like the BENE—Berlin Programme on Sustainable Development (Germany), implemented since 2015, or the National Strategy for Inner Area (SNAI—Italy) [59,60]. More in detail, the Re-creation of Lake Karla in Thessaly [61,62] was seen as an opportunity to enhance the water supply, restore the ecosystem and improve the quality of the soil that was in danger of overexploitation. The Enjoy Waltham Forest program has also been positively seen because it has delivered a series of micro-interventions (e.g., segregated cycle lanes, planting trees) aiming at promoting a more environmentally oriented approach. More oriented towards spatial and social regeneration, the Piano Periferie 1 and 2, introduced in Italy since 2015, aim to recover abandoned and deprived areas by investing in environmental and social, as well as economic sustainability, by allocating 4 billion EUR (two have been already activated) for the improvement of the cities' peripheries by prioritizing urban requalification and the regeneration of abandoned areas. In this respect, several initiatives have been financed and some of them are already implemented, while others are expected to be concluded in the coming years. Finally, the success of the Berlin Program on Sustainable Development (BENE), is evidenced by the amount of funds allocated (234 million EUR), the number of projects put in place and the integration of existing development programs, and a similar assessment concerns the Italian SNAI, aiming at integrating the use of EU and domestic resources in rural areas.

4.2.5. Projects

Projects are individual ad hoc initiatives with a given timeframe, which can be used for the implementation of permanent or provisional transformations of sites. They are extremely heterogeneous in terms of nature, objectives, design and level of success. Various examples show how projects can contribute to regenerate abandoned areas, like the Dublin Docklands (Ireland) which started in 1997, the South Harbour in Copenhagen (Denmark) started in 1995 and the Royal Seaport in Stockholm (Sweden) started in 2008. The same has been done in other parts of Europe, like the Vila d'Este in Vila Nova de Gaia (Portugal) works concluded in 2015, the Industrial Park Borská Pole in the City of Plzeň (Czech Republic) in 1992 and the Miasteczko Wilanów initiative implemented in Warsaw (Poland) since 2002. Although diverse in some aspects, all the projects deal with recovering, eco-designing and promoting a healthy life-style. Efforts at reducing the human footprint have been made in the case of the Eco-Viikki project in Helsinki (Finland) implemented between 1999 and 2010, which demonstrates how new living standards can be successfully combined with a minimal impact on the environment. Similarly successful was the Caserne de Bonne in Grenoble (2003–2009), the first eco-district in France. From the sustainable land-use perspective, the crucial factor is that the shapes of the buildings were compact to reduce land consumption and urban sprawl. More community-oriented, but also successful, are the transformation of Vacant Urban Areas (1996) in Berlin (Germany) into attractive parks and vibrant public spaces [63], and the case of Rotterdam (Netherlands), where houses in deprived neighborhoods (since 2014) were simply bought up by the municipality and given away for free to anyone willing to invest a certain amount in renovation and promising to live there for at least five years [64].

However, projects can also fail or create unexpected or unwanted effects. Regeneration initiatives can produce gentrification like the Urban Development Project of Hyllie developed between 2007 and 2013 in Malmö (Sweden) that ended up with an image of housing "wealthy white westerners" [65]. If not well-designed, regeneration projects may channel a pro-market authoritarian approach, as the cases of Skopje 2014 (North Macedonia) and the Belgrade Waterfront of 2015 in Serbia demonstrate. While both pursue the rehabilitation of strategic urban areas, local community interests take a back seat vis-à-vis private investors. Finally, some projects explicitly provide for overexploitation of natural resources like the Nessebar and Sunny Beach seaside development in Bulgaria since 1958, the Ranca Resort implemented since 1990 in Romania and the third Istanbul Bosphorus Bridge Canal Project in Istanbul in Turkey (2013–2016) [66].

5. Concluding Remarks

On the basis of the analysis of the various interventions collected in the framework of the ESPON SUPER project, it is possible to develop a tentative set of recommendations and warnings for decision and policy makers aiming at promoting a more sustainable urbanization of their territories. This concluding section rounds off the contribution by presenting these recommendations and warnings, with particular reference to the variable degree of success that actors may achieve when putting in place interventions aiming at different goals and adopting different types of instruments.

In particular, when looking at the scope and the different objectives of the analyzed interventions, the presented evidence shows that land use can be addressed in different ways, none of which, however, are either fully sustainable or unsustainable (Table 4). *Densification* can potentially contribute to achieving sustainable land use if opportunely addressed. For instance, interventions aiming at it have the potential to promote further social equity by reducing car dependency and journey distances [67]. According to the project's results, successful factors of densification are, among others, the adoption of a long-term perspective (e.g., up zoning and measures for infill development), as well as the introduction of legally binding instruments. As shown in the literature [68], densification does not always imply sustainable land use. In some cases, it may contribute to increasing traffic congestion if not opportunely designed [69]; in others, it has been shown to increase housing prices, while it also contributes to reducing green public areas in favor of buildings [70].

Similarly, some of the analyzed examples show that sustainable land use has been successfully promoted by regenerating abandoned areas. *Regeneration* of brownfields requires a paradigmatic shift that makes operative the concepts of reuse and of integrated sustainable development, thereby facilitating a circular use of land [71]. Even regeneration, however, cannot be taken for granted, as it may become more expensive than transforming greenfield sites [72] and thus not economically attractive for market operators due to the cost–benefit logic that development may give rise to. Another inhibitive factor of promoting regeneration is the fact that it may be intended as a tabula rasa without considering local specificity (and community needs) [73], thus paving the way for gentrification phenomena that can lead to social exclusion [74]. *Containment* oriented interventions are among the most common approaches in addressing sustainable land use. For instance, containment can be promoted by restricting the development of city edges, introducing policies to better contain urban expansion [75] and, in so doing, preserving agricultural land from being converted [76]. The information gathered by SUPER seems to suggest that one of the key factors in the success of containment initiatives is the presence of effective political will, since the spatial effect of these initiatives usually takes time to be visible. They also require the establishment of an effective and efficient normative apparatus (e.g., legally binding instruments) that can limit speculative market mechanisms (i.e., increased land prices, exclusion of certain social categories, concentration of development benefits, etc.). However, containment also brings side effects when it comes to sustainable development, such as traffic congestion and an increase in housing prices. In particular, unclear containment strategies may pave the way to increasing land and houses prices, thus forcing individuals and businesses to relocate to areas where more space is available. This kind of spatial competition may reduce the development pressure in one area but drastically increase it in others, making it inconvenient (or undesirable) in terms of sustainable land use [77].

Table 4. Successful factors and pitfalls when it comes to promoting sustainable land use (authors' own elaboration).

Scope and Objectives	Successful Factors	Pitfalls and Warnings
Densification	The adoption of a long-term perspective (e.g., up-zoning and measures for infill development). The inclusion and cooperation with private partners, as well as a balance between public and private interests. The adoption of legally binding instruments often improves the success of such interventions.	Densification may contribute to increasing traffic congestion if not opportunely designed. In some cases, densification has been shown to increase housing prices, which has a negative impact on affordable housing. Densification may contribute to reduction of green public areas in favor of buildings.
Regeneration	The adoption of a long-term vision (e.g., enhancing the economic, environmental and social quality of the area and of the local community). The application of the concept of reuse and of integrated sustainable development. Addressing environmental, economic and social issues at the same time.	Regeneration may become more expensive than transforming greenfield sites and thus not economically attractive for market operators. Regeneration may be intended as a tabula rasa without taking care of local specificity (and community needs). Regeneration may—in some cases—pave the way for gentrification and social exclusion.
Containment	Effective political will is needed since the spatial effect of containment initiatives usually takes time to be seen. The establishment of an effective and efficient normative apparatus (e.g., legally binding instruments) guarantees a certain level of success. The limitation of speculative market mechanisms (i.e., increased land price, exclusion of certain social categories, concentration of development benefits, etc.)	Unclear containment strategy may increase costs of land (and houses). If not carefully drafted, containment may force individuals and businesses to relocate to areas where more space is available (spatial competition).
Governance	Integrating public priorities with private (corporate or individual) interests. Establishing an adaptive multilevel collaboration and governance models: each context is different, as well as the contingencies where the political choices are taken. Implementation should be accompanied and supported by cooperative governance mechanisms able to include different scales (optimally both top-down and bottom-up approaches).	Uncoordinated governance models may act against sustainable development. Poorly defined responsibilities (or overlappings) are at the basis of uncontrolled development.
Sectoral policies	The adoption of an integrated approach and long-term sustainable perspective taking into consideration a multiplicity of sectoral interests. Stronger collaboration between the various stakeholders seems to be fundamental for achieving of a good level of sectoral integration and coordination. Support of soft initiatives that have direct and immediate impacts: long-term projects usually require more time to show their advantages.	The adoption of sectoral policies may lead to excessive policy fragmentation. Uncoordinated sectoral strategies may pave the way for unsustainable development.

The mechanism of implementation and models of *governance* are also important in terms of addressing sustainable land use. The most successful ones seem those that integrate public priorities with private (corporate or individual) interests. Effective public and private partnership seems to limit eventual negative externalities that development initiatives may give rise to. According to the research's results, another important factor of successful governance is the establishment of adaptive multilevel collaboration, taking into account that each context is different, as well as the contingencies where the political choices are made. These multilevel governance relations should take care to achieve an optimum balance between top-down and bottom-up approaches. Conversely, uncoordinated governance models and the overlapping of responsibilities seem to act against sustainable development. Due to this complexity, land use can also be addressed by *sectoral initiatives*. As shown, there are a series of examples, throughout Europe, that illustrate how sectoral policies support sustainable land use. In this respect, the success of this kind of initiative may depend on the adoption of an integrated approach and long-term sustainable perspective taking into consideration a multiplicity of sectoral interests. A strong collaboration between the various stakeholders also seems to be fundamental for achieving a good level of sectoral integration and coordination. Accordingly, sectoral authorities should be further integrated in the planning process [78], since sectoral strategies have proven to impact on land use although their impact is not always positive.

The type of instrument to be adopted in order to pursue further sustainable urbanization trajectories is also a highly relevant factor and, in this case too, no one-size-fits-all solution seems available to policy makers (Table 5). For example, the use of *visions and strategies* have proven to be successful when they support common territorial perspectives for territories that share the same needs and challenges and activate cooperative decision-making mechanisms. They benefit, moreover, from the establishment of a strong, stable and future-oriented political will that in the long run makes the difference. On the other hand, visions and strategies may fail when the required leadership and/or institutional capacity to translate them into effective measures is missing or when the targets identified are too ambitious and not realistically implementable. That is why decision and policy makers should establish tailored targets in line with territorial needs and effective institutional readiness to translate them into practice. According to the information gathered, *rules and legal devices* have proven successful when they are clear in their final objective (e.g., limit land consumption, protect valuable natural areas, monitor the housing and rental markets) and normatively solid. This is particularly important considering their technical feasibility and the link with their social acceptability. On the contrary, these tools are often less effective when they envisage a large window of flexibility as a consequence of the possibility to interpret the norms discretionally. Failure may also depend on their capacity to address sustainable development holistically. In this respect, decision and policy makers should guarantee an acceptable equilibrium between the various sustainability dimensions (e.g., social, economic, and environmental). If visions and legal devices set the "rules of the game", *land use regulations* are often used to translate them into practices. Through the implementation of regulative plans, decision and policy makers have the opportunity to convert political will and technical capacity into effective land use transformation. That is why it is important to be aware of the factors that have been shown to successfully address sustainable land use. According to the sample, successful examples show an optimum balance between the need for development and the need to achieve sustainable land use. This can be obtained by reorienting planning decisions in order to promote sustainable land use, for instance by reconverting buildable areas into agriculture ones, or protecting land instead of allowing its exploitation. Conversely, planning tools are subject to failure if they directly legitimate speculative phenomena when it comes to facilitating private investments and real estate (gentrification, exclusion of disadvantaged social groups, etc.), while in certain cases they may indirectly facilitate illegal initiatives when plans are hard to implement (lack of effective implementation mechanism).

Table 5. Successful factors and pitfalls when it comes to promoting sustainable land use (authors' own elaboration).

Type of Instruments	Successful Factors	Pitfalls and Warnings
Visions and strategies	Supporting common territorial perspectives for territories that share the same needs and challenges. Decisions are based on cooperative mechanisms; otherwise, visions and strategies could remain on paper without any chance of being effectively implemented. A strong, stable and future-oriented political will makes a difference.	There are no institutional capabilities to translate into effective measures. Targets identified are too ambitious, wide in their content and not realistically implementable. There is a lack of political perseverance.
Rules and legal devices	Should be clear in their final objective (limit land consumption, protect valuable natural areas, monitor the rental and housing markets). Should be normatively strict and adapted to their different institutional contexts. Should be technically feasible (coherent set of norms and regulations that may guarantee the applicability of interventions). Should be socially acceptable (sustained by social legitimacy).	Legal devices are not strict but envisage some windows of flexibility (not mandatory). Legal devices do not consider sustainability in a holistic perspective privileging one of its dimensions at the expense of the others.
Land use regulations	Optimum between the need for development and the need to achieve sustainable land use. Reorienting planning decisions in order to promote sustainable land use by reconfiguring (reconverting) buildable areas into agricultural ones. They are used as instruments of land protection instead of land exploitation. These can be implemented by promoting measures of urbanization containment and protection of agricultural/natural land.	May address the various sustainability dimensions only to a partial extent. In particular, in many cases the environmental dimension appears more prominent than the economic and the social ones. May give legitimacy to speculative phenomena when it comes to facilitating private and real estate investments; May indirectly facilitate illegal initiatives when plans are hard to implement.
Programmes	Should be well-integrated with existing instruments and spatial planning tools and policies. Should be operative-oriented by indifferently promoting mega-projects or small-scale initiatives. Their design should integrate all the thematic dimensions of sustainability.	There is a gap between ambition and effective achievement possibilities (overestimation of economic capabilities). They are too development-oriented instead of focusing on environmental protection. They are not institutionally and economically well-coordinated with the rest of the programmes.
Projects	When they are part of a long-term territorial vision without, however, losing sight of short-term objectives. When they incorporate simultaneously economic priorities (being cost-efficient), environmental needs (promoting pro-environmental solutions) and social aspects (supporting citizens' involvement).	Regeneration (and densification) sites are viewed as a tabula rasa for facilitating real-estate and speculative initiatives. Projects are used for achieving political legitimacy or exercising political power. Projects produce side effects like increasing inequalities, gentrification, segregation, etc. Projects explicitly promote the overexploitation of natural resources since they follow pro-growth market logics.

Moreover, the analyzed interventions have shown that even the most concrete strategy or plan may fail if it is not properly supported by effective *programming instruments*. These instruments have proven to be proactive in addressing land use, when well-integrated with existing spatial planning tools and policies. The capacity to mobilize funds effectively is one of the key factors of any initiative towards sustainable urbanization. Mobilizing funds also means implementing real land transformation by developing *projects*. Even though often underestimated, projects are the operative instruments that effectively transform space. That is why it is important for decision and policy makers to know which are the successful factors that make projects work. In particular, projects are proactive in sustainable urbanization when they are part of a long-term territorial vision without, however, losing sight of short-term objectives. They help to make a strategy visible and concrete thereby creating social legitimacy. Yet, they may only prove fully successful when simultaneously incorporating economic priorities (being cost-efficient), environmental needs (promoting pro-environmental solutions) and social aspects (supporting citizens' involvement). At the same time, projects are often subject to market and political manipulation. Among other factors, policy and decision makers should be aware that in some cases the regeneration (and densification) of sites might facilitate speculative real-estate initiatives.

In conclusion, it is important to recall once again that urbanization processes are a combination of factors that cannot simply be replicated from one context to another, but require a tailored approach [25]. In this view, land use policies cannot be intended as pre-packaged, but should be contextualized according to territorial, institutional, and cultural specificities [79]. Sustainable land use is a polymorphic concept, whose approach can shift from a more ecological and environmental perspective by promoting reconversion of land, establishing ambitious target and strategies, thus promoting a densification of urban structures through the rehabilitation of industrial areas or applying a wide range of incentives and disincentives. In this light, there are a number of messages that decision and policy makers should take into account, namely: (i) to avoid "one size fits all" solutions and thus each policy recommendation should be assessed according to territorial specificities; (ii) to avoid stand-alone initiatives when addressing complex issues like sustainable land use (multi-dimensional, multi-sectoral and multi-stakeholder approaches are preferable); and (iii) to ensure that sustainable land use is a shared responsibility and the identified solutions should be carefully evaluated and shared with all the relevant actors. As pointed out in the Introduction, making careful and prudent decisions on land use is not only a political and technocratic decision but, as the COVID-19 pandemic has dramatically highlighted, also one with highly significant societal consequences [80].

In short, this paper emphasizes the current and future opportuneness of comparative land use studies in a world which is coming to terms with the crucial need to face increasingly challenging issues such as climate change and sustainability as pointed out in the UN Sustainable Development Goals [81]. Nevertheless, it is important to reiterate that, even though there is no "right instrument" or "right target" for all European regions, "right attitudes" exist that can be adopted to promote a more sustainable urbanization, and we hope that the present contribution may constitute a useful support in that direction.

Author Contributions: G.C. designed the project and supervised its implementation. A.S. and E.B. carried out data collection and analysis, under G.C.'s supervision. All sections of the paper were written and revised by all three authors. All authors have read and agreed to the published version of the manuscript.

Funding: The research was carried out as part of the ESPON SUPER 2019–2020 project (https://www.espon.eu/super (accessed on 15 March 2021)).

Acknowledgments: The research project SUPER (Sustainable Urbanization and Land-Use Practices in European Regions) has been carried out within the framework of the European Territorial Observatory Network (ESPON—https://www.espon.eu/ (accessed on 15 March 2021)). The consortium responsible for the project is coordinated by PBL (the Dutch Environmental Agency) and composed of Politecnico di Torino, BBSR (German Federal Institute for Research on Building, Urban Affairs, and Spatial Development), OIR (Austrian Institute for Regional Studies and Spatial Planning), University of Valencia, University of Warsaw and Urbanex. Additional information concerning the project is available at: https://www.espon.eu/super (accessed on 15 March 2021). The authors would like to thank all the members of the ESPON SUPER team for their proactive cooperation throughout the project.

Conflicts of Interest: The authors declare no conflict of interest.

References

1. Cotella, G.; Vitale Brovarone, E. Questioning Urbanisation Models in the Face of Covid-19. *TeMA J. Land Use Mobil. Environ.* **2020**, 105–118. [CrossRef]
2. Filho, W.L.; Azul, A.M.; Brandli, L.; Salvia, A.L.; Wall, T. *Life on Land*; Encyclopedia of the UN Sustainable Development Goals; Springer: Berlin/Heidelberg, Germany, 2021; ISBN 978-3-319-95980-1.
3. Solly, A.; Berisha, E.; Cotella, G.; Janin Rivolin, U. How Sustainable Are Land Use Tools? A Europe-Wide Typological Investigation. *Sustainability* **2020**, *12*, 1257. [CrossRef]
4. Cotella, G. The Urban Dimension of EU Cohesion Policy. In *Territorial Cohesion. The Urban Dimension*; Medeiros, E., Ed.; Springer: Berlin/Heidelberg, Germany, 2019; pp. 133–151.
5. Science for Environment Policy. *No Net Land Take by 2050? Future Brief 14, Produced for the European Commission DG Environment by the Science Communication Unit, UWE, Bristol*; European Commission: Brussels, Belgium; Luxembourg, 2016.
6. Sikora, A. European Green Deal—Legal and Financial Challenges of the Climate Change. *ERA Forum* **2021**, *21*, 681–697. [CrossRef]
7. Bottero, M.; Caprioli, C.; Cotella, G.; Santangelo, M. Sustainable Cities: A Reflection on Potentialities and Limits Based on Existing Eco-Districts in Europe. *Sustainability* **2019**, *11*, 5794. [CrossRef]
8. Paniagua, A. Geographies of Differences (and Resistances) in Urbanized and Depopulated Remote Rural Areas. In *Life on Land*; Leal Filho, W., Azul, A.M., Brandli, L., Lange Salvia, A., Wall, T., Eds.; Springer: Cham, Switzerland, 2020; pp. 1–11. ISBN 978-3-319-71065-5.
9. Vitale Brovarone, E.; Cotella, G. Improving Rural Accessibility: A Multilayer Approach. *Sustainability* **2020**, *12*, 2876. [CrossRef]
10. Ali-Toudert, F.; Ji, L.; Fährmann, L.; Czempik, S. Comprehensive Assessment Method for Sustainable Urban Development (CAMSUD)—A New Multi-Criteria System for Planning, Evaluation and Decision-Making. *Prog. Plan.* **2020**, *140*, 100430. [CrossRef]
11. European Commission. Directorate General for Regional and Urban Policy. In *My Region, My Europe, Our Future: Seventh Report on Economic, Social and Territorial Cohesion*; Publications Office: Luxembourg, 2017.
12. Berisha, E.; Cotella, G.; Janin Rivolin, U.; Solly, A. Spatial Governance and Planning Systems in the Public Control of Spatial Development: A European Typology. *Eur. Plan. Stud.* **2021**, *29*, 181–200. [CrossRef]
13. Block, T.; Paredis, E. Four misunderstandings about sustainability and transitions. In *Sustainable Development Teaching: Ethical and Political Challenges*; Van Poeck, K., Östman, L., Öhman, J., Eds.; Routledge: London, UK, 2019; pp. 15–27. ISBN 978-1-351-12434-8.
14. World Commission on Environment and Development. *Report of the World Commission on Environment and Development*; Oxford University Press: Oxford, UK, 1987.
15. Koroneos, C.J.; Rokos, D. Sustainable and Integrated Development—A Critical Analysis. *Sustainability* **2012**, *4*, 141–153. [CrossRef]
16. Bulkeley, H. Urban Sustainability: Learning from Best Practice? *Environ. Plan. A* **2006**, *38*, 1029–1044. [CrossRef]
17. Held, M. Sustainable Development from a Temporal Perspective. *Time Soc.* **2001**, *10*, 351–366. [CrossRef]
18. Evers, D.; van Schie, M.; van den Broek, L.; Nabielek, K.; Ritsema van Eck, J.; van Rijn, F.; van der Wouden, R.; Schmidt-Seiwert, V.; Hellings, A.; Binot, R.; et al. *ESPON SUPER—Sustainable Urbanization and Land Use Practices in the European Regions*; Final Report. Version 06/11/2020; ESPON EGTC: Luxembourg, 2020.
19. Nulkar, G. *Ecology, Equity and the Economy: The Human Journey*; Ecological Society: Columbus, OH, USA, 2018; ISBN 978-81-935577-0-9.
20. Gallagher, V.C.; Hrivnak, M.W.; Valcea, S.; Mahoney, C.B.; LaWong, D. A Comprehensive Three-Dimensional Sustainability Measure: The 'Missing P' of 'People'—A Vital Stakeholder in Sustainable Development. *Corp. Soc. Responsib. Environ. Manag.* **2018**, *25*, 772–787. [CrossRef]
21. Seghezzo, L. The Five Dimensions of Sustainability. *Environ. Politics* **2009**, *18*, 539–556. [CrossRef]
22. Campbell, S.D. The Planner's Triangle Revisited: Sustainability and the Evolution of a Planning Ideal That Can't Stand Still. *J. Am. Plan. Assoc.* **2016**, *82*, 388–397. [CrossRef]
23. Pfahl, S. Institutional Sustainability. *IJSD* **2005**, *8*, 80. [CrossRef]
24. Baker, S.; Kousis, M.; Richardson, D.; Young, S. Introduction: The theory and practice of sustainable development in EU perspective. In *The Politics of Sustainable Development: Theory, Policy, and Practice within the European Union*; Baker, S., Kousis, M., Richardson, D., Young, S., Eds.; Global Environmental Change Series; Routledge: London, UK; New York, NY, USA, 1997; pp. 1–40.
25. Cotella, G.; Evers, D.; Janin Rivolin, U.; Solly, A.; Berisha, E. *ESPON SUPER—Sustainable Urbanisation and Land-Use Practices in European Regions. A Guide to Sustainable Urbanisation and Land Use*; ESPON EGTC: Luxembourg, 2020.
26. Kostof, S. *The City Shaped: Urban Patterns and Meanings through History*; Little, Brown and Company: Boston, MA, USA, 1991.
27. EEA; FOEN Urban Sprawl in Europe. *Joint EEA-FOEN Report*; European Environment Agency and Swiss Federal Office for the Environment; Publications Office of the European Union: Luxembourg, 2016.
28. Lord, A. *The Planning Game: An Information Economics Approach to Understanding Urban and Environmental Management*; Routledge: London, UK, 2012; ISBN 978-0-415-59906-1.
29. Cotella, G.; Janin Rivolin, U.; Berisha, E.; Solly, A. Governo del territorio e controllo pubblico delle trasformazioni: Una tipologia europea. *Territorio* **2020**, 140–148. [CrossRef]

30. Nadin, V.; Fernández Maldonado, A.M.; Zonneveld, W.; Stead, D.; Dabrowski, M.; Piskorek, K.; Sarkar, A.; Schmitt, P.; Smas, L.; Cotella, G.; et al. *ESPON COMPASS—Comparative Analysis of Territorial Governance and Spatial Planning Systems in Europe*; Final Report. Version 10/10/2018; ESPON EGTC: Luxembourg, 2018.
31. Cotella, G.; Evers, D.; Janin Rivolin, U.; Solly, A.; Berisha, E. *ESPON SUPER—Sustainable Urbanization and Land Use Practices in the European Regions. Annex 2—Evidence on Interventions*; Version 06/11/2020; ESPON EGTC: Luxembourg, 2020.
32. Holmstedt, L.; Brandt, N.; Robèrt, K.-H. Can Stockholm Royal Seaport Be Part of the Puzzle towards Global Sustainability?—From Local to Global Sustainability Using the Same Set of Criteria. *J. Clean. Prod.* **2017**, *140*, 72–80. [CrossRef]
33. Humer, A.; Sedlitzky, R.; Brunner, D. When Does Population Growth Pay off? A Case Study of Suburban Land Consumption to Assess the Lower Austrian Infrastructural Cost Calculator. *J. Hous. Built Environ.* **2019**, *34*, 331–344. [CrossRef]
34. Schroepfer, T.; Hee, L. Emerging Forms of Sustainable Urbanism: Case Studies of Vauban Freiburg and SolarCity Linz. *J. Green Build.* **2008**, *3*, 65–76. [CrossRef]
35. Byrne, M. Entrepreneurial Urbanism After the Crisis: Ireland's "Bad Bank" and the Redevelopment of Dublin's Docklands. *Antipode* **2016**, *48*, 899–918. [CrossRef]
36. Shaw, K.; Robinson, F. Centenary Paper: UK Urban Regeneration Policies in the Early Twenty-First Century Continuity or Change? *Town Plan. Rev.* **2010**, *81*, 123–149. [CrossRef]
37. Rotondo, F.; Abastante, F.; Cotella, G.; Lami, I.M. Questioning Low-Carbon Transition Governance: A Comparative Analysis of European Case Studies. *Sustainability* **2020**, *12*, 10460. [CrossRef]
38. Boatti, A. La Pianificazione Urbanistica in Lombardia Alla Prova Dei Piccoli Comuni. Due "Comuni Virtuosi. *Territorio* **2009**, 74–80. [CrossRef]
39. Bottero, M.; Bragaglia, F.; Caruso, N.; Datola, G.; Dell'Anna, F. Experimenting Community Impact Evaluation (CIE) for Assessing Urban Regeneration Programmes: The Case Study of the Area 22@ Barcelona. *Cities* **2020**, *99*, 102464. [CrossRef]
40. Cassatella, C. The 'Corona Verde' Strategic Plan: An Integrated Vision for Protecting and Enhancing the Natural and Cultural Heritage. *Urban Res. Pract.* **2013**, *6*, 219–228. [CrossRef]
41. Leiner, M.; Mollay, U.; Tordy, J. *Territories and Low-Carbon Economy: Rheintal, Austria. Case Study Report*; Version 17/11/2017; ESPON EGTC: Luxembourg, 2017.
42. Slaev, A.D.; Nedovic-Budic, Z. The Challenges of Implementing Sustainable Development: The Case of Sofia's Master Plan. *Sustainability* **2017**, *9*, 15. [CrossRef]
43. Paulsson, A. The City That the Metro System Built: Urban Transformations and Modalities of Integrated Planning in Stockholm. *Urban Stud.* **2020**, *57*, 2936–2955. [CrossRef]
44. Mueller, N.; Rojas-Rueda, D.; Khreis, H.; Cirach, M.; Andrés, D.; Ballester, J.; Bartoll, X.; Daher, C.; Deluca, A.; Echave, C.; et al. Changing the Urban Design of Cities for Health: The Superblock Model. *Environ. Int.* **2020**, *134*, 105132. [CrossRef] [PubMed]
45. Scudellari, J.; Staricco, L.; Vitale Brovarone, E. Implementing the Supermanzana Approach in Barcelona. Critical Issues at Local and Urban Level. *J. Urban Des.* **2020**, *25*, 675–696. [CrossRef]
46. Greyl, L.; Healy, H.; Leonardi, E.; Temper, L. Stop That Train! Ideological Conflict and the TAV. *Econ. Policy Energy Environ.* **2012**, 193–218. [CrossRef]
47. Marincioni, F.; Appiotti, F. The Lyon-Turin High-Speed Rail: The Public Debate and Perception of Environmental Risk in Susa Valley, Italy. *Environ. Manag.* **2009**, *43*, 863–875. [CrossRef] [PubMed]
48. Tønnesen, A.; Krogstad, J.R.; Christiansen, P.; Isaksson, K. National Goals and Tools to Fulfil Them: A Study of Opportunities and Pitfalls in Norwegian Metagovernance of Urban Mobility. *Transp. Policy* **2019**, *81*, 35–44. [CrossRef]
49. Sørensen, E.; Torfing, J. The Copenhagen Metropolitan "Finger Plan": A Robust Urban Planning Success Based on Collaborative Governance. In *Great Policy Successes*; Compton, M., Hart, P., Eds.; Oxford University Press: Oxford, UK, 2019; pp. 218–243. ISBN 978-0-19-884371-9.
50. Skayannis, P. The (Master) Plans of Athens and the Challenges of Its Re-Planning in the Context of Crisis. *Int. J. Archit. Res.* **2013**, *7*, 192–205.
51. Tulumello, S.; Cotella, G.; Othengrafen, F. Spatial Planning and Territorial Governance in Southern Europe between Economic Crisis and Austerity Policies. *Int. Plan. Stud.* **2020**, *25*, 72–87. [CrossRef]
52. Archibugi, F. *Rome: A New Planning Strategy*; Routledge: London, UK, 2005.
53. Campos, I.; Guerra, J.; Gomes, J.F.; Schmidt, L.; Alves, F.; Vizinho, A.; Lopes, G.P. Understanding Climate Change Policy and Action in Portuguese Municipalities: A Survey. *Land Use Policy* **2017**, *62*, 68–78. [CrossRef]
54. Kaczmarek, T. Soft Planning for Soft Spaces. Concept of Poznań Metropolitan Area Development—A Case Study. *Misc. Geogr.* **2018**, *22*, 181–186. [CrossRef]
55. Adobati, F.; Garda, E. Soil Releasing as Key to Rethink Water Spaces in Urban Planning. *City Territ. Archit.* **2020**, *7*, 9. [CrossRef]
56. Hall, P. *Urban and Regional Planning*, 4th ed.; Routledge: London, UK; New York, NY, USA, 2002.
57. Cotella, G.; Berisha, E. Inter-municipal spatial planning as a tool to prevent small towns' competition. The case of the Emilia-Romagna Region. In *The Routledge Handbook of Small Towns*; Bansky, J., Ed.; Routledge: London, UK, forthcoming.
58. Gollopeni, B. Socio-Urban Developments in Kosovo: Study Case Pristina. *Geo Inf.* **2016**, *13*, 81–93.
59. Cotella, G.; Vitale Brovarone, E. The Italian National Strategy for Inner Areas: A Place-Based Approach to Regional Development. In *Dilemmas of Regional and Local Development*; Bański, J., Ed.; Routledge: London, UK; New York, NY, USA, 2020; pp. 50–71. ISBN 978-0-429-43386-3.

60. Cotella, G.; Brovarone, E.V. La strategia nazionale per le aree interne: Una svolta place-based per le politiche regionali in Italia. *Arch. Studi Urbani Reg.* **2020**, 22–46. [CrossRef]
61. Karanikola, P.; Tampakis, S.; Zafeiriou, E.; Akrivouli, K. Local People Attitudes towards Wetland Management. The Case of Lake Karla in Greece. *J. Environ. Prot. Ecol.* **2017**, *18*, 1268–1276.
62. Panagopoulos, Y.; Dimitriou, E. A Large-Scale Nature-Based Solution in Agriculture for Sustainable Water Management: The Lake Karla Case. *Sustainability* **2020**, *12*, 6761. [CrossRef]
63. Mariko, I. Temporary Use of Vacant Urban Spaces in Berlin: Three Case Studies in the Former Eastern Inner-City District Friedrichshain. *Geogr. Rev. Jpn. Ser. B* **2018**, *91*, 1–16. [CrossRef]
64. Snel, E.; Aussen, S.; Berkhof, F.; Renlo, Q. Views of Gentrification from below: How Rotterdam Local Residents Experience Gentrification? In Proceedings of the The Struggle to Belong Dealing with Diversity in 21st Century Urban Settings, Amsterdam, The Netherlands, 7–9 July 2011.
65. Baeten, G. Normalising Neoliberal Planning: The Case of Malmö, Sweden. In *Contradictions of Neoliberal Planning: Cities, Policies, and Politics*; Tasan-Kok, T., Baeten, G., Eds.; GeoJournal Library; Springer Netherlands: Dordrecht, The Netherlands, 2012; pp. 21–42. ISBN 978-90-481-8924-3.
66. Fox, T. Erdoğan's 'crazy Project': New Istanbul Canal to Link Black and Marmara Seas. *The Guardian*, 17 February; 2020.
67. Burton, E. Housing for an Urban Renaissance: Implications for Social Equity. *Hous. Stud.* **2003**, *18*, 537–562. [CrossRef]
68. Millward, H. Urban Containment Strategies: A Case-Study Appraisal of Plans and Policies in Japanese, British, and Canadian Cities. *Land Use Policy* **2006**, *23*, 473–485. [CrossRef]
69. Nelson, A.C.; Dawkins, C.J.; Sanchez, T.W. *The Social Impacts of Urban Containment*; Ashgate Publishing Ltd.: Farnham, UK, 2008; ISBN 978-0-7546-7008-7.
70. Giezen, M.; Balikci, S.; Arundel, R. Using Remote Sensing to Analyse Net Land-Use Change from Conflicting Sustainability Policies: The Case of Amsterdam. *ISPRS Int. J. Geo Inf.* **2018**, *7*, 381. [CrossRef]
71. Ghisellini, P.; Cialani, C.; Ulgiati, S. A Review on Circular Economy: The Expected Transition to a Balanced Interplay of Environmental and Economic Systems. *J. Clean. Prod.* **2016**, *114*, 11–32. [CrossRef]
72. Bruegman, R. *Sprawl*; University of Chicago Press: Chicago, IL, USA, 2006.
73. Gordon, D.L.A.; Nicholson, M. Beyond the Tabula Rasa: Gordon Stephenson and Urban Renewal in Kingston, Ontario. *Town Plan. Rev.* **2012**, *83*, 337–354. [CrossRef]
74. Ali, L.; Haase, A.; Heiland, S. Gentrification through Green Regeneration? Analyzing the Interaction between Inner-City Green Space Development and Neighborhood Change in the Context of Regrowth: The Case of Lene-Voigt-Park in Leipzig, Eastern Germany. *Land* **2020**, *9*, 24. [CrossRef]
75. Jehling, M.; Hecht, R.; Herold, H. Assessing Urban Containment Policies within a Suburban Context—An Approach to Enable a Regional Perspective. *Land Use Policy* **2018**, *77*, 846–858. [CrossRef]
76. Perrin, C.; Clément, C.; Melot, R.; Nougarèdes, B. Preserving Farmland on the Urban Fringe: A Literature Review on Land Policies in Developed Countries. *Land* **2020**, *9*, 223. [CrossRef]
77. Berli, J. Competition in Local Land Use Planning? *J. Public Policy* **2018**, *38*, 27–56. [CrossRef]
78. Vigar, G. Towards an Integrated Spatial Planning? *Eur. Plan. Stud.* **2009**, *17*, 1571–1590. [CrossRef]
79. Cotella, G.; Janin Rivolin, U.; Santangelo, M. Transferring 'good' territorial governance across Europe: Opportunities and barriers. In *Territorial Governance across Europe: Pathways, Practices and Prospects*; Schmitt, P., Van Well, L., Eds.; Routledge: London, UK, 2015; pp. 238–253. ISBN 978-1-315-71622-0.
80. Cotella, G.; Vitale Brovarone, E. Rethinking Urbanisation after COVID-19: What Role for the EU Cohesion Policy? *Town Plan. Rev.* **2021**, 1–8. [CrossRef]
81. Solly, A. Territorial Inequality and Spatial Justice. How Level Is the Sustainable Development Playing Field? *Europa XXI* **2020**, *39*. [CrossRef]

land

MDPI

Article

The Role of Land Use Transition on Industrial Pollution Reduction in the Context of Innovation-Driven: The Case of 30 Provinces in China

Yanjun Meng [1], Kun Wang [2] and Yuanyuan Lin [3,*]

[1] School of Economics, Sichuan University, Chengdu 610064, China; 2015321010014@stu.scu.edu.cn
[2] Department of Accounting and Corporate Finance, Business School, Sichuan University, Chengdu 610064, China; liam_wang@stu.scu.edu.cn
[3] Department of International Economics and Trade, Finance and Economics School, Jimei University, Xiamen 361031, China
* Correspondence: yylinxm@jmu.edu.cn; Tel.: +86-189-5108-2866

Abstract: With the world calling for environmental protection, China has to follow an innovation-driven development path in order to achieve its own high-quality and sustainable development. During this period, the problem of inefficient land use resulting from rapid progress in urbanisation is difficult to ignore. This study uses data from 30 provinces in mainland China to analyse the environmental protection effects of land use transition towards innovation-driven development, using spatial econometric models and entropy method. The results show that the innovation-oriented land use transition in four dimensions, human capital, material capital, urban function and government, is conducive to reducing industrial pollution emissions in the region, but this effect does not have a spillover effect. The results of this study provide some insights into the "triple-win" (environmental protection, innovation and land-use optimisation) approach to economic development in China.

Keywords: land use transition; innovation agglomeration; industrial pollution; environmental protection; innovation-driven development

Citation: Meng, Y.; Wang, K.; Lin, Y. The Role of Land Use Transition on Industrial Pollution Reduction in the Context of Innovation-Driven: The Case of 30 Provinces in China. *Land* **2021**, *10*, 353. https://doi.org/10.3390/land10040353

Academic Editors: Maciej J. Nowak, Giancarlo Cotella and Przemysław Śleszyński

Received: 8 March 2021
Accepted: 21 March 2021
Published: 1 April 2021

1. Introduction

Since the industrial revolution, it seems that human development has inevitably led to environmental pollution. "London Fog", "greenhouse effect", "nuclear leak" and other words related to pollution are familiar. Many studies have found that the harm of environmental pollution to human is unexpected and its impact is far-reaching. Dolk and Vrijheid found that water and industrial pollution induce infant congenital anomalies [1]. Grönqvist et al. found that even at a low exposure, the early lead exposure still has a long-term negative impact on children's non cognitive ability [2]. Even plastic particles resulting from human misuse of plastics have been all over the world's land, sea and air ecological cycle (including human body) [3–5]. Nowadays, more and more social organizations and individuals are calling for environmental protection. The *Rio Declaration* provides the basis for the world's environmental protection. Industrial pollution, as the largest proportion of a kind of pollution, has a wide range of impacts [6] and can be deadly [7], making it difficult to be ignored. The focus of the academic community on industrial pollution has never been relaxed. There are studies on the calculation of industrial pollution emissions [8], studies on the reasonable formulation of pollution emission quota [9], and studies on industrial pollution and its driving factors, such as GDP [10], city size [11], openness [12–14], industrial agglomeration [15,16], financial subsidies [17], and environmental protection laws and regulations [18], etc. In recent years, scholars have shifted their research to innovation and environmental protection [19–21]; however, there is little studies on the role of land use transition in environmental protection.

China is in the era of innovation-driven development. As the second largest developing country in the world in terms of total economic output, China has responded positively to the call of the world. Since the "Ninth Five-Year Plan" period (1996–2000), the Chinese government has been consciously reducing energy consumption and emissions. In the "the 11th Five-Year Plan" (2006–2010), energy saving and emission reduction were made binding targets for the local government. For a developing country which is developing rapidly, energy saving and emission reduction are incompatible with economic development in the short term [22]. To address this issue, the Chinese government has made a decisive effort to transform its economy from a factor-input-driven sloppy growth model to an innovation-driven intensive growth model. Innovation is the first driving force leading development and the prevention front-end of green development [23]. Innovation can improve the efficiency of energy utilization, bring cleaner energy, and improve the return on capital, so that enterprises can save energy and reduce emissions and obtain profits. Schumpeter first defined innovation as an unprecedented combination of production factors and production conditions. From the subject level, innovation can be divided into national innovation, regional innovation, industrial innovation and enterprise innovation [24]. Compared with other concepts of innovation, the scope of innovation agglomeration is broader, which emphasizes the concentration of innovation level in a region. On the other hand, the contradiction between China's growing economic development needs and inadequate land use efficiency has further prompted factories to promote innovative development and achieve energy saving and emission reduction. As one of the main elements of production and operation, the constraints of land resources on the current urban economic growth in China are increasing [25,26]. According to NUMBEO data, China's housing price income ratio will be 28.4 in 2020, ranking eighth in Asia and more than 2 times of the world average. Soaring land price and exaggerated housing price income ratio declare innovation or bankruptcy with cruel facts. The land finance problem originated from the sub-loan crisis is one of the biggest obstacles to China's economic development. In addition, land and property prices remain high because of price rigidity and immediate consumer demand. Therefore, in the context of an overall innovation-driven development pattern, China urgently needs to improve its land use and get rid of land constraints, i.e., to achieve an innovation-oriented transition of land use. Land use comprehensively reflects the degree of material circulation and energy exchange among various elements in the urban system, the overall system and the external environment and is the direct manifestation of land value realization in the process of economic development [27]. Land use transition is a manifestation of land use and is also a major research focus of land system science. Scholars have mostly focused on land use in terms of measurement methods and their spatial and temporal distribution characteristics [28–30]. Some scholars have optimised land use efficiency through innovation in management practices [31,32]. However, few studies have focused on the relationship between land use transition and environmental protection, and no studies have yet focused on the role of innovation-oriented transition of land use on industrial pollution.

In addition, spatial factors play an important role that cannot be ignored in the study of environmental economic issues [33,34]. Natural geographic factors such as water flow and wind direction allow environmental problems in a region to spread outwards. Not only that, but because knowledge is partly non-exclusive, there are inevitable spillovers in the process of trade and learning exchange between knowledge subjects [35,36]. Therefore, it is logical that there are spatial spillovers from innovation agglomerations. Previous studies have also confirmed the existence of spatial spillovers in urban land use [37,38]. Therefore, the assumption of inter-regional environmental independence in this study is inconsistent with reality and justifies the use of a spatial econometric model.

In summary, it is clear that China needs to improve insufficient land use, promote innovation and reduce industrial pollution emissions. This article runs through these seemingly separate issues, proposing a four-dimensional approach of human capital, material capital, urban function and government to drive land use transition. It also examines whether this land use transition that enhances innovation agglomeration can reduce industrial pollution. The aim of this study is to test whether a "triple-win" approach to land use transition, innovation and industrial pollution reduction can be achieved in a rational manner. Based on the above analysis, the paper makes 4 hypotheses. Hypotheses H3 and H4 are preliminary hypotheses only. Section 3.2 will illustrate the 4 dimensions of land use transition driven by innovation agglomeration and present further hypotheses. Figure 1 shows the mechanistic route of this study.

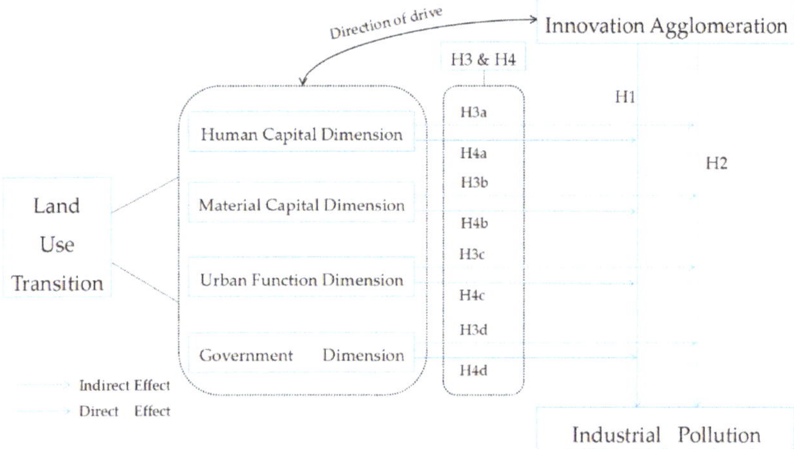

Figure 1. Mechanistic route.

Hypothesis 1 (H1). *Innovation agglomeration helps to reduce industrial pollution emissions on the region.*

Hypothesis 2 (H2). *Innovation agglomeration helps to reduce industrial pollution emissions on the surrounding regions.*

Hypothesis 3 (H3). *The land use transition in the direction of innovation agglomeration can reduce industrial pollution emissions on the region.*

Hypothesis 4 (H4). *The land use transition in the direction of innovation agglomeration can reduce industrial pollution emissions on the surrounding regions.*

The rest of this article is as follows. Section 2 introduces the various research methods mentioned in the study, including the spatial weight matrix, Moran test, spatial econometric model and entropy weight method. Section 3 details the variables of the study and designs the empirical model. Section 4 depicts the spatio-temporal evolution patterns of industrial pollution and innovation agglomeration and the results of the model regressions and performs a series of robustness tests on the conclusions of the paper. Section 5 discusses the findings of the study. Section 6 concludes the paper with a series of recommendations for accelerating innovation-oriented land use transition and thus reducing industrial pollution emissions.

2. Methodology

2.1. Spatial Weight Matrix

The spatial weight matrix is an indispensable element in the spatial econometric model. The spatial weight matrix can incorporate the unique spatial relationships of variables into the econometric model. Common spatial weight matrices are first-order contiguity matrix, geographical distance matrix and economic distance matrix.

2.1.1. First-Order Contiguity Matrix

First order adjacency matrix is a type of adjacency matrix, which mainly reflects the relationship between the local area and surrounding areas, that is, there is a common vertex or boundary between the two regions (Figure 2). The matrix limits the effective range of spillover effect and emphasizes that only the queen contiguity regions have obvious spillover effect. For example, the effective range of knowledge spillover effect is within 300 km (generally beyond the scope of a province in China) [39]. The expression of the first-order adjacency matrix is as follows:

$$W_{ij}^{C} = \begin{cases} 1, & \text{i and j are queen contiguity relations} \\ 0, & \text{others} \end{cases} \quad (1)$$

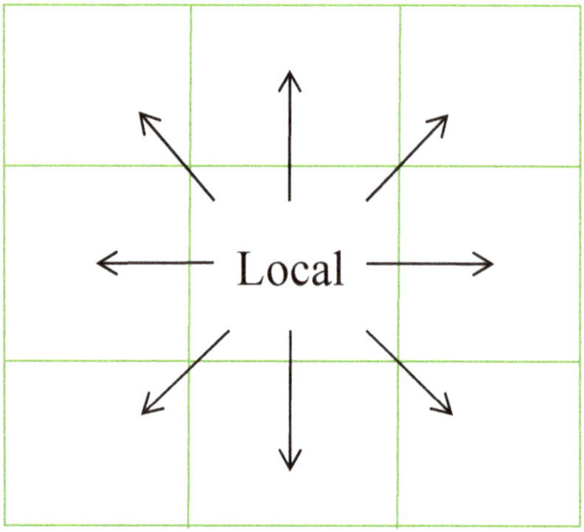

Figure 2. Queen contiguity.

2.1.2. Geographical Distance Matrix

Tobler's First Law of Geography pointed out "Everything is related to everything else, but near things are more related to each other" [40]. The geographic distance matrix best reflects this idea. Although this matrix does not limit the scope of spillover effects, it is believed that spillover effects weakens with increasing geographic distance. The expression of geographical distance matrix is as follows:

$$W_{ij}^{D} = \begin{cases} 1/d^2, & i \neq j \\ 0, & i = j \end{cases} \quad (2)$$

2.1.3. Another Matrix

With the popularity of spatial econometric method, adjacency matrix and geographical distance matrix have been unable to meet the needs of economic research, and more and more new spatial weight matrices have appeared. For example, technological distance matrix reflects the impact of technological consistency between regions on spillover effects [41], institutional distance matrix reflects the impact of institutional disparity on spillover effects [42], and economic distance reflects the impact of economic disparity on spillover effects [43], etc. Among them, the economic distance matrix is used most frequently.

2.2. Moran's I Test

Spatial econometric models require that there must be significant spatial autocorrelation of the explained variables. A commonly used test is the Moran's I Test, specifically, the global Moran's I test and the local Moran's I test.

2.2.1. Global Moran's I Test

The global spatial autocorrelation test tests the spatial autocorrelation degree of the whole sample, which reflects the spatial dependence of attribute values. Global Moran's I test is the most commonly used method, which can visualize the spatial aggregation characteristics of attribute values [44]. Formula (3) shows the calculation process of global Moran's I value.

$$I_t^G = \sum_{i=1}^{n}\sum_{j=1}^{n} W_{ij}\left(X_{i,t} - \overline{X_t}\right)\left(X_{j,t} - \overline{X_t}\right) \Big/ S^2 \sum_{i=1}^{n}\sum_{j=1}^{n} W_{ij} \tag{3}$$

where i and j are individual labels; n is the number of samples; t is the time; X_i, X_j and $\overline{X}$ are the attribute value of i, j and average; W_{ij} is the spatial weight matrix; S^2 is the variance of the attribute value. The value of Moran's $I \in [-1,\ 1]$. When $0 < I^G < 1$, there is a positive spatial agglomeration; when $I^G = 0$, there is no spatial agglomeration, which means the attribute value is randomly distributed; when $-1 < I^G < 0$, there is a negative spatial agglomeration.

2.2.2. Local Moran's I Test

Global spatial autocorrelation test can only test whether there is spatial autocorrelation in the whole sample, but it cannot judge the spatial autocorrelation characteristics of attribute values. We need to use the local spatial autocorrelation test to further explore the spatial autocorrelation characteristics of each attribute value (high-high agglomeration, low-low agglomeration, high-low agglomeration and low-high agglomeration). Moran scatter plot is one of the methods commonly used to test the characteristics of local regional aggregation. Formula (4) shows its calculation process.

$$I_{i,\,t}^L = \left(X_{i,t} - \overline{X_t}\right) \sum_{j=1}^{n} W_{ij}\left(X_{j,t} - \overline{X_t}\right) \Big/ S^2 \tag{4}$$

The meaning of each symbol is the same as above. In addition, when $I^L > 0$, there is H-H or L-L agglomeration characteristics in adjacent areas; when $I^L < 0$, there is L-H or H-L agglomeration characteristics in adjacent areas; when $I^L = 0$, there is no local agglomeration characteristics in adjacent areas.

2.3. Description of Spatial Econometric Model

Common spatial econometric models include spatial lag model (SLM), spatial error model (SEM), and spatial Durbin model (SDM). SLM refers to the spatial lag of the explained variable, rather than the traditional time lag. The combination of the spatial lag and the explained variable is used as an explanatory variable to reflect the influence of the explained variable in other regions in the whole on the local. SEM can deal with spatial spillover effects caused by missing important variables or unobservable random shocks, that is, assuming that the disturbance term has spatial dependence. The characteristic of SDM is to add a combination of explanatory variables and spatial lags as new explanatory variables to reflect the influence of explanatory variables in other regions in the whole on the local. Formulas (5)–(7) are the general forms of SLM, SEM and SDM, respectively:

$$Y = \alpha WY + \beta X + \varepsilon \tag{5}$$

$$Y = \alpha WY + \beta X + \delta WX + \varepsilon \tag{6}$$

$$\begin{aligned} Y &= \beta X + \mu \\ \mu &= M\mu + \varepsilon \end{aligned} \tag{7}$$

where W and M are spatial weight matrices; α, β and δ are coefficients of corresponding variables, and ε is a random error term.

2.4. Entropy Method

Too many variables will likely lead to multicollinearity problems, and in this study, we will develop a multidimensional, innovation agglomeration-based indicator system that can facilitate land use transition. The entropy method is an effective method for evaluating comprehensive indicators. It can effectively reduce the dimensionality of indicators and give higher weights to secondary indicators with greater entropy (degree of variation), thus obtaining an efficient composite indicator. A brief calculation of the entropy method is as follows:

Step 1. A standardised matrix of indicator evaluation systems ($c'_{ab,t}$) is created. where a is the cross-sectional individual a ($1 \leq a \leq n$); b is the indicator b ($1 \leq b \leq k$), and t is the period t.

$$c'_{ab,t} = c_{ab,t} - \min_k |c_{ab,t}| \Big/ \max_k |c_{ab,t}| - \min_k |c_{ab,t}| \tag{8}$$

Step 2. Formula (9) is the calculation of the information entropy ($E_{b,t}$) for the indicator b in period t, and Formula (10) is the calculation of the weight for the indicator b in period t ($\text{weight}_{b,t}$).

$$\begin{gathered} E_{b,t} = -\ln(n)^{-1} \sum_{a=1}^{n} (P'_{ab,t}) \ln(P'_{ab,t}) \\ \text{s.t. } P'_{ab,t} = c'_{ab,t} / \textstyle\sum_{a=1}^{n} c'_{ab,t} \end{gathered} \tag{9}$$

$$\text{weight}_{b,t} = 1 - E_{b,t} \Big/ b - \sum E_{b,t} \tag{10}$$

3. Design of Variables and Models

3.1. Explained Variable

Industrial pollution covers a wide range, but in this study, it refers specifically to "three wastes" (industrial effluent, industrial waste gas and industrial waste residue) pollution. Considering the availability of data, this study uses industrial effluent emissions, industrial SO_2 emissions and industrial soot emissions to measure the discharge of "three wastes", respectively. Due to the different scales of regions, the absolute value data is easy to make the research conclusion "unfair". Therefore, with reference to the design logic of location quotient, this study reduces the dimension of these 3 types of data into a kind of relative value data. The process is as follows:

Step 1. $e_{it,p}$ is the total emission of industrial pollution p (p = 3) of province i in period t; Y_{it} is the actual total industrial output value of province i in period t, and $E_{it,p}$ is the economic efficiency of industrial pollution emission.

$$E_{it,p} = e_{it,p} / Y_{it} \tag{11}$$

Step 2. $NE_{it,p}$ is the economic efficiency of national industrial pollution emission in China. The 30 cross-section samples are represented by "30".

$$NE_{it,p} = \sum_{i=1}^{30} e_{it,p} / Y_{it} \tag{12}$$

Step 3. Calculate the relative value of industrial pollution emission variables (Ind_pol_{it}). The higher the Ind_pol_{it} is, the greater and the more serious the industrial pollution is; otherwise, the smaller the industrial pollution is, the lighter the industrial pollution is.

$$\text{Ind\_pol}_{it} = E_{it,p} / NE_{it,p} \tag{13}$$

3.2. Explanatory Variables

This study uses innovation agglomeration to represent the background of innovation-driven, so the moderate variable is innovation agglomeration (Inno_agg). The core explanatory variables reflect land use transition in the direction of innovation agglomeration and contain human capital dimension, material capital dimension, urban function dimension and government dimension. In addition, we have further set further Hypotheses H3 and H4 in this section.

3.2.1. Innovation Agglomeration

According to the above, innovation agglomeration emphasizes the concentration of innovation level in a region. Due to the type of available data and in order to reduce the potential for multicollinearity, this study uses the number of granted patents, which is processed to remove the effect of economic volume, to reflect more realistically the level of innovation agglomeration in the region. The processing steps are as follows:

$$\mathrm{Inno\_agg}_{it,p} = \sum_{i=1}^{30} e_{it,p}/G_{it} \tag{14}$$

where, $\mathrm{Inno\_agg}_{it,p}$ represents level of innovation agglomeration of province i in period t. G_{it} is GDP of province i in period t.

3.2.2. Human Capital Dimension

Knowledge is the original force of innovation-driven, and people are the carrier and core of knowledge. On the one hand, the higher the human capital of a region, the higher the innovation development of the region, the higher the rate of return on capital, thereby promoting land use transition and achieving energy conservation and emission reduction. On the other hand, higher levels of human capital will require a higher quality of life. These will force the local government to improve their infrastructure and beautify the environment to retain talents and elites. Accordingly, this study selects the following three variables to reflect the level of human capital and makes further hypotheses. (I) Population density. People are agglomerated and will gather in areas with more employment opportunities, a more developed economy and a higher living environment. Observing domestic and foreign cities, it can be found that the population density of such high-quality cities is usually high (of course, it does not mean that cities with higher population density must be high-quality). (II) Average educational level. Education is a medium for passing on knowledge and the basis for generating new knowledge. Innovative agglomeration will attract more highly educated people to settle here, which will increase the average education level of local residents [45]. Average educational level is proportion of (population of college and above * 16 + population of high school * 12 + population of junior high school * 9+population of elementary school * 6) in population over 6 years old. (III) Full-time equivalent of R & D personnel. It reflects the degree of hard work of scientific researchers in the region. R & D is a time-consuming and labour-intensive process, and a large number of valuable innovations are based on the work of scientific researchers day and night. The average weights corresponding to urban population density, average educational level and full-time equivalent of R & D personnel are 0.2907, 0.2280 and 0.48124, respectively (Appendix A Table A1 for the complete data).

Hypothesis 3a (H3a). *The land use transition driven by human capital dimension can reduce industrial pollution emissions on the region.*

Hypothesis 4a (H4a). *The land use transition driven by human capital dimension can reduce industrial pollution emissions on surrounding regions.*

3.2.3. Material Capital Dimension

Just as production and operation are inseparable from material capital investment, innovation requires a lot of capital support (such as the development of COVID-19 vaccines). In terms of innovation agglomeration, it will gather a large amount of material capital (mainly capital). On the one hand, money capital has a certain degree of speculation. Therefore, high capital clusters often have a higher rate of return on capital, thereby accelerating land use transition. On the other hand, the agglomeration of material capital cannot only speed up the progress of scientific research but also clear its funding barriers, thereby improving various pollution emission, also alleviating the problem of "financing difficulties" for companies using environmental protection equipment. Accordingly, this study chooses the following three variables to reflect level of material capital and makes further hypotheses. (I) Internal expenditure of R & D funds. It refers to the actual expenditure of enterprises and institutions for internal R & D activities (including basic research, applied research and experimental development). This is the most intuitive capital investment directly used for scientific research. (II) Financial institutions density. Financial institutions can promote the financing, which is the inevitable outcome of financial development to a certain period. High financial institutions density is the inevitable product of innovation development. It can not only improve the investment and financing efficiency of enterprises but also form a competitive environment, thus reducing the investment and financing costs [46]. The average weights corresponding to internal expenditure of R & D funds and financial institutions density are 0.6072 and 0.3928, respectively (Appendix A Table A2 for the complete data).

Hypothesis 3b (H3b). *The land use transition driven by material capital dimension can reduce industrial pollution emissions on the region.*

Hypothesis 4b (H4b). *The land use transition driven by material capital dimension can reduce industrial pollution emissions on surrounding regions.*

3.2.4. Urban Function Dimension

Urban function refers to the role and division of labour that a city plays in the economic and social development of a certain area, and it can also be simply described as the characteristics of a city. Urban development often has a significant negative impact on ecosystems [47], especially in developing countries that need to develop industries to improve their economic levels. After the reform and opening-up, the industrial-based development mode has brought "miracle growth" to China, but it has also been accompanied by many environmental problems. At that time, developing industry and increasing GDP were the main theme of most cities. Nowadays, with China's national power is becoming stronger and stronger, people's requirements for the quality of the living environment are constantly increasing, and China's economic development has new requirements, that is, an innovation-driven development mode. In the process of innovation agglomeration, the urban functions need to be improved, and land use transition gradually is taking shape. On the one hand, the industrial structure of the city has changed, and the proportion of the secondary industry has decreased, while the proportion of the tertiary industry has increased year by year, which reduces the industrial pollution emissions. On the one hand, the industrial structure of cities has undergone changes, the proportion of the secondary industry has decreased, and the proportion of the tertiary industry has increased year by year, reducing industrial pollution emissions. On the other hand, as the government's focus gradually shifts to the quality of life of residents, the city's infrastructure will be improved accordingly. In the context of innovation agglomeration, local governments will build more humane and better infrastructure to meet the development needs of innovation, thereby accelerating land use transition and reducing industrial pollution emissions. Accordingly, this study chooses the following two variables to reflect level of urban function and makes further hypotheses. (I) Industrial structure evolution. Kuznets defines the industrial structure evolution as a re-allocation process of economic resources among agriculture, industry and service industries [48,49]. With the increase in economic development and the level of innovation agglomeration, the trend of economic servitization has accelerated, and the proportion of tertiary industry in GDP has also increased, thereby reducing the level of industrial pollution emissions. Although the industrial structure evolution is a comprehensive process, this study mainly focuses on the change phenomenon of the primary, secondary, and tertiary industries. Therefore, the ratio of tertiary industry's GDP to total

GDP is used to measure it. (II) Urban road area per capita. With the deepening of urbanization and the adjustment of urban functions, infrastructure is developing in the direction of convenience. Urban road area per capita directly reflects the city's traffic convenience and indirectly reflects the city's tendency to improve the life quality of residents. The average weights corresponding to industrial structure evolution and urban road area per capita are 0.6961 and 0.30392, respectively (Appendix A Table A3 for the complete data).

Hypothesis 3c (H3c). *The land use transition driven by urban function dimension can reduce industrial pollution emissions on the region.*

Hypothesis 4c (H4c). *The land use transition driven by urban function dimension can reduce industrial pollution emissions on surrounding regions.*

3.2.5. Government Dimension

The government dimension reflects what the government has done to strengthen the role of innovation agglomeration in industrial pollution reduction. China's special national conditions and development history determine that the position and authority of the Communist Party of China as the ruling party are recognized [50], and the behaviour of local governments has a strong influence on social development [10]. On the one hand, innovation agglomeration urges the government to further increase the investment in science and technology expenditure in the general government budget, promote innovation and development, so as to promote land use transition and reduce industrial pollution emissions. On the other hand, under the requirement of sustainable development, the local government has restricted the pollution emission of enterprises with large industrial pollution emission, and gradually controlled the total industrial pollution emission from the total amount. Accordingly, this study chooses the following two variables to reflect the government dimension and makes further hypotheses. (I) Proportion of technology expenditure. Similar to internal expenditure of R & D funds, this variable is the proportion of science and technology expenditure in the general government budget, which reflects the government's support and attitude to science and technology research. (II) Green coverage. Since it is difficult to directly measure the degree of government restrictions on industrial pollution emissions from enterprises, this study uses green coverage to indirectly reflect the government's focus on the environment. The average weights corresponding to proportion of technology expenditure and green coverage are 0.7636 and 0.2364, respectively (Appendix A Table A4 for the complete data).

Hypothesis 3d (H3d). *The land use transition driven by government dimension can reduce industrial pollution emissions on the region.*

Hypothesis 4d (H4d). *The land use transition driven by government dimension can reduce industrial pollution emissions on surrounding regions.*

3.3. Control Variables

There are many factors that affect industrial pollution. The core explanatory variable of this article is only to filter out variables that can promote land use transition from the perspective of innovation agglomeration. Therefore, control variables should also be selected from the following aspects to prevent endogenous problems caused by omission of important explanatory variables. (I) Per capita GDP (Per_GDP). Buryn et al. found a close relationship between economic development and pollution emissions [51]. On the one hand, the higher the per capita GDP of a region, the higher the residents' requirements for the quality of life and living environment. On the other hand, companies that can support a high level of per capita GDP often have a higher rate of return on investment, which is difficult for traditional industrial companies to achieve. (II) Foreign direct investment (FDI). In the early period of reform and opening-up, China had cheap labour, raw materials and land, which was extremely attractive to foreign manufacturers. They can use cheap production factors and perform corporate social responsibilities with low standards. However, with the increase in the cost of setting up manufactures in China and the Chinese awareness of environmental protection, the role of FDI in increasing industrial pollution emissions may weaken or even reverse [52]. This is not the focus of this article. However, it is undeniable that FDI in this study is a good control variable reflecting foreign influence. (III) Energy structure. Wang et al. found that there is a highly positive correlation between the proportion of coal energy and industrial pollution [53]. When the proportion of traditional coal energy drops, it indicates that the proportion of other relatively clean energy (wind power, hydroelectric power, etc.) in China has risen, thereby affecting industrial pollution emissions. Accordingly, this study uses the ratio of total electricity generation to total energy consumption to measure the energy structure. In addition, the converted standard coal coefficient (1.229 tonnes of standard coal/10,000 kWh) is used to convert the units of electricity generation into million tonnes of standard coal. Table 1 summarizes the indicator system.

Table 1. Variable description.

Type	Variable	Unit	Obs	Mean	Std.	Label
Explained variable	Industrial pollution	-	390	4.4162	0.7752	Ind_pol
Moderate variable	Innovation agglomeration	item	390	9.0124	1.5499	Inno_agg
Explanatory variables (Human capital dimension)	Urban population density	person/km^2	390	7.8374	0.4484	Human
	Average educational level	year/person	390	2.1703	0.1067	
	Full-time equivalent of R & D personnel	10,000 man-year	390	10.9526	1.1148	
Explanatory variables (Material capital dimension)	Internal expenditure of R & D funds	10,000 yuan	390	14.1989	1.4054	Material
	Financial institutions density	Unit/km^2	390	−5.6902	0.4764	
Explanatory variables (Urban function dimension)	Industrial Structure Evolution	%	390	3.7468	0.1932	Urban
	Urban road area per capita	m2/person	390	2.5838	0.3305	
Explanatory variables (Government dimension)	Proportion of technology expenditure	%	390	−1.0851	0.4764	Government
	Green coverage	%	390	3.6197	0.1338	
Control variables	Per capita GDP	yuan/person	390	10.4694	0.5826	Per_GDP
	Foreign direct investment	10,000 dollar	390	12.5964	1.6338	FDI
	Energy structure	%	390	2.6562	0.4717	Ener_stru

Mean and Std. are both values in logarithmic form.

3.4. Data Resource

Since 2006 (the starting point of the 11th Five-Year Plan), China has strictly controlled pollution emissions and strengthened its efforts to carry out green development. Therefore, this study uses the panel data of 30 provinces in China after 2006 (2006–2018) for research. In view of the integrity and availability of the data, the Tibet Autonomous, Hong Kong, Macao and Taiwan were excluded. All raw data comes from China Statistical Yearbook, China statistical yearbook on Science and technology, provincial statistical yearbook. Some of the missing data are supplemented using the moving average method.

3.5. Model Design

This study takes the form of the Cobb-Douglas production function and considers industrial pollution emissions as an "output". By taking the logarithm of both sides of the C-D production function, we transform the equation into a linear function and at the same time mitigate the heteroskedasticity generated by the panel data. ε_{it} is the random perturbation term.

$$\ln Y_{it} = \theta_{it} + \beta \ln X_{it} + \gamma \ln Control_{it} + \varepsilon_{it} \tag{15}$$

Since the spatial Durbin model has the widest range of applicability, we transform Formula (15) into the form of SDM.

$$\ln Y_{it} = \beta \ln X_{it} + \delta_1 W \ln X_{it} + \gamma \ln Control_{it} + \delta_2 W \ln Control_{it} + \varepsilon_{it} \quad (16)$$

Panel models usually use either fixed effects or random effects. Random effects assume that all regression variables containing individual random effects are exogenous and are often used to "see the big picture". Fixed effects, on the other hand, assume that the variables containing the effects of individuals are endogenous. [53] Therefore, as the study is for 30 provinces in China, fixed effects are used in this paper. There are three forms of fixed effects in the spatial panel model: spatial fixed effect, time-period fixed effect and spatial and time-period (S&T) fixed effect. The spatial fixed effect reflects characteristics that do not vary with time but vary with individuals (σ_i), while the time-period fixed effect reflects characteristics that do not vary with individuals but vary with time (τ_t). Since industrial pollution emissions have distinct regional characteristics and Yu et al. found that smog pollution has a time-varying trend and diffusivity [34], the S&T fixed effect model was used in this study and the spatial lag term of the explanatory variable (Ind_pol) was added to control for this (see Formula (17)).

$$\ln Y_{it} = \alpha W \ln Y_{it} + \beta \ln X_{it} + \delta W \ln X_{it} + \gamma \ln Control_{it} + \omega W \ln Control_{it} + \sigma_i + \tau_t + \varepsilon_{it} \quad (17)$$

Finally, substituting the variables mentioned in the article into Formula (17), get Formula (18). In which, $Explanatory_{v,it}$ represents the explanatory variables for period t of province i in dimension v, that is, human capital dimension, material capital dimension, urban function dimension and government dimension.

$$\begin{aligned} \ln Ind\_pol_{it} = \; & \alpha W \ln Ind\_pol_{it} + \beta_1 W \ln Inno\_agg_{it} \\ & + \beta_2 \ln\left(Explanatory_{v,it} * \ln Inno\_agg_{it}\right) \\ & + \delta_1 W \ln Inno\_agg_{it} \\ & + \delta_2 W \ln\left(Explanatory_{v,it} * \ln Inno\_agg_{it}\right) \\ & + \gamma_1 \ln Per\_GDP_{it} + \gamma_2 \ln FDI_{it} + \gamma_3 \ln Ener\_stru_{it} \\ & + \omega_1 W \ln Per\_GDP_{it} + \omega_2 W \ln FDI_{it} + \omega_3 W \ln Ener\_stru_{it} \\ & + \sigma_i + \tau_t + \varepsilon_{it} \end{aligned} \quad (18)$$

4. Results

4.1. Analysis of Spatial-Temporal Evolution

4.1.1. Industrial Pollution

Figure 3 shows that the regions of medium and low industrial pollution are mostly the more economically developed regions, and there is a clear distribution characteristic—the eastern coastal region have less industrial pollution, while some parts of central and western China have more. However, over time, the eastern region solidified its low industrial pollution levels, while the central region generally maintained medium industrial pollution levels and northern China clearly behaved in a high industrial pollution trend.

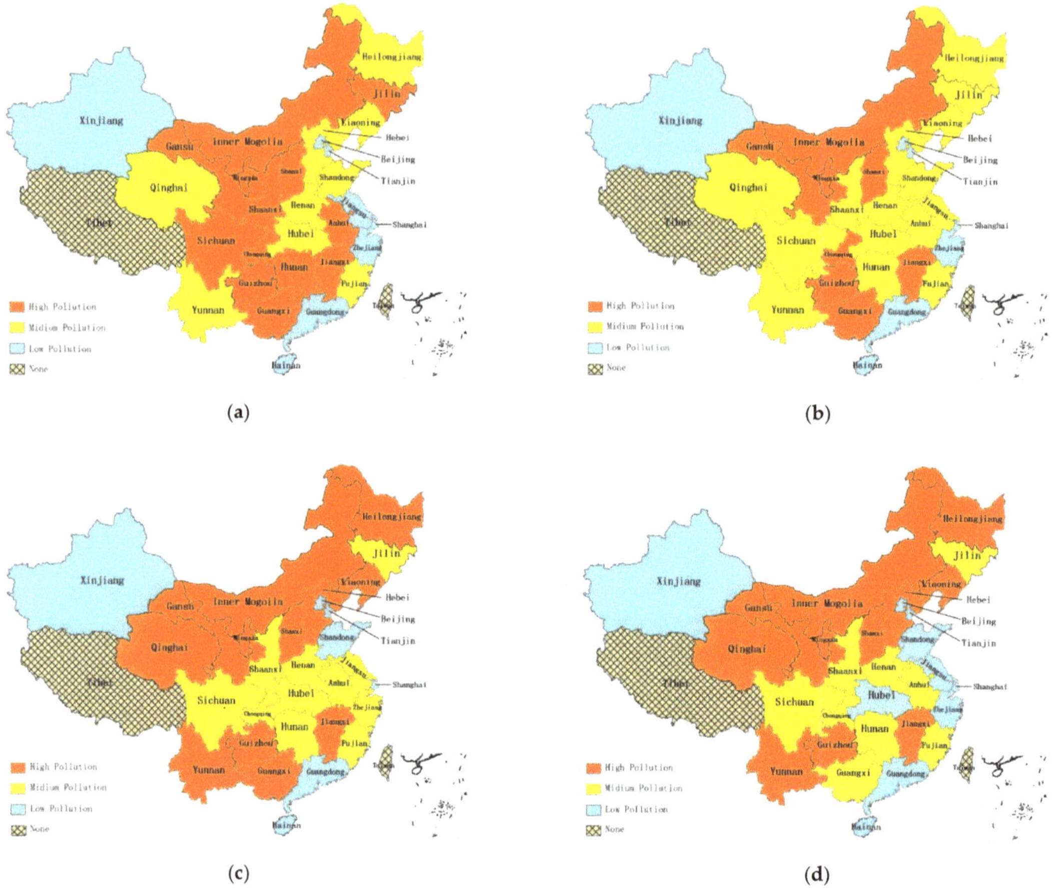

Figure 3. Industrial pollution distribution. (**a**) Industrial pollution in 2006. (**b**) Industrial pollution in 2010. (**c**) Industrial pollution in 2014. (**d**) Industrial pollution in 2018.

4.1.2. Innovation Agglomeration

Figure 4 shows that, Overall, innovation agglomeration is more extreme across China's provinces—there are fewer regions of high agglomeration and more regions of medium and low agglomeration. Analysing the spatial distribution pattern, it is clear that innovation agglomeration is high in the eastern region and low in the western region, with Sichuan Province standing out as the core province in western China. Combined with the time evolution pattern, it can be found that the divisional pattern has not changed significantly during the 13 years, indicating that the spatial distribution pattern has further solidified and behaved with obvious high and high agglomeration characteristics.

4.2. Spatial Regression Results

Table 2 presents the regression results for the direct and indirect effects of the five regression in this study. Model I test Hypotheses H1 and H2. Models II, III, IV, and IV test hypotheses H3 and H4.

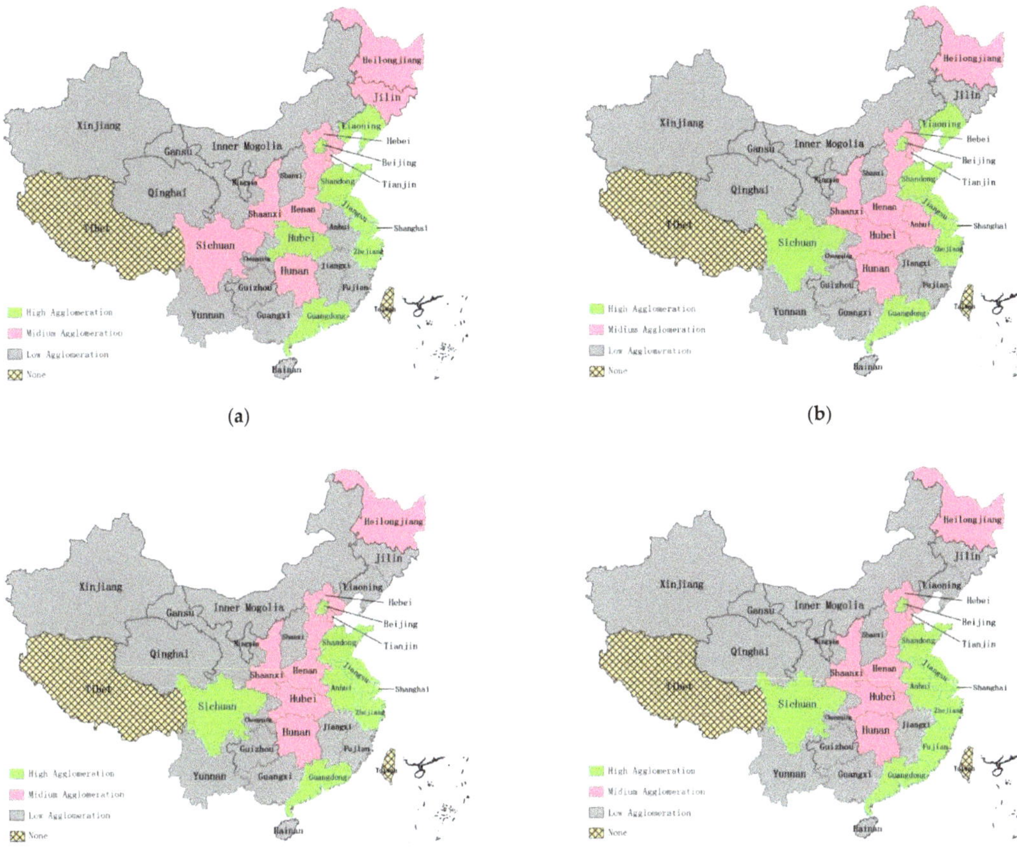

Figure 4. Innovation agglomeration distribution. (**a**) Innovation agglomeration in 2006. (**b**) InnovaTable 2010. (**c**) Innovation agglomeration in 2014. (**d**) Innovation agglomeration in 2018.

From Model I, the direct effect coefficient of innovation agglomeration is −0.2315 (significant), while its indirect effect coefficient is 0.2287 (insignificant). Therefore, hypothesis H1 holds, but Hypotheses H2 does not, i.e., innovation agglomeration helps to reduce industrial pollution emissions on the region, but it does not have a spillover effect.

In Models II–V, Hypotheses H3 and H4 can be tested by the direct and indirect effect coefficients of the interaction terms of innovation agglomeration and the explanatory variables (Human, Material, Urban and Government). The direct effect coefficients of the four models are −0.0627, −0.0152, −0.0018 and −0.0104, respectively, and all of them pass the 10% significance level test, indicating that Hypotheses H3 (H3a, H3b, H3c and H3d) holds, but the indirect effects are not significant, indicating that Hypotheses H4 (H4a, H4b, H4c and H4d) does not.

4.3. Robustness Tests

4.3.1. Spatial Autocorrelation Test

Spatial autocorrelation is the basis for spatial econometric model. Although industrial pollution is inherently spillover in nature, it is logical to use a spatial econometric model for the study. However, in order to be rigorous, this study still measured the spatial autocorrelation of industrial pollution between 2006 and 2018, and visualised the results using global Moran's I statistics and Moran scatter. Table 3 shows the global Moran's I statistics in 2006–2018, which shows that the majority of *p*-values are less than 0.10, indicating that industrial pollution in China has spatial autocorrelation at the provincial level. Figure 5 shows that there are obvious agglomeration characteristics in the distribution of industrial pollution in China, among which, low-low agglomeration is predominant. In summary, it is reasonable to use spatial econometric models in this study.

Table 2. Regression results.

Explanatory Variables	I	II	III	IV	V
Inno_agg	−0.2315 **	−0.3096 **	−0.2340 *	−0.2214 *	−0.2193 *
Human	0.0655 ***	-	-	-	-
Material	−0.1296 **	-	-	-	-
Urban	0.0264	-	-	-	-
Government	0.0828 **	-	-	-	-
Inno_agg * Human	-	−0.0627 ***	-	-	-
Inno_agg * Material	-	-	−0.0152 *	-	-
Inno_agg * Urban	-	-	-	−0.0018 *	-
Inno_agg * Government	-	-	-	-	−0.0104 *
Per_GDP	−0.4558 *	−0.4325 *	−0.4865 *	−0.4871 *	−0.4903 *
FDI	−0.1439 *	−0.1374 *	−0.1341 *	−0.1329 *	−0.1309 *
Ener_stru	−0.3496 *	−0.3658 *	−0.3709 *	−0.3784 *	−0.3693 *
W * Inno_agg	0.2287	0.1623	0.1853	0.2215	0.2171
W * Human	0.0424	-	-	-	-
W * Material	0.0076	-	-	-	-
W * Urban	0.0248	-	-	-	-
W * Government	−0.0382	-	-	-	-
W * Inno_agg * Human	-	−0.0403	-	-	-
W * Inno_agg * Material	-	-	−0.0390	-	-
W * Inno_agg * Urban	-	-	-	0.0185	-
W * Inno_agg * Government	-	-	-	-	−0.0145
W * Per_GDP	−0.6703 **	−0.7312 **	−0.7095 **	−0.7450 **	−0.7369 *
W * FDI	0.1292	0.1382	0.1372	0.1531	0.1467
W * Ener_stru	−0.8653 **	−0.8275 **	−0.8191 **	−0.8171 **	−0.8204 **
R-square	0.2320	0.2611	0.2625	0.2509	0.2594
Log-L	53.6512	48.3867	45.2893	44.0831	44.2472
rho	−2.51 **	−2,24 **	−2.35 **	−2.25 **	−2.32 **

***, **, and * respectively indicate statistical significance at the 1%, 5%, and 10% levels.

Table 3. Global Moran's I value.

Year	Moran's I	*p*-Value	Year	Moran's I	*p*-Value
2006	2.356	0.018	2013	1.192	0.117
2007	2.451	0.014	2014	1.762	0.078
2008	2.317	0.021	2015	1.690	0.091
2009	2.316	0.021	2016	1.794	0.073
2010	2.205	0.027	2017	1.624	0.096
2011	2.992	0.003	2018	1.523	0.128
2012	1.687	0.090			

4.3.2. Model Applicability Test

To test the superiority of SDM over SAR, we made the hypothesis that the spatial lag of the explanatory variables in the model, WX = 0. It was found that all regression models rejected the null hypothesis, i.e., SDM should be used for research rather than SAR.

To test the superiority of SDM over SEM, we made the hypothesis that the spatial lag of the explanatory variable in the model, WX = −rho * X. It was found that all regression models rejected the null hypothesis, i.e., SDM should be used for research rather than SEM.

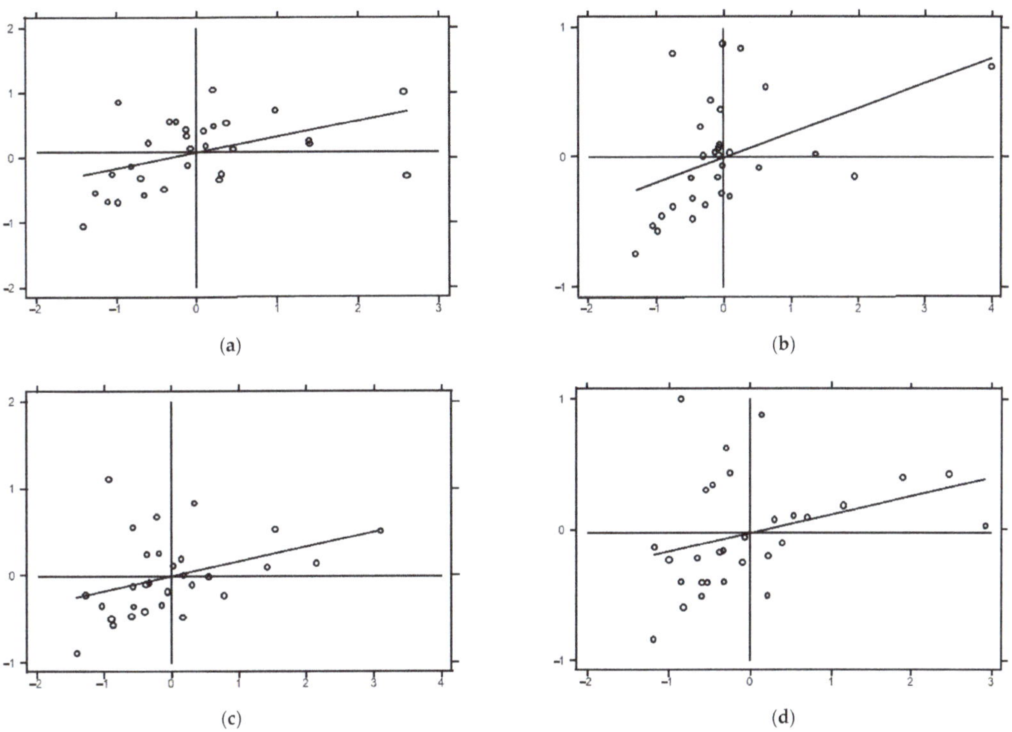

Figure 5. Moran scatters. (a) Local Moran's I in 2006. (b) Local Moran's I in 2010. (c) Local Moran's I in 2014. (d) Local Moran's I in 2018.

In order to verify that the S&T fixed effect model outperforms the time-period fixed effect model and the spatial fixed effect model in this study, all regression models were tested using the F-test and the null hypothesis was rejected. (Table 4).

Table 4. F statistic value.

	I	II	III	IV	V
Spatial fixed effect	115.86 ***	121.47 ***	120.71 ***	126.13 ***	119.75 ***
Time-period fixed effect	22.55 ***	36.54 ***	35.92 ***	37.86 ***	34.89 ***

*** indicate statistical significance at the 1% levels.

5. Discussions

Table 2 proves that Hypotheses H1 and H3 (H3a, H3b, H3c and H3d) are valid, while H2 and H4 (H4a, H4b, H4c and H4d) are not. This suggests that (1) innovation agglomeration contributes to the reduction of industrial emissions in the region but does not have a significant effect on its surrounding regions; (2) it is feasible to enhance the effect of innovation agglomeration on industrial pollution reduction by land use transition on the region, but this effect does not have a significant influence on the surrounding regions. Specifically: hypothesis H3a holds, which suggests that an increase in the human capital dimension will, on the one hand, help to drive land use transition and thus strengthen the reduction of industrial pollution emissions from innovation agglomeration; on the other hand, the government will be more active in implementing strategies to reduce emissions and retain elite talent. Based on the weight of the secondary indicators of human capital dimension, it can be further argued that full-time equivalent of R & D personnel plays the greatest role, followed by population density and finally average educational level.

This enlightens us that increasing the workload of R & D personnel and attracting the inflow of foreign population can bring greater benefits. Hypothesis H3b holds, which suggests that an increase in the material capital dimension will help to remove financial barriers to research, ease the "difficulty of financing" the use of environmental equipment by firms, accelerate land use transition and reduce industrial pollution emissions. In addition, the demand of capitalists for adequate returns on capital will also increase the level of land use in the region, thus promoting land use change and reducing industrial pollution emissions. Based on the weight of the secondary indicator of material capital dimension, it can be further argued that although the role of internal expenditure of R & D funds in reducing emissions is stronger than that of financial institutions density, both are very important. This reveals to us that although R & D expenses are important, the role of financial institutions in financing should not be neglected, which reduces the difficulty of innovative enterprises in obtaining funds. Hypothesis H3c holds, indicating that the upgrading of the urban function dimension is conducive to the transition and upgrading of industries in the region, achieving land use transition while also reducing industrial pollution emissions and, on the other hand, encouraging the government to build more humane and innovative infrastructure, thus accelerating land use transition. Based on the weight of the secondary indicators of the urban function dimension, it can be further argued that industrial structure evolution is the main force in promoting innovation and achieving industrial pollution reduction, which reveals to us that promoting industrial structure upgrading and accelerating the service-oriented economy is a triple-win path of accelerating land use transition, promoting innovation and achieving environmental protection. Hypothesis H3d holds that the government's efforts help to accelerate land use transition and reduce industrial pollution emissions. Based on the weights of the secondary indicators of the government dimension, it can be further argued that, on the one hand, the government, by supporting innovation development, has the guidance to promote land use transition and strengthen innovation agglomeration, thus reducing industrial pollution; on the other hand, the government's greening efforts help retain elites and provide an environmental basis for innovation agglomeration, which also indirectly curbs industrial pollution emissions.

For other variables, the direct effect coefficient of Per_GDP is negative and passes the 10% significance level test. The indirect effect coefficient was also negative and passed the 10% significance level test. This indicates that an increase in per capita GDP within a region not only helps to reduce industrial pollution emissions in the region but also helps to reduce emissions in neighbouring regions. This is consistent with the findings of Buryn et al. [51]. The coefficient of the direct effect of FDI is negative and passes the 10% significance level test. However, its indirect effect is not significant. This suggests that as the Chinese and the government have become more environmentally conscious, the role of foreign investors in increasing emissions has been reversed and has instead helped to reduce industrial pollution, which is consistent with Jorgenson's findings [52]. This is because China is focusing on bringing in high quality FDI (advanced production technologies) and gradually abandoning its role as a "processing plant". The direct effect coefficient of energy structure is negative and passes the 10% significance level test. The indirect effect coefficient is also negative and passes the 10% significance level test. This indicates, when the proportion of traditional coal energy drops, that the proportion of other relatively clean energy (wind power, hydroelectric power, etc.) in China has risen, thereby affecting industrial pollution emissions. This is consistent with the results of Wang et al.'s study [53], implying the importance of energy structure transformation in reducing industrial pollution.

6. Conclusions

Innovation and environmental protection are the main themes of China's development today, and the lack of efficient land use is one of the main problems of China's development. This paper analyses the relationship between innovation agglomeration, land use transition and industrial pollution, and subtly investigates the question of whether innovation-oriented land use transition can reduce industrial pollution emissions. Using provincial-level data from 2006–2018, the paper draws conclusions through a spatial econometric model and proposes a series of targeted policy implications based on an analysis of the spatio-temporal evolution of industrial pollution and innovation agglomeration, in the hope of providing theoretical support for China's triple-win development (innovation, land use transition and environmental protection).

The conclusions are as follows:

(1) Both industrial pollution and innovation agglomeration have a clear spatial and temporal distribution. In eastern China, the level of industrial pollution is lower, while in northern China it is higher. Moreover, this distribution characteristic has become increasingly evident over time; innovation agglomeration is more extreme across China's provinces—there are fewer regions of high agglomeration and more regions of medium and low agglomeration. Analysing the spatial distribution pattern, it is clear that innovation agglomeration is high in the eastern region and low in the western region. Moreover, this distribution characteristic has not changed significantly over time.

(2) The land use transition towards an innovation-driven direction contributes to the reduction of industrial pollution emissions on the region but has no significant impact on the surrounding regions. In human capital dimension, full-time equivalent of R & D personnel plays the greatest role, followed by population density and finally average educational level; in material capital dimension, the role of internal expenditure of R & D funds is stronger than that of financial institutions density; in urban function dimension, the role of industrial structure evolution is significantly stronger than that of urban road area per capita, due to the high level of infrastructure development in China and the limited variation in urban road area per capita across regions; in government dimension, the role of proportion of technology expenditure is significantly stronger than that of green coverage for the same reasons as above.

(3) In line with existing research, increasing per capita GDP and FDI and improving energy structure can help reduce industrial pollution. Moreover, increasing per capita GDP and improving energy structure can also generate positive spillover effects and promote the reduction of industrial pollution in neighbouring provinces.

Based on the above, we have obtained some inspiration on policy making:

(1) Adhere to the policy of compulsory education, continue to strengthen the training of talents, improve the mechanism of training talents, and improve the treatment of talents, especially R & D personnel. For the eastern regions with a high degree of innovation agglomeration, various policies should be formulated for the introduction of talents to attract the inflow of more innovative talents.

(2) Encourage and subsidise enterprises to undertake R & D; especially northern China, where the degree of innovation agglomeration is weak, should not be neglected because of its weak innovation agglomeration, but should instead be supported more vigorously, as these regions are heavily polluted by industry and their potential for improvement is enormous. Improve the distribution of financial institution outlets and ensure that a certain number of financial institutions are maintained throughout China to facilitate investment and financing for enterprises and to help them break down the barriers to financing.

(3) Continue to improve supply-side reforms in order to promote the industrial structures. This is especially true for the more polluted regions of western and northern China. For the eastern regions, where pollution is low and the industrial structure is more advanced, there should be a targeted move towards demand-side reform. In addition, maintain or reduce the investment in road infrastructure, especially in the central and eastern regions, but infrastructure development in the western regions should be further strengthentened.

(4) Strengthen financial support for science and technology research and development, and build a platform for cross-regional, cross-university and cross-disciplinary collaboration to increase the utilisation of research funds. At the same time, the government should continue to maintain the level of green coverage in all regions.

Author Contributions: Conceptualization, Y.M., K.W. and Y.L.; formal analysis, Y.M. and Y.L.; methodology, K.W.; writing—review and editing Y.M., K.W. and Y.L. All authors have read and agreed to the published version of the manuscript.

Funding: This research was funded by Fujian Innovation Strategy Joint Project: Research on the Integration Mechanism of Fujian High Tech Industry Innovation Chain and Industry Chain, grant number 2020R0143.

Institutional Review Board Statement: Not applicable.

Informed Consent Statement: Not applicable.

Data Availability Statement: All data comes from the statistical yearbook published by the government.

Conflicts of Interest: The authors declare that they have no conflict of interest.

Appendix A

Table A1. Weight of human capital dimension.

Year	Urban Population Density	Average Educational Level	Full-Time Equivalent of R & D Personnel	Year	Urban Population Density	Average Educational Level	Full-Time Equivalent of R & D Personnel
2018	0.311	0.295	0.394	2011	0.183	0.169	0.647
2017	0.285	0.288	0.428	2010	0.307	0.197	0.496
2016	0.175	0.160	0.665	2009	0.326	0.204	0.470
2015	0.458	0.222	0.320	2008	0.338	0.293	0.369
2014	0.364	0.219	0.417	2007	0.228	0.213	0.559
2013	0.177	0.152	0.670	2006	0.240	0.245	0.515
2012	0.389	0.307	0.304				

Table A2. Weight of material capital dimension.

Year	Internal Expenditure of R & D Funds	Financial Institutions Density	Year	Internal Expenditure of R & D Funds	Financial Institutions Density
2018	0.561	0.439	2011	0.644	0.356
2017	0.610	0.390	2010	0.531	0.469
2016	0.696	0.304	2009	0.695	0.305
2015	0.580	0.420	2008	0.770	0.230
2014	0.451	0.549	2007	0.508	0.492
2013	0.629	0.371	2006	0.595	0.405
2012	0.624	0.376			

Table A3. Weight of urban function dimension.

Year	Industrial Structure Evolution	Urban Road Area Per Capita	Year	Industrial Structure Evolution	Urban Road Area Per Capita
2018	0.680	0.320	2011	0.725	0.275
2017	0.715	0.285	2010	0.641	0.359
2016	0.737	0.263	2009	0.615	0.385
2015	0.771	0.229	2008	0.669	0.331
2014	0.800	0.200	2007	0.639	0.361
2013	0.777	0.223	2006	0.533	0.467
2012	0.748	0.252			

Table A4. Weight of government dimension.

Year	Proportion of Technology Expenditure	Green Coverage	Year	Proportion of Technology Expenditure	Green Coverage
2018	0.793	0.207	2011	0.767	0.233
2017	0.755	0.245	2010	0.865	0.135
2016	0.677	0.323	2009	0.743	0.257
2015	0.792	0.208	2008	0.660	0.340
2014	0.849	0.151	2007	0.854	0.146
2013	0.673	0.327	2006	0.750	0.250
2012	0.751	0.249			

References

1. Dolk, H.; Vrijheid, M. The impact of environmental pollution on congenital anomalies. *Br. Med. Bull.* **2003**, *68*, 25–45. [CrossRef]
2. Grönqvist, H.; Nilsson, J.P.; Robling, P.-O. Understanding How Low Levels of Early Lead Exposure Affect Children's Life Trajectories. *J. Polit. Econ.* **2020**, *128*, 3376–3433. [CrossRef]
3. Juan, B.; Ana, C.; Jean-Paul, V.; Omer, C.; Muriel, C. Protected areas in the Atlantic facing the hazards of micro-plastic pollution: First diagnosis of three islands in the Canary Current. *Mar. Pollut. Bull.* **2014**, *80*, 302–311.
4. Desforges, J.-P.W.; Galbraith, M.; Dangerfield, N.; Ross, P.S. Widespread distribution of microplastics in subsurface seawater in the NE Pacific Ocean. *Mar. Pollut. Bull.* **2014**, *79*, 94–99. [CrossRef]
5. Evangeliou, N.; Grythe, H.; Klimont, Z.; Heyes, C.; Eckhardt, S.; Lopez-Aparicio, S.; Stohl, A. Atmospheric transport is a major pathway of microplastics to remote regions. *Nat. Commun.* **2020**, *11*, 1–11. [CrossRef]
6. Olayinka, K.; Alo, B. Studies on Industrial Pollution in Nigeria: The effect of Textile effluents on the quality of Groundwater in some parts of Lagos. *Niger. J. Health Biomed. Sci.* **2004**, *3*, 44–50. [CrossRef]
7. Lloyd, O.L.; Smith, G.; Lloyd, M.M.; Holland, Y.; Gailey, F. Raised mortality from lung cancer and high sex ratios of births associated with industrial pollution. *Occup. Environ. Med.* **1985**, *42*, 475–480. [CrossRef]
8. Cameron, J.F. Radioisotope Techniques for Measurement and Control of Industrial Pollution. *Meas. Control* **1971**, *4*, 303–307. [CrossRef]
9. Ebiefung, A.A.; Udo, G. An industrial pollution emission control model. *Comput. Ind. Eng.* **1999**, *37*, 371–374. [CrossRef]
10. De Bruyn, S.; Bergh, J.V.D.; Opschoor, J. Economic growth and emissions: Reconsidering the empirical basis of environmental Kuznets curves. *Ecol. Econ.* **1998**, *25*, 161–175. [CrossRef]
11. Glaeser, E.L.; Kahn, M.E. The greenness of cities: Carbon dioxide emissions and urban development. *J. Urban Econ.* **2010**, *67*, 404–418. [CrossRef]
12. Cole, M.A. Trade, the pollution haven hypothesis and the environmental Kuznets curve: Examining the linkages. *Ecol. Econ.* **2004**, *48*, 71–81. [CrossRef]
13. Managi, S.; Hibiki, A.; Tsurumi, T. Does trade openness improve environmental quality? *J. Environ. Econ. Manag.* **2009**, *58*, 346–363. [CrossRef]
14. Ozturk, I.; Acaravci, A. The long-run and causal analysis of energy, growth, openness and financial development on carbon emissions in Turkey. *Energy Econ.* **2013**, *36*, 262–267. [CrossRef]
15. Su, Y.; Yu, Y.-Q. Spatial agglomeration of new energy industries on the performance of regional pollution control through spatial econometric analysis. *Sci. Total Environ.* **2020**, *704*, 135261. [CrossRef]
16. Zeng, D.Z.; Zhao, L. Pollution havens and industrial agglomeration. *J. Environ. Econ. Manag.* **2009**, *58*, 141–153. [CrossRef]
17. Han, L.; Kung, J.K.S. Fiscal incentives and policy choices of local governments: Evidence from China. *J. Dev. Econ.* **2015**, *116*, 89–104. [CrossRef]
18. Dean, J.M.; Lovely, M.E.; Wang, H. Are foreign investors attracted to weak environmental regulations? Evaluating the evidence from China. *J. Dev. Econ.* **2009**, *90*, 1–13. [CrossRef]
19. Zhu, C.; Lee, C.-C. The internal and external effects of air pollution on innovation in China. *Environ. Sci. Pollut. Res.* **2021**, *28*, 9462–9474. [CrossRef]
20. Ahn, S.J.; Yoon, H.Y. 'Green chasm' in clean-tech for air pollution: Patent evidence of a long innovation cycle and a technological level gap. *J. Clean. Prod.* **2020**, *272*, 122726. [CrossRef]
21. Omri, A.; Hadj, T.B. Foreign investment and air pollution: Do good governance and technological innovation matter? *Environ. Res.* **2020**, *185*, 109469. [CrossRef] [PubMed]
22. Ghosh, S. Examining carbon emissions economic growth nexus for India: A multivariate cointegration approach. *Energy Policy* **2010**, *38*, 3008–3014. [CrossRef]
23. Brunnermeier, S.B.; A Cohen, M. Determinants of environmental innovation in US manufacturing industries. *J. Environ. Econ. Manag.* **2003**, *45*, 278–293. [CrossRef]
24. Schumpeter, J.; Backhaus, U. *The Theory of Economic Development*; Springer: Boston, MA, USA, 2006; pp. 61–116.
25. Taylor, M.S.; Copeland, B.R. *Trade, Growth and the Environment*; NBER Working Paper; National Bureau of Economic Research: Cambridge, MA, USA, 2003; p. 9823.

26. Ji, X.; Wang, K.; Ji, T.; Zhang, Y.; Wang, K. Coupling Analysis of Urban Land Use Benefits: A Case Study of Xiamen City. *Land* **2020**, *9*, 155. [CrossRef]
27. Ji, Z.H.; Zhang, P. Spatial Difference and Driving Mechanism of Urban Land Use Efficiency Under the Environmental Constraints: Based on 285 Cities in China. *China Land Sci.* **2020**, *34*, 72–79. [CrossRef]
28. Huang, J.; Xue, D. Study on Temporal and Spatial Variation Characteristics and Influencing Factors of Land Use Efficiency in Xi'an, China. *Sustainability* **2019**, *11*, 6649. [CrossRef]
29. Yu, J.; Zhou, K.; Yang, S. Land use efficiency and influencing factors of urban agglomerations in China. *Land Use Policy* **2019**, *88*. [CrossRef]
30. Li, J.; Lewis, J.; Rowland, J.; Tappan, G.; Tieszen, L. Evaluation of land performance in Senegal using multi-temporal NDVI and rainfall series. *J. Arid. Environ.* **2004**, *59*, 463–480. [CrossRef]
31. Chen, C.-L. Establishing Urban Industrial Parks to Drive Regional Innovation System. *Int. J. Autom. Smart Technol.* **2012**, *2*, 283–286. [CrossRef]
32. Yun, W.; Zhu, D.; Tang, H. Reshaping and innovation of China land consolidation strategy. *Trans. Chin. Soc. Agric. Eng.* **2016**, *32*, 1–8.
33. Anselin, L. Spatial Effects in Econometric Practice in Environmental and Resource Economics. *Am. J. Agric. Econ.* **2001**, *83*, 705–710. [CrossRef]
34. Yu, X.; Shen, M.; Shen, W.; Zhang, X. Effects of Land Urbanization on Smog Pollution in China: Estimation of Spatial Autoregressive Panel Data Models. *Land* **2020**, *9*, 337. [CrossRef]
35. Romer, P.M. Increasing Returns and Long-Run Growth. *J. Polit. Econ.* **1986**, *94*, 1002–1037. [CrossRef]
36. Romer, P. Endogenous Technological Change. *J. Polit. Econ.* **1989**, *98*, 71–102. [CrossRef]
37. Motlagh, Z.K.; Lotfi, A.; Pourmanafi, S.; Ahmadizadeh, S.; Soffianian, A. Spatial modeling of land-use change in a rapidly urbanizing landscape in central Iran: Integration of remote sensing, CA-Markov, and landscape metrics. *Environ. Monit. Assess.* **2020**, *192*, 1–19. [CrossRef] [PubMed]
38. Tian, F.; Li, M.; Han, X.; Liu, H.; Mo, B. A Production–Living–Ecological Space Model for Land-Use Optimisation: A case study of the core Tumen River region in China. *Ecol. Model.* **2020**, *437*, 109310. [CrossRef]
39. Bottazzi, L.; Peri, G. Innovation and spillovers in regions: Evidence from European patent data. *Eur. Econ. Rev.* **2003**, *47*, 687–710. [CrossRef]
40. Tobler, W.R. A Computer Movie Simulating Urban Growth in the Detroit Region. *Econ. Geogr.* **1970**, *46*, 234. [CrossRef]
41. Jaffe, A.B. Real effects of academic research. *Am. Econ. Rev.* **1989**, *46*, 957–970.
42. Xu, D.; Shenkar, O. Note: Institutional Distance and the Multinational Enterprise. *Acad. Manag. Rev.* **2002**, *27*, 608–618. [CrossRef]
43. Conley, T.G.; Topa, G. Socio-economic distance and spatial patterns in unemployment. *J. Appl. Econ.* **2002**, *17*, 303–327. [CrossRef]
44. Pianta, M.; Archibugi, D. Innovation Surveys and Patents as Technology Indicators: The State of the Art. 1996. Available online: https://www.irpps.cnr.it/pubblicazioni/innovation-surveys-and-patents-as-technology-indicators-the-state-of-the-art/ (accessed on 22 March 2021).
45. Wang, L.M.; Wang, N. The Interactive Effects of Talent Agglomeration, Technological Innovation and High-quality Economic Growth: Empirical Analysis of VAR Model based on Provincial Panel Data. *J. Henan Norm. Univ.* **2021**, *48*, 88–94. [CrossRef]
46. Alberti, M. The Effects of Urban Patterns on Ecosystem Function. *Int. Reg. Sci. Rev.* **2005**, *28*, 168–192. [CrossRef]
47. Kuznets, S. Quantitative Aspects of the Economic Growth of Nations: II. Industrial Distribution of National Product and Labor Force. *Econ. Dev. Cult. Chang.* **1957**, *5*, 1–111. [CrossRef]
48. Kuznets, S. Modern economic growth: Findings and reflections. *Am. Econ. Rev.* **1973**, *63*, 247–258.
49. Zhang, S.G. Promoting financial reform and adjusting monetary policy in accordance with the requirements of Marketization. *J. Financ.* **1996**, *5*, 8–10.
50. Taylor, C.; Pollard, S.; Angus, A.; Rocks, S. Better by design: Rethinking interventions for better environmental regulation. *Sci. Total Environ.* **2013**, *447*, 488–499. [CrossRef]
51. Jorgenson, A.K. Foreign direct investment and the environment, the mitigating influence of institutional and civil society factors, and relationships between industrial pollution and human health: A panel study of less-developed countries. *Organ. Environ.* **2009**, *22*, 135–157. [CrossRef]
52. Wang, L.P.; Li, T.T.; Hu, Y.W. Economic Growth, Energy Structure and Industrial Pollution—Empirical Analysis Based on Spatial Panel Metering. *J. Ind. Technol. Econ.* **2016**, *8*, 3–11.
53. Mundlak, Y. On the Pooling of Time Series and Cross Section Data. *Econom. J. Econom. Soc.* **1978**, *46*, 69. [CrossRef]

land

Article

Research on the Peer Behavior of Local Government Green Governance Based on SECI Expansion Model

Hongda Liu, Pinbo Yao, Xiaoxia Wang, Jialiang Huang and Liying Yu *

School of Management, Shanghai University, Shanghai 200444, China; liuhoda@shu.edu.cn (H.L.); yaopinbo@shu.edu.cn (P.Y.); charmian@shu.edu.cn (X.W.); HuangJL@shu.edu.cn (J.H.)
* Correspondence: yuliying@shu.edu.cn

Abstract: Exploring the cohort behavior of local governments in green governance from the perspective of knowledge management can help promote the implementation of new development concepts. This article firstly explains the differentiation logic of local governments' green governance cohort behavior based on the SECI expansion model. Secondly, by constructing a dynamic evolutionary game model, the conditions for the formation of positive and negative cohorts are analyzed. Finally, corresponding countermeasures are proposed. The results show that under the effect of knowledge management, the explicit and tacit knowledge, such as green governance ability and willingness of local government transform into each other, finally differentiates into four kinds of peer behavior states. Willingness stimulation, learning effect perception, complementary knowledge stock, knowledge synergy income, cooperation value-added income, punishment and reputation loss increase, which promotes local government green governance into a positive-peer state. Knowledge learning effect only exists in the early and middle stages of green governance, while the knowledge spillover effect has a more significant impact in the later stage of green governance; a higher gap between explicit knowledge and tacit knowledge, and a lower level of tacit knowledge and explicit knowledge, are conducive to the formation of positive-peer status.

Keywords: SECI expansion model; local government; green governance; peer behavior; green development

Citation: Liu, H.; Yao, P.; Wang, X.; Huang, J.; Yu, L. Research on the Peer Behavior of Local Government Green Governance Based on SECI Expansion Model. *Land* **2021**, *10*, 472. https://doi.org/10.3390/land10050472

Academic Editors: Maciej J. Nowak, Giancarlo Cotella and Przemysław Śleszyński

Received: 19 March 2021
Accepted: 28 April 2021
Published: 1 May 2021

1. Introduction

Implementing the 'new development concept' is the key to the high-quality development of China's economy [1]. With the increasing downward pressure on China's economy and the gradual emergence of ecological adverse effects, the extensive economic growth mode is challenging to meet the requirements of China's high-quality economic transformation, and green governance has become a meaningful way to solve the problem of green development [2]. Green governance is a community of green governance based on the principles of mutual trust and mutual reliance and sharing, guided by the concept of green development, to cooperate and govern public affairs. In order to achieve a harmonious and sustainable governance process of economy, politics, society, culture, and ecology, the grassroots government is the core subject of green governance [3–6]. However, green governance has many characteristics, such as thorny subjects and broad fields, which require the effective promotion of government subjects [7]. Based on such a realistic background, the research of green governance based on the level of local government will help implement top-level design into the practical level and provide reference ideas for standardizing local government behavior and realizing scientific and rational decision-making.

The green governance work of local government has gradually deepened from a point to an area. At the beginning of the 13th five-year plan, the development concept of innovation, coordination, green, open, and sharing laid the thinking and focus of China's future development. It solved the problems of regional ecosystem degradation and low-quality economic development to a great extent. Green governance has become a vital integration practice of the new development concept [8]. The demonstration experience of ecological and green integration development in the Yangtze River Delta shows that green governance is the critical measure for building a modern economic system, optimizing the economic structure and transforming the development mode and power. The realization of efficient green governance will win significant opportunities for the region to seize future development opportunities [9]. In the middle and late period of the 13th five-year plan, successful attempts in some areas have made green governance a tool to promote backward area economic development to 'overtake' and improve quality and efficiency. Local governments show prominent characteristics of 'mutual competition' and 'mutual observation', which leads to the formation of green governance peer behavior [10]. Nevertheless, there is an economic question implied here: Why do local governments have assertive peer behavior in green governance? There are two main reasons: first, under the premise of the central government's strong emphasis on the 'new development concept', local governments have less room for decision-making, so peer behavior is more pronounced. Secondly, under the role of 'scale competition', the local government's individual behavior is more affected by group behavior. The successful cases of green governance significantly 'intervene' in the decision-making of local government behavior. Therefore, the local government's peer behavior in green governance is stronger than the convergence of previous decision-making, and its motivation and evolution logic are more worthy of attention and discussion. In particular, green governance cannot be achieved overnight. Blind conglomeration and perceptual decision-making may cause more economic losses to local governments, which is incomparable with the previous government management peer behavior. In view of this, this paper intends to build a systematic analysis framework, use knowledge management theory to analyze the logic of local government green governance, and put forward the peer effect and different peer types. Finally, based on the evolutionary game model, this paper clarifies the impact of knowledge management on the green governance peer behavior of the local government, promotes the local government's reasonable peer behavior, and enhances the peer effect.

2. Theoretical Analysis

2.1. Formation Logic of Peer Behavior of Green Governance

After the reform of the tax-sharing system, China's economic development entered a new era. Local governments now undertake more social responsibilities while fulfilling their economic construction responsibilities. Protecting the interests of the jurisdiction and realizing the balance of power and responsibility have become the local governments' action logic. Under the guidance of this action logic, the dynamic mechanism of social operation has become the critical element of effective, healthy, and sustainable management action of local governments [11]. Local governments achieve orderly and efficient social management through the external core links of power source development, power conversion, power distribution, power feedback, and other mechanisms [12]. As the local government's dynamic response to comprehensively deepen reform and optimize governance capability, green governance has a robust local government distinctive brand. Green governance exists in the form of system design and is regarded as a combination of 'package' behavior and capability [13]. Under the social operation dynamic mechanism, green governance takes the local government as the main body and the construction of regional ecological civilization environment as the power source. Based on the extension of 'package' behavior and ability and the integration or exclusion of the interest demands of various subjects, it forms the dynamic mechanism operation field of gravitation, thrust, resistance, and pressure [11].

Through the guidance of four force fields of gravitation, thrust, resistance, and pressure, local governments gradually form the cooperative or autonomous social operation dynamic mechanism of green governance. The action's feedback is characterized by cooperative or autonomous governance action. Based on the evolutionary stability of cooperative or autonomous governance action, green governance peer behavior is formed. From the perspective of gravity, the common interests of local governments lead the two sides to strengthen the cooperation relationship, and the increase of cooperation income leads to the strengthening of the green governance cooperation dynamic mechanism [14]. Unlike the endogenous gravitation caused by internal interests, the thrust comes more from the external environment of green governance. On the one hand, the guidance of macro value and the implementation of the top-level system bring great guidance to the practice of green governance. It ensures the development of green governance through the mechanism of error correction and fault tolerance [15,16]. On the other hand, with the promotion of the green governance culture system, the participation of green governance subjects and the flow of various elements break the resource and administrative barriers of green governance among governments and promote the stability of the green governance cooperation dynamic mechanism [17,18]. As the key field of the formation of the green governance cooperation dynamic mechanism, gravity and thrust are a positive force. However, due to the differences in the basis of green governance and the contradictions in the distribution of government benefits, the characteristics of the 'rational economic man' of local governments are increasingly obvious. The resistance conflict between the maximization of local interests and cooperative benefits is becoming more and more acute [11]. Simultaneously, the differentiation of co-construction, co-governance, and sharing of green governance is serious, and the independent dynamic mechanism of local government green governance gradually dominates the government management behavior [19]. This kind of governance resistance becomes the reverse force of the formation of the green governance cooperation dynamic mechanism. Whether it is to protect the interests of the jurisdiction optimization or out of rational decision-making, local governments need to promote green governance. However, there is a practical problem: the real change brought by green governance is not yet expected, but the local government has been burdened with higher governance pressure. On the one hand, this kind of pressure makes the local governments choose to follow other districts' management modes, trying to share the pressure and reduce the difficulty of decision-making. On the other hand, it causes some local officials to make narrow decisions, compressing the production cycle of governance achievements with expansionary governance to realize subversive development. Pressure causes local government green governance to be more competitive and observant, tends to form a cooperative dynamic mechanism of green governance, or reverses and solidifies the independent dynamic mechanism of green governance, which is reflected as an uncertain force. The action mechanism of each force field is shown in Figure 1.

With the shaping of the four force fields and the stability of local government's cooperation or autonomous governance, local government's green governance presents the peer behavior. That is to say, local governments with similar geographical location, decision-making, and institutional environments form defensive administrative concepts, learn from each other or imitate each other in the process of green governance, and become a 'peer' collective.

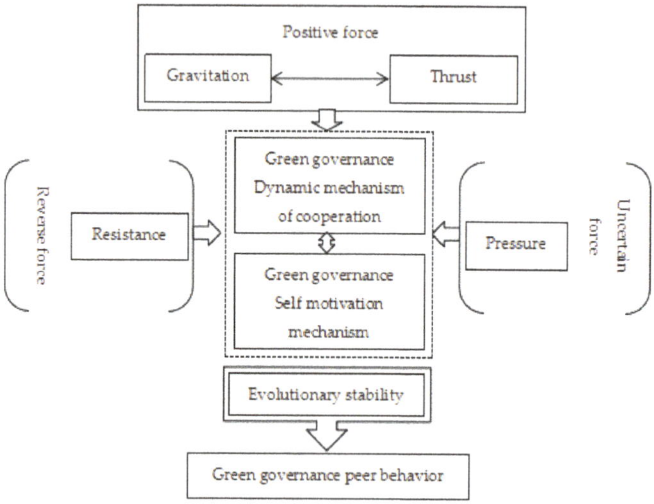

Figure 1. Logic diagram of the formation of the same peer behavior of green governance.

2.2. The Necessity of Knowledge Management in Green Governance

As a kind of management activity, the green governance of the local government needs substantial knowledge to assist in ensuring correct and effective decision-making. Scholars are concerned about the role of knowledge management in improving government work efficiency, and the research focuses on knowledge transfer and knowledge absorption and application [20]. Bonaccorsi [21] found that knowledge transfer has a positive effect on government—industry-university-research collaboration, and the process of knowledge transfer across organizations is the process of the government leading the industry-university-research collaboration. Koschatzky [22] tested the dynamic relationship between the knowledge transfer model and government collaborative innovation performance. He believes that the active transfer of knowledge, the coordination of objectives, and the correct transfer mode's determination will help improve the innovation output of collaborative organizations. Sun [23] discussed the path of knowledge heterogeneity and absorptive capacity on organizational performance from the perspective of organizational connection strength and believed that no matter what state the organization is in, it will accept heterogeneous knowledge resources. Horvat [24] used the knowledge absorption model to establish the corresponding index system, analyzed the coupling coordination of external knowledge absorption and utilization by government organizations, and emphasized knowledge acceptance. After the knowledge chain construction of knowledge transfer (output), knowledge absorption (input), and knowledge application (practice output) is completed, the expansion of sharing background further extends the knowledge chain and opens up the link of knowledge sharing [25] (input-output collaboration). Further integration of social attributes promotes the birth of a collaborative development knowledge sharing model [26], reducing the loss and capital cost in the process of knowledge transfer. Ahmed and Zhang analyzed the dilemma of knowledge sharing from social media [27] and alliance networks [28], respectively, and affirmed the positive contribution of knowledge sharing with alliance building. He emphasized the problem of knowledge embezzlement and unequal distribution of performance within the group and believed that the critical collaboration and breakthrough of knowledge is conducive to the stable development of the government collaborative development network.

To be sure, knowledge management not only promotes the scientific green governance of local governments but also promotes the formation of a government-led green governance collaborative system. However, there are many problems in the collaborative system: many organizations use the chain of knowledge transfer and knowledge sharing to carry out free riding actions [29] and conceal their destructive behaviors. On the one hand, enterprises use the collaborative system to reduce decision-making costs [30] and show their social decision-making as a positive transformation, but in fact they are not separate from the sequence of inefficient innovation and ineffective decision-making. On the other hand, with the enhancement of local government autonomy and self-interest, the conflicts of interests among regions and institutional environments pose challenges to green governance. Many local governments choose their behaviors to keep consistent with 'successful groups'. Therefore, although the green governance under this collaborative system reflects regional enterprises' collaborative development, it inevitably causes problems such as repeated construction and collective irrationality [31]. Although it has increased green social performance to a certain extent, negative-peer effects gradually emerge in areas with a poor institutional environment and weak innovation foundation [32]. Given the homogenization, inefficiency, and irrationality of local government's green governance, it is necessary to investigate the evolutionary logic of local government's green governance peer behavior from the perspective of knowledge management and explore how to use knowledge management to improve local government's green governance and enhance the decision-making efficiency of local government's peer behavior.

3. The Differentiation Logic of Green Governance Peer Behavior Based on Knowledge Management

3.1. *Local Governments and Their Green Governance Responsibilities*

From the perspective of heterogeneous government, this paper divides the local government into two types: focus local government (referred to as 'focus government') and non-focus local government (referred to as 'non-focus government') [33,34]. The focus government refers to the key actors and essential leaders in the development of regional linkage; non-focus government refers to the main participants with follow-up in regional linkage development. In Chinese practice, focus government is a local government with a high degree of regional development, a high level of central government attention, and a more prominent government capacity. Non-focus governments are local governments where regional development is relatively backward and government capacity is more limited. Focus and non-focus governments basically cover the main types of government in a metropolitan area or economic zone. In the Yangtze River Economic Belt, for example, the focus governments of Shanghai, Jiangsu, and Zhejiang have become the development leaders in the economic belt, while the non-focus governments of Yunnan, Guizhou, and Jiangxi generally undertake tasks such as industrial transfer and are in a state of development following.

As a significant project and action direction of local government development and transformation, green governance tends to be a kind of instrumental behavior and contains value [35]. This concept is embodied in the concept of 'green' and 'sustainable' development and tries to promote the society to form a 'green' development value orientation. Due to the high threshold of green development and the difficulty of implementation, local government governance behavior's 'instrumental' characteristics are strengthened. For example, the local government improved the corresponding democratic decision-making, administrative approval, social supervision, and other links and tried to support society in carrying out green transformation with more relaxed policies and softer ways.

3.2. *Mechanism of Knowledge Management on Green Governance of Local Government*

3.2.1. Knowledge Management Promotes Green Governance Peer Behavior

Due to the liquidity of knowledge, local governments are connected through the knowledge chain. In the process of the knowledge chain transmitting knowledge (knowledge transfer, knowledge absorption, and knowledge application), local governments' behaviors and ideas influence and act on each other. The feedback is characterized by the changes of the four major fields of dynamic social mechanism. From the perspective of gravity, there is a significant gap in economic and political resource endowment among local governments, which leads to differences in willingness and ability of green governance [11]. Through the moderating role of knowledge management, we can guide the matching orientation of green governance's will and ability, amplifying or reducing the gravitational effect and determining whether green governance is in the state of cooperation or autonomous dynamic mechanism. In the thrust field, the local government's external ability is limited, the system normative and rigid binding force are not strong, and the management efficiency and sustainable role are limited [11]. The moderating effect of knowledge management can guide the direction of explicit knowledge such as local government management ability, that is, enlarge or reduce the thrust effect and determine the final state of local government green governance. In the pressure field, local governments will be subject to the severe pressure of the central government's 'hierarchical pressure and key focus' institutional structure, resulting in the low willingness of green governance [11]. Moreover, the effective period of green governance is long, which may produce potential internal pressure on governance activities. The moderating effect of knowledge management can guide the direction of tacit knowledge such as local government's management intention, that is, amplify or reduce the pressure effect and ultimately affect the evolution and stability of green governance. As far as resistance is concerned, knowledge management's effectiveness will have an impact on the benefits of green governance of local governments. Through the dynamic balance between cooperative benefits and independent benefits of green governance, the leading dynamic mechanism of green governance is determined by amplifying or reducing the role of resistance. Therefore, knowledge management determines the trend of green governance peer behavior through the platform of four major fields.

3.2.2. Knowledge Management Content of Green Governance

In reality, in the face of mobile green development boundaries and diversified green governance demands, many local governments find it difficult to consider the unity of behavior idea and are forced by 'pressure cognition' and 'responsibility cognition' [36], leading to the conglomeration of green governance. In fact, the imbalance of local government's behavior idea is more manifested in the lack of knowledge management. As an essential means to promote the green governance of local governments, knowledge management undertakes the critical task of clarifying local government behavior and planning governance concepts. To some extent, the behavior and idea of local government is essentially a kind of knowledge resource. In green governance, some local governments' behaviors to society are presented in explicit forms such as policy planning and procedures, which is a kind of explicit knowledge. In contrast, local governments' ideas are presented in implicit forms such as management experience, willingness to green development, and value orientation, which are kinds of tacit knowledge. The local government's management of the two kinds of knowledge reflects its willingness and ability for green governance.

At present, the most classic knowledge transformation model in academia is the SECI model proposed by Nonaka, which contains four models for the mutual transformation of tacit knowledge and explicit knowledge. Most scholars at home and abroad have extended and expanded on this basis when doing relevant research in the field of knowledge management [37–40]. The SECI model can better explain the operation of knowledge [41], and the IDE-SECI extension model [42] can reflect the dynamic transformation process of internal and external knowledge in an organization. With this model's help, this paper describes the local government's knowledge management and explains the role of knowledge management in promoting green governance peer behavior. Generally speaking, knowledge is divided into four stages: socialization (S), externalization (E), combination (C), and internalization (I) [43].

In green governance, there is a knowledge collaborative transformation relationship among local governments, as shown in Figure 2. Knowledge can be divided into internal knowledge and external knowledge. Internal knowledge is the explicit and tacit knowledge of local governments, while external knowledge is the explicit and tacit knowledge of other local governments. The hidden knowledge reflects the concept of green governance of local government, including the attitude and attention to green governance. Explicit knowledge reflects the green governance behavior of the local government, including policy planning, management experience, technology orientation, human resources allocation ability, etc. The internal knowledge follows the IDE-SECI transformation mode. The four stages of knowledge circulation connect the knowledge interaction activities between local governments and enterprises within their jurisdiction, laying the foundation for the internal and external transformation of knowledge.

In the internal and external transformation of knowledge, there are two main types of local governments: social transformation and combinatorial transformation.

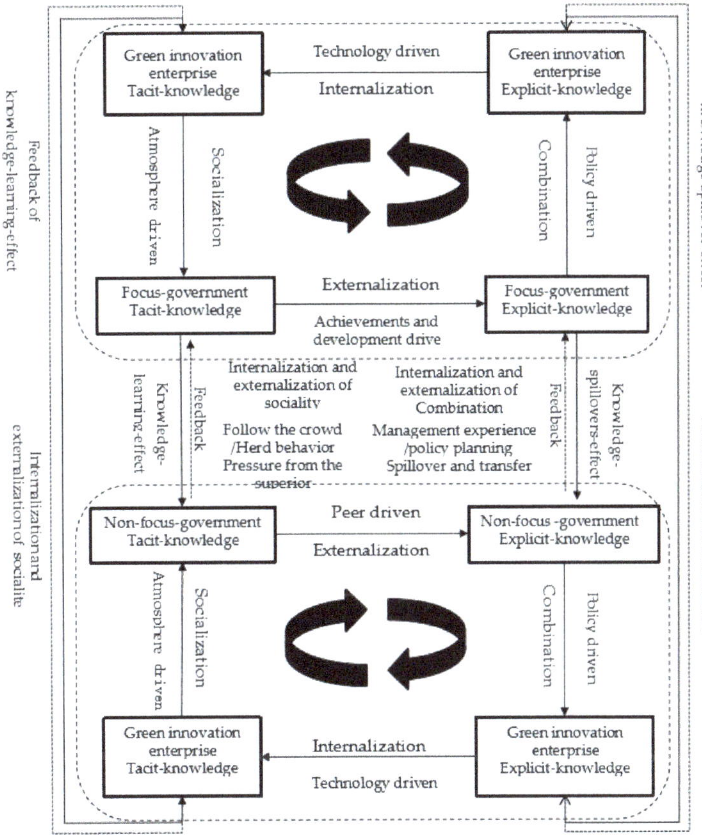

Figure 2. IDE-SECI simplified model of green governance peer behavior.

Social Transformation: Taking the non-focus government as an example, its green governance will be affected by the focus government. Non-focus governments often follow the focus government's development strategy, which is essentially the result of the tacit knowledge function of emotion and willingness [44]. This is defined as the relatively low organizational knowledge level and the relatively high level of organizational learning [45]. For the focus government, the output process of tacit knowledge is the social externalization of knowledge, which shows the 'low latitude' mobility of knowledge. In the process of knowledge output from focus government to non-focus government, the difference of governments' 'knowledge pool' will lead to feedback from the non-focus government to the focus government. In local development, there are leading or superior departments in non-focus government, which will produce crisis or stimulation to focus government and guide the focus government to strengthen green promotion willingness in weak departments. This process is social externalization of non-focus government knowledge. In Chinese practice, social transformation includes realistic forms such as regional government research missions and government exchange meetings. Based on these platform activities, local governments interoperate to achieve the will for green governance.

Combinatorial transformation: Non-focus government has some problems, such as lack of management experience, imperfect government systems, etc. Due to the knowledge spillover effect, the focus government will guide the non-focus government to supplement the explicit knowledge of green governance through industrial transfer, assistance, and docking, and will promote the development of regional green integration as the 'leader of the economic belt.' This knowledge flow process is the combined internalization of non-focus government knowledge [31]. In the process of capacity spillover, the non-focus government will also give feedback to complementary knowledge to make up for some deficiencies of the focus government and to realize the combined externalization of knowledge [24]. In Chinese practice, the combined transformation includes the signing of regional specific policies, the establishment of cooperation parks, the construction of green high-tech interoperable development zones, and other realistic forms. Through these opportunities for cooperation, local governments are able to interact with each other to achieve green governance capacity.

When the green governance cooperation dynamic mechanism is formed among local governments under the joint action of social transformation and combinatorial transformation, the knowledge learning effect and knowledge spillover effect promote local governments to build green governance collaborative networks and form knowledge synergy effects. In the interactive process of the knowledge synergy effect, local governments further obtain the reciprocal effect of knowledge. The knowledge learning effect, knowledge spillover effect, knowledge synergy effect, and knowledge reciprocity effect constitute the cooperative benefits of local government green governance and promote the stable development of cooperative governance.

3.2.3. Differentiation Process of Green Governance Conglomeration Behavior under Knowledge Management

In green governance, the focus government and non-focus government, through the relationship of social transformation and combinatorial transformation of knowledge given by knowledge management, form the knowledge learning effect, knowledge spillover effect, knowledge synergy effect and knowledge reciprocity effect based on the stages of internalization of external knowledge, externalization of internal knowledge, and internal knowledge transformation. Based on the moderating effect of knowledge management, all kinds of knowledge effects adjust the level of explicit and tacit knowledge of local governments, which are characterized by the change of four major fields of dynamic social mechanism. Under the comprehensive action of gravity, thrust, pressure, and resistance, local governments eventually form green governance cooperation or autonomous power mechanisms and produce two strategies of cooperative governance or autonomous governance. Among them, the strategy of independent governance means that the subject is affected by resistance and refuses to transform knowledge in order to maintain the local 'rational interests'; the strategy of cooperative governance means that the subject is affected by gravity and thrust and chooses to transform knowledge and obtain the benefits of the knowledge effect. Due to the differences between focus government and non-focus government, focus government usually actively leads non-focus government to transform knowledge in cooperative governance. Non-focus governments generally take an active part in knowledge transformation, and both sides realize knowledge flow and change their own explicit and tacit knowledge level. The formation of cooperative or autonomous governance strategies stems from the specific practices of different countries. Based on the analysis of the literature, it is evident that the United States is a country with a federal government where local governments have more power and are less influenced by the dynamics of social operations, which in turn can lead to autonomous dynamics [46–48]. In developed countries such as Europe, where the central government power is more centralized and more influenced by the dynamics of social operations, local governments tend to adopt more cooperative governance strategies [49–51]. In developing countries such as India, Brazil, the Philippines, and Malaysia, government power appears to be centralized but is actually relatively decentralized, with weak governance capacity in both central and local governments in green governance activities [52–55]. On the basis of the above research, this paper uses the Chinese government's green governance experience as a reference to analyze four cohort states formed by focus and non-focus governments based on the combination of governance strategies and the role of pressure fields.

- In the negative-peer state, both parties choose the self-governance strategy. Due to the development ladder, the interaction between the two sides is not strong, while independent governance can retain local characteristics. In this state, both sides' knowledge is only transformed by the internal knowledge chain, and the green development gap is further expanded due to the difference in the knowledge base.
- In the reverse-peer state, the focus government chooses the active leadership strategy, while the non-focus government keeps the independent governance strategy. Due to the high willingness of the focus government, they hope to promote the flow of green governance knowledge and promote green governance of non-focus government. However, due to the lack of initiative and low level of willingness, non-focus governments generally maintain the state of autonomous governance. In this state, the focus government 'follows' the non-focus government's green governance, and the decision-making is in the opposite direction.
- In the positive-peer state, the focus government chooses the active leadership strategy, and the non-focus government chooses the active participation strategy. Because of both sides' complementary ability and willingness, through cooperative governance they can use the knowledge learning effect, knowledge spillover effect, knowledge synergy effect, and knowledge reciprocity effect to improve their abilities or wishes. In this state, the gap of green development is gradually narrowing.
- In the consistent-direction peer status, the focus government chooses the strategy of self-governance, and the non-focus government chooses the strategy of active participation. Because of the low willingness level of some focus governments, they choose independent governance to keep the competitive advantage of the jurisdiction and avoid the risk of cooperation. The non-focus government is willing to seek cooperative governance to realize the internal and external transformation of knowledge. In this state, the non-focus government 'catches up' the focus government's green governance, and the decision-making is in a positive direction. It is worth noting that due to the existence of a basic gap, non-focus government will continue to 'fall behind,' and regional green development differentiation may exist.

The generation of all kinds of green governance peer behavior, the realization of peer behavior adapting to the regional environment, and the generation of peer benefits need knowledge management regulation (as shown in Figure 3). The specific embodiment is as follows: first, the level of green governance ability and willingness of various local governments must be adjusted to make them enter the appropriate group state; secondly, all kinds of the same group state must be guided to the positive-peer state to produce the peer effect.

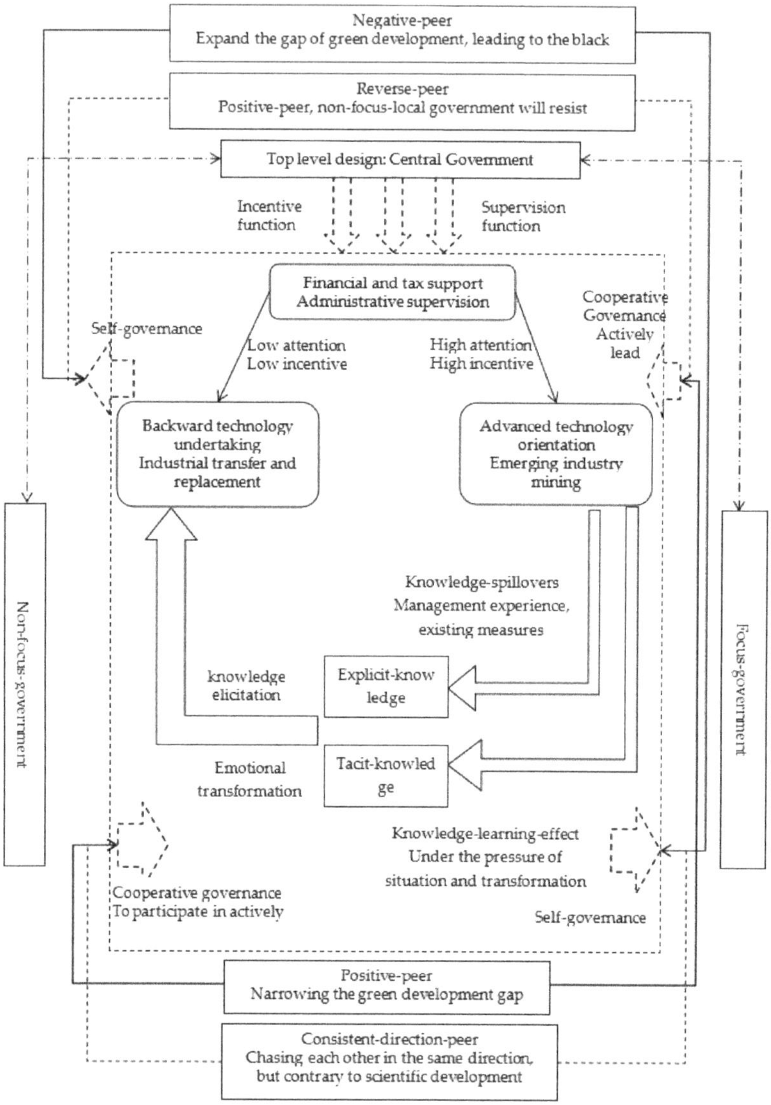

Figure 3. Relationship between green governance and peer behavior.

4. Evolutionary Game Model of Green Governance Peer Behavior of Local Government

Under the effect of knowledge management, explicit knowledge, and tacit knowledge, such as green governance ability and willingness, focus governments and non-focus governments are transformed into each other. Because of the interest and the necessity of green governance, the two sides have generated a game relationship of green governance in the collaborative knowledge transformation. Among them, the focus government and non-focus government have two strategies of cooperative governance and autonomous governance, respectively. According to the direction of decision-making and the effect of strategy, they form four conglomeration states: positive-peer (cooperation cooperation), negative-peer (autonomy autonomy), consistent-direction-peer (autonomy cooperation), and reverse-peer (cooperation autonomy). As a stable result of the evolutionary game of local government's green governance, peer state is essentially the result of knowledge management regulation on the level of local government's explicit and tacit knowledge. It is also the degree of influence of various knowledge effects on local government's cooperation or autonomous strategy in the stages of internalization of external knowledge, externalization of internal knowledge, and transformation of internal knowledge.

This paper constructs the evolutionary game model and analyzes the ultimate stability strategy of the green governance peer behavior of local government, namely, the final peer state. This paper discusses the influence of each knowledge effect on the stable strategy in each stage of knowledge management and identifies the key factors contributing to the formation of the knowledge effect. On this basis, considering that the goal of knowledge management regulation is the level of explicit and tacit knowledge of local government, the difference of the explicit and tacit knowledge level is related to the same group state. Therefore, numerical evolution and simulation analysis have studied the influence of the local government's explicit and tacit knowledge level on the final peer state. By analyzing the evolutionary stability and the influence of various factors on the peer state, the evolution trend of green governance peer behavior of local government is intuitively displayed and depicted, which provides theoretical guidance for guiding and controlling peer behavior and forming a positive-peer state.

4.1. Basic Assumptions

According to the game relationship between the focus government and the non-focus government in green governance, the following assumptions are put forward:

- The focus government adopts two strategies: 'actively leading' or 'autonomous governance'. The probability of choosing 'active leadership' is x, and the probability of 'independent governance' is $1-x$. There are two green governance strategies of non-focus government: 'active participation' and 'autonomous governance', the probability of 'active participation' is y, and the probability of 'autonomous governance' is $1-y$.
- Both 'social internalization' and 'combinatorial internalization' are the internalization process of external knowledge, and also the process of knowledge appreciation and coordination [56]. The abstract reflection is the influence of the knowledge learning effect and knowledge spillover effect on the behavior of the subject.

a. In the knowledge learning effect, the green governance willingness level (tacit knowledge level) of focus government and non-focus government is E_1 and E_2, respectively. The reality is characterized by internal meetings of local governments on green communication, media campaigns on green governance, etc. When they transform knowledge, they are influenced by each other's will. The incentive coefficients of focus government and non-focus government are a_1 and a_2, respectively. Indicates the frequency and acceptance of interaction between the parties in reality. Due to the knowledge base gap, non-focus government needs to effectively perceive tacit knowledge in the process of 'learning' from the focus government, so the perception coefficient of the learning effect of non-focus government is set as c.

b. In the knowledge spillover effect, the knowledge stock (explicit knowledge level) of green governance of focus government and non-focus government is K_1 and K_2, respectively. The reality is characterized by green summary reports and green experiences of local governments. When the two sides interact with each other, they absorb the spillover part of the management experience (government management ability, planning arrangement, etc.) to acquire the other side's knowledge. The knowledge spillover effect among subjects is affected by the proportion of complementary knowledge among subjects, the degree of knowledge protection, the ability of autonomous learning, and the ability of transformation and landing [57]. It is assumed that the proportion of complementary knowledge between focus government and non-focus government is α_1 and α_2, the degree of knowledge protection is β_1 and β_2, the coefficient of autonomous learning ability is λ_1 and λ_2, and the ability of knowledge transformation is θ_1 and θ_2.

c. Under the influence of the knowledge learning effect and knowledge spillover effect, focus government and non-focus government construct the knowledge collaborative network of green governance, forming the knowledge collaborative effect. Let h and i be the elasticity coefficients of complementary knowledge stock shared by focus government and non-focus government, respectively, and $h + i = 1$. The perceived relationship of trust between the two sides will affect the knowledge synergy effect. The learning effect perception coefficient c reflects the perception relationship. The knowledge synergy effect benefit created by the focus government and the non-focus government is $c(\alpha_1 K_1)^h(\alpha_2 K_2)^i$. In the repeated game of knowledge coordination, the focus government and non-focus government will also be affected by the knowledge reciprocity effect [58]. The open part of the knowledge system realizes the cooperative value added to the original knowledge system through knowledge interaction. Assuming that ξ is the cooperative value-added coefficient, the reciprocal effect of knowledge is inversely proportional to the degree of knowledge protection.

Based on the second hypothesis, we get that the benefits of the knowledge learning effect of the focus government and non-focus government are $E_2 a_1$ and $E_1(a_2 + c)$, respectively. The return of the knowledge spillover effect income is $K_2\alpha_2(1 - \beta_2)\lambda_1 K_1\theta_1$ and $K_1\alpha_1(1 - \beta_1)\lambda_2 K_2\theta_2$. Because of the difference of regional foundation and the knowledge synergy effect input, the income of the knowledge synergy effect is not evenly distributed but determined by the proportion of knowledge synergy effect income distribution z_1 and z_2. Therefore, the income of the focus government and non-focus government through the knowledge synergy effect is $z_1 c(\alpha_1 K_1)^h(\alpha_2 K_2)^i$ and $z_2 c(\alpha_1 K_1)^h(\alpha_2 K_2)^i$, respectively. In the knowledge reciprocity effect, the focus government and non-focus government obtain value-added benefits, which are $K_1(1 - \beta_1)\xi$ and $K_2(1 - \beta_2)\xi$, respectively.

- 'Social externalization' and 'combinatorial externalization' are both internal knowledge externalization processes. In the process of knowledge external transfer, each subject has to bear the corresponding expenditure costs, mainly including emotional willingness expenditure, the loss of private value of knowledge, and the use cost of knowledge platform. In the process of social externalized tacit knowledge transfer, there are activity expenses such as collaborative docking and negotiation, assuming that the tacit knowledge expenditure coefficients of focus government and non-focus government are m_1 and m_2, respectively. Therefore, the cost of each knowledge learning effect is $m_1 E_1$ and $m_2 E_2$. In the explicit knowledge transfer of combinatorial externalization, the private value of knowledge of all governments is impaired, and the management experience, policy guidance, and other activities need to rely on effective channels or places. The higher the occupation rate of knowledge transformation platform, the higher the cost of human and material resources. Assuming that the value coefficient of explicit knowledge of the focus government and non-focus government is b_1 and b_2, respectively, and the occupancy rate of knowledge transformation platform is d_1 and d_2, respectively, the cost of the knowledge spillover effect is $K_1(b_1 + d_1)$ and $K_2(b_2 + d_2)$, respectively. In the knowledge synergy effect, in order to build a knowledge collaborative network, the focus government and non-focus government bear the cooperation costs of $n_1\alpha_1 K_1$ and $n_2\alpha_2 K_2$, respectively, and n_1 and n_2 are the respective cooperation cost coefficients.
- In self-governance, knowledge is only transformed internally. At this time, the focus government and non-focus government rely on their own explicit and tacit knowledge to form internal knowledge income $(K_1 + E_1)R_1$ and $(K_2 + E_2)R_2$, where R_1 and R_2 are fixed income coefficients. There are differences in the development basis between focus government and non-focus government, and their own governance will further expand the green development gap: $R_1 > R_2$. At the same time, the focus government and the non-focus government rely on the ability of self-learning and knowledge transformation, tap the potential knowledge benefits, and can obtain the knowledge

value-added benefits of self-governance: $\Delta K_1\lambda_1\theta_1$, $\Delta K_2\lambda_2\theta_2$, where ΔK_1, ΔK_2 are the knowledge increments obtained by both sides through focused learning. Because of the idle spillover knowledge resources and knowledge closure, the focus government and non-focus government will lose the opportunity of spillover knowledge: $K_1(1-\beta_1)\gamma_{11}$, $K_2(1-\beta_2)\gamma_{21}$. γ_{11}. γ_{21} is the opportunity loss coefficient of the focus government and non-focus government, respectively. The focus government and the non-focus government are punished for the loss of knowledge protection: $K_1\beta_1\gamma_{12}$ and $K_2\beta_2\gamma_{22}$. γ_{12} and γ_{22} are the penalty coefficients of knowledge protection for the focus government and non-focus government, respectively.

- There are external constraints in knowledge management. When the focus government actively leads and the non-focus government actively participates in green governance, the central government will give corresponding incentive support R_{g1} and R_{g2}. The central government tries its best to promote the integration of regional green development. When the non-focus government has the will to actively participate and the focus government governs independently, it will give the focus government F punishment. The focus government will eliminate the backward industries to the non-focus government, so the focus government will get the industry elimination income G_1, and the non-focus government will get the industry transfer income G_2. Considering the lack of the initial development ability of the non-focus government, when the focus government actively leads and the non-focus government governs independently, the central government will not punish the non-focus government temporarily. Any party who refuses to cooperate in governance will suffer credit loss T.

4.2. Payment Matrix and Dynamic Equation of Replication

When the focus government and non-focus government are positive peers, the corresponding strategy combination is active leadership and active participation. Each subject realizes the internal and external transformation of knowledge, keeps the internal knowledge benefits, and undertakes the cost of the knowledge learning effect, knowledge spillover effect and knowledge spillover effect. Each subject obtains the benefits of the knowledge learning effect, knowledge spillover effect, knowledge synergy effect, knowledge reciprocity effect, and the incentive support given by the central government. In the case of negative peers corresponding to the combination of strategies of autonomous governance and autonomous governance, knowledge only transforms internally. Each subject undertakes the opportunity to lose spillover knowledge and the penalty loss of knowledge protection, gains internal knowledge benefits, and gains value-added benefits through self-governance. In the case of consistent direction peers, the strategy combination is autonomous governance and active participation. The focus government bears the loss of knowledge opportunity and knowledge protection punishment and suffers from external punishment and reputation loss, but gains internal knowledge income, value-added income, and industry elimination income. At this time, the non-focus government bears the cost of the knowledge learning effect and knowledge spillover effect. Because the cooperative relationship cannot be constructed, it can only obtain internal knowledge benefits, industrial transfer benefits, and the central government's incentive. In the case of reverse peers, the corresponding strategy combination is active leadership and autonomous governance. The focus government bears the cost of knowledge learning and spillover. Because of the blocking of knowledge transformation, they only gain internal knowledge benefits and incentive benefits. The non-focus government loses the knowledge opportunity income and bears the punishment of knowledge protection and faces the reputation loss but gains the internal knowledge income and value-added income.

According to the above assumptions and the profit and loss analysis, the payment matrix of the game is obtained, as shown in Table 1.

Table 1. Payment matrix of the game between the Non-focus government and non-focus government.

		Non-Focus-Government Active Participation	Autonomous Governance
Focus govenment	active leadership	$E_2a_1 + K_2\alpha(1-\beta_2)\lambda_1K_1\theta_1 + z_1c(\alpha_1K_1)^h(\alpha_2K_2)^i + (K_1+E_1)R_1 + R_{g1} + K_1(1-\beta_1)\xi - m_1E_1 - K_1(b_1+d_1) - n_1\alpha_1K_1$; $E_1(a_2+c) + K_1\alpha(1-\beta_1)\lambda_2K_2\theta_2 + z_2c(\alpha_1K_1)^h(\alpha_2K_2)^i + (K_2+E_2)R_2 + R_{g2} + K_2(1-\beta_2)\xi - m_2E_2 - K_2(b_2+d_2) - n_2\alpha_2K_2$	$(K_1+E_1)R_1 + R_{g_1} - K_1(b_1+d_1) - m_1E_1$; $(K_2+E_2)R_2 + \Delta K_2\lambda_2\theta_2 - T - K_2(1-\beta_2)\gamma_{21} - K_2\beta_2\gamma_{22}$
	autonomous governance	$(K_1+E_1)R_1 + G_1 + \Delta K_1\lambda_1\theta_1 - F - T - K_1(1-\beta_1)\gamma_{11} - K_1\beta_1\gamma_{12}$; $(K_2+E_2)R_2 + G_2 + R_{g2} - m_2E_2 - K_2(b_2+d_2)$	$(K_1+E_1)R_1 + \Delta K_1\lambda_1\theta_1 - K_1(1-\beta_1)\gamma_{11} - K_1\beta_1\gamma_{12}$; $(K_2+E_2)R_2 + \Delta K_2\lambda_2\theta_2 - K_2(1-\beta_2)\gamma_{21} - K_2\beta_2\gamma_{22}$

According to the revenue matrix in Table 1, we can calculate the expected revenue and average revenue when the focus government and non-focus government choose different strategies. The expected benefits of active leadership U_{11}, autonomous governance U_{12}, and average income U_1 of the focus government can be expressed as:

$$\begin{aligned}U_{11} &= y[E_2a_1 + K_2\alpha(1-\beta_2)\lambda_1K_1\theta_1 + z_1c(\alpha_1K_1)^h(\alpha_2K_2)^i + (K_1+E_1)R_1 + R_{g1} + K_1(1-\beta_1)\xi - m_1E_1 - K_1(b_1+d_1) - n_1\alpha_1K_1] \\ &+(1-y)[(K_1+E_1)R_1 + R_{g1} - K_1(b_1+d_1) - m_1E_1]\end{aligned}$$

$$U_{12} = y[(K_1+E_1)R_1 + G_1 + \Delta K_1\lambda_1\theta_1 - F - T - K_1(1-\beta_1)\gamma_{11} - K_1\beta_1\gamma_{12}] + (1-y)[(K_1+E_1)R_1 + \Delta K_1\lambda_1\theta_1 - K_1(1-\beta_1)\gamma_{11} - K_1\beta_1\gamma_{12}]$$

$$U_1 = xU_{11} + (1-x)U_{12}$$

Similarly, the expected benefits of non-focus government U_{21} (active participation), U_{22} (autonomous governance), and U_2 (average benefits) can be expressed as follows

$$\begin{aligned}U_{21} &= x[E_1(a_2+c) + K_1\alpha(1-\beta_1)\lambda_2K_2\theta_2 + z_2c(\alpha_1K_1)^h(\alpha_2K_2)^i + (K_2+E_2)R_2 + R_{g2} + K_2(1-\beta_2)\xi - m_2E_2 - K_2(b_2+d_2) - n_2\alpha_2K_2] \\ &+(1-x)[(K_2+E_2)R_2 + G_2 + R_{g2} - K_2(b_2+d_2) - m_2E_2]\end{aligned}$$

$$U_{22} = x[(K_2+E_2)R_2 + \Delta K_2\lambda_2\theta_2 - T - K_2(1-\beta_2)\gamma_{21} - K_2\beta_2\gamma_{22}] + (1-x)[(K_2+E_2)R_2 + \Delta K_2\lambda_2\theta_2 - K_2(1-\beta_2)\gamma_{21} - K_2\beta_2\gamma_{22}]$$

$$U_2 = yU_{21} + (1-y)U_{22}$$

From the above expressions, the replication dynamic equations of the focus government and non-focus government can be calculated.

The dynamic replication equation of the focus government's choice of active leadership strategy is as follows:

$$\begin{aligned}F(x) = \tfrac{dx}{dt} = \; & x(U_{11} - U_1) = x(1-x)\left\{y[E_2a_1 + K_2\alpha_2(1-\beta_2)\lambda_1K_1\theta_1 + z_1c(\alpha_1K_1)^h(\alpha_2K_2)^i + K_1(1-\beta_1)\xi \right. \\ & \left. -n_1\alpha_1K_1 - G_1 + F + T] + [R_{g1} - K_1(b_1+d_1) - m_1E_1 - \Delta K_1\lambda_1\theta_1 + K_1(1-\beta_1)\gamma_{11} + K_1\beta_1\gamma_{12}]\right\}\end{aligned}$$

The dynamic replication equation of the non-focus government's choice of active participation strategy is as follows:

$$\begin{aligned}F(y) = \tfrac{dy}{dt} = \; & y(U_{21} - U_2) = y(1-y)\left\{x[E_1(a_2+c) + K_1\alpha_1(1-\beta_1)\lambda_2K_2\theta_2 + z_2c(\alpha_1K_1)^h(\alpha_2K_2)^i + K_2(1-\beta_2)\xi \right. \\ & \left. -n_2\alpha_2K_2 - G_2 + T] + [R_{g2} + G_2 - K_2(b_2+d_2) - m_2E_2 - \Delta K_2\lambda_2\theta_2 + K_2(1-\beta_2)\gamma_{21} + K_2\beta_2\gamma_{22}]\right\}\end{aligned}$$

In order to solve the equilibrium point-of-evolution game, let $F(x) = 0$ and $F(y) = 0$, five local equilibrium points can be obtained: a (0,0), B (0,1), C (1,0), D (1,1) and E (x^*, y^*). Where x^*, y^* are:

$$x^* = \frac{K_2(b_2+d_2) + m_2E_2 + \Delta K_2\lambda_2\theta_2 - R_{g2} - G_2 - K_2(1-\beta_2)\gamma_{21} - K_2\beta_2\gamma_{22}}{E_1(a_2+c) + K_1\alpha_1(1-\beta_1)\lambda_2K_2\theta_2 + z_2c(\alpha_1K_1)^h(\alpha_2K_2)^i + K_2(1-\beta_2)\xi - n_2\alpha_2K_2 - G_2 + T}$$

$$y^* = \frac{K_1(b_1+d_1)+m_1E_1+\Delta K_1\lambda_1\theta_1-R_{g1}-K_1(1-\beta_1)\gamma_{11}-K_1\beta_1\gamma_{12}}{E_2a_1+K_2\alpha_2(1-\beta_2)\lambda_1K_1\theta_1+z_1c(\alpha_1K_1)^h(\alpha_2K_2)^i+K_1(1-\beta_1)\xi-n_1\alpha_1K_1-G_1+F+T}$$

4.3. Equilibrium Stability Strategy Analysis

According to Hirshleifer theory [59], the Jacobian matrix can be used to analyze the local stability of the evolutionary system at the above five equilibrium points. According to the dynamic replication equation, the Jacobian matrix is obtained.

$$J = \begin{bmatrix} \frac{\partial F(x)}{\partial(x)} \frac{\partial F(x)}{\partial(y)} \\ \frac{\partial F(y)}{\partial(x)} \frac{\partial F(y)}{\partial(y)} \end{bmatrix} = \begin{bmatrix} AB \\ CD \end{bmatrix}$$

Among them,

$$\begin{aligned} A \; &= (1-2x)\Big\{y\big[E_2a_1+K_2\alpha_2(1-\beta_2)\lambda_1K_1\theta_1+z_1c(\alpha_1K_1)^h(\alpha_2K_2)^i+K_1(1-\beta_1)\xi \\ &-n_1\alpha_1K_1-G_1+F+T\big]+\big[R_{g1}-K_1(b_1+d_1)-m_1E_1-\Delta K_1\lambda_1\theta_1+K_1(1-\beta_1)\gamma_{11}+K_1\beta_1\gamma_{12}\big]\Big\} \end{aligned}$$

$$B = x(1-x)\big[E_2a_1+K_2\alpha_2(1-\beta_2)\lambda_1K_1\theta_1+z_1c(\alpha_1K_1)^h(\alpha_2K_2)^i+K_1(1-\beta_1)\xi-n_1\alpha_1K_1-G_1+F+T\big]$$

$$C = y(1-y)\big[E_1(a_2+c)+K_1\alpha_1(1-\beta_1)\lambda_2K_2\theta_2+z_2c(\alpha_1K_1)^h(\alpha_2K_2)^i+K_2(1-\beta_2)\xi-n_2\alpha_2K_2-G_2+T\big]$$

$$\begin{aligned} D = \; &(1-2y)\Big\{x\big[E_1(a_2+c)+K_1\alpha_1(1-\beta_1)\lambda_2K_2\theta_2+z_2c(\alpha_1K_1)^h(\alpha_2K_2)^i+K_2(1-\beta_2)\xi \\ &-n_2\alpha_2K_2-G_2+T\big]+\big[R_{g2}+G_2-K_2(b_2+d_2)-m_2E_2-\Delta K_2\lambda_2\theta_2+K_2(1-\beta_2)\gamma_{21}+K_2\beta_2\gamma_{22}\big]\Big\} \end{aligned}$$

Then the trace of the matrix is: $trJ = A + D$.

The determinant of the Jacobian matrix and the sign of trace can determine when the above five equilibrium points are stable strategies (ESS). When $trJ < 0$ and $\det J = |J| > 0$ are satisfied, the equilibrium point reaches a stable state and finally becomes a stable strategy.

Because $x^*, y^* \in [0,1]$, we get

$$K_1(b_1+d_1)+m_1E_1+\Delta K_1\lambda_1\theta_1-R_{g1}-K_1(1-\beta_1)\gamma_{11}-K_1\beta_1\gamma_{12} > 0$$

$$K_2(b_2+d_2)+m_2E_2+\Delta K_2\lambda_2\theta_2-R_{g2}-G_2-K_2(1-\beta_2)\gamma_{21}-K_1\beta_1\gamma_{22} > 0$$

That is, when both sides choose to govern independently, the benefits are greater than those of one party seeking cooperation with the other. It shows that if the two sides cannot reach a cooperation agreement, the active participants will suffer a great loss. The overall benefit of the consistent direction peers or reverse peers is less than that of negative peers. Under this condition, the local stability results of the five equilibrium points are shown in Table 2.

Table 2. Local stability analysis of equilibrium point.

Equilibrium Points	*trJ*	det*J*	Local Stability
A (0,0)	−	+	ESS
B (0,1)	+	+	Instable
C (1,0)	+	+	Instable
D (1,1)	−	+	ESS
E (x^*, y^*)	/	0	Saddle point

It can be seen from Table 2 that there are two unstable points B (0,1) and C (1,0) in the evolution system of green governance peer behavior of the focus government and non-focus government. Point E (x^*, y^*) is the saddle point and point A (0,0) and point D (1,1) are the stable points of the system. Therefore, the evolution phase diagram of the system is shown in Figure 4.

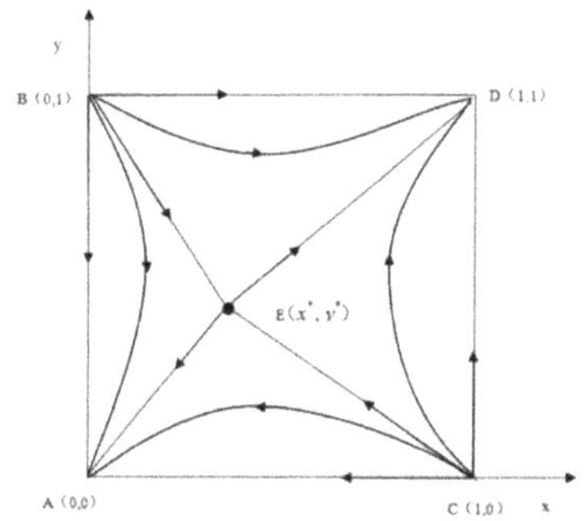

Figure 4. Phase diagram of system evolution.

It can be seen from Figure 4 that the saddle point position determines the stable strategy and the final partner state of the focus government and the non-focus government. Taking the broken line connected by points B, C, and E as the convergence critical line of the system, at the top right of the broken line (BECD) the system converges to the positive-peer state. In the lower left part of the broken line (ABEC part), the system converges to the negative-peer state. The larger the area of convergence region (BECD or ABEC), the closer the system is to the stable point (points D, A).

4.4. *Influence of Knowledge Management on the Evolution Trend of Peer Behavior*

4.4.1. The Evolution Trend of Peer Behavior in the Internalization Stage of External Knowledge

From the expressions of x^* and y^*, we can see that:

- The effect of knowledge learning promotes the focus government and non-focus government to actively participate in knowledge transformation activities to achieve a positive-peer state. Willingness stimulus coefficient a_1, a_2 and learning effect perception coefficient c are the decreasing functions of x^* and y^*. With the higher stimulation degree of the two kinds of government to the knowledge learning effect, the stronger the relationship between perception and trust. Saddle point e gradually transfers to equilibrium point A, and the system is stable in the positive-peer state of active leadership and active participation.
- The knowledge synergy effect plays a positive role in promoting the focus government and non-focus government to achieve positive-peer status. With the increase of elasticity coefficient, h, i of complementary knowledge stock and distribution ratio z_1, z_2 of knowledge synergy income, BECD area increases significantly. This shows that the higher the elasticity of complementary knowledge stock of focus government and non-focus government, the higher the income of the knowledge synergy effect transformation, which is greater than the income of their own governance and promotes both sides of the game to stay in a positive-peer state. At the same time, the higher the distribution coefficient of synergy benefits, the stronger their willingness to participate, but it is possible for both sides to fall into a bad situation of competing for interests. Because the elasticity coefficient of complementary knowledge stock has a relationship of $h + i = 1$ and the focus government knowledge stock is significantly higher than that of non-focus government, the complementary knowledge stock elasticity coefficient of the focus government has a stronger effect on the overall knowledge synergy effect income.
- The reciprocal effect of knowledge promotes the evolutionary system to a positive-peer state. The cooperative value-added coefficient ξ is decreasing with x^* and y^*, which indicates that under the knowledge collaborative network, the focus government and non-focus government gain value-added benefits, and the system will converge to a stable state of active leadership and active participation.

Conclusion 1: The stronger the trust relationship between the two types of governments, the closer the exchange of management will be, and the knowledge learning effect will promote the two sides to enter into a positive-peer state. The two types of government should intensify the frequency of communication, actively align their willingness to green governance and strengthen the positive-peer effects.

Conclusion 2: In the process of knowledge synergy, if the two types of government knowledge structure are complementary and the non-focus government is willing to give part of the synergy benefits to the focus government, this will contribute to the stability of the positive-peer state of both sides. At this point, non-focal governments should focus on the long-term benefits of green governance and avoid short-term horizons that limit the positive-peer effects.

Conclusion 3: If the ability of knowledge cooperation and development is strong, it will obtain a higher knowledge reciprocity effect to maintain a positive-peer state. Therefore, the two types of governments should dovetail their spatial governance policies to jointly promote green industry development to avoid the excessive losses of a single development.

4.4.2. Evolution Trend of Peer Behavior in Internal Knowledge Externalization Stage

From the expressions of x^* and y^*, we can see that:

- The input cost of the knowledge learning effect suppresses the participation enthusiasm of the focus government and non-focus government. Tacit knowledge expenditure coefficients m_1 and m_2 are increasing functions of x^* and y^*. With the increase of parameter value, saddle point e gradually approaches equilibrium point D, and the ABEC region expands continuously. The system converges to the negative-peer state of autonomous governance and autonomous governance.
- The knowledge protection behavior and cost input in the knowledge spillover effect have negative effects on the evolution system. The degree of knowledge protection β_1, β_2, the value coefficient of explicit knowledge b_1, b_2, the occupation rate of knowledge transformation platform d_1, d_2 and x^*, y^* showed an increasing relationship. With the increase of parameter value, the ABEC region increased significantly. This shows that the increase of the value coefficient of explicit knowledge leads to the two kinds of governments paying more attention to the protection of knowledge. On the one hand, it increases the cost of knowledge spillover, on the other hand, it reduces the knowledge that can be shared and used, which makes both sides more likely to self-governance. At the same time, due to the increase of the occupation rate of the knowledge transformation platform, the load of knowledge transformation increases and the efficiency of knowledge spillover decreases, which is not conducive to the construction of a knowledge collaboration network.

Conclusion 4: The higher the cost of the tacit knowledge exchange between the two types of government, the weaker the knowledge learning effect acquired by both sides, which leads to a negative-peer state for both sides.

Conclusion 5: The higher degree of protection for the two types of government will lead to higher value knowledge and the overcrowding of the knowledge transformation platform will lead to the closure of knowledge activities, which will make it difficult for both sides to obtain the knowledge spillover effect. This tends to lead to a negative-peer state.

4.4.3. Peer Behavior Evolution Trend in Internal Knowledge Transformation Stage

From the expressions of x^* and y^*, we can see that:

- The increment of autonomous governance knowledge ΔK_1 and ΔK_2 are positively correlated with x^* and y^*. With the increase of parameter value, the system converges to the negative-peer state. This shows that when the two players choose the self-governance strategy, the value-added benefits brought by self-focused development are higher than that of knowledge collaborative transformation, so they tend to choose the negative-peer state. There is no doubt that in this development mode, both focus government and non-focus government can construct a green governance mode with local characteristics and expand the stock of government knowledge. However, due to the weak foundation of non-focus government, the knowledge increment of the two is obviously not at the same level, which leads to the further widening of the development gap. This is also the 'negativity' of the negative-peer state. From the perspective of revenue, the knowledge incremental revenue of both sides is obviously greater than the knowledge synergy effect revenue in the short term. Because the latter needs continuous investment and stable knowledge exchange channels (low knowledge protection, low platform occupancy rate, etc.), the two types of governments tend to choose autonomous governance.

- The chance loss coefficient γ_{11}, γ_{21} and knowledge protection penalty coefficient γ_{12}, γ_{22} are negatively correlated with x^*, y^*. With the increase of the parameter value, the system converges to a positive-peer state. The higher the value of knowledge opportunity utilization and the greater the punishment to knowledge protection forces both sides to choose the actively lead and actively participate strategy. As a rational decision, when one party is idle or the redundant knowledge is too much, the other party needs corresponding knowledge to make up for it. The knowledge collaborative transformation activity can not only enlarge the value of knowledge, but also reduce punishment by opening knowledge and promoting the green collaborative development of the region.

Conclusion 6: The stronger the ability of the two kinds of governments to mine their own knowledge, the lower their willingness to participate in knowledge interaction, which leads to the formation of a negative-peer state.

Conclusion 7: The increase of opportunity and income of knowledge will enhance the willingness of the two types of government to participate in knowledge interaction. The increase of knowledge protection punishment will further promote the formation of a positive-peer state.

4.4.4. Influence of External Constraints of Knowledge Management on the Evolutionary Trend of Behavior of the Peer

From the expressions of x^* and y^*, we can see that the loss of credit T and punishment F are decreasing functions of x^* and y^*. When the value of T or F is increased, saddle point E tends to be stable point A. This shows that the greater the loss of government image or reputation, the more the government external expenditure caused by breach of contract and the resulting loss makes the organization tend to choose positive behavior. Considering that the central government is not willing to lead the focus government, the greater the exit penalty of the focus government is, the more the focus government will choose to actively lead. Therefore, in the consistent direction peer, punishment F suppresses the formation of the consistent-direction-peer state, while reputation loss T promotes the non-focus government to expand internal expenditure, avoid the occurrence of the adverse peer state, and finally guide both sides of the game to stabilize in the positive-peer state.

Conclusion 8: Stronger punishment and stronger binding forces of the intergovernmental cooperation contract will promote the two types of governments to maintain a positive-peer state.

4.5. The Influence of Explicit and Tacit Knowledge Level on the Final Peer State

In order to investigate the influence of explicit and tacit knowledge level of the focus government and non-focus government on knowledge transformation behavior and final peer state more intuitively, this paper used MATLAB to carry out numerical simulation. The initial parameter assignment is shown in Table 3, and the initial behavior probability was set as (0.5,0.5). In this regard, the initial data were modelled and selected from government reports on the Yangtze River Economic Zone, and the corresponding indicators that could be drawn upon were transformed to the same order of magnitude. For example, K1 is the average number of green governance policies made public by the three focus governments of Jiangsu, Zhejiang, and Shanghai over the years, while K2 is the average number of green governance policies of non-focus governments such as Anhui. Other indicators were similarly compared to ensure the validity of the simulation.

Table 3. Initial parameter assignment.

Related Parameters	Parameter Value	Related Parameters	Parameter Value	Related Parameters	Parameter Value	Related Parameters	Parameter Value
K_1	5	K_2	4	E_1	5	E_2	4
a_1	0.5	a_2	0.8	b_1	2.4	b_2	2
d_1	0.6	d_2	0.5	F	0.2	G_1	5
G_2	1	h	0.5	i	0.5	c	0.5
m_1	0.6	m_2	0.5	n_1	3	n_2	2
R_{g1}	0.2	R_{g2}	1	T	1.8	z_1	0.6
z_2	0.4	ΔK_1	3	ΔK_2	2	α_1	0.4
α_2	0.6	β_1	0.8	β_2	0.5	λ_1	0.6
λ_2	0.5	θ_1	0.6	θ_2	0.5	γ_{11}	3
γ_{21}	2	γ_{12}	2	γ_{22}	1	ξ	5

The effect of the willingness level of green governance (tacit knowledge level) on peer status was analyzed. With other parameters unchanged, it can be seen from Figure 5 that:

- (1) In Figure 5a, when the tacit knowledge level of the focus government and non-focus government is low as a whole ($E < 10$), both sides eventually tend to be in a negative-peer state (0,0). Among them, the non-focus government's willingness to actively participate will first have a small increase, and with the evolution of time, the willingness to participate will decline. The willingness of the focus government to actively lead will first decline significantly, then decline steadily and stay in the state of self-governance. Therefore, both sides experience the evolution process from consistent direction peer to negative peer. (2) When E_2 is constant and E_1 is higher, the speed of non-focus government converging to the state of self-governance slows down but accelerates the decline of focus government's willingness to actively lead. When E_1 remains unchanged and E_2 is lower, the willingness of non-focus government to actively participate is stronger, and the decline speed of willingness further slows down and the convergence speed of focus government to self-governance is also slower than that of the higher E_1 state. (3) In the early stage of knowledge transformation, the benefit of the non-focus government's knowledge learning effect is greater than the expenditure of knowledge externalization, so its willingness to actively participate has increased. The larger the knowledge gap and the lower the level of tacit knowledge, the lower the decline rate of willingness to participate. For the focus government, the higher the level of tacit knowledge, the higher the cost of knowledge externalization and the faster the decline of participation willingness. The increase of the knowledge gap further enlarges the imbalance of the focus government, which leads to its choice of independent governance strategy.
- In Figure 5b, (1) when the tacit knowledge level of the focus government and non-focus government is higher as a whole ($E > 20$) or the tacit knowledge gap is larger, both sides tend to be in a negative-peer state (0,0). Different from the feedback in Figure 5a, when the level of tacit knowledge is high, the willingness of active participation of the focus government and non-focus government rapidly declines and the speed of convergence to a negative-peer state (0,0) accelerates, and there is no transition period of a consistent-direction-peer state. (2) As the tacit knowledge level of the non-focus government is higher than that of the focus government, the willingness of the non-focus government to actively participate in the decline is faster, while the decline rate of the focus government is slower. (3) When the level of tacit knowledge on both sides is high, the benefits of learning and imitation will narrow. When the

knowledge gap increases significantly, the positive will of the focus government and the non-focus government will first increase slightly.

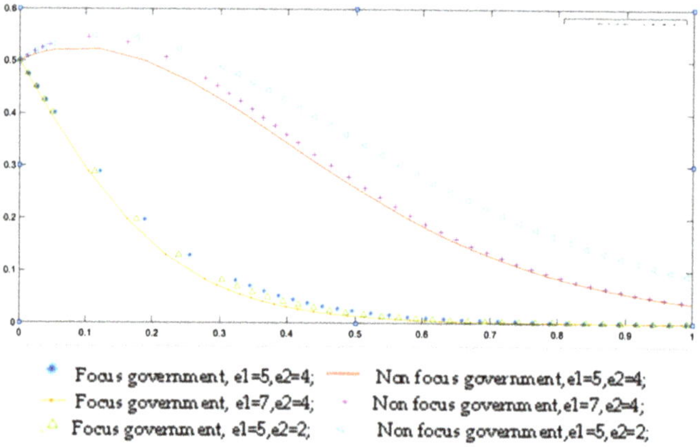

(**a**) E < 20

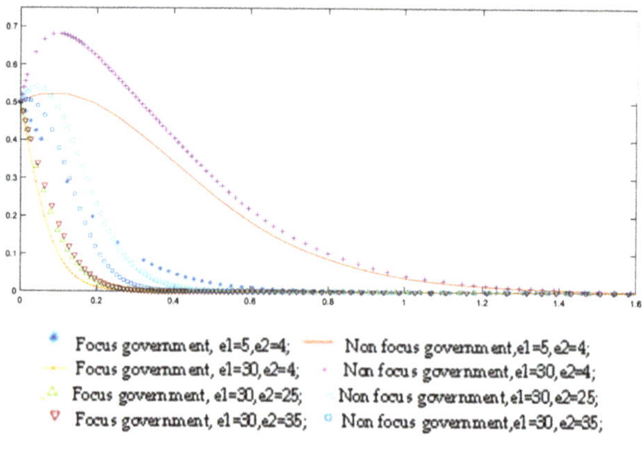

(**b**) E > 20

Figure 5. Evolution of the same peer state of both sides of the game when the tacit knowledge level changes.

The effect of knowledge stock (explicit knowledge level) of green governance on peer status was analyzed. With other parameters unchanged, it can be seen from Figure 6:

- In Figure 6a, (1) when the explicit knowledge level of focus government and non-focus government is low as a whole ($K < 10$), both sides eventually tend to be in a negative-peer state (0, 0). Among them, the willingness of non-focus governments to actively participate increases slightly at first and then decreases slowly. The focus government's willingness to actively lead continues to decline, and the decline rate gradually slows down. Similar to the mechanism of tacit knowledge, with the increase of knowledge, the focus government's willingness to lead decreases and increases rapidly, and the expansion of the knowledge gap also leads to the decline of leadership intention. However, the willingness of non-focus government to participate in the process of change is different. When the knowledge gap is large, the willingness of non-focus government to participate in the process of change is low. (2) With the decrease of their explicit knowledge level, the willingness curve of active participation rises. However, when the knowledge gap expands, the role of the knowledge spillover effect on non-focus government is reduced, and it is difficult for non-focus government with a weak foundation to obtain favorable resources and generate substantial benefits through the knowledge spillover effect. In the background there are external investments but as profits and the focus government's active will are not strong, the non-focus government tends to finally move to autonomous governance mode. It can be seen that the knowledge gap limits the role of the knowledge spillover effect, leading to a negative-peer state of the system.

- In Figure 6b, (1) when the explicit knowledge level of the focus government and non-focus government is higher as a whole ($K > 20$) or the explicit knowledge gap changes, the final state of both side changes. With the obvious increase of the explicit knowledge gap, the positive will of both sides continues to decrease, which is faster than that in Figure 6a. This reflects the existing problems of regional green development: In order to build better and faster in the green advantage industry and give play to the 'first mover' advantage, the focus government will speed up the pace of independent development, leading to the widening gap of explicit knowledge, such as the management experience of local governments among regions. (2) When both sides are in a state of a high level of explicit knowledge, the benefit of the knowledge spillover effect is significantly higher than that of external expenditure. At this time, although the focus government undertakes more external investment due to the rise of the stock of non-focus government knowledge, the focus government can also accept part of the spillover knowledge and make up for its own shortcomings. The two sides present the collaborative situation of mutual benefits and a win-win relationship, forming a (1,1) positive-peer state.

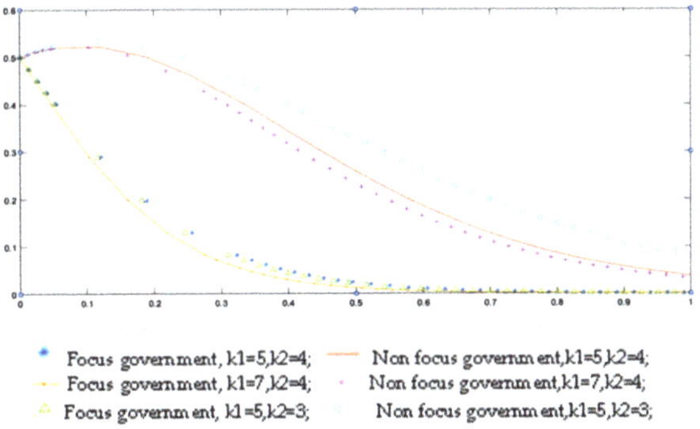

(a) K < 20

Figure 6. *Cont.*

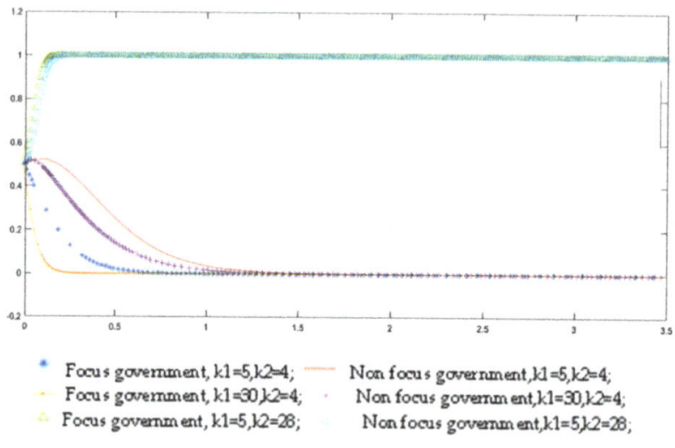

(**b**) K > 20

Figure 6. Evolution of the same peer state of both sides of the game when the level of explicit knowledge changes.

5. Conclusions and Suggestions

Based on the improved SECI model, this paper constructs a dynamic evolutionary game model of local government green governance peer behavior and further explains the mechanism of knowledge management on local government green governance peer behavior. It also considers the effects of knowledge learning, knowledge spillover, knowledge synergy, and knowledge reciprocity in the process of knowledge internal and external transformation. The results show that:

- Good trust and communication between governments are the basis of the knowledge learning effect. The key to the formation of the knowledge synergy effect is to enhance the complementarity of the knowledge structure among governments and give way to the interests of non-focus governments. The two kinds of government ability of cooperative knowledge development determine the strength of the knowledge reciprocity effect. With the increase of the knowledge effect, focus governments and non-focus governments will maintain a positive-peer state.
- The increase of tacit knowledge exchange cost will restrain the effect of knowledge learning. If the two kinds of governments form a relatively closed concept of knowledge utilization, overemphasize higher-value knowledge, enhance protection, and the infrastructure of knowledge utilization is not in place and the knowledge transformation platform is overcrowded, it will lead to the weakening of the knowledge spillover effect. With the attenuation of the two kinds of knowledge effects, focus government and non-focus government will stabilize the negative-peer state.
- The more active the knowledge transformation activities within the two types of government, the stronger the ability to mine their knowledge, which will inhibit the willingness of knowledge interaction and lead to the formation of a negative-peer state.
- The higher the opportunity income of the two types of intergovernmental external knowledge transformation activities, the greater the restriction of knowledge protection, and the higher the degree of punishment of the central government on knowledge closure behavior, the stronger the binding force of intergovernmental cooperation contract will be, promoting the formation of a positive-peer state.
- The knowledge learning effect only exists in the early and middle stages of green governance. When the willingness to manage is high, the effect of learning is limited. When the difference of management intention is large, both sides' enthusiasm to

participate in the collaborative transformation of knowledge increases, but because the high willing side bears too much cost, the collaborative relationship may break down.

- The knowledge spillover effect plays an important role in the later stage of green governance. With the increase of the capacity gap, the knowledge acceptance and transformation of non-focus government spillovers are limited, limiting the knowledge spillover effect. When peer interaction is positive, knowledge spillover will bring benefits.

Therefore, the following suggestions were put forward in this paper:

- Improve the efficiency of external knowledge absorption and strengthen the perception of external knowledge. The non-focus government should take the initiative to get close to the focus government, learn from the other party's green governance will, optimize the knowledge structure of management ability, and improve the elasticity of complementary knowledge stock. The non-focus government should make the proportion of low knowledge cooperative income distribution and the flexibility of knowledge stock properly and gain more knowledge income through increased overall interests. The non-focus government should actively absorb the focus government's management talents, open the exchange of posts and enterprises, and improve the absorption capacity of external explicit and tacit knowledge.
- Reduce the cost of knowledge outflow and avoid the collaborative crisis caused by knowledge 'private possession.' In knowledge learning, the cost of observation and communication should be controlled reasonably. In knowledge spillover, optimize the knowledge docking channels and platform space, reduce the occupancy of knowledge conversion platforms, share common experience, planning, and schemes, and enhance all governments' behavior enthusiasm. The regional government should form a unified program document and build a platform for knowledge transformation across regions. The green development policies of local governments can be seamlessly linked and a shared government platform can be established to gradually eliminate the constraints of geography on development.
- Correctly guide the internal knowledge transformation process. Through internal knowledge transformation, some governments increase knowledge increment significantly and obtain more knowledge increment benefits. However, the government should take a long-term view, reasonably evaluate the situation of its knowledge increment in the region and clarify the opportunity loss of knowledge investment and the damage of knowledge protection punishment to its interests. As far as the green development environment is concerned, restrictive punishment measures can be implemented to reduce the bad behaviors of 'free-riding' and the belief that 'knowledge is not open'.
- Create an excellent positive-peer environment and improve the local government audit and guidance mechanism. The central government should assess the local government's decision-making situation in time and regulate the bad behavior reasonably. The government should pay attention to the good government images and reputations, encourage local cooperation, and curb the relatively closed government behavior and refusal to exchange knowledge.
- Local governments should be encouraged to choose the appropriate group state, ensuring that their development is not biased, decisions are not blind, and management is followed. The non-focus government, if it is not encouraged, can enter into a positive-peer state. Non-focus government can use the knowledge learning effect in the early stage to increase the willingness of green governance, promote the improvement of management ability with the help of the transfer of internal tacit knowledge to explicit knowledge, and then enter the period of rapid green development with the help of the knowledge spillover effect. As for the focus governments, they are not encouraged to choose to lead actively. In the early stage, the non-focus government's awareness of green governance is weak, relying on the focus government's unilateral wake-up effect, which is low and easy to undermine their own positive will. The non-focus government can gradually lead the regional collaborative governance and take the

initiative to carry out knowledge spillover in the middle and later stages by following independently. Therefore, this paper encourages the formation of negative-peer, consistent-direction-peer, reverse-peer, and positive-peer development paths. All kinds of companion states are reasonable and necessary. The government should rationally analyze the path of green governance decision-making to formulate appropriate development plans.

The article examines green governance in China from the perspectives of central and local governments, focus and non-focus governments, but the following shortcomings still exist: (1) The ultimate landing point of the government's green governance is still on the green innovative enterprises. The article only considers the impact of the peer effects among local governments on green governance, and subsequent studies can add the role of enterprises. (2) In terms of methodology, the article adopts a two-party evolutionary game approach. In subsequent studies, green innovation enterprises can be added to build a three-party evolutionary game model to analyze the government's green governance behavior more comprehensively.

Author Contributions: H.L. proposed the topic, designed the research content, and revised the final version of the paper. P.Y. participated in revising and editing the paper. X.W. and J.H. were involved in the simulation analysis and writing of the thesis. L.Y. provided guidance during the writing of the paper. All authors have read and agreed to the published version of the manuscript.

Funding: This research was funded by Program of Shanghai Planning Office of Philosophy and Social Science of China (No. 2020BGL023).

Institutional Review Board Statement: Not applicable.

Informed Consent Statement: Not applicable.

Data Availability Statement: Not applicable.

Conflicts of Interest: The authors declare no conflict of interest.

References

1. Rong, L.; Bi, K. A study on the comprehensive carrying capacity and spatial optimization under the new development concept-an empirical study of shandong province. *E3S Web Conf.* **2020**, *199*, 00005. [CrossRef]
2. Li, W.; Zhang, Y. Family control, political connection, and corporate green governance. *Sustainability* **2020**, *12*, 7068. [CrossRef]
3. Dieng, B.; Pesqueux, Y. On 'green governance'. *Int. J. Sustain. Dev.* **2017**, *20*, 111. [CrossRef]
4. Kusis, J.; Brokane, L.; Miltovica, B. Green Governance Principles in the Development of Environmental Educational Infrastructure. *Auzina Rural Dev. Entrep. Bioecon. Prod. Co-Oper. Agric.* **2017**, *4*, 256–266.
5. Mackenzie, A.; Pearson, L.J.; Pearson, C.J. A framework for governance of public green spaces in cities. *Landsc. Res.* **2019**, *44*, 444–457. [CrossRef]
6. Yuan, L.; Cui, X. Green Governance Innovation in Government: Connotations, Situation and Strategic Options. *Chin. Public Adm.* **2016**, *11*, 151–154.
7. Yang, L.; Liu, H. Green Governance: The Way to Build a Beautiful China. *Chin. Public Adm.* **2014**, *29*, 291–314.
8. Fay, M.; Wang, J.Z.; Draugelis, G.; Deichmann, U. Role of green governance in achieving sustainable urbanization in china. *China World Econ.* **2014**, *22*, 19–36. [CrossRef]
9. Liao, K.; Dai, S.; Duan, X. Research on the Coordination Effect Evaluation and Dynamic Relationship of Technological Innovation and Green Governance. *Sci. Technol. Prog. Policy* **2019**, *36*, 34–43.
10. Huang, Y.; Aguilar, F.; Yang, J.; Qin, Y.; Wen, Y. Predicting citizens' participatory behavior in urban green space governance: Application of the extended theory of planned behavior. *Urban For. Urban Green.* **2021**, *1*, 127110. [CrossRef]
11. Wang, C. A Study of the Cooperative Dynamic Mechanism among Governments for Transregional Green Governance. *Shandong Soc. Sci.* **2020**, *6*, 124–129.
12. Tan, H.; Thurbon, E.; Kim, S.Y. Overcoming incumbent resistance to the clean energy shift: How local governments act as change agents in coal power station closures in China. *Energy Policy* **2021**, *149*, 112058. [CrossRef]
13. He, S. A study on the Coordination Mechanism and Policy System of Environmental Governance and Green Development in the Yangtze River Economic Belt. *Contemp. Econ. Manag.* **2019**, *41*, 57–63.
14. Jain, M.; Siva, V.; Hoppe, T. Assessing governance of low energy green building innovation in the building sector: Insights from Singapore and Delhi. *Energy Policy* **2020**, *145*, 111752. [CrossRef]
15. Pineda-Guerrero, A.; Escobedo, F.J.; Carriazo, F. Governance, Nature's Contributions to People, and Investing in Conservation Influence the Valuation of Urban Green Areas. *Land* **2020**, *10*, 14. [CrossRef]

16. Ding, G. Green Development and Modernization of National Governance Capacity–A Review of the Third Forum on the Construction of National Governance System and Governance Capacity. *J. Huazhong Univ. Sci. Technol. (Soc. Sci. Ed.)* **2017**, *31*, 138–140.
17. Li, W.; Zhang, Y.; Zheng, M. Research on Green Governance of Chinese Listed Companies and Its Evaluation. *Manag. World* **2019**, *35*, 126–133+160.
18. Poier, S. Clean and Green–The Volkswagen Emissions Scandal: Failure of Corporate Governance? *Probl. Ekorozw.* **2020**, *15*, 33–39. [CrossRef]
19. Wang, Y.; Chen, H. Leading Green Governance with Green Development: Change of Concepts, Reasons for Transformation and Selection of Strategies. *J. Sichuan Univ. (Philos. Soc. Sci. Ed.)* **2019**, *3*, 45–52.
20. Torres, C.; Olvera-Vargas, L.A.; Gómez, J.S. Discovering innovation opportunities based on SECI model: Reconfiguring knowledge dynamics of the agricultural artisan production of agave-mezcal, using emerging technologies. *J. Knowl. Manag.* **2020**, *6*, 1–12. [CrossRef]
21. Bonaccorsi, A.; Piccaluga, A. A Theoretical Framework for the Evaluation of University–Industry Relationships. *R D Manag.* **1994**, *24*, 229–247. [CrossRef]
22. Koschatzky, K. Networking and Knowledge Transfer Between Research and Industry in Transition Countries: Empirical Evidence from the Slovenian Innovation System. *J. Technol. Transf.* **2002**, *27*, 27–38. [CrossRef]
23. Sun, C.; Li, C. The influence of Trans-industry Organizational Ties on Innovation Performance——Double Moderating of Heterogeneity of Knowledge and Absorptive Capacity. *Soft Sci.* **2019**, *33*, 42–46+59.
24. Horvat, D.; Dreher, C.; Som, O. How Firms Absorb External Knowledge—Modelling and Managing the Absorptive Capacity Process. *Int. J. Innov. Manag.* **2019**, *23*, 217–230. [CrossRef]
25. Carayannis, E.G.; Alexander, J.; Ioannidis, A. Leveraging knowledge, learning, and innovation in forming strategic government–university–industry (GUI) R&D partnerships in the US, Germany, and France. *Technovation* **2000**, *20*, 477–488.
26. Xing, Q.; Shangguan, D.; Liang, X. Knowledge Sharing Considered the Multidimensional Attributes of Knowledge and Its Governance Model in Collaborative Innovation. *Soft Sci.* **2016**, *30*, 50–54+59.
27. Ahmed, Y.A.; Ahmad, M.N.; Ahmad, N. Social Media for Knowledge-Sharing: A Systematic Literature Review. *Telemat. Inform.* **2018**, *37*, 72–112. [CrossRef]
28. Zhang, J.M.; Jiang, H.; Wu, R. Reconciling the Dilemma of Knowledge Sharing: A Network Pluralism Framework of Firms' R&D Alliance Network and Innovation Performance. *J. Manag.* **2019**, *45*, 2635–2665.
29. Zhou, M.; Govindan, K.; Xie, X.B. How fairness perceptions, embeddedness, and knowledge sharing drive green innovation in sustainable supply chains: An equity theory and network perspective to achieve sustainable development goals. *J. Clean. Prod.* **2020**, *260*, 120950. [CrossRef]
30. Pan, H.; Chen, J.; Yang, C. Peer Effect of Family Business Violation. *J. Shanxi Univ. Financ. Econ.* **2020**, *42*, 87–98.
31. Curtius, H.C.; Hille, S.L.; Berger, C. Shotgun or snowball approach? Accelerating the diffusion of rooftop solar photovoltaics through peer effects and social norms. *Energy Policy* **2018**, *118*, 596–602. [CrossRef]
32. Feng, G.; Wang, J. The Peer Effect of Corporate Innovation in Social Network. *Chin. J. Manag.* **2019**, *16*, 1809–1819.
33. Anonymous. Hot technologies: Focusing government resources for more effective innovation. *Strateg. Dir.* **2008**, *24*, 32–34. [CrossRef]
34. Kong, Y.; Feng, C.; Yang, J. How does China manage its energy market? A perspective of policy evolution. *Energy Policy* **2020**, *147*, 111898. [CrossRef]
35. Khan, S.A.R.; Sharif, A.; Golpra, H. A Green Ideology in Asian Emerging Economies: From Environmental Policy and Sustainable Development. *Sustain. Dev.* **2019**, *27*, 1063–1075. [CrossRef]
36. Loughran, K. Urban parks and urban problems: An historical perspective on green space development as a cultural fix. *Urban Stud.* **2018**, *57*, 2321–2338. [CrossRef]
37. Hoe, S.L. Tacit Knowledge, Nonaka and Takeuchi SECI Model and Informal Knowledge Processes. *Int. J. Organ. Theory Behav.* **2006**, *9*, 490–502. [CrossRef]
38. Shao, C.; Ding, D.H. Study on Schroumldinger's Cat in SECI Model and Its Theoretical Explanation. *China Ind. Econ.* **2009**.
39. Harorimana, D. The Impact of Culture on the Application of the SECI Model. *BioMed Central* **2010**, *8*, 152–161.
40. Sakellariou, E.; Karantinou, K.; Goffin, K. "Telling tales": Stories, metaphors and tacit knowledge at the fuzzy front-end of NPD. *Creat. Innov. Manag.* **2017**, *26*, 353–369.
41. Farnese, M.L.; Barbieri, B.; Chirumbolo, A. Managing Knowledge in Organizations: A Nonaka's SECI Model Operationalization. *Front. Psychol.* **2019**, *10*, 2730. [CrossRef] [PubMed]
42. Richtnér, A.; Ahlstrom, P.; Goffin, K. "Squeezing R&D": A Study of Organizational Slack and Knowledge Creation in NPD, Using the SECI Model. *J. Prod. Innov. Manag.* **2014**, *31*, 1268–1290.
43. Nonaka, I.; Toyama, R.; Konno, N. SECI, Ba and Leadership: A Unified Model of Dynamic Knowledge Creation. *Long Range Plan.* **2000**, *33*, 5–34. [CrossRef]
44. Wu, Y.; Senoo, D.; Magnier-Watanabe, R. Diagnosis for organizational knowledge creation: An ontological shift SECI model. *J. Knowl. Manag.* **2010**, *14*, 791–810. [CrossRef]
45. Sarin, S.; Mcdermott, C. The Effect of Team Leader Characteristics on Learning, Knowledge Application, and Performance of Cross-Functional New Product Development Teams. *Decis. Sci.* **2003**, *34*, 707–739. [CrossRef]

46. Post, C.; Rahman, N. Green governance: Boards of directors' composition and environmental corporate social responsibility. *Bus. Soc.* **2011**, *12*, 58–72. [CrossRef]
47. Hsieh, H.C.; Claresta, V.; Bui, T. Green building, cost of equity capital and corporate governance: Evidence from us real estate investment trusts. *Sustainability* **2020**, *12*, 3680. [CrossRef]
48. Bush, L.; Kring, T.J.; Ruberson, J.R. Suitability of greenbugs, cotton aphids, and heliothis virescens eggs for development and reproduction of orius insidiosus. *Entomol. Exp. Appl.* **2011**, *67*, 217–222. [CrossRef]
49. Gea-Bermúdez, J.; Jensen, I.G.; Münster, M.; Oivisto, M.K.; Ravn, H. The role of sector coupling in the green transition: A least-cost energy system development in northern-central europe towards 2050. *Appl. Energy* **2021**, *289*, 116685. [CrossRef]
50. Khovanskaia, M.; Ivanyi, Z. Possibilities and options for the clean development mechanism and the green investment scheme in central and eastern europe: Macedonian and romanian perspectives. *Nat. Resour. Forum* **2010**, *31*, 1–10. [CrossRef]
51. Sano, J.; Inami, S.; Seimiya, K.; Ohba, T.; Sakai, S.; Takano, T. Effects of green tea intake on the development of coronary artery disease. *Circ. J.* **2003**, *68*, 665–670. [CrossRef] [PubMed]
52. Shah, K.U.; Arjoon, S.; Rambocas, M. Aligning corporate social responsibility with green economy development pathways in developing countries. *Sustain. Dev.* **2016**, *24*, 237–253. [CrossRef]
53. Tupas, F.P. Green governance-an integrated programs of local government units: A case of northern iloilo, philippines. *Indian J. Sci. Technol.* **2020**, *13*, 2686–2699. [CrossRef]
54. Radzi, A.; Darus, F.; Yusoff, H.; Hermawan, A. Green-based governance and external pressure: Do they influence environmental disclosure? empirical evidence from ISO 14001 companies in malaysia. *Humanit. Soc. Sci. Rev.* **2020**, *8*, 974–984.
55. Lin, G. Promoting green electricity development from industrial to developing countries: What needs to be done? *Environ. Politics* **2002**, *11*, 184–191.
56. Phillip, H.P.; Theodore, P. Knowledge Creation in Strategic Alliances: Another Look at Organizational Learning. *Asia Pac. J. Manag.* **2000**, *17*, 201–222.
57. Claudine, S.; Paul, H. Exploration and exploitation: The interplay between knowledge and continuous innovation. *Int. J. Technol. Manag.* **2008**, *42*, 1–2.
58. Liu, L.; Zhang, T. The Evolution Game Analysis on Organization Tactic Knowledge Transferring——Based on the Reciprocal E nterprise Environments. *J. Tech. Econ. Manag.* **2011**, *21*, 38–41.
59. Coll, J.C.M.; Hirshleifer, J. The Limits of Reciprocity: Solution Concepts and Reactive Strategies in Evolutionary Equilibrium Models. *Ucla Econ. Work. Pap.* **1989**, *3*, 1378–1379. [CrossRef]

land

MDPI

Article

Rule by Law, Law-Based Governance, and Housing Prices: The Case of China

Jie Chen [1,2], Haiyong Zhang [1,3,*] and Qian Zhou [4]

1 School of International and Public Affairs, Shanghai Jiao Tong University, Shanghai 200030, China; chenjie100@sjtu.edu.cn
2 China Institute for Urban Governance, Shanghai Jiao Tong University, Shanghai 200030, China
3 School of Mathematics and Finance, Chuzhou University, Chuzhou 239000, China
4 Economics School, Zhongnan University of Economics and Law, Wuhan 430073, China; Z0005072@zuel.edu.cn
* Correspondence: haiyongzhang@sjtu.edu.cn

Abstract: Although some attempts have been made to elucidate the relationship between law-based governance and housing prices, the existing literature still provides limited knowledge about the mediating mechanisms through which law-based governance correlates with housing prices. This study specifically investigates how the association between the rule of law and housing prices is sensitive to public satisfaction, and how the connection is heterogeneous across geographic and socioeconomic groups. Using panel data of Chinese cities over the period 2014–2017, our econometric estimation results indicate that law-based governance may enlarge financial loans and foreign investment and then raise housing prices, which is robust to different specifications. Moreover, the relationship is heterogeneous across city groups and sensitive to the degree of satisfaction with the rule of law quality. Additionally, we demonstrate that the mediating role of financial loans is larger than that of foreign investment. In the stage of emerging economies' pursuit of the rule of law, our findings have useful implications for local governments to control rapidly rising housing prices by reducing loans and foreign investment.

Keywords: rule by law; law-based governance; housing price; sensitivity; heterogeneity; mediating mechanism

Citation: Chen, J.; Zhang, H.; Zhou, Q. Rule by Law, Law-Based Governance, and Housing Prices: The Case of China. *Land* **2021**, *10*, 616. https://doi.org/10.3390/land10060616

Academic Editors: Maciej J. Nowak, Giancarlo Cotella and Przemysław Śleszyński

Received: 26 April 2021
Accepted: 7 June 2021
Published: 9 June 2021

1. Introduction

It is widely agreed that the quality of governance matters for economic prosperity [1–3], but the linkage between specific aspects of governance quality and economic prosperity has not been sufficiently studied in the literature yet. In the World Bank's first series of publications that stress "governance matters for development", the notion of "good governance" was built on four components that include the competence of the public sector to manage the economy and deliver public services, accountability of public officials, transparency of policy frameworks, and a legal framework for development [4–6]. However, the literature has not reached a consensus on what type of legal framework performs better in facilitating development [7,8]. In the World Bank's publication, only the legal framework satisfying the principle of "the rule of law" can create a sufficient stable setting for efficient use of resources and productive investment [5]. Nevertheless, "the rule of law is notoriously difficult to define and measure" [9]. Meanwhile, the connection between the rule of law and economic prosperity is still under extensive debate [10,11]. In several emerging economies, a low or even, sometimes, a negative association between the rule of law and economic development is observed [12,13]. In addition, as far as the authors are aware, to date, all the existing analyses on the law–development nexus have been conducted at a national level and none have been based on subnational or city-level data.

Over the last few decades, the Chinese ruling party (Chinese Communist Party, CCP) has made constant efforts towards "governing the country according to the law" [14]. Just recently, the fourth plenary session of the 19th CCP Central Committee that ended in Oct. 2019 again reiterated the importance of "ensuring law-based governance in all areas, building a country of socialist rule of law" [15]. However, several scholars have stressed that the Chinese state's attempts to use laws as a means to exercise the rule do not fit the universal notion of the "rule of law" but instead are better interpreted as pursuing a governance model of "rule by law" [16–19]. In this paper, we do not plan to get involved in the debate on whether and how the Chinese institutionalization efforts in its legal framework are different from the universal notion of the "rule of law". We hereby use the term "law-based governance" to refer to the law aspect of governance, as this term is the standard word used in the English versions of the Chinese government's official documents for promoting legal development [20] and also the translated copy of President Xi Jinping' related works [21]. While "law-based governance" appears to mainly emphasize the functional use of law in the spirit of "governing according to law" [22] or "rule-based regulation" and "law-based control" [17], it is, however, open to wider interpretations. For example, we presume that the notion of law-based governance is compatible with the World Bank's Worldwide Governance Indicators project team's conception of the rule of law: "perceptions of the extent to which agents have confidence in and abide by the rules of the society, and in particular the quality of contract enforcement, property rights, the police, and the courts, as well as the likelihood of crime and violence" [23].

This paper describes the relationship between average city-level housing prices and law-based governance, or the law aspect of governance, in Chinese cities. In this analysis, housing prices are chosen as a proxy to reflect both contemporary prosperity and people's confidence in future economic prosperity [24]. According to classical urban economics literature, people choose where to dwell by "voting with their feet" and their competition for desirable urban amenities including the quality of urban governance is well capitalized in housing prices [25–27]. Exploring the cross-city variations of the linkage between housing prices and law-based governance in China can provide rich information on how Chinese people value the law aspect of governance quality in their location choices. Such work will then contribute to bridging the knowledge gap regarding the heterogeneous associations between legal development and economic prosperity within a given political regime.

Our research work is premised on three unique advantages. First, we have the chance to utilize city-level indicators of law-based governance, which are rarely available in the empirical literature. The rule of law or quality of law-based governance is generally assessed on the country level but its city-level variations within a country are rarely explored in the literature. Second, compared to advanced economies, the Chinese housing market is still nascent and sensitive to the quality of the law aspect of governance. Launched formally in 1998 on the basis of the abolishment of a welfare housing system that served the needs of the central planning economy, the Chinese housing market has just roughly two decades of development history and many institution buildings are still evolving [24,28]. It will thus be of great interest to discover how people's confidence in the future prospects of local property is associated with the law aspect of governance in a nascent housing market. Third, China is a vast country with significant regional variations in both housing market development and the quality of governance, particularly its law aspect. These significant regional variations make it possible to detect the detailed heterogeneity of the relationship between housing market booms and law-based governance.

By investigating the correlations between law-based governance and housing prices, especially the mediating mechanisms, sensitivity, and heterogeneity of the relationship, this paper contributes to the literature in four aspects. First, for the first time, we demonstrate that a higher degree of law-based governance in one city is on average associated with higher average city-level housing prices. This relationship remains consistent in different subsamples, various model settings, and is robust when applying instrument variable (IV) estimators to alleviate potential endogeneity bias. In particular, we construct a weighted distance as an instrument for law-based governance using distances between different levels of government. Second, we find evidence that the effect of law-based governance can work through expanding the supply of banking loans and stimulating more foreign investment and, further, we find that the mediating role of loans is greater than that of foreign investment. Third, we find that the correlation of law-based governance and housing prices is stronger when the public has higher satisfaction with the quality of the law aspect of governance. This suggests that the extent that the law aspect of governance can be felt and accredited by the public is the key for law-based governance to affect people's confidence in asset prices. Fourth, the size of the association between law-based governance and housing prices is heterogeneous across different city groups. In particular, we find the association is greater in the first- and second-tier cities, and presume this is because housing is expensive in these cities and thus buyers and investors are more sensitive to the security of property rights and guarantee of contract outcomes.

The remainder of this study is structured as follows. Section 2 explores the mechanisms through which law-based governance correlates with housing prices, reviews the relevant literature, discusses potential research gaps, and proposes research hypotheses of this paper; Section 3 displays the methodology and constructs the empirical model used in this study; Section 4 introduces the variables and data; Section 5 presents the estimation results and shows robustness checks and other extensions. Finally, we conclude this study with policy suggestions in Section 6.

2. Analytic Framework and Hypothesis Development

In this section, we first discuss the literature relevant to the general relationship between law-based governance and housing prices, China's pursuit of law-based governance, and Chinese housing market development. Based on the insights and theoretic arguments from the existing literature, we derive the main hypotheses to be tested in the study.

2.1. Governance, Law, and Economic Development

Since the World Bank's 1992 publication of the booklet "Governance and Development", the roles of governance in development and economic prosperity have been extensively studied worldwide [2,3,29–31]. For example, governance is said to affect economic growth via many direct and indirect channels, but the central role is its function in the formation of an institutional environment that is friendly to investment and capital accumulation [32]. Alternatively, good governance can be considered as the existence of an appropriate set of institutions that reward efforts to develop economic performance [33].

From the beginning of the World Bank's call for "good governance", the rule of law, alongside accountability and transparency, is one of the central elements of governance institutions [6]. The World Bank itself deemed that "some elements of rule of law are needed to create a sufficient stable environment for economic actors to make investments and transact business" [5], and further proposed that "good governance is epitomized ... by all behaving under the rule of law" [6]. The build-up of "good governance" has always been closely blended with the concept of the "rule of law" as they are believed to mutually reinforce each other [3]. Although with a wide or sometimes, arguably, an all-embracing meaning, the "rule of law" is perhaps one of the most universally appealing political concepts. For example, the principle of the "rule of law" has been interpreted as "man is governed by law, and not by whims of men" [5]. Meanwhile, the rule of law is also said to mean that "the state should exercise power under the authority of law; government officials should be subject to law just as private citizens" [5]. As the United Nations put it, "the rule of law is a principle of governance in which all persons, institutions and entities, public and private, including the State itself, are accountable to laws" [34]. In empirical work, the rule of law is one of the six ingredients in the World Bank's Worldwide Governance Indicators [35], and the World Development Report 2017 also stresses the importance of the linkage between governance and law [36].

However, the connection between the degree of the rule of law and economic prosperity involves much controversy [10]. Taking the case of China as an example, China's performance of the rule of law is generally assessed as inferior in Western literature [37,38], and consistently ranks low in most international rankings, e.g., China was ranked 100 in 2014 and 87 of 177 countries and regions in 2018 on the Corruption Perceptions Index (CPI). Nonetheless, despite the persistence of low international assessment of its degree of rule of law, China has not only achieved a stunning miracle of economic growth since 1978 but also continued to maintain the economic boom after four decades of rapid development. This phenomenon has been called the China paradox, between the low degree of rule of law and high economic growth, in the literature [39]. A similar association is also observed in several other new emerging economies [12,40]. It has been suggested that in the case of China, the disinterested government, i.e., a government that not captured by any interest group, is impartial towards different sections of the population and prioritizes the long-term welfare of the whole society [41], acting as a substitute for the rule of law to constrain the pitfalls of "entrenched special interest groups" and underpinning China's economic success [42]. However, the exact relationship between Chinese-style rule of law and economic performance has not received much empirical investigation.

2.2. China's Pursuit of Law-Based Governance

Since 1978, accompanying the shift towards a market-oriented economic system, the Chinese party-state has pledged to move forward with "ruling the country by law", the professionalization of the judiciary, and the expansion of legal practitioners, and many new laws have been passed [18,38,43]. Table 1 shows the major events in China's pursuit of law-based governance during the period 1997–2010.

Table 1. Major events in China's pursuit of law-based governance.

Date	Event	Source
Sept. 1997	President Jiang Zemin called for "ruling the country according to the law" and deemed "constructing the socialist state in accordance with the law" as one of basic policy strategies of the Chinese Communist Party (CCP) at the opening speech of the 15th National Congress of the CCP.	[44]
Mar. 1999	The slogan "ruling the country according to the law" was added to the Constitution when the 9th National People's Congress of the People's Republic of China passed the constitutional amendment.	http://www.npc.gov.cn/zgrdw/npc/dbdhhy/content_9508.htm (accessed on 26 April 2021)
Nov. 1999	The State Council issued the *Decision of the State Council on Comprehensively Promoting Administration According to Law.*	SC[1999]23
Mar. 2004	The State Council promulgated the *Implementation Outline for Comprehensively Promoting Administration by Law*, which established the objective of constructing a law-based government.	SC[2004]10
Aug. 2008	The State Council issued the *Decision on Strengthening the Administration of Municipal and County Governments by Law*, and made special arrangements for the construction of law-based government at the municipal and county levels.	SC[2008]17
Nov. 2010	The State Council promulgated the *Opinions on Strengthening the Construction of a Government Ruled by Law*, which made a comprehensive arrangement and raised overall demand for the construction of a law-based government.	SC[2010]33

In the Xi Jinping era, in 2012, the 18th Congress of the Chinese Communist Party and two important decisions adopted subsequently in the 3rd and 4th Plenum in 2013 and 2014, respectively, opened new phases of China's instrumentalist legal-based governance [38]. Particularly, the fourth plenary session of the 18th CCP Central Committee that convened in Oct. 2014 was exclusively devoted to a theme "concerning comprehensively advancing the law-based governance of China". The Plenum called for making "coordinated efforts to promote law-based governance, law-based exercise of state power, and law-based administration of government", and emphasized that "justice is administered impartially, the law is observed by everyone", in order to "ensure that everyone is equal before the law" [45]. The Plenum also pointed out that "to exercise state power based on law, the Party not only has to govern the country in accordance with the Constitution and laws, but also has to ensure that its self-governance is in line with its own rules and regulations", and therefore "to ensure judicial impartiality and improve judicial credibility" [45]. It was clearly stated at this Plenum that "the law is an instrument of great value in the governance of a country and good laws are a prerequisite for good governance" [45].

The pronouncements on socialist law-based governance at the Congresses and Plenums, together with the legal dimensions of Xi Jinping's anticorruption campaign, signify China's localization of international standard of rule of law discourses including substantial modifications to fit Chinese circumstances and the party-state's ambitions [22,46]. According to the *Implementation Outline for Constructing Law-based Government* (2015–2020), jointly issued by the Central Committee of the Communist Party of China (CPC) and the State Council on Dec. 2015, the law-based governance structure that ensures all the government's work complies with the law should be basically established by 2020. The fulfillment of this aim, however, requires not only major institutional developments but also sufficient legal service capability. The data from China's Ministry of Justice suggest that, by the end of 2019, in China there were 473,000 practicing lawyers, including 393,300 full-time lawyers, 43,300 public lawyers, and 10,900 corporate lawyers; Beijing, Guangdong, Jiangsu, and Shandong are the four provincial-level region units that host more than 30,000 lawyers [47]. However, in terms of registered lawyers per capita, the gap between China and the advanced economies is still very large.

2.3. *Evolution and Differentiation of Chinese Housing Market*

The Chinese housing market plays an important role in the economy and society [24]. In July 1998, the State Council formally abolished the in-kind distribution of welfare housing in urban areas. Between 1999 and 2016, the Chinese government considered the commodity housing sector as an engine to promote investment, expand domestic demand, and boost economic growth [48]. During this period, the scale of real estate investment was over-inflated and prices rose fast. According to the data released by the National Bureau of Statistics, the phase of fastest-rising housing prices in China was 2004–2009, with an average annual growth rate of 12.4% and a more pronounced phenomenon of investment and speculation. In November 2008, China proposed an economic stimulus package totaling about four trillion RMB in response to the financial crisis, and housing prices grew by as much as 23.2% in 2009. Since 2010, in order to stabilize housing prices and alleviate the unaffordability crisis that has threatened social stability, the Chinese government has intensively introduced a series of regulatory policies to dampen the speculative demand. During the study period of this paper, 2014–2017, data from the National Bureau of Statistics show that the average annual growth rate of housing prices in China fell to 6.1%, which is lower than the average growth rate of 8% over the past 20 years. Based on this, the regulatory policies during this period were relatively loose, mainly in the form of interest rate and tax rate reductions. Since 2017, the Chinese government emphasized the residential nature of housing and insisted on the position that houses were for living in, not for speculation, and attempted to promote a steady development of the housing market [49]. This seems to be a return to the original intent of the market-oriented housing reform in 1998.

During both the socialist planned economy era and the early stage of the economic reform era, housing in Chinese cities was considered as part of the welfare provision package, while population mobility was constrained, and thus the spatial differentiation of housing was insignificant [50]. However, during the market-oriented development process of the housing sector, the widening regional economic inequality amplified by the massive urban–rural migration, as well as increasing city-to-city mobility, has led housing market conditions and institutional settings to rapidly exhibit substantial spatial variations across cities [24]. In particular, housing prices have shown increasingly significant spatial differences across different tiers of cities [51]. Figure 1 shows the spatial distribution of mean housing prices between 2014 and 2017 in 100 large and medium-sized sample cities.

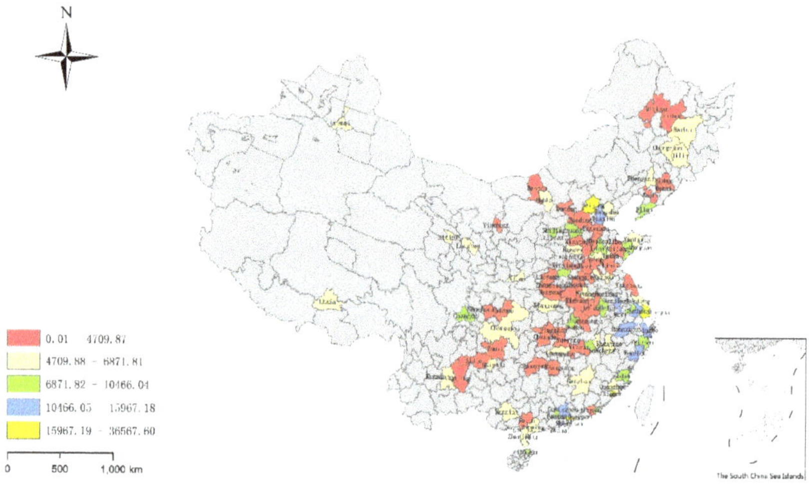

Figure 1. Housing price distribution.

It can be seen that the cities falling into the two highest housing price categories are mainly concentrated in the eastern region of China, such as Shenzhen, Beijing, Xiamen, Shanghai, Hangzhou, Zhuhai, Guangzhou, etc. Meanwhile, the cities with lower housing prices are primarily located in the central and western regions of China. Therefore, regional differences in housing prices are evident in China's real estate market.

2.4. Mechanism Discussions and Hypothesis Development

A "fair" legal framework plays an important role in the housing market. Both housing investments made by developers and housing purchases made by households are capital intensive, and thus very sensitive to legal non-transparency or legal uncertainty. A business climate of predictability that features economic agents' certainty in exercising their rights and high confidence in the restraint of arbitrary behavior of government officials can help greatly to attract stable capital investment and promote a sustainable boom in the housing market. The market confidence would be upheld with the availability of an independent and credible judicial system that can give impartial judgement in conflict solving even when the private agents confront the state. Over the last two decades, significant changes have been made to property-related laws as well as legal procedural frameworks of property-related dispute settlement as the state needs to respond to intensifying conflicts in the booming Chinese real estate market [52]. There is also a growing awareness among the execution branches of Chinese local authorities of governing the growing rights-based disputes through law [53], and increasing compliance with the law.

In addition, a high level of law-based governance may promote the housing market through better information disclosure. Evidently, the law aspect of governance strengthens information disclosure by improving the legal system, whereas liquid and credible information disclosure boosts buyers'/investors' confidence and facilitates capital circulation [54]. In fact, China has placed a lot of emphasis on the disclosure of government affairs and government information, which can improve public participation in decision making [55]. For example, the Opinions on Comprehensively Promoting the Government Affairs Disclosure Work, issued by the General Office of the Central Committee of the CPC and the General Office of the State Council in 2016, provide the directions for work on government affairs disclosure. In addition, the Implementation Outline for Constructing Law-based Government (2015–2020) states clearly that information disclosure shall become a regular government practice [56]. Moreover, the disclosure of government affairs and government information in the pursuit of a law-based government may alleviate the problem of information asymmetry in the housing market.

In a credit market, information asymmetry between transaction parties and the resulting moral hazard is a major obstacle for financial business. Without reliable legal enforcement to punish cheating and curtail opportunistic behaviors, financial institutions have to invest heavily in investigating the creditability quality of potential borrowers before deciding whether to release loans [57]. The existence of serious information asymmetry and the failure to curb cheating would cause high financing costs, the prevalence of credit constraints, and weaker borrowing capacity. These problems can further accelerate the default of borrowers and in turn reduce the quantities of credit supply. Eventually, reduced availably of financial loans, to both developers and buyers, leads to a more depressed housing market [58]. In contrast, housing markets that with less information asymmetry through a better legal arrangement for information disclosure can attract more credit inflow and have a greater chance to experience and sustain a boom.

Further, nations with highly transparent legal system can attract more foreign investment because a "level playing field" exists between foreign and local investors [59]. In international investment, foreign investors particularly demand good local governance and strong law enforcement in the housing market [60]. Therefore, it is reasonably expected that a nation/region with better law aspect of governance may attract more foreign investment, which may then boost the local housing market through both the direct injection of external demand for properties and indirect but more important shifts from the improvement of the long-term economic outlook.

In sum, a high level of the law aspect of governance can reduce uncertainty and ambiguousness in conflict solving, strengthen information disclosure to mitigate information asymmetry, and attract foreign investors. Further, reducing uncertainty and ambiguity in conflict resolution can guarantee housing-related rights, such as access to public services in China, which boosts the desire to buy houses. Additionally, strengthening information disclosure enables homebuyers to obtain more loans, which, combined with foreign investment, ultimately increases demand for home ownership. Finally, these aspects can raise housing demand and then cause housing prices to rise. Based on the analysis, we propose hypothesis 1 as follows:

Hypothesis 1. *Higher level of law-based governance is associated with higher housing prices, holding other things equal.*

Nevertheless, if the public is not cognitively aware of the exact level of law-based governance, then the relationship between law-based governance and housing prices may not be strong. It is quite likely that there may exist a large gap between the public's awareness of governance quality and researchers' measurements of such quality. We thus explore the satisfaction level of the public with respect to law-based governance as it is based on the public's perspective of the quality of law-based governance. Thus, we propose hypothesis 2 as follows:

Hypothesis 2. *The more satisfied the public is with law-based governance, the greater the positive association between law-based governance and housing prices.*

In addition, it is reasonable to expect that the relationship between law-based governance and housing prices could be very heterogeneous across city groups. For example, housing is much more expensive in first- and second-tier cities, which thus implies great asset value and requires a significant amount of financial credit; both investors and buyers in these cities are thus more sensitive to local law-based governance. On the contrary, investors and buyers of housing in small and less developed cities may give less attention to the quality of local law-based governance. Based on these arguments, hypothesis 3 is proposed as follows:

Hypothesis 3. *The correlation between the law-based governance and housing prices is greater in the first- and second-tier cities.*

3. Methodology

We first use a series of pooled cross-sectional regressions to obtain the initial relationship between law-based governance and housing prices. Then, in order to mitigate the estimation bias caused by the endogeneity problem, we construct an instrument for the rule of law. Finally, the causal steps approach is applied to test the mediating effects.

3.1. Model Specification

The econometric model used in this study is expressed as:

$$y_{it} = \alpha + \sum_{j=1}^{k} \beta_j x_{ijt} + dummy_{region} + dummy_{year} + \varepsilon_{it} \quad (1)$$

where y_{it} is the dependent variable for city i in year t, α is the constant term. x_{ijt} denotes the j_{th} explanatory variable for city i in year t, which may be the key variable of interest or other control variables. β_j denotes the coefficient to be estimated for the j_{th} explanatory variable. $dummy_{region}$ includes the regional submarket dummy variables, $dummy_{year}$ includes the year dummy variables. ε_{it} is the random error term for city i in year t. To increase explanatory power, the regional dummy is introduced into Equation (1) [61]. We control for the general time trend effect by employing a time dummy for each year.

3.2. Instrument for Law-Based Governance

Although we try to include a considerable number of control variables in Equation (1), it is still possible that we omit some relevant variables, especially those unobservable variables that influence housing prices and law-based governance simultaneously. In this case, law-based governance may be correlated with the residual errors, leading to biased estimates of the coefficient. To alleviate any possible endogeneity bias, previous studies generally resorted to constructing various exogenous instrumental variables.

We construct a weighted geographical distance as an instrument for law-based governance using the distance from local government to provincial government and the distance from provincial government to central government. In China, spatial distance deeply affects the degree and efficiency of top-down supervision and monitoring from higher-level government [62]. According to the top-down governmental management system in China, local government is directly supervised by provincial government. Thus, the closer the local government is to the provincial government, the more likely it is that the local construction of law-based government should be regulated. Meanwhile, the supervision of central government over provincial government may have an indirect impact on the local construction of law-based government. However, this impact should be less than the impact of the supervision of provincial government over local government. Therefore, we specify the weight of the distance from local government to provincial government to be 0.8, and the weight of the distance from provincial government to central government to be 0.2. Furthermore, the weighted geographical distance should be uncorrelated with the error term.

3.3. Causal Steps Approach

The methodology classically used to identify the mediating role of an interested variable is testing the regression coefficients step by step (causal steps approach) [63,64]. To conveniently describe the principle of this approach, we use the following simplified models.

$$y = \alpha_1 + \beta_1 x + \varepsilon_1 \quad (2)$$

$$m = \alpha_2 + \beta_2 x + \varepsilon_2 \quad (3)$$

$$y = \alpha_3 + \beta_3 x + \beta_4 m + \varepsilon_3 \tag{4}$$

where y is the dependent variable, α_i (I = 1, 2, 3) is the constant term. x denotes the independent variable. β_j (j = 1, 2, 3, 4) denotes the coefficient to be estimated. m is the mediating variable for x to influence y. ε_i (I = 1, 2, 3) is the random error term.

To identify the mediating role of m, the significance of β_1 should be tested in the first step. If β_1 is statistically significant, then β_2 and β_4 should be tested. If β_2 and β_4 are both statistically significant, then the mediating role of m is significant. Further, if β_3 is not statistically significant, then the mediating effect is in full force.

4. Variables and Data

In this study, we are interested in how the law aspect of governance of one city is related to housing prices in that city. The housing price indicator uses the average annual price of new residential housing sold in a city, because there are is no reliable price data for second-hand housing unit sales for a large number of cities in China. A reliable measure of law-based governance is crucial for the credibility of the estimation results. While there is a large number of efforts measuring the degree of rule of law globally [9,65], few studies have attempted to assess the rule of law or law-based governance at the city level. In this paper, the data of city-level indicators of the quality of the law aspect of governance are collected from the Annual Assessment Report on China's Law-based Government that issued by the School of Law-based Government, China University of Political Science and Law (CUPL) [66]. Since 2014, the report has been successively released five times with annual assessment results for 100 cities, which include four major municipalities that are under the state's direct administration, twenty-seven provincial capitals, twenty-three large cities (according to the category set by the State Council), and forty-six medium-sized cities. These cities have a good representation of the levels of law-based governance in China. The report's assessment index system has nine first-level indicators, including "comprehensively performing government functions by law", "organizational leadership", "system construction", "administrative decision", "administrative law enforcement", "government information disclosure", "supervision and accountability", "solving social conflicts and administrative disputes", and "public satisfaction", of local law-based administration. Due to its professionality and independence, the assessment report has earned a good reputation in Chinese society and is widely cited in the media as well as Chinese academic research [66].

As "comprehensively performing government functions by law" has been placed at the most prominent position in the Implementation Outline for Constructing Law-based Government (2015–2020), we use the scores of this indicator in the assessment report to measure the quality of law-based governance. This core indicator is specified to capture the situation of administration by law including aspects of institution setting, leadership design, public services, administrative approval, emergency response, etc. [66]. It has a full score of 100 in the annual assessment report, and the score can be expressed as:

$$\text{LAWGOV} = \text{IS} + \text{LD} + \text{PS} + \text{AA} + \text{ER} \tag{5}$$

where LAWGOV is the score of "comprehensively performing government functions by law", IS denotes the score of "institution setting", LD is the score of "leadership design", PS is the score of "public services", AA denotes the score of "administrative approval", and ER is the score of "emergency response". Figure 2 shows the spatial distribution of mean law-based governance quality between 2014 and 2017 across the sample cities. It can be seen that the cities falling into the highest quality category are mainly located in the eastern region of China. To ensure the robustness of our main findings, we also use the sum of the scores of other auxiliary aspects as an alternative indicator of law-based governance. Additionally, the two types of indicators (the core indicator and the mix of auxiliary indicators) enable us to describe the different law-based governance models well.

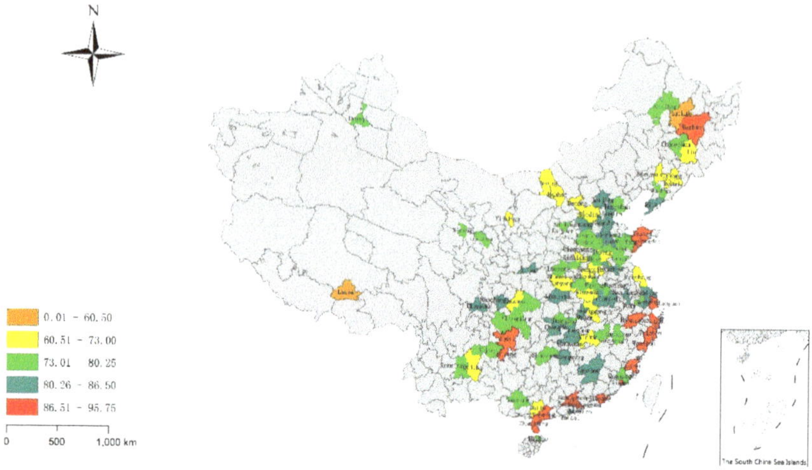

Figure 2. The distribution of law-based governance quality.

In addition to the law aspect of governance, many other factors may also affect city-level housing prices. Guided by findings of the existing literature, we select a large number of control variables that reflect the characteristics of the economic, humanistic, ecological, and geographic environment of cities. Two indicators are utilized to reflect the economic environment, including per capita disposable income of urban households and the ratio of tertiary industry's output value in GDP. For the humanistic environment, we include eight indicators of traffic, educational, medical, and cultural facilities (details in Table 1). Greenness ratio and the emission ratio of industrial soot and dust are used to reflect the ecological environment. Finally, we apply the distance to the coastline to capture the features of the geographic environment.

In addition, as discussed in Section 2.4, law-based governance affects the housing market through the mediating variables of financial loans and foreign investment. We use per capita personal housing purchase loans from banks and non-bank financial institutions to reflect financial loans. The foreign investment indicator is per capita foreign investment. Additionally, per capita loans from housing provident funds are used as an alternative indicator of financial loans to check the robustness of their mediating role between housing prices and law-based governance. In accordance with the suggestions of [67], to improve the estimation results, we incorporate economic regional submarket dummy variables into OLS equations, which can also alleviate the problem of heteroscedasticity [68]. Meanwhile, to control for the time trend effect, we include the time dummy variables for each year.

The data of housing provident fund loans are collected from housing provident fund management centers in each city. The data of the distance to the coastline are calculated by ArcGIS software, which is the shortest straight-line distance from the geometric center of each city to the coastline. The data of city-level housing prices, mediating variables, and control variables are collected from the Bureau of Statistics of each city, the data of the RMB/USD exchange rate come from the People's Bank of China. As the original unit of foreign investment is the dollar, we need to convert dollars to yuan using the exchange rate. The eastern, central, western, and northeastern economic regions are divided by the National Bureau of Statistics of China. The division of first-, second-, third-, fourth-, and fifth-tier cities is based on a research report from Shanghai YiCai Media Co., Ltd. (https://www.yicai.com (accessed on 26 April 2021)). It issues the classification of Chinese cities every year based on the commercial store data of mainstream consumer brands, the user behavior data of internet companies, and urban big data. This type of classification changes the traditional classification of cities based on administrative hierarchy. China's cities are classified according to five dimensional indices: business resource concentration, urban hub, urban activity, lifestyle diversity, and future plasticity, using expert scoring and principal component analysis. The data used in this study cover all the 100 cities in the report over the period 2014–2017 and take their natural logarithm forms in the analysis, except dummy variables. Table 2 describes details of the variables and shows the descriptive statistics.

Table 2. Definitions of variables and descriptive statistics.

Variable	Definition	Unit	Mean	SD	Min	Max	Source
HOUPRI	City-level average price of urban residential housing	yuan/m^2	6814.77	5256.203	1497.69	45818.83	City's Bureau of Statistics
LAWGOV	Score of comprehensively performing government functions by law	—	79.23	10.165	37	98	China University of Political Science and Law
MULVAR	Sum of the other scores of constructing law-based government including organizational leadership, system construction, administrative decision, administrative enforcement of law, government information disclosure, supervision and accountability, and solving social conflicts and administrative disputes	—	369.34	59.994	160.5	506.3	China University of Political Science and Law
LOAN	Per capita personal housing purchase loan from banks and non-bank financial institutions	yuan/person	2115.04	3018.626	16.97	27075.82	City's Bureau of Statistics
HOPRFU	Per capita loans from housing provident funds	yuan/person	782.83	708.421	63.67	4812.74	City's Bureau of Statistics
FOINV	Per capita foreign investment	yuan/person	1489.57	1821.362	0.5	12684.79	City's Bureau of Statistics
SATISFY	Indicator of the degree of satisfaction with law aspect of governance quality	—	125.54	14.918	80.29	184.45	China University of Political Science and Law
INCOME	Per capita disposable income of urban households	yuan/person	30830.32	8482.858	15680.74	59328.92	City's Bureau of Statistics
INDSTR	Ratio of tertiary industry's output value in GDP	%	46.54	9.936	25.42	80.56	City's Bureau of Statistics
POPDEN	Population density	persons/km^2	621.54	405.751	17.86	2648.11	City's Bureau of Statistics
SCHDEN	School density	schools/100 km^2	12.13	12.432	0.34	112.65	City's Bureau of Statistics
HOSDEN	Hospital density	hospitals/100 km^2	2.42	2.073	0.09	18.79	City's Bureau of Statistics
TROBUS	Number of buses per 10,000 people	buses/10^4 people	4.51	4.146	0.22	29.29	City's Bureau of Statistics
ROAD	Per capita area of paved roads	m^2/person	5.54	4.649	0.46	37.55	City's Bureau of Statistics
BOOK	Books in public library per capita	volume/person	0.75	0.707	0.06	4.47	City's Bureau of Statistics
GRERAT	Green ratio	%	2.42	6.366	0.02	49.01	City's Bureau of Statistics
LANSUP	Per capita area of residential construction land launched by the government	m^2/person	13784.20	43740.631	43.58	456260.2	City's Bureau of Statistics
UNEMRA	Unemployment rate	%	2.95	0.771	0.9	4.3	City's Bureau of Statistics
DISCOA	Shortest distance to coastline	km	416.78	514.594	1.13	3435.23	ArcGIS

Table 2. *Cont.*

Variable	Definition	Unit	Mean	SD	Min	Max	Source
DUSOOT	Emission ratio of industrial soot and dust	%	2.56	5.663	0.02	81.3	City's Bureau of Statistics
WEIDIS	Weighted distance using the distance from local government to provincial government and the distance from provincial government to central government	km	321.53	175.561	6.58	1344.38	ArcGIS
EAST	Regional dummy variable: 1, if the city is in Eastern China; 0, otherwise	—	0.46	0.499	0	1	National Bureau of Statistics
CENTRE	Regional dummy variable: 1, if the city is in Central China; 0, otherwise	—	0.26	0.439	0	1	National Bureau of Statistics
WEST	Regional dummy variable: 1, if the city is in Western China; 0, otherwise	—	0.18	0.385	0	1	National Bureau of Statistics
NORTHEAST	Regional dummy variable: 1, if the city is in Northeastern China; 0, otherwise	—	0.10	0.300	0	1	National Bureau of Statistics
FIRST	Dummy variable: 1, if the city is among first-tier cities in China; 0, otherwise	—	0.04	0.196	0	1	https://www.yicai.com (accessed on 26 April 2021)
SECOND	Dummy variable: 1, if the city is among second-tier cities in China; 0, otherwise	—	0.38	0.486	0	1	https://www.yicai.com (accessed on 26 April 2021)
THIRD	Dummy variable: 1, if the city is among third-tier cities in China; 0, otherwise	—	0.32	0.467	0	1	https://www.yicai.com (accessed on 26 April 2021)
FOURTH	Dummy variable: 1, if the city is among fourth-tier cities in China; 0, otherwise	—	0.22	0.415	0	1	https://www.yicai.com (accessed on 26 April 2021)
FIFTH	Dummy variable: 1, if the city is among fifth-tier cities in China; 0, otherwise	—	0.04	0.196	0	1	https://www.yicai.com (accessed on 26 April 2021)

Note: — indicates that corresponding variable is unitless.

5. Research Findings and Discussions

The economy is sensitive to housing [69], and fluctuations in housing markets have long been recognized as leading indicators of an economy [70]. This study aims to investigate the correlation between the law aspect of governance and the economy in China using housing prices as a proxy for economic prosperity [24]. On the other hand, the data released by the National Bureau of Statistics show that the average annual growth rate of housing prices was 8% over the past 20 years in China, and the growth rate of GDP was 9%. The difference between them is not significant. Furthermore, in the sample period, 2014–2017, the average annual growth rate of housing prices was 6% and the growth rate of GDP was 7%. There is still no big difference between the two growth rates. To test whether the hypotheses developed above can be supported, we use Equation (1) to explore the association between law-based governance and housing prices. We first use the method of ordinary least squares (OLS) to perform baseline estimation. Then, in order to avoid possible biased estimates, we test the endogeneity of law-based governance. Thereafter, we discuss the sensitivity, heterogeneity, and robustness of the relationship between the rule of law and housing prices.

5.1. Baseline Estimates

The baseline estimates are shown in Table 3. To compare the results of models with/without dummies, column (1) in Table 3 shows the results of the model without regional dummies and yearly dummies, column (2) includes yearly dummies, and column (3) includes both regional dummies and yearly dummies.

Table 3. Baseline estimates.

	(1) HOUPRI	(2) HOUPRI	(3) HOUPRI
LAWGOV	0.32580 ***	0.32191 ***	0.29648 ***
	(0.10999)	(0.11182)	(0.11207)
INCOME	0.45266 ***	0.41980 ***	0.39392 ***
	(0.07352)	(0.07665)	(0.07714)
INDSTR	0.42731 ***	0.40893 ***	0.40263 ***
	(0.09722)	(0.09966)	(0.09969)
POPDEN	0.00324	0.00496	−0.02143
	(0.04142)	(0.04156)	(0.04285)
SCHDEN	0.06304 *	0.05885 *	0.04798
	(0.03370)	(0.03384)	(0.03480)
HOSDEN	0.01862 **	0.02257 **	0.02676 ***
	(0.00843)	(0.00873)	(0.00916)
TROBUS	0.05808 **	0.06098 ***	0.06752 ***
	(0.02280)	(0.02284)	(0.02298)
ROAD	0.01089 ***	0.01128 ***	0.00997 **
	(0.00387)	(0.00387)	(0.00387)
BOOK	0.08992 ***	0.09513 ***	0.11087 ***
	(0.02340)	(0.02373)	(0.02445)
GRERAT	0.01228	0.00862	0.01487
	(0.02469)	(0.02474)	(0.02472)
LANSUP	−0.02756 ***	−0.03125 ***	−0.03425 ***
	(0.01057)	(0.01072)	(0.01079)
UNEMRA	−0.11651 **	−0.12029 **	−0.11885 **
	(0.04763)	(0.04782)	(0.04954)
DISCOA	−0.06975 ***	−0.07104 ***	−0.08056 ***
	(0.00996)	(0.01002)	(0.01227)
DUSOOT	−0.02622 **	−0.02671 **	−0.01469
	(0.01320)	(0.01354)	(0.01435)
Constant	1.40760	1.86315 *	2.44558 **
	(0.88928)	(0.95404)	(0.97881)
Regional Dummies	No	No	Yes
Yearly Dummies	No	Yes	Yes
N	400	400	400
Root MSE	0.23522	0.23484	0.23254
R^2	0.80705	0.80918	0.81437

Note: *, **, and *** indicate statistical significance at the 10%, 5%, and 1% levels, respectively. Standard errors are in parentheses.

The coefficient of LAWGOV in each column is statistically significantly positive, suggesting the law aspect of governance is positively associated with housing prices. Additionally, the signs of the coefficients of the control variables are basically as expected. Neither population density (POPDEN) nor green ratio (GRERAT) have significant effects on housing prices. However, the effects of other control variables on housing prices are all significant. Per capita disposable income of urban households (INCOME) and the ratio of tertiary industry's output value in GDP (INDSTR) have greater effects on housing prices than other control variables do. Not surprisingly, the effects of the per capita area of residential construction land launched by the government (LANSUP), unemployment rate (UNEMRA), the shortest distance to the coastline (DISCOA), and the emission ratio of industrial soot and dust (DUSOOT) on housing prices are negative. Compared to columns (1) and (2), column (3) shows that the root MSE becomes lower and the R2 rises to a higher level. This indicates that when economic region submarket dummy variables are introduced into the OLS model, its explanatory power increases [61]. We use the model with both regional and yearly dummies to undertake further analysis.

5.2. Endogeneity Test

If the rule of law has potential endogeneity issues, it can lead to biased estimates. To decrease the inaccuracy of the coefficients to be estimated, we first perform a weak instrument test and Durbin–Wu–Hausman test [71,72], and the results are shown in Table 4.

Table 4. Endogeneity test.

	(4) OLS HOUPRI		(5) 2SLS HOUPRI
LAWGOV	0.47390 ***		1.04783 **
	(0.10693)		(0.44295)
Control variables	Yes		Yes
Constant	2.12933 **		−1.66614
	(0.93171)		(2.08097)
Regional dummies	Yes		Yes
Yearly dummies	Yes		Yes
F value of weak instrument test		29.474 ***	
F value of Durbin–Wu–Hausman test		2.25092	
N	400		400
Root MSE	0.22317		0.24711
R^2	0.82903		0.77876

Note: *, **, and *** indicate statistical significance at the 10%, 5%, and 1% levels, respectively. Standard errors are in parentheses. The control variables are the same as in Table 3.

In Table 4, the F value of the weak instrument test for columns (4) using OLS and (5) using 2SLS is significantly greater than 10, indicating that the weighted geographical distance is not a weak instrument [73]. Additionally, the F value of the Durbin–Wu–Hausman test for these two columns is not statistically significant, implying that the law aspect of governance may be exogenous. Therefore, the endogeneity problem of the rule of law may not be paid special attention in doing so. This may imply that we could estimate our model using OLS.

5.3. Mediating Mechanism Test

Mediating mechanism analysis can provide a more detailed understanding to figure out how an interested variable affects the dependent variable [74]. We check the mediating roles of financial loans and foreign investment through testing the regression coefficients step by step [63,64]. The relevant test results are shown in Tables 5 and 6.

Table 5. Correlation between law-based governance and financial loans, and correlation between law-based governance and foreign investment.

	(6) LOAN	(7) FOINV
LAWGOV	0.81186 ***	0.84155 *
	(0.20525)	(0.48367)
Control variables	Yes	Yes
Constant	−7.95179 ***	−21.17797 ***
	(1.84999)	(4.10219)
Regional dummies	Yes	Yes
Yearly dummies	Yes	Yes
N	400	400
Root MSE	0.44171	1.01283
R^2	0.82475	0.52420

Note: *, **, and *** indicate statistical significance at the 10%, 5%, and 1% levels, respectively. Standard errors are in parentheses. The control variables are the same as in Table 3.

Table 6. Correlation between financial loans and housing prices, and correlation between foreign investment and housing prices.

	(8) HOUPRI	(9) HOUPRI
LOAN	0.20088 ***	
	(0.02314)	
FOINV		0.04515 ***
		(0.01059)
LAWGOV	0.21916 **	0.24164 **
	(0.09464)	(0.09862)
Control variables	Yes	Yes
Constant	3.44314 ***	3.55998 ***
	(0.82104)	(0.94096)
Regional dummies	Yes	Yes
Yearly dummies	Yes	Yes
N	400	400
Root MSE	0.19413	0.20930
R^2	0.87096	0.85001

Note: *, **, and *** indicate statistical significance at the 10%, 5%, and 1% levels, respectively. Standard errors are in parentheses. The control variables are the same as in Table 3.

5.3.1. Mediating Role of Financial Loans

First, in Table 3, we show that the law aspect of governance is positively related to housing prices. Second, it is easy to see that the rule of law is significantly positively correlated with financial loans in column (6) of Table 5. Third, we can see in column (8) of Table 6 that both the law aspect of governance and financial loans are significantly positively related to housing prices. Therefore, the mediating role of financial loans is statistically significant according to the step-by-step approach, which implies that improving the quality of the rule of law may enlarge loans and then raise housing prices. Hypothesis 1 is supported.

5.3.2. Mediating Role of Foreign Investment

Similarly, column (7) in Table 5 shows that the law aspect of governance is significantly positively connected with foreign investment. In addition, both the rule of law and foreign investment are significantly positively associated with housing prices in column (9) of Table 6. Based on the results in Table 3 and the step-by-step approach, the positive mediating role of foreign investment is statistically significant, indicating that raising the quality of the law aspect of governance may attract foreign investment and then boost housing prices. Hypothesis 1 is also confirmed.

5.3.3. Robustness Test of Mediating Role of Loans

In order to ensure the credibility of the positive mediating role of loans, we replace financial loans from banks and non-bank financial institutions with loans from housing provident funds to check the robustness. The test results are in Table 7.

Table 7. Robustness test of the mediating role of financial loans.

	(10) HOPRFU	(11) HOUPRI
LAWGOV	0.42804 **	0.22448 **
	(0.20647)	(0.10940)
HOPRFU		0.06432 **
		(0.02787)
Control variables	Yes	Yes
Constant	−2.51929	2.79558 ***
	(1.64530)	(1.02577)
Regional dummies	Yes	Yes
Yearly dummies	Yes	Yes
N	400	400
Root MSE	0.43228	0.23308
R^2	0.75362	0.81398

Note: *, **, and *** indicate statistical significance at the 10%, 5%, and 1% levels, respectively. Standard errors are in parentheses. The control variables are the same as in Table 3.

It is shown in column (10) of Table 7 that the rule of law is significantly positively associated with loans from housing provident funds. Additionally, both housing provident fund loans and the law aspect of governance significantly and positively link with housing prices in column (11) of Table 7. In according with the results in Table 3 and the step-by-step approach, the positive mediating role of housing provident fund loans is statistically significant. Therefore, the mediating role of loans in the relationship between the rule of law and housing prices is very robust.

5.4. Sensitivity Analysis

To elaborate on how the association between the rule of law and housing prices changes with the degree of public satisfaction with the quality of the law aspect of governance, we consult with respondents on a series of different questions, such as "How well does the local government listen to the opinions and suggestions of the people when making major decisions?", "What about the integrity of the local government?", "How effective is the local government in fighting corruption?", "How about the propaganda of law-based governance?", etc. The final score for this indicator is equal to the sum of the scores for responses to each question. We add the interaction term of the rule of law and the degree of satisfaction, LAWGOV×SATISFY, in Equation (1). The estimation result is displayed in Table 8.

Column (12) in Table 8 shows that the coefficient of the interaction term is significantly positive. We also drop the variable LAWGOV from the regressions to eliminate the possible collinearity between it and the interaction term, finding that the estimate of the interaction term is still significantly positive in column (13) of Table 8. This finding implies that, if the public has high satisfaction with the quality of the law aspect of governance, then the correlation between the rule of law and housing prices would be greater. Therefore, hypothesis 2 is supported.

Table 8. Sensitivity and heterogeneity of the relationship between law-based governance and housing prices.

	(12) HOUPRI	(13) HOUPRI	(14) HOUPRI
LAWGOV	0.06259		0.17454 *
	(0.15232)		(0.09765)
LAWGOV × SATISFY	0.05207 **	0.05928 ***	
	(0.02365)	(0.01586)	
Control variables	Yes	Yes	Yes
LAWGOV × FIRST			0.16205 ***
			(0.02434)
LAWGOV × SECOND			0.06075 ***
			(0.01611)
LAWGOV × THIRD			−0.00281
			(0.01467)
LAWGOV × FOURTH			0.00491
			(0.01486)
Constant	2.68313 ***	2.80369 ***	5.11483 ***
	(0.88353)	(0.83248)	(0.81852)
Regional dummies	Yes	Yes	No
Yearly dummies	Yes	Yes	Yes
N	400	400	400
Root MSE	0.21171	0.21148	0.19214
R^2	0.84653	0.84647	0.87360

Note: *, **, and *** indicate statistical significance at the 10%, 5%, and 1% levels, respectively. Standard errors are in parentheses. The control variables are the same as in Table 3.

5.5. Heterogeneity Analysis

In order to elucidate the heterogeneity of the relationship between law-based governance and housing prices across city groups, we add the interaction terms, LAWGOV × FIRST, LAWGOV × SECOND, LAWGOV × THIRD, and LAWGOV × FOURTH, in Equation (1). We drop the regional dummy variables to eliminate the possible collinearity between them and the interaction terms. The estimation result is displayed in column (14) of Table 8, suggesting that the association between the rule of law and housing prices in the first- and second-tier cities is significantly greater than that in other cities. Thus, hypothesis 3 is confirmed.

5.6. Robustness Test of the Effect of Rule of Law Quality on Housing Prices

In China, "comprehensively performing government functions by law" is the core of the construction of law-based government. In addition to this critical variable, some other auxiliary variables are also available to measure the quality of the rule of law in the Annual Assessment Report on China's Law-based Government. Each of the auxiliary variables reflects a special aspect of law-based governance. To ensure the trustworthiness of the correlation between the law aspect of governance and housing prices, we construct another variable, MULVAR, to replace LAWGOV. Each indicator score of other auxiliary aspects of law-based governance can be obtained like LAWGOV. Then, we combine these indicators into one indicator to alternatively describe law-based governance, of which the score can be expressed as:

$$\text{MULVAR} = \text{OL} + \text{SC} + \text{AD} + \text{AE} + \text{GI} + \text{SA} + \text{CD} \quad (6)$$

where MULVAR denotes the score of the alternative indicator, OL is the score of "organizational leadership", SC denotes the score of "system construction", AD is the score of "administrative decision", AE denotes the score of "administrative law enforcement", GI is the score of "government information disclosure", SA is the score of "supervision and accountability", and CD denotes the score of "solving social conflicts and administrative disputes". The robustness test results are displayed in Table 9.

Table 9. Robustness test of the relationship between law-based governance and housing prices.

	(15) HOUPRI	(16) HOUPRI
MULVAR	0.19954 **	0.14891 *
	(0.09845)	(0.08836)
Control variables	Yes	Yes
FIRST × MULVAR		0.12198 ***
		(0.01796)
SECOND × MULVAR		0.04945 ***
		(0.01147)
THIRD × MULVAR		−0.00032
		(0.01066)
FOURTH × MULVAR		0.00504
		(0.01079)
Constant	2.21459 **	5.64530 ***
	(0.88288)	(0.80838)
Regional dummies	Yes	No
Yearly dummies	Yes	Yes
N	400	400
Root MSE	0.21486	0.19189
R^2	0.84151	0.87393

Note: *, **, and *** indicate statistical significance at the 10%, 5%, and 1% levels, respectively. Standard errors are in parentheses. The control variables are the same as in Table 3.

Obviously, the coefficient of the alternative indicator of the rule of law is still significantly positive in column (15) of Table 9, and the characteristic of the heterogeneity in column (16) is consistent with that in column (14) of Table 8. Therefore, the relationship between the law aspect of governance and housing prices is robust.

In addition, we construct a 0–1 spatial weight matrix (**W**) to calculate Moran's I of housing prices in our sample cities, Moran's I is 0.24314 and the p-value is less than 2.2e-16, suggesting that there is significant spatial autocorrelation in housing prices. Therefore, we next test whether the relationship between law-based governance and housing prices can still be robust in spatial models after dropping regional dummies. The estimates of the spatial lag model and spatial error model are shown in Table 10.

Table 10. Maximum likelihood (ML) estimation of spatial models.

	(17) Spatial Lag Model HOUPRI	(18) Spatial Error Model HOUPRI
LAWGOV	0.29187 ***	0.23523 **
	(0.10906)	(0.10491)
W × HOUPRI	0.19766 ***	
	(0.04429)	
W × ERROR		0.39975 ***
		(0.06565)
Control variables	Yes	Yes
Constant	1.08814	2.52113 ***
	(1.04273)	(0.97105)
Yearly dummies	Yes	Yes
N	388	388
Wald chi^2	1890.01	1639.34
Prob > chi^2	0	0
R^2	0.8183	0.8297

Note: *, **, and *** indicate statistical significance at the 10%, 5%, and 1% levels, respectively. Standard errors are in parentheses. The control variables are the same as in Table 3. To avoid the emergence of cities without neighbors, Urumqi, Kashgar, and Lhasa are dropped.

It can be seen from Table 10 that the estimated coefficients of law-based governance are both significantly positive in the spatial lag model and spatial error model. This implies that our main findings are still supported after taking into consideration spatial autocorrelation.

6. Conclusions

With the increasing role of law in governance [75], there is a growing emphasis on law-based governance worldwide, and China expects to build itself into a socialist country with Chinese characteristics under the rule of law. In conventional terms, the rule of law necessarily has a positive correlation with the economic growth and the overall economic prosperity of any country [76]. For example, law-based environmental governance boosts employment [77]. Therefore, the pursuit of law-based governance is closely related to economic development, including the real estate market [53]. Although some studies have noted that a certain law can have a significant impact on housing prices [54], and the revised "Japanese Tenant Protection Law" affects housing rent [78], there is still limited knowledge about how the rule of law and housing prices are related across cities in a given country. In the current context of China's efforts to raise the quality of the law aspect of governance, a lack of awareness of such liaising mechanisms may not contribute maximally to economic development and may lead to less efficient regulation of possible rapid increases in housing prices. Our study bridges this cognitive gap by analyzing the ways in which the law aspect of governance is associated with housing prices, and the focus is the roles played by the factors of public satisfaction and socioeconomic groups.

This study finds that improving the quality of the law aspect of governance can enlarge loans, attract foreign investment, and then significantly raise housing prices. However, the relationship between the rule of law and housing prices is sensitive to public satisfaction. Additionally, considering the geographic and socioeconomic factors, the present paper shows that the correlation between the law aspect of governance and housing prices is greater in the first- and second-tier cities. These findings provide new insights into the pursuit of the rule of law with high quality in contemporary China.

In fact, China has made various efforts to raise the quality of the law aspect of governance in order to establish a socialist state under the rule of law. This pursuit in practice necessarily contributes to economic prosperity. Nevertheless, housing prices may increase additionally in the pursuit, which is an unwanted and concerning outcome for the government. Inspired by our findings, local governments could promulgate measures to reduce financial loans and foreign investment to curb the possible rapid rise in housing prices when improving the law aspect of governance quality, especially for emerging economies in the world.

Author Contributions: Conceptualization, H.Z.; methodology, H.Z.; software, H.Z.; validation, J.C. and H.Z.; formal analysis, H.Z.; investigation, H.Z.; resources, H.Z.; data curation, H.Z. and Q.Z.; writing—original draft preparation, H.Z.; writing—review and editing, J.C.; visualization, H.Z.; supervision, J.C.; project administration, J.C.; funding acquisition, J.C. All authors have read and agreed to the published version of the manuscript.

Funding: This research was funded by National Natural Science Foundation of China, grant number NSFC71974125, NSF71661137004, NSF71573166; China Postdoctoral Science Foundation, grant number 2019M651511, Provincial Natural Science Foundation of Anhui, grant number 2008085MG237; and Scientific Research Foundation of Chuzhou University, grant number 2018qd12. The APC was funded by the Provincial Natural Science Foundation of Anhui.

Data Availability Statement: Data that support the findings of this study are available from the corresponding author upon reasonable request.

Conflicts of Interest: The authors declare no conflict of interest.

References

1. Boeninger, E. Governance and development: Issues and constraints. *World Bank Econ. Rev.* **1991**, *5* (Suppl. S1), 267–288. [CrossRef]
2. UNDP. Governance for Sustainable Human Development. Quezon City, the Philippines. 1997. Available online: https://digitallibrary.un.org/record/261618 (accessed on 18 March 2019).
3. United Nations. Governance and Development: Thematic Think Piece. New York, 2012. Available online: https://www.un.org/millenniumgoals/pdf/ThinkPieces/7_governance.pdf (accessed on 6 November 2019).
4. World Bank. *Sub-Saharan Africa: From Crisis to Sustainable Growth, a Long-Term Perspective Study*; World Bank Group: Washington, DC, USA, 1989; Available online: https://documents.worldbank.org/en/publication/documents-reports/documentdetail/498241468742846138/from-crisis-to-sustainable-growth-sub-saharan-africa-a-long-term-perspective-study (accessed on 28 December 2020).
5. World Bank. *Governance and Development*; World Bank Group: Washington, DC, USA, 1992.
6. World Bank. *Governance: The World Bank's Experience*; World Bank Group: Washington, DC, USA, 1994; Available online: https://documents.worldbank.org/en/publication/documents-reports/documentdetail/711471468765285964/governance-the-world-banks-experience (accessed on 13 August 2019).
7. Posner, R.A. Creating a legal framework for economic development. *World Bank Res. Obs.* **1998**, *13*, 1–11. [CrossRef]
8. Davis, K.; Trebilcock, M. The relationship between law and development: Optimists versus skeptics. *Am. J. Comp. Law* **2008**, *56*, 895–946. [CrossRef]
9. WJP. *World Justice Project Rule of Law Index 2020*; World Justice Project: Washington, DC, USA, 2020; Available online: https://worldjusticeproject.org/rule-of-law-index/ (accessed on 30 December 2020).
10. Haggard, S.; MacIntyre, A.; Tiede, L. The rule of law and economic development. *Annu. Rev. Political Sci.* **2008**, *11*, 205–234. [CrossRef]
11. Xu, G. The role of law in economic growth: A literature review. *J. Econ. Surv.* **2011**, *25*, 833–871. [CrossRef]
12. Weingast, B.R. Why developing countries prove so resistant to the rule-of-law. In *Global Perspectives on the Rule of Law*, 1st ed.; Heckman, J.J., Nelson, R.L., Cabatingan, L., Eds.; Routledge: Oxfordshire, UK, 2013; pp. 28–52. [CrossRef]
13. Tiede, L.B. The rule of law, institutions, and economic development. In *Handbook on the Rule of Law*; May, C., Winchester, A., Eds.; Edward Elgar Publishing: London, UK, 2018; pp. 405–418. [CrossRef]
14. Cho, Y.N. 'Governing the country according to the law': China's rule of law policy as political reform. *J. Int. Area Stud.* **2014**, *21*, 21–36. Available online: http://www.jstor.org/stable/43111522 (accessed on 25 July 2020).
15. CGTN. Graphics: All You Need to Know about China's Rule of Law. China Global Television Network. 2019. Available online: https://news.cgtn.com/news/2019-11-28/Graphics-All-you-need-to-know-about-China-s-rule-of-law-LZpW0KeM8w/index.html (accessed on 23 April 2020).
16. Li, E. China and the rule of law. *Am. Aff.* **2019**, *3*, 133–154.
17. Li, A.H.F. Centralisation of power in the pursuit of law-based governance: Legal reform in China under the Xi Administration. *China Perspect.* **2016**, 63–68. Available online: http://journals.openedition.org/chinaperspectives/6995 (accessed on 27 November 2019). [CrossRef]
18. Peerenboom, R. *China's Long March toward Rule of Law*; Cambridge University Press (CUP): Cambridge, UK, 2002. [CrossRef]
19. Li, L. Rule by law and governance by law. In *Building the Rule of Law in China*; Elsevier: Berlin, Germany, 2017; pp. 145–215. [CrossRef]
20. MOJ. Minister of Justice: Further Advancing Overall Law-Based Governance. The Official Website of Ministry of Justice of PRC, 2020. Available online: http://en.moj.gov.cn/2020-05/29/c_496509.htm (accessed on 26 December 2020).
21. Xi, J. The Law-Based Governance of China. Beijing: Central Compilation & Translation Press. 2017. Available online: https://www.amazon.com/law-based-governance-china-Xi-Jinping/dp/7511732267 (accessed on 17 September 2019).
22. Peerenboom, R. Fly high the banner of socialist rule of law with Chinese characteristics! *Hague J. Rule Law* **2015**, *7*, 49–74. [CrossRef]
23. WGI. Worldwide Governance Indicators Homepage. 2018. Available online: http://info.worldbank.org/governance/wgi/ (accessed on 19 July 2020).
24. Glaeser, E.; Huang, W.; Ma, Y.; Shleifer, A. A real estate boom with Chinese characteristics. *J. Econ. Perspect.* **2017**, *31*, 93–116. [CrossRef]
25. Kuminoff, N.V.; Smith, V.K.; Timmins, C. The new economics of equilibrium sorting and policy evaluation using housing markets. *J. Econ. Lit.* **2013**, *51*, 1007–1062. [CrossRef]
26. Roback, J. Wages, rents, and the quality of life. *J. Political Econ.* **1982**, *90*, 1257–1278. Available online: http://www.jstor.org/stable/10.2307/1830947 (accessed on 22 December 2019). [CrossRef]
27. Tiebout, C.M. A Pure Theory of Local Expenditures. *J. Politician Econ.* **1956**, *64*, 416–424. [CrossRef]
28. Chen, J.; Han, X. The evolution of the housing market and its socioeconomic impacts in the post-reform people's Republic of China: A survey of the literature. *J. Econ. Surv.* **2014**, *28*, 652–670. [CrossRef]
29. Leftwich, A. Governance, democracy and development in the Third World. *Third World Q.* **1993**, *14*, 605–624. [CrossRef]
30. Sundaram, J.K.; Chowdhury, A. *Is Good Governance Good for Development? United Nations Series on Development*; United Nations Department of Economic and Social Affairs: New York, NY, USA, 2014. [CrossRef]

31. Bardhan, P. Decentralization of governance and development. *J. Econ. Perspect.* **2002**, *16*, 185–205. Available online: http://www.jstor.org/stable/info/3216920 (accessed on 11 March 2019). [CrossRef]
32. Acemoglu, D.; Johnson, S.; Robinson, J. Institutions as the fundamental cause of long-run growth. In *Handbook of Economic Growth*; Aghion, P., Durlauf, S., Eds.; Elsevier: Amsterdam, The Netherlands, 2005; pp. 386–472. Available online: http://economics.mit.edu/files/4469 (accessed on 29 November 2019).
33. North, D.C. *Institutions, Institutional Change, and Economic Performance*; Cambridge University Press: Cambridge, UK, 1991; Available online: http://www.cambridge.org/gb/knowledge/isbn/item1139799/?site_locale=en_GB (accessed on 19 September 2020).
34. United Nations. What Is the Rule of Law: United Nations and Rule of Law. The Official Website of United Nations, 2020. Available online: https://www.un.org/ruleoflaw/what-is-the-rule-of-law/ (accessed on 18 December 2020).
35. Kaufmann, D.K.; Kraay, A.; Mastruzzi, M. The worldwide governance indicators: Methodology and analytical issues. *Hague J. Rule Law* **2011**, *3*, 220–246. [CrossRef]
36. World Bank. World Development Report 2017: Governance and the Law. New York, 2017. Available online: https://www.worldbank.org/en/publication/wdr2017 (accessed on 19 March 2020).
37. Biddulph, S.; Cooney, S.; Zhu, Y. Rule of law with Chinese characteristics: The role of campaigns in lawmaking. *Law Policy* **2012**, *34*, 373–401. [CrossRef]
38. Delisle, J. Law in the China Model 2.0: Legality, developmentalism and leninism under Xi Jinping. *J. Contemp. China* **2016**, *26*, 68–84. [CrossRef]
39. Rothstein, B. The Chinese paradox of high growth and low quality of government: The cadre organization meets Max Weber. *Governance* **2015**, *28*, 533–548. [CrossRef]
40. Heckman, J.J.; Nelson, R.L.; Cabatingan, L. (Eds.) *Global Perspectives on the Rule of Law*; Routledge: Oxfordshire, UK, 2009. [CrossRef]
41. Yao, Y. The disinterested government: An interpretation of China's economic success in the reform era. In *Achieving Development Success: Strategies and Lessons from the Developing World*; Oxford University Press: Oxford, UK, 2013; Available online: https://global.oup.com/academic/product/achieving-development-success-9780199671557?cc=cn&lang=en&# (accessed on 8 May 2020).
42. Mazur, J.; Ursu, A.-E. China's Disinterested Government and the Rule of Law. *Asia Pac. Policy Stud.* **2017**, *4*, 376–382. [CrossRef]
43. Diamond, L. The rule of law as transition to democracy in China. *J. Contemp. China* **2003**, *12*, 319–331. [CrossRef]
44. Jiang, Z. Hold High the Great Banner of Deng Xiaoping Theory for an All-Round Advancement of the Cause of Building Socialism with Chinese Characteristics' into the 21st Century–Report Delivered at the 15th National Congress of the Communist Party of China. Beijing Review. 1997. Available online: http://www.bjreview.com.cn/document/txt/2011-03/25/content_363499.htm (accessed on 25 July 2019).
45. CTB. Communique of the Fourth Plenary Session of the 18th Central Committee of the Communist Party of China. Translated by Compilation and Translation Bureau (CTB) of the Central Committee of the Communist Party of China. 2014. Available online: http://www.china.org.cn/china/fourth_plenary_session/2014-12/02/content_34208801.htm (accessed on 24 November 2019).
46. Chen, A.H.Y. China's long march towards rule of law or China's turn against law? *Chin. J. Comp. Law* **2016**, *4*, 1–35. [CrossRef]
47. MoJ. Statistical Analysis of Lawyers and Grassroots Legal Services in 2019. The Official Website of Ministry of Justice, 2020. Available online: http://www.moj.gov.cn/organization/content/2020-06/24/574_3251377.html (accessed on 30 December 2020).
48. Chen, K.; Wen, Y. The great housing boom of China. *Am. Econ. J. Macroecon.* **2017**, *9*, 73–114. [CrossRef]
49. Fang, Y.; Liu, Z.; Chen, Y. Housing inequality in urban China: Theoretical debates, empirical evidences, and future directions. *J. Plan. Lit.* **2020**, *35*, 41–53. [CrossRef]
50. Li, Z.; Wu, F. Socio-spatial differentiation and residential inequalities in Shanghai: A case study of three neighborhoods. *Hous. Stud.* **2006**, *21*, 695–717. [CrossRef]
51. Funke, M.; Leiva-Leon, D.; Tsang, A. Mapping China's time-varying house price landscape. *Reg. Sci. Urban Econ.* **2019**, *78*, 103464. [CrossRef]
52. Qiao, S.; Upham, F. The evolution of relational property rights: A case of Chinese rural land reform. *Iowa Law Rev.* **2015**, *100*, 2479–2506. [CrossRef]
53. Shih, M. Legal geographies–Governing through law: Rights based conflicts and property development in Shanghai. *Urban Geogr.* **2010**, *31*, 973–987. [CrossRef]
54. Nanda, A.; Ross, S.L. The impact of property condition disclosure laws on housing prices: Evidence from an event study using propensity scores. *J. Real Estate Financ. Econ.* **2009**, *45*, 88–109. [CrossRef]
55. Li, Z.; Ouyang, X.; Du, K.; Zhao, Y. Does government transparency contribute to improved eco-efficiency performance? An empirical study of 262 cities in China. *Energy Policy* **2017**, *110*, 7. [CrossRef]
56. Li, L.; Tian, H.; Lv, Y. China's rule of law index 2017. In *Research Series on the Chinese Dream and China's Development Path*; Li, L., Tian, H., Lv, Y., Eds.; Springer: Singapore, 2018. [CrossRef]
57. La Porta, R.; Lopez-De-Silanes, F.; Shleifer, A.; Vishny, R.W. Law and finance. *J. Political Econ.* **1998**, *106*, 1113–1115. [CrossRef]
58. Rose, M.J. Origination channel, prepayment penalties and default. *Real Estate Econ.* **2012**, *40*, 663–708. [CrossRef]
59. Jain, P.K.; Kuvvet, E.; Pagano, M.S. Corruption's impact on foreign portfolio investment. *Int. Bus. Rev.* **2017**, *26*, 23–35. [CrossRef]

60. He, C.; Wang, J.; Cheng, S. What attracts foreign direct investment in China's real estate development? *Ann. Reg. Sci.* **2011**, *46*, 267–293. [CrossRef]
61. Goodman, A.C.; Thibodeau, T.G. Housing market segmentation and hedonic prediction accuracy. *J. Hous. Econ.* **2003**, *12*, 181–201. [CrossRef]
62. Li, L.; Pang, B.; Wu, Y. Isolated counties, administrative monitoring, and the misuse of public funds in China. *Governance* **2019**, *32*, 779–797. [CrossRef]
63. Baron, R.M.; Kenny, D.A. The moderator–mediator variable distinction in social psychological research: Conceptual, strategic, and statistical considerations. *J. Pers. Soc. Psychol.* **1986**, *51*, 1173–1182. [CrossRef]
64. Judd, C.M.; Kenny, D.A. Process analysis. *Eval. Rev.* **1981**, *5*, 602–619. [CrossRef]
65. Dougherty, A.; Gryskiewicz, A.; Ponce, A. Measuring the rule of law: The world justice project's rule of law index. In *The Palgrave Handbook of Indicators in Global Governance*; Springer International: Cham, Switzerland, 2018; pp. 255–276. [CrossRef]
66. CUPL. Introduction about the Annual Assessment Report on China's Law-Based Government. The Official Website of Institute of Law-Based Government, China University of Political Science and Law, 2018. Available online: http://en.fzzfyjy.cupl.edu.cn/Assessment_Report_of_China_s_Law_Based_Government_/About_the_Report.htm (accessed on 20 October 2020).
67. Bourassa, S.C.; Cantoni, E.; Hoesli, M. Spatial dependence, housing submarkets, and house price prediction. *J. Real Estate Finance Econ.* **2007**, *35*, 143–160. [CrossRef]
68. Stevenson, S. New empirical evidence on heteroscedasticity in hedonic housing models. *J. Hous. Econ.* **2004**, *13*, 136–153. [CrossRef]
69. Loutskina, E.; Strahan, P.E. Financial integration, housing, and economic volatility. *J. Financ. Econ.* **2015**, *115*, 25–41. [CrossRef]
70. Huang, Y.; Li, Q.; Liow, K.H.; Zhou, X. Is housing the business cycle? A multiresolution analysis for OECD countries. *J. Hous. Econ.* **2020**, *49*, 101692. [CrossRef]
71. Fernández-Avilés, G.; Román, J.; Montero, J.M. Geostatistical air pollution indexes in spatial hedonic models: The case of Madrid, Spain. *J. Real Estate Res.* **2012**, *34*, 243–274. Available online: https://ssrn.com/abstract=2029826 (accessed on 27 December 2019). [CrossRef]
72. Simons, R.A.; Seo, Y.; Rosenfeld, P. Modeling the effects of refinery emissions on residential property values. *J. Real Estate Res.* **2015**, *37*, 321–342. [CrossRef]
73. Stock, J.H.; Yogo, M. Testing for weak instruments in linear IV regression. In *Identification and Inference for Econometric Models*; Andrews, D.W.K., Stock, J.H., Eds.; Cambridge University Press: Cambridge, UK, 2005; pp. 80–108. [CrossRef]
74. MacKinnon, D.P.; Fairchild, A.J. Current Directions in Mediation Analysis. *Curr. Dir. Psychol. Sci.* **2009**, *18*, 16–20. [CrossRef]
75. Cosens, B.A.; Craig, R.K.; Hirsch, S.L.; Tony Arnold, C.A.; Benson, M.H.; DeCaro, D.A.; Garmestani, A.S.; Gosnell, H.; Ruhl, J.; Schlager, E. The role of law in adaptive governance. *Ecol. Soc.* **2017**, *22*, 30. [CrossRef]
76. Avbelj, M. Rule of law and the economic crisis in a pluralist European Union. *Hague J. Rule Law* **2016**, *8*, 191–203. [CrossRef]
77. Zhong, S.; Xiong, Y.; Xiang, G. Environmental regulation benefits for whom? Heterogeneous effects of the intensity of the environmental regulation on employment in China. *J. Environ. Manag.* **2021**, *281*, 111877. [CrossRef]
78. Seko, M.; Sumita, K. Japanese housing tenure choice and welfare implications after the revision of the tenant protection law. *J. Real Estate Financ. Econ.* **2007**, *35*, 357–383. [CrossRef]

land

MDPI

Article

Land Economic Efficiency and Improvement of Environmental Pollution in the Process of Sustainable Urbanization: Case of Eastern China

Binbin Chang [1] and Lei Chen [2,*]

[1] School of Finance and Accounting, Henan University of Animal Husbandry & Economy, Zhengzhou 450046, China; 201012@hnuahe.edu.cn
[2] School of Finance and Economics, Jimei University, Xiamen 361023, China
* Correspondence: 200661000207@jmu.edu.cn

Abstract: Economic development, environmental protection and land resources are important components in sustainable cities. According to the environmental Kuznets curve, developing countries are prone to environmental pollution problems while developing their economies. At the same time, as urbanization progresses, the problem of inadequate land resources and land use efficiency in China is coming to the fore. Although China is a developing country, it began to actively implement environmental protection measures years ago in an effort to transform itself into an innovative country. Therefore, as an economic and policy pioneer region, can eastern China benefit from all three aspects of land–economy–environment at the same time? Or will the increase in land economic efficiency (Land_EcoE) and the improvement of environmental pollution occur simultaneously? With the characteristics of land use efficiency and other concepts, this study combines economic factors and land factors to establish a Land_EcoE evaluation system. On the basis of mapping the spatio-temporal evolution of carbon emissions and Land_EcoE, and discussing the spatio-temporal evolution characteristics and correlation between them initially and visually by means of geographic data visualization, this study uses the data of 84 prefecture-level cities and municipalities directly under the central government in eastern China from 2011 to 2017 to test the research hypotheses from a quantitative perspective. Specifically, this study analyzes the correlation between Land_EcoE and environmental pollution by constructing a panel regression model. The conclusions show that, in general, the increase in Land_EcoE in eastern China is associated with the increase in carbon emissions. For a group of prefecture-level cities with the most developed economies in eastern China, the increase in Land_EcoE is correlated with the decrease in carbon emissions. Based on this research, this study proposes a series of policy implications on how to promote simultaneous economic–land–environmental benefits.

Keywords: land economic efficiency; environmental pollution; carbon emissions; sustainable cities; eastern China

Citation: Chang, B.; Chen, L. Land Economic Efficiency and Improvement of Environmental Pollution in the Process of Sustainable Urbanization: Case of Eastern China. *Land* **2021**, *10*, 845. https://doi.org/10.3390/land10080845

Academic Editors: Maciej J. Nowak, Giancarlo Cotella and Przemysław Śleszyński

Received: 22 June 2021
Accepted: 11 August 2021
Published: 12 August 2021

1. Introduction

Although the industrial revolution liberated human productivity, it was destined to intensify the conflict between human development and the natural environment. The development of industry over the centuries has brought people an abundance of material resources, but at the same time has created serious environmental hazards. For example, industrial water pollution induces infant congenital anomalies [1]; plastic particles have entered the human body through the ecological cycle of land, sea and air [2,3]. The dangers of pollution have awakened humankind to the need to protect the environment and to promote sustainable development. In 2007, 50% of the world's population was urban, and by 2025 it is expected to be 60%. There is no doubt that cities will be the main carrier of human life [4], and the construction of sustainable cities is of great importance to sustainable development [5,6].

Sustainable cities were first formally proposed at the Second United Nations Conference on Humanity in 1996 and have a rich connotation: social connotation [7], resource connotation [8], economic connotation [9] and environmental connotation [10]. Sustainable cities are one of the current research hotspots. Although the research on sustainable cities in China started late, it has been relatively fruitful. The literature on sustainable cities in China from the perspective of economics is distinctive. There are studies from the perspective of scientific landscape of smart cities [11], applied case studies [12], studies based on the perspective of eco-cities and low-carbon cities [13] and studies measuring the level of sustainable cities [14]. In addition, there are many studies focusing on the environmental factors of sustainable cities, such as green infrastructure and urban living environment [15] and territorial spatial planning [16]. The environmental Kuznets curve (EKC) was originally used to explain the existence of an inverted U-shaped relationship between income and the environment [17,18], while scholars later extended the connotation of the EKC to the interrelationship between the economy and the environment [19]. Recently, many scholars have extended its connotation to the interrelationship between the economy and the environment. When a country has a low level of economic development, the growth of the economy brings environmental pollution due to the scale effect [20,21]. Additionally, because industrial development requires a large amount of energy, and one of the main sources of energy in China is carbon-based energy [22,23], this leads to the fact that economic development in China in the past was inevitably polluting the environment. Studies by Christmann and Taylor and Li and Gong have proved this view [24,25].

Land urbanization has a negative impact on urban eco-efficiency [26]. Thus, China's rapid urbanization [27,28] has left China with some hidden problems and contradictions: between the scarcity of land resources [29] and the growing demand for urban building land, and between the lack of land use efficiency and the growing demand for environmental protection [30–32]. Since land resources, economic development and environmental protection are all important for the development of sustainable cities, can they all benefit at the same time? Terrell found that economic growth can influence land use and thus reduce carbon emissions through the EKC [33]. Pontarollo and Muñoz found an inverted U-shaped curve relationship between land consumption and economic growth [34]. Pontarollo and Serpieri discussed EKC from the perspective of urban architecture [35]. In China, Chen examined the presence of EKC using CO2 emissions [36]. However, Wang and Ye argued that the increase in income cannot directly reduce pollution, but it needs to be achieved by improving energy efficiency and implementing carbon taxes [37]. There are scholars have also focused their perspectives on cities and found that smart cities have environmental improvement effects [38]. Liao et al. measured urban land use efficiency in the framework of sustainable cities [39]. Dong et al. clarified the interaction between LUE, industrial transformation and carbon emissions [40]. To some extent, these studies confirm that the triad of economy, land and environment can benefit simultaneously. However, there is a paucity of literature on the study of China, and their conclusions cannot be strongly supported.

In order to study land, economy and environment in the same framework, this study proposes and measures the land economic efficiency (Land_EcoE) index based on the characteristics of the concepts of "economic benefit of land use" and "land use efficiency" (LUE). Economic benefit of land use emphasizes the value of goods and services that may be produced within a limited amount of land [41], focusing on the output dimension. Land use efficiency integrally reflects the degree of material circulation and energy exchange between the elements in the urban system, the overall system and the external environment, and is a direct reflection of the realization of land value in the process of urban economic development [42]. Based on the two concepts, Land_EcoE not only contains the connotation of economic output, but also has the connotation of economic rationality (economic structure dimension) and economic growth potential (economic quality dimension).

In fact, the Communist Party of China and the Chinese government have promptly realized that the past crude factor-driven development model cannot meet the needs of China's development in the new era and that green, healthy and sustainable development is the choice of the times. The "Ninth Five-Year Plan" period (1996–2000) put limits on energy consumption and pollution emissions. The "11th Five-Year Plan" (2006–2010) made environmental regulation a binding target for local governments. Innovation is the first driving force for development. For many years, China has been actively pursuing an economic transformation strategy towards an innovation-driven, intensive development model. Wang et al. measured the low-carbon development quality of 259 cities in China and found that the quality level was generally higher in the eastern region [43]. According to the above, the synergistic development of economy–land–environment is achievable. Then, is the synergistic development of economic–land–environmental aspects possible in eastern China, which is the first place to go for policies and economically developed regions [44]? Or will the increase in land economic efficiency and the improvement of environmental pollution occur simultaneously?

Through the aforementioned literature, it can be found that: first, sustainable cities are a current research hotspot, but in China, research on sustainable cities is relatively weak, and research from the economic and land dimensions still needs to be improved; second, there are abundant studies on the EKC, but there are few studies on LUE from multiple dimensions from an economic perspective, in order to study the land economic efficiency and environmental pollution improvement. Therefore, combining the abovementioned realistic background and the questions raised, this study includes the following hypotheses:

Hypothesis 1 (H1). *There is a positive correlation between the increase in land economic efficiency and the improvement of environmental pollution in eastern China.*

At the same time, Chong et al. emphasize the close correlation between China's economy and carbon emissions [23], considering that the eastern part of China was chosen as the subject of this study because it is the most prosperous. However, in reality, there are still some prefecture-level cities in eastern China that are relatively less developed. Therefore, on the basis of H1, this study further proposes the hypothesis that:

Hypothesis 2 (H2). *There is a positive relationship between the increase in land economic efficiency and the improvement of environmental pollution in the most economically developed group of cities in eastern China.*

The possible contributions of this paper are: first, with the changing situation in China, earlier studies on the interrelationship between the economy and the environment are no longer appropriate for the current China, and this paper complements this study. Second, few studies have examined the relationship between land use efficiency (i.e., land economic efficiency) and environmental improvement from an economic perspective. Third, unlike other indicator evaluation methods, this study empowers the land economic efficiency evaluation system with the help of the entropy method, which enables a multi-layered discussion of what Land_EcoE is all about. Fourth, this study uses a combination of qualitative (data visualization) and quantitative (econometric modeling) methods to make the conclusions of the article more convincing.

The remainder of the paper is as follows: Section 2 provides a brief description of the subject of this paper and describes the methods that emerged from this study. Section 3 shows the variables involved in this study and their sources. The spatio-temporal evolution of carbon emissions and land economic efficiency is plotted and analyzed. Section 4 describes the empirical process and results of this study. Section 5 discusses the findings of the study. Section 6 concludes the paper and presents the policy implications of the study.

2. Materials and Methods

2.1. Study Area

Located on the eastern edge of the East Asian continent and the western coast of the Pacific Ocean, eastern China is the most economically developed region in China due to its unique natural harbor cluster and geographical environment. Eastern China includes Hebei Province, Beijing, Tianjin, Shandong Province, Jiangsu Province, Shanghai, Zhejiang Province, Fujian Province, Guangdong Province, Hainan Province, Taiwan Province, Hong Kong and Macau (See Figure 1). Considering the issue of data integrity and statistical consistency, Taiwan, Hong Kong and Macau will be excluded from this study. Hainan Province is also considered to be significantly less developed than the other regions and does not meet the requirement of this study to be a prosperous region, so it is excluded. The following is a basic description of the regions studied:

Figure 1. Eastern China.

Hebei Province is located in northeastern China (113°27′–119°50′ E, 36°05′–42°40′ N), surrounded by Beijing and bordered by Tianjin and the Bohai Sea to the east. Hebei Province has a complex and diverse landscape, mainly mountainous, with a total area of 188,800 km^2 as of 2020. As of 2019, Hebei Province has 11 prefecture-level cities: Shijiazhuang, Tangshan, Qinhuangdao, Handan, Xingtai, Baoding, Zhangjiakou, Chengde, Cangzhou, Langfang and Hengshui, with a resident population of 75,919,700. In 2020, Hebei's GDP was RMB 3,620.69 billion, ranking 13th in China.

Beijing is located in northern China (115.7°–117.4° E, 39.4°–41.6° N), bordering Tianjin to the east and Hebei Province to the west. Beijing is predominantly mountainous and plain, with a total area of 16,410.54 km^2 by 2020. As of 2019, Beijing's resident population is 21.536 million. In 2020, Beijing's GDP was RMB 361.026 million, ranking 12th in China.

Tianjin is located in northern China (116°43′–118°04′ E, 38°34′–40°15′ N), is bordered by the Bohai Sea to the east and Beijing to the west. Tianjin is dominated by plains and depressions, with a total area of 11,966.45 km^2 as of 2020. As of 2019, Tianjin has a resident population of 15,618,300 people. In 2020, Tianjin's GDP was RMB 140,837,300, ranking 23rd in China.

Shandong Province, located on the eastern coast of China (114°47.5′–122°42.3′ E, 34°22.9′–38°24.01′ N), shares borders with Hebei, Henan and Anhui as well as Jiangsu. Shandong Province is predominantly hilly and mountainous, with a total area of 157,900 km^2 as of 2020. As of 2019, Shandong province has 16 prefecture-level cities: Jinan, Qingdao, Zibo, Zaozhuang, Dongying, Yantai, Weifang, Jining, Tai'an, Weihai, Rizhao, Binzhou, Dezhou, Liaocheng, Linyi and Heze, with a resident population of 100,702,100 people. In 2020, the GDP of Shandong province was RMB 73,129,000, ranking 3rd in China.

Jiangsu Province, located on the eastern coast of China (116°21′–121°56′ E, 30°45′–35°08′ E), bordered by the Yellow Sea to the east, shares borders with Shanghai, Zhejiang, Anhui and Shandong Provinces. Jiangsu Province is predominantly a plain, with a total area of 107,200 km^2 as of 2020. As of 2019, Jiangsu Province has 13 prefecture-level cities: Nanjing, Wuxi, Xuzhou, Changzhou, Suzhou, Nantong, Lianyungang, Huai'an, Yangzhou, Zhenjiang, Taizhou, Suqian and Yancheng, with a resident population of 80.7 million. In 2020, Jiangsu Province had a GDP of RMB 102,719,000, ranking 2nd in China.

Shanghai, located in eastern China (120°52′–122°12′ E, 30°40′–31°53′ N), is bordered by Jiangsu and Zhejiang Provinces. Shanghai is predominantly a plain, with a total area of 6,340.5 km^2 as of 2020. As of 2019, the resident population of Shanghai is 24,281,400. In 2020, Shanghai's GDP was RMB 387,058,000, ranking 10th in China.

Zhejiang Province, located on the southeast coast of China (118°01′–123°10′ E, 27°02′–31°11′ N), is bordered by the East China Sea to the east, Fujian Province to the south, Anhui and Jiangxi Provinces to the west and Jiangsu Province and Shanghai to the north. Zhejiang Province is mainly hilly, supplemented by plains, with a total area of 105,500 km^2 as of 2020. As of 2019, Zhejiang province has 11 prefecture-level cities: Zhoushan, Hangzhou, Jiaxing, Wenzhou, Ningbo, Shaoxing, Huzhou, Lishui, Taizhou, Jinhua and Quzhou, with a resident population of 58.5 million people. In 2020, Zhejiang's GDP was RMB 646.13 million, ranking 4th in China.

Fujian Province, located on the southeast coast of China (115°50′–120°40′ E, 23°33′–28°20′ N), is adjacent to Zhejiang Province in the northeast, bordered by Jiangxi Province in the northwest and connected to Guangdong Province in the southwest and Taiwan in the southeast. Fujian Province is predominantly mountainous and hilly, with a total area of 121,400 km^2 as of 2020. As of 2019, Fujian Province has nine prefecture-level cities: Fuzhou, Putian, Quanzhou, Xiamen, Zhangzhou, Longyan, Sanming, Nanping and Ningde, with a resident population of 39.73 million. In 2020, Fujian Province's GDP was RMB 434,348,900, ranking 7th in China.

Guangdong Province, located in the southernmost part of China (109°39′–117°19′ E, 20°13′–25°31′ N), shares borders with Hong Kong, Macau, Guangxi, Hunan, Jiangxi and Fujian Provinces. Guangdong Province is dominated by plains and hills, with a total area of 179,725 km^2 as of 2018. As of 2019, Guangdong Province has 21 prefecture-level cities: Guangzhou, Shenzhen, Foshan, Dongguan, Zhongshan, Zhuhai, Jiangmen, Zhaoqing, Huizhou, Shantou, Chaozhou, Jieyang, Shanwei, Zhanjiang, Maoming, Yangjiang, Yunfu, Shaoguan, Qingyuan, Meizhou and Heyuan, with a resident population of 115.21 million. In 2020, Guangdong's GDP was RMB 110,760.94 million, ranking 1st in China.

2.2. Methods

2.2.1. Entropy Method

The entropy method is one of the common composite indicator measures. The entropy method assigns weights based on the degree of variation between variables, and the greater the variation, the greater the weight. The entropy method has the feature of reducing the dimensionality of variables and mitigating the presence of multicollinearity between variables [45]. The entropy method is calculated as follows:

Step 1. Obtain a standardized matrix of indicators ($E_{it,k}$) where $e_{it,k}$ is the matrix of unprocessed indicators, i indicates the region i, t indicates the year t, k indicates the kth indicator, with a total of K indicators.

$$E_{it,k} = \frac{e_{it,k} - \underset{K}{min}|e_{it,k}|}{\underset{K}{max}|e_{it,k}| - \underset{K}{min}|e_{it,k}|} \quad (1)$$

Step 2. Calculate the information entropy ($I_{t,k}$). Calculate $E\prime_{it,k}$ by Equation (2), where n is the total number of regions. Additionally, calculate $I_{t,k}$ by Equation (3).

$$E\prime_{it,k} = \frac{E_{it,k}}{\sum_{i=1}^{n} E_{it,k}} \quad (2)$$

$$I_{t,k} = -ln(n)^{-1} \sum_{i=1}^{n} E\prime_{it,k} * ln(E\prime_{it,k}) \quad (3)$$

Step 3. Calculate the weight matrix ($W_{t,k}$) by Equation (4).

$$W_{t,k} = \frac{1 - I_{t,k}}{K - \sum I_{t,k}} \quad (4)$$

2.2.2. Map Visualization of Data

Map visualization of data is a type of exploratory spatial data analysis (ESDA), whose main purpose is to present spatial geographic attributes and data information more clearly to the reader, usually through software such as ArcGIS [46], where spatial data are embedded in a geographic map. However, traditional studies of regional economics, geography economics, etc. usually analyze data through such visualization methods, which are qualitative in nature and have a certain non-objectivity. Moreover, this method cannot verify the causal relationship between the dependent and independent variables. For example, in this study, we are only able to theorize that there is a causal relationship between economic efficiency of land and environmental pollution improvement, and we are unable to obtain quantitative support.

2.2.3. Econometric Model

Econometric models are able to analyze the correlation between data, the degree of association, etc., and are the most common methods used in economics research. In this study, econometric models are used to investigate the correlation and significance of pollution data in relation to land economic efficiency. Econometric models can be classified into time series regression models, cross-sectional regression models and panel regression models, depending on the type of data [47]. As panel data are used in this paper, a panel regression model is used. Econometric modeling is able to reflect the correlation between variables in a holistic manner and test the research hypothesis by quantifying them. However, it tends to ignore the unique performance of each region. For example, in this study, we can determine the relationship between land economic efficiency and environmental pollution improvement through econometric models, but this conclusion is presented based on the full sample, while the specific performance of each region is not known. This makes the study conclusions less fleshed out.

2.3. Research Idea

This study uses a combination of qualitative and quantitative methods to obtain richer and more convincing conclusions. On the one hand, this study visualizes the spatio-temporal evolution of carbon emission and land economic efficiency to obtain preliminaries conclusions; on the other hand, this study uses an econometric model to verify the above conclusions from a quantitative perspective and to obtain richer conclusions. Figure 2 is the methodological framework of the research idea of this study.

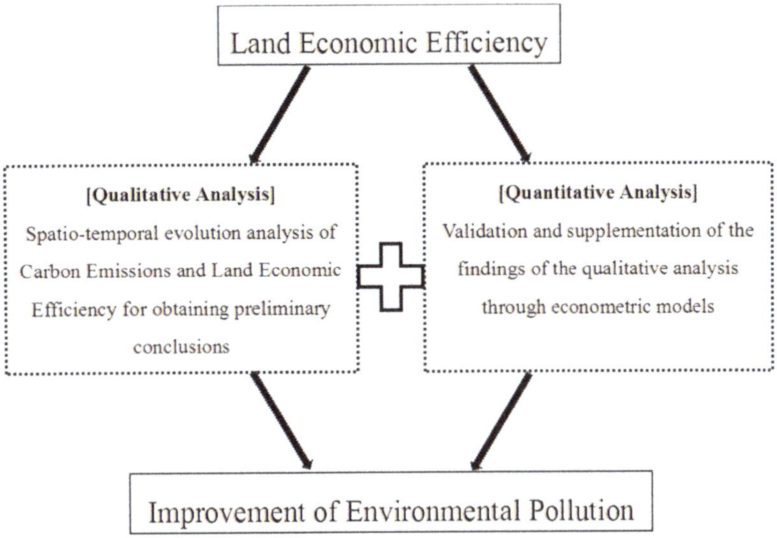

Figure 2. Methodological framework.

3. Variable Design and Analysis

3.1. Explained Variable

The explained variable in this study is the environmental pollution variable, as measured by carbon emissions (Carbon) at the city level. On the one hand, with the popularity of "carbon neutrality" and "carbon capping", carbon emissions are undoubtedly an important element of current social and environmental issues, and are highly representative [48]. On the other hand, China is still dominated by carbon-based energy sources [49], and using carbon emissions can more accurately cover the environmental impact of energy factors.

3.2. Explanatory Variables

3.2.1. Core Explanatory Variable

Land economic efficiency (Land_EcoE) is the core explanatory variable in this study. Most scholars use comprehensive indicators to measure Land_EcoE, for example, traditional data envelopment analysis (DEA), the slacks-based measure (SBM) model [50], land and output intensity [51] and principal component analysis [52]. As a matter of course, different measurement methods and research objectives yield different results [53,54]. Among them, DEA and SBM methods can measure input–output values better, but cannot show the different dimensions of indicators better. Principal component analysis can show multiple dimensions of indicators, but its explanatory power of different dimensions is weaker. The entropy method is based on the degree of variation among variables to different dimensions of indicators. The entropy method is able to explain the importance of each dimension of an indicator and extract the maximum information from the variables. Therefore, this study uses Matlab 2019a software to measure Land_EcoE using the entropy method.

The aim of this study is to investigate whether there is a win-win situation between the "economy" and the "environment" in the development process of sustainable cities in eastern China, i.e., whether an increase in Land_EcoE can improve environmental pollution. Therefore, this study constructs land economic efficiency indicators only at the level of economic development. Economic development generally consists of three dimensions: the economic growth dimension, the economic structure dimension and the economic quality dimension. Based on this, the indicator evaluation system of Land_EcoE is described as follows (Table 1):

(1) Economic growth. Economic growth is the basis of economic development. This study uses GDP growth rate and industrial production intensity (gross industrial output value above scale/land area) to measure it. GDP growth rate visually reflects the growth rate of the region's production capacity. The gross industrial output value above scale reflects the level of industrial production in the region, and when divided by its urban area, the industrial production intensity obtained excludes the effect caused by the size of the city.

(2) Economic structure. Economic structure includes industrial structure, population structure, etc. A reasonable economic structure is conducive to economic development. In this study, we use the share of tertiary output (tertiary industry output value/GDP), tertiary industry production intensity (tertiary industry output value/land area) and employment density (urban employment population/land area) to measure it. Tertiary industrial output reflects the development of the service sector in the region. The development of sustainable cities leads to changes in urban functions [55], most notably a decline in the share of secondary industrial output and an increase in the share of tertiary industrial output over the years [56,57]. Dividing tertiary industrial output by GDP and land area, respectively, controls for the impact of the size of the economy and the size of the city on it. Labor is a necessary element of production, and a city without employed people will struggle to support economic development. In this study, we divide urban employment by land area to exclude the effect of city size.

(3) Economic quality. Economic quality is not only reflected in the current economic development achievements, but also in the potential for economic development of the region. This study uses GDP per capita, R&D intensity (science and technology expenditure in the general public budget/land area) and road density (urban road area/land area) to measure this. GDP per capita visually reflects the average production capacity and indirectly shows the income level of the residents, and can better measure the current economic development achievements of the region. Innovation is the first driving force of development and a key factor in escaping the middle-income trap. On the one hand, science and technology expenditure reflects the importance the government attaches to innovation development and judges whether the government's economic development course is reasonable [58]. On the other hand, science and technology expenditure promotes innovative development and has long-term significance in optimizing production methods, increasing production efficiency and improving product competition [59]. Urban road density is a direct reflection of the accessibility of a city. Convenient transport is an important component of economic development and can reduce commuting times and improve the quality of life of residents.

Table 1. Indicator evaluation system of land economic efficiency.

Core Explanatory Variable	Dimension	Indicator	Unit	Average Weight (2011–2017)	Impact Ranking
Land economic efficiency (Land_EcoE)	Economic growth	GDP growth rate	%	4.38%	7
		Industrial production intensity	RMB 10,000/km^2	22.62%	2
	Economic structure	Share of tertiary output	%	3.87%	8
		Tertiary industrial production intensity	RMB 10,000/km^2	14.40%	3
		Employment density	People/km^2	12.71%	4
	Economic quality	GDP per capita	RMB/people	7.29%	6
		R&D intensity	RMB 10,000/km^2	24.41%	1
		Road density	%	10.32%	5

3.2.2. Control Variables

In this study, the explained variable is carbon emissions and the explanatory variable is land economic efficiency (Land_EcoE). To increase the validity of the empirical results and to avoid endogeneity problems arising from omitted variables, the following control variables are added: (I) Chen and Ouyang et al. both found that foreign investment has a significant impact on environmental improvement [60,61]. Therefore, the foreign capital utilization intensity (amount of actual foreign investment utilized/land area) is used, controlling for the impact from abroad. (II) There is no doubt that innovation can have a relationship with the environment [62–64]. This study uses innovation intensity (number of non-descript patent applications/employment), controlling for the impact from domestic innovation.

3.3. Data Resource and Processing

This study uses the eastern region of China as the sample for this study. Considering the statistical caliber and completeness of the data, Taiwan Province, Hong Kong and Macau are excluded from this study. Hainan Province is excluded due to its relatively underdeveloped economy and because it does not meet the requirement of being a more economically developed region. The initial time point for this study is set at 2011 as China has developed and implemented a rich and stringent environmental governance policy since the starting point of the 12th Five-Year Plan (2011). As the latest city-level carbon emission data were only updated to 2017, the end point of this study is set at 2017. In summary, this study uses data from 2011–2017 for 84 prefecture-level cities in eastern China. The main data for this study were obtained from the China City Statistical Yearbook, and all of them were from the statistical scope of municipal districts. City-level carbon emissions data were obtained by aggregating county-level data from Carbon Emission Accounts & Datasets (CEADs) [65]. For some of the missing data, the moving average method was used to complete the study. Table 2 reports the descriptive statistics of the main variables in the study. In this case, all values are in logarithmic form, except for land economic efficiency. It can be found that the standard deviations of the variables are small and there are no extreme values that are several orders of magnitude higher than the other variables, indicating that the data are suitable for use in the regression model.

Table 2. Variable description.

Type	Variable	Unit	Obs	Mean	Std.	Min	Max	Label
Explained variable	Carbon emission	Million tons	588	3.5417	0.6873	1.7576	5.4235	Carbon
Explanatory variable	Land economic efficiency	-	588	1.1905	1.4061	0.1079	13.8653	Land_EcoE
Control variables	Foreign capital utilization intensity	USD million/km^2	588	2.8392	1.6474	−4.8793	5.9149	Fore_CUI
	Innovation intensity	Items/10,000 people	588	4.8430	0.8303	2.4417	6.8811	Inno_I

3.4. Analysis of Spatio-Temporal Evolution of Key Variables

3.4.1. Carbon Emissions

In this section, three periods, 2011, 2014 and 2017, are taken to map the distribution pattern of carbon emissions. These maps will provide a better picture of the spatio-temporal evolution of carbon emissions in eastern China. In addition, carbon emissions are classified into three classes—high, medium and low emissions—based on the "expectation $\pm$ 1 times standard deviation" (data processed by Winsor 95%). Figures 3–6 depict the spatial and temporal evolution of carbon emissions at the prefecture level in eastern China. It can be found that:

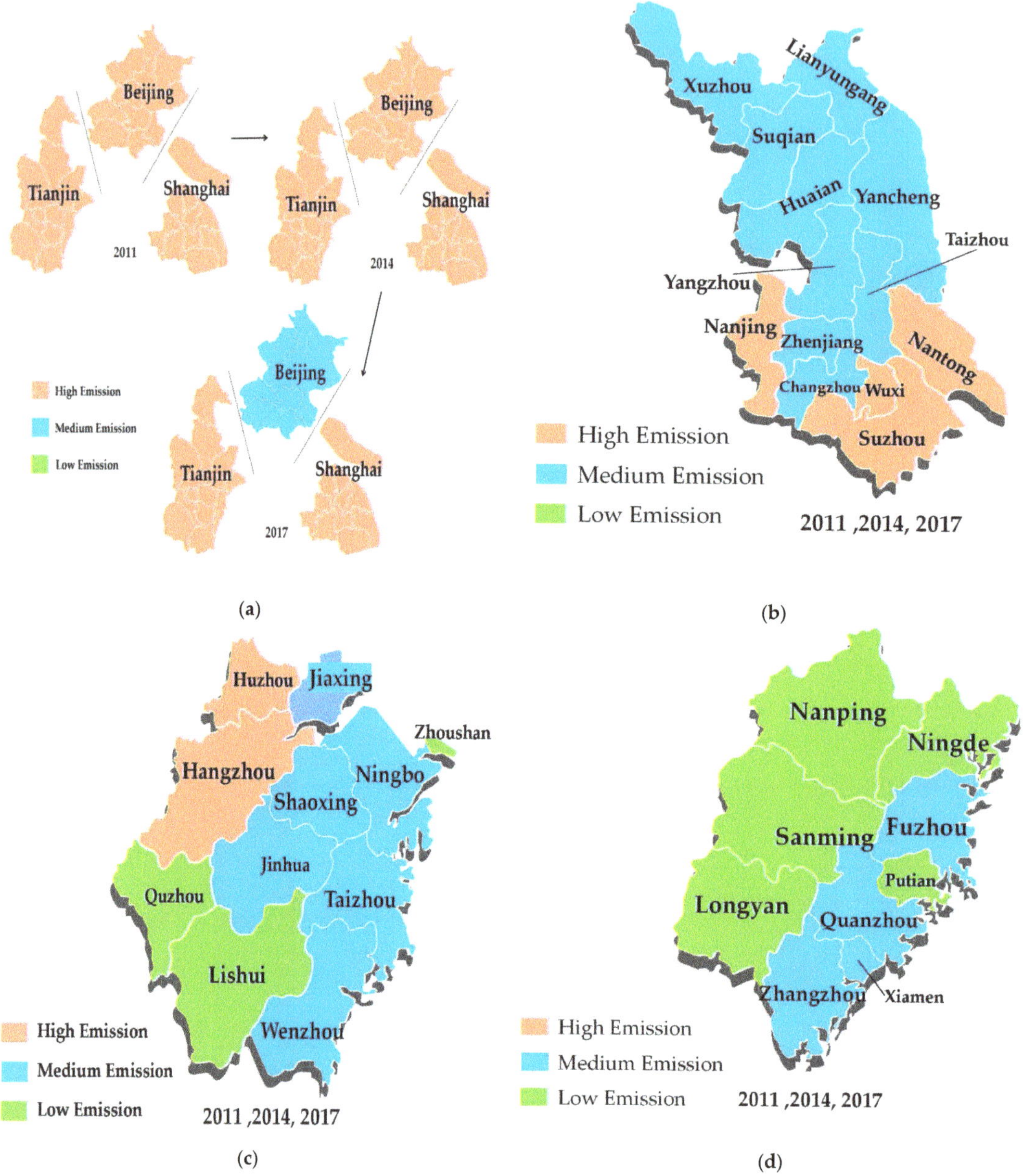

Figure 3. Spatio-temporal evolution map of carbon emissions. (**a**) Beijing, Tianjin and Shanghai. (**b**) Jiangsu Province. (**c**) Zhejiang Province. (**d**) Fujian Province.

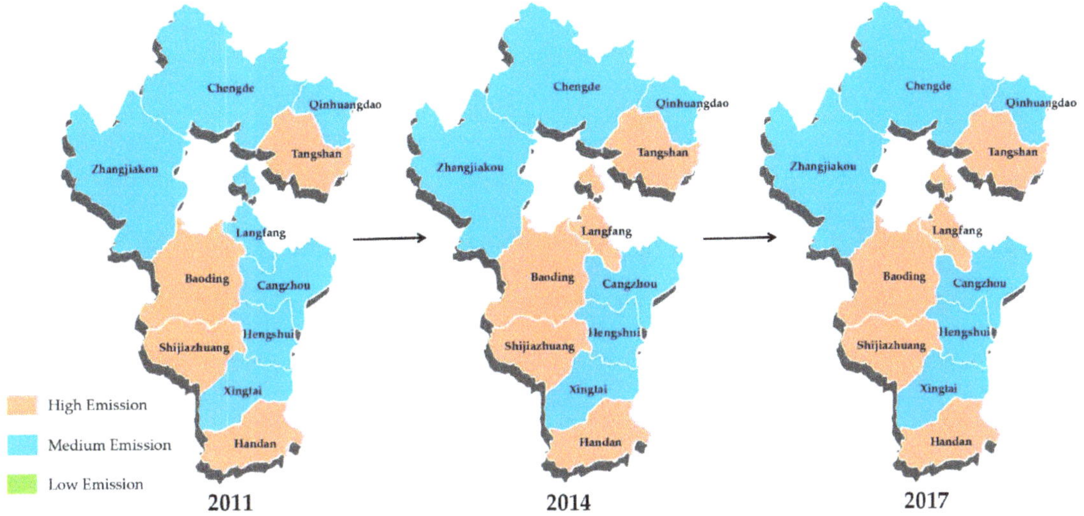

Figure 4. Spatio-temporal evolution map of carbon emissions in Hebei Province.

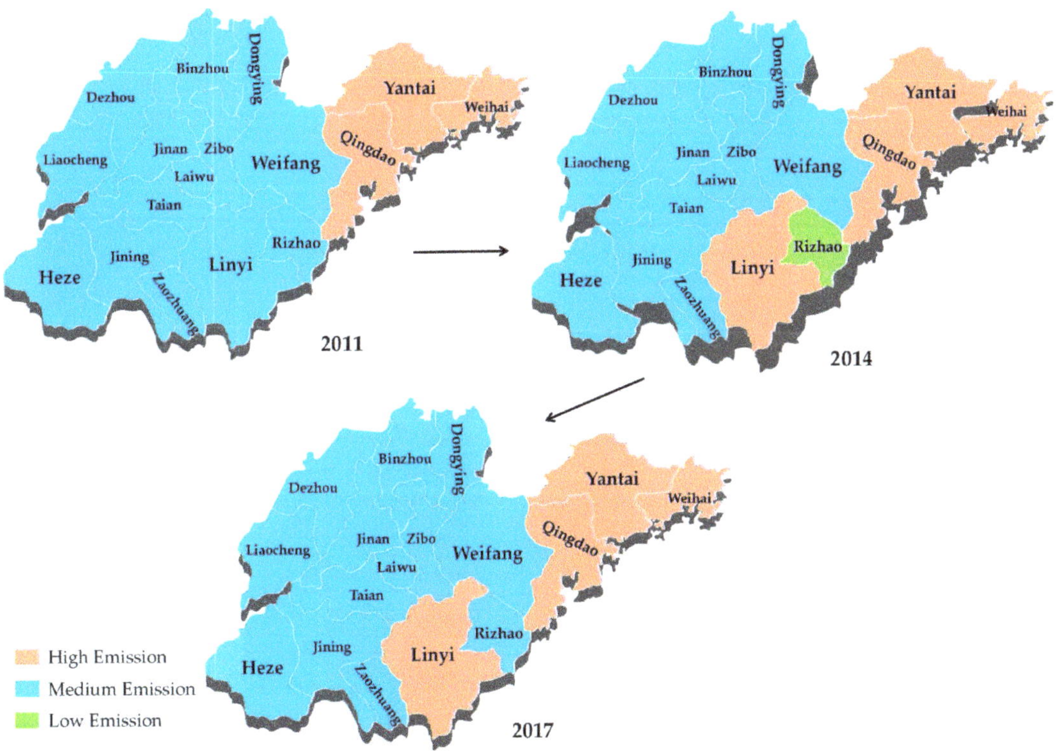

Figure 5. Spatio-temporal evolution map of carbon emissions in Shandong Province.

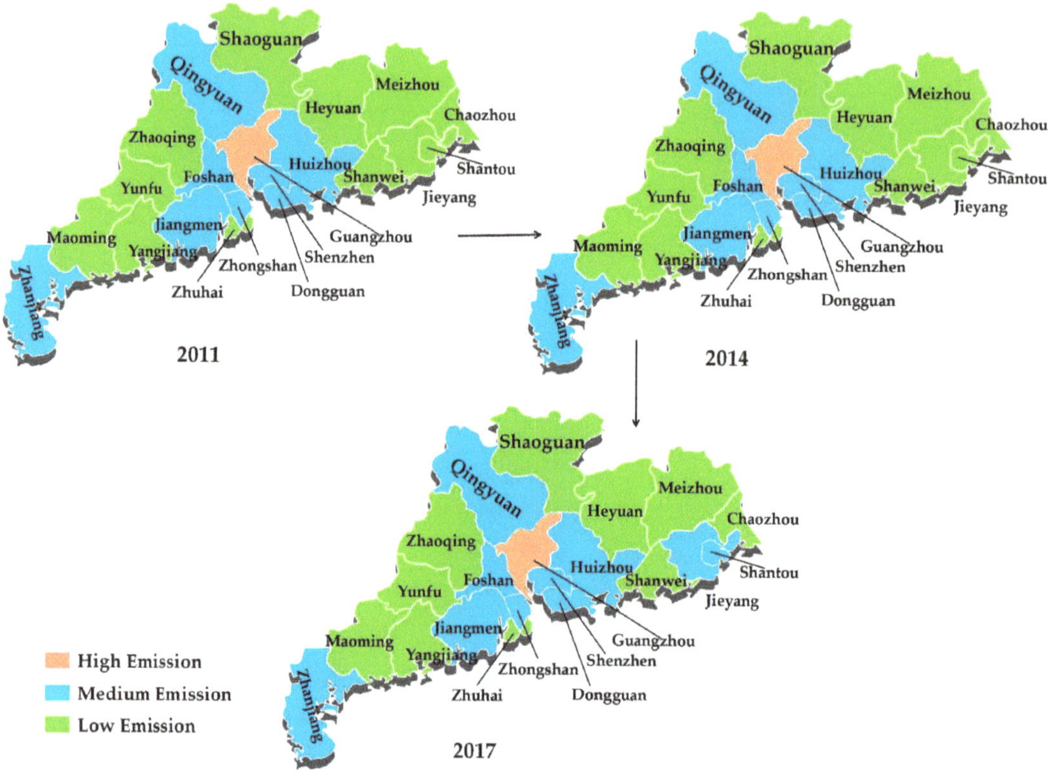

Figure 6. Spatio-temporal evolution map of carbon emissions in Guangdong Province.

In Figure 3, the relative levels of carbon emissions in Fujian, Zhejiang and Jiangsu Provinces have not changed at any of the three time points (2011, 2014, 2017). From Figure 3a, we can see that the relative levels of carbon emissions in Beijing, Tianjin and Shanghai are all at a high level and have not changed over time, with the exception of Beijing. Figure 3b shows that the overall level of carbon emissions in Jiangsu Province is high, with the northern part at an intermediate level, but the southern part is at a high level. Figure 3c shows that Hangzhou and Huzhou have high carbon emissions, while the southeastern part of Zhejiang Province has moderate emissions. Figure 3d shows that Fujian Province has a low overall level of carbon emissions, with its relatively less economically developed northwestern region having low carbon emissions, while its southeastern coastal region has relatively higher carbon emissions.

In Figure 4, the overall level of carbon emissions in Hebei Province is moderate and the relative emission levels of the other prefecture-level cities have not changed over time, except for Lanfang where the level of carbon emissions has increased.

In Figure 5, the overall level of carbon emissions in Shandong Province is moderate, with the western region having lower levels than the eastern region. At the same time, it can be found that the carbon emission levels in its southeastern region (Rizhao, Linyi) are reduced.

In Figure 6, the overall level of carbon emissions in Guangdong Province is low, where the level of carbon emissions decreases in all directions with Guangzhou as the strongest center. At the same time, it can be noticed that the carbon emission levels of Shantou and Jieyang, which are located in the southeast of Guangdong Province, have increased as time progressed.

3.4.2. Land Economic Efficiency

Similarly, according to the method in Section 3.4.1, Figures 7–10 present maps of the spatio-temporal evolution of land economic efficiency (Land_EcoE) in 2011, 2014 and 2017. It can be found that:

In Figure 7a, the Land_EcoE levels in the three municipalities of Beijing, Tianjin and Shanghai are all high, with the exception of Tianjin, which dropped to a moderate level in 2017, while the other two remained unchanged. In Figure 7b, the Land_EcoE in Shandong Province is at a moderate level overall, with only Qingdao at "high efficiency". In addition, the relative levels of Land_EcoE in Shandong Province did not change as time progressed, and the trend was stable. In Figure 7c, the overall Land_EcoE in Zhejiang Province is at a moderate level. Among them, Quzhou and Lishui are "low efficiency" and Hangzhou and Shaoxing are "high efficiency". However, as time progresses, the Land_EcoE levels of all regions in Zhejiang Province are at the "medium efficiency" stage and tend to be homogeneous. In Figure 7d, the overall Land_EcoE in Fujian Province is at a low to moderate level. The relative efficiency of Nanping and Longyan is low, while the relative efficiency of Xiamen is high. Overall, the efficiency of southeastern Fujian Province is higher than that of northwestern Fujian Province, and although there is a tendency to assimilate towards "medium efficiency" over time, the pattern of higher efficiency in eastern Fujian Province is still evident.

In Figure 8, the overall Land_EcoE in Hebei Province is at a moderate to high level, with the southern and northern parts showing lower levels of efficiency than the central regions. In addition, three regions (Baoding, Zhangjiakou and Qinhuangdao) have seen their relative efficiency levels degrade over time, while the rest of the regions remain unchanged.

In Figure 9, the overall Land_EcoE in Jiangsu Province is at a moderate level, with higher levels of efficiency in Changzhou, Wuxi and Suzhou and lower levels in Suqian. It is clear that Land_EcoE in southern Jiangsu is higher. As time progresses, the efficiency levels of each region in Jiangsu tend to homogenize, with Suqian's efficiency level increasing and Suzhou's decreasing.

In Figure 10, the relative efficiency of land in Guangdong Province is at a low to medium level. The efficiency of Yunfu, Qingyuan, Shaoguan and Meizhou is low, while the efficiency of Guangzhou, Shenzhen, Zhongshan and Dongguan is high. It can be seen that Land_EcoE in Guangdong Province is centered on Shenzhen and radiates downwards in all directions, reflecting the central position of Shenzhen and the "siphon effect". As time progresses, Land_EcoE in Guangdong does not change significantly, and three regions—Yunfu, Qingyuan and Meizhou—are still "low efficiency".

3.4.3. Comprehensive Discussion

The above analysis of the spatio-temporal evolution of carbon emissions and land economic efficiency in each region shows that regions with high land economic efficiency generally do not have low carbon emissions (for example, Figures 3a and 7a). This suggests that even in eastern China, it is difficult to achieve better land–economy–environment synergy. Such a conclusion contradicts hypothesis H1. However, this may not be the case as the map analysis requires a quantitative analysis of the econometric model. Furthermore, the study shows that the level of land economic efficiency in each region does not usually get worse as time progresses, but rarely breaks through to "high efficiency". This suggests that the level of land economic efficiency in eastern China tends to be at the same level, indirectly reflecting the fact that each region in eastern China is actually improving its own land economic efficiency.

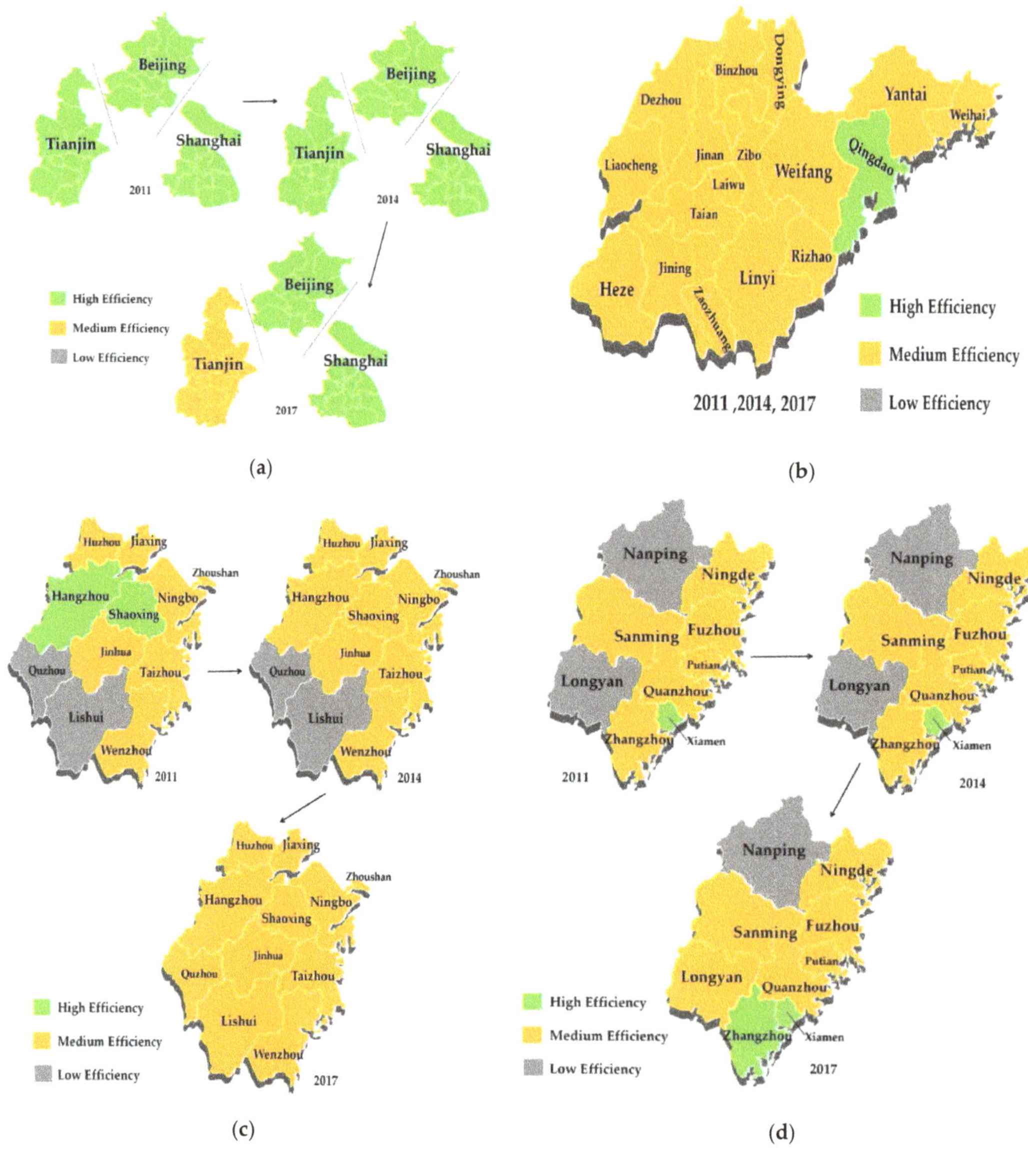

Figure 7. Spatio-temporal evolution map of land economic efficiency. (**a**) Beijing, Tianjin and Shanghai. (**b**) Shandong Province. (**c**) Zhejiang Province. (**d**) Fujian Province.

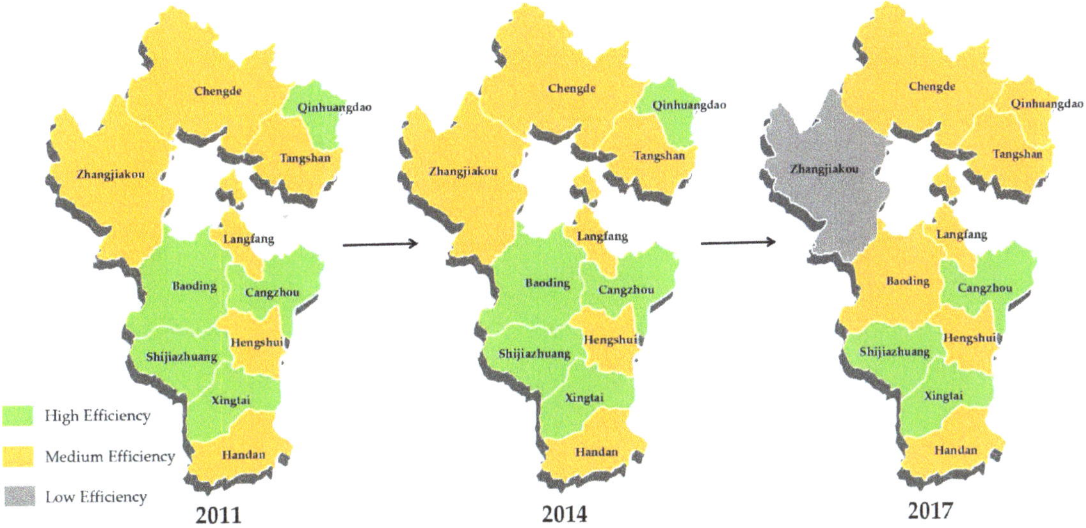

Figure 8. Spatio-temporal evolution map of land economic efficiency in Hebei Province.

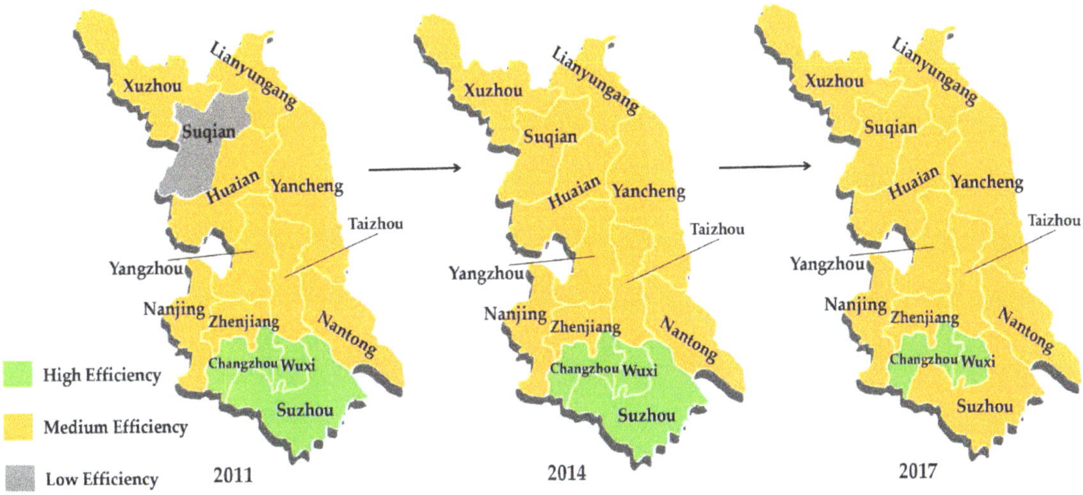

Figure 9. Spatio-temporal evolution map of land economic efficiency in Jiangsu Province.

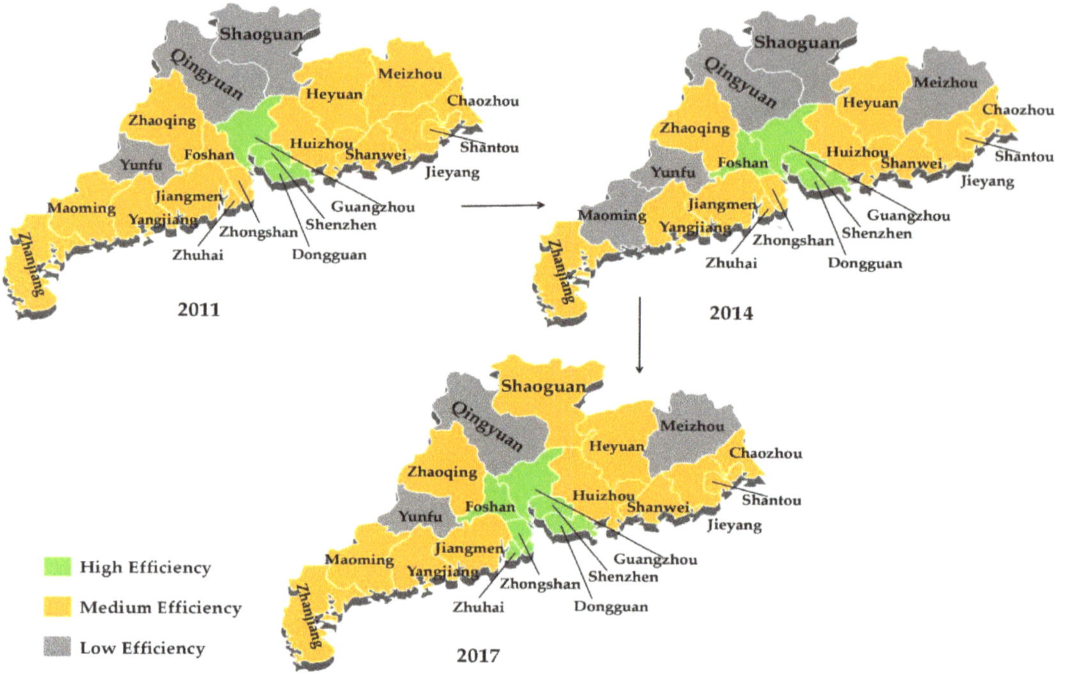

Figure 10. Spatio-temporal evolution map of land economic efficiency in Guangdong Province.

4. Empirical Design and Results

4.1. Model Design

This study involves data from 84 prefecture-level cities and municipalities from 2011–2017, and therefore uses a panel regression model. Referring to the C-D production function [66], the main regression model (Equation (5)) is developed.

$$lnCarbon_{it} = \alpha + \beta Land\_\ EcoE_{it} + \gamma lnControl_{it} + \varepsilon_{it} \quad (5)$$

where i denotes prefecture-level city i and t denotes year. $Carbon_{it}$ denotes carbon emissions, $Land\_\ EcoE_{it}$ denotes land economic efficiency and $Control_{it}$ denotes control variables, which in this study refer to foreign capital utilization intensity (Fore_CUI) and innovation intensity (Inno_I). ε_{it} denotes the random disturbance term.

Each region in the study has its own unique underpinnings, such as policies and culture, and these unique attributes may change over time. Therefore, in this study, θ_t and σ_i are added to Equation (5). θ_t, which can control for changes over time, represents time fixed effects, and σ_i, which controls for regional idiosyncrasies, represents spatial fixed effects.

$$lnCarbon_{it} = \alpha + \beta Land\_\ EcoE_{it} + \gamma \ln Control_{it} + \theta_t + \sigma_i + \varepsilon_{it} \quad (6)$$

Equation (6) is used to test hypothesis H1, and this study proposes hypothesis H2 on the basis of hypothesis H1. In order to implement the process, this study constructs dummy variables (D), where, if region i belongs to the most economically developed group of regions in eastern China, $D = 1$; otherwise, $D = 0$. The specific equation is as follows:

$$lnCarbon_{it} = \alpha + \beta_1 Land\_\ EcoE_{it} + \beta_2 D * Land\_\ EcoE_{it} + \gamma lnControl_{it} + \theta_t + \sigma_i + \varepsilon_{it} \quad (7)$$

4.2. Regression Results

In this study, the regression of the model of Equation (6) was performed using Stata15SE software, and the results are shown in Table 3. Table 3(I), (II) and (III) show the regression results of Equation (6) controlling for random effects, fixed effects and two-way fixed effects, respectively. It can be found that all three fail the 10% significance test, indicating that there is no definite relationship between land economic efficiency and carbon emissions in eastern China and hypothesis H1 is not valid. However, there are regional differences in carbon emissions, and the more economically developed regions are more "green" [44]. The essence of this study is to investigate the impact of land economic efficiency on carbon emissions in economically prosperous regions. Although the overall economic level of eastern China is higher than that of central and western China, there are still some provinces and prefecture-level cities with average economic levels.

Table 3. Regression results for the spatio-temporal fixed effects of land economic efficiency *.

Explanatory Variables	I	II	III
Land_EcoE	0.0006	−0.0008	−0.0003
Control	YES	YES	YES
Time fixed effects	YES	-	YES
Spatial fixed effects	-	YES	YES
R-sq	0.3709	0.0411	0.2120
Obs	588	588	588

* indicate statistical significance at the 10% levels.

4.3. Further Analysis

In this study, the regression of the model of Equation (7) was performed using Stata15SE software, and the results are shown in Table 4. This study screens out regions with high economic levels in eastern China by comparing the averages of regional GDP from 2011–2017. Two groups of regions were screened using "expectation + 1 times standard deviation" and "expectation" as the bounds. A-group: Beijing, Tianjin, Shanghai, Nanjing, Hangzhou, Guangzhou, Shenzhen and Foshan, a total of eight prefecture-level cities. B-group: on the basis of A-group, 10 prefecture-level cities, Tangshan City, Wuxi City, Changzhou City, Suzhou City, Ningbo City, Xiamen City, Jinan City, Qingdao City, Zibo City and Dongguan City, are added, to a total of 18 prefecture-level cities. Table 4 reports the regression results for both groups and it can be found that the third column has the best regression effect in both A-group and B-group. In Table 4(III), the coefficient of Land_EcoE is significantly positive, indicating that for most regions in eastern China, the increase in land economic efficiency promotes carbon emissions and pollutes the environment. However, the coefficients of (D_A * Land_EcoE) and (D_B * Land_EcoE) are both negative and extremely significant, suggesting that the cities in eastern China with the most prosperous economies have been able to reduce carbon emissions and thus improve environmental pollution by increasing land economic efficiency. Therefore, hypothesis H2 holds.

Table 4. Further regression for the spatio-temporal fixed effects of land economic efficiency.

A-group Explanatory Variables	I	II	III
Land_EcoE	0.0130 **	0.0121 **	0.0127 ***
D_A * Land_EcoE	−0.0239 ***	−0.0249 ***	−0.0252 ***
Control	YES	YES	YES
Time fixed effects	YES	-	YES
Spatial fixed effects	-	YES	YES
R-sq	0.2319	0.0622	0.2333
Obs (A-group)	56	56	56
Obs	588	588	588
B-group Explanatory Variables	I	II	III
Land_EcoE	0.0133 **	0.0132 **	0.0138 ***
D_B * Land_EcoE	−0.0229 ***	−0.0251 ***	−0.0252 ***
Control	YES	YES	YES
Time fixed effects	YES	-	YES
Spatial fixed effects	-	YES	YES
R-sq	0.2709	0.0627	0.2332
Obs (B-group)	126	126	126
Obs	588	588	588

***, ** and *, respectively, indicate statistical significance at the 1%, 5% and 10% levels. Obs (A-group) and Obs (B-group) refer to observations where the dummy variable is 1.

5. Discussion

This paper first discusses the spatio-temporal evolution patterns of carbon emissions and land economic efficiency to form a basic understanding of the research content and preliminary conclusions. On this basis, this study further verifies and supplements the preliminary conclusions quantitatively by means of econometric models. By combining qualitative and quantitative methods, this study aims to conduct a more detailed study of the problem and draw more convincing conclusions. In addition, this study enriches the findings with the specificity of the entropy method of weight assignment. In this section, the findings of the study are analyzed and discussed in detail.

5.1. Discussions of Spatio-Temporal Evolution

5.1.1. Carbon Emissions

From spatial distribution patterns, the overall carbon emissions of coastal cities in eastern China are higher. In 2011, among the 84 prefecture cities in eastern China, there were 20 "low-emission" areas, 46 "medium-emission" areas and 18 "high-emission" areas. In 2014, the figures were 21, 43 and 20, respectively, and in 2017 they were 18, 46 and 20, respectively. It can be seen that the three categories of high-, medium- and low-emission regions do not obviously change, with "medium-emission" regions accounting for more than half of the overall distribution and the remaining two categories accounting for about a quarter each. When categorized by province and municipality, we can see that Beijing (12th), Shanghai (10th), Tianjin (23rd) and Hebei Province (13th) have higher carbon emissions, while Zhejiang Province (4th), Shandong Province and Jiangsu Province (2nd) have medium emissions, and Guangdong Province (1st) and Fujian Province (7th) have lower emissions, where the national ranking of the regional GDP is shown in brackets. It can be found that there is no strong positive correlation between carbon emissions and GDP. However, it cannot be denied that, with the exception of the special case of Guangdong Province, the rest of the regions that are economically developed are generally not low in carbon emissions. Among them, Beijing, Tianjin and Shanghai, which are the only municipalities directly under the central government, are ranked highly and therefore do not affect this conclusion.

From temporal trends, 77 regions, accounting for 91.67%, had unchanged carbon emission levels in 2011, 2014 and 2017, while only seven regions had changed their carbon emission levels. Of the seven regions that changed, only Beijing saw a decrease in carbon emissions. The decline in Beijing's carbon emissions is due to the relocation of a large number of factories from Beijing to Hebei Province in recent years. At the same time, in 2017, Beijing launched a "coal-to-gas" strategy, using natural gas, a clean energy source, to replace coal as the main source of energy for winter heating. The analysis in this paragraph shows that the distribution of carbon emissions in eastern China has not changed obviously over time.

5.1.2. Land Economic Efficiency

From spatial distribution patterns, the land economic efficiency (Land_EcoE) of coastal cities in eastern China is significantly higher than that of other regions, but there is no significant difference between the north and the south. In 2011, among 84 municipal areas in eastern China, there were 18 "high-efficiency" areas, 57 "medium-efficiency" areas and 9 "low-efficiency" areas. Similarly, in 2014, the number was 17, 57 and 10, respectively. In 2017, it was 16, 62 and 6, respectively. It can be observed that the number of "high-efficiency" areas is slowly decreasing, the number of "medium-efficiency" areas is significantly increasing and that of "low-efficiency" areas is decreasing. Overall, the number of medium-Land_EcoE areas is higher, about 70%, and the number of "high-efficiency" areas is also significantly higher than that of "low-efficiency" areas, which is in line with the expectation of this study when selecting the more economically developed region of eastern China as the research target.

From temporal evolution trends, 66 regions, or 78.57% of the total, had a constant Land_EcoE level over the three time points 2011, 2014 and 2017. There were 18 regions where the level of efficiency changed, of which seven regions saw a decrease and 11 regions saw an increase. In addition, in 2017, for example, 12 of these 18 regions became "medium-efficiency" areas, while only two regions were downgraded. This indicates that the distribution of Land_EcoE in eastern China has gradually converged over time (becoming a "medium-efficiency" region) as Land_EcoE indicators in this study are relative indicators. This is in line with China's development strategy of "common prosperity", whereby some regions get rich first and then help others to get richer, thus achieving common prosperity.

5.2. Discussion of the Empirical Results

The aim of this study is to investigate whether the current economically developed regions of China can achieve synergistic environmental and economic development. Considering the current low land use efficiency in China [67], the purpose of the study is analyzing the correlation between land economic efficiency and environmental pollution (carbon emissions). Therefore, this study establishes the first hypothesis: there is a positive correlation between the increase in land economic efficiency and the improvement of environmental pollution in eastern China. However, the results of Table 3 show that there is no significant correlation between Land_EcoE and carbon emissions in eastern China. This may be due to the fact that even in economically developed eastern China, there are still some economically underdeveloped municipal areas. Accordingly, this study sets up a second hypothesis: there is a positive relationship between the increase in land economic efficiency and the improvement of environmental pollution in the most economically developed group of cities in eastern China. The results in Table 3 clearly show that the eastern regions of China, as a whole, still do not show co-development of land economic efficiency and environmental pollution improvement. However, in the most economically developed cities of eastern China, there is an extremely significant negative correlation between Land_EcoE and carbon emissions (Table 4). This indicates that these economically developed regions have achieved synergistic development in economy–land–environment, indirectly indicating the effectiveness of China's existing economic development plans.

In addition, the evaluation system of land economic efficiency (Table 1) shows that R&D intensity (24.41%) and industrial production intensity (22.62%) contribute the most to the composite indicator of land economic efficiency, while with tertiary industrial production intensity (13.40%) and employment density (12.71%), the total contribution reaches 74.14%. This figure does not reflect their "importance" for land economic efficiency, but rather implies the degree of variation between regions in the other four secondary indicators (GDP growth rate, share of tertiary output, GDP per capita and road density) is relatively low. Therefore, this study argues that there is a need for regions with low land economic efficiency to pay more attention to the economic content of the first four indicators.

6. Conclusions

In the context of the world's call for "peak carbon" and "carbon neutral" efforts, China is faced with the choice between economic development and environmental protection. In addition, China's rapid urbanization as a developing country has led to problems such as inefficient land use. Under these conditions, the Chinese government is adjusting its approach to development and transforming itself into an innovative powerhouse. Therefore, after years of transformation and development, are China's prosperous regions able to alleviate the conflict between economy and environment? Exploring the spatio-temporal evolution patterns of land economic efficiency and environmental pollution, and the interrelationship between the two, is an important guide to promote the synergistic development of land use efficiency, economic development and environmental governance. Using data from 84 prefecture-level cities and municipalities directly under the central government in eastern China from 2011–2017, this study measures the relative levels of land economic efficiency through the entropy method and plots the spatio-temporal evolution of carbon emissions and land economic efficiency to analyze the spatio-temporal characteristics of the two. Based on this, the study further identifies the relationship between land economic efficiency and carbon emissions through a general panel model, and obtains some insights on how to reconcile economic, land and environmental development.

The conclusions are as follows:

(1) From 2011–2017, carbon emissions in eastern China were generally more spatially distributed along the coast than inland, and more to the north than to the south, and this pattern did not change over time. Only Beijing achieved a significant downgrade in carbon emissions in 2017 due to its special strategy ("factory relocation" and "coal-to-gas") [68,69].
(2) From 2011–2017, the land economic efficiency in eastern China was generally characterized by higher coastal than inland efficiency, but there is no significant difference between the north and the south. At the same time, according to the number of high-, medium- and low-efficiency areas in the three time points (2011, 2014 and 2017), the land economic efficiency in eastern China has been changing towards "medium efficiency" over time. This suggests that the differences between regions are narrowing and that most regions were upgraded from "low efficiency" to "medium efficiency".
(3) From Table 3, eastern China as a whole is still unable to achieve synergistic development of land economic efficiency and the environment. However, the further findings of Table 4 demonstrate that the 18 most economically developed cities in eastern China (Section 4.3 for a list of these cities) have been able to achieve synergistic development of land economic efficiency and the environment. Furthermore, according to this study, there are four important factors that contribute to the low land economic efficiency (R&D intensity, industrial production intensity, tertiary sector production intensity and employment density).

Based on the above, this study can provide some inspiration for policy making:

(1) China has been implementing a sustainable development and innovation strategy for many years, and is now seeing results. Eastern China's prosperous region is already moving closer to the goal of synergistic economic–environmental–land development,

and has stepped off the path of socialist economic development with Chinese characteristics. The findings of this study provide support for the validity of China's economic policies and environmental regulation policies.

(2) Maintain the strengths of regions with high science and technology expenditure, and increase support for weaker regions to balance the progress of science and technology research and development across regions. Additionally, encourage enterprises, and fund their R&D to promote their innovative transformation and development, so as to strengthen the overall competitiveness of the region.

(3) Promote the optimization of industrial structure and encourage and improve the industrial transfer strategy. Optimize the industrial structure by promoting the development of tertiary industries, and at the same time transfer some important factories to less economically developed areas in order to promote the economic development of the area and allow the pollution emissions to be shared by more areas.

(4) Adhere to the policy of compulsory education without wavering, further improve the training mechanism for all types of talents, and raise the bar for scientific research and treatment of innovative talents. In particular, strengthen the introduction of talents and the treatment of ordinary workers in the less economically developed inland regions in order to attract the inflow of labor, promote innovation and development and enhance economic potential. At the same time, promote cross-regional cooperation so that wealthy regions can drive the development of less developed regions.

Prospects and shortcomings of this study include, first, that environmental pollution problems often have spatial effects, but they have not been studied here. Second, due to the type of data, there is still much room for improvement in the evaluation system of land economic efficiency. Thirdly, due to the limitation of space and the research purpose, this study only includes the prefecture-level cities in eastern China as a whole, and lacks a more detailed study of a particular province.

Author Contributions: Conceptualization, B.C. and L.C.; formal analysis, B.C. and L.C.; methodology, B.C.; writing—review and editing, B.C. and L.C. All authors have read and agreed to the published version of the manuscript.

Funding: This research received no external funding.

Data Availability Statement: Publicly available datasets were analyzed in this study. These data can be found here: https://pan.baidu.com/s/1eUHhvDqcxy9E30e7rjMqqw/Extraction (accessed on 1 June 2021) code: land.

Conflicts of Interest: The authors declare that they have no conflict of interest.

References

1. Grönqvist, H.; Nilsson, J.P.; Robling, P.O. Understanding How Low Levels of Early Lead Exposure Affect Children's Life Trajectories. *J. Political Econ.* **2020**, *128*, 3376–3433. [CrossRef]
2. Desforges, J.P.W.; Galbraith, M.; Dangerfield, N.; Ross, P.S. Widespread distribution of microplastics in subsurface seawater in the NE Pacific Ocean. *Mar. Pollut. Bull.* **2014**, *79*, 94–99. [CrossRef]
3. Evangeliou, N.; Grythe, H.; Klimont, Z.; Heyes, C.; Eckhardt, S.; Lopez-Aparicio, S.; Stohl, A. Atmospheric transport is a major pathway of microplastics to remote regions. *Nat. Commun.* **2020**, *11*, 3381. [CrossRef]
4. Shen, L.; Cheng, S.; Gunson, A.J.; Wan, H. Urbanization, sustainability and the utilization of energy and mineral resources in China. *Cities* **2005**, *22*, 287–302. [CrossRef]
5. Brelsford, C.; Lobo, J.; Hand, J.; Bettencourt, L.M. Heterogeneity and scale of sustainable development in cities. *Proc. Natl. Acad. Sci. USA* **2017**, *114*, 8963–8968. [CrossRef] [PubMed]
6. Seto, K.C.; Golden, J.S.; Alberti, M.; Turner, B.L. Sustainability in an urbanizing planet. *Proc. Natl. Acad. Sci. USA* **2017**, *114*, 8935–8938. [CrossRef]
7. Yiftachel, O.; Hedgcock, D. Urban social sustainability: The planning of an Australian city. *Cities* **1993**, *10*, 139–157. [CrossRef]
8. Walter, B.; Arkin, L.; Crenshaw, R.W. (Eds.) *Sustainable Cities: Concepts and strategies for Eco-City Development*; Eco-Home Media: Los Angeles, CA, USA, 1992.
9. Tjallingii, S.P. *Ecopolis: Strategies for Ecologically Sound Urban Development*; Backhuys Publishers: Amsterdem, The Netherlands, 1995.
10. Nijkamp, P.; Perrels, A. *Sustainable Cities in Europe*; Routledge: London, UK, 2018.

11. Janik, A.; Ryszko, A.; Szafraniec, M. Scientific landscape of smart and sustainable cities literature: A bibliometric analysis. *Sustainability* **2020**, *12*, 779. [CrossRef]
12. Zhan, C.; De Jong, M.; De Bruijn, H. Funding sustainable cities: A comparative study of sino-singapore tianjin eco-city and shenzhen international low-carbon city. *Sustainability* **2018**, *10*, 4256. [CrossRef]
13. Fu, Y.; Zhang, X. Planning for sustainable cities? A comparative content analysis of the master plans of eco, low-carbon and conventional new towns in China. *Habitat Int.* **2017**, *63*, 55–66. [CrossRef]
14. Zhao, J. An Assessment Indicator System and a Comprehensive Index for Sustainable City. In *Towards Sustainable Cities in China*; Springer: New York, NY, USA, 2011; pp. 37–47.
15. Fan, X.M.; Liu, Y.F. Exploring Ways to Create Sustainable Urban Habitat. *City House* **2020**, *7*, 160–161. Available online: https://t.cnki.net/kcms/detail?v=-j_lVuKOk7otYpFUsZjewrqwWvKs7UgAoLOH5QrsgMpTynrhpNmCjz6cAhGmsE1jepw6R-K31H3vNpK8MpdWXlfAnhQhYWXZXv0-38iHYOT0FZDgXC11a_qyTFLZ-R8_&uniplatform=NZKPT (accessed on 1 June 2021).
16. Qi, F.; Xie, H.X.; Wang, G.Z. The Delineation and Management of the Three Control Lines in Territorial Spatial Planning. *China Land* **2019**, *2*, 26–29. [CrossRef]
17. Panayotou, T. *Empirical Tests and Policy Analysis of Environmental Degradation at Different Stages of Economic Development (No. 992927783402676)*; International Labour Organization: Geneva, Switzerland, 1993.
18. Panayotou, T. Demystifying the environmental Kuznets curve: Turning a black box into a policy tool. *Environ. Dev. Econ.* **1997**, *2*, 465–484. [CrossRef]
19. Kaika, D.; Zervas, E. The Environmental Kuznets Curve (EKC) theory—Part A: Concept, causes and the CO_2 emissions case. *Energy Policy* **2013**, *62*, 1392–1402. [CrossRef]
20. Fujii, H.; Iwata, K.; Chapman, A.; Kagawa, S.; Managi, S. An analysis of urban environmental Kuznets curve of CO_2 emissions: Empirical analysis of 276 global metropolitan areas. *Appl. Energy* **2018**, *228*, 1561–1568. [CrossRef]
21. Ghosh, S. Examining carbon emissions economic growth nexus for India: A multivariate cointegration approach. *Energy Policy* **2010**, *38*, 3008–3014. [CrossRef]
22. Tu, Z.G.; Luo, Z. Strategic Measures to Reduce China's Carbon Emissions: Based on an Index Decomposition Analysis of Carbon Emissions in Eight Industries. *Soc. Sci. China* **2014**, *3*, 158–173. [CrossRef]
23. Chong, W.H.B.; Guan, D.; Guthrie, P. Comparative analysis of carbonization drivers in China's megacities. *J. Ind. Ecol.* **2012**, *16*, 564–575. [CrossRef]
24. Christmann, P.; Taylor, G. Globalization and the environment: Determinants of firm self-regulation in China. *J. Int. Bus. Stud.* **2001**, *32*, 439–458. [CrossRef]
25. Li, J.W.; Gong, F.H. Energy, Environment and China's Economic Growth. *J. Quant. Tech. Econ.* **1994**, *1*, 3–14.
26. Tang, M.; Li, Z.; Hu, F.; Wu, B. How does land urbanization promote urban eco-efficiency? The mediating effect of industrial structure advancement. *J. Clean. Prod.* **2020**, *272*, 122798. [CrossRef]
27. Wang, H.; He, Q.; Liu, X.; Zhuang, Y.; Hong, S. Global urbanization research from 1991 to 2009: A systematic research review. *Landsc. Urban Plan.* **2012**, *104*, 299–309. [CrossRef]
28. Michael, F.L.; Noor, Z.Z.; Figueroa, M.J. Review of urban sustainability indicators assessment—Case study between Asian countries. *Habitat Int.* **2014**, *44*, 491–500. [CrossRef]
29. Yu, J.; Zhou, K.; Yang, S. Land use efficiency and influencing factors of urban agglomerations in China. *Land Use Policy* **2019**, *88*, 104143. [CrossRef]
30. Yuan, J.; Bian, Z.; Yan, Q.; Pan, Y. Spatio-temporal distributions of the land use efficiency coupling coordination degree in mining cities of western China. *Sustainability* **2019**, *11*, 5288. [CrossRef]
31. Taylor, M.S.; Copeland, B.R. *Trade, Growth and the Environment*; National Bureau of Economic Research: Cambridge, MA, USA, 2003.
32. Ji, X.M.; Wang, K.; Ji, T.; Zhang, Y.H.; Wang, K. Coupling analysis of urban land use benefits: A case study of Xiamen city. *Land* **2020**, *9*, 155. [CrossRef]
33. Terrell, T.D. Carbon flux and N-and M-shaped environmental Kuznets curves: Evidence from international land use change. *J. Environ. Econ. Policy* **2021**, *10*, 155–174. [CrossRef]
34. Pontarollo, N.; Muñoz, R.M. Land consumption and income in Ecuador: A case of an inverted environmental Kuznets curve. *Ecol. Indic.* **2020**, *108*, 105699. [CrossRef] [PubMed]
35. Pontarollo, N.; Serpieri, C. Testing the Environmental Kuznets Curve hypothesis on land use: The case of Romania. *Land Use Policy* **2020**, *97*, 104695. [CrossRef]
36. Chen, H.; Zhang, X.; Wu, R.; Cai, T. Revisiting the environmental Kuznets curve for city-level CO2 emissions: Based on corrected NPP-VIIRS nighttime light data in China. *J. Clean. Prod.* **2020**, *268*, 121575. [CrossRef]
37. Wang, Z.; Ye, X. Re-examining environmental Kuznets curve for China's city-level carbon dioxide (CO_2) emissions. *Spat. Stat.* **2017**, *21*, 377–389. [CrossRef]
38. Yao, T.; Huang, Z.; Zhao, W. Are smart cities more ecologically efficient? Evidence from China. *Sustain. Cities Soc.* **2020**, *60*, 102008. [CrossRef]
39. Liao, C.X.; Gao, A.G.; Huang, E.H. Enlightenment of Rainwater Management in Foreign Countries to Sponge City construction in China. *Water Resour. Prot.* **2016**, *32*, 42–45. Available online: https://t.cnki.net/kcms/detail?v=b7NF9JV5R2v2AW2i2JpSB2FKNCJr3uPWWjAM7A7SrQ4nF7omxwa9sef-bRYpCuh4x6r_hsjlQo-EN8TTwpeLQq4uhHQ8FnPp0KZ9L30AKWsk-kVw3hpw8lgodBPDx8-I&uniplatform=NZKPT (accessed on 1 June 2021).

40. Dong, Y.; Jin, G.; Deng, X. Dynamic interactive effects of urban land-use efficiency, industrial transformation, and carbon emissions. *J. Clean. Prod.* **2020**, *270*, 122547. [CrossRef]
41. Yang, Z.R.; Wu, C.F.; Jin, X.M.; Yao, Q.P. Comparative study on urban land use economic benefit based on DEA. *Resour. Environ. Yangtze Basin* **2009**, *18*, 14–18.
42. Xu, X.; Huo, H.; Liu, J.; Shan, Y.; Li, Y.; Zheng, H.; Guan, D.; Ouyang, Z. Patterns of CO_2 emissions in 18 central Chinese cities from 2000 to 2014. *J. Clean. Prod.* **2018**, *172*, 529–540. [CrossRef]
43. Wang, Y.; Fang, X.; Yin, S.; Chen, W. Low-carbon development quality of cities in China: Evaluation and obstacle analysis. *Sustain. Cities Soc.* **2021**, *64*, 102553. [CrossRef]
44. Feng, K.; Siu, Y.L.; Guan, D.; Hubacek, K. Analyzing drivers of regional carbon dioxide emissions for China: A structural decomposition analysis. *J. Ind. Ecol.* **2012**, *16*, 600–611. [CrossRef]
45. Tang, Y.; Chen, Y.; Wang, K.; Xu, H.; Yi, X. An Analysis on the Spatial Effect of Absorptive Capacity on Regional Innovation Ability Based on Empirical Research in China. *Sustainability* **2020**, *12*, 3021. [CrossRef]
46. Shen, W.; Zhang, J.; Zhou, X.; Li, S.; Geng, X. How to Perceive the Trade-Off of Economic and Ecological Intensity of Land Use in a City? A Functional Zones-Based Case Study of Tangshan, China. *Land* **2021**, *10*, 551. [CrossRef]
47. Chen, Q. *Advanced Economic Economics with Stata Applications*, 2nd ed.; Higher Education Press: Beijing, China, 2014.
48. Shan, Y.; Huang, Q.; Guan, D.; Hubacek, K. China CO_2 emission accounts 2016–2017. *Sci. Data* **2020**, *7*, 54. [CrossRef]
49. Ji, Z.H.; Zhang, P. Spatial Difference and Driving Mechanism of Urban Land Use Efficiency Under the Environmental Constraints: Based on 285 Cities in China. *China Land Sci.* **2020**, *34*, 72–79. [CrossRef]
50. Meng, Y.; Wang, K.; Lin, Y. The Role of Land Use Transition on Industrial Pollution Reduction in the Context of Innovation-Driven: The Case of 30 Provinces in China. *Land* **2021**, *10*, 353. [CrossRef]
51. Van Zanten, H.H.; Mollenhorst, H.; Klootwijk, C.W.; van Middelaar, C.E.; de Boer, I.J. Global food supply: Land use efficiency of livestock systems. *Int. J. Life Cycle Assess.* **2016**, *21*, 747–758. [CrossRef]
52. Zitti, M.; Ferrara, C.; Perini, L.; Carlucci, M.; Salvati, L. Long-term urban growth and land use efficiency in Southern Europe: Implications for sustainable land management. *Sustainability* **2015**, *7*, 3359–3385. [CrossRef]
53. Xianzhi, F. On the index system of evaluating land utility efficiency. *Syst. Eng.* **2004**, *12*, 22–26.
54. Bao, X.Z.; Liu, C.; Zhang, J.B. Comprehensive appraise to the efficiency of urban land use. *Urban Probl.* **2009**, *165*, 46–50. [CrossRef]
55. Huo, T.; Li, X.; Cai, W.; Zuo, J.; Jia, F.; Wei, H. Exploring the impact of urbanization on urban building carbon emissions in China: Evidence from a provincial panel data model. *Sustain. Cities Soc.* **2020**, *56*, 102068. [CrossRef]
56. Kuznets, S. Quantitative aspects of the economic growth of nations: II. industrial distribution of national product and labor force. *Econ. Dev. Cult. Chang.* **1957**, *5*, 1–111. [CrossRef]
57. Kuznets, S. Modern economic growth: Findings and reflections. *Am. Econ. Rev.* **1973**, *63*, 247–258.
58. Wallsten, S.J. The effects of government-industry R&D programs on private R&D: The case of the Small Business Innovation Research program. *RAND J. Econ.* **2000**, *31*, 82–100.
59. Jaffe, A.B. *Technological Opportunity and Spillovers of R&D: Evidence from Firms' Patents, Profits and Market Value*; National Bureau of Economic Research: Cambridge, MA, USA, 1986.
60. Chen, D.K. Trade Barrier Reduction and Environmental Pollution Improvement: New Evidence from Firm-level Pollution Data in China. *Econ. Res. J.* **2020**, *12*, 98–114. Available online: https://kns.cnki.net/kcms/detail/detail.aspx?dbcode=CJFD&dbname=CJFDLAST2021&filename=JJYJ202012006&v=x7X5dmdiedO9fs8fieE9hww1c0L%25mmd2BGksRK%25mmd2FUyiZbhJJtdr9Xl3Qpi1MNI5cLfCiFB (accessed on 1 June 2021).
61. Ouyang, Y.Y.; Huang, X.F.; Zhong, L.M. The Impact of Outward Foreign Direct Investment on Environmental Pollution in Home Country: Local and Spatial Spillover Effects. *China Ind. Econ.* **2020**, *2*, 98–121. [CrossRef]
62. Ahn, S.J.; Yoon, H.Y. 'Green chasm' in clean-tech for air pollution: Patent evidence of a long innovation cycle and a technological level gap. *J. Clean. Prod.* **2020**, *272*, 122726. [CrossRef]
63. Omri, A.; Hadj, T.B. Foreign investment and air pollution: Do good governance and technological innovation matter? *Environ. Res.* **2020**, *185*, 109469. [CrossRef]
64. Brunnermeier, S.B.; Cohen, M.A. Determinants of environmental innovation in US manufacturing industries. *J. Environ. Econ. Manag.* **2003**, *45*, 278–293. [CrossRef]
65. Chen, J.; Gao, M.; Cheng, S.; Hou, W.; Song, M.; Liu, X.; Liu, Y.; Shan, Y. County-level CO_2 emissions and sequestration in China during 1997–2017. *Sci. Data* **2020**, *7*, 391. [CrossRef] [PubMed]
66. Cobb, C.W.; Douglas, P.H. A theory of production. *Am. Econ. Rev.* **1928**, *18*, 139–165.
67. Wang, K.; Tang, Y.; Chen, Y.; Shang, L.; Wang, P. The Coupling and Coordinated Development from Urban Land Using Benefits and Urbanization Level: Case Study from Fujian Province (China). *Int. J. Environ. Res. Public Health* **2020**, *17*, 5647. [CrossRef] [PubMed]
68. Wang, Q.; Zhou, B.; Zhang, C.; Zhou, D. Do energy subsidies reduce fiscal and household non-energy expenditures? A regional heterogeneity assessment on coal-to-gas program in China. *Energy Policy* **2021**, *155*, 112341. [CrossRef]
69. Liang, J.; He, P.; Qiu, Y.L. Energy transition, public expressions, and local officials' incentives: Social media evidence from the coal-to-gas transition in China. *J. Clean. Prod.* **2021**, *298*, 126771. [CrossRef]

land

MDPI

Article

Beijing's First Green Belt—A 50-Year Long Chinese Planning Story

Lu Sun, Christian Fertner and Gertrud Jørgensen *

Department of Geosciences and Natural Resource Management, University of Copenhagen, 2000 Frederiksberg, Denmark; lusun@ign.ku.dk (L.S.); chfe@ign.ku.dk (C.F.)
* Correspondence: gej@ign.ku.dk

Abstract: This article traces the development process of Beijing's First Green Belt from its origins in the 1950s, to its reinterpretation in the 1980s/1990s and its implementation in the 1990s/2000s. We identify three-time phases and important milestones, which kept the green belt idea alive, developed it and contextualized it in relation to the historical background. This article shows that the first green belt project in Beijing was a continuing process of changing functions and ranges. Its adaptability to variations followed the political changes and reflected the socio-economic dynamics, which secured its longevity. Different ideas shaped the plan and its link to mega events like the Olympic Games and environmental problems accelerated the implementation, but the shortage of funding and absence of legislation led to a compromised result. The case is an interesting example of how a long-term project transforms over and with time, but also for the gap between planning ambitions and actual urban development, illustrating past and contemporary urban planning in the context of a fast-developing country.

Keywords: green belt; master plan; planning history; planning policy; urban containment

Citation: Sun, L.; Fertner, C.; Jørgensen, G. Beijing's First Green Belt—A 50-Year Long Chinese Planning Story. *Land* **2021**, *10*, 969. https://doi.org/10.3390/land10090969

Academic Editors: Przemysław Śleszyński, Maciej J. Nowak and Giancarlo Cotella

Received: 2 July 2021
Accepted: 11 September 2021
Published: 15 September 2021

1. Introduction

1.1. Planning for the Rapid Growth of Beijing

Beijing has experienced a tremendous urban growth in the past century, growing from 4.2 million inhabitants in 1949 to 21.7 million inhabitants in 2015. In parallel with that, the built-up area of the city expanded and increased its size by more than 12 times in that period, from 109 to 1401 km^2 [1]. Regulating urban development of the capital was always a major focus of planning and spatial policies during all these years. One of the key planning ideas of the past was the development of a green belt around the city, now referred to as the 'first green belt', as a second one, further out from the centre, also came up later.

The design and development of the first green belt in Beijing covered a long period since 1949. Six successive master plans were formulated for Beijing from 1949 to 2004, and from the 1958 master plan, the green belt took a place in the comprehensive plan. The green belt was influenced by various policies and plans, and its size fluctuated up and down following the policy changes.

Previous studies worked on this case from various aspects. Ouyang et al. [2] evaluated its ecological function and species composition. Yang and Jinxing [3] analysed the administrative framework as well as temporal spatial changes. Zhao [4] assesses the performance of urban containment strategies in Beijing over between 1990 and 2009. Han [5] discussed the possibility to convert the green belt into greenways. Ma and Jin [6] analysed the possible scenarios under alternative levels of green belt interventions. Han and Long [7] listed the disadvantages of the first green belt policies and discussed the impacts. However, a comprehensive investigation of the planning history has not been written yet, despite that the case provides the possibility to deep insides into the urban development of the Chinese capital and its accompanying planning ideas and practices through the decades.

1.2. The Green Belt Concept and the Chinese Context

The idea of a green belt surrounding the city goes back to the nineteenth century and planning ideas in British and other European cities [8]. Today it is a widely used planning instrument. A green belt is a physical area of open space, e.g., farmland, forest, or other greenspace, that surrounds a city or metropolitan area and connects with the wider urban green infrastructure. The content in a green belt can be different, but essential characteristics of green belts, i.e., the openness and permanence, as, for example, stated by the UK planning department [9], can be found in most cases. Elson [10] described a green belt as a special policy defining an area within which only a highly restrictive schedule of changes constituting development under the planning acts will normally be permitted. Therefore, it is to be a permanent barrier to urban expansion and thus recognized as the most restrictive form of urban containment policy [11].

A globally famous example is London, with a green belt firstly put in place in the interwar period, soon to be positioned as an instrument to nature close to the city and limit urban sprawl [12]. Green belts since then occupied a central position in England's planning system. The first green belt in London drew worldwide attention because of its success in containing urban growth in existing and planned communities, preserving agricultural land, and protecting the environment [13]. Since then, green belts were applied in many other cities in different countries [14]. In Tokyo, green belts were used to create open space for air defence [15], in Moscow to provide clean air and recreation for the city core [16].

The ambitions were though not always met and green belts have also been criticised for a number of negative effects, e.g., urban land shortages, increased housing prices, decreased green belt land prices, increased urban congestion, or leapfrog development [8,11,13]. Several scholars analysed the role of different factors for the success of green belts. Ali [13] proposed four framing factors: political will, public support, plans, and legislation. Amati and Yokohari [17] highlighted the importance of flexibility with regulations and support from landowners. Bengston and Youn [11] stated the impact of social and economic contexts, cost and benefit, and policy reform.

As we will see later, similar factors played a decisive role for Beijing's first green belt. Today, some kind of green belt is employed in many Chinese cities, often as a measure to contain urban growth and improve the environment [18,19]. This wide coverage has a young history though, as, for example, urbanization was not recognized as an issue in China until the openness and economic reform in the late 1970s [20]. However, urbanization happened rapidly, far beyond calculation and soon out of control. Between 1978 and 2015, China's urbanization rate increased from 18% to 56% [21] and is expected to continue [22]. The unprecedented scale of urbanization has caused social and economic challenges, for examples, loss of agricultural land threatening the food security, and housing shortage for immigrant workers [23,24], but was also linked to environmental and health problems. Beijing struggled with sandstorms and smog pollution in recent decades [25,26], but it is not a unique case: In 2012, less than 1% of the 500 largest cities in China met the air quality standards recommended by WHO [27].

Urbanisation in Chinese cities was often accompanied by a fairly high population density, especially in some fringe villages [18], which resulted in a vulnerable urban fringe zone under strong pressure since the 1980s. Most of the population increase happened in the closest suburban areas [28]. Between 1982 and 1990, population growth in Beijing was 3% in the urban centre, 40% in the near suburbs and 13% in the far suburbs [29,30].

The disordered urban growth and consequent challenges called for corresponding approaches, and green belts were one of the most popular ways to tackle urban sprawl and contain urban growth in the country's cities [31]. Green belts were heavily introduced in the mid-1990s, when the economic development boosted urbanisation, including the biggest cities such as Shanghai and Shenzhen [32,33]. Many cities developed their tailored schemes including green belt(s) as a part of the city's master plan. Guangzhou designed a system of green corridors and nodes [19] and Jinan planned an integrated green network system consisting of green belts and green wedges [34]. Moreover, Beijing's green belt got renewed attention in the 1990s. Its roots can though be traced back to the 1940s.

2. Materials and Methods

In this paper, we analyse the making of the first green belt, from the first ideas and plans in the 1950s until it was officially declared as finished in 2004. How did the green belt idea evolve over time, how was it put into practice, and how was it influenced by contemporary political and socio-economic agendas?

To answer these questions and establish the construct validity and reliability of the case study, we collected multiple sources of evidence, including document study, direct observations, and interviews. Through desk-based and fieldwork studies, we have collected multiple sources of evidence to support the analysis, as shown in the Figure 1 below.

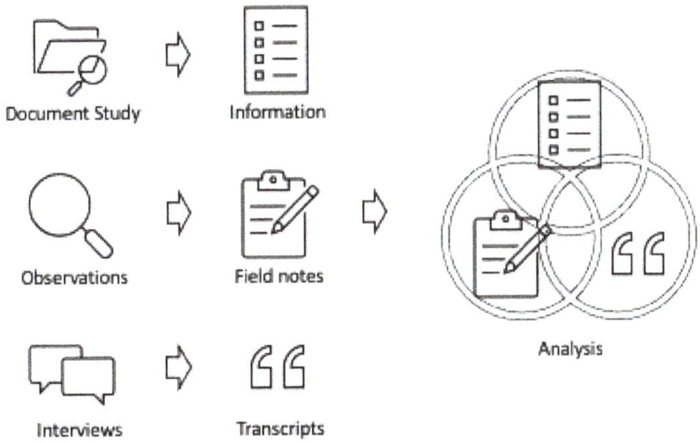

Figure 1. Research methods and process.

First, we give an in-depth account of the important planning documents and events related to the green belt since the proclamation of the P.R. China in 1949. The most important documents include the several City Master Plans of Beijing that we will discuss in the next section, as well as the green belt related official documents listed in Table 1 below. Many materials were acquired from official archives and planning institutions, including national and local policies, regulations and plans.

We have also visited the case areas multiple times which gave us the opportunity for direct observations of the current status of the green belt. Besides site visits, the fieldwork included semi-structured interviews with 4 experts: 2 with former senior officials from the municipal government and the City's Planning Institute and 2 with active planners in the City's Planning Institute. The interviews were especially helpful to get hold of unpublished documents and insights into discussions and debates at the time. We are aware that our source material mainly refers to official documents and planners' perspectives which is caused by the historical and contextual nature of the case. We will critically discuss that at the end of the paper. Moreover, before going deeper into the case we will provide a short review of the general idea of a green belt, which we later use to discuss the case's specificities.

We have used a mixed methods approach for data collection and analysis which permits a synergistic utilisation of data from various sources. The document study provided a good collection of quantitative data which are supplemented by qualitative data from site observations and interviews. We have compared and analysed findings with quantitative and qualitative data sources which provided validation for each other. The consolidated results are presented in the next section.

Table 1. Relevant official documents beyond the Master Plans.

Date	Title of Document	Authority
31.07.1993	Emergency notice about strict control on the development and construction in green belt areas	Formulated by Capital Planning & Construction Commission, forwarded by Beijing Government office
20.01.1994	Request for instructions on greening in green belt areas	Formulated by Capital Planning & Construction Commission, authorized by Beijing Government
25.11.1996	Request for instructions on relevant policies during the construction of green belt	Formulated by Beijing Municipal Commission of Urban Planning, authorized by Beijing Government
29.02.2000	Notice on the establishment of leadership group and general headquarters of green belt construction	Released by Beijing Municipal Government Office
20.03.2000	Suggestions for accelerating the construction of green belt	Released by Beijing Municipal Government
29.03.2000	Interim measures on accelerating the construction of green belt	Formulated by Beijing leadership group of green belt construction, forwarded by Beijing government office
27.10.2000	Notice on the implementation of boundary markers in green belt area	Formulated by Beijing leadership group of green belt construction and planning committee, forwarded by Beijing government office
20.04.2001	Notice on accelerating the renovation and construction of new villages in green belt area	Formulated by Beijing leadership group of green belt construction, forwarded by Beijing government office
23.05.2001	Suggestions to improve the economic development in green belt area	Formulated by Beijing agriculture committee, forwarded by Beijing government office
06.07.2001	Suggestions on implementation of master plan for green space system in green belt area	Formulated by Capital Greening Office, forwarded by Beijing government office
14.08.2001	Regulations on protection and management of boundary markers in green belt area	Formulated by Beijing Municipal Commission of Urban Planning, forwarded by Beijing Government office
26.09.2001	Notice on personnel adjustment of leadership group and general headquarters of green belt construction	Released by Beijing Municipal government office
30.12.2001	Regulations on land use replacement in green belt area	Formulated by the Beijing Municipal Bureau of Land and Housing Management, forwarded by Beijing government office

3. Results

The development of the first green belt in Beijing was a prolonged project covering the first semi-century of P. R. China. This half a century witnessed a constantly transforming period in the country, along with which the green belt was initiated and developed step by step.

3.1. A First Hint of the Green Belt

> *"On 16 September [1949], a group of Soviet experts in municipal administration arrived in Beijing. They were supposed to help the new government in its work to plan the city's development. In reality, however, they were to have absolute say in everything."* [35], p. 38, authors' translation

When Beijing became the capital of the People's Republic of China in 1949, there was a debate about the location of the administrative centre: should the old town be renovated, or a new town be built? Two factors finally lead to the success of the old town strategy and a monocentric plan for Beijing was finally determined as a guideline for future city development [36]. Firstly, the new-born Chinese government was significantly influenced by the Soviet Union. In 'Report on Beijing's Development Plan in the Future' in 1949, Soviet Planner M. G. Barannikov suggested the expansion of Tiananmen Square as the city centre, like the Red Square in Moscow. Secondly, another plan for building a new administrative centre in a western suburb was denied by the government, because of the larger expenses for new construction costs. There were 1.65 million residents and about 20 million m^2 of buildings in the old town, but only tens of thousands m^2 in the proposed new centre, Gongzhufen [37]. After this debate, the 1954 master plan for Beijing was set as a monocentric structure aiming to a megacity with 5 to 6 million population.

The political condition changed dramatically after 1954 and the changes had immediate impact on planning. Because of political movements and economic recession, evacuating urban population to the suburbs and countryside became an order from the central government [38]. However, at that time, the city had already expanded to a vast area with a very low density as a side product of the radical growth movement "Great Leap Forward", and built-up areas were spread out in several suburban centres. In 1954, there were 4.5 million m^2 (floor area) new buildings spread out of the city centre [39]. Later in 1958, the "National Landscaping and Gardening Movement" started and aimed at turning the whole country into a "big beautiful park" [40] and then as an immediate consequence, the city was asked to offer its territory for greening. In the recast 1958 master plan, the pattern of "decentralized groups" became a dominant feature (see Figure 2) [36]. The idea of this plan aimed to decentralise city development so as to keep a green belt between the centre and suburbs. The "decentralized groups" were a compromise between reality and future development expectations, keeping flexible for the future [39]. The designated vacant land between the decentralized urbanized groups was thought to be productive land, supplying vegetables to the city [36].

Apparently, the green belt was not the priority in this plan, as it was not even drawn on the plan map, but only left blank to highlight the pattern of the decentralized groups (see Figure 2). However, it is widely believed that the idea of "decentralized groups" in 1958 firstly indicated the conception for a green belt [2,41].

3.2. New Urban Planning Ideas and Challenges Lead to a New Proposal of the Green Belt

> *"The size and population of the city was uncertain during the dramatic development. In this situation, only a proper layout plan could keep the space for future development. The "decentralized groups" was a reasonable model to achieve this purpose. It was generated from history, with the feature of flexibility."* [39], p. 11, own translation

While the 1958 master plan was being formulated, China went into a long phase of political turmoil. The Sino-Soviet Split, started in 1958, resulted in the loss of aid from the Soviet Union; meanwhile, radical communism reform movements led to more serious economic recession and food shortages, followed by migration from the city to the countryside [42]. The direct consequence was the reduction of urban populations, especially in big cities.

During the Cultural Revolution (1966–1976), most of the governmental operations were interrupted, including planning. A master plan was published in 1973 (Figure 2), which mainly followed the 1958 plan, though with considerable reductions of urban land in the outskirts of the city. The plan, however, never got implemented. Still, it is notable that the idea of the 'decentralized groups' was kept alive, at least in the planners' heads.

Only after the "economic reforms and openness" in 1978, China returned gradually to normality and economic development became the priority. The population in Beijing increased rapidly along with the economic boost [43], which soon triggered the wild urban development.

The rapid—and sometimes disordered—development turned lots of green areas into built-up areas. According to the master plans, 314 km^2 green belt areas was planned between the decentralized groups in 1958, but it decreased to 260 km^2 in 1983, and then to 240 sq. km in 1993 (see Table 2). Meanwhile, environmental problems, especially air pollution and sandstorms appeared in parallel with the rapid urbanization, thus the causality between pollution and development was widely discussed [44–46]. The green belt was back on the table and considered as a green cushion to protect the city against sandstorms while also improving air quality [19].

Table 2. Changes in planned urban area and planned green belt area in Beijing, Sources: [36,39,47,48].

Year of Master Plan	Planned Urban Area in City Centre (km^2)	Planned Green Belt Area (km^2)	Main Focus in the Green Belt
1954	600	N/A	No green belt in this master plan.
1958	600	314	Restricted areas between city centre and decentralized groups.
1978	600	314	Same as 1958.
1983	440 (750 in whole municipality)	260	Restricted areas between city centre and decentralized groups, 60% to be planted trees.
1993	610 (900 in whole municipality)	240	Restricted areas between city centre and decentralized groups. Forests and parks. Certain percentage of the land could be used as cultural and recreation facilities upon approval.
2004	778 (1650 in whole municipality)	240	Restricted areas between city centre and decentralized groups. Recreation and ecological protection. Green and high-tech industries are prioritized to promote employment.

The green belt approach was reinstated from the former plans (i.e., the 1958 master plan) and given much attention in the 1993 master plan. So although the green belt was designed several decades ago, it was not implemented as a belt until new problems occurred along with economic development.

3.3. Implementing the Green Belt in a Time of Rapid Urban Growth and New Ambitions

> *"No fund but only supporting policies from the government; this was the precondition. Could we implement the green belt with the help of real estate development? And don't forget, the farmers needed to be resettled and reallocated."* (Former official at Beijing Planning Institute, interview with author, own translation)

Suffering from a bad reputation due to air pollution and sandstorms, Beijing failed in the competition for hosting the Olympic Games in 1993, which hit the city badly. Solving the environmental problems got great political attention and various actions, among them the implementation of the green belt, followed. The green belt was implemented through a series of policies and regulations, released in the following years. A main tool was the establishment of parks and tree planting which already started in 1993, when a new master plan was announced. As lots of building construction had already happened in the green belt area, the 1993 Beijing master plan [47] stated a reduced but more realistic target of 140 km^2 of greening areas out of the 240 km^2 green belt area. Figure 3 shows the green belt and the location of 19 pilot villages and surrounding green areas, indicating the area of the first green belt between the city centre and ten suburban towns. The second green belt outside of the fifth ring road was also proposed in the 1993 master plan.

The implementation of the green belt was supported by several executive orders from the city government. One of the most important was published in 1994, executive order 1994 [7] "The proposal of greening construction in green belt". According to this order, the actual green area in the green belt was only 20 km^2 in 1994, far less than the target of 140 km^2 [50]. In the same order, another policy was announced, "Green Supports Green", which soon became a guiding principle. This policy responded to the new condition in the area and was considered as the actual start of the green belt development. As the land price rose sharply along with the economic growth in the 1990s [51], the cost of purchasing land for building the green belt became much higher, beyond the affordability of the governments. This policy aimed at raising funding by a real estate approach, without acquiring financial support from the government. The basic idea was that the sub-local governments (mainly villages and a few towns) got the permission to operate real estate development and built high-rise settlements in certain limited areas. The newly built housing should be used mainly for allocating farmers and the rest for sale in order to cover the cost for maintaining the green belt. After that, the land in former villages and farmland became state-owned and transferred to be part of the green belt.

Figure 2. Master plans from 1958, 1983, and 1993, from the top down. The red/black line is added to indicate the green belt as planned in 1993 [49].

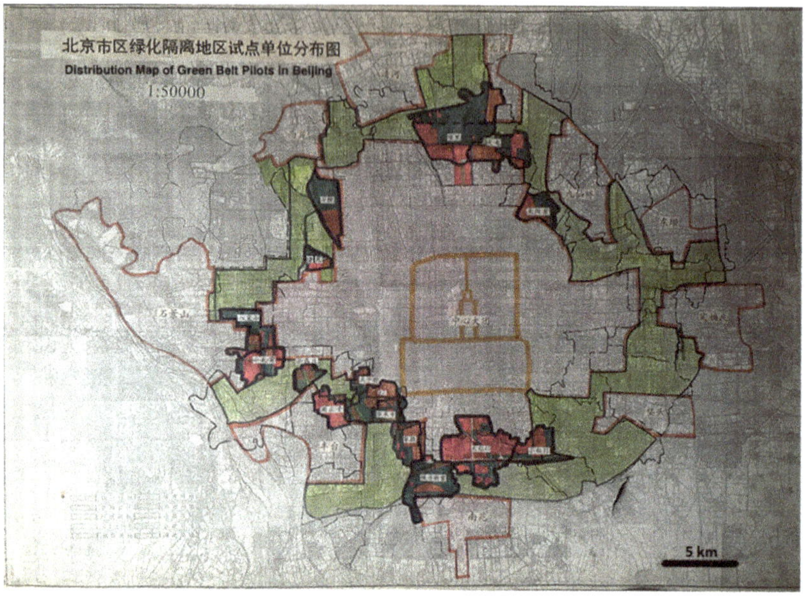

Figure 3. The 1993 plan map for first green belt in Beijing, showing the green belt (light green) and the location of 19 pilot villages (red) and surrounding green areas (dark green), indicating the area of the first green belt between the city centre (orange lines in the middle) and ten suburban towns (pink lines out of the green belt). Source: Private collection of a former planner, photo by author.

This approach was later summarized as a slogan, "Green attracts investment, investment drives development, development builds green, green supports green" [36].

The mode of cooperation and profit distribution was set based on the actual situation in different villages or towns, with the supervision of Beijing municipal government. The sub-local governments would get 30–50% of the newly built housing, without any financial investment, and developers got the rest as return on investment [53].

This policy was supposed to be a win-win solution for the three parties: the government received funds for building and maintaining the green belt, the residents got their living conditions improved, and the developers acquired land in a fine location, without problems with demolition and resettlement.

However, a hidden conflict between farmland acquisition and the state land law soon disrupted this policy [54]. The farmland in the green belt area was protected by the state land law. Therefore, the land acquisition by sub-local government was stopped as it was against the land protection law. A nationwide survey of cultivated land in China in 1996 revealed the rapid reduction of cultivated land and caused the project to be set on hold [36].

The green belt project was suspended until 1999, when Beijing was preparing a new bid for hosting the 2008 Olympic Games. It was recommissioned as a way of improving the terrible environmental pollution in Beijing. The measures from executive order no. 7 in 1994 were partly adopted, but the previous method of land acquisition was abandoned. Instead, farmlands were rezoned as economic forests and financially supported by the government. Subsequently, detailed measures were formulated, e.g., financial subsidies, compensation, and investment management. There were also financial subsidies for maintaining the green areas for the first time [55].

In 2000, the successful bid for the 2008 Olympic Games accelerated the green belt construction to a large extent. A high-level joint committee was established as a leadership group for green belt construction [56]. Meanwhile, boundary markers were established around the green belt [57,58], which were anticipated to guard the green belt. These measures showed the government's determination on implementing the green belt during that time. Then finally, Beijing's first green belt was announced as finished in 2004, well before the 2008 Olympic Games.

After the first green belt project finished, a study [2] shows that the green space increased in the green belt areas in 2005, compared to 1992. However, although the tree cover increased, the agriculture land and water area decreased, meanwhile the built-up area also increased.

4. Discussion and Perspectives

Following the milestone planning documents, it is clear that there were important factors putting the plan into practice.

4.1. The Idea Evolves with the Master Plans from 1958 and 1993

The green belt idea got through times of crisis and prosperity in China. Looking back, three important planning phases culminating in important planning documents and milestones can be identified:

The first years for the PRC up to the adoption of the 1958 master plan. The green belt was, for the first time, proposed in an official document; even though not implemented specifically, the concept kept alive in all following master plans.

The years of rapidly increasing urbanization pressure since the 1970s and 1980s, finally reinstating a strong green belt concept in the master plan of 1993.

The years of implementation with numerous practical regulations released up to the time when it was declared finished in 2004.

The focus of the policies in different periods varied during the process, indicating the change of expected functions of the green belt (see also Table 2). Seen as 'isolation areas' in 1958, as well as in 1973 and 1983, the green belt was considered as a buffer zone to separate the city centre and suburban towns, which can be clearly recognized on the master plans in Figure 2; however, the idea followed no specific action towards implementation. Only with the pressure of rapid urban development and severe air pollution, the green belt was brought up again as a mitigation instrument in 1990s. The 1993 master plan finally initiated the implementation and special policies for the green belt were announced. The process was interrupted in 1996 because of its conflict with farmland reservations but restarted in 1999 to assist in the Olympic Games bid [36]. New policies abandoned the approach from the 1994 order but paid more attention to strict control and financial subsidies.

Over the decades the green belt changed from being a buffer zone between satellite towns ('decentralized groups') and the city centre, to an area for recreation with air cleaning functions combined with green industries. The adaptability of the concept to changing situations contributed to its longevity. However, the green belt was lacking concrete formulated goals or criteria, e.g., regarding the containment of urban growth, green infrastructure for recreation, or air improvement. This uncertainty left space for flexible operations at the sub-local level. The immediate result was that a large part of the green belt was converted to become, for example, golf courses or even built-up areas.

4.2. Putting the Green Belt into Practice-Regulations and Legislation, and the Sub-Local Level

Pollution and the Olympic Games raised the political will for the green belt, but this will only exist at the higher-level authorities, i.e., the central and municipal governments. The loose connection between the initiator (municipal government) and the implementation at the sub-local level (village and town governments) became a problem in practice. Several municipal governmental departments played the role as supervisors, but no single player was able to get the overall control. This left the programme soon to become a free play by the sub-local governments and companies.

The municipal government's reaction to this was a series of regulations and policies. There were several policies and measures created for the green belt project, which were innovative and different from other cases. The collective land ownership in China made land acquisition and compensation rather complicated, as the villages and towns which own the land must find a balance between many interests when changing land rights. The "green supports green" policy was a response to this issue and facilitated several pilot projects [36], but its legal validity was questioned, and the policy was suspended after a short experimental period. The substitute policy in 1999 paid more attention to legal validity but did not provide an economically sustainable solution for maintenance, although temporary financial subsidies supported the implementation. However, the green belt lacked at comprehensive law specifying rules and regulations and taking account for the special land ownership. Moreover, the ongoing policy changes in the 1990s resulted in a mosaic of regulations effective in different areas of the green belt. With this dilemma, the consequent challenges for maintaining the green belt seemed to be unavoidable.

4.3. Political and Socio-Economic Dynamics-Pollution and Olympic Games Finally Made it Happen, but as a Compromise Far from the Original Vision

In the rapid growth years with urbanization and environmental pollution, the green belt got strong political and public attention again, peaking in 1993 when Beijing failed the first bid for hosting the Olympic Games. The environment pollution was considered as an important factor for this failure and the green belt became an iconic project coping with the environmental problems. There was also a wide discussion in the newspapers and on TV and the green belt was among the most popular solutions in response to those problems [25]. The public pressure as expressed in media increased the political will for improvements. Meanwhile, the tight deadline before Olympic Games pushed the implementation of the green belt to progress much faster than normal.

The implementation also fell in a dynamic period regarding the urban political economy in China. Economic globalisation accelerated the decade after 1993. Foreign investments doubled from 1992 to 1993 and almost doubled again in 1994 [59]. To attract and accommodate these foreign investments, local governments in China established exclusive zones called "economic and technological development zones" (ETDZs). Soon the premium of land leasing in these ETDZs became a large source of government revenue [60], which left the local and sub-local governments at a weak position in the negotiations with foreign investment. The foreign investments and foreign tourists also stimulated the need for new types of entertainment, including and increasing demand for golf courses [61].

This dynamic period also witnessed the rocketing of land price in Beijing, following the increase of investment. Funding to purchase land, implement the green infrastructure, and maintain it became a hard nut to crack. Cooperation with external developers within the "Green Support Green" policy provided funding in the beginning, but a conflict with the state land law forfeited this approach. The strong political will resulted in subsidies for land acquirement, but the unexpected boom of land price made it impossible to continue. A sustainable mechanism for financial support with consideration of future changes was missing.

Under these pressures the urban area increased, and the green belt area decreased (see Table 2). The focus in the green belt was also adjusted several times opening doors for commercial operations in disguised form. The green belt located in the "blank" areas was a feasible plan back in 1958. However, after decades of development, the plan in 1993 was a quite ambitious project compared to the constructed reality in the 1990s, not to say an unrealistic vision at that time. On a satellite image from 2006, two years after the declared completion, the green belt area can hardly be recognized (Figure 4) and many of the remaining green areas are not connected [5].

4.4. Lessons to Draw for Future Green Belt Planning

It is rare to see that a planning idea like the green belt could live through for half a century in China, especially in its quick-changing capital city. Through its ups and downs, we get a chance to investigate the political, social, and economic changes and its relation to planning and policy transfer.

This study gives a thorough review of the process and reveals it was a pragmatic decision to keep, adapt and finally implement the green belt in Beijing. In the first years, a green belt between the city centre and suburbs was to keep some flexibility for the future development, while the belt shape was adapted to the existing city structure well. Later, beside the function for urban containment, the green belt was expected to tackle environmental problems and ambitions for the city development in regards the Olympic Games, which led to a range of concrete policies in 1990s and 2000s, aiming at realising the green belt.

Our source material is, however, limited to mainly official views from Beijing's municipal planning. Considering the complex background especially in the implementation phase, views from sub-local governments or private developers may had offered different perspectives for the interpretation of the development process. Taking the "Green Support Green" policy as an example, it was considered as an innovative and effective approach by the planners but could potentially be economic unsustainable for sub-local governments and private developers.

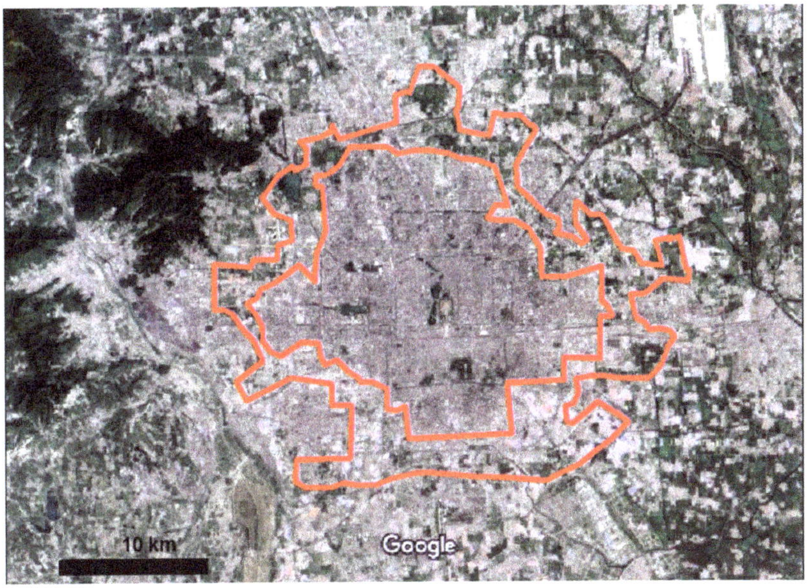

Figure 4. Satellite image of Beijing in 2006 (Source: Google). The red line indicates the first green belt in Beijing as planned in the 1993 master plan.

The case of the first green belt in Beijing shows the importance of several influencing factors, including political will and funding support, legislation and regulation, concrete goals and comprehensive planning, social and economic context. This is similar to studies from other green belt cases. Our case shows that there are significant synergies between the factors, and they can hardly be looked at isolated. The case also shows that a strong planning vision with a certain flexibility fitting the local context can remain over a long period of time. Beijing's planners kept the green belt, despite no possibilities for its realisation, in the plans over the decades until the city's development required its implementation. However, it also shows that planning ideas can be somehow far from the actual development on the ground, which was also reflected in the policy transfer in between as descripted previously. When the green belt was taken seriously finally in the 1990s, much of it was already lost to development.

One of the green belt idea's strengths lies in its clear spatial vision of having a continuous "belt" shape. As shown by other studies, this can though increase housing prices in the remaining areas and lead to a housing shortage [11]. The proposal to down scale the green belt to be a "belt of parks" was a response to that, which reduced the possibilities to control urban growth [62]. A belt is, however, not the sole way for a strong green infrastructure vision. Green wedges, green hearts, green corridors, etc., have been implemented successfully with similar strong spatial vision, and plans for the second green belt in Beijing also consider other spatial models [63,64]. The impact on social justice in relation to housing affordability and public accessibility to green space should be considered when making policies, which can be improved in the Beijing case. A way to mitigate the growth challenges is working with land supply mechanisms on a larger scale. The master plan initiative is one of Beijing's strengths and has the potential to better integrated the green belt needs with other plans of the municipality, as e.g., the land resource plan or the greening plan, in the future.

Author Contributions: Conceptualization, L.S., C.F. and G.J.; Writing—original draft, L.S.; Writing—review & editing, C.F. and G.J. All authors have read and agreed to the published version of the manuscript.

Funding: This research was funded by China Scholarship Council (CSC), grant number [2014]3026.

Institutional Review Board Statement: Not applicable.

Informed Consent Statement: Not applicable.

Data Availability Statement: The data presented in this study are openly available as listed in References section.

Conflicts of Interest: The authors declare no conflict of interest.

References

1. MOHURD. *Statistical Yearbook of City Development 2015*; Ministry of Housing and Urban-Rural Development: Beijing, China, 2015.
2. Ouyang, Z.; Wang, R.; Li, W.; Juergen, P.; Li, D.; Xiao, Y.; Wang, X. Ecological planning on greenbelt surrounding mega city, Beijing. *Acta Ecol. Sin.* **2005**, *25*, 965–971.
3. Yang, J.; Jinxing, Z. The Failure and Success of Greenbelt Program in Beijing. *Urban For. Urban Green.* **2007**, *6*, 287–296. [CrossRef]
4. Zhao, P. Managing Urban Growth in a Transforming China: Evidence from Beijing. *Land Use Policy* **2011**, *28*, 96–109. [CrossRef]
5. Han, X. From Green Belt to Green Corridor: Case Study from Beijing Green Belt. *Urban Probl.* **2004**, *2*, 5.
6. Ma, M.; Jin, Y. What If Beijing Had Enforced the 1st or 2nd Greenbelt?—Analyses from an Economic Perspective. *Landsc. Urban Plan.* **2019**, *182*, 79–91. [CrossRef]
7. Han, H.; Long, Y. Green or Green Space?—Effect Analysis of the First Green Belt of Beijing. *Beijing Plan. Rev.* **2010**, *3*, 59–63.
8. Amati, M. *Urban Green Belts in the Twenty-First Century*; Ashgate Publishing Ltd.: Farnham, UK, 2012; ISBN 1-4094-8790-3.
9. DCLG. *National Planning Policy Framework*; UK Department of Communities and Local Government: London, UK, 2012.
10. Elson, M.J. *Green Belts: Conflict Mediation in the Urban Fringe*; Heinemann: Portsmouth, NH, USA, 1986; ISBN 978-0-434-90532-4.
11. Bengston, D.N.; Youn, Y.-C. Urban Containment Policies and the Protection of Natural Areas: The Case of Seoul's Greenbelt. *Ecol. Soc.* **2006**, *11*. [CrossRef]
12. Miller, M. The Elusive Green Background: Raymond Unwin and the Greater London Regional Plan. *Plan. Perspect.* **1989**, *4*, 15–44. [CrossRef]
13. Ali, A.K. Greenbelts to Contain Urban Growth in Ontario, Canada: Promises and Prospects. *Plan. Pract. Res.* **2008**, *23*, 533–548. [CrossRef]
14. Taylor, J.; Paine, C.; FitzGibbon, J. From Greenbelt to Greenways: Four Canadian Case Studies. *Landsc. Urban Plan.* **1995**, *33*, 47–64. [CrossRef]
15. Yokohari, M.; Takeuchi, K.; Watanabe, T.; Yokota, S. Beyond Greenbelts and Zoning: A New Planning Concept for the Environment of Asian Mega-Cities. *Landsc. Urban Plan.* **2000**, *47*, 159–171. [CrossRef]
16. Boentje, J.P.; Blinnikov, M.S. Post-Soviet Forest Fragmentation and Loss in the Green Belt around Moscow, Russia (1991–2001): A Remote Sensing Perspective. *Landsc. Urban Plan.* **2007**, *82*, 208–221. [CrossRef]
17. Amati, M.; Yokohari, M. The Actions of Landowner, Government and Planners in Establishing the London Green Belt of the 1930s. *J. Jpn. Inst. Landsc. Archit.* **2004**, *67*, 433–438. [CrossRef]
18. Wang, H.; Li, H.; Ming, H.; Hu, Y.; Chen, J.; Zhao, B. Past Land Use Decisions and Socioeconomic Factors Influence Urban Greenbelt Development: A Case Study of Shanghai, China. *Landsc. Ecol.* **2014**, *29*, 1759–1770. [CrossRef]
19. Yu, X.J.; Ng, C.N. Spatial and Temporal Dynamics of Urban Sprawl along Two Urban–Rural Transects: A Case Study of Guangzhou, China. *Landsc. Urban Plan.* **2007**, *79*, 96–109. [CrossRef]
20. Wu, Y. Socialist Urbanization of China. *City Plan. Rev.* **1979**, *5*, 13–25.

21. Yang, J.; Wu, T.; Gong, P. Implementation of China's New Urbanization Strategy Requires New Thinking. *Sci. Bull.* **2017**, *62*, 81–82. [CrossRef]
22. Shen, L.; Cheng, S.K.; Gunson, A.J.; Hui, W. Urbanization, Sustainability and the Utilization of Energy and Mineral Resources in China. *Cities* **2005**, *22*, 287–302. [CrossRef]
23. Bai, X.; Shi, P.; Liu, Y. Society: Realizing China's Urban Dream. *Nature* **2014**, *509*, 158. [CrossRef]
24. Zhou, Y. Opinions on the Speed of Urbanization in China. *City Plan. Rev.* **2006**, *30*, 32–35.
25. Li, M. Reasons of the Four Sandstorms in Beijing in March. *Beijing Evening News*, 29 March 2000.
26. Zhu, K. 100 billion for Better Environment Supporting Bid for Olympics. *Chin. J. Environ. Eng.* **2001**, *1*, 95.
27. Zhang, Q.; Crooks, R. *Toward an Environmentally Sustainable Future: Country Environmental Analysis of the People's Republic of China*; Asian Development Bank: Mandaluyong, Philippines, 2012.
28. Yan, X.; Jia, L.; Li, J.; Weng, J. The Development of the Chinese Metropolis in the Period of Transition. In *The New Chinese City*; Blackwell Publishers Ltd.: Oxford, UK, 2008; pp. 37–55. ISBN 978-0-470-71286-3.
29. Zhou, Y. On the Suburbanization of Beijing. *Sci. Geogr. Sin.* **1996**, *3*, 198–206.
30. Zhou, Y.; Meng, Y. Suburbanization in Big Chinese Cities. *Urban Plan. Forum* **1998**, *3*, 22–27.
31. Liu, J.; Zhan, J.; Deng, X. Spatio-Temporal Patterns and Driving Forces of Urban Land Expansion in China during the Economic Reform Era. *AMBIO J. Hum. Environ.* **2005**, *34*, 450–455. [CrossRef]
32. Hong, W.; Guo, R. Indicators for Quantitative Evaluation of the Social Services Function of Urban Greenbelt Systems: A Case Study of Shenzhen, China. *Ecol. Indic.* **2017**, *75*, 259–267. [CrossRef]
33. Leading Group Office of Shanghai Master Plan. *Shanghai Master Plan 2016–2040*; Leading Group Office of Shanghai Master Plan: Shanghai, China, 2016.
34. Kong, F.; Nakagoshi, N. Spatial-Temporal Gradient Analysis of Urban Green Spaces in Jinan, China. *Landsc. Urban Plan.* **2006**, *78*, 147–164. [CrossRef]
35. Wang, J. *Beijing Record*; SDX Joint Publishing: Beijing, China, 2003; ISBN 978-7-108-01816-8.
36. Beijing Municipal Commission of Urban Planning. *Echoes of the Years—Record of the 60 Years of Planning for the Capital City*; Urban Planning Society of Beijing: Beijing, China, 2009.
37. Liang, S.; Chen, Z. *Liang-Chen Plan and Beijing*; Liaoning Education Press: Shenyang, China, 2005.
38. Zhu, T. Nationalism and Chinese Foreign Policy. *China Rev.* **2001**, *1*, 1–27.
39. Chen, G. *Jinghuadaisilu: Anthology of Chen Gan*; Beijing Municipal Institute of City Planning & Design: Beijing, China, 1996.
40. Zhao, J. A Historical Review of "Land Gardenization Movement". *Chin. Landsc. Archit.* **2010**, *10*, 56–60.
41. Li, F.; Wang, R.; Paulussen, J.; Liu, X. Comprehensive Concept Planning of Urban Greening Based on Ecological Principles: A Case Study in Beijing, China. *Landsc. Urban Plan.* **2005**, *72*, 325–336. [CrossRef]
42. Gooch, E. Estimating the Long-Term Impact of the Great Chinese Famine (1959–1961) on Modern China. *World Dev.* **2017**, *89*, 140–151. [CrossRef]
43. Golley, J.; Wei, Z. Population Dynamics and Economic Growth in China. *China Econ. Rev.* **2015**, *35*, 15–32. [CrossRef]
44. Amsden, A.H.; Dongyi, L.; Xiaoming, Z. China's Macroeconomy, Environment, and Alternative Transition Model. *World Dev.* **1996**, *24*, 273–286. [CrossRef]
45. Cao, S.; Chen, L.; Liu, Z. An Investigation of Chinese Attitudes toward the Environment: Case Study Using the Grain for Green Project. *AMBIO J. Hum. Environ.* **2009**, *38*, 55–64. [CrossRef] [PubMed]
46. Liu, X.; Mu, R. Public Environmental Concern in China: Determinants and Variations. *Glob. Environ. Chang.* **2016**, *37*, 116–127. [CrossRef]
47. BICP. *Beijing Master Plan 1991–2010*; Beijing Municipal Institute of City Planning & Design (BICP): Beijing, China, 1992.
48. BICP. *Beijing Master Plan 2004–2020*; Beijing Municipal Institute of City Planning & Design (BICP): Beijing, China, 2005.
49. Compilation Committee of Beijing Records. *Beijing Records: Urban and Rural Planning Volume. Planning Records*; Beijing Publishing House: Beijing, China, 2009; ISBN 978-7-200-06807-8.
50. Capital Planning and Construction Commission. *Request for Instructions on Greening in Green Belt Areas*; Capital Planning and Construction Commission: Beijing, China, 1994.
51. Zhang, X.Q. Urban Land Reform in China. *Land Use Policy* **1997**, *14*, 187–199. [CrossRef]
52. Tian, Y.; Yin, K.; Lu, D.; Hua, L.; Zhao, Q.; Wen, M. Examining Land Use and Land Cover Spatiotemporal Change and Driving Forces in Beijing from 1978 to 2010. *Remote Sens.* **2014**, *6*, 10593–10611. [CrossRef]
53. Zhao, Z. Opinions on the Construction of the Green Belt in Beijing. *Beijing City Plan. Constr. Rev.* **2003**, *C00*, 27–28.
54. Hu, W. Household Land Tenure Reform in China: Its Impact on Farming Land Use and Agro-Environment. *Land Use Policy* **1997**, *14*, 175–186. [CrossRef]
55. Beijing Leadership Group of Green Belt Construction. *Interim Measures on Accelerating the Construction of Green Belt*; Beijing Leadership Group of Green Belt Construction: Beijing, China, 2000.
56. Beijing Government Office. *Notice on the Establishment of Leadership Group and General Headquarters of Green Belt Construction*; Beijing Government Office: Beijing, China, 2000.
57. Beijing Leadership Group of Green Belt Construction and Planning Committee. *Notice on the Implementation of Boundary Markers in Green Belt Area*; Beijing Leadership Group of Green Belt Construction and Planning Committee: Beijing, China, 2000.

58. Beijing Municipal Commission of Urban Planning. *Regulations on Protection and Management of Boundary Markers in Green Belt Area*; Urban Planning Society of Beijing: Beijing, China, 2001.
59. State Statistical Bureau. *China Statistical Yearbook 1998*; China Statistical Press: Beijing, China, 1998.
60. Wu, F. China's Recent Urban Development in the Process of Land and Housing Marketisation and Economic Globalisation. *Habitat Int.* **2001**, *25*, 273–289. [CrossRef]
61. Deci, Z. The Open Door Policy and Urban Development in China. *Habitat Int.* **1996**, *20*, 525–529. [CrossRef]
62. Guo, Z.; Xu, B.; Zhong, J. Opinions on building "belt parks" in Beijing green belt area. *Beijing Landsc. Archit.* **2009**, *4*, 7–11.
63. Kühn, M. Greenbelt and Green Heart: Separating and Integrating Landscapes in European City Regions. *Landsc. Urban Plan.* **2003**, *64*, 19–27. [CrossRef]
64. Lemes de Oliveira, F. Green Wedges: Origins and Development in Britain. *Plan. Perspect.* **2014**, *29*, 357–379. [CrossRef]

land

Article

It's All about Details. Why the Polish Land Policy Framework Fails to Manage Designation of Developable Land

Tomasz Zaborowski

Urban Geography and Spatial Planning, Faculty of Geography and Regional Studies, University of Warsaw, 00-927 Warszawa, Poland; t.zaborowski@uw.edu.pl

Abstract: Since the introduction of the current legal planning system, Polish land policy has failed to manage the designation of developable land. The oversupply of developable land designated in land-use plans and resulting from various weaknesses of auxiliary planning permissions undermines the creation of compact urban settlements. The article argues that, theoretically, the Polish legal framework of developable land designation management conforms with its more effective European counterparts. What makes it not work properly are the detailed regulations and their interpretation. In order to support this argument, the Polish land policy framework will be analysed and assessed by comparing it with the key common features of its German and Spanish counterparts.

Keywords: land policy; planning system; land-use planning; land development; urban development; legal framework; containment; Poland; Germany; Spain

Citation: Zaborowski, T. It's All about Details. Why the Polish Land Policy Framework Fails to Manage Designation of Developable Land. *Land* **2021**, *10*, 890. https://doi.org/10.3390/land10090890

Academic Editors: Maciej J. Nowak, Giancarlo Cotella and Przemysław Śleszyński

Received: 8 July 2021
Accepted: 16 August 2021
Published: 25 August 2021

1. Introduction

Managing the designation of developable land is definitely one of the key tasks of land policy. The decision on which land may be developed has an impact on both the quality and efficiency of the settlement structure and the natural environment [1] (p. 211). The developable land designation management involves two main practical questions: *how much* land should be designated for development, and *where* should that land be located? While considering the issue of *how much* land should be assigned for development, everyone should agree that there should be neither too little nor too much land designated. A sufficient quantity of developable land is needed to provide various urban land uses such as housing, industrial, commercial development, public buildings, social and technical infrastructure, etc. On the other hand, an overestimated quantity of land for development threatens both qualities of urban patterns and the natural environment. If there is too much developable land, inconsistent and dispersed settlements may arise [2]. Such patchy, chaotic developments form invalid, unstructured urban patterns [3], [4] (p. 224), [5] (p. 91), [6]. A side effect of such an urban growth pattern is overconsumption of open land followed by a decrease of natural areas, arable and recreational land, forests, etc. [7] (p. 123), [8] (pp. 36–38), [9] (p. 16).

Excessive land development has been a serious problem worldwide [10]. Between 1990 and 2000, at least 275 ha of land was converted to built-up land in Europe per day [11], [12] (p. 186). The extent of residential areas in Europe has been growing disproportionately faster than the population (ca. 20% vs. ca. 6% between 1995 and 2015) [13] (p. 220). Uncurbed land consumption resulting in dispersed suburban development was observed in many European countries, especially in the 1990s (e.g., in Norway [12] (p. 186), [14], Spain [15] (p. 54), [13] (p. 238) and Eastern Germany [16] (p. 640)). Immoderate urban land expansion is a problem specifically in rapidly developing countries [12] (p. 186), [17], e.g., China [18] (p. 253), Iran [19] (p. 593), Turkey [19], (p. 594) [20] and Mexico, where land-use plans designated land for development that far exceeds predicted long-term needs [21] (p. 79). The pace of urban sprawl is notably great in Eastern Europe [22], [23] (p. 114).

Natural and farmland consumption due to unsustainable urban growth processes is a widely recognised research problem [12,24–32].

Bearing in mind the regrettable effects of allowing too much land to be developed [33], in many countries, *land thrift* [34,35] policies and instruments aimed at limiting land being built upon have been developed and adopted [36–38], [39] (p. 16). In Israel, agricultural land preservation was established as a national objective already in 1965 [39] (p. 18), [40,41]. Among various land thrift policies [23], the Norwegian Parliament established a national target to limit farmland conversion [12] (p. 186). In 2002, the German Strategy for Sustainable Development (*Nachhaltigkeitsstrategie*) [42] set an ambitious goal to reduce the daily amount of developed land from 129 ha to 30 ha by 2020 (30% target) [42] (s. E.VII), [43,44]. Now, the 0% target is advocated [34,45]. In 1956, the Spanish Land Act (*Ley de Suelo*) ordered that the general urban plan divides the stock of land into urban, to be urbanised and not to be urbanised. The same simple distinction still exists in the Spanish autonomous region of Valencia [46] (art. 28).

To reconcile the above-mentioned objectives of providing land for urban development with the objective of limiting land take, urban containment strategies evolved. The notion of *urban containment* [34] is based on the premise that urban growth should be contained in a limited area [34] in order to both decrease the quantity of built-up land and to produce compact urban nodes. The latter aim shifts our reasoning to the second question involved with the developable land designation management that is *where* the developable land ought to be designated.

The crucial question in that respect is how far from existing developments should the new developable land be allocated? An answer to this question impacts the density of urban settlements. The only thing we can be sure of is that urban structures, regardless of what scale they are looked at from, should be neither too concentrated nor too dispersed. The widely appreciated notion of *polycentricity* reflects the striving for the development of an expanded network of compact towns and cities. It involves a relative dispersion of settlements at the supra-regional and regional levels and concentration of settlements at the local level to form reasonably compact urban nodes of limited size. Compact cities, in contrast to sprawled [47], [48] (pp. 78–79), [33] (p. 89), [49], [50] (p. 142) and fragmented [51–53] (p. 118) ones are considered to be both efficient [23] (p. 119), [54] (p. 71) and effective in providing high-quality living environments [53] (p. 119) in an egalitarian way. However, some academics suggest that there may be significant welfare costs of urban compactness [55]. The polycentric approach to urban development attempts to balance economies [56], [57] (p. 69) and diseconomies of scale [58], [59] (pp. 65–72) that occur in urban patterns [57] (p. 69). Its advantages include qualities of urban, rural and natural environments [15], [60] (p. 115), [61].

The professional and academic discussion regarding how to better contain urban growth has been thriving for several years [34,62–65]. The question of *where* to designate developable land has been addressed by planning policies [38], [39] (p. 16), [66] in many countries around the world.

In England, the Kate Barker Review of Land Use Planning [67] coined the notion of *containment policy* aimed at increasing the efficiency of using the already urbanised land to protect the openness of rural areas [9] (p. 163). Among various measures to achieve this goal, the well-known *green belt policy* has been used as a tool for urban containment at least since 1955. Another important measure may be considered the *previously developed land policy* (PDL-Policy) [68] (s. 10, 38, 44), [69] (s. 2.3, 2.4, 2.51), [70] followed by the *sequential approach in site designation* [69] (s. 2.44), [71] (p. 210). The PDL-Policy established a preference to re-use the previously developed land (i.e., *brownfield*) over open land (i.e., *greenfield*) development. The policy was complemented by a measurable goal to allocate 60% of new housing developments on PDL (60% target) [72], [68] (s. 41). Similarly, as in England, in Valencia, there is a priority given to *brownfield* over *greenfield* development [46] (art. 7.2). There is a *sequential approach*-like policy in sites designation established, too, that gives a preference to the coherent development of existing urban areas [46] (art. 7.2).

In Germany, the *decentral concentration policy* (*dezentrale Konzentration*) aimed at deconcentrating the settlement at the national and regional levels and concentrating it at the local level had been implemented for many years. The policy of *land stock management* (*Flaechenhaushaltspolitik*) embraces both the questions of *where* and *how much* land should be allocated for development in order to strive for compact and land–economic settlement structures [73].

In 2005, the deconcentrated concentration policy was implemented in Israel [39] (p. 20), in particular, to resist low density, dispersed development. In recent decades, many countries introduced compact city policies [74,75]. For instance, Norway and Sweden entered a period of re-urbanisation [23] (p. 114). The Chinese Twelfth 5-Year Plan requires establishing boundaries of urban development, increasing densities of urban areas and limiting further expansion of mega-cities [18] (p. 260).

Nevertheless, there are countries where this issue has not been addressed in a consistent and effective way—e.g., Poland. Polish land-use planning designates vast quantities of developable land [2] (p. 5), [6] (p. 36) that are not possible to be utilised in a consistent manner to deliver well-planned urban structures [76] (p. 161). Instead, dispersed, suburban or semi-rural settlements that lack quality urban infrastructure are produced [2] (p. 5), [77]. In effect, sprawled development encroaches upon environmentally valuable open land [78] (p. 191), [79–82]. Due to a huge demand for investment areas [83], [84] (p. 169), extensive amounts of land are converted from natural or agricultural uses to settlement uses [83], [84] (p. 170), [85]. According to data retrieved in 2015 [86], this process was much faster in Poland than in other European countries [30] (p. 2240). As the problem is of great importance, a lot of research and papers have been produced on these issues that analyse the phenomenon from geographic [87–89], urban planning [9,90–94], sociological [88,95] and economic [6,96,97] points of view.

One can argue that the most prominent reason for the Polish sprawled urban growth pattern is the lack of proper management of the designation of land for development. Moreover, an even further-reaching thesis may be posed that the legal framework that governs this management was tailored to enable extensive, unplanned urban growth. As it will be argued in this paper, in theory, the Polish land policy framework is very similar to other continental frameworks. However, its detailed provisions, in contrast to its Western European counterparts, cause the Polish framework to foster overconsumption of open land and create dispersed urban development patterns. This is why it is worth examining foreign land policies to search for decisive differences that, in the case of model legal frameworks, allow them to better manage developable land designation to increase the rationality of the allocation of developments and to protect open land from expansive development.

There are three hypotheses of this research. The first one is that, in theory, the Polish legal framework of developable land designation management follows key features of two model frameworks—the German and Spanish frameworks (H1). The second and the third hypotheses say that due to a distortion of the original idea, the Polish legal framework of developable land designation management:

- In fact, does not conform to the key features of the two model frameworks (H2);
- Neither rationalises the allocation of settlements nor protects open land from expansive development (H3).

2. Aims, Scope and Methods

The aims of this research are:

- To identify key common features of the two model legal frameworks of developable land designation management (A1);
- To identify and structure the Polish legal framework of developable land designation management (A2);
- To compare the Polish framework with the key features of the two model frameworks (A3);

- To describe the problem of ineffectiveness of the Polish legal framework of developable land designation management (A4);
- To formulate recommendations for the Polish legal framework of developable land designation management (A5).

The model legal frameworks analysed are German and Spanish ones. They are examples of institutional toolsets adopted to counteract excessive consumption of greenfield land that in the past could be observed in both countries. Both frameworks are based on an official, clear distinction between land to be urbanised and not to be urbanised. They both share similarities with the Polish legal planning system as being founded on civil law. The German spatial planning framework has been the role model for the Polish one since its establishment after 1918. As Germany and Spain are federally organised countries with distinct elements of planning law in different autonomous regions or states, legal frameworks of Region Hannover in Lower Saxony and Comunidad Autonoma de Valencia—respectively—have been taken into account. All legal enactments identified as constituting the respective three frameworks of developable land designation management have been analysed (see reference list).

The substantial scope of this research is limited to ordinary urban development. It means that extraordinary development cases (e.g., infrastructure, special plants, agriculture or forestry-related buildings, etc.) have not been considered.

The research mainly consists of a qualitative institutional analysis of legal enactments (aims A1 and A2). Theses of the author are supported by empirical results of his own quantitative and qualitative research or literature (A4). Aim A3 required international comparative research. Basing on the results of the institutional, comparative and empirical research, some normative propositions have been formulated (A5).

The article is structured as follows. The next Section 3.1, analyses and describes two model frameworks for managing the designation of developable land. The German and Spanish frameworks have been identified, structured and then compared to indicate their key common features. Two graphic diagrams, one for each framework, have been produced. The aim of the next Section 3.2 is to present the basic presumptions of the Polish legal framework of developable land designation management. Section 3.3 analyses and discusses details of the respective Polish framework. The aim of this section is to state if and to what extent the Polish framework practically matches the key features of the two model counterparts indicated in Section 3.1. The outcome of this section is a graphic diagram of the identified Polish framework that follows the same pattern used to depict the complexity of the two model frameworks. In the fourth section, the results of the conducted research are discussed. Basing on conclusions of the research completed, key recommendations for reshaping the Polish legal framework were formulated in Section 5.

3. Results

3.1. Model Frameworks of Developable Land Designation Management

3.1.1. German Framework of Developable Land Designation Management

In Germany, the designation of developable land is regulated by all levels of land-use planning. The federal and state planning (*Raumordnung*) states general rules (*Grundsaetze der Raumordnung*) of urban development to be followed by lower-level planning bodies. Two main federal enactments regulating planning at distinct scales, namely, the Spatial Planning Act (*Raumodnungsgestz* (ROG)) [98] and the Building Code (*Baugesetzbuch* (BauGB)) [99] recognise the problem of overconsumption of open land for construction purposes. Minimising the quantity of open land consumed (*Inanspruchnahme der Freiflaechen*) for the purposes of settlement and transport, as well as the rule of using land in a thrifty way (*sparsame Flaechenutzung*), are embedded in the overarching Spatial Planning Act [98] (art. 2.2.6) and the Building Code that provides rules for urban planning at the local scale [99] (art. 1a.2, 9.1.3).

The most important regulations are assigned to subregional and municipal levels, including rules of admissibility of developments. The first step of designating developable land is linked to subregional (city-regional) spatial plans (*regionale Raumordnungsprogramme*[1]). These plans determine detailed planning objectives (*Ziele der Raumordnung*) that have to be consistent with upper levels general planning rules (*Grundsaetze der Raumordnung*), e.g., reducing the land take (*Verringerung der Flaecheninanspruchnahme*), concentration of development (*Konzentration der Siedlungstaetigkeit*) and orientating it on *central places* (*zentralle Orte*) [98] (art. 2.2.2). The settlement pattern advocated by the *central places policy* is based on a premise of focusing urban growth in selected urban nodes of sufficient size and qualities [100]. According to both regional (Lower Saxony) and subregional (Region Hannover)[2] plans, urban growth has to concentrate primarily in central places. Additionally, the subregional plan of Hannover Region assigns subsidiary urban development functions (e.g., housing) to some rural settlements that are intended to accommodate urban growth, too. Other villages are subject to *self-development* (*Eigenentwicklung*) [101] that assumes only 5% increase of the settlement area (*Siedlungsflaeche*) during the period of the subregional plan validity [102] (s. 2.1.4.03). Subregional plans set the city-regional settlement structure, greenbelts and other areas designated for preservation of open spaces [16] (p. 641), [103,104]. Detailed planning objectives set in the subregional plan have to be followed by local planning bodies that issue general land-use plans (*Flaechennutzungsplaene*).

The municipalities designate land for urban growth purposes in their general land-use plans. New areas foreseen for development, located on open land or on inconsistently developed areas (*outer areas* (*Aussenbereich*)) are assigned to the category of new development areas (*Neubaugebiete*) and become *expected development areas* (*Bauerwartungsland*). Generally, these areas must not be developed until a detailed, legally binding development plan (*Bebauungsplan*) is adopted. Thus, in Germany there is a general rule that new greenfield developable land is designated by legally binding plans. However, there are some minor exceptions from this rule that will be explained further.

Let us first introduce the crucial distinction between two categories of land: consistently developed areas (*inner areas* (*Innerbereich*)) and other areas (*outer areas* (*Aussenbereich*)). The *inner areas* are completely urbanised areas, i.e., consist of sufficient quantity and *Gewicht* (weight, importance) of interconnected buildings that are equipped with sufficient urban infrastructure. All remaining areas, that is open land, dispersed rural settlements and inconsistently urbanised settlement areas, are categorised as *outer areas*. The municipality sets boundaries of the *inner area* (*Innerbereich*) in a by-law [99] (art. 34.4.1). The aim of this distinction is to prevent scattered development (*Splittersiedlung*) on rural and suburban areas. In general, *inner areas* together with areas covered by detailed development plans are the only places where ordinary urban growth is admissible.

In the case of consistently developed areas a development is allowed if it fits into the surrounding built environment, following important features of developments and if the site is equipped with necessary technical infrastructure including a road[3].

Only extraordinary developments (e.g., agricultural or technical ones) are admissible on the *outer areas*. Any development has to follow provisions of the general land-use plan and should not create an increase in scattered development, nor reinforce or extend it [99] (art. 35.3.7).

The municipality may extend the boundaries of the *inner area* (*Innenbereich*) issuing one of the special by-laws called *Innenbereichsatzungen* that are treated as an alternative detailed development plan (*Ersatzplan*). They may create development rights that normally are absent on the *outer areas* (*Aussenbereich*) thus they are an exception from the general designation of new greenfield developable land in the detailed development plan (*Bebauungsplan*) only. Their advantages are simpler form and simpler procedure than in the case of the standard development plan. Among several types of such by-laws, the most important one from the point of view of the designation of developable land is the *development by-law* (*Entwicklungssatzung*) aimed at extending the *inner area*. It may be completed under two conditions—the development must be dense enough and the area must be designated in the general land-use plan as land for development (*Bauflaeche*).

Despite the general ban on developing *outer areas*, the municipality may issue another special by-law to enable extension of existing housing or small business development on *outer areas* without time consuming adoption of a detailed development plan. The *outer areas by-law* (*Aussenbereichsatzung*) may state that such development does not infringe the general local land-use plan and does not threaten to produce or extend scattered development [99] (art. 35.6). This instrument is controversial because it may be used to circumvent tough restrictions of developing *outer areas* [9] (p. 135). However, according to Greiving [105] this by-law requires an approval by a higher planning authority.

To sum up, there are two main land classes in Germany: consistently developed (urbanised) areas (i.e., *inner areas*) and other areas that consist of open land and scattered settlements (i.e., *outer areas*). The *outer areas* are generally protected from ordinary development. General local land-use plans indicate *inner areas* (precisely delimitated in municipal by-laws) and an extent of *outer areas* that may be subject to prospective urban development. There are two possibilities to urbanise such land: either issuing a detailed development plan or an auxiliary by-law. These instruments are not required to obtain the development permit on *inner areas*. Municipal general land-use plans have to follow concrete objectives of subregional spatial plans as well as national and regional planning policy (see Scheme 1).

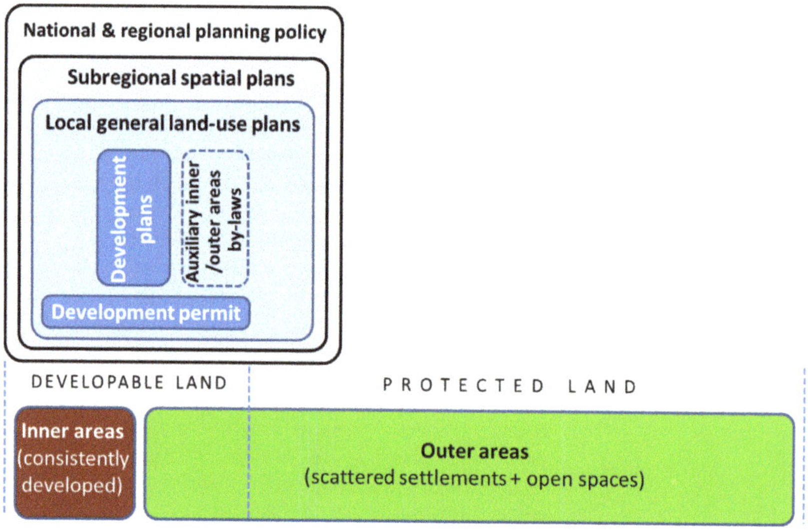

Scheme 1. German legal framework of developable land designation management.

3.1.2. Spanish Framework of Developable Land Designation Management

There is no universal Spanish spatial planning system. The legal power to establish it belongs to autonomous regions. In the autonomous Community of Valencia the planning enactment is the *Ley de Ordenación del Territorio, Urbanismo y Paisaje, de la Comunitat Valenciana* [46]. However, the national legislation sets legal foundations of property rights in spatial management. Such enactment is the Land Act (*Ley de Suelo*) [106].

As there is no national spatial plan, the only significant planning policy is set by regional acts and strategies issued by autonomous regions, in accordance with their legislative power in the field of spatial planning. In the autonomous Community of Valencia the regional strategy is called *Estrategia Territorial de la Comunidad Valenciana* [107]. Along with the planning act it provides for planning policies in the autonomous Community of Valencia.

The planning policy is aimed at concentrating housing development in the network of cities, strengthening the polycentric urban pattern of the region, reaching compact urban structures, maintaining open spaces between them, including green belts, consolidating and extending existing urban nodes and reusing vacant land [46] (art. 7.2.), [107] (s. 78.1). The land-use and urban planning must prefer compact urban patterns over scattered ones [46] (art. 7.2). To implement this rule, limits of residential density were increased from 75 to 100 units per ha [46] (art. 36.3). Creation of new isolated urban structures as well as monofunctional residential ones, especially in municipalities with a high share of discontinuous urban fabric, should be avoided [107] (s. 89). The planning policy strives at maintaining continuity of the open land network by demanding to provide for definite urban borders. Where feasible, there has to be a minimum of 500 m of open space left between each urban node to avoid a merging of settlement entities [46] (art. 7.2), [107] (s. 90). Priority is given to brownfield over greenfield development as well as to the extension of existing urban structures over the creation of new ones [46] (art. 7.2).

There are detailed guidelines for estimating the necessary land to be provided to respond to the demands on urban growth. The planning act [46] (art. 7.1) sets out that the supply of *urban land* (*suelo urbano*) and *land to be urbanised* (*suelo urbanizable*) has to reflect the real demand and refers to detailed rules of estimating it, established in the regional territorial strategy. According to them, the demand should be estimated based on demographic prognoses provided for each county (*comarca*) by the Statistical Office of Valencia. The strategy sets detailed mathematic formulas to calculate the demand for residential and commercial land within the period of a maximum of 20 years. The strategy enables an increase in the calculated demand by 25% maximum depending on local circumstances [107] (s. 86) and even more in case of listed specific cases in accordance with justified public interest (e.g., localisation of supra-municipal services, densifying low density towns, etc.). On the other hand, rural municipalities have to decrease the reference numbers of growth that derive from the accounts for the whole county by 0.5 in the case of residential needs and 0.6 in the case of employment [107] (s. 108.1). Estimating quantities and locations of the land designated for economic activities undergoes similar guidelines and framework of rules as in the case of the residential use.

Subregional spatial plans, i.e., *spatial action plans* (*planes de acción territiorial*) in many places do not exist. If they do, they provide no co-ordination to and between general local plans. The *Plan de Acción Territorial del Área Metropolitana de Valencia* does not give any important guideline for local planning.

The Land Act (*Ley de Suelo*) [106] sets the basic categorisation of land as *rural* (*suelo rural*) or *urbanised* (*suelo urbanizado*) [106] (art. 21.1). According to the law *urbanised land* has to form an integral part of a settlement that is connected to networks of roads, services and parcels and be urbanised according to one of the planning instruments (*instrumento de ordenación*) or be sufficiently equipped with urban infrastructure according to legal requirements, or conform with requirements set by relevant planning instrument. All other land is considered to be *rural*, including *land planned to be urbanised* in land-use plans until *urbanisation activities* (*actividades de urbanización*) have been completed.

An important term in this respect is a notion of *urbanisation* (*urbanización*) defined by the *Ley de Suelo* as a transformation of a rural land into an *urbanised* one by forming one or more parcels suitable for development, equipped with the necessary infrastructure and services required by the spatial and urban planning [106] (art. 7.1.a.1).

The basic conditions of land (*rural* or *urbanised*) set by the Land Act are complemented by Valencian spatial planning law. Article 28 of the Spatial, Urban and Landscape Planning Act [46] indicates that planning instruments classify land as *urban land* (*suelo urbano*), *land to be urbanised* (*suelo urbanizable*) and *land not to be urbanised* (*suelo no urbanizable*). The default plan that classifies land is the general local structure plan (*plan general estructural*). In the region of Valencia, the general local structure plan designates three types of areas that correspond with these land classes: rural areas (*land not to be urbanised*), urbanised areas (*urban land*), areas of new development or urban expansion (*land to be urbanised*) [46] (art. 25).

Land not to be urbanised consists of two subtypes: *ordinary rural land* and *rural land of special protection*. The *ordinary rural land* is protected by the general local structure plan via various regulations (e.g., minimal, indivisible surfaces of plots) from uncontrolled subdivision and development. The *rural land of special protection* is additionally protected according to the provisions of sectoral legislation.

Urbanised areas are those equipped with urban services plus adjacent plots (one block of houses maximum) that may complement the existing urban tissue by small *urban development activities* (*actuaciones urbanísticas*) [46] (art. 25.2). An important notion that derives from the term of *urbanisation* is the *building plot* (*solar*). In line with art. 177 of [46], *solares* are urbanised and formed or legally subdivided parcels, suitable to be used in accordance with the provisions of the plan. The necessary services to have a status of *solar* are immediate access to public, paved road and walkway, waterworks, electric energy line and sewerage. There are two conditions of legal possibility to develop a parcel. Either it has the status of a *building plot* (thus is already urbanised), or it would be simultaneously urbanised and developed. Complete urban development (*urbanisatión*) is a necessary legal condition to make use of buildings [46] (art. 178.2).

The default way of developing the *land to be urbanised* (*suelo urbanizable*) is the *partial plan* (*plan parcial*) [46] (art. 40.1) aimed at structuring new urban expansion and consistently urbanise greenfield land [46] (art. 29.1.a). The equivalent of the *partial plan* envisaged for restructuring already urbanised areas is the *reform development plan* (*plan de reforma interior*) [46] (art. 29.1.b). Buildings on the *land not to be urbanised* have to follow a rural, touristic or extraordinary function. In exceptional cases, plans may allow building a house there if it is sufficiently isolated (minimal statutory requirements are a plot of a minimum of 1 ha per house and the built-up area is 2% of the plot maximum) [46] (art. 197.b) and conforms to relevant planning regulations [46] (art. 196.1) (in most cases, the *plan de ordenación pormenorizada* [46] (art. 35.1.d)). Ribbon development [46] (art. 196.3) as well as groups of houses [46] (art. 197.b.5) are prohibited.

To sum up, in the Spanish region of Valencia, it is possible to develop, in an ordinary way (e.g., housing), *urbanised land*, *land to be urbanised* and *ordinary rural land*. However, the urban expansion is only possible on the *land to be urbanised* (*suelo urbanizable*). The default way to do this is by issuing the *partial development plan* (*plan parcial*). Further development of the *urbanised land* (*suelo urbanizado*) is possible according to the *reform development plans* (*planes de reforma interior*) or, in the case of *building sites* (*solares*), without any plan. *Land not to be urbanised* (*suelo no urbanizable*) is protected from large scale urban development, but isolated housing development is possible. The categorisation of land is completed by the municipal general structure plan (*plan general structural*). All ordinary development activities along with detailed plans (*partial and reform development plans*) have to follow provisions of *plans of detailed order* (*planes de ordenación pormenorizada*) (see Scheme 2).

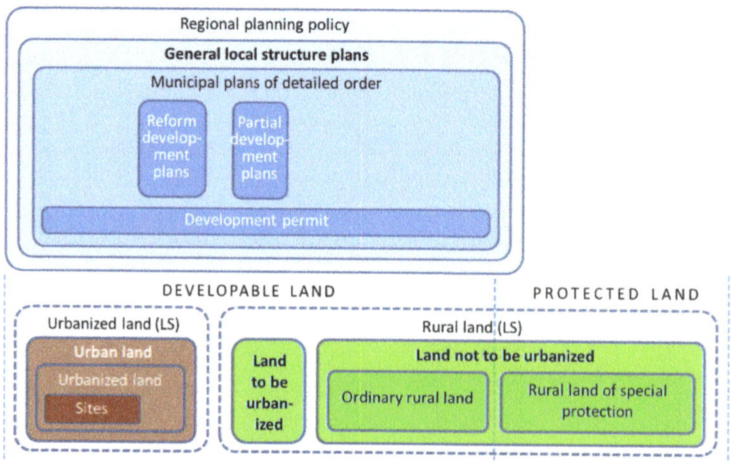

Scheme 2. Spanish legal framework of developable land designation management.

3.1.3. Key Common Features of the Two Model Frameworks

Based on the above descriptions, key features of the two analysed frameworks of developable land designation management may be indicated as follows:

- Supra-municipal guidelines for the developable land designation;
- General local plan that designates a reasonable amount of urban growth areas;
- Detailed development plan as a primary tool of greenfield land development;
- Urban development without a plan or a by-law only allowed in the case of infilling urbanised areas;
- Distinction between land to be urbanised and land not to be urbanised.

The first hypothesis of the following research is that the respective Polish legal framework theoretically shares these features (H1).

3.2. General Premises of the Polish Framework of Developable Land Designation Management

3.2.1. Supra-Municipal Guidelines for Developable Land Designation Management

The overarching Polish planning enactment is the Spatial Planning and Development Act [108]. It encompasses several legally binding principles that affect the policy of designating developable land in both distinguished aspects, i.e., *how much* land should be designated for development and *where* that land should be located. One of the issues to be considered in *spatial planning and development* (*planowanie i zagospodarowanie przestrzenne*) is the protection of forest and agricultural land [108] (art. 1.2.3). This principle implies a thrifty approach to the designation of greenfield developable land. There are more detailed guidelines for allocating settlements that affect the question of the location of developable land. The act requires that the planning should strive for allocating new developments on comprehensively urbanised areas[4] within boundaries of existing settlement entity, specifically by refilling existing urban fabric. Other lands may only be developed if such areas, suitable for a specific type of development, are lacking. Nevertheless, in such a situation, a priority is given to areas with the best access to technical infrastructure (transport, waterworks, sewerage, electricity, gas, heating and telecommunication networks) [108] (art. 1.4.4). These rules may be called a sequential approach in sites designation, similar to the English counterpart mentioned in the Introduction.

The act provides for a detailed procedure of estimating right amounts of land to be designated for urban growth in general local plans (*studia uwarunkowań i kierunków zagospodarowania przestrzennego*) (see the next section).

There is a framework of supra-municipal spatial plans and strategies that are to be followed by the local planning. The regional plan (*plan zagospodarowania przestrzennego województwa*) provides general guidelines for spatial management and indicates supra-local investments to be obligatorily included in local plans. For functional urban areas of provincial capital cities, a supplementary subregional plan may be issued as a part of the regional plan [108] (art. 39.6). Additionally, at the subregional level, there is an institution of the *strategy of supra-local development* (*strategia rozwoju ponadlokalnego*) [108] (art. 11.3) that may be issued by neighbouring municipalities and, if created, includes a *model of functional–spatial structure* (*model struktury funkcjonalno-przestrzennej*).

3.2.2. General Local Plan That Designates Reasonable Amount of Urban Growth Areas

When issuing the general local plan (*studium uwarunkowań i kierunków zagospodarowania przestrzennego*), the municipality has to follow detailed legal instructions on how to estimate the amount of land to be designated for urban growth. This estimation has to be completed on the basis of an account of demand and capabilities [108] (art. 10.5). The account consists of six steps. Firstly, a maximal municipal demand on new development (for each land-use function separately) should be estimated on the basis of economic, environmental and social analyses as well as demographic prognoses. Secondly, the absorbency of comprehensively urbanised areas[5] located within boundaries of settlement entities has to be estimated. In the third step, the absorbency of other areas designated for development in legally binding detailed development plans (*miejscowe plany zagospodarowania przestrzennego*) is assessed. The fourth step is a comparison of the calculated maximal demand with the aggregated absorbency of the two mentioned kinds of areas. Only if the calculated demand exceeds the absorbency, the municipality is allowed to indicate new settlement land. The fifth step is an assessment of transport and social infrastructure needed to urbanise all areas already designated and eventually indicated for development. In the last step, the scope of necessary investments is compared with the financial potential of the municipality. If the investment needs exceed the financial capabilities, the demand is to be adjusted to the capabilities; thus, the whole procedure is to be repeated.

3.2.3. Detailed Development Plan as Primary Tool of Greenfield Land Development

There are two ordinary legal bases for issuing the *building permit* (*pozwolenie na budowę*) for constructing an ordinary building[6]. The default option is the legally binding detailed development plan (*miejscowy plan zagospodarowania przestrzennego* (MPZP)) [108] (art. 4.1). The second option is an auxiliary ad hoc planning permission (*decyzja o waunkach zabudowy i zagospodarowania terenu*)[7]. The latter was invented to enable development without the necessity of long-lasting and costly production of the detailed development plan. The original idea was to enable an infill development in already urbanised areas (see the next section). According to this premise, the only ordinary way to develop non-urbanised land should be by the adoption of a detailed development plan.

3.2.4. Urban Development without a Plan or a By-Law Only Allowed in the Case of Infilling Urbanised Areas

The general idea of the auxiliary instrument of ad hoc planning permission (DWZ) was to enable infill development on already urbanised areas. The requirements to issue this permission are:

- There is a neighbouring developed site;
- There is access to a public road;
- There is sufficient technical infrastructure (existing or planned);
- Consent of an authority to change the land status from agricultural or forest land to development land is not required [108] (art. 61).

This set of requirements, if literally interpreted, reflects the premise that the development to be allowed by the ad hoc planning permission (DWZ) has to take place in an urbanised area.

3.2.5. Distinction between Land to Be Urbanised and Land Not to Be Urbanised

In Poland, there is an official distinction between the following land classes:

- Agricultural land;
- Forest land;
- Developed and urbanised land;
- Ecological sites;
- Land under water bodies;
- Miscellaneous areas [109] (§ 67).

There is a general premise that the agricultural and forest land may be designated for development by a detailed development plan (MPZP). However, a change of the land status, in the case of some subclasses, requires the *consent* of a higher authority. Besides this generic premise, there are some cases in which agricultural and forest land may be developed without a plan.

The land classes supplement the above-mentioned requirements to issue the auxiliary planning permission (DWZ). If one of those requirements relates to the land class, and the general premise of the auxiliary planning permission is that it should only be issued to extend existing urbanised areas, one could assume that the only class of land allowed to be developed without a detailed development plan is the *developed and urbanised land* class. Such land, by definition, fulfils the requirement that *consent* of an authority to change the land status from agricultural or forest one to development land is not required [108] (art. 61).

To conclude, all distinguished key common features of the analysed two foreign frameworks of the developable land designation management generally exist in the Polish legal framework. Therefore, it is sound to state that the first research hypothesis (H1) has been positively verified. However, as this statement deliberately bases on a general perception of the analysed framework, a detailed analysis of its specific provisions may shed new light on that issue.

3.3. Detailed Regulations, Their Assessment and Outcomes

3.3.1. Weakness of Supra-Municipal Guidelines for Developable Land Designation Management

The national guidelines provided by the planning act are legally binding requirements of *spatial planning and development* (see Section 3.2.1). They should be assessed as strong material regulations that clearly indicate objectives of the management of the designation of developable land that are in line with contemporary knowledge, current needs and the paradigm of sustainable development. However, the requirements are put into context by the art. 56 and 64.1 of the planning act [108]. According to them, not conforming with the statutory guidelines may not be the only reason to reject to issue the auxiliary planning permission (DWZ). It means that in the case of this planning permission which is the dominant basis of obtaining the building permit, these laudable guidelines have no real power and thus remain purely theoretical.

Another deficiency of the supra-municipal framework of land policy-making is a weakness of regional and subregional planning. The regional plan (*plan zagospodarowania województwa*) is a very weak tool (see [110] (pp. 77–101), [111] (p. 97), [112]). In practice, it does not provide any concrete provisions on the settlement structure to be strived for and no guidance on estimating allowable urban growth rates for each municipality[8]. These regional plans are made for whole provinces (normally NUTS 2 level). Supplementary city-regional plans may only be issued for functional areas of provincial capitals. As hitherto practice shows, even these city-regional plans are very general, too. Unlike their German counterparts, they do not assign settlement entities with specific functions (e.g., growth centre or rural settlement). Therefore, in practice, the regional plan may not be regarded as a real tool of developable land designation management.

As far as the subregional (city-regional) planning is concerned, the afore-mentioned supra-municipal strategy (see Section 3.2.1) is a new tool introduced in 2020; thus, it is still impossible to evaluate its relevance in the discussed field. However, its two deficits may already be indicated. Firstly, it is just a strategy, not a plan; hence, the level of accuracy of the *model of functional–spatial structure* might not be high enough to deliver real control on the rates of urban growth of municipalities. Secondly, adoption of the strategy is not obligatory. It may be assumed that most municipalities will not be willing to be bound by any external directions that would limit their land-use planning power.

3.3.2. Overestimated Urban Growth Areas in the General Local Plans

Strict rules of estimating municipal demand on settlement land delivered by the planning act are unquestionably a good step towards rationalising the developable land designation management. Nevertheless, some concerns regarding the details of these rules may be raised. The first one is related to the premise of estimating the *maximal* demand for settlement growth. It seems logical that if the *maximal* demand is calculated, any uncertainty of development processes, indicated by the legislator, may only produce a state that the maximal demand would not be attained. Consequently, taking into account this uncertainty as a ground for increasing the estimated demand by 30%, as the planning act allows [108] (art. 10.7.2), may be claimed a logical fault. It would not occur if, instead of the maximal demand, a most probable one was required to be estimated, such as in the region of Valencia, where the demand is based on prognoses of the statistical office. Nevertheless, even in such a case, the possibility to increase the estimated demand by as much as 30% seems to be unjustified because of the aim of the regulations that is to decrease the current oversupply of developable land [6], [9] (p. 26).

The strict statutory rules of estimating the amount of urban land designated in the general local plans were introduced by the amendment of the planning act on 9 October 2015. Before that date, according to the research of Kowalewski et al.[2], the number of people that could settle on urban growth areas indicated in the general local plans was estimated as 167–229 million, while the population of Poland is ca. 38 million. There are rural municipalities located in metropolitan areas that plan for 70% of their area (Siechnice next to Wrocław, where the current percentage of urbanised land equals ca. 16% [113] (p. 128)). Lesznowola, located next to Warsaw, is well known for its policy aimed at extensive expansion of developments on farmland [114]. Only small pieces of greenfield (mostly natural) land were excluded from a designation for development [7] (p. 126). It is the lack of or unreliable estimations of demand for settlement areas that experts blame for this situation [2], comp. [115] (p. 331).

An illustrative example of the oversupply of land to be prospectively developable indicated in the general local plans[9] is a case study[10] on the Radom functional urban area (ROF)[11] and the municipality of Kowala[12].

The conducted research has shown that the relationship between newly prescribed and existing residential areas in the Radom functional urban area (ROF) accounts for 212%, but taking into account the suburban zone[13], 243%. The highest rate is in the municipality of Iłża, which indicates residential areas as large as 362% of the current residential areas. As far as the number of residents that could find a dwelling in there is concerned, an additional 167% (267,000) could settle in the suburban zone of the Radom functional urban area (ROF). It means that the whole city of Radom (ca. 212,000 inhabitants), and 55,000 people additionally, could move to the suburban municipalities. Meanwhile, in the years 1989–2019, only 23,938 people moved from Radom to the suburban zone of ROF [116]. By extrapolating the trend line, a total number of foreseen migration from Radom to other municipalities of ROF has been calculated as 14,503 persons within a perspective of 30 years[14]. The difference between the number of people that could settle on areas foreseen in analysed general plans in the suburban zone and the forecasted migration rate is more than 17-fold.

One of the leaders in stimulating the oversupply of developable land in the Radom functional urban area (ROF) is the municipality of Kowala that planned in its former general local plan [117][15] residential areas that could allow increasing the number of inhabitants 3.5 times (from ca. 12,000 to ca. 44,000). In 2020, Kowala adopted a new general plan [118], this time based on the new planning law. The new plan does not revise the overestimated amount of urban growth areas, although the number of inhabitants of the municipality is expected to only rise in the next 30 years by 5000 to reach 17,000. The new general local plan, theoretically made following the rigorous rules established in 2015 (described in Section 3.2.2), repeated the described oversupply of residential land.

The key to understanding the reason for this approach of the plan-makers seems to be their interpretation of the term *new development* as development that exceeds the prospective development foreseen on urban growth areas designated by the previous general plan[16]. In line with the enactment, however, the *new development* is any prospective development likely to occur in the municipality. Its estimated amount should derive from an account of the demand that is based on demographic and economic prognoses.

The interpretation applied by the plan-makers of the Kowala municipality makes mutually inconsistent (thus deprived of any sense) regulations of Article 10 Section 5 of the Spatial Planning and Development Act [108]. It seems that if the legislator defined the *new development* in the same way as these plan-makers, there would not be required any tedious accounting of the capacity of the comprehensively urbanised areas and development areas designated in the legally binding detailed development plans. They would just demand to count the number of settlement areas designated in the previous general local plan and compare it with the estimated demand for new development. Multiplying provisions of previous plans by the general plans is considered by some academics to be extremely harmful and contradictory to the intention of the legislator [119], [120] (p. 77).

The amendment of the planning law in 2015 was aimed at changing the previous unregulated methods of making general local plans that led to the vast overestimation of land indicated for development. Legitimising old plans by new ones distorts that idea and makes adopted legal changes irrelevant. The conducted research has shown that the current statutory rules of estimating the quantities of developable land in the general local plans have not always been followed.

3.3.3. Detailed Development Plan as Secondary Tool of Greenfield Land Development

Although the ad hoc planning permission (*decyzja o warunkach zabudowy i zagospodarowania terenu* (DWZ)) should have been an auxiliary planning instrument, not undermining the primacy of the legally binding detailed development plan (MPZP) as the default way of approving and defining conditions of development, it became the main planning tool regulating urban development in Poland. In fact, most new buildings are authorised through this instrument (in 2012, ca. 80% of all buildings) [2] (p. 9). The general lack of detailed development plans is often blamed for this situation (31.2% of the country area was covered by these plans in 2019 [121]). However, the main reasons for this situation seem to be rather lenient rules of obtaining permission, depicted and explained further in Sections 3.3.4 and 3.3.5.

Besides the relatively weak position of the detailed development plan (MPZP), there is an issue whether or not the plan may be considered a tool for controlling the quantities of land designated for development. Theoretically, it allows designating both development and open land. Nonetheless, due to legal rules of compensating landowners who lose their development rights, it is quite costly for municipalities to designate non-developable areas. The ease of obtaining the ad hoc planning permission (DWZ) implies that almost everywhere next to existing settlement areas, there are some development rights associated with the real property. The problem is that the municipality, in the case of banning development in the plan, has to compensate landowners at the market value of their land that derives from any prospective development rights to be obtained via DWZ.

Additionally, as the detailed development plan must follow provisions of the general local plan, the extensive urban growth areas indicated in the general plans have to be translated into development rights if the legally binding detailed plan is issued. In effect, on all areas designated for development in legally binding detailed development plans (MPZP), 62 million people could settle [2]. There are rural municipalities located in metropolitan areas that designate for settlement purposes in their detailed development plans the majority of their areas. According to Topczewska and Maliszewski [122], [7] (p. 126), 62% of the rural municipality area of Lesznowola is formally designated as developable. The resulting oversupply of developable land designated in the detailed plans [6], [9] (p. 26) makes it impossible to urbanise and develop them in a consistent manner because it is unachievable to manage settlement processes that occur in so vast areas [2].

3.3.4. Common Development without the Detailed Development Plan

The requirements to issue the auxiliary ad hoc planning permission, described in Section 3.2.4, have been relativised by little details.

The first requirement—there is a neighbouring developed site—has been relativised by an interpretation of the term *neighbouring*. It may seem that *neighbouring* means *adjacent*, but it is not the case. According to some courts judgements, if there is a term of a *direct* neighbourhood, there ought to be an *indirect* neighbourhood distinguished, too [123]. A secondary law provides detailed instructions on how to assess whether there is a neighbouring developed site. The minimal area to be examined accounts for three times the width of the investment site but not less than 50 m. There is no maximal distance indicated.

Following the logic of jurisprudence, the neighbouring area may be very large. This logic undermines the premise of compactness as one of the features of quality urban patterns that could be infilled without a plan.

The second condition—access to a public road—is quite relative, too. No *direct* access to a public road is required to have the right to develop a site without a plan. The access may be via a private road (namely, an *internal road*) or a service road established on adjacent sites. According to jurisprudence [124–127], the term *access* should be interpreted widely. Both the accessed public road and the auxiliary ones do not have to be paved. They may just theoretically exist on a detailed development plan and cadastral map. This approach widens the scope of areas qualifying to development that may occur several hundred meters or even further away from a public paved road.

The third prerequisite—sufficient technical infrastructure—is relativised in the way that the infrastructure does not have to exist at the moment of issuing permission. It may be just planned, and it has to be affirmed by an administrator of a network that they are capable and willing to provide the necessary technical infrastructure. Additionally, there are no standards of required infrastructure necessary to obtain the planning permission. It is possible to obtain it in the case of sites lacking access to gas, waterworks and sewerage networks. Individual wells, septic tanks or domestic sewage treatment systems are allowed not only in the case of distant rural settlements but are common solutions in the case of suburban and sometimes even urban single-family housing as well. There are no preconditions for necessarily any service by non-technical urban infrastructure such as schools, recreational areas or greenery [77].

The last condition to obtain the ad hoc planning permission relates to the status of the land. The snag is the term *consent* of a higher authority to change the land status from agricultural or forest land to development land that must not be required to issue the planning permission. According to Article 7 of the Agricultural and Forest Land Protection Act [128], *consent* is not required in the case of the majority of rural land (it will be explained in detail in the next Section 3.3.5). Thus, the planning permission may be obtained even on agricultural land.

Additionally, the planning permissions do not have to follow provisions of the general local plans. Therefore, and because of the vague requirements described above, it is not possible to estimate the extent of land developable through this instrument. To sum up, in practice, it is possible to issue the planning permission for developments on open greenfield land, on inconsistently developed and non-urbanised areas that are lacking urban infrastructure [77,129]. The conclusion is that the instrument of the ad hoc planning permission (DWZ) cannot be considered as an effective tool of land policy. In line with this conclusion, the tool of DWZ is commonly perceived to be detrimental [111] (p. 97), [130] (p. 90), [131] (pp. 157–190).

3.3.5. Equivocal Distinction between Land to Be Urbanised and Land Not to Be Urbanised

As explained above (Sections 3.3.3 and 3.3.4), due to vague rules of obtaining the planning permission (DWZ), it is not possible to estimate the quantity of developable land in Poland. There is neither an official classification of land as *urbanised*, *to be urbanised* and *not to be urbanised*, nor a rule that the *land to be urbanised* is designated by the general local plans. The only classification of land is provided by the Agricultural and Forest Land Protection Act [128] (see Section 3.2.5). Among six classes of land, there is one definitely suitable for ordinary development (i.e., *developed and urbanised land*). However, it does not mean that other land classes must not be developed.

Scheme 3 shows in a schematic, simplified way the developability of distinct land classes.

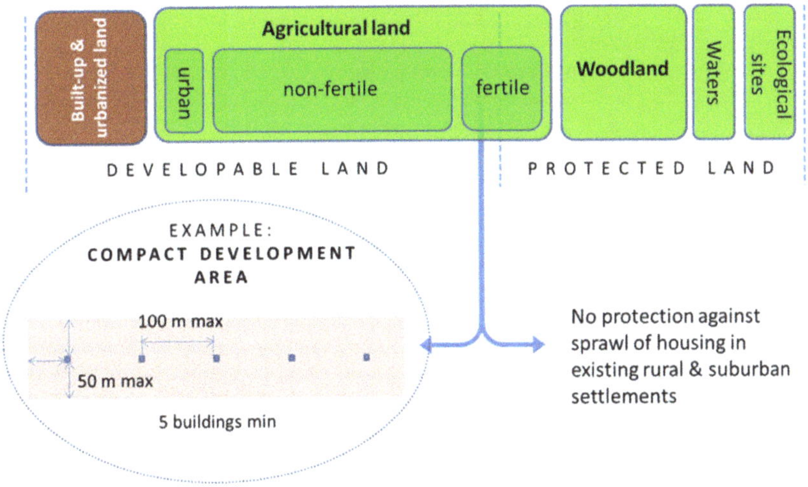

Scheme 3. Polish land classes and their developability.

Land categories generally protected from development are ecological sites, water bodies, woodland and fertile agricultural land. However, plan-makers may obtain the consent of a higher authority to designate woodland in the detailed development plan for urban development. In the case of the agricultural land, besides the same possibility to reclassify the land to urban use in the legally binding plan (MPZP), there are some possibilities to develop it via ad hoc planning permission (DWZ). The key precondition is whether the *consent* of a higher authority is required or not.

The consent is required to reclassify all woodland and the most fertile agricultural land (subclasses I-III) [128] (art. 7.2). However, there are some exceptions in the latter case. The consent is not required if the respective land satisfies the following conditions[17]:

- At least a half of it is located in *compact development areas*;
- It is located not further than 50 m from a developed site;
- It is located not further away than 50 m from a public road;
- Its area does not exceed 0.5 ha [128] (art. 7.2a).

To estimate the extent of areas that satisfy these requirements, a definition of *compact development areas* is of crucial significance. Such areas are a minimum of five non-auxiliary buildings spaced not more than 100 m from each other plus 50 m envelope [128] (art. 4.30, 4.29) (see Scheme 3). Additionally, there is no consent required in the case of agricultural land located within administrative boundaries of towns and cities, regardless of whether the land is fertile or non-fertile.

If the consent of a higher authority is required to reclassify the agricultural land, plan-makers must obtain it before the adoption of the detailed development plan (MPZP). If no consent is required, auxiliary planning permission (DWZ) may be issued. Along with all agricultural land located within cities' and towns' boundaries, and the non-fertile land, the option to reclassify fertile agricultural land relativises the protection of rural land from an expansion of ordinary developments. Besides that, there are financial incentives for housing development in agricultural areas. Normally, in order to exclude land from agricultural or forest use, which is a requirement to obtain the building permit [128] (art. 12a), the investor has to pay a fee [84] (p. 170). However, in the case of residential developments, if the area of land does not exceed 500 m^2 (one-family housing) or 200 m^2 (for each unit in multi-family housing), no payment is involved.

According to estimations, the total amount of agricultural and forest land in which the class was changed to the *developed and urbanised* one by provisions of legally binding development plans (MPZP) has accounted for ca. 600,000 ha since 2003, which is 1.9% of the country area [132]. In comparison to the number of residential areas, which accounted for 1.1% of the total country area in 2017, the reclassified area is almost twice as large [132] (p. 28). Moreover, it is worth stressing that this number does not reflect the total scope of the phenomenon as it does not include the amount of rural land converted to developed land due to consumed planning permissions (DWZ).

The problem of extensive reclassification of agricultural and forest land for urban purposes raises serious concerns that are reflected in research and articles produced on this topic [133,134]. The problem is especially severe in suburban areas, and the rural land is consumed mainly for residential purposes [134]. In 2016, 24% of developments were carried out, and 23% were planned outside of *developed and urbanised areas*, mainly on agricultural land [78] (p. 168). Practitioners in land-use planning confirm that private investors push for reclassifying agricultural land by issuing a development plan [135] (p. 337).

Vast amounts of land reclassified from the *agricultural* or *forest* land classes to *developed or urbanised* one indicate that the land classification may not be considered a proper tool to effectively manage the designation of developable land.

To sum up, the *development permit* (*pozwolenie na budowę*) may be obtained on the basis of the detailed development plan (MPZP) or by the auxiliary planning permission (DWZ). Provisions of the detailed development plan have to follow the guidance of the general local plan. Auxiliary planning permissions do not have to conform to it. However, both documents have to follow national and regional planning policies. The regional planning guidance is weak, whereas the national planning act regulates in detail the issuing of both land-use plans at the local level and auxiliary planning permissions. Detailed development plans may be issued for all classes of land and may make them developable (except for land protected on the basis of other enactments) (the diagram does not depict it). Auxiliary planning permissions may be issued only for areas not covered by the detailed development plan. It is possible to obtain permissions on urbanised land, agricultural land located within boundaries of urban municipalities, non-fertile agricultural land and, if some conditions are fulfilled (see Scheme 3), on fertile land, too (see Scheme 4).

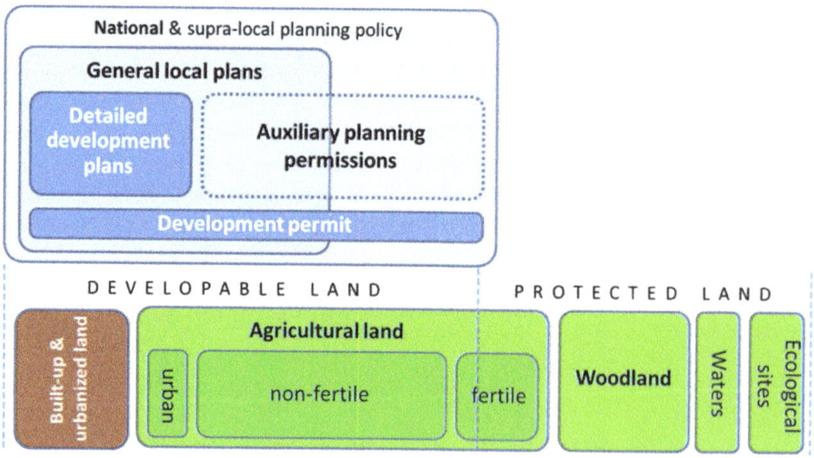

Scheme 4. Polish legal framework of developable land designation management.

4. Conclusions and Discussion

Table 1 depicts the most important features of the three investigated frameworks of developable land designation management.

Table 1. The comparison of the key features of the investigated frameworks of developable land designation management.

Key Features of the Model Frameworks	Germany	Spain	Poland	
			Theory	Practice
Supra-municipal guidelines for the developable land designation	Statutory principles in the federal spatial planning act	Statutory principles in the autonomous region's spatial planning act	Statutory principles in the national spatial planning act	Relativised by the planning act
	Statutory principles and binding objectives in the state spatial plan	Planning guidelines in the autonomous region's spatial strategy	Planning guidelines in the regional spatial plan	Very general
	Legally binding objectives in the subregional plan	Planning guidelines in the subregional plan, very general	Planning guidelines in the subregional plan	The subregional plan is not obligatory, for selected cities only and very general
	Inter-municipal general local plan, not obligatory	Inter-municipal general local plan, not obligatory	Supra-municipal strategy	The supra-municipal strategy is not obligatory
General local plan that designates reasonable amount of urban growth areas	Municipal growth rates follow subregional objectives	Detailed statutory guidelines on estimating urban growth rates, accounts made by the municipality	Detailed statutory guidelines on estimating urban growth rates, accounts made by the municipality	Assumed growth rates may by far exceed the most probable amounts
Detailed development plan as primary tool of greenfield land development	Detailed development plan is the default tool of greenfield urban development	Detailed development plan is the default tool of greenfield urban development	Detailed development plan is the default tool of greenfield urban development	Majority of developments are legitimised by the auxiliary planning permissions
	Out-of-plan greenfield urban development requires a municipal by-law			Greenfield urban development located on rural land lacking infrastructure is possible without the detailed development plan
Urban development without a plan or a by-law only allowed in the case of infilling urbanised areas	Urban development without a plan or a special by-law is allowed only in the case of infilling comprehensively urbanised areas	Urban development without a plan is allowed in the case of comprehensively urbanised areas only	Urban development without a plan is allowed in the case of infilling urbanised areas only	
Distinction between land to be urbanised and land not to be urbanised	Land classes embedded in the planning framework: urbanised areas, areas to be urbanised by detailed development plans, areas not to be urbanised	Land classes embedded in the planning framework: urbanised land, land to be urbanised, land not to be urbanised	Key land classes distinction: developed and urbanised land vs. agricultural and forest land	It is allowed to develop non-fertile agricultural land. Fertile land may be developed in line with some restrictions
	Urban development on the land not to be urbanised allowed by issuing a by-law	Isolated rural housing is allowable on the land not to be urbanised		

As it can be seen in Table 1 and as was evidenced in Section 3.2, theoretically, the Polish legal framework of developable land designation management shares key features with analysed model German and Spanish frameworks (H1). Therefore, it can be assumed that the first hypothesis of this paper has been positively verified. However, when looking into details of the analysed Polish land policy system (Section 3.3), one can conclude that because of the distortion of original ideas, in practice, the Polish legal framework of developable land designation management does not conform to identified key features of the model legal frameworks (H2). Presented research on the outcomes of the Polish land policy supports the further conclusion that it neither rationalises the allocation of settlement nor protects open land from expansive development (H3). It seems reasonable, therefore, to assume that the second (H2) and third (H3) hypotheses of this article have been positively verified, too.

Key similarities and differences between the three analysed frameworks, along with their implications for the Polish land policy framework, will be further discussed.

Theoretically, supra-municipal guidelines for the developable land designation are present in all of the three frameworks. All of them are regulated by statutory principles fixed in respective enactments that express striving for the protection of greenfield land and urban containment. The Polish planning act, however, puts them into context, stating that not conforming to the statutory guidelines may not be the only reason to reject to issue the auxiliary planning permission, which is the most common way to obtain the development permit. Additionally, lacking effective implementation by proper planning and land management tools, the statutory guidance on a sustainable land policy does not bring any significant results. The role model for it can be the strict German rules of focusing growth in central places. This general principle, embedded in the German Spatial Planning Act (ROG), is implemented by hierarchically subsequent regional and subregional plans. The central places system is considered to be extremely effective in controlling and managing urban development [16] (p. 649).

Both German federal states and Spanish autonomous regions dispose of strong regional level plans or strategies that include planning policies to control the designation of developable land. In contrast to them, the Polish regional plan is a weak tool unsuitable to effectively manage urban growth processes inside the region (see Table 1). Nevertheless, the most prominent deficiency of the Polish supra-municipal planning framework is the practical lack of plans at the functional city-region level that should manage the allocation of settlement in line with the comprehensive land policy of the entire city region. In Poland, subregional plans are not obligatory and may only be issued for functional urban areas of provincial capitals. Even if produced, usually, they are not specific. These deficiencies of the Polish framework are shared with the Spanish one (see Table 1). In contrast to them, the analysed subregional planning of the Hannover Region, which disposes of prerogatives of issuing legally binding regulations, may serve as a role model.

The need to regulate urban growth processes at the city-regional level is advocated by academics and planners both in Poland [30] (p. 2247) and in other countries, too [13] (p. 240), [16] (p. 639), [136] (p. 52). The city-regional scale of planning is considered to be the most appropriate governance level to avoid harmful inter-jurisdictional competition [137], see [138] (p. 23) and to curb self-oriented municipal planning that otherwise can produce negative spillover effects affecting adjacent municipalities and the city region as a whole [16] (p. 639). However, in order to effectively avoid undesirable downscaling urban governance [23] (p. 134), [139], the planning at the city-regional scale should follow a top–down model (see [16] (p. 652)). In line with these arguments, municipal growth rates in Hannover Region have to follow subregional objectives, whereas, both Spanish and Polish frameworks assign the municipalities with the prerogative to estimate them independently (see Table 1). However, in the case of Valencia region, the estimations have to be based on real demographic prognoses, while in Poland, relevant statutory regulations may be considered as inconsistent and enable assuming excessive municipal growth rates.

Polish municipalities strive for their own economic development, hence profile their vague demographic prognoses and assess their needs in line with a principle of everlasting growth. Every new inhabitant and business brings additional tax revenues to the municipal budget [88]. Nevertheless, as evidenced, such planning, in the long run, implies extensive expenditures on infrastructure [2], [7] (p. 123) and threatens the quality of the local urban pattern. Still, this short-sighted approach is not unique to Poland but is noticed in Spain as well [13] (p. 221), [140]. Jędraszko [135] (p. 73) described this problem as a symptom of an *absolutisation of municipal sovereignty* that, in the case of Poland, went further than in the majority of EU countries. Based on the results of the conducted research, it seems to be sufficiently justified to pose a thesis that one of the factual aims of the post-Communist Polish spatial planning system has been an absolutisation of planning sovereignty of municipalities that enables them to permit and promote unrestrained urban growth. After the 44-year period of the Communist regime, associated with restrictive top–down planning, Polish society perceived democracy and capitalism as unrestricted freedom based on the free market principle. Since the administrative reform in 1990, the municipality has been considered as an emanation of democracy and bottom-up governance. However, this controversial aim of the spatial planning system could not be openly articulated because of the paradigmatic foundations of the Polish spatial planning, expressed in the planning act, that are spatial order and sustainable development [108] (art. 1.1).

Theoretically, two main local planning instruments—the general local plan (*studium uwarunkowań i kierunków zagospodarowania przestrzennego*) and the detailed development plan (*miejscowy plan zagospodarowania przestrzennego* (MPZP))—should be aimed at rationalising the allocation of settlement and the protection of open land from expansive development. In practice, however, they became tools of the planned expansion of settlements. Instead of preventing diffusion of dispersed urban patterns and safeguarding open land for the sake of far-reaching public interest, both instruments are used to stimulate unsustainable peri-urban growth [2] (pp. 6–7) for the benefit of particular interests of landowners and investors [88].

The ongoing discussion on the optimal level of the general local plan's intervention in the development rights [120] (p. 77), [141] and protection of nature [120] (p. 77), [142–144] denotes its intrinsic deficient legal construction. The Polish general local plan is considered to be an ineffective instrument in terms of providing for sustainable spatial development [145] and implementing planning policy [120] (pp. 89–90). Vast settlement areas designated in detailed development plans imply high municipal financial commitments of acquiring land for public purposes. For instance, in the municipality of Lesznowola, they tenfold exceed its annual budget [7] (p. 123), [146].

In all investigated land policy frameworks, the detailed development plan is the default tool of greenfield urban development (see Table 1). In Germany, it is the *development plan* (*Babauungsplan*) that is the default legal basis of urban expansion. However, it is possible to enable ordinary greenfield development (e.g., housing) without the legally binding development plan by issuing a special municipal by-law. In Spain, the only legal way of urban expansion is issuing the *partial development plan* (*plan parcial*), which is envisaged for comprehensive urbanisation of the *land to be urbanised*. Nevertheless, housing development is allowed on the *land not to be urbanised,* too. However, it has to be sufficiently isolated from each other and follow requirements of the municipal *plan of detailed order* (*plan de ordenación pormenorizada*). Therefore, such kind of land development cannot be considered unplanned urban expansion. In contrast, the Polish instrument of ad hoc auxiliary planning permission (*decyzja o warunkach zabudowy*) allows both dispersed and dense urban development in both urban and rural areas. Therefore, the tool of the auxiliary ad hoc planning permission (DWZ) is the most questionable Polish planning instrument [111] (p. 97), [130] (p. 90), [131] (pp. 157–190) that may be blamed for the majority of the current amount of developable land. Furthermore, this instrument makes it impossible to assess the total amount of developable land. Due to the nuances of respective legal regulations and their debatable judicial interpretation, an indefinable quantity of land may be deemed developable upon a request by potential investors that apply for the ad hoc planning permission (DWZ).

However, there are some aspects that differentiate the evaluation of the instruments of the auxiliary planning permission (DWZ) and the two local land-use plans (the general and the detailed ones). The ad hoc planning permission (DWZ), as actually legally constructed, is malicious per se. In contrast, the detailed development plan (MPZP) and the general local plan are suitable tools to properly manage the designation of developable land. The problem is that they have the potential to damage the land-use pattern, too. The practical problem with them seems to be twofold. Firstly, there is no political will to use them properly. A lucrative possibility to change the land use from agricultural or forest ones to development one is too tempting to landowners and politicians [7] (p. 122), [88]. Secondly, restricting the developability of land is costly to municipalities. Due to costly compensation requirements [77] that cannot be rewarded by increments from planned urbanisation initiated by municipalities, they are reluctant to adopt and implement a strong land policy. The imbalance of losses and profits that derive from urban planning [77] makes municipalities passively react to initiatives of private developers [7] (p. 121), [147], in line with principles of avoiding immediate problems and minimising direct costs.

Whereas in Europe, municipalities actively manage development processes—prepare investment land, regenerate neglected areas, etc.—in Poland, authorities are passive. Habitually, the initiative belongs to private investors that just *obtain the change of land status for developable and consent to develop it* [53] (p. 77).

Probably the most prominent reason why the Polish system of protecting rural areas from urban development does not function properly is a lack of clear division of the land stock into three land classes: *urbanised land, land to be urbanised* and *land not to be urbanised*. In Poland, instead, there are separate regulations aimed at protecting agricultural and forest land. As evidenced, this protection does not work well. The legal framework practically does not protect non-fertile agricultural land from development. The fertile land is not protected either from housing development to be located in urban municipalities or within the boundaries of so-called *compact development areas* that have been defined in a ridiculous way from the point of view of containment policies.

The protection of the land class *not to be urbanised* is not perfect in the investigated foreign legal frameworks either (see Table 1). However, their approach is very different to the Polish one. The German framework enables encroaching the *outer areas* only by issuing a special municipal by-law. Admittedly, the Spanish regulations allow encroaching the *land not to be urbanised* by housing development, but they set a *minimum* surface of a plot per house. Although this approach may cause detrimental dispersion of developments over the countryside, it does not allow dense or large scale urban development there, as it is common in the Polish case. The Polish rural land protection framework, setting *maximum* surfaces standards per development, incentivises relatively dense housing development on agricultural land.

Bearing in mind all presented arguments, it seems to be justified to pose the second summarising thesis, that the Polish land policy framework was tailored to enable lucrative conversion of agricultural land into development land.

Depicted aspects of mismanagement of developable land designation reflect a more general problem of perceiving real property rights. Land-use planning is generally not popular in Poland as it is seen as an obstacle in the development process. It is perceived as an incursion in *the holy property right* (*święte prawo własności*) (see [148]). According to the Polish Constitution, *the property may be limited by means of a statute only and only within a scope that does not infringe the essence of the property right* [149] (art. 64.3). Does it imply that the property right is protected to a greater extent than other values? On the one hand, this provision entitles the parliament to limit property rights by issuing enactments. Such an example is the Spatial Planning and Development Act that, in fact, restricts rights to make use of real property. On the other hand, however, it is not easy to determine what is *the essence of real property rights*. For sure, development rights are limited by the planning law. Nevertheless, in Poland, the development right is perceived as a default attribute of real property. The *freedom of development* (*wolność budowlana*) [150], [151] (p. 65) seems to reflect the overriding approach of the Polish society to the urban planning issues that has prevailed since the fall of Communism in 1989. The objective of the spatial economy ever since has been to foster urban growth as a factor of economic development, regardless of where it occurs and how it looks. This research and reasoning make it justified then to state that the Polish post-Communist land policy has been characterised by an absolutisation of the real property right [135] (p. 73) that has been equated with the development right [148]. The paradigm of *development freedom* applies even at the expense of irrational land-use patterns (see [7] (p. 123), [111] (p. 97), [150] (pp. 1–10)).

In contrast to the described Polish situation, in Spain, the right to develop a real property is created by regulations of land-use plans. Additionally, according to the Land Act [106] (art. 11.2), the developability of a plot, if assigned by land-use planning, is not considered a property right. The right to develop the land depends on the fulfilment of obligations imposed on the landowner by the land-use and urban planning.

Although none of the investigated legal frameworks is perfect, the German and Spanish examples may be considered attempts to create clear institutional frameworks of developable land designation management. However, as the conducted research has shown, detailed regulations and their interpretation may significantly change the system's performance. This research was focused on the Polish framework. Further research is needed to assess outcomes and nuances of the German and Spanish as well as other land policy systems in a similar way.

5. Recommendations

On the basis of the conducted research, some recommendations for the Polish land policy framework may be formulated. They follow the examined models of Germany (Region Hannover) and Spain (Comunidad Valenciana). The first recommendation is based specifically on the German example: it is the subregional planning that should define the quantity of developable land for each municipality. The subregional level is deemed to be the functional city-region that encompasses an urban node (the city), suburban area and rural areas functionally bound with the urban agglomeration [135] (p. 269)[18]. The city-regional planning level is low enough to grasp, thoroughly consider and effectively manage all significant spatial phenomena that occur in and around a big city. On the other hand, it is high enough to avoid involvement in particularities that happen at the municipal level and hinder proper comprehensive land-use planning. Instead of estimating the prospective demand for housing and commercial development by municipalities themselves, growth allowances balanced at the city-regional level ought to be assigned to each municipality according to its supra-municipal function.

The second recommendation is that land classes should be embedded in the spatial planning system. The current distinction between urbanised land and various classes of rural land is separate from the core Polish planning framework. Besides, the rural land classes do not imply protection from urban development. Based on the analysed foreign experience, one can conclude that there should be unequivocal classes of *urbanised land*, *land to be urbanised* and *land not to be urbanised*. This classification should be tailored to protect rural land from urban growth. Additionally, concentrating urban growth on clearly indicated areas would significantly help to obtain rational settlement patterns. The land classes should be assigned in general local plans.

Both model frameworks agree that the *urbanised land* has to be adequately equipped with all necessary urban infrastructure. Additionally, in line with the German concept of *inner areas* (*Innenbereich*), it is recommended that the *urbanised land* has to be consistently developed in terms of density, form and layout of buildings. It is especially important in Polish circumstances, where inconsistently semi-urbanised areas are widespread and require comprehensive restructuring. Such a definition of *urbanised land* makes it suitable to continue its development without the necessity of plan adoption. Subsequently, development without a plan should be permissible only in the case of consistently urbanised land. Only such an approach would allow for stopping the present extension of chaotically developed areas.

A logical consequence of the last recommended rule is that the *land to be urbanised* should become developable only by regulations of the detailed development plan. Following such a rule, urban extension or infilling of inconsistently developed areas would be possible only if there is a development plan that allows it.

In contrast to the current Polish regulations, complete urbanisation should be regarded as a prerequisite for ordinary land development. In both of the countries referred to, the necessary infrastructure must exist before completion or the occupation of the buildings. If a provision of all mandatory infrastructure was a requirement to develop land, the quantity of developable land would decrease, and its location would be more rational. Such a precondition may thus be considered one of the tools of developable land designation management.

All recommended regulations would help to implement a land policy that attempts to correctly respond to the two key planning questions: *how much* and *where* should developable land be designated? Consequently, the recommended regulations would directly or indirectly assist to rationalise the allocation of settlements and to protect open land from expansive development.

Funding: This research received no external funding.

Acknowledgments: The author would like to thank Janet Askew and David Amborski as well the anonymous Reviewers for helping to significantly improve the article.

Conflicts of Interest: The authors declare no conflict of interest.

Notes

1 Names of planning documents used in different federal states slightly vary. The default names used in this article are taken from Lower Saxony and Region Hannover. In other federal states (*Laender*), these plans are usually called *Regionale Raumordnungsplaene*.

2 The German terminology of spatial plans has been translated as follows: the federal state spatial plan (*Landesraumordnungsprogramm*)—regional spatial plan, the city-regional spatial plan (*Regionales-Raumordnungsprogramm*)—subregional plan, *Flaechennutzungsplan*—local general land-use plan, *Bebauungsplan*—detailed development plan.

3 Additionally, the new development may not negatively impact the townscape and must guarantee healthy living conditions [99] (art. 34.1).

4 The exact term used: *areas of fully developed compact functional–spatial structure* (*obszary o w pełni wykształconej zwartej strukturze funkcjonalno-przestrzennej*) [108] (art. 1.4.4).

5 *Areas of fully developed compact functional–spatial structure* (*obszary o w pełni wykształconej zwartej strukturze funkcjonalno-przestrzennej*).

6 Extraordinary cases of admissibility of specific kinds of buildings on the basis of special enactments have not been considered.

7 There are two types of this planning permission: permission for public purposes investments (*decyzja o lokalizacji inwestycji celu publicznego*) and a permission for other developments (*decyzja o warunkach zabudowy*) (DWZ) [108] (art. 4.2). Legal conditions to issue both of them are very similar. As the latter is the one to be issued in the case of private development that constitutes the majority of cases, the ad hoc planning permission will be further referred to as *decyzja o warunkach zabudowy* (DWZ).

8 On the weakness of the Regional Development Plan of Mazovia Province (*Plan zagospodarowania przestrzennego województwa mazowieckiego*), see [112].

9 Provisions of the general local plan (*studium uwarunkowań i kierunków zagospodarowania przestrzennego*) become binding in case of adoption of the legally binding detailed development plan (*miejscowy plan zagospodarowania przestrzennego* (MPZP)).

10 The amounts of settlement land were estimated on the basis of municipal general local plans that were in force in 2019. All of them were adopted before the 2015 legal amendments, when strict rules of designating urban growth areas in general local plans were introduced.

11 The amounts of settlement land were estimated on the basis of municipal general local plans that were in force in 2019. All of them were adopted before the 2015 legal amendments, when strict rules of designating urban growth areas in general local plans were introduced.

12 Kowala is a rural municipality in the Radom functional urban area, neighbouring the city of Radom from the south. It undergoes extensive suburban growth processes.

13 The suburban zone is the area of ROF, excluding the core city of Radom.

14 Due to the poor economic situation, the overall population of the Radom functional urban area (ROF) has not been growing recently. That is why only migrations from the core city to the suburbs have been taken into account. It has been assumed that the potential number of people moving into the suburban zone of ROF from outside of Radom would equalise the number of people migrating from there outside ROF.

15 This plan was adopted before the amendment of the planning act that introduced strict rules for estimating the number of urban growth areas [117].

16 The plan-makers refer to a letter of the Ministry of Infrastructure and Construction from 28th April 2016 that contains such an interpretation.

17 The description of these conditions was slightly simplified to make it easier to comprehend.

18 Region Hannover is considered to be one of the best innovative examples of planning organisations at that level [9] (pp. 114–115).

References

1. Friedman, T.L. *Gorący, Płaski i Zatłoczony. Dlaczego Potrzebna Jest Nam Zielona Rewolucja i Jak Może Ona Odmienić Amerykę?* Dom Wydawniczy Rebis: Poznań, Poland, 2009.
2. Kowalewski, A.; Mordasiewicz, J.; Osiatyński, J.; Regulski, J.; Stępień, J.; Śleszyński, P. Ekonomiczne straty i społeczne koszty niekontrolowanej urbanizacji w Polsce—Wybrane fragmenty rapoFrtu. *Samorząd Terytorialny* **2014**, *4*, 5–21.
3. Chmielewski, T.J.; Chmielewski, S.; Kułak, A. Wpływ bezładu przestrzennego na krajobrazowe systemy ekologiczne. *Studia KPZK* **2018**, *182*, 317–340.
4. Goryński, J. *Polityka Przestrzenna*; Państwowe Wydawnictwo Ekonomiczne: Warsaw, Poland, 1982.
5. Górczyńska, M. Wskaźniki zagospodarowania i ładu przestrzennego w miastach i na obszarach silnie zurbanizowanych. *Biuletyn KPZK PAN* **2013**, *259*, 87–109.
6. Śleszyński, P. Społeczno-ekonomiczne skutki chaosu przestrzennego dla osadnictwa i struktury funkcjonalnej terenów. *Studia KPZK PAN* **2018**, *182*, 29–80.
7. Mantey, D. Potencjalne konflikty przestrzenne w strefie podmiejskiej z perspektywy potrzeb mieszkańców na przykładzie podwarszawskiej gminy Lesznowola. *Studia Regionalne i Lokalne* **2016**, *3*, 117–140. [CrossRef]
8. Bański, J. Strefa podmiejska—Już nie miasto, jeszcze nie wieś. In *Gospodarka Przestrzenna w Strefie Kontinuum Miejsko-Wiejskiego*; Jezierska-Thoele, A., Kozłowski, L., Eds.; Wydawnictwo Naukowe Uniwersytetu Mikołaja Kopernika: Toruń, Poland, 2008.
9. Zaborowski, T. *Polityka Przestrzenna Kształtowania Koncentracji Osadnictwa Anglii i Niemiec. Cele i Instrumentarium Planistyczne*; Wydawnictwa Uniwersytetu Warszawskiego: Warsaw, Poland, 2017.
10. Seto, K.C.; Fragkias, M.; Güneralp, B.; Reilly, M.K. A meta-analysis of global urban land expansion. *PLoS ONE* **2011**, *6*, e23777. [CrossRef]
11. European Comission. Overview of best practices for limiting soil sealing or mitigating its effects in EU-27. In *Final Report Contracted by the European Commission*; Prokop, G., Jobstmann, H., Schönbauer, A., Eds.; DG Environment: Brussels, Belgium, 2011; Volume 23.
12. Skog, K.L.; Steinnes, M. How do centrality, population growth and urban sprawl impact farmland conversion in Norway? *Land Use Policy* **2016**, *59*, 185–196. [CrossRef]
13. Gómez-Antonio, M.; Hortas-Rico, M.; Li, L. The causes of urban sprawl in Spanish urban areas: A spatial approach. *Spat. Econ. Anal.* **2016**, *11*, 219–247. [CrossRef]
14. Saglie, I.L.; Falleth, E.I.; Bloch, V.V.H.; Bye, A.S.; Steinnes, M. *Scattered Building and Protection of Farmland. The Scale and the Causes of Scattered Building on Agricultural Land*; NIBR-Report; NIBR: Vienna, Austria, 2006; Volume 6.
15. Duarte Marmolejo, C.; Tornés Fernández, M. The influence of urban structure on commuting: An analysis for the main metropolitan systems in Spain. *Procedia Eng.* **2017**, *198*, 52–68. [CrossRef]
16. Schmidt, S.; Siedentop, S.; Fina, S. How effective are regions in determining urban spatial patterns? *Evid. Ger. J. Urban Aff.* **2018**, *40*, 639–656. [CrossRef]
17. Gardi, C.; Panagos, P.; van Liedekerke, M.; Bosco, C.; de Brogniez, D. Landtake and food security: Assessment of land take on the agricultural productionin Europe. *J. Environ. Plan. Manag.* **2015**, *58*, 898–912. [CrossRef]
18. Fan, J.; Zhang, Y. A preliminary analysis of land resource constraints on urban expansion of Beijing based on land supply and demand. *J. Resour. Ecol.* **2012**, *3*, 253–261.
19. Dadashpoor, H.; Salarian, F. Urban sprawl on natural lands: Analyzing and predicting the trend of land use changes and sprawl in Mazandaran city region, Iran. *Environ. Dev. Sustain.* **2020**, *22*, 593–614. [CrossRef]
20. Doygun, H. Effects of urban sprawl on agricultural land: A case study of Kahramanmaraş, Turkey. *Environ. Monit. Assess.* **2009**, *158*, 471–478. [CrossRef] [PubMed]
21. Morales Schechinger, C.H. Cure or vaccinate, two contrasting policies: Regularisation vs. *land reserve in sustainable urban development. Bull. Latin Am. Res.* **2019**, *38* (Suppl. S2), 77–94. [CrossRef]
22. Schwedler, H.U. *Greenfield Development Versus Inward Urban Development—Challenges in Sustainable Development in Central and Eastern Europe*; European Academy of the Urban Environment: Berlin, Germany, 1999.
23. Næss, P.; Næss, T.; Strand, A. Oslo's farewell to urban sprawl. *Eur. Plann. Stud.* **2011**, *19*, 113–139. [CrossRef]
24. Xin, Y.; Zheng, X.; Lv, L. A spatiotemporal model of land use change based on ant colony optimization, Markov chain and cellular automata. *Ecol. Model.* **2012**, *233*, 11–19.

25. Yue, W.; Zhang, L.; Liu, Y. Measuring sprawl in large Chinese cities along the Yangtze River via combined single and multidimensional metrics. *Habitat Int.* **2016**, *57*, 43–52. [CrossRef]
26. Zaborowski, T. Suburbanization in the light of sustainable spatial development principles. In *Suburbanization Versus Peripheral Sustainability of Rural-Urban Areas Fringes*; Czerny, M., Hoyos Castillo, G., Eds.; Nova Science Publishers: New York, NY, USA, 2014; pp. 1–38.
27. Ferrara, A.; Salvati, L.; Sabbi, A.; Colantoni, A. Soil resources, land cover changes and rural areas: Towards a spatial mismatch? *Sci. Total Environ.* **2014**, *478*, 116–122. [CrossRef]
28. Rienow, A.; Goetzke, R. Supporting SLEUTH—Enhancing a cellular automaton with support vector machines for urban growth modeling. *Comput. Environ. Urban Syst.* **2015**, *49*, 66–81. [CrossRef]
29. Colantoni, A.; Grigoriadis, E.; Sateriano, A.; Venanzoni, G.; Salvati, L. Cities as selective land predators? A lesson on urban growth, deregulated planning and sprawl containment. *Sci. Total Environ.* **2016**, *545*, 329–339.
30. Szewrański, S.; Kazak, J.; Żmuda, R.; Wawer, R. Indicator-based assessment for soil resource management in the Wrocław Larger Urban Zone of Poland. *Pol. J. Environ. Stud.* **2017**, *26*, 2239–2248. [CrossRef]
31. Puertas, O.; Henríquez, C.; Meza, F. Assessing spatial dynamics of urban growth using an integrated land use model. Application in Santiago Metropolitan Area: 2010–2045. *Land Use Policy* **2014**, *38*, 415–425. [CrossRef]
32. Martellozzo, F.; Ramankutty, N.; Hall, R.J.; Price, D.T.; Purdy, B.; Friedl, M.A. Urbanization and the loss of prime farmland: A case study in the calgary-edmonton corridor of Alberta. *Reg. Environ. Chang.* **2014**, *15*, 881–893. [CrossRef]
33. Wolf, J. *Nachhaltige Raumentwicklung. Ein Beitrag zu Einem Neuen Leitbild der Raumordnung*; VWF Verlag fuer Wissenschaft und Forschung: Berlin, Germany, 1996.
34. Jehling, M.; Hecht, R.; Herold, H. Assessing urban containment policies within a suburban context—An approach to enable a regional perspective. *Land Use Policy* **2018**, *77*, 846–858. [CrossRef]
35. Davy, B. Flächenhaushalt reconsidered: Alternatives to the German federal thirty hectares goal. In *Regional Planning for Open Space*; van Valk, A., van Dijk, T., Eds.; Routledge: London, UK; New York, NY, USA, 2009; pp. 279–300.
36. Koomen, E.; Dekkers, J.; van Dijk, T. Open-space preservation in the Netherlands: Planning, practice and prospects. *Land Use Policy* **2008**, *25*, 361–377. [CrossRef]
37. Han, H.Y.; Lai, S.K.; Dang, A.R.; Tan, Z.B.; Wu, C.F. Effectiveness of urban construction boundaries in Beijing: An assessment. *J. Zhejiang Univ. Sci. A* **2009**, *10*, 1285–1295. [CrossRef]
38. Ingram, G.K.; Carbonell, A.; Hong, Y.H.; Flint, A. *Smart Growth Policies: An Evaluation of Programs and Outcomes*; Lincoln Institute of Land Policy: Cambridge, MA, USA, 2009.
39. Frenkel, A.; Orenstein, D.E. Can urban growth management work in an era of political and economic change? International lessons from Israel. *J. Am. Plan. Assoc.* **2012**, *78*, 16–33. [CrossRef]
40. Alterman, R. The challenge of farmland preservation: Lessons from a six-nation comparison. *J. Am. Plan. Assoc.* **1997**, *63*, 220–243. [CrossRef]
41. Hananel, R. Zionism and agricultural land: National narratives, environmental objectives, and land policy in Israel. *Land Use Policy* **2010**, *27*, 1160–1170. [CrossRef]
42. Die Bundesregierung. *Nachhaltigkeitsstrategie. Perspektiven Fuer Deutschland. Unsere Strategie Fuer Eine Nachhaltige Entwicklung*; Die Bundesregierung: Karlsruhe, Germany, 2002.
43. Joerissen, J.; Coenen, R. *Sparsame und Schonende Flaechennutzung. Entwicklung und Steuerbarkeit des Flaechenverbrauchs*; Edition Sigma: Berlin, Germany, 2007.
44. Davy, B. Freiraumsicherung durch Bodenpolitik: Was passieren müsste, wenn wir das Ziel-30-ha ernst nähmen. In *Siedlungsflächen Entwickeln—Akteure. Interdependenzen, Optionen*; Klemme, M., Selle, K., Eds.; Edition Stadt-Entwicklung 2010, 9–16; Rohn: Detmold, Germany, 2010; pp. 258–271.
45. Impulse für Eine Integrative Umweltpolitik. SRU Umweltgutachten. 2016. Available online: http://www.umweltrat.de/DE/Publikationen/Umweltgutachten/umweltgutachtennode.html (accessed on 20 August 2016).
46. Valencian Community. *Ley 5/2014, de 25 de Julio, de la Generalitat, de Ordenación del Territorio, Urbanismo y Paisaje*; DO 7329 de 31.07.2014; Valencian Community: Valencia, Spain, 2014.
47. Domański, R. *Gospodarka Przestrzenna*; Wydawnictwo Naukowe PWN: Warszawa, Poland, 2002.
48. Chmielewski, J.M. *Teoria Urbanistyki w Projektowaniu i Planowaniu Miast*; Oficyna Wydawnicza Politechniki Warszawskiej: Warsaw, Poland, 2001.
49. Urban sprawl in Europe. The ignored challenge. *Eur. Environ. Agency Rep.* **2006**, *10*, 5–56.
50. Gilg, A.W. *Planning in Britain: Understanding and Evaluating the Post-War System*; Sage Publications: Thousends Oaks, CA, USA, 2005.
51. Foster, S.R. The city as an ecological space: Social capital and urban land use. *Notre Dame Law Rev.* **2006**, *82*, 527–582.
52. Farber, S.; Li, X. Urban sprawl and social interaction potential: An empirical analysis of large metropolitan regions in the United States. *J. Transp. Geogr.* **2013**, *31*, 267–277. [CrossRef]
53. Brown, Z.S.; Oueslati, W.; Silva, J. Links between urban structure and life satisfaction in a cross-section of OECD metro areas. *Ecol. Econ.* **2016**, *129*, 112–121. [CrossRef]
54. Kagermeier, A.; Miosga, M.; Schussmann, K. Die Region Muenchen—Auf dem Weg zu regionalen Patchworkstrukturen. In *Suburbanisierung in Deutschland: Aktuelle Tendenzen*; Branke, K., Dangschat, J., Herfert, G., Eds.; Springer: Berlin/Heidelberg, Germany, 2001.

55. Garcia, D.; Riera, P. Expansion versus density in Barcelona: A valuation exercise. *Urban Stud.* **2003**, *40*, 1925–1936. [CrossRef]
56. Wheeler, J.; Muller, P.; Thrall, G.; Fik, T. *Economic Geography*; John Wiley & Sons Inc.: New York, NY, USA, 1998.
57. Malisz, B. *Podstawy Gospodarki i Polityki Przestrzennej*; Zakład Narodowy im Ossolińskich: Wrocław, Poland, 1984.
58. Isard, W. *Location and Space-Economy*; John Wiley & Sons: New York, NY, USA, 1956.
59. Malisz, B. *Zarys Teorii Kształtowania Układów Osadniczych*; Arkady: Warsaw, Poland, 1981.
60. Zuziak, Z.K. *O Tożsamości Urbanistyki*; Politechnika Krakowska: Kraków, Poland, 2008.
61. Schwanen, T.; Dieleman, F.M.; Dijst, M. Travel behaviour in Dutch monocentric and policentric urban systems. *J. Transp. Geogr.* **2001**, *9*, 173–186. [CrossRef]
62. Henger, R.; Bizer, K. Tradable planning permits for land-use control in Germany. *Land Use Policy* **2010**, *27*, 843–852. [CrossRef]
63. Bock, S.; Hinzen, A.; Libbe, J. (Eds.) *Nachhaltiges Flächenmanagement—Ein Handbuch für die Praxis*; Difu: Berlin, Germany, 2011.
64. Bizer, K.; Cichorowski, G.; Henger, R.; Stephenson, N. Vom Leitbild der Flaechenkreislaufwirtschaft zur Implementation. *Zeitschrift für Angewandte Umweltforschung* **2009**, *16*, 38–55.
65. Lieber, M.; Preuss, T. Flächenrecycling—Neue Ergebnisse aus der REFINA-Forschung. *Informationen zur Raumentwicklung* **2010**, *1*, 59–70.
66. Frenkel, A. The potential effect of national growth-management policy on urban sprawl and the depletion of open spaces and farmland. *Land Use Policy* **2004**, *21*, 357–369. [CrossRef]
67. Barker, K. *Barker Review of Land Use Planning Final Report—Recommendations*; Her Majesty's Stationery Office: London, UK, 2006.
68. Office of the Deputy Prime Minister. *Planning Policy Statement 3: Housing, Communities and Local Government*; Office of the Deputy Prime Minister: London, UK, 2006.
69. Office of the Deputy Prime Minister. *Planning Policy Statement 6: Planning for Town Centres*; Office of the Deputy Prime Minister: London, UK, 2005.
70. English Partnerships. *Towards a National Brownfield Strategy*; English Partnerships: London, UK, 2003.
71. Cullingworth, B.; Nadin, V. *Town and Country Planning in the UK*, 14th ed.; Routledge: London, UK, 2006.
72. Ganser, R. Quantifizierte Ziele flaechensparsamer Siedlungsentwicklung im englischen Planungssystem: Ein Modell fuer Raumordnung und Bauleitplanung in Deutschland? In *Schriften zur Stadtplanung*; Technical University in Kaiserslautern: Kaiserslautern, Germany, 2005; Volume 3.
73. Scholich, D. Flaechenhaushaltspolitik. In *Handwoerterbuch der Raumordnung*; Verlag der ARL: Hannover, Germany, 2005; pp. 308–314.
74. Litman, T. *An Alysis of Public Policies That Unintentionally Encourage and Subsidize Urban Sprawl in Cities—Sprawl Subsidy Report*; The New Climate Economy, The Global Commision on the Economy and Climate; Victoria Transport Policy Institute: British Columbia, VIC, Canada, 2015.
75. Hoftun, S. The Emergence of a Sustainable Urban Form: A Study of the Different Factors Influencing What Is Considered the Best Strategy for Urban Sustainability in Norway. Master's Thesis, University of Oslo, Oslo, Norway, 2002.
76. Zaborowski, T. Polityka kształtowania koncentracji osadnictwa. Propozycja konceptualizacji i instrumentalizacji na podstawie polityk przestrzennych Anglii i Niemiec. *Studia KPZK PAN* **2015**, *161*, 131–139.
77. Zaborowski, T. Land acquisition and land value capture instruments as determinants of public urban infrastructure provision: A comparison of the Polish legal framework with its German counterpart. *Geogr. Polonica* **2018**, *91*, 353–369. [CrossRef]
78. Gibas, P.; Heffner, K. Społeczne i ekonomiczne koszty bezładu przestrzeni—Osadnictwo obszarów wiejskich. *Studia KPZK PAN* **2018**, *182*, 163–195.
79. Wesołowska, M. Rozwój budownictwa mieszkaniowego a przemiany przestrzenne wsi województwa lubelskiego. In *Studia Obszarów Wiejskich*; Polska Akademia Nauk: Warsaw, Poland, 2005; Volume 10.
80. Kistowski, M. Problemy zrównoważonego rozwoju terenów wiejskich—Między rozkwitem, peryferyzacją a degradacją. In *Jak Zapewnić Rozwój Zrównoważony Terenów Otwartych?* Instytut na Rzecz Ekorozwoju: Warsaw, Poland, 2009; pp. 6–17.
81. Niedźwiecka-Filipiak, I.; Borcz, Z. Zmiany krajobrazu wiejskiego zagrożeniem dla zachowania tożsamości miejsca. *Acta Scientiarum Polonorum Administratio Locorum* **2010**, *9*, 85–97.
82. Gibas, P. (Ed.) *Analiza Zmian i Prognoza Przyrostu Zabudowy Mieszkaniowej na Obszarze Polski do 2020 Roku*; Bogucki Wyd Naukowe: Poznań, Poland, 2017.
83. Prus, B. Kierunki zmian przeznaczenia gruntów rolnych i leśnych w Polsce. *Acta Sci. Polonorum Geod. Descr. Terr.* **2012**, *11*, 27–40.
84. Prus, B. Exclusion of lands from agricultural production and urban pressure—Case study. *Geomat. Landmanag. Landsc.* **2016**, *4*, 169–182. [CrossRef]
85. Mrozik, K.; Wiśniewska, A. Miejscowe plany zagospodarowania przestrzennego jako instrument zarządzania procesem suburbanizacji na terenach wiejskich na przykładzie obrębu geodezyjnego Skórzewo. *Rocznik Ochrony Środowiska* **2013**, *15*, 2126–2141.
86. Stathakis, D.; Tselios, V.; Faraslis, I. Urbanization in European regions based on night lights. *Remote Sens. Appl. Soc. Environ.* **2015**, *2*, 26–34. [CrossRef]
87. Lisowski, A.; Grochowski, M. Procesy suburbanizacji. Uwarunkowania, formy i konsekwencje. In *Ekspertyzy do Koncepcji Przestrzennego Zagospodarowania Kraju 2008–2033*; Saganowski, K., Zagrzejewska-Fiedorowicz, M., Żuber, P., Eds.; Ministerstwo Rozwoju Regionalnego: Warsaw, Poland, 2009; pp. 217–280.
88. Mantey, D. *Żywiołowość Lokalizacji Osiedli Mieszkaniowych na Terenach Wiejskich Obszaru Metropolitalnego Warszawy*; Wydział Geografii i Studiów Regionalnych UW: Warsaw, Poland, 2011.

89. Kurek, S.; Gałka, J.; Wójtowicz, M. *Wpływ Suburbanizacji na Przemiany Wybranych Struktur Demograficznych i Powiązań Funkcjonalno-Przestrzennych w Krakowskim Obszarze Metropolitalnym*; Wyd Instytutu Geografii UP: Kraków, Poland, 2015.
90. Bieńkowska, M.; Korpetta, D. Rozlewanie się zabudowy a planowanie przestrzenne w strefie podmiejskiej miasta Płocka. *Acta Scientiarum Polonorum Administratio Locorum* **2015**, *14*, 7–28.
91. Lorens, P. (Ed.) *Problem Suburbanizacji*; Towarzystwo Urbanistów Polskich, Wydawnictwo Akapit: Warsaw, Poland, 2005; Volume 7.
92. Solarek, K. Struktura przestrzenna strefy podmiejskiej Warszawy. Determinanty współczesnych przekształceń. *Prace Naukowe Politechniki Warszawskiej Seria Architektura* **2013**, *13*, 7–283.
93. Staszewska, S. *Urbanizacja Przestrzenna Strefy Podmiejskiej Polskiego Miasta*; Bogucki Wyd. Naukowe: Poznań, Poland, 2013.
94. Śleszyński, P. Procesy suburbanizacji w Polsce a polityka przestrzenna i regionalna. In *Centra i Peryferie w Okresie Transformacji Ustrojowej*; Wolaniuk, A., Ed.; Wydawnictwo UŁ: Łódź, Poland, 2014; pp. 11–26.
95. Kajdanek, K. *Suburbanizacja po Polsku*; Zakład Wyd. "Nomos": Kraków, Poland, 2012.
96. Drejerska, N.; Chrzanowska, M.; Pomianek, I. *Strefa Podmiejska Warszawy. Wybrane Zagadnienia*; Wyd. SGGW: Warsaw, Poland, 2014.
97. Majewska, A.; Denis, M.; Jaroszewicz, J. Procesy rozpraszania zabudowy w strefie podmiejskiej Warszawy. *Mazowsze Studia Regionalne* **2015**, *16*, 73–85.
98. *Raumordnungsgesetz* vom 22. Dezember 2008 (BGBl. I S. 2986), das zuletzt durch Artikel 5 des Gesetzes vom 3. Dezember 2020 (BGBl. I S. 2694) geändert worden ist.
99. *Baugesetzbuch* in der Fassung der Bekanntmachung vom 3. November 2017 (BGBl. I S. 3634), das zuletzt durch Artikel 1 des Gesetzes vom 16. Juli 2021 (BGBl. I S. 2939) geändert worden ist.
100. Blotevogel, H. *Fortentwicklung des Zentrale-Orte-Konzepts*; Verlag der ARL: Hannover, Germany, 2002.
101. Greiving, S.; Dappen, C.; Schlegelmilch, F.; Selk, A. *Regionalplanerische Instrumente Zur Reduzierung der Flächeninanspruchnahme*; Bundesministerium für Verkehr, Bau und Stadtentwicklung: Bonn, Germany, 2012.
102. *Regionales Raumordnungsprogramm Region Hannover 2016*; Satzung vom 27 September 2016 der Regionsversammlung der Region Hannover.
103. Domhardt, H.J.; Braun, S.; Proske, M.; Scheck, C.; Schiller, H.; Theis, M. Freiraumschutz in regionalplänen. hinweise für eine zukunftsfähige inhaltliche und strukturelle ausgestaltung. In *Werkstatt: Praxis*; Bundesamt für Bauwesen und Raumordnung: Bonn, Germany, 2006; Volume 40.
104. Siedentop, S.; Fina, S.; Krehl, A. Greenbelts in Germany's regional plans—An effective growth management policy? *Landsc. Urban Plann.* **2016**, *145*, 71–82. [CrossRef]
105. Greiving, S. Ergaenzende instrumente zur bauleitplanung. In *Handwoerterbuch der Raumordnung*; Verlag der ARL: Hannover, Germany, 2005; pp. 220–227.
106. Real Decreto Legislativo 7/2015, de 30 de Octubre, Por el Que se Aprueba el Texto Refundido de la *Ley de Suelo y Rehabilitación Urbana* (BOE-A-2015-11723).
107. Decreto 1/2011, de 13 de enero, del Consell, por el que se aprueba la *Estrategia Territorial de la Comunitat Valenciana* (DOGV núm. 6441 de 19.01.2011).
108. *Ustawa z dnia 27 marca 2003 r. o planowaniu i zagospodarowaniu przestrzennym* (t.j. Dz. U. 2021 poz. 741, ze zm.).
109. *Rozporządzenie Ministra Rozwoju Regionalnego i Budownictwa w sprawie ewidencji gruntów i budynków* (t.j. Dz. U. z 2019 r. poz. 393, ze zm.).
110. Nowak, M.; Mickiewicz, P. *Plan Zagospodarowania Przestrzennego Województwa Jako Instrument Zarządzania Rozwojem Regionalnym*; CeDeWu: Warsaw, Poland, 2012.
111. Nowak, M.J. Niesprawność władz publicznych a polityka przestrzenna w Polsce. *Zarządzanie Publiczne* **2016**, *2*, 94–106. [CrossRef]
112. Zaborowski, T. Miejskie obszary funkcjonalne w projekcie Planu zagospodarowania przestrzennego województwa mazowieckiego z 24.07.2018 r—Krytyka w oparciu o praktykę zagraniczną. *Samorząd Terytorialny* **2019**, *7*, 31–45.
113. Hełdak, M.; Raszka, B. Evaluation of the spatial policy of a commune with regard to planned land use. *Pol. J. Environ.Stud.* **2013**, *22*, 125–130.
114. Topczewska, T.; Maliszewski, C. Suburbanizacja a jakość dokumentów planistycznych gmin—Na przykładzie gmin podwarszawskich. *Człowiek i Środowisko* **2014**, *38*, 23–43.
115. Stacherzak, A.; Hełdak, M.; Kazak, J. Obciążenia finansowe gmin kosztami realizacji dróg. *Res. Pap. Wrocław Univ. Econ* **2014**, *331*, 201–212. [CrossRef]
116. Śleszyński, P. *Wariantowe Szacunki Wybranych Kosztów Zewnętrznych Rozwoju Radomia*; Expertise (Unpublished); Miejska Pracownia Urbanistyczna w Radomiu: Radom, Poland, 2020.
117. Uchwała nr VII/40/09 Rady Gminy w Kowali z dnia 31.08.2009 r. w sprawie uchwalenia zmiany Studium uwarunkowań i kierunków zagospodarowania przestrzennego gminy Kowala.
118. Uchwała nr XXIV.175.2020 Rady Gminy Kowala z dnia 28 września 2020 r. w sprawie studium uwarunkowań i kierunków zagospodarowania przestrzennego gminy Kowala.
119. Izdebski, H.; Zachariasz, I. *Ustawa o Planowaniu i Zagospodarowaniu Przestrzennym—Komentarz*; Wolters Kluwer: Warsaw, Poland, 2013.
120. Nowak, M.J.; Śleszyński, P.; Ostrowska, A. Orzeczenia sądów administracyjnych dotyczące studiów uwarunkowań i kierunków zagospodarowania przestrzennego gmin. *Perspektywa polityki publicznej i geograficzna. Studia Regionalne i Lokalne* **2021**, *2*, 75–92.
121. Główny Urząd Statystyczny. 2021. Available online: https://bdl.stat.gov.pl/BDL/dane/podgrup/tablica (accessed on 29 June 2021).

122. Topczewska, T.; Maliszewski, C. Plany miejscowe gmin podwarszawskich. Sposób realizacji polityki urbanizacji. *Człowiek i Środowisko* **2015**, *39*, 5–17.
123. The Highest Court's resolution, Poland; Wyrok SN z dnia 10 stycznia 1969 r. (II CR 506/68, OSNC 1969, nr 9, poz. 166).
124. The Provincial Administrative Court's resolution; Wyrok WSA w Rzeszowie z dnia 4 września 2013 r. (II SA/Rz 282/13)).
125. The Provincial Administrative Court's resolution; Wyrok WSA w Gdańsku z dnia 13 lutego 2008 r. (II SA/Gd 514/07).
126. The Provincial Administrative Court's resolution; Wyrok WSA w Warszawie z dnia 29 listopada 2009 r. (IV SA/Wa 1433/09).
127. The Provincial Administrative Court's resolution; Wyrok WSA w Opolu z dnia 7 kwietnia 2009 r. (II SA/Op 43/09).
128. *Ustawa z dnia 3 lutego 1995 r. o ochronie gruntów rolnych i leśnych* (t.j. Dz.U. 2017 poz. 1161, ze zm.).
129. Izdebski, H.; Nelicki, A.; Zachariasz, I. *Zagospodarowanie Przestrzenne: Polskie Prawo na tle Standardów Demokratycznego Państwa Prawnego*; Ernst & Young: Warsaw, Poland, 2007.
130. Nowak, M. Decyzje o warunkach zabudowy i zagospodarowania terenu—Instrument, czy wyłącznie bariera rozwoju? *Studia Regionalne i Lokalne* **2012**, *2*, 77–91.
131. Foryś, I.; Nowak, M. *Zarządzanie Przestrzenią w Gospodarowaniu Nieruchomościami*; Poltext: Warsaw, Poland, 2014.
132. Śleszyński, P.; Deręgowska, A.; Kubiak, Ł.; Sudra, P.; Zielińska, B. *Analiza Stanu i Uwarunkowań Prac Planistycznych w Gminach w 2017 roku*; IGiPZ PAN, Departament Polityki Przestrzennej Ministerstwa Inwestycji i Rozwoju: Warsaw, Poland, 2018.
133. Kwartnik-Pruc, A.; Parzych, P.; Bydłosz, J. Problemy przeznaczania, na terenach wsi, gruntów rolnych i leśnych na cele inwestycyjne. *Infrastruktura i Ekologia Terenów Wiejskich* **2011**, *4*, 97–108.
134. Bielecka, E.; Całka, B. Analiza procesu wyłączeń gruntów z produkcji rolnej i leśnej na terenach wiejskich. *Infrastruktura i Ekologia Terenów Wiejskich* **2012**, *2*, 163–173.
135. Jędraszko, A. *Zagospodarowanie Przestrzenne w Polsce—Drogi i Bezdroża Regulacji Ustawowych*; Unia Metropolii Polskich: Warsaw, Poland, 2005.
136. Jiménez, V.B.; Malheiros, J.; Campesino, A.-J.F. La función residencial en la regulación del suelo no urbanizable de la Península Ibérica. *Finisterra* **2019**, *54*, 37–54.
137. Rusk, D. *Cities without Suburbs: A Census 2010 Perspective*, 4th ed.; Woodrow Wilson Center Press: Washington, DC, USA, 2013.
138. Markowski, T. Zintegrowane planowanie rozwoju—Dylematy i wyzwania. *Studia KPZK PAN* **2015**, *161*, 12–26.
139. Næss, P. Nyliberalisme i byplanlægningen. In *Dansk Nyliberalisme*; Lundkvist, A., Ed.; Frydenlund Publishers: Copenhagen, Denmark, 2008; pp. 231–264.
140. Hortas-Rico, M. Urban sprawl and municipal budgets in Spain: A dynamic panel data approach. *Pap. Reg. Sci.* **2014**, *93*, 843–864. [CrossRef]
141. Asman, T. Określanie kierunków i wskaźników dotyczących zagospodarowania oraz użytkowania terenów, w tym wyłączonych spod zabudowy w studium zagospodarowania przestrzennego gminy—Wybrane zagadnienia prawne. *Biuletyn KPZK PAN* **2010**, *245*, 30–36.
142. Baran-Zgłobicka, B. *Środowisko Przyrodnicze w Zarządzaniu Przestrzenią i Rozwojem Lokalnym na Obszarach Wiejskich*; Wydawnictwo UMCS: Lublin, Poland, 2017.
143. Giedych, R. Ochrona przyrody w polityce przestrzennej miast. *Studia KPZK PAN* **2018**, *190*, 5–252.
144. Szulczewska, B. Zielona infrastruktura—Czy koniec historii? *Studia KPZK PAN* **2018**, *189*, 6–211.
145. Stanek, L. Studium uwarunkowań i kierunków zagospodarowania przestrzennego gminy jako narzędzie równoważenia rozwoju obszarów wiejskich. *Infrastruktura i Ekologia Terenów Wiejskich* **2011**, *1*, 91–102.
146. Olbrysz, A.; Koziński, J. Raport o finansowych efektach polskiego systemu gospodarowania przestrzenią. In Proceedings of the Conference: Finansowe Skutki Polskiego Systemu Gospodarowania Przestrzenią, Warsaw, Poland, June 2011.
147. Pawłowska, K. (Ed.) *Zanim Wybuchnie Konflikt: Idea i Metody Partycypacji Społecznej w Ochronie Krajobrazu i Kształtowaniu Przestrzeni, t. A: Dlaczego?* Fundacja Partnerstwa dla Środowiska: Kraków, Poland, 2010.
148. Gzell, S. Doktryna urbanistyczna w czasach zarazy. *Przegląd Urbanistyczny* **2010**, *1–2*, 10–14.
149. The Constitution of the Republic of Poland, *Konstytucja Rzeczypospolitej Polskiej*. Tekst uchwalony w dniu 2 kwietnia 1997 r. przez Zgromadzenie Narodowe.
150. Koziński, J. Doktryna swobody budowlanej. Aspekty ekonomiczne i urbanistyczne. In Proceedings of the Problemy Planistyczne—Wiosna 2012, Zeszyt Zachodniej Okręgowej Izby Urbanistów, Wrocław, Poland, 21–22 May 2012; Volume 1, pp. 5–24.
151. Niewiadomski, Z. (Ed.) *Prawna Regulacja Procesu Inwestycyjno-Budowlanego. Uwarunkowania, Bariery, Perspektywy*; LexisNexis: Warsaw, Poland, 2009.

land

MDPI

Article

Singapore vs. the 'Singapore of Africa'—Different Approaches to Managing Urban Agriculture

Ada Górna * and Krzysztof Górny

Faculty of Geography and Regional Studies, University of Warsaw, 00-927 Warsaw, Poland; krzysztofgorny@uw.edu.pl
* Correspondence: ada.gorna@uw.edu.pl

Abstract: Through structured comparison, this article seeks to present the different approaches to urban agriculture in the cities of Singapore and Kigali. The former is seen as a model 'smart city' worth following worldwide, while the latter is frequently referred to as the 'Singapore of Africa'. The research conducted was divided into two stages. The first one was desk-based and included the analysis of satellite and aerial images along with the analysis of legal documents regarding land ownership and urban agriculture management. The second one was based on field work carried out in 2019 in both cities and comprised the mapping of areas encompassed by urban agriculture, the collection of photographic documentation, field observations, as well as semi-structured interviews. The research was summarized in line with a comparative analysis of institutional and legal framework of urban agriculture and policy towards its development; spatial features of urban agriculture, including distribution, location, and area; as well as inherent features of urban agriculture, including systems of production, main crops, production methods, and functions. The process makes it clear that despite the fact that urban agriculture is considered in planning documents of both cities, the scale of the activity and the approach towards it differ markedly. In Singapore, the authorities support mainly the high-technology and land-efficient solutions, with other, low-profit forms of agricultural activity being pushed out from the urban space. In turn, in Kigali, where the scale of agricultural activity is incomparably greater, the inhabitants enjoy a certain freedom to make use of unused land in cultivation, which increases their food security and enhances their ability to cope with external stresses.

Keywords: urban agriculture; Kigali; Singapore; land-use policy; urban development

Citation: Górna, A.; Górny, K. Singapore vs. the 'Singapore of Africa'—Different Approaches to Managing Urban Agriculture. *Land* **2021**, *10*, 987. https://doi.org/10.3390/land10090987

Academic Editors: Przemysław Śleszyński, Maciej J. Nowak and Giancarlo Cotella

Received: 10 July 2021
Accepted: 15 September 2021
Published: 18 September 2021

1. Introduction

The work underpinning this article entailed a systematic comparison of the urban agriculture in the cities of Singapore and Kigali. Rwanda is one of the most dynamically developing African countries, with its capital Kigali being increasingly referred to as the 'Singapore of Africa'. The use of the term, most common in media discourse [1–5], results from the rapid economic growth and ease of doing business as well as the introduction of modern urban policies similar to those implemented in Singapore. As urban agriculture constitutes an important element of Kigali's urban tissue, it becomes valid to compare the follower and the precursor also in this aspect of urban life, which is more frequently discussed with regard to sustainable and smart development as well as urban resilience (see, for instance, [6–11]). The examples analyzed allow an assessment of the future prospects for urban agriculture in different economies, and different sociocultural and political contexts. Does the approach to managing urban agriculture in Kigali mirror that in Singapore? Are the patterns of urban agriculture development similar? In order to answer these questions, one should characterize and confront the policies toward urban agriculture in both cities. In the paper, we point to differences and similarities between Kigali and Singapore from the point of view of how the institutional and legal framework shapes the distribution and inherent features of urban agriculture, as set in the natural, socioeconomic and political context. Such a framework is particularly important, given the general direction and rate of development of urban agriculture as well as the determining of its place and significance for the urban system. Beyond that, based on qualitative methods and an exploratory approach, the article determines the main features of urban agriculture in the two cities with regard to the methods and organization of production and distribution processes. The identified set of features in question also helps present how different forms of urban agriculture develop in Kigali and Singapore. The comparative analysis comprised the following:

- Institutional and legal framework of urban agriculture and policy toward its development, including land ownership and land use policy, institutions governing urban agriculture, and planning documents;
- Spatial features, including distribution and location, and area (total, mean, minimum, maximum);
- Inherent features, including systems of production (animal and/or plant), main crops, production methods, and functions.

Thus far, the scientific literature has not offered a presentation of this kind, even if the two cities have indeed been the frequent topic of discussion from the point of view of Kigali aspiring to become 'the Singapore of Africa'.

Though far apart in terms of their economic development, the two cities are linked by issues of geography, history and politics. For a start, Singapore and Kigali are at almost identical distances from the Equator, albeit in two different directions. This means that a very humid tropical climate holds sway in both (even if Singapore is more under a maritime influence, while Kigali is affected by altitude). Under the circumstances, similar conditions for the development of plants are present, mainly in terms of precipitation, high temperatures and length of the growing season (agricultural activity is possible year-round). Singapore and Rwanda are also relatively small—the former is a microstate and a city-state, while the latter is one of Continental Africa's smallest countries. Beyond these considerations, both states are constitutional republics governed in a similar fashion, on the basis of a unitary system with a dominant parliamentary party, while the whole economic system in each is founded upon the free-market economy, albeit one in which the state enjoys a strong position. Finally, the politics of both states are making use of 'smart' solutions at present.

Concepts such as *smart city*, *resilient city* or *soft city* that, albeit in different ways, stress the urgency for in-depth change of the prevailing paradigm of urban development, have gained in importance not only in the two cities selected, but also worldwide.

The term smart city was born in the 1990s, when the concept was linked with the incorporation of new information and communications technology (ICT) into urban infrastructure [12]. Currently, this kind of technocratic approach is criticized to the extent that modern technological solutions are no longer treated as the concept's central element [12–14]. Therefore, today, 'smart' is taken to denote a city that draws benefit from high technology, as it seeks to raise the level of sustainability, and improve living conditions for inhabitants, as well as the quality of the natural environment, while also generating better economic prospects [13]. Key emphasis is also placed on support for community-building among urban inhabitants, as well as investment in human and social capital [12]. The relevant literature thus mentions six characteristics of smart cities, i.e., a smart economy, smart mobility, smart governance, smart environment, smart living and smart people [13]. D. Maye [14] in an article linking smart city planning and urban food systems (which also include urban agriculture), came up with the term 'smart food city'. The author notes that 'smart food city' modes of governance assume consideration to be given both to modern technologies and innovative methods of food production being deployed in the city as well as to social and civil forms of innovation, in line with the traditions of the urban food system. On the other hand, the resilient city concept refers to the ability of a city system, understood in environmental, economic, social and human terms, to cope with stresses and disturbances [15,16]. Although the term is rooted in ecological studies, it is considered a complex and multidisciplinary phenomenon [16]. Not only is a resilient city able to mitigate and adapt to effects of climate change, but it is also one with less social inequalities, a fairer distribution of resources and inclusive decision-making processes. Finally, the soft city concept assumes improving the quality of life of residents and building sustainable and resilient communities not through development based on modern technologies, but on simple, low-cost, low-tech and human-centered solutions that increase urban densities and multifunctionality [17].

Urban agriculture, which constitutes the subject matter of this article, might serve as a solution to tackle many of the problems faced by modern cities, such as social inequalities, uneven and unfair distribution of food or even air pollution, and has increasingly been taken up by scientists, planners and city decisionmakers. The production of food within urban areas is considered to have many benefits for both the inhabitants and the whole urban system. When managed well, urban agriculture provides for the sustainable use of urban resources, increases the share of city space that is greenspace, improves living conditions for inhabitants and ensures the shortening of certain value and supply chains, bringing tangible economic profit [18–21]. It is also an important livelihood strategy in times of crisis and serves to maintain the adaptive capacities of cities [11]. Due to the benefits resulting from its integration within urban systems, it is often linked with the concept of sustainable development [7,8,20,22], and it also complies with assumptions where the smart, resilient and soft city concepts are concerned. The role of local food production in increasing urban resilience and sustainability in Asian and African cities has been analyzed by other authors, e.g., in Ilorin (Nigeria) [23], Tamale (Ghana) [24], and Ho Chi Minh City (Vietnam) [25]. J. Padgham et al. [26] provided a multi-stressor analysis of urban and peri-urban agriculture in nine cities of the two continents, namely the following: Addis Ababa (Ethiopia); Chennai (India) Dakar (Senegal); Dar es Salaam (Tanzania); Dhaka (Bangladesh); Ibadan (Nigeria); Kampala (Uganda); Kathmandu (Nepal); and Tamale (Ghana).

Urban agriculture, however, is not arbitrarily advantageous. Poorly managed, it can lead to irreversible damage to the natural environment and pose a threat to the health of the inhabitants [27–29]. In order to maximize the positive effects of urban agriculture, it is necessary to include it in spatial planning and a long-term urban development strategy [20,21]. Considering the increased competition for space in both Kigali and Singapore, integrated actions that take into account both city authorities, planners and residents can contribute to building sustainable food systems in the city while reducing the risk of exacerbation of local conflicts. The future and role of agriculture in the city space are thus often in the hands of decisionmakers in the field of urban spatial planning [21,30,31]. It is worth mentioning a number of case studies that prove how important the institutional response is for shaping the directions of urban agricultural development. In Havana, urban agriculture appeared in the city as a grassroots response to the economic crisis in the early 1990s but the rapid institutionalization of this activity had a key impact on the maintenance of urban gardens in the urban space, and even their growing role in the spatial and functional structure [32–34]. On the other hand, A. P. Bopda, and L. Awono [35], based on the research carried out in Yaoundé, indicated that despite the omnipresence of agriculture in the capital of Cameroon, the lack of institutional response is a serious barrier to the creation of effective structures of its management. In turn, G. W. Nasinyama et al. [36], using the positive example of Kampala, emphasized that the cooperation between urban farmers and municipal policymakers can be beneficial for effectively managing urban agriculture and improving the health of urban populations. Finally, Diehl, J. A et al. [37], with regard to Singapore, also discussed in this paper, highlighted the important role of state policy, especially based on a cross-agency approach, in building sustainable forms of urban agriculture.

We argue that the institutional and legal framework plays an important role in shaping the distribution of urban agriculture across the space of two cities selected. The framework is considered to comprise legal regulations in force, especially regarding land ownership as well as planning documents that steer directions of spatial management in cities. These reflect the policies that central and urban authorities are pursuing, conferring rights of ownership or leaseholder rights, and the drawing up of planning documents indicating those urban areas in which it is possible to engage in agricultural activity. Legal regulations also have a direct influence on the internal features of urban agriculture, such as the selection of methods and techniques of production. Therefore, authorities are in a position to shape the presence, features and role of urban agriculture in the urban system, overall. However, they can do this solely in the given natural, socioeconomic and political conditions. The spatial distribution of urban agriculture, though steered by the authorities, depends on access to such natural resources as land and water, with this being a product of natural and economic factors.

Given the above issues, it is important to stress that urban agriculture in the two cities selected takes various forms and performs different functions. What is more, its prestige as well as the scope of its preservation in the city space differs and depends on local socio-economic and political conditions. Therefore, the comparison of Singapore and Kigali, the cities of dissimilar socio-economic characteristics, is justified, as it will enable an illustration of the full spectrum of functions performed by urban agriculture and the role it plays in achieving urban sustainability and resilience. Moreover, since the adoption of smart development is emphasized by decisionmakers in both Singapore and Kigali, this article presents different approaches toward the activity that is considered to be compliant with the concept.

The structure of the text is as follows. We start with the characteristics of the materials analyzed and the methods applied. Then, there is a presentation of the results of the research conducted in the two cities chosen. First, we characterize the socio-economic and political conditions as well as the legal and institutional framework shaping the role and position of urban agriculture in the spatial and functional structure. Secondly, we present the spatial distribution and inherent features of urban agriculture in both cities selected. Summary conclusions are then offered in the last part of the paper, where also the validity of the comparison of Singapore and Kigali is verified.

2. Materials and Methods

The research, based mainly on qualitative methods, was carried out in two stages—firstly, desk-based and then in-the-field. In order to present and compare the institutional and legal framework of urban agriculture and the policy toward its development, the analysis of legal documents regarding land ownership and urban agriculture management in both cities was conducted. Among the documents analyzed, the most important ones are the Singapore Master Plan 2019 and Kigali Master Plan 2013 (together with its updated version from 2020) [38–40]. They are the latest strategic planning documents that present the authorities' vision of the future of both cities and the place and role of urban agriculture in it. Then, a satellite and aerial imagery (available via Google Earth) analysis (manual and visual interpretation) was conducted in order to locate agricultural areas and urban farms in the two cities. Thanks to the high level of spatial resolution of the images provided by Google Earth, the method in question has already proved to be suitable for research on urban agriculture, where there is a diversity of plant cover [41–44]. The study area in Singapore comes within the city limits and was taken to exclude smaller islands, which are uninhabited, serve recreational functions (as is the case with Sentosa), or are industrial (like the artificial island of Jurong). In contrast, in Kigali, where the administrative limits encompass extensive rural-type areas and even undeveloped heights, the research area was deliberately limited to the continuously built-up area.

The second stage involved fieldwork carried out in January and February 2019 in Singapore, as well as in July 2019 in Kigali. It entailed the mapping of areas encompassed by urban agriculture and the collection of photographic documentation as well as semi-structured interviews (described in more detail below). Field observations represent a very important element of the work done in this case, taking in particular farms and agricultural areas, and their surroundings. As a result, it becomes possible to determine the features specific to places in which urban agriculture in the two cities is located.

In Singapore, semi-structured interviews based around a list of topics prepared in advance were held with representatives of 18 city farms, including either owners or employees. Due to a possibility (built into the method of research) for new subject-matter to be introduced by either the respondent or the researcher, comprehensive information on the operations of different farms was obtained and augmented by matters relating to the problems and challenges faced by actors in Singaporean urban agriculture. What is more, via the internet, an interview was also held with the Executive Manager of the Food Supply Resilience Group coming under the Agri-Food & Veterinary Authority of Singapore.

On account of the universality of urban agriculture in Kigali's urban space as well as difficulties with identifying those responsible for particular plots, it was decided to resign from semi-structured interviews with producers. An interview was, however, held with a representative of the Kigali City Hall responsible for implementing Kigali's 2013 Master Plan. The talk held allowed for a broader perspective on the role urban agriculture plays in the city's spatial and functional structure as well as policy directions in line with prospects for development.

In Singapore, the detailed research took place in 36 urban farms. Semi-structured interviews were run in 18 of these, while in the remainder, the work was confined to field observation and the gathering of photographic documentation. In turn, where Kigali was concerned, some 98 areas occupied by urban agriculture were analyzed in the course of the fieldwork.

3. Results

Research material obtained during the work in Singapore and Kigali was compiled, and then subjected to the comparative analysis, which is presented in the following part of this article.

3.1. Singapore—City of the Future

In international smart city rankings, Singapore has for years been presented as one of the smartest. According to the IMD Smart City Index 2019 developed by the IMD World Competitiveness Center, Singapore took first place in the ranking [45]. The Asian city-state owes this very favorable position not only to the application of modern solutions as regards ICT and the high rate of economic growth, but first and foremost to the way citizens are assured a high quality of life [46]. Nonetheless, the technocratic-style solutions introduced by the authorities of Singapore are sometimes criticized and regarded as activities directed at the consolidation of power in authoritarian governments as well as the reinforcement of a pragmatic and rather depoliticized ethos in Singaporean society [47], which is contradictory to the smart city concept.

Once independent in 1965, Singapore very quickly set off along the track of dynamic (but also sustainable) development, with matters of environmental protection thus being taken account of in the spatial planning process from the very outset. This was necessary in the aftermath of a colonial period whose legacy was an almost total lack of natural plant cover [48]. Further decades of urban greening followed, ensuring the current status of Singapore as an exemplar of a metropolis in which vegetation forms a foundation for the whole urban ecosystem [49]. Moreover, thanks to the introduction of vegetation on roofs and building walls along with broad reforms seeking to restore the original structure of the urban ecosystem (a priority i.a. taken into account in The Singapore Green Plan 2012) Singapore is regarded as a pioneer of the new 'biophilic urbanism' [50].

While the above activities can be regarded as a spectacular example of the effective implementation of the sustainable development concept, Singapore is faced with the need to achieve a greater density of built-up area, due to steady growth of the population in a very limited amount of space [51]. In spite of actions to preserve greenspace within the city, Singapore's built-up areas doubled between 1965 and 2000, at the expense of forests and farmland [52]. On account of the cut-throat rivalry for land, activity not efficient from the economic point of view cannot be continued within the city space. What first and foremost fell victim to built-up areas was the urban agriculture analyzed in this paper. On account of Singapore being compelled to import almost all of its food [53], local production should be a priority for today's authorities. However, as resources of land are lacking and as there is a great deal of competition for land exerted by other, more profitable forms of land use, there are many urban gardens and farms unable to remain on the market. Urban agriculture in Singapore is, thus, faced with a difficult situation engendered by an existing institutional and legal framework that necessitates the restructuring of land use for the benefit of built-up areas.

3.1.1. Spatial Policy and Urban Agriculture Management

Once independence was gained, power passed to the People's Action Party, which has remained in power to date. Key policy at once focused on acquiring control over the use of land, allowing for very effective steering of the economic activity—agricultural activity included—pursued within the borders of Singapore. As early as 1966, the Land Acquisition Act (LAA) did much to further facilitate the purchase of land by the state [54]. Currently, all transactions, along with those concerning land intended for cultivation, are managed by state institutions, such as the Singapore Land Authority and Urban Redevelopment Authority [54,55]. The level of state ownership of land in 1992 was 80% [56], as compared with 90% now [55]. Such wide-ranging remits in the hands of the authorities not only ensure income for the Treasury, but also allow for a very centralized system of spatial planning that is now proving to be of model importance, and therefore gaining application in the Global South, where serious development challenges are faced [54]. Moreover, the land tenure system is critical to the decision-making process regarding the spatial distribution of agricultural activity within the city limits.

In Singapore, the main institution governing urban agriculture was, until recently, the Agri-Food & Veterinary Authority of Singapore (AVA). However, on 1 April 2019, this organization split into the Singapore Food Agency (SFA) providing 'food-related services', and the Animal & Veterinary Service (AVS) providing 'non-food related animal, plant and wildlife management services' [57]. These institutions extend technical and technological support, as well as provide for strategic collaboration over research and development. Local farmers can avail of the services of a dedicated advisor when it comes to their introduction and testing of modern technology, as well as the development of business and receipt of funding under the Agriculture Productivity Fund (APF). Until June 2016, the permissible period of land lease for agriculture in Singapore was a maximum of 10 years, with the possibility of extension for another 10 years. This constituted a serious obstacle for the operation of Singaporean farms, which were not able to achieve financial stability in such a short time. After much contradictory information from the representatives of the authorities, the AVA's decision was announced to extend this period to 20 years. It is worth emphasizing, however, that it is the Singaporean government that decides to extend the lease agreement and has full authority in this regard. According to the documents posted on the website of the Singapore Land Authority—the institution responsible for land management—the government's policy in this regard is unambiguous. Although it is possible to extend the lease period, this practice is rarely used, and each case is considered individually [58].

The main argument for the regular review of municipal land ownership is the scarcity of land resources and the need to adapt the methods of its use to the changing needs of the Singaporean economy [58]. In the case of agriculture, the lease term can only be extended if the tenants have made substantial investments in land or real estate and their activities are essential to 'strategic national needs'. This means that farms that are not profitable enough or do not fit in with the development directions promoted by the authorities may be moved, or, if they fail to obtain land use rights elsewhere, closed. The Singapore Food Agency also offers another form of lease—short-term land lease for agriculture—

lasting from 1 to 3 years. In this case, urban agriculture is considered a temporary activity that can hardly be regarded as strategic for urban development. In addition to the time-limited lease term, city-state authorities can also control agricultural deployment through a farm license system. Residents interested in such activities, with the right to use a given area, are required to submit a business plan to the Singapore Food Agency, which then undergoes a comprehensive assessment [59]. The above practices show that authoritarian authorities limit the freedom and decision making of Singaporeans in the shaping of urban space. The government inhibits the bottom-up initiatives of residents as long as they do not fit into the chosen policy. Short-term solutions that change urban space indeed only temporarily comply with the concept of the soft city and provide for the city space dynamic character. Nevertheless, strict control of the residents' activities limits their influence on the nature of changes taking place in the city, and the concepts of the soft city, smart city and resilient city include the participation of residents in the decision-making process. In the context of the future of urban agriculture in Singapore, a matter of importance are the provisions contained in the latest Singapore Master Plan [38]. Firstly, according to the document, agricultural activity is considered to embrace units enjoying the status of agrotechnology park, aquaculture farm, plant nursery, hydroponics farm or agricultural research/experimental station. The Master Plan therefore does not take into account the soil-based cultivation that actually dominates in the farms studied here. Secondly, in line with the document, the only areas designated for agriculture are in the Lim Chu Kang district as well as the area between Tengah and the Peng Siang River [38]. However, this is not an extensive area and does not coincide with that occupied by urban farms at the present time.

Thus, the Singaporean authorities have a number of tools to control and steer the directions of urban agriculture development. The conducted field research confirms that institutional and legal structures have a key impact on the distribution and inherent features of urban farms in the city state. Strong centralization, however, prevents grassroots initiatives and inhabitants' agency, whose individual needs are usually not taken into account in the strategies implemented by state institutions. Considering the fact that, currently in the smart city concepts, emphasis is also placed on support for community-building among urban inhabitants as well as investment in human and social capital [12], Singapore should not be set as an example to follow in this area.

3.1.2. Contemporary Urban Agriculture in Singapore

Spatial Distribution of Urban Agriculture

In the context of the present research, locations represent important carriers of information. On the one hand, a location reflects the activity of authorities within the existing institutional and legal structures as well as such external factors exerting an influence as the availability of land with particular desirable attributes, and the socioeconomic situation. On the other hand, the location influences agriculture's internal features, such as methods of production and forms of organization. It thus carries with it a series of aspects making up the broader picture where the presence of agriculture in a city is concerned. The location of 36 Singaporean urban farms analyzed in this paper is presented in Figure 1.

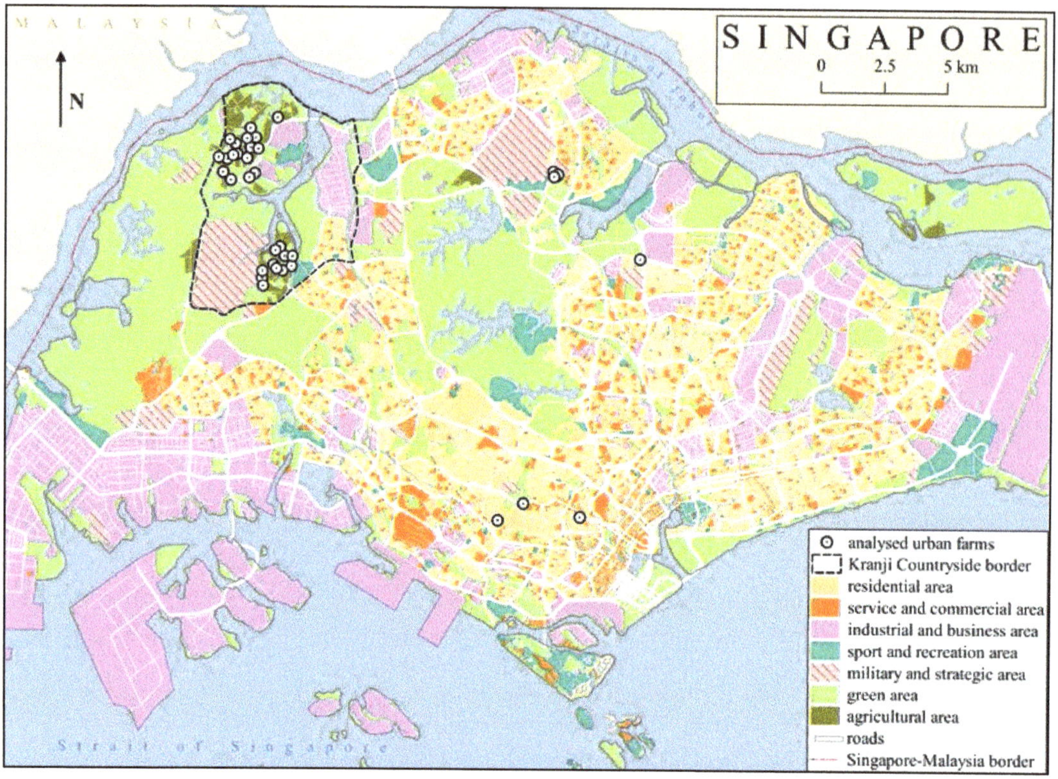

Figure 1. Land use and spatial distribution of urban farms in Singapore.

The 36 urban farms in Singapore (of total area 188.8 ha and mean area 5.24 ha) analyzed in this text may be categorized into two main groups. The first, comprising 28 farms of total area 178.76 ha and mean area 6.39 ha, includes the growing of plants and the raising of animals ongoing in the northwestern part of the island, named the Kranji Countryside (Figure 2). This area, in which two nature reserves (the Sungei Buloh Wetland Reserve and the Kranji Marshes) are also located, is characterized by a limited share of residential neighborhoods and is promoted as a place of recreation in the bosom of nature for Singaporeans tired of the city. However, despite the name, it is rather a stretch to consider this an area that is particularly rural in character. While it does indeed include a rather large number of urban farms, most of these exemplify 'industrial' farming, whereby cultivation and animal husbandry often take place behind walls or in greenhouses. In essence, the Kranji Countryside is a productive hinterland for Singapore located rather far from the city center. The urban farms here do produce food of both plant and animal origin, but their neighbors include defense establishments and enterprises dealing with the production of ornamental plants and pond fish. As a consequence, a specific kind of industrial and agricultural landscape is shaped here.

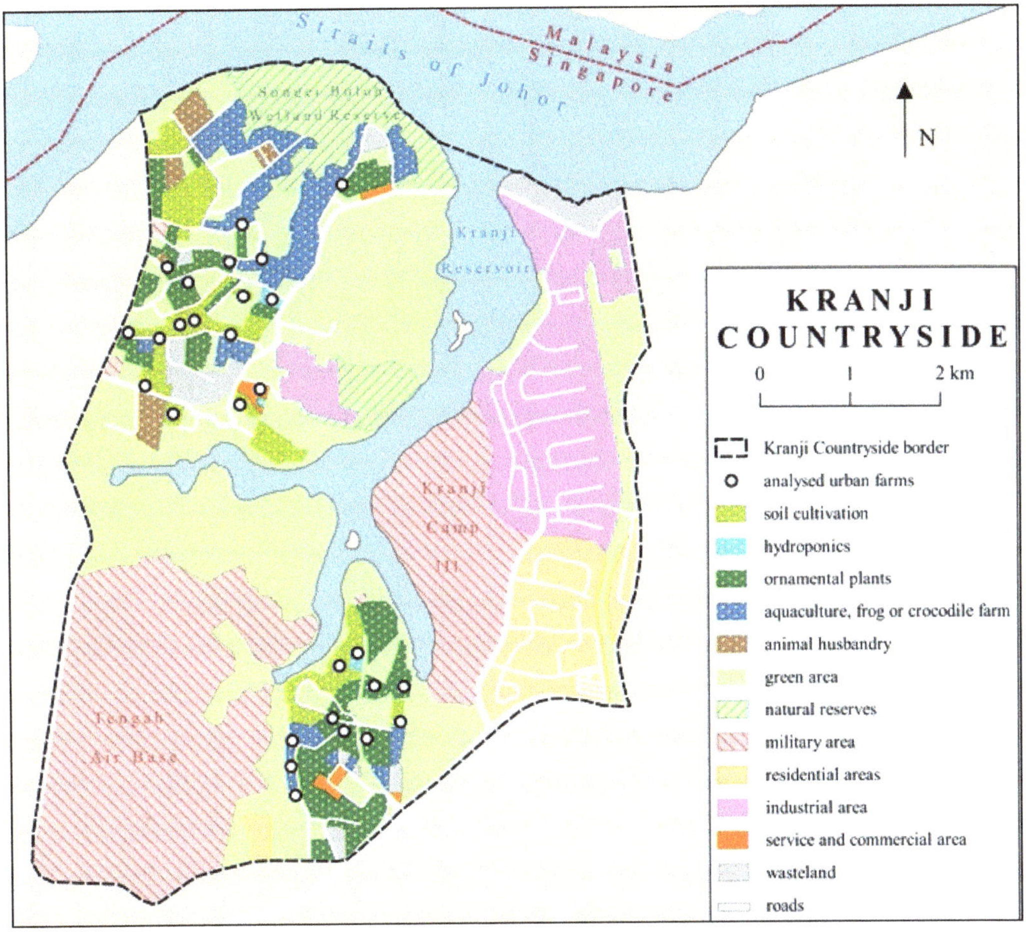

Figure 2. Land use and spatial distribution of urban farms within the Kranji Countryside.

The second group of farms in Singapore coming under study comprises eight sites of a total area of 10 ha and mean area of 1.25 ha, located in the central districts where transport links are good. Three are located in the south of the island and five in the north, on either side of the Lower Seletar Reservoir. On account of the high-density built-up area, sitting urban farms in central parts of Singapore is very much hindered and requires appropriate adaptive measures. Thus, for example, one of the farms—owned by Comcrop—is on the roof of the *SCAPE Mall, less than 200 m from one of Singapore's main transport arteries, Orchard Road (Figures 3 and 4a,b). A rooftop location denotes appropriate methods of production that revolve around soil-free hydroponics.

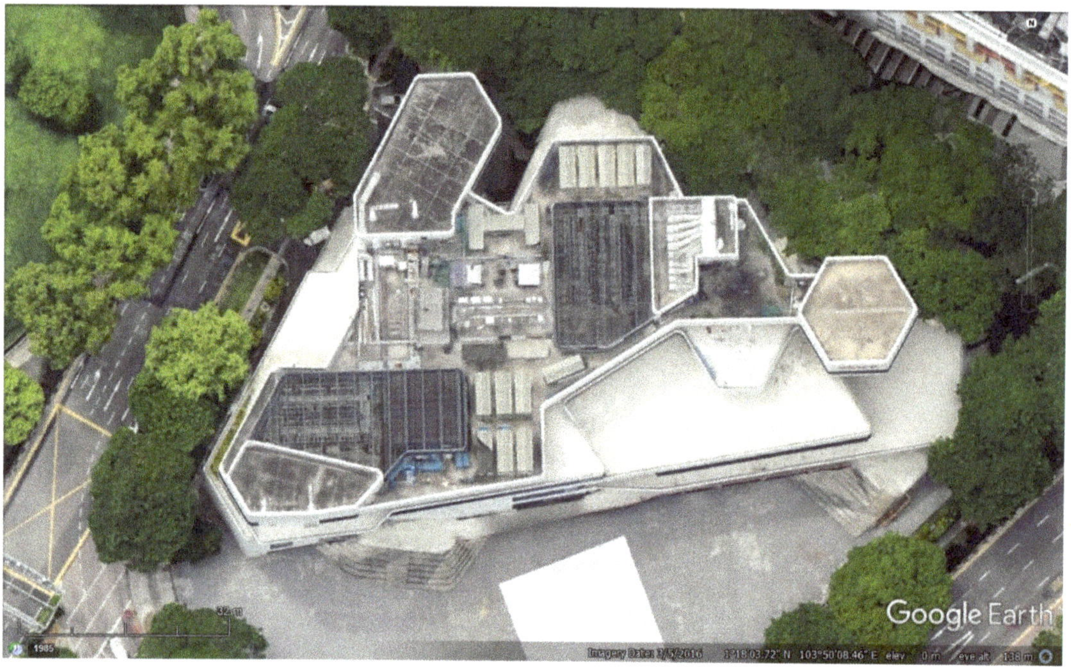

Figure 3. Satellite imagery of the Comcrop farm located on the roof of the *SCAPE building, map data: Google Earth ©2016.

(a) (b)

Figure 4. (a) Hydroponic modules visible from the ground floor of the *SCAPE building and (b) rows of hydroponic modules placed on the rooftop.

In the second case, the owners of the firm Citizen Farm, which is located in the Queenstown district of southern Singapore, noted the ever-greater density of construction in their area, assumed that they might need to move sooner or later, and therefore decided on the use of port containers in plant production. Thanks to that decision, the farm is, indeed, almost completely mobile and thus, ready for its probable transfer elsewhere. Limited space and current land-use policy therefore have an impact on the application of innovative solutions in the field of urban agriculture in Singapore. Ability to adapt to changing economic conditions is in line with the concepts of smart, resilient and soft cities.

Nevertheless, the need to change locations emerged as one of the key challenges facing many individual farms, and hence, urban agriculture in Singapore in general. During the course of interviews with farm employees and owners, seven respondents indicated that the upcoming expiration of their lease was a problem they were having to face up to, with the attendant prospects of either moving elsewhere or closure. This is mainly true of farms not producing food on an industrial scale, such as Bollywood Veggies and Onesimus Garden, as well as farms located more favorably—in the north (the Oh Chin Huat Hydroponic Farm and Green Valley Farm) or in the island's central part (Citizen Farm). The system of land management in Singapore is based mainly around a 20 year lease period, which will end in the coming years in the above cases. It will depend on the state authorities whether this period is prolonged or not. It is likely that farms not profitable enough will be moved, or, if they prove unable to acquire the right to use land elsewhere, will most probably be closed down. The situation of two analyzed farms, which had been still operating in the course of the fieldwork—Oh Chin Huat Hydroponic Farm and Onesimus Garden—was recently settled. The former was closed shortly after the fieldwork in 2019. The plot it had leased is now intended for the development of housing. The latter was most probably shut down too, as the website of the farm is no longer available. That complies with what the respondent of the farm had stated during the interview, that the farm would be closed before long.

As, in line with the Master Plan published in 2019, the area designated for agriculture is limited, the closure of other farms needs to be anticipated. Moreover, by the end of 2021, the Singaporean authorities plan to allocate significant areas within the Kranji Countryside for military purposes [60]. The sites that will have to be relocated, including the 14 farms analyzed in this paper, with a total area of 84.8 hectares, were offered 60 hectares of land adjacent to the Sungei Tengah Reserve (Figure 2). Taking into account the fact that in this study, not all farms within the Kranji Countryside were examined, the area of land proposed by the government will most likely be insufficient (the area of only the farms examined is already larger by almost 25 ha). The militarization of areas so far occupied by agriculture is another form of legal and administrative pressure toward urban farmers who have no possibility of any objections. Out of 36 farms researched here, only 13 (of a total area of 79.6 ha) are located in areas in which, according to the Master Plan, it is possible to engage in agricultural activity. The location of the remaining 23 farms of a total area of 109.2 ha (including 14 within the Kranji Countryside) is not consistent with the provisions of the document, and therefore, they will be relocated or closed.

Although the situation of urban farms in Singapore is difficult and volatile, the government's 2019 Master Plan includes an alternative to traditional cultivation that could become an opportunity for the development of agriculture in the city. The document promotes the adaptation to produce food of the space hitherto unused but present, inter alia on roofs, and even inside buildings [38]. In line with the work conducted by L. Y. Astee and N. T. Kishnani [61], public housing estates in Singapore are suitable to apply rooftop farming based around soil-less hydroponics, with this obviously doing much to increase the output locally. The authors estimate that, in terms of yields, such farms could satisfy approximately 31% of Singapore's vegetable needs. This is then a possible direction that the development of the urban agriculture on the island could take, while being in line with the current policy on the part of the authorities. It requires, however, extensive activities in the cooperation of state, cooperative and private entities. The potential of the development of rooftop farms was also studied in other cities, e.g., Guangzhou [62,63], Hong Kong [64,65], Malaysian George Town [66], Bologna [67] and Dhaka [68]. Y-L Su et al. [63] proved on the basis of their research that sufficient roof space is available in Guangzhou for vegetable crop self-sufficiency. This shows that investments in roof farming can be an opportunity for the development of local food production also in other cities of the world.

Features of Urban Agriculture

The new policy of the authorities in Singapore takes the defined direction of investment in modern, intensive, income-generating agriculture, with simultaneous efficient use of limited space. The production of food is to be based around high technology, thanks to which the city is to move up to a new level of 'smartness'.

Only a few forms of agricultural activity are included in the Master Plan from 2019. Thus, in the future, the document will have a significant impact on the changes of inherent features of urban farms in Singapore. Moreover, the Singapore Food Authority and Singapore Land Authority also have a wide scope of control over farming practices within the city. Obtaining the land use rights for the purpose of agricultural production depends on the decision of these institutions. In an interview, the executive director of the Food Supply Resilience Group, an organizational unit of the AVA (former SFA), emphasized that the Singaporean government is committed to promoting highly productive and innovative commercial agriculture, based on high technology and production carried out in a controlled environment, enabling the generation of maximum profits. As such practices are approved by the government, it might be assumed that farms will be willing to implement them, in order to gain the state's support. Technologically advanced practices are, therefore, most likely to become ever more popular in Singapore. The changes are already taking place, which was proved during the fieldwork.

Among the 36 farms studied, a clear majority (28 farms—77.8%) are based exclusively around plant production. It is mainly vegetables that are grown, including so-called Asian leafy vegetables (e.g., bok choy, Chinese lettuce, butterhead lettuce, Korean lettuce) cultivated on 21 farms (58.3% of all farms analyzed and 70% of farms specialized in plant production). The other 6 farms (16.7%) are specialized in animal production, while 2 (5.5%) combine crops and livestock. Among the farms in which crops are cultivated, the prevailing methods are not the modern hydroponics that the authorities promote (although this is present at 7 farms, 19.4%), but rather, the more traditional soil-based cultivation that characterizes 14 of the places studied (38.9%). In regard to the two cases in which the methods are present side by side, respondents (representing Orchidville, as well as the Kok Fah Technology Farm) noted that hydroponic was only a supplementary method, not proving efficient enough at present, with the soil-based output thus representing the main source of income for both. The owners of both farms, however, are ready for further investment in hydroponics as well as aquaponics (Orchidville).

Four of the farms visited (11.1%) are also trying organoponics, which is to say cultivation in raised container beds, a production method that is widespread in Cuban cities, especially Havana [31,32,43]; Pacific Agro Farm involved in growing plants in growbags, as well as pots and other containers. Eight sites (22.2%) are involved in the growing of ornamental plants.

Two study sites stand out from the others in the diversity of their methods of production. The first of these is Citizen Farm, which applies soil-cultivation methods, hydroponics, organoponics, aquaponics, mushroom-growing and the raising of poultry. However, as may be imagined, this wide spectrum of forms of agricultural activity is a deliberate choice based around the idea of the techniques being presented (i.a. for educational and also trial purposes). Activity here includes workshops for Singapore's inhabitants in regard to sustainable food production, as well as research pursued to further perfect the modern methods on show. The second example is that of Green Valley Farm on Bah Soon Pah Road. This area actually belongs to the AVA, hence the presence here of more than 80 separate greenhouses that individuals are able to rent. Different greenhouses thus play host to various production methods, including soil-cultivation, hydroponics, organoponics or container growing. Six of the studied farms—located in the Kranji Countryside—are engaged in aquaculture, producing both ornamental pond fish and edible fish. The Jurong Frog Farm raises American Bullfrogs (*Lithobates catesbeianus*), while Hay Dairies engages in goat keeping. It is worth noting that 33 analyzed farms (91.7%) are private companies, and the food they produce is intended for sale. In the remaining three facilities, the products are intended solely for the community members or for the restaurant operating on the farm. In addition, 12 farms (33.3%) also offer educational and recreational services. Taking into account the difficult financial situation of a large part of the surveyed Singaporean farms, income diversification may be an opportunity to keep them on the market. Expanding their activities to include educational or recreational events may stimulate sales and at the same time, increase the farm's revenues.

On the urban farms researched, there were 14 respondents who, upon interviewing, recalled the assistance of state institutions. In 7 cases (those of the Kok Fah Technology Farm, Orchidville, the Nippon Koi Farm, Oh Chin Huat Hydroponic Farms, Pacific Agro Farm, Green Valley Farm and Comcrop), representatives said they had been supported by the AVA. The assistance extended mainly took the form of expert opinions, as well as the testing of new technology and the quality of food produced. In turn, representatives of the remaining 7 farms noted how they were not taking advantage of support from the authorities, as that was either unnecessary or deemed too expensive. According to the representatives of both Bollywood Veggies and Onesimus Garden, the state only supports high-income farms that deploy the latest technologies.

In essence, their opinion overlaps with what was said in an interview by the manager of the Food Supply Resilience Group (AVA). Farms like Bollywood Veggies and Onesimus Garden, whose operations depend in large measure on education and social activity (and whose methods of cultivation should be regarded as traditional), do not fit in with the model of modern urban agriculture that the authorities are backing. Units of this kind must, therefore, rely on the assistance of a different kind, which is cooperation between producers within the framework of the Kranji Countryside Association. This brings together 40 operating farms, not only in the Kranji Countryside, but also in other parts of the city. The association offers a platform for the exchange of experience, technology transfers, joint promotion of local output and agritourism, and also coordinated activity, seeking to improve the performance of public transport [69]. Interviews held showed that farm owners and employees at various locations know one another and cooperate on a regular basis. Examples might be the composting of wastes from the Seng Choon Farm poultry breeders at the Onesimus Garden and Farm 85 in the Kranji Countryside. This is the way in which farms create the foundations of a sustainable and self-supplying system, limiting any loss of resources.

3.2. *Kigali—'The Singapore of Africa'*

At the other extreme, our considerations turn to Kigali, the capital of Rwanda and a city of over a million inhabitants. On account of the observed dynamic development, the 'Singapore of Africa' epithet was first applied by The Economist in 2012 [1], and was taken to reflect the rapid development of the services sector and pro-environmental solutions introduced by local authorities. Rwanda offers an example of a very radical policy as regards the fight with plastic. Citizens also participate in unpaid work for the community, comprising, for instance, monthly cleaning of streets [70,71]. Due to this activity, Rwanda's capital has come to be known as 'the cleanest city in Africa' [72]. The term is taken to refer to the country as a whole, as much as to its capital, with references being made to a smart city model, African style. As one aspect of the smart city entails skillfully managed resources of urban greenspace (including areas set aside for agriculture), it is worth comparing and contrasting this capital city in Central Africa with a southeast Asian city it often seems to be compared with. Verification (or otherwise) of this point of view, often repeated in media discourse, in relation to urban agriculture has constituted a key task of the work presented here.

In general terms, a genuine resemblance between Kigali and Singapore—at least at moments—reflects the large share of urban greenspace within the city as well as (first and foremost) a level of cleanliness on the streets that stands out when comparisons are made with other African metropolises. However, a matter of much wider significance is the fact that the Rwandan authorities have for years drawn directly on Singapore's example and experience when it comes to spatial planning. Indeed, Lee Kuan Yew, co-founder of the People's Action Party and first long-term Premier of Singapore (1959–1990), spent part of his time in the first decade of the 21st century as an advisor to President of Rwanda, Paul Kagame, in matters of effective governance [73]. What is more, Kigali is an example of an African metropolis in which, similar to Singapore, the assumptions of the smart, sustainable and resilient city concepts are being pursued [74].

It is worth looking at the transformation that Kigali went through, from being a subordinate colonial city to being a model vis-à-vis spatial planning [73,75]. The city was a minor trading center dominated by low-rise, informal housing, with most of the area taken by marginal districts [73]. The situation began to change slowly after 1962, when Kigali became the capital of an independent state. Three decades later, the population had exceeded 200,000. However, the genocide in 1994 led to the city being abandoned, with its infrastructure left devastated. In spite of the marked decline in population that occurred, several years on from the genocide, a major increase in population had already taken place in the capital. Kigali authorities, faced with the explosive population growth typical for so many metropolises in the region, and with the resulting sprawl of an informally built suburb, were not in a position to meet the inhabitants' increasing basic needs. The result was a succession of conflicts over spatial resources [75–77]. In addition, one of the major problems was how to provide the growing population with a sufficient amount of food with most of the farmland being destroyed or abandoned. That is when Kigali's residents started to turn wastelands into cultivated plots. Soon after, urban agriculture was implemented in the city's long-term development strategy.

3.2.1. Spatial Planning and Urban Agriculture Management

An important issue influencing the effectiveness of spatial planning is the system of land ownership in Rwanda, which differs from that in Singapore. In the period immediately after the genocide, in the face of returning refugees again settling in Kigali, the city authorities had to deal with the problem of claims for building plots. The inadequate supply and then-dominant system of land distribution were not in a position to meet the needs of a dynamically growing number of urban residents. The population flowing in was forced to purchase land belonging to the state prior to gaining a right to use or right of ownership [78].

This kind of situation prevailed for a decade until 2005, when the Organic Law was introduced [79]. This ensured a possibility for land to be purchased and rights of ownership to be acquired, irrespective of ethnic affinities or gender [79]: Article 4. Moreover, a possibility of 'expropriation due to public interest' was introduced, albeit on the basis of prior compensation at an appropriate level [79]: Article 3. This provision aroused considerable controversy, especially on account of the flexible approach to what are regarded as 'public interest projects' [73]. In turn, the Land Governing Law assumed a need for the purchase of land to be registered in line with the Land Tenure Regularization (LTR) Program [80]. Though, unlike in Singapore, it is not the authorities that are the main landowners, in Rwanda, like in the Asian city state, the whole process is the subject of close scrutiny on the part of state institutions that are, at the same time, the main decisionmakers.

The comparison between Kigali and Singapore may also involve the directions taken by spatial development policy in both. Work on the devising of the Kigali Master Plan 2013 was i.a. a matter for foreign specialists associated with the Singaporean consulting firm Surbana Jurong Private Limited, whose services relate to infrastructure and planning in urban areas, and the drawing up of planning documents for various different cities, including Singapore itself [39]. The same firm took part in work to draw up detailed area plans following the 2007 publication of the earlier Kigali Conceptual Master Plan prepared by the American firm Oz Architects [73]. The Master Plan 2013 introduced zoning, and thus regulated the means of land use, the heights of buildings and permissible densities of population in each area. A further assumption is that people living in hazardous areas will be resettled [75,81], and this may be a serious matter for the most vulnerable groups, with such negative socioeconomic consequences as loss of means of upkeep and reduced food security, the severing of social ties, marginalization, or even induced homelessness [82,83]. Resettlements therefore lead to the exclusion of the most vulnerable city residents, which is in contradiction with the concepts of smart, resilient and soft cities that comprise solutions aimed at social inclusion.

As early as 2009, urban agriculture gained incorporation in the Kigali Conceptual Master Plan as an element to a strategy whereby the level of food security of inhabitants of the Rwandan capital was to be raised [84]. According to the cited document, 47,000 ha (or 65% of the city's administrative area) was to be deemed natural, i.e., subject to safeguarding against regular construction. Within that area, some 3481 ha was designated for urban agriculture. At the same time, a 10-people-per-hectare limit was set on permissible population densities in these areas [84]. The Master Plan 2013 encompasses integrated activity to ensure the retention of agriculture across the city-space, an improvement in its level of efficiency, and a curbing of any negative influences on the natural environment. The document assumes conservation measures on cultivated land adjacent to wetlands in areas where slopes are of less than 15% as well as restrictions on mechanized intensive agriculture on the steeper slopes. Beyond that, to safeguard against erosion where slopes are of 15–25%, there is an effort to promote agroforestry using slope terracing, while slopes in excess of 25% should only be used for forestry. Two districts are associated with priority cultivation of certain crops, i.e., maize, vegetables, legumes, fruit, rice and soybeans in the Gasabo District as well as coffee and fruit in the Kicukiro District [39].

The document that in the nearest future will shape the spatial distribution of agricultural activities in Kigali is the Master Plan 2020 [40]. Its provisions are, however, ambiguous. On the one hand, according to the document, the area designated to agriculture is 165 km^2, which constitutes 22.7% of the city's total area. Therefore, the projected share of agricultural land is lower compared to the one presented in the 2013 version of the document, where it amounted to 192.9 km^2 and 26.4%, respectively [39,40]. Thus, in both Kigali and Singapore, there is a tendency to reduce the area occupied by agriculture. On the other hand, one of the objectives of the latest Kigali Master Plan is the reclamation and conservation of agricultural land as well as the promotion of sustainable production methods that would allow the preservation of high-quality soil. As part of the document, zones of 'Zero Net Loss of Agricultural Areas' are to be designated in the city; horticulture is to be integrated in the urban design; and kitchen gardens as well as rooftop farms are to be promoted. However, unlike in the case of Singapore, the Kigali Master Plan does not include modern production methods, such as hydroponics or aquaponics. The implementation of the above provisions of the document is to be possible thanks to the development of the Urban Agriculture Development Plan, the Urban Agriculture Extension Manual and the Integrated Urban Agriculture Management Plan. Moreover, the document also provides for the organization of a series of awareness-raising trainings on sustainable agricultural techniques aimed at city residents. In contrast to Singapore, in Kigali, there is no institution that can provide financial support, especially in the implementation of innovative agrotechnical solutions.

The Kigali Master Plan provides for integrated measures to protect urban agriculture in some valleys and in areas with a slight slope as part of a strategy of increasing the food security of residents. However, crops from most of the valleys within the city limits are to be moved to the highlands in order to protect naturally valuable wetlands. Therefore, the actions contained in the document indicate the will to preserve agriculture in Kigali's space. It turns out, however, that most of the above protective provisions refer to rural areas within the administrative boundaries of Kigali. In line with the division of the city into different land use zones, agriculture is to be maintained only in rural areas in the northern part of Gasabo and in the south of Nyarugenge. However, the planned share of agriculture in central parts of the city is small. It is to occupy only a limited part of the valleys in the Kicukiro district (south and north of the airport), on the border of densely built-up areas [40]. Taking into account the fact that agriculture is currently present also within the urbanized zone, even in the central districts of the city, it should be expected that, in the nearest future, similar to Singapore, large-scale agriculture will be pushed to peripheral areas. However, contrary to the Asian city-state, the planning documents do not include wide-ranging implementation of innovative urban production methods based on modern technologies that could serve as an alternative to traditional agriculture.

In comparison to Singapore, the Kigali authorities adopted a slightly different policy with regard to small, cultivated plots in wastelands. A common practice mentioned in the interview with a representative of the Kigali City Hall is the granting of a temporary right to lease unused plots of land (both state-owned and privately owned land) for the purpose of food production. A sole condition here is that this activity should not be pursued on an industrial scale but should rather serve to meet people's own nutritional needs, albeit with the possibility also envisaged of surplus produce being sold. Nonetheless, when the original owner expresses their will to develop a plot of land, local farmers must change their location. Such a practice allows for the temporary use of wastelands while supporting the local population in improving their food security. As it is based on a grassroots initiative of residents, it also fits into the concepts of sustainable, smart, resilient and soft cities. A similar practice has been used since the 1990s in Havana. In the Cuban capital, however, agricultural activity that was originally intended to be temporary turned out to be long term, as gardens founded almost three decades ago continue to operate today [33,44]. In turn, in Singapore, even though it is possible to obtain a short-term license or land lease for urban agriculture, such permits are rarely issued. In addition, in order to obtain them, residents must meet a number of administrative requirements, and their applications are subject to prior scrutiny by the authorities [57,58].

Another practice that is part of the policy against malnutrition in Kigali is the promotion of the so-called kitchen gardens (Kinyarwanda: *akarima k'igikoni*). The city authorities support the cultivation of fruit and vegetables for the needs of individual households. The campaign named 'Promoting Diversified Diet and Innovative Urban Farming for a better and Well-Nourished City' implemented in 2017 by the City Hall of Kigali in cooperation with the International Potato Center is one of the examples of actions taken by the city authorities to increase the food security of residents and to enrich and diversify the diet, especially among children. The action involved a series of trainings aimed at educating the population in the field of organic fruit and vegetable cultivation and healthy nutrition. Similar initiatives are not undertaken or even supported by the Singaporean authorities. Urban farms that focus on educational and social activity, if they are not economically viable, are unlikely to survive on the market or to have their lease agreement prolonged.

Based on the abovementioned policy, significant changes in the distribution and characteristics of urban agriculture in Kigali are to be expected in the following decades. It is worth emphasizing that, despite the fact that, as in Singapore, the city authorities are the main decisionmaker in shaping the spatial policy of the Rwandan capital, including the spatial distribution of agricultural areas, the existing institutional and legal framework gives residents a certain degree of agency in this respect. As a result of the possibility of using wastelands for cultivation, urban dwellers have a chance to transform their immediate surroundings in a bottom-up manner in accordance with their needs, even if these changes are only of a short-term nature.

3.2.2. Contemporary Urban Agriculture in Kigali

Spatial Distribution of Urban Agriculture

The total number of agricultural areas identified with Google Earth tools in Kigali was 780.98 (of total area 1170.4 ha and mean area 11.9 ha), which were further analyzed during fieldwork. They will be discussed in detail in this article (initially 100 sites were planned to be visited, but due to the limited time of the research and difficult access to two of the selected arable plots, 98 of them were analyzed during fieldwork). The largest number of agricultural sites, 48, is located in the Gasabo district. In the two remaining districts, the number is two times smaller—23 in Kicukiro and 17 in Nyarugenge. In addition,

5 agricultural areas are located on the border of Nyarugenge and Gasabo districts, 2 on the border of Nyarugenge and Kicukiro, and 3 on the border of Gasabo and Kicukiro.

Features of spatial distribution of urban agriculture in Kigali differ markedly from those in Singapore. First of all, there is no concentration in particular parts of the city, but rather a presence in all districts. Unlike in Singapore, whose relief is not very varied, differences in altitude in Kigali can reach 300 m, and it is largely this factor that determines the distribution of urban agriculture mainly present, where the development of built-up areas is either impossible or very much hindered. The places involved are either extensive and humid valley bottoms between hills, or else the steep slopes of the latter. Among the 98 agricultural sites examined, 35 (of total area 1011.49 ha and mean area 28.9 ha) are located in valleys. Due to high humidity, the use of valley bottoms for development is very difficult and therefore, they are intended for agricultural activities. Often, large areas occupied by agriculture are adjacent to densely built-up residential neighborhoods, occupying the slopes of the valleys. The two contiguous forms of land use create a clear sharp border in space. Otherwise, the vicinity of residential buildings and urban agriculture in the valleys compose a specific rural–urban landscape. It is characteristic of even the most central parts of Kigali (for instance, the area on the border of Nyarugenge and Kicukiro districts). It is worth noting that agricultural areas are adjacent to both densely built-up informal neighborhoods inhabited by the poorest social groups, as well as the formal ones, having a slightly lower building density occupied by the middle and upper–middle classes. The second group of agricultural sites analyzed during fieldwork consists of 63 (of total area 158.89 ha and mean area 2.52 ha), located on the hill slopes. They usually take the form of small, cultivated plots or vegetable gardens and are situated between residential buildings. They are present in all surveyed districts. Figure 5 presents the distribution of urban agriculture in Kigali, both of the 98 agricultural sites examined during fieldwork and the remaining 682 previously identified in Google Earth.

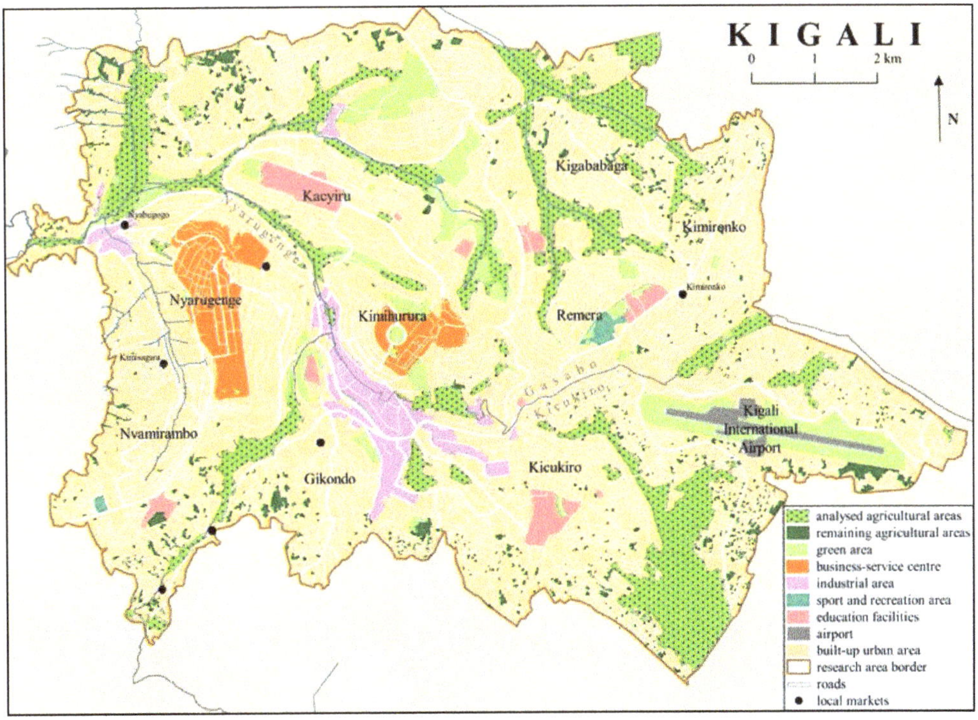

Figure 5. Land use and spatial distribution of urban agriculture in Kigali.

In the central parts of Kigali, small, cultivated plots on slopes and hilltops are less frequent. The agriculture is concentrated here mainly in vast valley bottoms. This is mainly due to high building density in central sectors. The short distances between buildings limit the possibility for cultivation and setting up vegetable gardens. However, the further away from the center of Kigali, the share of micro-scale agricultural sites located on slopes and hilltops increases significantly. This results from the decline in the building density toward the outskirts of the city. The majority of small, cultivated plots are located on the outer parts of the research area, characterized by the least compact spatial form. In turn, in Singapore, farms of a small total area dominate in the central parts of the city, while large-scale farming is concentrated in the periphery, mainly within the Kranji Countryside.

In Kigali, the spatial distribution of agriculture is, in part, a manifestation of the needs of the capital city's inhabitants. Unlike in Singapore, farming is mainly carried out in the immediate vicinity of residential buildings, sometimes taking the form of the so-called 'kitchen garden' in a person's backyard. What can be regarded as a spatial similarity between Kigali and Singapore is that urban agriculture is present alongside green areas that are highly valuable from the natural point of view. In the case of Singapore, these are the natural wetlands in the Kranji Countryside, while in Kigali, they take the form of wetlands in valley bottoms. In addition, in neither of the cities does agriculture appear commonly in areas in which the services sector or administration hold sway. Hence, the small number of urban farms in Singapore's downtown, and their absence from the summits of the Nyarugenge and Kimihurura heights in Kigali (which, according to spatial planning documents, are to become prestigious service–business centers).

A key practice underpinning the ubiquitous nature of urban agriculture in the city space of Kigali is the transformation of even the smallest wasteland into arable plots. Although this practice is based on a grassroots initiative and enables the participation of residents in the shaping of the city space, it also poses a significant threat. The use of land unsuitable for cultivation, for example, too-steep slopes of hills, leads to the intensification of soil erosion and, consequently, to mass movements hazards. In addition, valuable natural wetlands located in the valley bottoms are also endangered, as they are turned into cultivated plots. The above problems were taken into account in the directions of spatial planning outlined by the Kigali authorities. According to the published master plans from 2009, 2013 and 2020, agriculture, mainly large-scale, is to gradually disappear from the central districts of the city. Additionally, most of the wetlands in the valleys, which are currently occupied by crops, are to be protected as naturally valuable areas where no agricultural activities are planned. The exceptions are agricultural areas in the valleys on the border of the Niboye and Kanombe sectors and the Nyarugunga sector in the Kacukiro district. Moreover, according to the latest 2020 document, agricultural activity is to be restricted in areas with steep slopes (more than 15%) in order to prevent soil erosion.

The dynamic in-fill development as well as spatial expansion of the residential neighborhoods are the factors that may significantly contribute to intensified displacement of agriculture from the central districts of the city in the following years. Kigali is an example of a city that, contrary to Singapore, has a relatively high share of wastelands in its space. However, due to the strong economic and political position of Rwanda as well as the increase in the number of foreign investments, gaps in the urban tissue in the central sectors, such as Nyarugenge, Kimihurura, Kacyiru, Kinyinya and Remera, are being filled by buildings. Due to the fact that, so far, these gaps have been occupied by crops and the land use rights granted to inhabitants are short-term in nature, the share of agricultural land in the fastest-growing parts of Kigali will decline. Similar processes took place in Singapore. Urban farms in favorable locations (such as Oh Chin Huat Hydroponic Farms analyzed above) were shut down in order to be replaced by residential neighborhoods.

An example illustrating both the situation of urban agriculture as well as the transformations occurring in Rwandan society is presented in Figure 6a,b. The June 2019 satellite image available in Google Earth clearly points to the plot of 23 ha in the Kinyinya sector in the Gasabo district being under cultivation (Figure 6a). The presence of agriculture in this area was also confirmed during fieldwork in July 2019. According to the March 2020 Google Earth image (Figure 6b), the plot was almost completely cleared and was recently turned into a golf course. The area allocated to cultivation was radically reduced to 4.9 ha. Agriculture was only preserved on the edge of the golf course. The fact that farmlands have been replaced by a luxury recreational facility demonstrates the increasing demand for similar leisure activities and may indicate the growing wealth of Rwandan society as well as the influx of foreign tourists and businessmen. The displacement of urban agriculture to the outskirts of the city was observed by M. Taguchi and G. Santini [85]. The authors point out that since the 1990s, when agriculture was included in the Kigali spatial planning policy on the advice of FAO, the city experienced a dynamic development. The Rwandan capital has become one of the fastest growing cities in the world, and agriculture—which was slowly losing its importance, similar to Singaporean urban farms—has begun to be replaced primarily by residential buildings. Our results also attest to what was stated by S. Reuther and N. Dewar [30] with regard to Khayelitsha in Cape Town, that very often land tensions occur between urban agriculture and the development of housing and other uses, such as ecological corridors and public open spaces.

(**a**) (**b**)

Figure 6. Area occupied by urban farming (limited by the red outline) in the Kinyinya sector in (**a**) June 2019; (**b**) in March 2020 during the construction of the golf course, map data: Google Earth ©2021/Maxar Technologies.

Features of Urban Agriculture

As in Singapore, location exerts an influence on the methods of production used as well as the species of plant cultivated. The valley bottoms are divided into smaller plots that are leased by the city or represent the property of individual farmers (Figure 7a). What are mainly grown here are bananas, maize, and tuberous crops, such as manioc, yams, sweet potatoes, as well as vegetables (e.g., cabbage, lettuce and tomatoes). Particular plots are also used in rice growing, even if this is more typical of suburban areas (Figure 7b). In contrast, on the slopes, the main cultivated species are resistant to the water stress arising due to the low level of the water table. Involved first and foremost is the growing of manioc, sweet potatoes and yams, whereas vegetables are rarely cultivated here. Moreover, bananas and maize are very widespread where slopes are steeper. Taking into account all the studied urban agriculture sites, the dominant crops are maize (68% of sites analyzed), bananas (48%), manioc (39%), yams (37%) and sweet potatoes (24%). In all of the agricultural areas visited, plants are grown directly in the ground, and only traditional production methods are applied. Despite the fact that Kigali follows the example of Singapore when it comes to the implementation of ICT, innovative methods of agricultural production are yet to be introduced.

(a) (b)

Figure 7. (**a**) Valley bottom divided into smaller cultivated plots in the Gasabo district, (**b**) rice plots in the valley on the border of Gasabo and Nyarugenge districts.

Nevertheless, it is not merely relief, natural conditions or the needs of inhabitants that influence crop cultivation in given areas, as the city authorities are also involved. Fieldwork shows, however, that it is difficult to observe the effects of implementation of provisions concerning the priority of certain crops included in the Kigali Master Plan 2013. There seems, in practice, to be no difference in what crops are being grown in the three districts. While Gasabo does indeed have dominant cultivation of maize, the document refers to (present at 29 sites) manioc also frequently being present (at 20), along with yams (14), bananas (13) or sweet potatoes (11). In Kicukiro—the area slated for coffee and fruit production under the Master Plan 2013—it is, again, maize that dominates (17 sites), as well as manioc (11), bananas (8) and yams (5). A similar situation applies to the Nyarugenge District. Taking into account the fact that 6 years have passed since the publication of the 2013 version of the Master Plan to the fieldwork conducted, some effects of its implementation can already be expected. According to the document, depending on the district, the species of plants cultivated should be different; in reality, however, fieldwork attested to them are quite similar.

The role of urban agriculture in Kigali differs greatly from that in Singapore. First and foremost, as subsistence agriculture predominates within the city limits, it is primarily aimed at ensuring food security for urban dwellers. Nevertheless, it is worth noting that in the face of the city's current development and the improvement of living standards of its inhabitants, the functions of agriculture are also changing. It is increasingly becoming an activity that provides additional income to those involved. Farmers sell their crops to intermediaries or distribute their products themselves at local markets. Moreover, taking into account the recent initiatives of the Kigali authorities to promote kitchen gardens, agriculture in the city is also expected to play a role in diversifying the inhabitants' diet and popularizing healthy eating.

In Singapore, some farms, in addition to selling food, also provided trips and educational services, which were an important part of their operation. In Kigali, agriculture mainly brings other social benefits, such as an improvement in the economic situation of inhabitants, as well as the inclusion of excluded social groups. However, these benefits are rather indirect and appear, as it were, alongside the basic function, which is food provision.

4. Discussion

4.1. Future of Urban Agriculture in Singapore

Agriculture in Singapore awaits a series of major changes, not only quantitative, but also spatial, in connection with the closure and/or relocation of certain farms, as well as qualitative (leading to a change of production methods). The policy that Singapore's authorities pursue as regards the smart city concept is a somewhat selective one. It supports actions integrating modern technology, while making it difficult for inhabitants to become involved in bottom-up initiatives that are less advanced technologically but do strengthen ties in society and help educate young people of school age, who usually lack contact with rural areas and do not have much idea of how the food goods that they consume every day are actually produced. The government of Singapore, in fact, takes a rather restrictive approach to civic activism, and that does much to limit the development of, say, community gardens [86]. On the other hand, the building of a contented and healthy community is an aspect of the smart, resilient and soft city concepts, and one intended to facilitate coping with the challenges that today's city poses.

Urban farming in Singapore is, thus, at a turning point, where the technocratic vision of an autocratic city of the future is beginning to win against grassroots initiatives as well as tradition, and low-profit forms of agricultural activity are being pushed out of the urban space. Investments in the latest technology and a drastic policy toward ineffective farms are the way of the Singapore's government to reach the goal set in March 2019 of achieving a 30% level of food self-sufficiency by 2030, known as 'the 30 by 30 goal' [87]. It comes, however, at the price of the seizure and development of the land previously allocated to traditional agriculture.

4.2. Future of Urban Agriculture in Kigali

Considering the fact that subsistence farming predominates in the capital of Rwanda, nutritional needs of the inhabitants constitute an important factor influencing its presence in the urban space. In order to improve the food security of Kigali's urban dwellers, who suffered from severe food shortages, agriculture was included in the city's spatial policy. Currently, however, its role is changing. First of all, given that the vast majority of households in Kigali have achieved food security (according to the Ministry of Agriculture in 2015, only 3% of urban households in Rwanda's capital were considered food insecure), agriculture is not so much a basis for livelihood as it is an additional source of income for the inhabitants, who sell agricultural produce, thereby improving their financial situation [88]. The fact that agriculture is slowly ceasing to be indispensable to secure livelihoods and provide food for families may work to its disadvantage. Once the food security of the inhabitants is achieved, local food production will no longer be a strategic activity and will be pushed out into peri-urban or rural areas, as demonstrated by the Singapore example. It should be noted, however, that the situation related to food security in the capital of Rwanda is still unstable, as almost 35% of households within the city are considered marginally food secure [88]. Urban agriculture, although slowly losing its importance, still serves as a kind of safety buffer for residents.

The urban tissue of Kigali is currently undergoing dynamic changes, similar to those that took place in Singapore. They result from the present urban planning policy as well as from increased foreign investment and hence, the inflow of foreign capital. Due to the gradual improvement of residents' economic status, urban farming will most likely become the first victim of the spatial expansion and in-fill development, the first cases of which are presented in this paper. Moreover, the government's policy toward agricultural activity in Kigali is ambiguous. On the one hand, urban agriculture is to be removed from the valleys in order to enable the restoration and protection of valuable natural wetlands. On the other hand, as part of the policy of food security improvement, the authorities allow residents to use wastelands for short-term cultivation.

As urban agriculture is not a highly profitable activity, and Kigali is one of the fastest growing cities in Africa, it is very important to ask not whether, but how long agriculture will be able to remain in the urban space. The Kigali authorities choose similar solutions regarding urban development to those currently being implemented in Singapore. While comparing the two documents—the Singapore Master Plan 2019 and Kigali Master Plan 2020—there are many noticeable similarities concerning the policy toward urban agriculture in both cities. Agricultural areas are to be concentrated mainly on the outskirts of the cities, and the area that they currently occupy is to be limited in both cases. Thus, will Kigali's urban agriculture, like that in Singapore, be gradually pushed out of the most central districts of the city, to finally disappear completely from the urban space? The results of the fieldwork conducted in Kigali lead toward a positive answer to the question posed.

As for the qualitative changes, according to the latest Kigali Master Plan, the priority action is the modernization and mechanization of urban agriculture as well as increasing productivity while reducing the use of artificial fertilizers and pesticides. These provisions regard, primarily, peri-urban areas though, as agriculture is to be removed from inner-parts of the city. As for the integration of modern cultivation methods, the document merely mentions rooftop farming. Nevertheless, considering the fact that Kigali, to a certain degree, follows Singapore's steps, some changes might be anticipated. The transformations projected in the Kigali Master Plan seek an optimization of land use that, at the same time, takes into account the inhabitants' nutritional needs. The limitation of traditional agricultural activity within central parts of the city requires innovative solutions that will sustain the level of food security; therefore, the methods implemented in Singapore, such as hydroponics, aquaponics and rooftop farming, might prove effective enough to catch the authorities' attention.

Table 1 presents a juxtaposition of the research results with regard to 36 farms studied in Singapore and 98 agricultural areas analyzed in Kigali.

Table 1. Research results for Singapore and Kigali.

Characteristic	Attribute	Singapore	Kigali
institutional and legal framework of urban agriculture and policy towards its development	land ownership and land use system	90% of land state-owned; the Singapore Land Authority—the institution responsible for land management; land lease for agriculture—a maximum of 20 years (extended from 10 years); 1–3 years lease and short-term farm license system; limited possibilities to extend the lease period due to centralized decision-making process	private ownership of the land allowed provided every purchase is registered in line with the Land Tenure Regularization; common practice—the granting of a temporary right to lease unused plots of land (both state-owned and privately owned land) for the purpose of food production (industrial scale excluded); centralized decision-making process
	institutions governing urban agriculture	Agri-Food & Veterinary Authority of Singapore (the Singapore Food Agency; the Animal & Veterinary Service)	no designated institution
	provisions of the planning documents	Singapore Master Plan 2019: planned reduction of the agricultural area; supported forms of agricultural activity: agrotechnology park, aquaculture farm, plant nursery, hydroponics farm or agricultural research/experimental station	Kigali Master Plan 2020 (and previous versions from 2009 and 2013): planned reduction of the agricultural land, preservation of agricultural land in the peri-urban area; support of kitchen gardens; planned development of the Urban Agriculture Development Plan, the Urban Agriculture Extension Manual and the Integrated Urban Agriculture Management Plan

Table 1. *Cont.*

Characteristic	Attribute	Singapore	Kigali
spatial features	distribution and location	main area of concentration of urban agriculture—the Kranji Countryside in the periphery of the city, where 28 out of 36 (77.8%) analyzed urban farms are located, the remaining 8 out of 36 (22.2%) farms scattered across the inner-city	concentration in vast valley bottoms—35 out of 98 (35.7%) agricultural sites analyzed; concentration on hill slopes 63 out of 98 (64.3%) agricultural sites analyzed; agriculture present in all districts: Gasabo (48 sites), Kicukiro (23), Nyarugenge (17), Nyarugenge/Gasabo (5), Nyarugenge/Kicukiro (2), Gasabo/Kicukiro (3)
	total area	188.82 ha (the Kranji Countryside—178.76 ha; other districts—10 ha)	1170.4 ha (valley bottoms—1011.49 ha; hill slopes—158.89 ha)
	mean area	5.24 ha (the Kranji Countryside—6.39 ha; other districts—1.25 ha)	11.9 ha (valley bottoms—28.9 ha; hill slopes—2.52 ha)
	minimum area	0.28 ha	0.009 ha
	maximum area	21 ha	284.59 ha
inherent features	systems of production	28 farms (77.8%)—plant production; 6 farms (16.7%)—animal production; 2 farms (5.5%)—plant and animal production (aquaculture included)	96 urban agriculture sites (98%)—plant production; 2 sites (2%)—plant and animal production
	main crops	Asian leafy vegetables—21 farms (58.3% of all farms analyzed and 70% of farms specialized in plant production)	maize (68% of sites analyzed), bananas (48%), manioc (39%), yams (37%) and sweet potatoes (24%), other crops: cabbage, lettuce, tomatoes, rice
	main production methods	14 farms (38.9%)—soil-based cultivation; 7 farms (19.4%)—hydroponics; other methods—organoponics, grow-bags	soil-based cultivation, only traditional production methods
	functions	primary: commercial; secondary: recreational, educational	primary: subsistence, secondary: commercial (sale of surpluses)

The two cities studied provide two distinct examples of how urban agriculture can develop and what forms it can take under different socio-economic, political and cultural conditions. The attributes of urban agriculture in both cases differ in terms of spatial and inherent features, as well as the scope of grassroots initiatives and inhabitants' agency in shaping urban space. Nevertheless, the analysis of the institutional and legal framework of urban agriculture and the policy toward its development proved that certain similar patterns may be observed. This mainly includes the planned reduction of farmland contained in the analyzed planning documents, as well as the process of large-scale urban agriculture being pushed out into the periphery of both cities. It should be noted, however, that in the case of Singapore, the alternative to limiting agricultural areas proposed by the authorities is the implementation of innovative production methods based on high technologies, while in Kigali such solutions have not been promoted so far, although they could prove to be an effective and sustainable solution to the problems with food security of the inhabitants.

5. Conclusions

The above case studies involving Singapore and Kigali offer two examples of cities in which urban agriculture differs markedly from the point of view of methods of production used and the role played in the spatial and functional structure. This reflects both the natural, socioeconomic and political context and the institutional and legal structures that are in place. A matter of significance for the latter is the scale of the presence of agriculture in the cities selected on which the nature of management is dependent. In the case of Singapore, this is currently, in fact, a marginal activity that does not represent a policy priority for the authorities, even in the context of the inhabitants' almost total dependence on imports for their food security. In turn, in Kigali, agriculture is an integral element of the city ecosystem, and one whose presence and role is sufficient to ensure consideration being given to it as the development policy in the Rwandan capital is pursued.

For many decades, urban agriculture was regarded by planners and government representatives in many countries as a form of resistance to urban development priorities and was, therefore, prohibited from the urban space [31]. Despite its role in poverty alleviation and food security improvement, there appeared to be little political will to support urban agriculture [89]. Nevertheless, progress is being made, and the attitude toward the activity is gradually changing. In many cities of the world, the legislative restrictions on urban agriculture have been removed and systems designed to support urban agriculture are even put in place [31]. In the case of the two cities analyzed in this paper, urban agriculture is indeed included in the land-use policy. Thus, while it takes into account the planning documents of both Singapore and Kigali (i.e., the Master Plan 2019 in the case of Singapore and the Kigali Master Plan 2013), the vision for the future situation looks quite dissimilar in the two metropolises. Moreover, in the two cases presented, the approaches toward urban agriculture to a different extent comply with the principles of smart, resilient and soft urban development. Certain solutions promoted by the cities' decisionmakers might be considered as being in line with the concepts, while others are quite the opposite. In the case of Singapore, the emphasis is on modern agriculture based around high-technology and not occupying the valuable and limited resource that space represents for the city. Its place, therefore, falls within a technocratic vision of the smart city, with inhabitants being encouraged to use modern technology in urban agriculture, while support is not forthcoming for initiatives based around the 'more conventional' community gardens or farms in general cultivating land in a traditional way. Bottom-up initiatives and participation of residents are limited, which is inconsistent with the assumptions of at least two pillars of the smart city concept, which are smart people and smart governance. Neglecting the grassroots and community activities of inhabitants as well as the social function of urban gardens is also inconsistent with the assumptions of the soft city, which is based on simple solutions developed by the citizens themselves. Innovative methods of agricultural production such as hydroponic modules often placed on rooftops or indoors, have several socio-economic benefits, as their presence increases the multifunctionality of the urban space and provides for the shortening of value chains, which falls within the smart, resilient and soft city concepts. At the same time, however, such high-technology production systems have fewer benefits in environmental and ecological terms, as they do not help preserve natural resources or increase the share of green areas. Moreover, the reduction in the agricultural land outlined in the current Singapore Master Plan will lead to a further decrease in the share of green areas within the city limits.

In Kigali, the authorities seek optimal means of using land whose geophysical features preclude it from being built on, yet urban agriculture is to be preserved almost exclusively in peri-urban areas. At the same time, authorities offer inhabitants a certain freedom to make use of unused land in cultivation, in line with their needs. This conferment of a right of initiative among citizens is in line with the smart city concept and its smart governance aspect, as well as the soft city concept, as it gives the inhabitants the possibility to create and shape their own urban space, according to their needs. Moreover, the creation of kitchen gardens and the transformation of small-scale wastelands into cultivated plots leads to the improvement of the residents' food security and enhances their ability to cope with stresses, such as a drastic increase in food prices, which is in line with the urban resilience concept. In Singapore, the authorities are more restrictive in these matters, with a large proportion of the farms studied, especially those performing social or community functions, not having their land leases prolonged.

While the two cities do clearly differ significantly where urban agriculture is concerned, it is possible to note certain similarities as well. In the first place, it is worth recalling the system of land ownership, wherein the authorities in both states are the main decision-makers when it comes to land management. While in Rwanda (unlike Singapore), they are not actually the main owners, Article 13 of the Organic Law confers very broad powers with regard to control over economic activity in general within the city. In neither case is it possible to regard urban agriculture as a priority activity. Though the issue appears in planning documents, with reference made to the significance from the point of view of inhabitants' food security and wellbeing, the activity is not important enough for the space of economic significance to be allocated. So, while the scale of urban agriculture in Kigali is incomparably greater than in Singapore, even here, the activity only takes in those areas incapable of being used in construction. Singapore simply has a smaller share of this kind of area unsuited to being built up. Furthermore, the fact that Rwanda is developing dynamically at present suggests that upcoming decades will see demands for land resources increase, just as it did in Singapore, which is, after all, a model for the Rwandan authorities. This should ensure urban agriculture's expulsion from whichever areas are capable of supporting more profitable types of economic activity. It remains in question whether the Kigali's authorities will further follow Singapore's footsteps and start supporting high-tech initiatives, enabling the efficient use of scarce land resources. As innovative methods of agricultural production are indeed gaining in importance in fast developing cities of the Global South, they may also prove effective and beneficial in the capital of Rwanda. Nevertheless, it is important to emphasize that, in contrast to Singapore, whose experience is quite consolidated, in Kigali, the policy agenda as well as the approach to managing urban agriculture might still evolve in a different direction. As Kigali's urban tissue is currently under dynamic transformation, solutions integrating urban agriculture into urban space planning can still be introduced. By combining innovative solutions with the grassroots initiatives of the inhabitants, Kigali could create sustainable urban food systems, while achieving a high level of urban resilience.

Author Contributions: Conceptualization, A.G. and K.G.; methodology, A.G.; validation, A.G., K.G.; formal analysis, A.G.; investigation, A.G. and K.G.; resources, A.G.; writing—original draft preparation, A.G.; writing—review and editing, A.G. and K.G.; visualization, A.G. and K.G; project administration, A.G.; funding acquisition, A.G. Both authors have read and agreed to the published version of the manuscript.

Funding: This research was funded by the Faculty of Geography and Regional Studies of the University of Warsaw (SOP-87/19; SOP-130/19; SOP-38/2020; SWIB 36/2021) and Rada Konsultacyjna ds. SRN of the University of Warsaw (20/II/2019).

Conflicts of Interest: The authors declare no conflict of interest.

References

1. The Economist. Africa's Singapore? Available online: https://www.economist.com/business/2012/02/25/africas-singapore (accessed on 10 July 2021).
2. Foreign Policy. Africa's Singapore Dream. Available online: https://foreignpolicy.com/2015/04/02/africas-singapore-dream-rwanda-kagame-lee-kuan-yew/ (accessed on 10 July 2021).
3. EJinsight. Rwanda: From Genocide to "Africa's Singapore". Available online: https://www.ejinsight.com/eji/article/id/2108427/20190411rwanda-from-genocide-to-africas-singapore (accessed on 10 July 2021).
4. Foreign Brief. Geopolitical Risk Analysis. Kagame and Kigali: Rwanda's Curious Rise to Africa's Envy. Available online: https://www.foreignbrief.com/africa/kagame-and-kigali-rwandas-curious-rise-to-africas-envy/ (accessed on 10 July 2021).
5. Polemics. The Magazine of Diplomatic Academy of Vienna. The Singapore of Africa? Available online: https://www.polemics-magazine.com/econ/rwanda-economic-miracle (accessed on 10 July 2021).

6. De Zeeuw, H.; Van Veenhuizen, R.; Dubbeling, M. The role of urban agriculture in building resilient cities in developing countries. *J. Agric. Sci.* **2011**, *149*, 153–163. [CrossRef]
7. Pearson, L.J.; Pearson, L.; Pearson, C.J. Sustainable urban agriculture: Stocktake and opportunities. *Int. J. Agric. Sustain.* **2010**, *8*, 7–19. [CrossRef]
8. Ferreira, A.J.D.; Guilherme, R.I.M.M.; Ferreira, C.S.S. Urban agriculture, a tool towards more resilient urban communities? *Curr. Opin. Environ. Sci. Health* **2018**, *5*, 93–97. [CrossRef]
9. Gulyas, B.Z.; Edmondson, J.L. Increasing city resilience through urban agriculture: Challenges and solutions in the Global North. *Sustainability* **2021**, *13*, 1465. [CrossRef]
10. Langemeyer, J.; Madrid-Lopez, C.; Beltran, A.M.; Mendez, G.V. Urban agriculture—A necessary pathway towards urban resilience and global sustainability? *Landsc. Urban Plan.* **2021**, *210*, 104055. [CrossRef]
11. Górna, A. Urban agriculture: An opportunity for sustainable development. In *Globalización y Desarollo Sostenible*; Czerny, M., Serna Mendoza, C.A., Eds.; Wydawnictwa Uniwersytetu Warszawskiego: Warszawa, Poland, 2018; pp. 129–142. [CrossRef]
12. Albino, V.; Berardi, U.; Dangelico, R.M. Smart cities: Definitions, dimensions, performance, and initiatives. *J. Urban Technol.* **2015**, *22*, 3–21. [CrossRef]
13. Monfaredzadeh, T.; Berardi, U. Beneath the smart city: Dichotomy between sustainability and competitiveness. *Int. J. Sustain. Build. Technol. Urban Dev.* **2015**, *6*, 140–156. [CrossRef]
14. Maye, D. "Smart food city": Conceptual relations between smart city planning, urban food systems and innovation theory. *City Cult. Soc.* **2019**, *16*, 18–24. [CrossRef]
15. Chelleri, L. From the «Resilient City» to Urban Resilience. A review essay on understanding and integrating the resilience perspective for urban systems. *Doc. D'anàlisi Geogràfica* **2012**, *58*, 287–306. [CrossRef]
16. Jabareen, Y. Planning the resilient city: Concepts and strategies for coping with climate change and environmental risk. *Cities* **2013**, *31*, 220–229. [CrossRef]
17. Sim, D. *Soft City: Building Density for Everyday Life*; Island Press: Washington, DC, USA, 2019.
18. Mougeot, L.J. *Urban Agriculture: Definition, Presence, Potentials and Risks, and Policy Challenges*; Cities Feeding People Series; IDRC: Ottawa, ON, Canada, 2000.
19. Bryld, E. Potentials, problems, and policy implications for urban agriculture in developing countries. *Agric. Hum. Values* **2003**, *20*, 79–86. [CrossRef]
20. De Bon, H.; Parrot, L.; Moustier, P. Sustainable urban agriculture in developing countries. A review. *Agron. Sustain. Dev.* **2010**, *30*, 21–32. [CrossRef]
21. Aubry, C.; Ramamonjisoa, J.; Dabat, M.H.; Rakotoarisoa, J.; Rakotondraibe, J.; Rabeharisoa, L. Urban agriculture and land use in cities: An approach with the multi-functionality and sustainability concepts in the case of Antananarivo (Madagascar). *Land Use Policy* **2012**, *29*, 429–439. [CrossRef]
22. Giradet, H. Urban agriculture and sustainable urban development. In *Continuous Productive Urban Landscapes*, 1st ed.; Viljoen, A., Howe, J., Eds.; Elsevier: Oxford, UK, 2005; pp. 32–39.
23. Ola, A. Building a food-resilient city through urban agriculture: The case of Ilorin, Nigeria. *Town Reg. Plan.* **2020**, *77*, 89–102.
24. Gyasi, E.A.; Fosu, M.; Kranjac-Berisavljevic, G.; Mensah, A.M.; Obeng, F.; Yiran, G.A.B.; Fuseini, I. *Building Urban Resilience Assessing Urban and Peri-Urban Agriculture in Tamale, Ghana*; United Nations Environment Programme (UNEP): Nairobi, Kenya, 2014; ISBN 978-92-807-3372-3.
25. Le, H.T.; Vo, T.H.L.; Chau, N.H. The role of urban agriculture for a resilient city. *J. Vietnam. Environ.* **2020**, *12*, 148–154. [CrossRef]
26. Padgham, J.; Jabbour, J.; Dietrich, K. Managing change and building resilience: A multi-stressor analysis of urban and peri-urban agriculture in Africa and Asia. *Urban Clim.* **2015**, *12*, 183–204. [CrossRef]
27. Smit, J.; Nasr, J.; Ratta, A. *Urban Agriculture: Food, Jobs and Sustainable Cities*; United Nations Development Programme: New York, NY, USA, 1996; ISBN 978-9-21126-047-2.
28. Chaudhuri, N. Using Participatory Education and Action Research for Health Risk Reduction Amongst Farmers in Dakar, Senegal. Available online: https://www.taylorfrancis.com/chapters/edit/10.4324/9781849770439-34/using-participatory-education-action-research-health-risk-reduction-amongst-farmers-dakar-senegal-nita-chaudhuri (accessed on 10 July 2021).
29. Maldonado Villavicencio, L. Urban Agriculture as a Livelihood Strategy in Lima, Peru. Available online: https://www.taylorfrancis.com/chapters/edit/10.4324/9781849770439-11/urban-agriculture-livelihood-strategy-lima-peru-luis-maldonado-villavicencio (accessed on 10 July 2021).
30. Reuther, S.; Dewar, N. Competition for the use of public open space in low-income urban areas: The economic potential of urban gardening in Khayelitsha, Cape Town. *Dev. S. Afr.* **2006**, *23*, 97–122. [CrossRef]
31. Redwood, M. *Agriculture in Urban Planning Generating Livelihoods and Food Security*; IRDC: Ottawa, ON, Canada, 2009; pp. 1–20. ISBN 978-1-84407-668-0.
32. Chaplowe, S.G. Havana's popular gardens: Sustainable prospects for urban agriculture. *Environmentalist* **1998**, *18*, 47–57. [CrossRef]
33. Altieri, M.A.; Companioni, N.; Cañizares, K.; Murphy, C.; Rosset, P.; Bourque, M.; Nicholls, C.I. The greening of the "barrios": Urban agriculture for food security in Cuba. *Agric. Hum. Values* **1999**, *16*, 131–140. [CrossRef]
34. Koont, S. The urban agriculture of Havana. *Mon. Rev.* **2009**, *60*, 44. [CrossRef]

35. Bopda, A.P.; Awono, L. Institutional development of urban agriculture–an ongoing history of Yaoundé. In *African Urban Harvest*; Prain, G., Karanja, N., See-Smith, D., Eds.; Springer: New York, NY, USA, 2010; pp. 71–94.
36. Nasinyama, G.W.; Cole, D.C.; Lee-Smith, D. Health impact assessment of urban agriculture in Kampala. In *African Urban Harvest*; Prain, G., Karanja, N., See-Smith, D., Eds.; Springer: New York, NY, USA, 2010; pp. 167–190.
37. Diehl, J.A.; Sweeney, E.; Wong, B.; Sia, C.S.; Yao, H.; Prabhudesai, M. Feeding cities: Singapore's approach to land use planning for urban agriculture. *Glob. Food Secur.* **2020**, *26*, 100377. [CrossRef]
38. Government of Singapore. The Planning Act Master Plan Written Statement, 2019. Available online: https://www.ura.gov.sg/Corporate/Planning/Master-Plan (accessed on 31 January 2021).
39. City of Kigali. Kigali City Master Plan Report. Available online: https://kigalicity.gov.rw/fileadmin/templates/Documents/reports/KIF_29.01.2014_Master_Plan_Presentation.pdf (accessed on 10 July 2021).
40. City of Kigali. Kigali Master Plan 2050. Master Plan Report. Available online: https://bpmis.gov.rw/asset_uplds/kigali_master_plan/1_Kigali%20Master%20Plan_Analysis%20&%20VisionLowRes.pdf (accessed on 10 July 2021).
41. Forster, D.; Buehler, Y.; Kellenberger, T. Mapping urban and peri-urban agriculture using high spatial resolution satellite data. *J. Appl. Remote Sens.* **2009**, *3*, 033523. [CrossRef]
42. Drechsel, P.; Dongus, S. Dynamics and sustainability of urban agriculture: Examples from sub-Saharan Africa. *Sustain. Sci.* **2010**, *5*, 69–78. [CrossRef]
43. Taylor, J.R.; Lovell, S.T. Mapping public and private spaces of urban agriculture in Chicago through the analysis of high-resolution aerial images in Google Earth. *Landsc. Urban Plan.* **2012**, *108*, 57–70. [CrossRef]
44. Górna, A.; Górny, K. Urban agriculture in Havana–evidence from empirical research. *Misc. Geogr.* **2020**, *24*, 85–93. [CrossRef]
45. IMD. Smart City Index 2019. Available online: https://www.imd.org/research-knowledge/reports/imd-smart-city-index-2019/ (accessed on 31 January 2021).
46. Woo, J.J. *Singapore's Smart Nation Initiative–A Policy and Organisational Perspective*; Lee Kuan Yew School of Public Policy, National University of Singapore: Singapore, 2017; Available online: http://www.smartnation.sg/initiatives/ (accessed on 31 January 2021).
47. Ho, E. Smart subjects for a Smart Nation? Governing (smart) mentalities in Singapore. *Urban Stud.* **2017**, *54*, 3101–3118. [CrossRef]
48. Kong, L.; Yeoh, B.S. Social constructions of nature in urban Singapore. *Jpn. J. Southeast Asian Stud.* **1996**, *34*, 402–423. [CrossRef]
49. Tan, K.W. A greenway network for Singapore. *Landsc. Urban Plan.* **2006**, *76*, 45–66. [CrossRef]
50. Newman, P. Biophilic urbanism: A case study on Singapore. *Aust. Plan.* **2014**, *51*, 47–65. [CrossRef]
51. Tan, P.Y.; Wang, J.; Sia, A. Perspectives on five decades of the urban greening of Singapore. *Cities* **2013**, *32*, 24–32. [CrossRef]
52. Roth, M.; Chow, W.T. A historical review and assessment of urban heat island research in Singapore. *Singap. J. Trop. Geogr.* **2012**, *33*, 381–397. [CrossRef]
53. Tey, Y.S.; Suryani, D.; Emmy, F.A.; Illisriyani, I. Food consumption and expenditures in Singapore: Implications to Malaysia's agricultural exports. *Int. Food Res. J.* **2009**, *16*, 119–126.
54. Shatkin, G. Reinterpreting the Meaning of the 'Singapore Model': State Capitalism and Urban Planning. *Int. J. Urban Reg. Res.* **2009**, *38*, 116–137. [CrossRef]
55. Haila, A. *Urban Land Rent: Singapore as a Property State*; John Wiley & Sons: Chichester, UK, 2016; ISBN 978-1-118-82767-3.
56. Han, S.S. Global city making in Singapore: A real estate perspective. *Prog. Plan.* **2005**, *2*, 69–175. [CrossRef]
57. Singapore Food Agency. Available online: https://www.sfa.gov.sg/ava (accessed on 31 January 2021).
58. Singapore Land Authority (2020). Available online: https://www.sla.gov.sg/state-land-n-property/land-sales-and-lease-management/lease-management/lease-policy (accessed on 31 January 2021).
59. Singapore Food Agency. Available online: https://www.sfa.gov.sg/food-farming/food-farms/starting-a-farm (accessed on 31 January 2021).
60. Dairy Reporter. Available online: https://www.dairyreporter.com/Article/2019/03/27/Singapore-farmers-hope-government-gives-clarity-on-the-future-of-their-lands (accessed on 10 July 2021).
61. Astee, L.Y.; Kishnani, N.T. Building integrated agriculture: Utilising rooftops for sustainable food crop cultivation in Singapore. *J. Green Build.* **2010**, *5*, 105–113. [CrossRef]
62. Liu, T.; Yang, M.; Han, Z.; Ow, D.W. Rooftop production of leafy vegetables can be profitable and less contaminated than farm-grown vegetables. *Agron. Sustain. Dev.* **2016**, *36*, 1–9. [CrossRef]
63. Su, Y.L.; Wang, Y.F.; Ow, D.W. Increasing effectiveness of urban rooftop farming through reflector-assisted double-layer hydroponic production. *Urban For. Urban Green.* **2020**, *54*, 126766. [CrossRef]
64. Hui, S.C.M. Green Roof Urban Farming for Buildings in High-Density Urban Cities. In Proceedings of the Hainan China World Green Roof Conference, Hainan, China, 18–21 March 2011; pp. 1–9.
65. Wang, T.; Pryor, M. Social Value of Urban Rooftop Farming: A Hong Kong Case Study. In *Agricultural Economics-Current Issues*; Kulshreshtha, S.N., Ed.; IntechOpen: London, UK, 2019. [CrossRef]
66. Hashim, N.H.; Mohd Hussain, N.H.; Ismail, A. The Rise of Rooftop Urban Farming at George Town, Penang. *Environ. Behav. Proc. J.* **2018**, *3*, 351–355. [CrossRef]
67. Orsini, F.; Gasperi, D.; Marchetti, L.; Piovene, C.; Draghetti, S.; Ramazzotti, S.; Gianquinto, G. Exploring the production capacity of rooftop gardens (RTGs) in urban agriculture: The potential impact on food and nutrition security, biodiversity and other ecosystem services in the city of Bologna. *Food Secur.* **2014**, *6*, 781–792. [CrossRef]

68. Safayet, M.; Arefin, M.F.; Hasan, M.M.U. Present practice and future prospect of rooftop farming in Dhaka city: A step towards urban sustainability. *J. Urban Manag.* **2017**, *6*, 56–65. [CrossRef]
69. Henderson, J.C. Agro-tourism in unlikely destinations: A study of Singapore. *Manag. Leis.* **2009**, *14*, 258–268. [CrossRef]
70. Uwimbabazi, P.; Lawrence, R. Indigenous Practice, Power and Social Control: The Paradox of the Practice of Umuganda in Rwanda. *Altern. J.* **2013**, *20*, 248–272.
71. Hasselskog, M.; Schierenbeck, I. National policy in local practice: The case of Rwanda. *Third World Q.* **2015**, *36*, 950–966. [CrossRef]
72. Cleanest City in Africa? Kigali Scrubs up, Reuters. Available online: https://www.reuters.com/article/us-rwanda-green-pollution/cleanest-city-in-africa-kigali-scrubs-up-idUSKBN1HR2F8 (accessed on 10 July 2021).
73. Goodfellow, T. Rwanda's political settlement and the urban transition: Expropriation, construction and taxation in Kigali. *J. East. Afr. Stud.* **2014**, *8*, 311–329. [CrossRef]
74. Masłoń-Oracz, A.; Mazurewicz, M. Smart Regions and Cities Supporting Cluster Development and Industrial Competitiveness in The European Union. Africa's Smart Region Development Influencing Global Competitiveness. In *Facing the Challenges in the European Union*; Latoszek, E., Proczek, M., Kłos, A., Pachocka, M., Osuch-Rak, E., Eds.; PECSA: Warsaw, Poland, 2015; pp. 335–345.
75. Goodfellow, T.; Smith, A. From urban catastrophe to 'model' city? Politics, security and development in post-conflict Kigali. *Urban Stud.* **2013**, *50*, 3185–3202. [CrossRef]
76. Musahara, H.; Huggins, C. Land reform, land scarcity and post-conflict reconstruction: A case study of Rwanda. *Eco-Conflicts* **2004**, *3*, 1–4.
77. Manirakiza, V. Promoting inclusive approaches to address urbanisation challenges in Kigali. *Afr. Rev. Econ. Financ.* **2014**, *6*, 161–180.
78. Bizimana, J.P.; Mugiraneza, T.; Twarabamenye, E.; Mukeshimana, M.R. Land Tenure Security in Informal Settlements of Kigali City. Case study in Muhima Sector. *Rwanda J.* **2012**, *25*, 86–100. [CrossRef]
79. Organic Law N° 08/2005 of 14/07/2005 Determining the Use and Management of Land in Rwanda. Available online: https://repositories.lib.utexas.edu/bitstream/handle/2152/4960/4063.pdf;sequence=1 (accessed on 1 May 2021).
80. Law N° 43/2013 of 16/06/2013 Governing Land in Rwanda. Available online: http://gmo.gov.rw/fileadmin/user_upload/laws%20and%20policies/Law_N43-2013_of_16-06-2013_governing_land_in_Rwanda.pdf (accessed on 1 May 2021).
81. Baffoe, G.; Malonza, J.; Manirakiza, V.; Mugabe, L. Understanding the concept of neighbourhood in Kigali City, Rwanda. *Sustainability* **2020**, *12*, 1555. [CrossRef]
82. Nikuze, A.; Sliuzas, R.; Flacke, J. Towards Equitable Urban Residential Resettlement in Kigali, Rwanda. In *GIS in Sustainable Urban Planning and Management*; van Maarseveen, M., Martinez, J., Flacke, J., Eds.; CRC Press: Boca Ranton, FL, USA, 2018; pp. 325–344. [CrossRef]
83. Nikuze, A.; Sliuzas, R.; Flacke, J. From Closed to Claimed Spaces for Participation: Contestation in Urban Redevelopment Induced-Displacements and Resettlement in Kigali, Rwanda. *Land* **2020**, *9*, 212. [CrossRef]
84. De Kigali, V. *Stratégie d'Appui à l'Agriculture Urbaine et Peri-Urbaine de la Ville de Kigali 2009–2012. Rapport Final*; FAO: Kigali, Rwanda, 2009.
85. Taguchi, M.; Santini, G. Urban agriculture in the Global North & South: A perspective from FAO. Field Actions Science Reports. *J. Field Actions* **2019**, *20*, 12–17.
86. Tan, L.H.; Neo, H. "Community in Bloom": Local participation of community gardens in urban Singapore. *Local Environ.* **2009**, *14*, 529–539. [CrossRef]
87. Singapore Food Agency. Available online: https://www.sfa.gov.sg/food-farming (accessed on 31 January 2021).
88. Rwanda 2015. Comprehensive Food Security and Vulnerability Analysis. Available online: https://documents.wfp.org/stellent/groups/public/documents/ena/wfp284395.pdf (accessed on 10 July 2021).
89. Sonneveld, B.G.J.S.; Houessou, M.D.; van den Boom, G.J.M.; Aoudji, A. Where Do I Allocate My Urban Allotment Gardens? Development of a Site Selection Tool for Three Cities in Benin. *Land* **2021**, *10*, 318. [CrossRef]

MDPI
St. Alban-Anlage 66
4052 Basel
Switzerland
Tel. +41 61 683 77 34
Fax +41 61 302 89 18
www.mdpi.com

Land Editorial Office
E-mail: land@mdpi.com
www.mdpi.com/journal/land

www.ingramcontent.com/pod-product-compliance
Lightning Source LLC
Chambersburg PA
CBHW061821210926
51850CB00006B/773
9783036523651